The Jews in the Soviet Satellites

The Jews in the Soviet Satellites

BY

Peter Meyer

Bernard D. Weinryb

Eugene Duschinsky

Nicolas Sylvain

Sponsored by The American Jewish Committee

Preface

In 1948 the Library of Jewish Information of the American Jewish Committee undertook a long-range research project on the situation of the Jews in the Soviet Union and its European satellite countries. Its purpose was to obtain an organized body of knowledge, based on a critical examination of all available sources, on the Communist attitude towards Jewish problems and the effect of the Soviet system on Jewish life. The American Jewish Committee initiated this study in line with its traditional policy of studying and making available the facts about the civic and political status of Jews in the contemporary world.

The first half of the study was completed in August 1951 with the publication by Syracuse University Press of *The Jews in the Soviet Union* by Solomon M. Schwarz. The American Jewish Committee has been gratified at the uniformly favorable reception this work has received both in the United States and abroad, and at the extensive use that has been made of it by scholars, publicists, journalists, and all those interested in Soviet affairs. Part II of this work, "Antisemitism in the Soviet Union," has been translated into the Russian and Hebrew languages and published in the United States and Israel; negotiations are currently under way for other foreign language editions.

The present volume marks the completion of this project. It consists of six separate studies dealing with the countries of Czechoslovakia, Poland, Hungary, Rumania and Bulgaria, together with a supplementary study of Eastern Poland after its occupation by the Soviets in 1939, and an Introduction which presents appropriate historical background and summarizes the principal conclusions of the studies. These studies were first completed for publication in 1951 but they have been brought up to date to include the developments of major importance up to the spring of 1953. Thus, chapters have been added dealing with the purge and trial of Rudolf Slansky in Czechoslovakia, and the deportations and purges in Hungary, while a brief postscript has been added to the study on Rumania. No new developments of major interest have taken place in Poland and Bulgaria since these studies were completed.

The principal sources used are the publications of the Communist parties in the various countries, especially the Communist-sponsored Jewish publications. Use has also been made of official documents, reports by emigrés, national committees-in-exile, escapees, the general press, and the Jewish press outside the Iron Curtain. Each of the studies on the satellite states contains brief summary chapters describing the pre-war Jewish communities and their fate under the Nazi occupation. These chapters are not intended to be comprehensive and definitive accounts of the periods covered, but rather introductory material to the postwar studies.

As director of this project, I wish to acknowledge the invaluable assistance rendered by the Advisory Committee of the Library of Jewish Information, and by the special subcommittee it set up to advise on this study; by Martin Greenberg, who edited most of the manuscripts; by Jacob Sloan of the Library of Jewish Information, who furnished valuable editorial assistance; and by Dora Cohen, Lucy S. Dawidowicz, Stella Ettlinger, and Bernice Sandler of the Library staff, who furnished useful research and technical aid. Acknowledgment is also made of the help of Mark Tabachnik, who prepared the material dealing with the internal problems of the Jewish community of postwar Rumania. I am especially grateful to Peter Meyer, noted authority on Central Europe and the Soviet system, who not only contributed three excellent studies to this volume and assisted in the preparation of the study on Rumania, but also provided invaluable scholarly guidance at every stage of the project.

MORRIS FINE, *Director*
Library of Jewish Information
of the American Jewish Committee

June 19, 1953

Contents

III. Polish Jews Under Soviet Rule, by Bernard D. Weinryb

IV. Hungary, by Eugene Duschinsky

V. Rumania, by Nicolas Sylvain

VI. Bulgaria, by Peter Meyer

Introduction

BY

PETER MEYER

Introduction

At the end of 1952 and the beginning of 1953, the democratic world was deeply shocked by the revival of open antisemitism in the Soviet Union and its satellite countries. The first blow fell in Czechoslovakia. In the Prague trial against Rudolf Slánský *et al.*, Jews were acused of every possible and impossible crime, allegedly perpetrated in the services of a world-wide "Zionist" conspiracy directed by Israel statesmen and "Jewish big business" in America. The indictment stressed the defendants' Jewish origin and the interrogation extracted admissions that their "criminal dispositions" were due to their Jewish background. Jews, allegedly acting on orders of this "conspiracy," were made responsible for treason and espionage, misplanning and sabotage, low productivity and starvation. The defendants, dishonored and vilified, were sentenced to death and executed. With very few exceptions, all persons of Jewish origin in the Communist party and the administration were demoted, and most of them were arrested. A hate campaign of unheard-of violence was conducted against Jewish "nationalists," "cosmopolitans," and "traitors."

A few weeks later, similar accusations and similar persecutions followed in East Germany, Hungary, Rumania, and throughout the satellite world. In the Soviet Union itself, nine doctors, six of them Jews, were accused of a murderous plot against Soviet statesmen and generals; again, the alleged crimes were said to have been committed in the framework of a world-wide Jewish conspiracy on orders of the philanthropic American Joint Distribution Committee. A campaign of vilification, reviving all kinds of anti-Jewish stereotypes, filled the columns of the Soviet press.

Even when the charges against the Moscow doctors were retracted after Stalin's death and officially admitted to have been fabricated by the Ministry of State Security, the accusations of a "Zionist conspiracy" were continued. They were reminiscent of the *Protocols of Zion* and their use proved that antisemitism had now become a weapon of Communist policy.

Mass deportations of Jewish populations from the border territories of the Soviet Union and from the cities of Hungary and Rumania, the systematic removal of persons of Jewish origin from all positions in administration, economy and professions, and a violent campaign of antisemitic slander left little doubt that the 2,500,000 Jews of Eastern and Central

Europe were threatened with a government-directed campaign of genocidal proportions. It became clear that in satellite Central Europe as well as in Soviet Russia itself Jews were again being considered members of a suspect minority, to be persecuted, denounced, and used as scapegoats for the crimes and failures of a discredited regime. At the same time, their persecution was being used to win new allies for Soviet anti-American policies among the unreconstructed Nazis, the Arab chauvinists, and other reactionary groups.

The turn to antisemitism came as a surprise to those who were not informed about the recent developments in Soviet Russia, or who failed to understand the workings of a totalitarian system and its impact on Central Europe. This introduction is intended to analyze these developments in the context of the social, ethnic, and political conditions in Central Europe.

Central Europe: Past and Present

The Soviet-dominated nations of Central and Southeastern Europe form a belt reaching from the Baltic to the Black and Aegean Seas, between the eastern borders of Germany, Austria, and Italy, and the western frontiers of the Soviet Union. Though not geographically exact, this area will be referred to in this discussion as Central Europe. Only Greece in the extreme south of this territory was saved from Soviet control. Yugoslavia ceased to be a satellite in 1948, but remained under a Communist dictatorship; although no study is made of Yugoslavia in this volume, it cannot be ignored in an introductory description of Satellite Europe's history.

The belt defined above is now often described as the western glacis of the Soviet empire. But throughout history it served the opposite purpose of defending the civilization of Western Europe against the attacks of the numerous invaders from the Asiastic steppes; in it they were caught, repelled, or absorbed. Through almost two millenia, in one wave after another, Huns, Avars, Magyars, Bulgars, Tatars, and Turks stormed the eastern ramparts of Europe. Some, like the Huns and Avars, were defeated and disappeared from history; others, like the Magyars and Bulgars, settled down and mixed with older populations, accepting European civilization; still others, like the Tatars in Russia and Turks in the Balkans, ruled for long periods over alien peoples until pushed back to Asia.

Contrary to popular belief, this territory is inhabited by nations possessing ancient histories and cultures. The Poles had a flourishing and independent state from the tenth to the end of the eighteenth century—in the fifteenth and sixteenth centuries it was one of the European Great Powers. The Czechs adopted Christianity and founded their first great state, the Great Moravian Empire, in the ninth century; their medieval kings were powerful princes and often rulers of the Holy Roman Empire. Bohemia in the fourteenth and fifteenth centuries was one of the richest and most advanced countries of Europe; the Hussite reformation shook Europe one hundred years before Luther. In the two centuries that followed, the Czech lands enjoyed a high degree of religious freedom and cultural development. The Hungarians can look back to one thousand years of political rule over the Middle Danube basin and to a continuous cultural achievement. The Serbs and Bulgarians converted to Christianity by the ancient Byzantine Empire, possessed powerful independent states and high civilizations before the Turkish conquest of the Balkans.

But each of these nations has in its history a "national catastrophe," followed by a period of "darkness." For the Poles, it is the partition of Poland; for the Czechs, the period of Counter Reformation after the Battle of White Mountain, which destroyed religious freedom, national independence, and the educated classes. The Danubian nations' catastrophe was the Turkish conquest. Strange national holidays were observed throughout this part of Europe: the anniversary of the Battle of White Mountain reminded the Czechs, the "Widows' Day" the Serbs, of their vanished independence and present servility. Most of these national catastrophes involved the destruction of all the higher and educated classes; only in Poland and Hungary did national aristocracies survive under foreign rule. The Central and Southeastern European nations were for the most part reduced to peasant populations. Although nations of a great and glorious past, they entered the modern age a people of peasants, small artisans, and servants, lacking urban centers of their own, institutions of higher education, and independent state organizations.

The nineteenth century was the period of their national renaissance. Its driving forces were those which transformed the entire European society of that time. The abolition of serfdom gave the peasants freedom of movement; modern industry created new needs and economic possibilities; into the cities poured a steady stream of country folk; growing markets and new means of transportation destroyed the old local and provincial isolation; elementary education became general, and higher education less the privilege of a few. New classes grew out of the old undifferentiated peasant and artisan population: an urban middle class, a class of industrial workers, and a native intelligentsia.

It is important to note that all these new classes came into being in the course of a struggle against "foreigners," against privileged strata of foreign origin and language.

Beginning in the early Middle Ages, many cities of the Danubian basin had been founded and settled by Germans. Rulers favored them for economic as well as political reasons. The German settlers brought arts and trades, foreign commodities, and money into the country, custom duties and taxes into royal treasuries, they also supported the monarch's power against the feudal lords. The native populations in many cases had invaded the cities, forming the lower urban strata, and in times of national upheaval (as in the Czech Reformation) temporarily overthrew the power of the German burghers. But after the loss of national independence, the German element recovered its domination of the cities; in addition, German freeholders settled on many stretches of land between the Alps and Carpathians. With the beginning of the industrial revolution, the class of manufacturers and business men was recruited from the German burghers; a modern bureaucracy, which came into being in the epoch of "enlightened despotism," was also recruited from the German burgher class, as well as from the small gentry; and in countries where the national aristocracy had been destroyed, a great part of the nobility was German or Germanized.

Thus, the native worker in the early days of industrialism confronted a foreign capitalist. The native middle class had to struggle against the competition of well-established foreigners. The land-hungry rural population confronted foreign landowners. The native intelligentsia had to re-create, in the process of its development, the very conditions of its existence—a national language and culture. And all the native classes were ordered about, victimized and humiliated by foreign officials, tax collectors, army officers, police chiefs—and monarchs. All these factors account for the extremism and pettiness of Central European nationalism.

The Central European notion of "nation" and "nationality" differs from the Western European (and American) notion. In Western Europe, there emerged in modern times large national states populated largely by people of the same language, culture, and tradition; the nation was to a great extent identified with the state, nationality with citizenship. In Central Europe, up to the beginning of the twentieth century, empires were founded by conquest and dynastic combination on the ruins of ancient national states. The motley conglomerations of peoples under such imperial rule could not consider themselves members of one nation. The notion of nationality was based not on citizenship, but on language, history, and culture.

A Pole did not consider himself a Russian though living in Tsarist Russia or a German though living in Prussian Silesia. A Serb or Bulgar did not consider himself a Turk because he was forced to endure Ottoman rule. A Czech was not an Austrian because his country made part of the territory ruled by the Hapsburg monarchy. On the contrary, the word "Austrian" became, for the modern Czech, a term of abuse. And all Slavonic languages have a proverb to the effect that there are no worse Turks than the "Turkified."

The Romantic Age's enthusiasm for language, folk poetry, popular customs, folklore, and ancient history was eagerly shared by the oppressed peoples, who defined "nationality" in terms of language and culture. The national awakening started everywhere with a revival of language and literature, and with a glorification of the mythological and historical past. The primary loyalty was not to the "foreign" state power, but to the native language, history, and culture. The state was considered something artificial, ethnic nationality something natural and organic.

It was in this part of Europe that long and bitter political struggles were fought over the question of which language should take precedence in the polyglot street signs. Cities often had three different names in three different languages. Workers conducted strikes and bloody demonstrations for the right to send their children to schools taught in their native language. Large organizations were maintained to secure minorities against the forced deprivation of their language (and to force this same language on some other minority). Manuscripts were faked in order to prove the existence of an ancient national poetry and history, disputes about their authenticity giving rise to long and bitter political struggles.

In modern times the struggle for national equality and autonomy inside the half-feudal and autocratic empires inevitably became part of the general struggle for democracy. The equality of all citizens, civil liberties, and universal suffrage and education were necessary for the development of underprivileged nationalities; no less democratic were demands for the employment of the native language in the schools, courts, civil administration, and election of officials from the native population. First the fight for political and social equality with the ruling nation; later the fight for different degrees of local, provincial, and national home rule; and finally the fight for national self-determination—such was the course of the struggle for democracy.

This is not to say that undemocratic elements did not take part in the struggle. In the beginning, the fight was often conducted under the standard of "historic rights and privileges," inherited from the past and disregarded by the centralizing administration of the empires. But as broader strata of the population entered the struggle, and democratic ideas from the West began to influence the developing national middle classes, workers' movements, and intelligentsia, the struggle for national equality and self-determination became a democratic one.

The struggle proceeded against a background of increasing social tension. First of all, there was the unsolved agrarian question. Serfdom had been abolished, but a great part of the land remained in the hands of a few large landowners. There were great masses of landless agricultural workers, forced to hire themselves out as seasonal workers on the great estates; there were millions of peasants whose holdings were too small to maintain their families and who had to seek employment in the cities as servants or occasional workers. The productivity of peasant labor was low; competition from overseas lowered the prices of agricultural products; the cultivation of marginal lands, necessary in densely populated countries, was made unprofitable by the lack of machines, livestock, and fertilizer. There was increasing agrarian overpopulation, which kept down living standards in the villages and depressed wages in the cities. Agricultural workers banded together under the influence of the labor movement, and peasants organized national parties of their own with democratic programs.

Where modern industry existed in Central Europe (western Poland, Bohemia, Moravia, the center of Hungary), it had to compete with that of the Western European countries. The poverty of the rural population limited the expansion of domestic markets. Although the Czech, Polish, and Hungarian workers developed skills matching those of their German colleagues, their standard of living remained much lower. Nevertheless, a modern working class, a labor union movement, and strong Social Democratic parties arose.

It was no accident that the Marxist and socialist mass parties of Central and Eastern Europe took the name of Social Democracy. However critical Marxism was of "bourgeois democracy," socialist parties found their first task to be the struggle for political democracy. They and the labor unions with which they were intimately connected of course pressed for such things as the eight-hour working day, higher wages, protective labor laws, and social security, and declared their final aim to be a socialist and classless society; but their main energies were engaged in the struggle for civil and political rights, for universal suffrage, for governments responsible to parliaments, and for democratic self-rule.

Social Democracy's greatest action was the campaign which it launched in Austria-Hungary in 1905, under the impact of the first Russian revolutionary upheaval, for "universal, equal, and direct suffrage with the secret ballot." Its aim was partly achieved when an Austrian parliament was elected for the first time by universal suffrage. But there remained an aristocratic upper house; governments were not responsible to the representatives of the people; and the lower chamber, having no stable majority, was soon reduced to impotence by the perpetual filibustering of different national groups. Moreover, provincial legislatures and local municipal councils were still elected by privileged minorities. Similar electoral systems prevailed in Prussia and in Hungary. And Turkey was still an absolute monarchy. The fight for democracy, far from being won, had just begun.

Although there now existed a democratically elected German Reichstag, Austrian parliament, and Russian Duma, prewar Germany, Austria-Hungary, Russia, and of course Turkey by and large remained autocratic empires. For this reason neither the complicated national question nor the great social problems presented by the peasantry and workers could be solved in a regular and peaceful way. The catastrophe of world war, with its mass suffering, starvation, atrocities, and national antagonisms, forced the national movements as well as Social Democracy to give up their program for peacefully transforming the empires into some kind of democratic federation of nations. National liberation could now be achieved only in a revolutionary way—the old empires had to be destroyed.

The Jews Among the Nations

It is against this historical background that we have to consider the situation of the Jewish communities, which in this part of the world were very ancient. They first emerged about the time when the native peoples, adopting Christianity, entered European civilization and formed their first state organizations. In the tenth century, a Jewish-Arabic merchant, Ibrahim ibn Jakub, was the first man to describe, in a famous travel report, the emerging nations of the Czechs and Poles. The Jewish communities of Prague and Gniezdno are first mentioned in the eleventh century. In Bulgaria, at the other end of the territory, there were Jews who probably came from Byzantium; they were already settled there in the times of the Bulgarian empire, long before the great migration of the Sephardim from Spain.

There is much evidence that these old Jewish communities were in large part integrated with the native population, and that they knew the native languages. The Hebrew works of Prague Jewish scholars of the thirteenth century preserve a large number of old Czech expressions in very exact transcription, and repeatedly mention Czech as the tongue spoken by Jews in everyday life.

But the bulk of Jewish population came to Eastern and Southeastern Europe as the result of two great Jewish migrations at the end of the Middle and beginning of the Modern Ages. The first was the migration of German Jews to Poland, and the second the settlement of Spanish and Portuguese Jews in the Balkans. Both migrations were mainly the result of mass expulsions and persecutions. The migration of German Jews to Poland proceeded through four dark centuries from the period of the Crusades to that of the Reformation and Counter-Reformation; the migration of Jews from the Iberian to the Balkan peninsula was compressed into a comparatively short period at the end of the fifteenth and beginning of the sixteenth centuries. The older Jewish communities in Poland and Turkey were inundated by the numerous and culturally more developed immigrants, who brought with them two Jewish vernaculars: Yiddish, which became the everyday language of Eastern European Jews, and Ladino, the tongue of the Balkan and Levantine Sephardim.

In the western part of Central Europe—Bohemia, Moravia, Western

Hungary (and neighboring Austria)—the history of the Jewish communities was more continuous, although punctuated by numerous pogroms, persecutions, and local expulsions, followed by readmissions. Here the Jews were forced into the position of helpless buffers between the German burghers and native rural population. Like the Germans, they lived in the cities, engaged in trade, and incurred the hatred of the native peasants who considered them their exploiters. Like the Germans, they were dependent on the protection of the rulers. But while the German burghers were a well-established part of feudal society, Jews were outside the pale of Christian society and civilization. They were not allowed to join the guilds, could not acquire land, were excluded from most trades, had to live in ghettos and wear distinctive badges, and were without civil rights; and they had to pay, for the protection of their lives, exorbitant and arbitrary taxes and ransoms to the rulers. Allowed to engage in pawnbroking, moneylending, the inferior sort of commerce, permanently overtaxed and periodically expropriated, the "serfs of the treasury" became, as the author of a book on Jewish life in the Middle Ages puts it, unwilling sponges, sucking in the wealth of the land only in order to be squeezed dry of it by unscrupulous rulers.

The majority of Jews lived on the verge of starvation. There were, of course, exceptions, famous "court Jews" who, for their services to the rulers, were allowed to acquire wealth and education and were exempted from the usual Jewish disabilities. Their careers, adventurous and brilliant, increased the hatred of the native rural population as well as of the German burghers, who despised and hated their Jewish competitors.

Finally, the Era of Enlightenment, the Industrial Revolution, and the French Revolution brought about the political emancipation of Jewry. This began, in the Austro-Hungarian monarchy, with the patent of religious tolerance issued by Joseph II in 1782, being consummated, however, only after the revolution of 1848. In this same period the native nationalities awoke, and Jews were immediately caught up in their struggle, which was, as we have seen, inseparably connected with the chief social antagonisms. The Jews, being an urban and commercial group, could now engage in trade, large-scale commerce and industry, and played an important role in the industrialization of the region. For the first time they were allowed to acquire a secular education and culture and to engage in the professions and arts and sciences.

The prevailing culture, however, was German. Forced to adopt German family names under the Germanizing regime of Joseph II, the Jews now had to send their children to German secular schools and to use the German language in commerce and in their dealings with the authorities. And they formed a part of the urban German "language islands" in the sea of native peasantry. Native workers went to work for German and German-Jewish manufacturers; native peasants sold their products through German-Jewish grain and cattle dealers; rising native middle classes competed with German and Jewish capital. Jewish intellectuals, journalists, lawyers, and writers contributed to the modern development of German culture in Vienna, Prague, and other cultural centers. "Germans and Jews" became an ominous linkage in the native political vocabulary.

Things began to change in the last quarter of the nineteenth century. The Czechs, Hungarians, Poles, and Croats now developed an urban culture of their own, higher classes, schools in the national language, their own literature and art, their own intelligentsia, a liberal and democratic ideology, and a labor movement. Everywhere an increasing part of the Jewish population became interested in and identified with the national culture. A Czech-Jewish movement was founded which was loosely connected with T. G. Masaryk's small liberal party of the intellegentsia; Jewish leaders came to the fore in the labor movements of the minority nations. Jews gained prominence in the national literatures, arts and sciences, and in political and economic life. But the majority of Jews in these regions continued to be identified with German culture up to 1918.

Matters developed differently in Poland. From the time of the Crusades Polish kings had welcomed Jewish refugees from Germany and settled them in towns and villages throughout the country. To a certain degree the Jews of Poland played a social and political role like that of the German settlers in the Danubian territories: they helped to develop trade and commerce and their revenues helped to support the royal power in its fight against the feudal nobles. The Jewish settlements, reinforced by successive waves of immigration, grew apace. Jews were not limited to moneylending and peddling; they could engage in every kind of productive enterprise and in rural vocations; in certain periods they played a role in the civil administration. What is most important, the Jews had a far-reaching autonomy, with their own courts, schools, and local administration, and with a central administrative body, the Council of Four Lands (Great Poland, Little Poland, Eastern Galicia, and Wolhynia). In this way the Polish Jews formed what Dubnow calls a stateless nation, "upholding and unfolding its own genuine culture."

There were, of course, periods of discrimination and persecution. But the situation was on the whole tolerable, and it was only natural that Jewish volunteers should take part in the Kosciusko uprising in 1794, and in the Warsaw revolt of 1830 against the Tsar.

Under Russian rule, the Jews of Poland as well as of other territories were confined to the overcrowded Pale of Settlement; had no civil rights; were mercilessly exploited by a corrupt officialdom; were made the scapegoats for every failure of the regime; and endured repeated waves of bloody pogroms.

The rapidly increasing Jewish population crowded the cities and villages to bursting. Large numbers were impoverished and proletarianized. Emigration to countries overseas could draw off only a part of the surplus population.

But the communal organization, the "stateless nation," survived. It was held together not only by religious traditions, but also by the Yiddish language and culture. It led a richly variegated life. Religion embraced talmudic orthodoxy, mystical hasidism, as well as reform tendencies, all of them confronted by the militant secularism of the younger generation. Politics ran the gamut from orthodox and conservative through liberal and populist tendencies to Marxist socialism; from assimilationism through national autonomy to Zionism. Socially, the old commercial class was joined by large numbers of artisans, a Jewish intelligentsia, a Jewish proletariat, and a mass of declassed *Luftmenschen.* The Jews of Poland (and of the neighboring Eastern European territories) were transforming themselves into a "nationality" in the Central European sense. It was a unique "nationality" without a continuous territory or rural basis, and with a decadent economy—a "ghetto nation" held together by outside pressure, but with a pulsating communal life.

In Hungary, the situation was different again. German urban settlement was important only along the western border and in Transylvania; the Hungarian nobility had survived Turkish and Austrian rule, and although its struggle for independence was beaten down in 1849 with the help of a Russian intervention, the country had achieved a large amount of autonomy under the Dual Monarchy in the Austro-Hungarian settlement of 1867. Hungarians were the ruling nation within the borders of historic Hungary,where a half of the population belonged to minority nationalities. The aristocracy was content to exploit its fertile landed estates, keep the peasant and agricultural workers in poverty and ignorance, and maintain its monopoly of political rule. Industry and commerce were considered necessary for maintaining national independence in a modern age, but to engage in them actively was beneath the dignity of the landowning and state-administering aristocracy. In this way, Jews came to play a prominent role in the economic life of the country, and a wealthy Jewish industrial and commercial class developed. It adopted the Hungarian language and contributed greatly to modern Hungarian culture. Along the northern and eastern border, in Slovakia, Carpatho-Russia, and parts of Transylvania, there were poor, traditional, Yiddish-speaking communities of the Polish type.

In the Balkans the Jews had found, under Turkish rule, just such a haven as in medieval Poland. The Ottoman rulers were content to exact taxes and levy troops for their armies from the peasant populations, who lived in primitive conditions of poverty and squalor. The Turks did not engage in commerce and allowed the Jews (as well as Greeks and Armenians) to develop prosperous trading and commercial communities. The Jewish newcomers from the Iberian peninsula absorbed the older Jewish communities and created a cultural life of their own, shut off from the life of the native peasants and undisturbed by the Turkish rulers. These communities survived, substantially intact, the setting up of the independent national states of Serbia, Bulgaria, and Greece on the ruins of the Ottoman empire. Considered as fulfilling limited but useful functions in the primitive Balkan conditions, they encountered relatively little antisemitism.

Thus, at the beginning of the twentieth century, there were Jews and Jewish communities of three distinct types in Central Europe. In the West—Bohemia, Moravia, western and central Hungary—there were wealthy, liberal Jewish communities, speaking the local languages and playing a large role in economic, political, and cultural life. In the East—Poland, Slovakia, Carpatho-Russia (and neighboring Lithuania, Ukraine, Bessarabia)—there were compact, Yiddish-speaking populations, deeply influenced by Jewish traditions, differentiated socially and politically, and forming a distinct Jewish nationality with a language and culture of its own. And in the Southeast—Serbia, Bulgaria, and Greece—there was a compact group of Sephardic Jews, speaking the Spaniolic dialect, living apart from the surrounding population, but rarely coming into conflict with them.

The Era of National States

The First World War marked the end of an epoch in the history of Central and Southeastern Europe. The old empires disappeared; Turkey was pushed out of Europe and transformed into an Asiatic national state, and Austria-Hungary was divided among the successor states. Germany was, for a period of time, eliminated as a great power. Russia, in the throes of social revolution, was successfully repelled by the most developed minority nationalities living along her western border. From the Arctic to the Mediterranean, from Finland to Greece, the struggle of small nations for national independence, together with the peace treaties, created a system of small and middle-sized "national" states.

This "Balkanization" of Central Europe has been blamed for all subsequent misfortunes and catastrophes, the peaceful imperial era of the second half of the nineteenth century being remembered with nostalgia. But in reality that epoch was idyllic only in comparison with what took place later on. The old empires bore within them the seeds of catastrophe, and the absence of democracy prevented the solution of pressing social and national problems.

The new states came into being at a time when complete national sovereignty was already in conflict with the imperative demands of the times, when economic and social conditions cried for European solutions. In Central Europe, it was a question of whether the independent nations could find a way to integrate successfully and carry out far-reaching reforms on a democratic basis.

All the new states were founded under the flag of political democracy. This was the result of the fact that the struggle for national independence had been conducted against semifeudal and autocratic monarchies, and had been supported and carried through to victory by the democratic Western powers. Everywhere democratic constitutions were adopted by the new republics or constitutional monarchies, universal suffrage was introduced, and civil rights and liberties were guaranteed by law. The affording of an elementary education in the native tongue to broader sections of the population, the involvement in politics of lower social strata, hitherto excluded from public life, the appearance of new educated elites of popular origin—all this seemed to augur well for the development of democracy.

But there were also serious drawbacks. In most of the countries of Central Europe there were no deep-rooted democratic traditions such as can develop only over long periods of time. The living standards of workers and peasants were too low to allow them to make full use of their newly acquired civil rights. There were too few self-sustaining and really independent farmers, and too many impoverished small peasants and landless agricultural proletarians; too few workers with skills, traditions, and political experience, and too great an industrial reserve of raw hands came to the cities from the overpopulated countryside to be alternately exploited in the busy seasons and thrown out of work in the slack.

The national middle classes were largely composed of *nouveaux riches* seeking to make up the lean past by rapaciously expanding their businesses with the help of the newly acquired state power. The new bureaucracies were eager to show their gratitude to their new masters, and their power to their new subjects. T. G. Masaryk, the liberal founder of the Czechoslovak Republic, coined the slogan of "de-Austrianization." To "de-Austrianize" meant to cease being servile to one's superiors, and brutal to one's inferiors; to substitute for the duplicity of clever serfs the citizen's sense of civic responsibility—in a word, to base democratic institutions on a truly democratic way of life. Even in Czechoslovakia, with its skilled workers, independent peasants, and high level of education, this goal was achieved only to a very limited extent. In most of the other countries progress was slight; it seemed as if several smaller "Austrias" had taken the place of the one imperial Austria of the past.

One of the reasons for this was the violent and romantic character of Central European nationalism. In the fight against the old empires, this nationalism had been a democratic force; now it created new problems which retarded the development of democracy, complicated the solution of social problems, and prevented a rational organization of the Central European area.

Before and during the First World War, the small peoples, notwithstanding their hostility to one another, combined to fight against the oppressive imperial rule. The Finns, Balts, Poles, and Ukrainians fought against Russia; Poles, Czechs and Slovaks, Slovenes, Croats and Serbs, Rumanians and Italians—all joined forces to oppose the Austro-Hungarian monarchy. Serbs and Montenegrins, Bulgars and Greeks, temporarily united against Ottoman rule.

After the defeat of the common enemy, the liberated territories were divided among states each of which insisted on complete political and economic independence, absolute sovereignty, and the greatest possible national and cultural homogeneity. Populations were so mixed that it was impossible to draw exact ethnic frontiers; often ethnic lines ran counter to the most elementary economic requirements, cutting off cities from agrarian markets, ports from their hinterland, industries from their sources of raw materials, seasonal labor from the places of their employment, and railroads and waterways from the regions they served.

Nationalist sentiment was based on a glorious past; now each nation chose from its past the period of its greatest territorial extension. But the "historical rights" thus advanced conflicted with those of neighboring states who based their claims on some other historical epoch. Nationality was identified with language; but there were, especially among Slavonic populations, intermediary linguistic groups which could be claimed with equal justice by two states. And even worse, there were disputes as to whether certain related tongues were merely dialects or independent languages, that made of those who spoke them separate "nationalities" with a claim to national independence. Ukrainians and Poles fought over Eastern Galicia, with its Polish (and Jewish) cities and Ukrainian villages. Czechs and Poles disputed the industrial Teschen area, with a mixed population part of which spoke an intermediary Silesian dialect. Transylvania was contested by Hungary and Rumania; Dobrudja by Rumania and Bulgaria; Macedonia by Bulgaria, Yugoslavia and Greece—not to speak of those who wanted an independent Macedonian republic. Both Greece and Albania laid claim to northern Epirus; Albania and Yugoslavia to Kosovo Pole; Rumania, Yugoslavia and Hungary to the Banat; Yugoslavia and Italy to Dalmatia, Fiume and Trieste; Yugoslavia and Austria to south Carinthia and Styria; Austria and Hungary to the Burgenland;

Czechoslovakia and Hungary to the mixed regions of southern and eastern Slovakia and Carpatho-Russia—the conflicts are too many to list.

Croats and Slovenes, and even Montenegrins and Macedonians, insisted on a separate ethnic existence of their own, whereas the Serbs considered all of them simply Yugoslavs. The Slovaks claimed to be a separate nationality, although the Czechs maintained that they were only a branch of the Czechoslovak language and nation. Inside these ethnic groups, separatists and autonomists fought against the advocates of unity.

According to official statistics, 22,000,000 of the 110,000,000 inhabitants of Central Europe belonged to national minorities. But the censuses greatly underestimated the size of the minority populations, counting disputed groups as members of the majority people. Without the Slovaks, the Czechs constituted scarcely a half of Czechoslovakia's population; without the Croats and Slovenes, the Serbs were a minority in Yugoslavia.

The consequences for the development of democracy were obvious: in order to maintain the "national character" of the states, the civic rights of minorities had to be curtailed, the state power highly centralized and strengthened, and large armies and police forces maintained. The parasitic character and high costs of this apparatus retarded social progress and often stopped it altogether.

As the whole region was predominantly agricultural with the peasantry forming in all countries (except Czechoslovakia) fifty to eighty per cent of the population, the greatest social problem was the agrarian one. Land reform was an urgent necessity everywhere except in Serbia and Bulgaria; in the latter countries small holdings were already the rule before the First World War and postwar agrarian reforms destroyed large estates completely. Characteristically, the most radical land reforms were carried out in Czechoslovakia and those parts of Yugoslavia formerly held by Austria, where there was no native nobility and the large landed estates were in the hands of a foreign aristocracy. In Poland a land reform was begun after the war, but it came to a halt in the thirties. In Hungary, with a native landowning aristocracy making up the ruling class, the great estates were left virtually intact. Reform was more extensive in Rumania, especially in Transylvania where Hungarian gentry owned the land. All these reforms favored the well-to-do peasants; the new (and old) smallholders were inadequately supplied with livestock, fertilizer, machines and credit, and went heavily into debt. In the depression of the thirties, agricultural prices fell more sharply than those of industrial products, the burden of debts and taxes increased, and the situation of the peasants became intolerable.

The backward state of agriculture pressed heavily on industry. Agrarian overpopulation and a steady influx of impoverished peasants and semi-proletarians kept down wages in the cities; peasant poverty prevented a rapid expansion of domestic markets. Industry, moreover, concentrated in the western part of Czechoslovakia and accustomed to work for Imperial Austria's large domestic market of fifty million inhabitants, was now cut off by the new frontiers and toll barriers. It was therefore especially hard hit by the depression. And as the most industrialized parts of Czechoslovakia were the border regions, inhabited by Sudeten Germans, mass unemployment and misery provided a fertile soil for the growth of the Nazi movement.

In the agrarian countries—Hungary, Rumania, Yugoslavia, Bulgaria—certain heavy industries, protected by the state and helped by foreign investments, made rapid advances. But this growth was inorganic, wages remained low, and the workers were heavily oppressed by the police regimes. A modern working class with a mode of life and outlook different from the peasantry existed only in the Czech lands, central and western Poland, central Hungary, and Slovenia.

Although the new Central European democracy was confronted from the beginning with huge obstacles, it would be a mistake to conclude that it lacked all means to surmount them.

There existed in its western half a labor movement with democratic traditions. Immediately following the First World War, large parts of this labor movement became radicalized. A large *Communist party* took shape in Czechoslovakia, and for a time Communist influence was strong in Yugoslavia, Bulgaria, and Poland. In their initial stages these Communist mass movements were an expression of simple discontent and social protest rather than of Bolshevik programs, tactics, and organization, which conflicted with the democratic and national traditions. The more the Russian leadership tried to bolshevize these parties, making them into docile instruments of Soviet policy, the more they lost ground among the people. In the early thirties, Social Democracy again had the support of the majority of Czechoslovak and Polish workers. The Czechoslovak Communist party was still able to muster a considerable vote, but its membership was declining, its position in the trade unions negligible, and its influence on the country's life small. Elsewhere the Communist parties were reduced to small and isolated underground groups.

Everywhere in Central Europe there also existed peasant movements of an essentially democratic character. In Czechoslovakia, the *Agrarians* were a leading party in a government coalition which included *Social Democrats*, Beneš Liberal party, and the *Democratic Catholics*. In Bulgaria, Poland, and Rumania, peasant parties held power for a short period, forming the core of the opposition to the subsequent reactionary regimes. In Hungary, the *Smallholders party*, kept down by the government, still carried the hopes of the impoverished peasants.

Moreover, in every country there was a liberal and democratic intelligentsia under the influence of Western ideas; though not very strong numerically, they exercised a large influence on culture and education.

These democratic forces were opposed by the big landowners, the reactionary wing of big business, by the extreme nationalists, and by the military bureaucracy. The task of the democratic forces, though difficult, was not in the end hopeless. What finally tipped the scales in favor of reaction were powerful influences from the outside.

The statesmen who helped create the belt of small, independent, and (as they hoped) democratic states between Germany and Russia, doubtless wished to set limits to German imperialism should it revive, and to Russian westward expansion should *it* revive. But this was possible only if Germany could be kept a democracy and integrated into the European community, and a democratic Russia could be brought to co-operate with the West. Both these hopes failed. When the Nazis overthrew the Weimar Republic and began their conquest of Europe; when Soviet Russia became a full-fledged totalitarian empire, Central Europe was bound once more to become a battlefield, its small states first the buffers between the contending powers and then the satellites of the victors. The "Central European problem" could be solved only as part of a general European solution.

Soviet Russia was the first power to disturb the precarious postwar balance. In 1919, in a moment of general panic after the defeat and partition of prewar Hungary, the Hungarian government handed power over to a small group of Communist agents. Lacking firm support in the country, the government of Bela Kun committed atrocities and engaged in adventures which quickly brought about its fall. The consequence was the installment of a military-aristocratic dictatorship that suppressed all the democratic forces in Hungarian society.

In 1920, the Bolsheviks, after repelling a Polish attack, tried to conquer Poland by military force. This attempt mobilized the Polish nation against them and strengthened the nationalist and military forces, which several years later in 1926 came to power by the *coup d'etat* of Marshal Pilsudski.

In 1923, when the Bulgarian democratic peasant movement of Alexander Stamboliski was struggling against the reactionary forces, the Communists remained neutral. But several months later they organized an uprising, followed by terroristic attempts, whose suppression led to the destruction of Bulgarian democracy. Yugoslavia, frightened by a strong though ephemeral wave of Communist influence, and torn by the internecine battles of its component national groups, first limited democratic rights in 1921 and then established the military dictatorship of King Alexander in 1929. Rumania followed a similar course. Thus, under the pretext of suppressing Communistic subversion and separatist trends in minority nations, democratic governments were replaced by reactionary dictatorships everywhere except in Czechoslovakia.

These regimes were certainly antidemocratic. But they were by no means fascist and totalitarian: genuine opposition parties were generally able to exist, even if they were heavily persecuted, and there were no totalitarian mass movements such as existed in Italy or Germany. Most of these regimes were dictatorships or semidictatorships of military-bureaucratic cliques, sometimes with a monarch at the top, maintained in power by big landowners and capitalist elements who feared to see democracy put an end to their privileges. Genuine fascist movements (which were usually overtly antisemitic), such as the Iron Guard in Rumania, the Arrow Cross in Hungary, and the Croatian Ustashi in Yugoslavia, often opposed these regimes; sometimes they were tolerated because they served to intimidate the democratic opposition.

All these regimes rested on a shaky base and were obliged to maneuver between contending social and national groups, to change their leadership periodically, and to make concessions to the opposition and sometimes to foreign opinion. Moreover, being extremely nationalistic, they were forever at each other's throats.

What saved them in the end from disintegration was the victory of Nazism in Germany in 1933. When Hitler came to power, the reactionary regimes began to court the Nazis and to divert German aggression towards their neighbors, in the hope of picking up some territorial spoils. At the same time, they strengthened their armies and police, and on the pretext that the nation was in danger increased the terror against the democratic opposition and non-German minorities. One of the easiest (and most profitable) ways of placating the Nazis was to mistreat the Jews, partly by officially expropriating and persecuting them, partly by tolerating violent antisemitic propaganda and rioting.

The Polish and Yugoslav regimes ended, after unsuccessful attempts to placate the Nazis, in the ranks of the Allies; those of Hungary, Rumania, and Bulgaria became, under compulsion, Hitler's satellites. All the satellites were unreliable; when the German hold weakened, they looked for an opportunity to break away. Rumanian and Bulgarian armies fought against Germany in the last months of the war; only the German occupation prevented the Hungarian government from concluding a separate peace and a part of its army capitulated in 1944; and in the same year the Slovak army took part in an anti-Nazi uprising.

The Jewish Communities Between the Wars

The Jewish situation in the inter-war period improved or worsened according to the rising and declining fortunes of liberal and democratic regimes. The period following the First World War was one of rosy hopes. The peace treaties guaranteed not only individual equality but also religious freedom, the free use of one's own language, and equality in education. Partly under pressure of international public opinion, partly because of democratic enthusiasm at home, these guarantees were embodied in the constitutions of the Central European states. Jews were now theoretically granted not only citizenship but equal rights, and theoretically had equal access to all schools, professions, and the civil service.

To what extent these rights were actually realized depended on two factors: the degree of democracy in the country, and the degree of Jewish cultural assimilation to the ruling nation.

In the western part of Central Europe, Jews now began to take a much more active part in public life. A new Jewish generation was educated in the native language and tradition. The Jewish intelligentsia shifted from a German to the new national cultural orientation, bringing to it a broader and more cosmopolitan outlook. Jews now played a prominent role in Czech and Hungarian, a modest but increasing role in Slovak and Croatian cultural life. Jews began to figure in the leadership of the liberal, democratic, Social Democratic, and also Communist parties. Last but not least, a rapidly increasing number of mixed marriages was an unmistakable sign of gradual assimilation.

The latter did not exclude increased tolerance of those Jews who refused to be assimilated and professed "Jewish nationality." The balance between majority and minority nationalities was often so precarious that the ruling nation had good reason to prefer "Jewish Jews" to those who swelled the ranks of the larger national minorities. Hebrew education and the Zionist movement were tolerated and sometimes favored even in countries where the majority of Jews considered themselves as being assimilated.

In the eastern part of this area, the participation of Jews in the life of the country was much smaller, social barriers were higher, and discrimination still rampant; but the Yiddish-speaking Jewish community developed a vital and various religious, cultural, and political life of its own. In the southeast, especially in Bulgaria, the Sephardic communities remained relatively cut off from their surroundings; but they were much influenced by Zionism and built up an elaborate structure of Hebrew educational and cultural institutions.

Everywhere, however, except in the western part of Czechoslovakia in the West and Bulgaria in the East, antisemitism was widespread. It had several sources. One was xenophobic nationalism. However assimilated Jews might be, they were still regarded as an unreliable "internationalist" element by extreme nationalists. Jews still speaking German were accused of exercising a "Germanizing influence." On the other hand, Slovaks and Carpatho-Ukrainians began to speak of "Czechs and Jews" as Czechs had spoken of "Germans and Jews" a generation earlier.

Another source was clerical. In Catholic antisemitism, old-fashioned religious prejudice was mixed with denunciations of Jewish atheists, liberals, and socialists who wished to "deprive the people of their Christian faith." Behind this lay the resentment of clerical groups seeing their influence wane in the secular atmosphere of democracy.

The middle-class and commercial character of the Jewish communities gave rise to an economically motivated antisemitism. Jews were accused of dominating economic life, and, through corruption, political and cultural life as well.

Socialism, Marxism, and Communism were increasingly depicted as Jewish conspiracies against the state, family, religion, and established social order. This was especially so in Hungary, where a number of commissars in Bela Kun's government had been Jewish, and in Poland, where Communism had some influence among Jewish workers and intellectuals.

The advent of Nazism brought racism with it. Except among the German minorities, however, it had no acceptance; in racist eyes the peoples of Central Europe themselves belonged to "inferior races" and "mongrel populations."

Although faced with many obstacles, the Jewish populations of Central Europe were able to take many strides forward. The general tendency in the western part seemed to be toward assimilation with the dominant nationality; and in the eastern part toward the development of a Jewish minority "nationality." But both of these "solutions of the Jewish question" were possible only under the conditions of democracy. When first Nazi and then Soviet imperialism overwhelmed Central Europe, all Jewish possibilites were destroyed.

Under the Nazi Yoke

Hitler's conquest of Central Europe began with the annexation of Austria in March 1938, followed by the Munich Pact in October, 1938, and the dismemberment of Czechoslovakia. Thus, the two most industrialized and potentially most democratic countries of Central Europe were in Nazi hands. The dictatorial regimes in the rest of the region tried to compromise with Hitler, and although two—the Polish and Yugoslav—in the end fought to preserve their independence, the Nazi conquest of Central Europe was relatively easy. In the late spring of1941, after a series of lightning campaigns, the entire area was under Nazi domination.

Strategically, the conquest of Central Europe and the Balkans was for the Nazis but a preparation for their great offensive against Russia and, ultimately, the Middle East. They exploited the region's economic resources and lines of transportation primarily for this purpose, postponing its "thorough reorganization" until after the war.

It was quite clear what the Nazis intended for Central Europe after the war. Already in the midst of the war they sought to exterminate the educated classes and transform large sections of the population into slave laborers. Plans were being prepared for the final elimination of the Czechs and Poles as ethnic units; parts of these peoples were to be dispersed and thoroughly Germanized, the rest deported and physically exterminated.

A national catastrophe much greater than any experienced in the past thus threatened the Central European nations. They were menaced not only by loss of their national independence and destruction of their culture, not only by the dispersion of their peoples, but also by sheer physical extermination. Not only the educated classes but also the free workers and independent peasants were marked for destruction.

All active elements of the population were aware of the danger in which they stood. In the first years of war, they were stunned by the rapid Nazi conquests and disorganized by Nazi terror. Knowing that they could not hope to overthrow the oppressor without outside help, they listened to London broadcasts and prayed for England's endurance and the entry of Russia and America into the war. When the tide began to turn, Central Europe became a cauldron seething with discontent and sabotage.

Except among the ethnic German minorities, the Nazi rulers had nowhere any significant popular support. The satellite regimes were hated by the people, maintaining their rule only with the help of German bayonets. Even among their leaders and supporters there were many prepared to desert at the first sign of German defeat. Even the "native" pro-fascist movements, made up of people who had considered themselves oppressed minorities before the war and who now enjoyed a fictive independence (like the Slovaks and Croats) were full of men ready to abandon the Germans whenever it would be profitable.

Only two of the satellites made substantial military contributions. Hungarian troops helped to attack Yugoslavia in 1941. Later, 150,000 fought in Russia, sustaining heavy losses and being withdrawn from the front to guard communications in the Ukraine. Rumania, claiming the province of Bessarabia, sent thirty divisions to fight against the Soviets in 1941-1944. It is interesting to note, however, that the same Rumanian army, in the same formations and under the same officers, fought with the Russians against the Germans after Rumania's capitulation to Russia in 1944, as did Bulgaria's satellite army after that country's capitulation.

On the other hand, exile armies, composed of refugees and emigrants, fought with the Allies against the Nazis all over the world. Polish flyers played a large part in the air defense of England; Polish and Czech troops distinguished themselves at Narvik, Tobruk, Montecassino, and Dunkirk, as well as in Russia. There were also army and navy units in the service of the Yugoslav and Greek governments-in-exile. Jews formed a considerable percentage of the exile soldiers. In some formations of the Czech army in exile, they probably were in the majority.

Nationalist as well as pro-Communist partisans waged guerilla warfare with increasing success in the mountains of Yugoslavia, Albania, and Greece. At the same time Polish and Ukrainian guerillas fought in the forests of eastern Poland, Wolhynia, eastern Galicia and the Ukraine. Their exploits, though less well-known than those of Tito, were by no means insignificant. In 1943 the Nazis admitted in secret documents that virtually all of Wolhynia was in the hands of Ukrainian nationalist partisans. The Poles organized an underground Home Government and Home Army; the latter, on August 1, 1944, took Warsaw in an uprising and fought off German attacks single-handed for two months. In September 1944 an uprising in Bánská Bystrica, in central Slovakia, involved numerous units of the Slovak satellite army and was suppressed only after weeks of fighting. In Prague, in May 1945, as in Paris in 1944, the uprising came only when Allied armies were approaching. But the American army under General Patton was ordered not to advance beyond the line agreed upon with Stalin, and the insurgents were left to the tender mercies of the Germans until the arrival of the Red Army.

At the same time the satellite governments were looking for an opportunity to jump off the German bandwagon. Rumanian, Bulgarian, and Hungarian emissaries were negotiating with the Allies. In August, 1944, Rumania's King Michael, in agreement with the leaders of the opposition parties, deposed and arrested the dictator Antonescu, then concluded an armistice which opened the Balkans to the Russian armies. A new Bulgarian government had already agreed to an armistice with the Western Allies. But the Soviet Union, until then at peace with Bulgaria, suddenly declared war, invaded Bulgaria and imposed a hand-picked government on it. Both Balkan countries now declared war on Germany, their armies advancing with the Russians into Serbia, Hungary, and Slovakia. The Hungarian government twice sought to capitulate; both attempts were thwarted by the Germans, who occupied the country with troops and arrested Regent Horthy. Even so, one army commander, General Miklos, succeeded in deserting to the Russians with his troops.

Both World Wars demonstrated that a strong foreign power can conquer Central Europe if the Central European nations are not united and effectively supported from outside. But the moment the oppressor is challenged from the outside, the nations of Central Europe will rise and help to overthrow him. They remain, at least so long as they are not destroyed as coherent ethnic units, a mighty revolutionary force.

The Jewish Catastrophe

The defeat of Nazism came in time to prevent the annihilation of the Czech and Polish peoples. But it came too late to save millions of European Jews. No appeal to economic and political expediency could stop or delay the massacre which Hitler considered "a matter of principle." Long before, the Führer had threatened that "in case of war" (the same he was actively preparing), the Jews would be exterminated. The decisions were made, plans prepared, preliminary measures of expropriation, isolation, and ghettoization taken, between 1938 and 1941. Mass extermination started in June 1941 when German armies, followed by special extermination squads, invaded the Soviet Union. Subsequently, death factories and gas chambers were established and the great massacre swept all Europe. Six million Jews were its victims.

Extermination was virtually complete in Czechoslovakia and Yugoslavia. Only a handful of Jews were able to save their lives by hiding underground or joining the partisans; relatively few were rescued from ghettos, concentration camps, and slave labor gangs by the advancing Allied armies. Some had, legally or illegally, left their countries in time; these returned with the Allied armies and exile governments. In this way 60,000 of the 360,000 Jews of Czechoslovakia and 15,000 of the 75,000 Jews of Yugoslavia were able to survive.

Of the Jews in Poland, a great part had lived in, or fled to, the Russian-occupied parts at the time of the Hitler-Stalin pact. Some found life so unsupportable that they tried to return to Nazi-occupied Poland, not suspecting that extermination awaited them in two or three years' time. Many were deported as laborers to eastern Russia before the Nazi-Soviet war started. But the great majority remained in eastern Poland until 1941. As the Russians took no special measures to evacuate the Jewish population, most of it was overtaken by the Nazi armies and subsequently exterminated. Nevertheless, several hundred thousand Jews fled to eastern and Asiatic Russia, joining those who had already been deported there. Those who survived the misery, starvation, cold, and hard labor, were allowed to return to Poland after the war. Most of these passed quickly on to the West or to Israel; those who stayed in Poland formed a part of its small postwar Jewish community.

In Hungary and Rumania, mass extermination started later, in the period when the Nazi defeats had already begun. It was slowed down by Allied threats of punishment, by the sabotage of satellite authorities, and even by negotiations with a few leading Nazis who were seeking to save their necks. Three hundred thousand Jews survived in Rumania, and 150,000 in Hungary. The Jewish community of Bulgaria, some 50,000 souls, survived persecution intact thanks to the resistance of virtually the entire Bulgarian nation.

But on the whole the slaughter of the Jews met with little resistance. The Nazis succeeded in isolating the Jews in ghettos and in disarming and starving them; they were terrorized by being held collectively responsible for every act of resistance. Under these conditions the Warsaw uprising of April 1943, and similar instances of collective and individual resistance in other ghettos and camps, were feats of almost supernatural heroism. These acts were doomed to remain isolated. The Nazis succeeded to a great extent in hiding the fact of extermination from the non-Jewish population and, until their turn came, from most of the victims as well. Extermination in the northern half of the area occurred at a time when the Nazis were advancing and resistance seemed hopeless. The fascist and collaborationist elements of the native population helped the Nazis to expropriate, deport, and murder Jews, whereas the majority of the population remained passive. There were examples of heroic sacrifices made in attempts to help the Jews, but they remained exceptions. And no relief came from the outside world. The Soviet government, which already had information about the mass extermination of Jews in 1941, did not publish it and glossed over the anti-Jewish character of German atrocities. Public opinion in the West found it hard to credit underground reports of crimes so lurid and immense.

President Roosevelt's declaration that war criminals would be held responsible for their crimes helped to retard and finally to stop the butchery in Hungary and the Eastern Balkans. But for most Russian, Ukrainian, Polish, Czech, Yugoslav (and German and Austrian) Jews, it was too late. The defeat of Hitler saved the bulk of the non-Jewish native populations; among the Jews, it saved only a small minority, but, as subsequent events showed, a minority of great vitality and recuperative power.

Postwar Hopes and Disillusions

The first period after the liberation from Nazi rule seemed to augur well. Once again, the nations of Central Europe seemed to be in a position to decide their own future. The reactionary, pro-fascist forces were hopelessly compromised by their capitulation to and collaboration with the Nazi foe. The military-bureaucratic dictatorships which had become German satellites collapsed with the downfall of Nazi Germany. No one was willing to defend the privileges of the big landowners or monopolistic cartels. The democratic parties of labor, peasantry, and the liberal intelligentsia were revived, having behind them the great majority of the population. The Communists, although considerably strengthened by their manipulation of the resistance movements, by the influence of the Soviet Union, and by the adherence of opportunist elements, were still everywhere in the minority and professed to respect democratic rules. Democracy seemed to be guaranteed by the international agreements made at Teheran, Yalta, and Potsdam, and by the power of the victorious Western democracies. The way seemed open to major social reforms, to be carried out peacefully and in a democratic fashion. Plans prepared by leaders of the governments-in-exile, and a certain rapprochement of the different nationalities in the common struggle against the Nazis at home, gave some hope that a way to the economic and political integration of Central Europe might be found.

All the countries of Central Europe adopted formally democratic constitutions. These, as well as the Teheran and Yalta agreements, guaranteed the civil rights of all, and "free and unfettered elections." The rights of national and religious minorities were set forth in many basic laws. Yugoslavia adopted a federal constitution. Czechoslovakia gave a *de facto* autonomy to the Slovaks.

The first postwar governments were coalitions and their first programs were relatively moderate. These called for a land reform which would have strengthened the independent peasantry, and for the nationalization of vital natural resources and major industrial enterprises. Protection, however, was promised to private property and initiative in other fields of economic life. Plans for economic reconstruction and industrialization were prepared, supposedly to be administered in a democratic way, under the control of democratic parliaments. A higher standard of living, social security, and free labor unions were promised to the working class. The economic system to be created was pictured as a kind of welfare state with a mixed economy, partly nationalized, partly private, and under democratic controls. The new regimes took the name of "people's democracy." This tautological title was interpreted as something different from the Soviet type of dictatorship, and was advertised in the West as a "synthesis of political and economic democracy." Economically, politically, and internationally, Central Europe was pictured as a "bridge between East and West."

National minorities were promised not only equal treatment, but also full freedom and autonomy for their communal and cultural life. Surviving Jews were to obtain, as a matter of course, full restitution of their Nazi-expropriated properties, and compensation for what they had been forced to endure. They were to enjoy equal civic rights, including complete religious freedom, and full opportunity to develop their culture and communal institutions. They were free to choose between joining the newborn Jewish nation in Palestine, or integrating themselves into the life of the Central European nations on the basis of complete equality and free cultural development. Antisemitism was not only to be outlawed and punished, but was to be completely extirpated at its social roots.

Six years later, nothing remained of these illusions. "People's democracy" was now identified with "proletarian dictatorship" in official theory, and with totalitarian slavery in ruthless practice. Coalition governments were everywhere replaced by Communist dictatorships. All non-Communist parties were liquidated, their leaders jailed, executed or driven into exile. Civil rights were completely abolished and the rule of law replaced by unmitigated terror. Urban middle classes were relentlessly expropriated and their remnants dispersed in slave labor camps. The peasantry groaned under the burden of forced deliveries, excessive taxation and steady threats of expropriation; continuous collectivization was transforming farmers into pauperized *kolkhoz* slaves. The labor unions were turned into organs of exploitation. Workers were mercilessly driven for long hours and a ruthless speed-up was introduced. At their back was a growing army of actual slaves, working in mines, on construction projects, and in concentration camps.

Cultural life was stifled and the intellectuals forced to serve as propagandists for the regime. A new class of Communist bureaucrats usurped all power, its members living in comparative luxury amid general misery. Free to suppress and punish, harass and exploit the rest of the population, they were themselves required to show complete subservience to Moscow. Never-ending purges suppressed not only every sign of actual or intended disobedience, but also every inclination toward independent thought or feeling. The entire area of Central Europe was reorganized and exploited according to Soviet Russian needs, becoming a Soviet colony. The "bridge between East and West" was transformed into a bulwark of aggressive Soviet power.

Jewish hopes collapsed with the destruction of democracy. The modest restitution claims of the Jews clashed, from the very beginning, with the vested interests of the nationalizing bureaucracy. Restitution laws were first sabotaged, then revised, and finally abolished. Those Jews who were able to establish private enterprises in the first years after the war were expropriated again in the subsequent waves of nationalization. Large sections of the Jewish population became unemployed and destitute, no effective effort being made to find work for them in the nationalized economy. Jewish welfare institutions and Jewish communal and cultural organizations, rebuilt with substantial help from abroad, were first taken over by the Communists and then either completely abolished, or transformed into organs of Communist propaganda. Antisemitism, nourished by new social antagonisms, sprang up again. Jews became a suspect minority, and vicious Soviet-sponsored campaigns against "Jewish nationalism" and "cosmopolitanism" reinforced antisemitic moods inherited from the past. The two democratic solutions of the Jewish question—organic integration of Jewish communities into the life around them, or cultural autonomy for a Jewish national minority—became impossible. Emigration, the only remaining way out, was either prohibited outright, or frustrated by bureaucratic regulations in several Central European states. In others, general exodus was the only way to Jewish survival.

Soviet Imperialism

The Sovietization of Central Europe was not the fruit of a domestic movement but the result of imperialistic pressure and conquest, aided and abetted by native Communist parties. To understand it we must understand something about the expansive force of Soviet totalitarianism.

Three decades before, the Bolsheviks had seized power as a small but disciplined minority, maintaining their dictatorial rule by an ever increasing terror. Their party claimed to represent the historical interests of the Russian working class, and also of all underprivileged classes and nations throughout the world. But it also taught that the masses by themselves could arrive only at a limited understanding of their "historical role." To fulfil that role the masses needed to be enlightened from the outside, to be led by a centralized, disciplined organization of professional revolutionaries. Having seized power, this organization, the Communist party, would exercise the dictatorship of the proletariat. It pretended that this was a "higher form of democracy"; but the dictatorship was of the proletariat in name only. From the beginning, the self-appointed "vanguard" substituted itself for the people; and inside its centralized organization, the centralized leadership soon usurped all power.

In the years of civil war and economic breakdown following the revolution, all democratic pretense was abandoned. The suppression of the non-Communist parties, complete abolition of civil liberties, merciless terror practiced against any opposition, originally rationalized as temporary wartime measures, became permanent features of the Soviet regime.

At the same time, the Communist "vanguard" changed its social character. In the absence of democratic controls, the nationalized economy supplied a solid basis for the absolute power of the new ruling class. A centralized hierarchy of commissars and administrators assumed control over the production and distribution of wealth, over economic as well as political and cultural life. Even the labor power of the entire population, who had to work in places and under conditions dictated by the rulers, was considered as belonging to the state. The state became the universal employer as well as omnipotent policeman, universal educator as well as supreme arbiter in matters of culture, science, art, and morals. It decided the conditions of work and standards of living of its subjects, as well as their opinions and tastes; how they lived and how they died.

The absolute power of the new ruling class found expression in its great economic privileges. Differences in income and living standards increased tremendously, the members of the ruling group living in luxury in the midst of general want. Advocacy of economic and social equality was proscribed and persecuted as "petty-bourgeois egalitarianism."

The urban middle classes were expropriated and their remnants exterminated. The great collectivization drive of the early thirties destroyed the independent peasantry. Millions of well-to-do or simply independent-minded farmers were deported and killed; the rest of the rural population were forced into kolkhozes to labor directly under the eye of the bureaucracy. The industrial workers, having lost the right to strike and to bargain for better conditions, having lost even their right to quit their jobs, were reduced to the status of industrial serfs. Finally, there was the ever increasing army of outright slave laborers, living and dying under the most inhuman conditions and replenished by repeated purges of suspect individuals and social and ethnic groups. In the second half of the thirties, the Great Purge, in which millions perished, was aimed at the elimination of all past, present or future, actual or potential, opponents of the regime, including members of the bureaucracy itself.

The "internal enemy" now seemed definitely liquidated, its very "social roots" destroyed. Yet the contradictions of Soviet society did not disappear. On the contrary, they were sharpened.

Despite all planning, tremendous disproportions appeared in the Soviet economy. A rational development of resources and a reconciliation of the interests of different social groups were impossible under a regime which could not tolerate free discussion, correction of mistakes and abuses by the pressure of an independent public opinion, and democratic bargaining among different groups. Mistakes in planning swelled to colossal proportions; wastage and duplication took place on an immense scale. Errors and abuses could not be corrected by the singling out of scapegoats. The existence of a privileged class possessed of unlimited power bred an immense parasitism. In an all-pervading atmosphere of terror, initiative became dangerous and unquestioning bureaucratic routine the safest course. The apparatus of suppression and terror placed an unbearable burden on the economy. The purges, by removing skilled workers and administrators, disrupted production and administration. In spite of every effort to sweat the working class, its productivity remained low. The Soviet economy was plagued by chronic shortages of consumers' goods, raw materials, machines, skilled workers and technicians, and labor power in general.

Until the thirties, each new crisis was weathered by expropriating still another economic group, and by increasing the degree of exploitation of the workers in the nationalized "sector." But the completion of collectivization left no one and nothing to expropriate, and there was a limit to what could be wrung out of the population by the speed-up and forced labor. However, many of the resources lacking in the Soviet Union were available in foreign countries—if the countries could be organized and exploited in the Soviet way. Across the border were raw materials and machines for Soviet industries; stocks of goods which could be transported to Russia to relieve acute shortages; whole industries which could be made to work for Soviet needs. There were skilled workers and technicians who coud be sent to Russia or forced to work for it at home. There was room for "social engineering," which would yield, in addition to material goods, new recruits for the army of forced labor.

From the Soviet point of view, the exploitation even of such relatively poor countries as Poland or Rumania promised rich returns, and the east German, Czechoslovak, and Hungarian factories seemed a veritable treasure trove of industrial power. Once in possession of the territory, manpower, armies, and economic resources of Central Europe, the rulers of the Soviet Union could hope to expand still farther into the European and Asiatic continents. Exploitation of foreign countries thus promised to solve many economic problems which the Soviet regime could not solve at home.

But expansion was a political necessity as well. Now fully established, the totalitarian order created social conditions which could not stand comparison with those of Western countries. Although the "internal enemy" was now liquidated, the promise of a better life could not be kept. While Communist theoreticians proclaimed that Russia, after having achieved socialism, was now entering the "higher stage of Communist society," which had always been envisaged as an economy of abundance, the majority of the population continued to live in squalid poverty. In this situation, the Soviet ruling class could explain the failures of the Soviet regime only by laying them at the door of "capitalist encirclement"; all social evils were blamed on foreign powers and their agents. Dictatorship and terror, the state power itself—supposed to "wither away" in the "higher stage of communism"—were necessary to defend the country against imminent danger from the world outside. An atmosphere of fear and crisis, of life-and-death struggle, was assiduously created. Free international intercourse, the free exchange of information and opinion were a threat to the dictatorship; an Iron Curtain guarding Soviet subjects against contact with the rest of the world had to be erected. And as long as freedom existed anywhere in the world, the dictatorship was in peril; in the eyes of the Soviet masters, the world could not long endure half totalitarian and half free.

The rulers of the Soviet Union could not admit that economic and social realities might set limits to their power to manipulate human life. Nothing seemed impossible to a group which concentrated all economic, political and social power in its hands, which felt that it could change not only social conditions, but also human nature and even past history. Believing themselves to be the agents and heirs of "historical necessity," proclaiming that "cadres decide everything"—i.e., all problems could be solved by administrative organization and the manipulation of social groups—the Soviet rulers grew vainglorious to an extent scarcely matched in history. Their system was not only superior to any other in the world, but the "new Soviet man" produced by it was superior to all other human beings. The Soviet superman was convinced of his "civilizing mission," which was to introduce the Soviet order everywhere, to "liberate" the world by transforming it into a totalitarian empire ruled from Moscow.

The Revival of Russian Nationalism

This conviction led to a revival of Russian nationalism. The Soviet regime had never succeeded in welding its numerous nationalities and ethnic groups into one nation. The promise of the right of self-determination for national minorities was not kept. Although their national aspirations for the most part went no further than a desire for local and cultural autonomy, and took the form of an appreciation of local history, traditions and folklore, these were considered dangerous to the rule of Moscow and persecuted with increasing violence. Purges in the thirties of "bourgeois nationalists," including many thousands of local Communist leaders, destroyed whole generations of the minorities' intelligentsia. The rights of the minorities were finally reduced to one of using their own language to parrot the official Moscow line and praise the leader Stalin. When sections of the minority population were deemed to have been unreliable during the Second World War, even the pretense of equality was dropped. The Russians were proclaimed by Stalin to be the "most outstanding" of the peoples of the Soviet Union. Their superiority was read back into the pre-Communist past. All men, movements and events which had contributed to the expansion of the Russian empire throughout the ages were now considered "progressive," and all those who had opposed it, "reactionary." Russians had always carried a higher civilization to their neighbors, had always defended the just cause, had always marched in the vanguard of mankind. All the great discoveries and inventions had been made by Russians. Anything less chauvinist than this was branded as "cosmopolitanism," identical with treasonable service to foreign imperialism.

The Jews, belonging to a group with world-wide cultural and emotional ties, internationalist traditions, and a Western cultural outlook, were charged with cosmopolitanism and bourgeois nationalism in the same breath. In fact, Jewish nationalism was stigmatized as a branch of cosmopolitanism, and in the postwar purges "rootless cosmopolitan" became virtually a synonym for "Jew." The complete destruction of all Jewish organizations and cultural life in the Soviet Union was followed by a purge of Jewish party leaders, officials, and intellectuals—the higher echelons of party and government were "cleansed" of Jews.

In foreign policy, the original Bolshevik idea of world revolution was transformed to suit the needs of Soviet expansion. When Stalin proclaimed, in the twenties, that Russia by its own efforts could achieve "socialism in one country," he did not renounce the thought of imposing this "socialism" on the rest of the world. He reiterated many times that the existence of two social systems in the world made a final clash inevitable, the building of socialism in the Soviet Union being simply a preparatory stage for this struggle. But the content of the words "socialism" and "world revolution" had changed. "Socialism" now meant the exploitation of society by a hierarchic bureaucracy wielding absolute economic, political, and social power. And "world revolution" signified the extension of this rule to take in the world.

To the leadership of the "Socialist Fatherland" Communists everywhere owed undivided allegiance. The victory of the theory of "socialism in one country" ushered in a period of "bolshevization" of Communist parties abroad that transformed them into tools of Soviet foreign policy. Communist policies were moderate one day, ultra-radical the next; revolutionary in one country, counter-revolutionary in another; now "patriotic," and now openly subversive, according as the winds of Moscow blew. Blind obedience to Russia was the first tenet of Stalinist theory; the world rule of the Soviet Union, the final goal.

Preparation for Expansion

As the Second World War approached, the Soviet Union prepared to re-enter upon the world scene. The liquidation of every independent class and possible opposition made this possible, the growing inner conflicts of totalitarian society made it desirable.

The struggle between Nazi Germany and the Western democracies provided the opportunity. Until then the Bolshevik leaders had been haunted by the nightmare of the non-Communist world uniting against them. In their foreign policy they had sought to foment and utilize dissensions among the different powers. Since 1922 they had been conspiring with the Reichswehr and lending their support to the secret rearmament of Germany. The disastrous policies of the German Communists, which contributed so much to the victory of Hitler in Germany, had been laid down in Moscow in the expectation that a Nazi assumption of power would lead to a conflict among the "imperialists." When the danger arose that Hitler would attack not the West but Russia, everything was done to secure Western aid to Russia through "collective security." But when

Hitler signified his readiness to negotiate an arrangement with Stalin, Litvinov's speeches about collective security abruptly ceased. With the Hitler-Stalin pact of August 1939, the Soviet Union entered the international arena as a full-fledged imperialist power.

The Hitler-Stalin pact was a typically imperialist one by which Russia, in one year, annexed the Ukrainian and White Russian provinces of Eastern Poland, occupied and then incorporated into itself the Baltic states, and forced Rumania to surrender Bessarabia and north Bukovina. It also sought to subjugate Finland. The Nazi-Soviet pact ended, as it was born, in a fight for imperialist spheres of influence. Russia's demands concerning the Danube region, Bulgaria, and the Turkish straits made further collaboration between Stalin and Hitler difficult. Behind these disagreements was of course each partner's understandable fear that the other was waiting for a suitable moment to cut his throat.

Stalin planned to snatch up Europe after Germany and the Western powers exhausted themselves in their war against each other. Hitler's onslaught forced him into a coalition with the Western powers, but his plans for Soviet expansion remained unchanged.

Even during the worst days of the Russo-German war, when German troops stood under the walls of Leningrad, Moscow and Stalingrad, the Soviets did not cease to claim southern Finland, the Baltic countries, eastern Poland and Bessarabia as integral parts of their territory, and Central Europe and the Balkans as their sphere of influence.

All wartime Soviet policies served to prepare for the future conquest of Central Europe. The first step was to isolate, compromise and break up Western-oriented exile governments and armies, and to destroy non-Communist resistance groups. After the Nazi invasion of Russia, it was discovered that 10,000 Polish officers had been massacred in the forest of Katyn. The Polish army of General Anders, recruited on Soviet soil, was sabotaged and finally had to leave Russia via Iran. The Polish government-in-exile, a coalition of democratic and nationalist parties, was denounced as "fascist," another Polish government being organized in Russia by Soviet agents. Polish demands for investigation of the Katyn murders were the pretext for breaking diplomatic relations with the London Polish government. Finally, an uprising of the underground Polish Home Army in August 1944 was allowed to burn itself out, the Red Army standing passively by at the gates of Warsaw.

In the same way, the Red Army allowed the Germans to crush the Slovak uprising of September 1944. Only a Czech brigade of parachutists was flown in—and left to perish in the struggle. The Czech Eastern Army, hastily organized in 1941 from prisoners and refugees working in slave labor camps, was bled white in the Carpathians. The Czechoslovak government-in-exile was forced to forswear co-operation with the Poles; before being allowed to return home it was "reorganized" in Moscow according to Communist wishes.

In Yugoslavia, Albania and Greece, Communist partisans, supplied with weapons by the Western Allies, neglected no opportunity to weaken, attack and, wherever possible, destroy Western-oriented or independent guerilla groups. The Yugoslav and Greek governments-in-exile were denounced as monarcho-fascist regimes and a revolt in the Greek navy was used for Communist purposes.

An interesting feature of Soviet policy was the care taken to frustrate all projects for a Central European federation or system of alliances. The Czech and Polish governments-in-exile agreed upon a federation with common parliamentary, executive, and economic organs. Similar negotiations were proposed between the exile Greeks and Yugoslavs. The broader idea of a Balkan federation also found much support. But all these plans were countermanded by Stalin. The Soviets insisted on absolute "national sovereignty." "Divide and rule" remained the watchword of Soviet imperialism. When, later, Tito and Dimitrov sought to promote a Communist Balkan federation, Stalin also put a stop to this. Any direct dealing among the satellites was treasonable; everything had to be cleared through Moscow.

Patterns of Conquest

At Teheran and Yalta, America and England recognized the right of the Soviet Union to secure its frontiers and to surround them by friendly, democratic governments which would respect legitimate Soviet interests and cooperate with Russia.

There was a fundamental ambiguity in these terms. By friendly governments, Western public opinion understood regimes which would not attack Russia and would cooperate with her; Russia meant regimes completely subservient to Moscow. By democratic governments the West meant administrations freely elected by, and responsible to the people, parliamentary rule and civil rights; the Russians meant the "higher democracy" of the Soviet regime. Economic cooperation meant for the Allies mutually profitable agreements; the Soviets understood it as exploitation of the entire area according to Soviet needs. Cultural collaboration meant in the West an exchange of cultural goods; in the East the acceptance of the Soviet and the liquidation of the "bourgeois" culture. Finally, "security" was, for the Soviet mind, attainable only after a complete social transformation and the extermination of any possible opposition. This was done when the Soviets "secured their borders" by annexing the Baltic countries, eastern Poland, and Bessarabia. This had now to be achieved in the entire area of Central Europe.

The Communist leadership in Moscow understood that Central Europe could not be profitably exploited and integrated into the Soviet order without reducing its higher living standards to something near the Russian level; that the population would necessarily resist such a reduction; and that new national movements would arise to combat imperialist exploitation. Only the complete suppression of freedom and thoroughgoing Sovietization of Central Europe could prevent this.

Sovietization began immediately after the liberation. Already in 1945, the situation was less hopeful than it appeared on the surface. The democratic constitutions remained largely dead letters. Many national, social and political groups were denied civil and political rights from the very beginning; others were afraid to assert them for fear of economic and police reprisals. People had seen the atrocities committed by the Red Army, witnessed how disobedient citizens were spirited away by illegal and semilegal Communist organizations, never to be seen again. Under German rule, everybody had to conform to some degree; now he could be accused of "collaboration" and destroyed if he failed to satisfy the Communists in any particular. Everybody trembled before the tremendous and omnipresent Soviet power. Democratic institutions served only as a cover for the all-pervasive terror.

The postwar coalitions were shot-gun marriages forced upon the democratic parties by the Russians with the acquiescence of the Western Allies. Non-Communist kings, presidents, and premiers were often only stalking horses for Communist vice premiers or ministers of the interior wielding the real power. Non-Communist parties were infiltrated by Communist agents and pro-Communist factions. Holding the key positions in the army, police, intelligence, propaganda service, central planning agencies, land reform offices, and labor unions, the Communists from the very beginning enjoyed far more power than appearances indicated.

Still, democratic forces in some measure continued to exist. Wherever relatively free elections were held, the anti-Communist parties carried the day, sometimes with overwhelming majorities. In agricultural countries the traditional peasant parties enjoyed the support of the great majority of the peasant population. The Social Democratic parties showed a desire to rid themselves of Communist-imposed leaderships. The popularity of Soviet Russia declined as people made the acquaintance of the Red Army and Soviet secret police. Nowhere could the native Communists come to power without the exertion of direct pressure by Soviet Russia.

It should not be forgotten that the Soviet march on Sofia was required to install the Communist-dominated Fatherland Front government in Bulgaria in September 1944. The direct intervention of Vishinsky, supported by the Russian army of occupation, and not a popular uprising, brought Groza's cabinet to power in Rumania in March 1945. Every step toward the Sovietization of Hungary was supported by threats of Marshal Voroshilov and direct interventions of the Soviet occupation power. The Polish pro-Communist regime was brought to Lublin and later to Warsaw by Soviet troops; the installation of Soviet Marshal Rokossovsky as virtual dictator of Poland took place in the shadow of Red Army bayonets. Only direct orders from Moscow prevented, in 1947, the acceptance of Marshall plan aid by Czechoslovakia and Poland. The Czechoslovak Communist coup of February 1948 was conducted under the command of the Soviet Deputy Minister of Foreign Affairs, Valerian Zorin.

No event did more to rouse the Western world from its ignorance and torpor concerning Central Europe than the Communist coup in Czechoslovakia, the most Westernized, advanced, and democratic country in the satellite area. But developments in Czechoslovakia did not differ essentially from those in other satellite countries.

Looking back, we are struck by the fact that substantially the same story was repeated in all the satellite countries. In the beginning, the Communists were everywhere a minority, often a small minority, and were not able to seize power alone. Soviet pressure was therefore exerted from Prague to Sofia to establish coalition governments, in which the Communists obtained the major positions of power: army, police, propaganda and education, and control of the offices for the expropriation and redistribution of property. Some of the democratic leaders were allowed to serve as figureheads in the government, and non-Communist partners in the coalition were allowed a limited freedom of expression and organization. But "enemies of the people" were denied all political and civil as well as the most elementary human rights from the start; the Communist leaders dominating the police and propaganda machines alone decided who the "enemies of the people" were. Together with authentic fascists, anti-Communist democrats were liquidated as "traitors" and "collaborators." Some national minorities were expropriated and expelled *en masse*. Individual citizens and entire political and social groups were terrorized into submission and collaboration by threats of being charged with "pro-fascism" or "antisocial behavior." Refusal to continue to collaborate with the Communists meant ultimate suppression. Continuing to collaborate meant accepting Communist dictation and abetting the suppression of other democratic groups. The democratic politicians who collaborated with the Communists thus became the latter's political prisoners. Step by step they were forced to dig their own graves.

Finally, the democratic coalition parties were eliminated by the "discovery" of "subversive plots" in their ranks; either they were outlawed right off, or, after purges of "unreliable" members, captured by Communist agents. It made little difference thereafter whether they were forced to merge with the Communist party, or were maintained as Soviet fronts.

The Communists were able to paralyze their adversaries, partly by intimidation, partly by promising them they would be spared if they did not oppose the liquidation of someone else. Thus the Communists destroyed the democratic opposition piecemeal.

The Social Transformation

The economic and social transformation of Central Europe followed a similar pattern. By nationalizing the big industries, transportation, banks and foreign trade and seizing the key positions for themselves, the Communists were able to establish their monopolistic control over the economy. Political and economic power was thus concentrated in the hands of one group. A new bureaucracy came into being wielding despotic power over industry, as well as over government and administration. The individual was placed at the mercy of this bureaucracy in every respect: on it he depended for his job, his wage, apartment, life itself.

The creation of the new bureaucratic class went faster and smoother in the satellite countries than in Soviet Russia thirty years before. The higher general level of education provided a larger reservoir from which to recruit bureaucrats than the Russian Bolsheviks had been able to draw upon. Under the old governments men had acquired experience as officials in the labor unions, cooperatives, municipal administrations and, not least, in the Communist apparatus. There was also an unemployed or underemployed intelligentsia which lent a ready ear to the spiritual and material blandishments of Stalinist state power. From the very beginning, great economic privileges were accorded those ready to serve the new masters. Communist administrators shamelessly possessed themselves of high salaries, luxurious homes, and big automobiles.

Until 1947-48, in the period when the Communist bureaucracy was occupying the most important points of political and economic power, other classes were neutralized by transitory concessions, as well as by false promises of economic security. Once the new ruling class was firmly in the saddle, the socio-economic transformation of the satellite countries entered a new stage. All pretense that people's democracy was different from the Soviet type of dictatorship was dropped, and all classes of society were brought under totalitarian control.

The urban lower middle classes were the first victims. At the beginning, they had been allowed to keep their property and to engage in small business. Those who behaved themselves were even allowed to share in the distribution of the expropriated properties of the "collaborators" and expelled minorities. Small entrepreneurs, business men, artisans, many of them Jews, made a considerable contribution to postwar recovery, organizing the exchange of commodities and rebuilding the smaller industries. Now, a new wave of expropriations cut the ground from under them. No adequate measures were taken to provide work for those who had been expropriated. Deprived of their livelihood, finding no place in the new economy, discriminated against because of their origin, the expropriated "petty bourgeois" were forced to engage in marginal, semilegal, or illegal economic activities, or to live off the sale of what remained of their belongings. A minority found work as manual workers in factories or as white-collar employees. The rest formed a "surplus population," slowly dying of starvation. Many were jailed for economic offenses. Finally, in 1951, thousands were deported to concentration and slave labor camps. Considered "unproductive" and "parasitic," these remnants of the middle classes, with a relatively large percentage of Jews in their ranks, were a favorite target for antisemitic demagogy.

At the same time, a new offensive was launched against the peasants, many of whom supported or tolerated the new regime because of the land it had given them. This land came from two chief sources. In countries where there had been no substantial land reform between the World Wars, the main source was the distribution of the large landed estates of the aristocracy. In countries where there had been a land reform, even middling estates were now divided up, much of the land, however, being simply taken from other peasants—members of expelled minorities or "collaborators." Not all the land was distributed: forests, pastures, and tracts of arable land were kept in the possession of the state. The available land fund was often insufficient to create viable farms for the numerous claimants. In Hungary, a substantial number of claimants received no land at all. And the new farms were often so small that they could not, without a more intensified system of cultivation, support the families of the new owners. All the means of agricultural improvement—machines, fertilizers, credits—now lay in the hands of the state. Peasant marketing and credit cooperatives, dominated by the Communists, were used to force the peasants to obey the state.

The urban economy, forced to deliver an ever increasing part of its product to Soviet Russia and to invest huge sums in armaments and heavy industry, could not satisfy the peasants' demand for consumer goods. The prices of agrarian commodities fell far below the level of industrial prices and the peasants were forced to deliver the major part of their crops at fixed prices in devaluated money. This, and insecurity of tenure, weakened incentives for higher production. Throughout the postwar years there were repeated crop failures and near-famine conditions, not only in Czechoslovakia and Poland, but even in Hungary and Rumania, once the breadbaskets of Central Europe. The Communists answered with increased pressure, expropriations of "saboteurs," liquidations of "kulaks," and accelerated collectivization. Although the "voluntary" character of collectivization was stressed in official resolutions, and "excesses" of bureaucratic zeal were sometimes condemned, there is no doubt that collectivization was being pushed by a combination of economic pressure and outright violence. The aim of Communist agrarian policies was clearly to reduce the peasants to agricultural laborers working in kolkhozes under direct supervision of the government. The peasants, knowing this, opposed the Communist regime by every passive means. In countries with a tradition of rural antisemitism their dissatisfaction often took an antisemitic form.

The industrial workers also became victims of totalitarian enslavement. In the first years after the war, when their support was needed to overcome the resistance of other social groups, they were granted higher wages and preferential rations protecting them from the worst consequences of inflation. Social security services were introduced where none had existed before, and labor unions were organized. More educational opportunities were offered to workers, and also opportunities for individual advancement into the new administrative class.

The workers were told that the factories were their "common property." Now that they were working "for themselves," they were admonished to work harder. But the furious tempo of industrialization, expensive apparatus of repression, administrative mismanagement, bureaucratic luxury, and steadily mounting Soviet demands left no room for an improvement of their living standards. Quite the contrary, the tendency was to depress standards to the Soviet level.

The hours of work were increased, many holidays abolished, and the working without pay of endless "voluntary shifts" was required. On top of this, workers were asked to make increasing "voluntary contributions" to all kinds of organizations. Payment by the piece and premium systems replaced payment by the hour. Minimum output norms were introduced everywhere and periodically revised upwards. "Socialist competition" served to stimulate output without regard to the danger to health and life—but the higher the records set, the higher general norms were raised. Paid vacations, social security benefits, and the visiting of health resorts were transformed into rewards for output records, informing and servility. Protests against bureaucratic privilege were punished as "counterrevolutionary agitation." The right to strike was virtually abolished. When the workers tried to defeat the speedup by passive resistance, job-changing and absenteeism, they were punished individually and collectively. Labor service was introduced for the working-class youth; compulsory assignments to jobs became frequent. Far from being master of the factories, the working class was reduced to a "living inventory," a mere means of production, learning in consequence to hate their "socialist" bosses.

The situation is well—if cautiously—described in an article (October 25, 1951) in the Prague magazine *Tvorba* by F. J. Kolar, Communist Party secretary in the mine district of Moravska Ostrava:

> Equalization of wages—this expression of petty-bourgeois and Social Democratic tendencies—became the main topic of conversation in the mines. Wrong and obnoxious comparisons of wages and salaries and petty criticisms of managers' automobiles influence the relations of some workers to the technical intelligentsia. . . . The complicated economic, political and ethnic conditions in Ostrava. . . . nourish Czech and Polish bourgeois nationalism, and a chauvinistic and racist attitude towards Slovaks and Gypsies.

These conditions were general in Central Europe and there is little doubt that they also bred antisemitism.

An army of forced laborers was created in all the satellite countries. Laws modelled on the Soviet example gave the authorities power to deport "unreliable" and "antisocial" elements by mere administrative decision. The forced labor camps were first filled with men suspected or guilty of opposition to the regime. These were soon joined by members of suspect social or ethnic groups. Terror, first used against political opponents, actual or potential, and against "hostile" national minorities, was now brought to bear against whole social classes. Expropriated members of the middle classes were deported as "profiteers," "speculators," or simply "unproductive elements"; well-to-do or independent peasants, as "kulaks"; recalcitrant workers, as "shirkers" and "saboteurs of socialist discipline"; independent-minded intellectuals, as "nationalists," "Westerners," or "cosmopolitans." The year 1951 saw mass deportations of such elements, among them many thousands of Jews, from Hungarian and Rumanian cities.

The situation was further complicated by a rift in the ranks of the Communist ruling class. After achieving absolute power, the native Communist bureaucracy found itself in a difficult position. On one hand, it could now exploit its own nation unopposed. On the other hand, it was more than ever dependent on Moscow. Russia's interests clashed with the most basic interests of its satellites. The latter were required to deliver goods to Russia at Soviet-dictated prices, and to trade with the rest of the world, and even among themselves, only under Russian supervision. They were required to pay Russia every kind of tribute and to allow "mixed" companies under complete Soviet control to exploit their natural resources. They had to produce what Russia needed and to revise their economic plans according to Soviet wishes. Soviet instructors, advisers, officers, and commissars had to be given unquestioning obedience. The satellites, in short, were forced to ruin their economies and depress living standards to the Russian level.

Native bureaucrats, because they must wring an increasing tribute from their countrymen, were more and more hated by them—but all attempts to moderate Soviet demands made them suspect in Soviet eyes. Is it any wonder, then, that the satraps dreamed of independence?

For special geographical and historical reasons, Tito's government in Yugoslavia was able to resist Moscow's demands. The Yugoslavs had always tried to keep a little more freedom for themselves within the Soviet empire. But the Kremlin, growing impatient, confronted them with an ultimatum. Capitulation meant destruction. Very much against their original intention, the Yugoslav Communists broke with Moscow. Thanks to the growing strength of the democratic West, Moscow was unable to attack Yugoslavia with troops; its economic pressures were withstood with the economic help of the West. Yugoslavia, remaining a Communist and totalitarian dictatorship, nevertheless shook off the foreign Soviet yoke.

For the reasons cited, Titoist tendencies existed in some degree in every satellite country. Tito's defiance strengthened them, and Moscow immediately started a campaign of preventive extermination. Beginning in 1948, one purge followed another and hundreds of thousands were expelled from Communist parties. "Titoist conspiracies" were discovered everywhere. High Communist leaders, such as Laszlo Rajk in Hungary, Koci Xoxe in Albania, and Traicho Kostov in Bulgaria, were arrested, forced to confess, and executed. Others, like the Greek guerilla General Markos and Lucretiu Patrascanu in Rumania, disappeared without a trace. The old Bulgarian Communist leaders, Georgi Dimitrov and Vasil Kolarov, died under suspicious circumstances. Wladyslaw Gomulka in Poland and Vlado Clementis in Czechoslovakia were demoted and arrested. In 1951, with the demotion and arrest of Rudolf Slánský, the purge took a new turn. His fall was the signal for the great anti-Semitic campaign mentioned at the beginning of this introduction.

All victims of the purge were accused of "bourgeois nationalism," "cosmopolitanism," "subservience to Western imperialism," and "striving to reintroduce capitalism"; from these ideological sources, crimes of espionage, sabotage and treason were said to have flowed. New ethnic minorities now became suspect: settlers of Yugoslav origin were deported from the border regions of Hungary and Rumania; Turks were expropriated and expelled from Bulgaria. All men who had been in Western exile, who had friends or relatives beyond the Iron Curtain, who were attached to or showed an interest in Western culture, were suspected of "bourgeois" and "Titoist" nationalism and trembled for their lives. Groups linked by origin, nationality, religion, spiritual outlook or any of the ties of human sympathy or solidarity with people outside the Soviet orbit, were especially suspect. Such is the background against which we must analyze the fate of Central Europe's Jews.

New Roots of Antisemitism

Communist theory had promised to solve the "Jewish question" once and for all by eliminating the social roots of antagonism between Jews and non-Jews. In a socialist society, there would be no class or national antagonisms, no hatred for any ethnic, religious or racial groups, and no need for scapegoats. Once the "abnormal economic composition" of the Jewish community was abolished, Jews would merge, as equal citizens, with the peoples around them. The final solution was assimilation, but this assimilation was to be a voluntary one, and for a transitory period the Jews were promised a free rein to develop their cultural and communal traditions and institutions.

Instead, the Soviet system stimulated, as we have seen, new social antagonisms and new tensions among national and ethnic groups. Far from removing the social causes of antisemitism, the new regime created them apace. These tensions were not relieved but rather sharpened by the fact that the Nazis had already expropriated all and exterminated most of the Jewish population.

The first upsurge of the new antisemitism was connected with the problem of restitution. The Jews had been expropriated by the Nazis, not only the "big capitalists" but everyone—down to widows living off their pensions; not only large enterprises were seized, but also small shops, homes, furniture, clothing, wedding rings, and even eyeglasses and dental fittings. The survivors emerged completely destitute from concentration camps and hiding places, many of them half starved, their health destroyed, clothed in rags, and with no means whatsoever of subsistence. They had a claim against the state for compensation and for restitution of as much of their property as could be identified. This claim was recognized in laws adopted by all the Central European countries. Of course, in the case of big enterprises, Jewish claims of ownership were superseded by that of the state, according to the laws of nationalization generally adopted in Eastern Europe. But at the time, small businesses, as well as homes, apartments, and personal belongings, were still private property. Their Jewish owners claimed no special privilege but only the right to repossess their property and enjoy it in the same way their neighbors possessed and enjoyed their property.

They met with resistance from two quarters. The "custodians" of Jewish property (who had acquired it either directly under the Nazis, or indirectly when the first German "Aryanizers" were in their turn expropriated and expelled after the war); the peasants holding former Jewish farms; the artisans and businessmen in possession of former Jewish shops; the people living in former Jewish apartments or who had undertaken to hide Jewish money or jewels—all had grown accustomed to thinking of the property as their own. Now they were shocked to see some survivors appear. It was from their midst that the infamous cry arose that Hitler should have been allowed more time to finish the job of extermination. As this group was numerous, the Communists and some of the opposition parties sought to woo their favor by confirming them in their possession of Jewish property. Thus it came about that the various governments sabotaged and then finally rejected Jewish claims to restitution of such properties, tolerating antisemitic agitation in this connection.

But a more formidable opponent of restitution was the well-entrenched Communist bureaucracy. It already considered all the property of the nation its own. Jews, however well founded their claims might have been in the law as it then stood, were considered "looters of national property" aiming at the "subversion of the socialist order" and "reintroduction of capitalist exploitation."

In Czechoslovakia, where in that period there still was a relatively free press, this struggle can be followed in detail. The study of Czechoslovakia shows how the restitution claims of Jews were denied on the pretext that they were "German" or "Hungarian"; how the bureaucracy sabotaged restitution proceedings; how Communist-led unions forced workers to strike against court decisions; how claimants were terrorized into abandoning their claims; and how restitution laws were finally revised in such a way as completely to destroy their force.

But here we are concerned with something more important than legal claims and disputed property: with the passions this clash generated. It was in connection with restitution that the Czech Communist deputy Kapoun declared in 1947 that one "cannot trust Jewish patriotism," adding that "the pot in which food once spoiled stinks even if it has been thoroughly scoured." The Communist Minister of Information Václav Kopecký spoke of Carpatho-Russian Jews as "these bearded Solomons," this "Jewish scum." An official organ of the Ministry of Education declared that the capitalists in Czechoslovakia had always been of foreign—Jewish—origin, and factory meetings adopted resolutions thanking the government for liberating them, through nationalization, "from Jewish and German exploiters." When the Jewish communities protested against a strike preventing restitution of a Jewish factory, the Central Union Council, headed by the Communist leader Antonín Zápotocký, warned "citizens of the Jewish faith" that "they would be committing the gravest possible error" if they joined the ranks of the "enemies of united labor." Four years later, the same Zápotocký, now Premier of Czechoslovakia, recalled the incident during the purge of the Jewish party leader Rudolf Slánský and other Communist "cosmopolitans," and spoke about Jewish capitalists and interference from Jerusalem in words scarcely different from those of antisemites. Now the charge of attempting to restore capitalism was preferred against high Communists of Jewish origin.

If the conflicts around restitution revived old and generated new antisemitic moods, the subsequent expropriation of the lower middle classes did nothing to mitigate them. On the contrary, expropriated Jews were hated even more by the antisemites. Forced to live by selling what personal possessions they had left and by marginal economic activities, the members of the surplus Jewish population were denounced as "black-marketeers," "shirkers," "unproductive elements" and "disrupters of the socialist economy." Those expropriated middle-class Jews who went to work in the factories were regarded as unwelcome competitors, especially if thanks to their education they advanced to supervisory or white-collar positions. Workers selected Jewish managers or supervisors as special targets of their wrath; peasants blamed their misery on "Jewish commissars" and "Jewish black-marketeers"; the bureaucrats, themselves resentful of Jewish colleagues, tried to divert the hate of the masses against "Jewish cosmopolitans" and "agents of the West."

It is a fallacy to believe that a totalitarian society eliminates competition. In the general misery and insecurity, competition for better jobs, rations, apartments, and the favor of superiors is murderous in the literal sense of the word. Racial hatred thrives in such an atmosphere of *bellum omnium contra omnes*. There is a deep significance in the fact that the great antisemitic riots in Bratislava in 1948 grew out of a dispute between two housewives over precedence in a shopping queue.

In prewar Central European society there had been two contradictory antisemitic images of the Jew: in the eyes of the impoverished peasant, uneducated worker, and needy white-collar worker, "the Jew" was "usurer," "unfair competitor," "parasitic capitalist exploiter." In the eyes of the native aristocracy, middle class, and bureaucracy, he was the "subversive," "internationalist," "rootless" revolutionary. In the new social order, two new Jewish stereotypes were substituted for those of the "Jewish capitalist" and "Jewish Communist" of prewar times: the bourgeois or petty-bourgeois "Jewish profiteer," hating the new order and working for the "imperialist West"; and the "Jewish commissar" in the service of Moscow. The old stereotypes were now reversed, the "capitalist" becoming the "subversive," and the "revolutionary" a representative of the ruling power. One thing, however, remained unchanged: the "alien," "rootless" and "antinational" traits imputed to the Jew. The "bourgeois Jew" was considered an agent of the United States, the "Jewish commissar," of Moscow; both were considered as subverting the character, homogeneity, and independence of the nation.

The Destruction of Jewish Life

Under totalitarian rule, any form of ethnic, religious, or communal solidarity, or cultural diversity is intolerable. For this reason all Jewish communal and cultural institutions were first taken over by the Communists and then either liquidated or transformed into sounding boards for Communist propaganda.

The regimentation and destruction of communal life, a long and painful process, is described in detail in the present volume. Here, it should be pointed out that Communist tactics in the Jewish field were substantially the same as in other fields. First, the consciously anti-Communist, staunchly democratic elements were eliminated, the Communists allying themselves with opportunistic or intimidated groups to achieve this end. When the proper time came, the allies of the Communists were in their turn persecuted and destroyed.

This tactic was employed by the Communist regimes especially against the Zionists. For many reasons Zionism was, in the postwar Jewish population, the strongest political and ideological force. Wartime suffering strengthened the bonds of Jewish solidarity, making even the most assimilated Jews conscious of their common Jewish fate. With their entire families exterminated, many survivors naturally wished to leave the scene of their sufferings, and Palestine was a principal haven. Many Jews were afraid of war and of new antisemitic outbreaks. And those who had some acquaintance with the Soviet regime were resolved to evade its grasp at any cost. Thus the Polish Jews who returned from Russian exile were the first to leave Central Europe *en masse*. Most of them considered Poland only a station on the way to the West or Israel. Others left at the first occurrence of antisemitic outbreaks. Finally, the establishment of Israel made the Zionist dream a reality and provided a refuge for the Jewish survivors.

The postwar coalition governments had no special policy with respect to the Jews. The revulsion against Nazi racist crimes was fresh, democratic traditions were still alive, and tolerance of Jews paid handsome dividends in material help from the Western democracies. The abolition of the Nuremberg laws, granting of legal equality to Jewish citizens, and enactment of indemnification and restitution laws were everywhere carried out as a matter of course.

But the Jewish problem soon began to vex the bureaucracy. The refusal to restore Nazi-confiscated Jewish property and the wholesale expropriation of the middle class created a surplus Jewish population deemed unreliable because of its "petty-bourgeois origin" and emotional ties with Jews of the West. In the eyes of many bureaucrats, emigration must have seemed the best solution, and one moreover out of which they could profit

—it is no secret that emigration permits were sold for handsome sums of money, the satellite governments picking up much needed dollars in this way, and also by charging exorbitant fares for the transportation of the emigrants.

Soviet Russia, which had outlawed Zionism and jailed its leaders in the twenties, tolerated this policy for reasons of its own. The Jewish fight for the independence of Israel weakened Britain in the East. Attempting to infiltrate the emigrants' ranks with its agents, Moscow also hoped to strengthen Soviet influence in Israel to the point of making the new state a Russian satellite.

Tolerance of Zionism and a liberal emigration policy were never, however, extended to Russia proper. In some satellite countries, Jews who wanted to go to Israel were free to do so. Those who remained were required to assimilate completely. Communist leaders in the Jewish communities who tried to oppose such "liberalism" were several times overruled by party heads. In this way most Bulgarian and Yugoslav, many Czech and Polish, and even some Rumanian and Hungarian Jews were allowed to emigrate.

A sudden change in attitude toward Israel and Zionism came in the fall of 1948, after the now famous article by Ilya Ehrenburg in the Moscow *Pravda*. Again, Zionism was declared a bourgeois, nationalist, and counter-revolutionary movement, an agency of Western imperialists, and the existence of any ties among Jews of different countries was denied.

It was a return to basic Communist policy. There were several reasons why it came at this point, and why it was followed by a violent campaign of denunciation and the suppression of all manifestations of Jewish life throughout the Soviet orbit.

Moscow's hope of extending its influence over the young state was disappointed with the emergence of Israel as a democratic country of the Western type; Russian foreign policy tended more and more to support and exploit the Arab nationalist movements. The ardent response of Soviet and satellite Jews to the establishment of Israel reawakened fears of Jewish "dual loyalty." At the same time, the Sovietization of the Central European satellites had reached the point where pretensions to democratic tolerance could be dropped. The campaign against "Zionism and Jewish nationalism," formed part of the general campaign against "bourgeois nationalism," which was intensified after Tito's defection.

But the main reason for the change in line was the cold war which developed on the international scene. All organizations and activities were brought under Communist control and thoroughly purged of individuals and ideas considered unreliable. The propaganda against democratic countries and against everything connected with Western influences, not only political, but also cultural, religious, artistic and scientific, assumed warlike proportions. Adherence to any group, culture, or tradition not Soviet Russian became "bourgeois nationalism"; adherence to any international ideals, "cosmopolitanism." Both were mortal sins, to be punished by purge, jail, and in serious cases by extermination.

As in other things, so here, Jews suffered like all others, only more so. They were not only a minority, but an unpopular and suspect one— because of their "petty-bourgeois" past, the individualism of their intelligentsia, their attachment to communal traditions, and because of the emotional solidarity of Jews the world over. An "international nation," they were accused of "Jewish nationalism" and "cosmopolitanism" in the same breath. In the end, "cosmopolitan" became synonymous with "Jew," and the drive against "Jewish nationalism" was extended to every manifestation of Jewish life. "Anti-Zionism" came very close to outright antisemitism.

First, Zionist organizations of every kind were disbanded or forced to dissolve. Then the offices of foreign Jewish welfare organizations were required to close. Domestic Jewish welfare organizations were liquidated and their properties and institutions "nationalized." Jewish schools were also taken over by the state and, with some exceptions, closed; what few remained were used for the anti-Zionist and "anti-nationalist" indoctrination of the younger generation. Only the religious communities, completely under the thumb of the Communists, remained legal, having to serve as Communist propaganda agencies.

After the liquidation of the Zionist organizations, Zionist leaders were purged from all positions of influence and in many cases arrested. Then came a purge of those not zealous enough in the opposition to Zionism and "Jewish nationalism," followed by a purge of the intellectual "cosmopolitans," among them many Jews. Finally, Communists of Jewish origin were purged.

For a long time, Communist leaders avoided the word "Jew" in official denunciations of the "enemies of the people." "Aliens," "people without roots," "cosmopolitans" served in its stead. But when the Secretary General of the Czechoslovak Communist Party, Rudolf Slánský, was arrested at the end of 1951, distinctly antisemitic pronouncements issued from the highest official places, accompanying an almost complete purge of Jews from the Communist party and government. The time had come for an open antisemitic policy which, after the Prague trial of November 1952, reached the proportions of a major government-directed campaign.

Meanwhile, middle-class people, among them a high percentage of Jews, were being deported from the cities of Hungary and Rumania to forced labor camps and places of internment, where death by disease and starvation awaited them. Understanding what was happening, some of the Jewish victims put on yellow stars preserved from Nazi times. The remaining Jews lived in an atmosphere of terror difficult to conceive for those who have never experienced life under a totalitarian regime.

The postwar history of Central Europe's Jews, narrated country by country in the following pages, will count among the most pathetic episodes in the long annals of Jewish suffering. It is a story of how thousands of widowers, widows, and orphans, the few survivors of once teeming communities limp back, sick, starved, and destitute from concentration camps and underground places of hiding; how they find their houses occupied by strangers, their property lost, their relatives exterminated, encountering hatred where they expected sympathy, and envy where they expected pity. With fierce energy they set about to recreate a personal and communal life for themselves, almost succeeding in the face of immense difficulties. Though oppressed by their memories, they begin to hope that it will be possible to rediscover a life of peace and security. And then all these hopes are abruptly blasted by new terror and oppression—the agony of persecution, so recently ended, begins anew. It is a story showing once again that for the Jews, as for other people, a secure, happy, and purposeful life is possible only under democracy.

I. Czechoslovakia

BY

PETER MEYER

Chapter 1

The Jewish Community Before World War II

There were about 360,000 persons of the Jewish faith in prewar Czechoslovakia, constituting a little less than 2½ per cent of the total population. The official censuses of 1921 and 1930 show that their absolute number remained fairly stationary, so that as the total population increased the percentage of Jews declined slightly. Table 1 shows their distribution among the Czechoslovak provinces (the so-called "lands"):

TABLE I

DISTRIBUTION OF JEWS IN CZECH PROVINCES, 1921, 1930

	1921		1930		1930
	Number	% of pop.	Number	% of pop.	% of all Czech Jews
Bohemia	79,777	1.19	76,301	1.07	21.39
Moravia	37,989	1.43	41,250	1.16	11.56
Silesia[1]	7,317	1.09			
Slovakia	135,918	4.53	136,737	4.11	38.32
Carpatho-Russia	93,341	15.39	102,542	14.14	28.73
Total	354,342	2.6	356,830	2.42	100.00

These statistics refer only to persons professing the Jewish religion.[2] In addition, there were baptized and non-professing Jews. The number of the latter in the eastern part of the country was negligible, but in Bohemia and Moravia they were more numerous.[3] The total number of "racial Jews" in Czechoslovakia can be estimated at about 380,000.

We can see that the density of Jewish population grew from west to east. Two-thirds of the Czechoslovak Jews were concentrated in the eastern provinces, Slovakia and Carpatho-Russia, which had been part of Hungary before 1918; only one-third lived in the historic lands of the Czech crown, i. e., Bohemia, Moravia, and Czechoslovak Silesia, which had belonged to the Austrian half of the former Austro-Hungarian realm.

Historical Background

There were great differences in historical background and social conditions between the Jews of Bohemia, Moravia, and Silesia and those of Slovakia and Carpatho-Russia. In the Middle Ages, the historic lands of the Czech crown were the center of a powerful independent state, and the Kings of Bohemia were, under the Luxemburg dynasty, Emperors of the Holy Roman Empire. Economically, politically, and culturally, the Czech lands belonged to the most developed section of Central Europe. The Czech Reformation in the fifteenth century preceded the German by a century, and for two hundred years Bohemia was the first country to enjoy a relative degree of religious freedom. Only in the Thirty Years War, when a counter reformation was forcibly imposed on the Czechs, did they lose their national independence; their upper classes were exterminated or expropriated and forced to emigrate. But even under the Hapsburg oppression in the subsequent "dark age," the Czechs, though reduced to a nation of peasants, managed to preserve their ethnic identity, and the historic lands had a certain degree of territorial autonomy within the structure of the Austrian Empire. At the end of the eighteenth and beginning of the nineteenth century, a remarkable revival of the Czech language, literature, and national consciousness took place. The country was industrialized, a Czech middle class and intelligentsia arose, and the Czech workers organized themselves into strong labor unions. Throughout the nineteenth century the Czechs waged a persistent struggle, first for their language rights and political and cultural equality; later for autonomy under the Hapsburg monarchy; and finally for complete national independence. When they entered the final phase of the struggle during the First World War, the Czechs had—except for political independence—all the attributes of a modern nation, and the historic lands were an advanced country where the soil was cultivated intensively, industry flourished, the standard of education was high, and democratic traditions were long established.

The Jewish communities in the historic lands belong to the oldest in Central Europe. According to some sources, there had been a Jewish community in Prague as far back as the tenth century; one indisputably existed in the eleventh century. In the thirteenth century, there were sixteen Jewish communities in Bohemia and Moravia. The situation of Jews improved during the era of the Hussite Reformation and of the succeeding period of religious freedom, and Jews from surrounding countries streamed into Bohemian and Moravian towns. At that time Jews were active in all fields of endeavor; they owned land, engaged in agriculture and trade, practised crafts, medicine, and were in the service of the court. They made important contributions to Jewish learning and literature.

Prague was an important cultural center of Jewish life.

After the loss of Czech independence the Jewish communities were able to preserve their position under Hapsburg rule. The beginnings of their political emancipation, however, were made before the Czech national revival. At that time the Czechs were still a nation of peasants, small artisans, and domestic servants. The cities and towns, courts and administrative authorities, higher schools and institutes of learning, were German, and the Austrian government followed a policy of conscious Germanization. The Jews had to adopt German family names, use the German language in business and when dealing with the authorities, and send their children to German schools. The rising upper middle class, the state bureaucracy, and municipal administrations were still German; Vienna was the great financial and administrative center of the Empire around which all economic life turned. The textile industry, where Jewish influence was greatest, was largely concentrated in those parts of the country inhabited by Germans, or in towns that formed German-language islands in a Czech countryside. The Jewish manufacturers, business men, and merchants became assimilated to the German milieu in which they lived. The Jewish intelligentsia, which was educated in German schools, played a considerable role in the cultural life of the German minority in Bohemia and Moravia; German-Jewish poets, writers, and scholars helped to make Prague an important center of German culture.

Under these circumstances, Jews were identified or considered to be allied with Germans in the eyes of Czech peasants and workers, as well as in the eyes of the Czech middle class, which had to make its way in competition against these already well-established German and German-Jewish middle classes. The phrase "Germans and Jews" was a standard one in the vocabulary of Czech politics.

But soon after 1848 some Bohemian Jews began to call for assimilation not to the German but to the Czech nation. This movement grew throughout the second half of the nineteenth century, and especially after the development of Czech institutions of higher learning, and a Czech cultural life brought a Czech-educated Jewish intelligentsia into being. Jewish and half-Jewish writers made valuable contributions to Czech literature; politically, many of the Czech Jews were active in the small Progressive Party of Professor Thomas G. Masaryk. At the end of the nineteenth century, 54 per cent of the Jews of Bohemia and 23 per cent of the Jews of Moravia declared in a census that Czech was the language of their daily life. The rest used German–Yiddish was no longer spoken in the historic lands of the Bohemian Crown.

Thus we had, in the historic lands, a Jewish community of the Western European type, with a wealthy middle class and a broad stratum of intelligentsia. It was preponderantly liberal in its politics, linguistically and culturally assimilated, and played an important economic, cultural and political role in the life of the Czech and German ethnic groups.

Conditions in Slovakia and Carpatho-Russia were different. The Slavonic inhabitants of these provinces had been under Hungarian rule for a thousand years and had no traditions of independent statehood; their lands were regarded simply as Hungarian "mountain territories." For the most part the country was poor, predominantly agrarian, with a primitive agriculture and forestry. There was scarcely any industry, and low standards of living and education prevailed. The Slovaks and Carpatho-Russians were mostly poor peasants; they had no native middle class and hardly any native intelligentsia. In the towns the middle class was Hungarian or German. Owners of big estates and government officials were Hungarian. There were no schools with Slovak or Russian as the language of instruction above the primary level. Social and cultural conditions at the beginning of the twentieth century were similar to those of the historic lands in the first half of the nineteenth century.

Except for a few old settlements, the Jewish communities in Slovakia were of recent date, having been founded by immigrants from Moravia and Galicia. Only Bratislava with its Yeshiva was an important center of Jewish cultural life. The Jews of Slovakia were generally engaged in commerce. Religious influence and Jewish traditions were much stronger here than in the historic lands. Yiddish was still spoken by a great part of the community. The younger generation, educated in Hungarian or German schools, spoke Hungarian and German and began to take part in the cultural life of these nations, but there was no assimilation to the Slovak nation or culture. In Carpatho-Russia, the majority of the Jews were Yiddish-speaking, orthodox, poor, and in appearance and way of life like the neighboring Jews of eastern Galicia.

Under the Republic

So matters stood in 1918 when the foundation of the Czechoslovak Republic brought these different Jewish groups together in one democratic state. The new republic enacted on February 29, 1920 a constitutional law concerning the language rights of minorities. According to this law, each minority had the right to use its own language in courts and in its dealing with the authorities in all districts where it constituted 20 per cent or more of the population. As there were no districts in which Yiddish-speaking Jews constituted 20 per cent of the population, Yiddish was not recognized an an official minority language; nor were there enough Yiddish-speaking children in most communities to warrant state-supported Yiddish minority schools. On the other hand, the Jewish ethnic nationality was officially recognized.

The old Austrian censuses knew only the language of communication (*Umgangssprache*). The Czechoslovak census also gave statistics about nationalities, i. e., ethnic groups. Mother tongue was considered the main criterion of nationality, but every citizen could register as a member of the nationality of his choice, his declaration being accepted in the absence of irrefutable objective considerations to the contrary. Persons of the Jewish faith had the right to profess "Jewish nationality." In territories with German or Hungarian minorities they were even encouraged to do so, in order to reduce the number of citizens registering as Germans or Hungarians and so reduce the number of districts where German or Hungarian enjoyed the status of official minority languages. Table II shows the professed nationality of persons of the Jewish faith according to the census of 1930:

TABLE II

NATIONALITY OF JEWS, 1930

Nationality	Bohemia	Moravia-Silesia	Slovakia	Carpatho-Russia	Total
Czechoslovak[4]	35,418	7,251	44,009	811	87,489
Russian[5]	161	39	178	708	1,086
German	23,660	11,997	9,945	130	45,732
Hungarian	802	407	9,728	5,870	16,807
Jewish	15,463	21,315	72,644	95,005	204,427
Polish	488	179	144	7	818
Other					471

Compared with the census of 1921, the number of Jews of Czech and Jewish nationality had substantially increased; the number of German and Hungarian Jews had declined. The percentage of Jews professing each nationality is shown in Table III.

TABLE III

NATIONALITY OF JEWS, BY PERCENTAGE, 1921, 1930

Nationality	1921	1930
Czechoslovak	21.84	24.52
Russian	1.10	0.30
German	14.26	12.82
Hungarian	8.45	4.71
Jewish	53.62	57.20
Other	0.73	0.75

Persons of the Jewish faith constituted 0.9 per cent of all ethnic Czechoslovaks, 0.19 per cent of the Russians, 1.38 per cent of the Germans, 2.34 per cent of the Hungarians, and 99.83 per cent of the persons of Jewish nationality. The rest of the members of the Jewish nationality were non-professing Jews and a few persons of the Christian faith.

More than 57 per cent of the Jews registered as of Jewish nationality in 1930; but the geographical distribution of these national Jews was very uneven. In Bohemia, only one-fifth of the Jews considered themselves members of the Jewish nationality; in Moravia-Silesia and Slovakia, the majority of Jews belonged to this group; in Carpatho-Russia, almost 95 per cent of the Jews registered as members of the Jewish nationality. In Bohemia and Moravia most persons who professed Jewish nationality spoke Czech or German and were to a large extent culturally assimilated. In the eastern parts of the country (eastern Slovakia and Carpatho-Russia), the language of "national" Jews was Yiddish, and religious and communal ties were strong.

Under the Austrian monarchy, there had been more German than Czech Jews, although, as we have said, a Czech nationalist movement among Jews existed throughout the second half of the nineteenth century; the majority of the older generation of Bohemian and Moravian Jews was educated in German schools and strongly influenced by German culture. The younger generation, growing up under the republic, went to Czech schools and took part in Czech cultural life. Many Jews were bilingual and could opt for either nationality. After 1918, there was a steady shift of Jews from the German to the Czech—or, as it was officially called—Czechoslovak nationality. In 1930, before Hitler took power in Germany, there were already, in absolute numbers, more Czech than German Jews, although the percentage of Jews among the Germans was still greater than among the Czechs.

This was true in even larger measure of the Hungarian and Slovak Jews in Slovakia. Although the number of Hungarian Jews declined rapidly (8.45 per cent of all Jews in 1921, and only 4.71 per cent in 1930), yet the percentage of Jews among the Hungarians was greater than among any other linguistic group in Czechoslovakia. In Carpatho-Russia, the assimilation of Jews to the Russian or Ukrainian peasant population was negligible.

An indication of the extent of assimilation in different parts of the country can be got from statistics on mixed marriages. The percentage of such marriages was very high in Bohemia, but declined rapidly as one passed from west to east. In the six-year period from 1928 to 1933 about 19 per cent of all new marriages in which at least one partner was Jewish were mixed marriages. This was the percentage for the entire republic. But in Bohemia, 43.8 per cent of such marriages were mixed; in Moravia,

30 per cent. In Slovakia, the percentage fell off to 9.2 per cent, and in Carpatho-Russia to 1.3 per cent.[6]

Of the Jewish men in Czechoslovakia who married in this period, 11.2 per cent took non-Jewish wives. In Bohemia, the percentage was 30 per cent; in Moravia, 19 per cent; in Slovakia 5 per cent; in Carpatho-Russia 0.4 per cent. Of the Jewish women who married, not quite 10 per cent took non-Jewish husbands. In Bohemia the percentage was 26 per cent; in Moravia 16.6 per cent; in Slovakia 4.8 per cent; in Carpatho-Russia 0.9 per cent. Only in Carpatho-Russia was the percentage of Jewish women making mixed marriages greater than the percentage of Jewish men making such marriages.

In these statistics Jew means a professing Jew, so that marriages of religious Jews to baptized or agnostic Jewish partners figure here as "mixed marriages." On the other hand, cases where Jewish partners were baptized or left the Jewish religious community before marrying a non-Jewish partner were not included in the statistics, so that the percentages of mixed marriages are rather under- than over stated.

More than half of all persons of the Jewish faith lived in cities and towns having 10,000 inhabitants or more (whereas only a quarter of the total population lived in such towns). Table IV gives the figures for Jews residing in the capital, Prague.

TABLE IV

JEWS RESIDING IN PRAGUE, 1921, 1930

Year	Total Population	Jews	Percentage of Jews
1921	676,657	31,751	4.69
1930	848,823	33,425	4.17

Table V shows the distribution of Jews in the principal occupations according to the census of 1921 (dependents being counted with their supporters).

In the historic lands (Bohemia and Moravia-Silesia), Jews constituted 0.1 per cent of all persons engaged in agriculture, forestry, and the fisheries; 0.7 per cent in industry and handicrafts; 9.2 per cent in commerce and banking; 0.6 per cent in transportation; 2.3 per cent in public administration and the professions; 0.2 per cent in the armed services; 2.2 per cent in household jobs; and 1.2 per cent of all persons engaged in "other or unknown occupations."

Table VI gives the distribution of Jews—and, for comparison, of the total population—by social classes in 1921 (without dependents).

TABLE V

DISTRIBUTION OF JEWS BY PRINCIPAL OCCUPATIONS, 1921

Occupation	No. of Jews	Percentage Distribution of Jewish Population in Occupation Classes	Percentage Distribution of Total Population in Occupation Classes
Agriculture, forestry, fisheries	43,261	12.21	39.57
Industry, handicrafts	78,992	22.29	33.80
Commerce, banking	145,814	41.15	5.78
Transportation	9,348	2.64	4.88
Public administration and the professions	25,538	7.21	4.34
Military	1,534	0.43	1.17
Household jobs	2,676	0.76	1.27
Others or unknown	47,179	13.31	9.19
Totals	354,342	100.00	100.00

TABLE VI

DISTRIBUTION OF JEWS BY SOCIAL CLASSES, 1921

Social Class	Distribution of Jews Gainfully Employed Among Classes	Distribution of All Gainfully Employed Among Classes
Independent owners and tenants	53.74	27.51
Officials (*Beamte*), public and private	19.36	8.13
Workers and clerks	20.76	47.88
Apprentices	3.60	4.84
Day laborers	2.54	11.64
Totals	100.00	100.00

According to the census of 1930 Jews constituted 4.21 per cent of the independents and tenants; 4.93 per cent of the public and private officials, 4.15 per cent of the clerks; 0.47 per cent of the workers; 1.8 per cent of the apprentices; and 0.6 per cent of the day laborers.

The Czechoslovak Republic undertook, by the Peace Treaty of St. Germain of September 10, 1919, to respect the rights of religious and national minorities. This obligation was reaffirmed in the text of the

Czechoslovak Constitution of February 29, 1920. No special provision concerning Jews was made. According to a report by Foreign Minister Beneš to the parliament in September 1919, the reason for this was that it was considered obvious that the republic would grant Jews the same rights it granted other minorities. So far as general human and civil rights were concerned, all citizens of the state possessed them equally.

Religious freedom was guaranteed by the constitution. Jewish religious communities were recognized and entitled to tax their members; in addition they received—as did other religious communities—some financial assistance from the state treasury for the maintenance of their clergy. The Law for the Protection of the Republic, promulgated in 1923, contained a paragraph punishing by fine and imprisonment persons inciting hatred or violence against groups because of their religion, race, or nationality.

There was some discrimination and chicanery against Jews at the lower levels of public administration, and the paragraph against incitement to hatred was seldom invoked to protect the Jews. In general, however, the juridical position of Jews was tolerable and much better than in any of the other states of Eastern Europe.

A certain amount of popular antisemitism had always existed. The last major antisemitic riots occurred at the end of the nineteenth century, in connection, significantly, with a constitutional conflict between Czechs and Germans. In 1897 the Austrian Premier Badeni, who had made considerable concessions to Czech language demands, was defeated by a German filibuster in the Vienna parliament. The Czech population reacted with demonstrations and riots which were aimed at German as well as Jewish institutions and individuals in Czech cities and towns. German and Jewish shops were demolished, German schools and Jewish synagogues attacked. The German nationalists retaliated with attacks on Czechs and Jews in places with German majorities. The excitement had not yet died down when the death of a Czech girl in the small town of Polná gave rise to rumors about a ritual murder. Leopold Hilsner, a Jew, was indicted and condemned by Czech juries; a new wave of antisemitic riots followed. But liberals among the Czech intelligentsia, under the leadership of Thomas G. Masaryk, fought back. There were meetings and counter-meetings, pamphlets and counter-pamphlets, and heated debates in parliament; the Polná affair divided the nation somewhat like the Dreyfus Affair did France. The final result was the discrediting of antisemitic agitation; it came to be looked upon as something contemptible. There were no major antisemitic riots among the Czechs after the beginning of the twentieth century.

Under the republic, whose president was Masaryk and whose major parties espoused a democratic and humanitarian program, there were no pogroms or major antisemitic excesses. Antisemitic moods still survived in sections of the population, especially among the peasants. These were expressed in slighting remarks, chalked inscriptions, broken windowpanes, small incidents, and some discrimination in social life. Of the Czech political parties and groups, only those of fascist or semifascist tendencies raised antisemitic slogans; they used antisemitic arguments in their fight against political democracy, against the equality of national minorities, and against the leadership of Masaryk and Beneš. Antisemitism was much stronger among the Slovaks, especially in the autonomist Slovak Catholic People's Party of Father Hlinka. In the ranks of the German minority, the National Socialist Party, which was older than the party of the same name in Germany, was antisemitic from the beginning. Before Hitler's rise to power in Germany it had only a small following. But after 1933 it began to grow rapidly. When the Czech authorities dissolved it, it was reorganized as the Sudeten German Party. Under the leadership of Konrad Henlein, the Sudeten German Party won over, in the years of depression and unemployment in the industrial Sudeten territories and under pressure from neighboring Nazi Germany, a great majority of the German population in Czechoslovakia. This was accompanied by a rise of overt antisemitism in the so-called Sudetenland, or German areas of Bohemia, Moravia, and Silesia, where, in the late thirties, only the protection of the Czech authorities saved Jews, and the remaining German democrats, from violent attacks.

In addition to the usual rationalizations of anti-Jewish attitude, connected with social antagonisms: "Jews are exploiters," "they make easy money," "they are Communists," antisemitism in Czechoslovakia used aspersions that reflected the incessant struggle of nationalities against each other under the Austrian monarchy and later under the Czechoslovak Republic.

For the Czech antisemites, the charge was Jewish Germanization. Under the Austrian crown, the Germans had dominated in many cities and towns which existed in purely Czech surroundings; thus the middle class was often German, the lower classes Czech. In these circumstances, as we have seen, many Jews, even in Czech regions, attended German schools and were obliged to use the German language in social life and business. Under the republic, some of them still belonged to German minorities in Czech cities and used German in daily life. The Czech nationalities reproached them for their "provocative use of German"; those Jews, who, being bilingual, professed Czech nationality were suspected of doing so for purely opportunist reasons.

Until 1918 the Jewish middle class in Slovakia sent their children to Hungarian schools for the simple reason that there were no Slovak high schools, not to speak of colleges. Speaking Hungarian (or German) in Slovak towns, these Jews were considered to be the main abettors of "Hungarization." Among the strongly Catholic peasants, antisemitism was reinforced by religious prejudices.

After the founding of the republic, national minorities began to consider the Jews living among them as agents of the Czechs. Among the Germans, this feeling existed even before the rise of Nazism. In Slovakia, and especially in Carpatho-Russia where centrifugal tendencies were strong, Jews were in fact the most loyal citizens of the republic and their children filled Czech schools in districts where there were no Czechs. The Slovak and Carpatho-Russian population consequently responded to slogans lumping "Czech oppressors and gendarmes" with "Jewish exploiters and opportunists." Nevertheless, the Carpathian Jews, situated between antisemitic Poland, antisemitic Rumania, and Horthy's Hungary, considered themselves fortunate to be living in Czechoslovakia. Thus the Jews were caught in the middle of contending nationalities, a fact which had—as we shall see—important postwar consequences.

Chapter II

Munich, War, and Deportation

More than 100,000 Czechoslovak Jews lived in territories that Czechoslovakia lost in consequence of the Munich agreement (the Sudetenland was ceded to Germany, the Těšín [Teschen] area in Silesia to Poland, and the southern regions of Slovakia and Carpatho-Russia to Hungary).

Table VII shows the distribution of the 356,830 Czechoslovak Jews recorded by the census of 1930 as between the ceded and non-ceded areas:

TABLE VII

DISTRIBUTION OF JEWS, 1930

Territory	Ceded Areas	Non-ceded Areas
Bohemia	20,838	55,463
Moravia-Silesia	9,600	31,650
Slovakia	45,108	91,629
Carpatho-Russia	33,015	69,527
Totals	108,561	248,269

According to an estimate of the Czechoslovak State Bureau of Statistics, Jews constituted the following percentages of the population of the remaining parts of the partitioned provinces: 1.24 per cent in Bohemia; 1.37 per cent in Moravia-Silesia; 3.8 per cent in Slovakia; and 12.75 per cent in Carpatho-Russia.

In reality, however, the number of Jews in the non-ceded areas was greater, for these estimates, being based on the census of 1930, did not include an influx of several thousand German and Austrian Jewish refugees in the late thirties.

Nor did the estimates take into account the movement of Jewish population at the time of the Munich pact. Fortunately, we possess three separate sets of population statistics for the period after Munich and before the commencement of the systematic slaughtering of Jews. These are the Slovak census of December 31, 1938; the Sudentenland census of May 17, 1939; and the Protectorate census of October 1, 1939.

In May 1939 there were almost no Jews left in the Sudetenland. Of the 27,037 Jews living in that area in 1930, only 1,534 remained.[1] The rest had fled to the Czech parts of Bohemia and Moravia at the time of Munich.

In the Protectorate (Bohemia and Moravia, less the Sudetenland and Těšín) we should expect to find almost all the 117,500 Jews recorded by the census of 1930 as resident in Bohemia and Moravia, plus the several thousand German and Austrian refugees who had come to Czechoslovakia in the thirties, plus a small natural increase. And in fact the postwar Association of Jewish Religious Communities of Bohemia and Moravia[2] gives the number of persons of the Jewish faith on December 31, 1938 as: Bohemia, 78,612, Moravia-Silesia, 42,899. This was three months after Munich, when several thousand Jews had already emigrated.

On March 15, 1939, the day the Germans occupied the Protectorate, there were 118,310 "racial" Jews, including 14,350 persons of "other than the Jewish faith."[3] Thus there were 104,000 professing Jews, which shows that an additional 17,500 had left the country in the first two and a half months of 1939.

Emigration continued during the first months of German rule, and the Protectorate census of October 1, 1939 recorded only 90,147 professing Jews.[4] This census was taken just before the first deportations, which began in October 1939.

The figures in Table VIII, published by the Association[5] show the progressive decline in the number of Jews in Bohemia and Moravia (apart from the camp in Terezín) during the war:

TABLE VIII
JEWS IN BOHEMIA AND MORAVIA, 1939-43

Date	Number of Jews	Of these, Non-professing Jews
March 15, 1939	118,310	14,350
December 31, 1939	97,961	
December 31, 1940	90,041	
June 30, 1941	88,686	13,088
December 31, 1941	74,190	
June 30, 1942	45,336	
December 31, 1942	16,661	
March 31, 1943	11,267	5,130
July 15, 1943	8,695	

The figure for July 15, 1943 includes 750 persons in prison and 350 whose whereabouts are unknown. After this date there remained only Jews married to non-Jewish partners, descendants of mixed marriages who were considered Jews according to the Nuremberg Laws, and some survivors of the personnel of Jewish organizations. Of these, 2,803 (including 820 of the Jewish faith) survived outside the camps until their liberation in May 1945. Thirty-eight per cent of these survivors were children of mixed marriages, under fourteen years, who were just about to be deported when the war ended.

After March 15, 1939, 26,111 Jews emigrated from Bohemia and Moravia. To these must be added the 17,500 emigrants who left the country between January 1 and March 15, 1939, and several thousand who had emigrated in 1938. The total number of Jews who left Bohemia and Moravia was something like 50,000.

The first mass deportation started in Moravská Ostrava in October 1939. All men between 16 and 70 were deported from that city and two smaller towns to Nisko in Poland. Their number was 1,291; some 460 of them came back in April 1940. Of the rest, some escaped to Russia and 123 returned as soldiers in the Czech army after the war.

The next big deportation started on October 16, 1941. By November 3, 1941, 7,000 Jews had been deported in seven transports directly to Minsk and Lodz. Of these, 265 returned after the war.[6]

The deportation to the ghetto in Terezín started on November 24, 1941. The total number of Jews deported to Terezín from Bohemia and Moravia during the war was 73,635.[7]

Of this total, 31,879 were deported to the East (Riga, Warsaw, Zamosc, Treblinka, etc.) in 15 transports between January 9 and October 22, 1942. Not one person from these transports came back.

Transports began to be sent from Terezín to Oswiecim (Auschwitz) on October 26, 1942, continuing until October 28, 1944. There were 29 such transports. A total of 28,551 Bohemian and Moravian Jews were sent to Oswiecim, only 2,747 of whom returned.

The number of Czechoslovak Jews who died in Terezín was 6,180, the number who survived, 6,850 (3,617 of these being the offspring of mixed marriages). Jews sent from Terezín to Switzerland in the first months of 1945 are not counted among the survivors; there may have been 200 Bohemian and Moravian Jews among the 1,613 persons so saved.

To summarize: Of 118,500 "racial" Jews present in Bohemia and Moravia in March 1939, about 72,000 were killed or died in the camps; 26,000 emigrated; about 5,000 died before being deported.[8] There were 13,000 survivors, more than 3,000 of them in the camps in the East, including Oswiecim; 7,000 in Terezín, including persons sent to Switzerland; and not quite 3,000 at home. This leaves only 2,500 persons not accounted for. Of the 82,000 deported, only 10,000 survived.

In what remained of Slovakia after the Munich cessions, there were, on December 31, 1938, 87,487 Jews,[9] who constituted 3.23 per cent of the entire population.[10] The decrease from 91,629 living in the same area in 1930 is not very great. It cannot be ascertained how many Jews of the areas ceded to Hungary fled to the rest of Slovakia, or vice versa, but the number was probably small as the treatment of Jews in both countries was about the same at that time. In 1941-1943, however, Jews fled from Slovakia to Hungary, where systematic extermination did not begin until 1944.

Statistical information in Table IX, published by the Slovak puppet government, shows the decline in the number of professing Jews in Slovakia.[11]

TABLE IX

PROFESSING JEWS IN SLOVAKIA, 1938-44

Date		Number
December 31, 1938		87,487
December 12, 1940		88,970
January 1, 1942	over	89,000
September 1, 1942		23,451
April 1, 1943	*ca.*	16,000
January 1, 1944	*ca.*	15,000

The first antisemitic measures were taken in Slovakia in 1939. In September 1940 the Slovak puppet parliament authorized the cabinet to order the expropriation of Jewish properties. By January 1941 half of all Jewish businesses were expropriated. In February 1941 a law for the distribution of Jewish-owned land among the peasants was adopted. Segregation measures followed. In April 1942 the last remaining Jewish organization, the Jewish Central Committee in Bratislava, was dissolved.

On May 18, 1942, the Quisling minister Šaňo Mach announced the impending deportation of 45,000 Slovak Jews to Poland, to be concluded by September. In July 1942 the newspaper *Gardista* declared that 56,000 Jews had already been deported from the country. In February 1943 Mach announced that the 20,000 remaining Jews would be deported to Poland. In the meantime, the distribution of Jewish-owned land had been completed with the transfer of 19,771 hectares to Slovak peasants. The value of all Jewish property expropriated in Slovakia was estimated at 160 million dollars.[12]

Among the Jews who still remained in Slovakia in the last years of the war were several thousand declared to be performing indispensable economic functions, as well as several thousand baptized Jews. (Many Protestant and some Catholic clergymen performed mercy baptisms.) As early as 1942,Šaňo Mach ordered a revision of the labor permits granted these "indispensable" Jews and a cancellation of newly acquired baptismal certificates. In July 1943 there were still about 3,000 indispensable Jews left, and about 5,000 holding recently issued baptismal certificates.

In addition to the deportations to Poland, the Slovak government organized forced labor camps on Slovak territory. On June 30, 1943, there were three such camps with 2,938 prisoners. On December 21, 1943, to these three camps six "centers" had been added with 3,768 prisoners.[13]

In the fall of 1944 several hundred Jews joined the Slovak armed uprising that took place in the region of Báňská Bystrica. After its defeat a new wave of deportations and killings began. Some of the remaining Jews went into hiding and were able to survive.

Only 87,000 of the 136,000 Jews of prewar Slovakia were living within the borders of the Slovak puppet state at the time of its setting-up; the rest were living in areas ceded to Hungary or else had emigrated. Of these 87,000, 70,000 were deported and 11,000 came back. In 1946, there were 31,000 Jews (professing and non-professing) in Slovakia. Two thousand of them were newcomers, mostly from Poland[14]; 11,000 were returned deportees; some 10,000 had survived in the country; the rest had returned from exile. There are no reliable data on wartime emigration.

The southern part of Carpatho-Russia, with the cities of Užhorod and Mukačevo, was occupied by Hungary in October 1938, and the remainder of the province in March 1939. The deportation of Carpatho-Russian Jews started in April 1944. Of 102,000 about 15,000 survived, some of them in concentration camps in Poland, others in Russia, whence they returned with the Czech army. All but a few hundred fled westward after the postwar annexation of the area by Russia. About 8,500 settled in Bohemia and Moravia. The rest journeyed on, some 4,000 going to France. It is impossible to ascertain how many Jews from other parts of Soviet Russia came to Carpatho-Russia after the Russian occupation.

To summarize: in 1946 there were about 56,000 "racial" Jews in Czechoslovakia (as against 380,000 before Munich). About 50,000 more were living in emigration. The rest had perished.

Jews in the Resistance at Home and Abroad

As far as can be ascertained, Jews played no independent role in the Czechoslovak resistance in the historic lands. In the first years of the war, before their segregation, individual Jews took part in the underground activities of Czech political parties and resistance groups. But segregation and deportation put an end to such Jewish activities. No cases of militant resistance against deportation were reported from Bohemia and Moravia.

There was one such case in Slovakia. On April 22, 1942, the Slovak puppet government reported that the military had been called out to quell resistance in two eastern Slovak towns against the deportation of

Jews.[15] A number of Jews also took part in the already noted Slovak armed uprising near Báňská Bystrica in September-October 1944.[16]

There was a high percentage of Jews in the small Czech military units fighting with the Allies abroad. There are no official statistics on the subject, and the Jewish estimates which we are about to quote may be exaggerated. But the units were recruited among Czech citizens in Allied countries, most of them refugees, and the number of Jews among the Czech refugees was considerable. Not all of the soldiers of these units were volunteers: Czech citizens of military age in Great Britain and France were drafted into the Czech army. Other Czech units, drawn from refugees on Polish territory, fled to Russia after the fall of Poland. There they were interned until 1941, when they were formed into the Eastern Czech Army which fought under Russian command. They were reinforced by other Czech refugees who had been working in factories and forced labor camps in Russia until that time. Many of these had come from eastern Slovakia or Carpatho-Russia and the percentage of Jews among them was high.

On April 17, 1947, the Vice Chairman of the Prague Jewish Religious Community, Mr. Fuchs, declared in a public meeting in Prague that almost 50 per cent of the Czechoslovak soldiers abroad were Jews.[17] Of the soldiers in the Eastern Army, organized by the Russians, Jewish sources repeatedly give 75 per cent as being Jewish.[18] Among its officers and soldiers receiving Soviet military decorations on April 17, 1943, there were many with Jewish names.[19] According to Jewish sources, more than 1,000 Jews joined the Czech military unit formed in Palestine which fought at Tobruk and Benghazi. Later this unit was transferred to England where it joined the Western Czech Brigade. The Czech Brigade attacked Dunkirk in the last months of the war. Of 51 Czech soldiers killed in battle before Dunkirk, 21 were Jews.[20] Even in remote Shanghai, 55 of the Czechoslovak citizens who joined the Shanghai Volunteer Corps were Jews.[21] The role of Jews in the military units abroad was repeatedly recognized by the Minister of National Defense, General Ludvík Svoboda, former commander of the Eastern Czech Army.

On November 18, 1941, Arnošt Frischer, a former member of the Czechoslovak parliament and leader of the Jewish Party, was appointed to the Czechoslovak State Council, a consultative body for the Czechoslovak Government-in-Exile in London; he served in this capacity until the end of the war.

Chapter III

The Survivors

After the war there were about 24,000 Jews in Bohemia and Moravia (including 5,000 not belonging to the religious community), and 31,000 in Slovakia. The 8,500 Jews who had fled from Carpatho-Russia to the western part of Czechoslovakia after the former's annexation by Soviet Russia are counted among the 24,000 Bohemian and Moravian Jews.

Statistics compiled by the Association of Jewish Religious Communities give the Jewish population of Bohemia and Moravia as of June 30, 1948,[1] (see Table X.)

TABLE X

JEWISH POPULATION OF BOHEMIA AND MORAVIA, JUNE 30, 1948

Region	Persons of the "Mosaic Faith"	Other Members of Jewish Communities	Total
Prague	7,572	3,188	10,760
Bohemia (exclusive of Prague)	8,547	1,147	9,694
Moravia-Silesia	3,004	937	3,941
Totals	19,123	5,272	24,395

For Slovakia the Bratislava *Cesta* (*Haderech*), organ of the Hashomer Hatzair, estimated the number of Jews (as of 1946)[2] as follows: Persons of the Mosaic faith 24,000; other Jews 6,000, total 30,000.

The Statistical Department (Evidenční *oddělení*) of the Association published the analysis[3] in Table XI of the types and numbers of surviving Jews in Bohemia and Moravia (as of 1947).

Of a total of 24,001 "racial" Jews, 10,338 lived in Prague and 13,663 in other, mostly Sudeten, towns. About 3,000 of the Jews lived in Moravia. Of the 8,455 Carpatho-Russian refugees, 2,233 lived in Prague and 6,222 in other, mostly the Sudeten, parts of Bohemia and Moravia.

A report by the Prague correspondent of the American Jewish Committee[4] gives occupational statistics for professing Jews in Bohemia and Moravia: (see Table XII, p. 68).

TABLE XI
CLASSES OF SURVIVORS (1947)

Class of Survivor		Professing Jews Male	Professing Jews Female	Other Jews Male	Other Jews Female	Totals	
1. Returned from prison	a)*	70	21	39	54	184	
	b)	125	68	25	22	240	424
2. Returned from deportations to the East	a)	562	718	283	224	1,787	
	b)	565	496	89	72	1,222	3,009
3. Returned from Terezín (AE Transports)	a)	283	762	123	344	1,512	
	b)	337	747	77	203	1,334	2,846
4. Returned from Terezín (except AE Transports)	a)	467	209	402	425	1,503	
	b)	445	223	264	333	1,269	2,768
5. Subcarpathian repatriates and optants	a)	859	1,140	134	100	2,233	
	b)	2,892	3,301	12	17	6,222	8,455
6. Returned with army	a)	625	93	70	9	824	
	b)	1,096	65	22	..	1,183	2,007
6a. Returned with army (persons deported to Nisko)	a)	52	..	7	..	59	
	b)	64	..	..	..	64	123
7. Returned from abroad	a)	201	317	41	54	613	
	b)	145	215	16	7	383	996
8. Never deported	a)	369	291	395	341	1,396	
	b)	400	440	290	423	1,553	2,949
9. Underground survivors and others	a)	74	70	41	42	227	
	b)	77	89	13	18	197	424
Totals		9,735	9,235	2,343	2,688	10,338	
						13,663	
Totals, male & female		18,970		5,031			24,001

*a) living in Prague, b) living elsewhere in Bohemia and Moravia.

Table XII cannot provide an exact comparison with prewar statistics. It puts dependants into separate categories (pre-school children, students, housewives), rather than counting them with their supporters. Nor are the categories defined in the same way as in prewar statistics. And, most important, it describes a decimated community. Still, a comparison can—with certain qualifications—roughly indicate current trends.[5]

If we subtract housewives, children, students, and persons of unregistered occupation, we get a figure of about 10,000 gainfully occupied.

"Independent owners" formed almost 69 per cent of gainfully occupied Jews before the war. Now, adding the 261 farmers and 789 professionals to the 906 businessmen, we get almost 2,000 "independents," or hardly 20 per cent of the total. On the other hand, there are about 3,600 workers, agricultural workers, and apprentices, who constitute more than 35 per cent of the occupational total (against 15 per cent before the war). Clerks and civil servants, including "national administrators," amount to 3,200, or more than 30 per cent (against the prewar figure of 12 per cent for "officials and clerks"). This was in 1947, before the second wave of nationalization, when small industry and the majority of commercial enterprises were still in private hands. The trend is toward a community consisting of a majority of "workers and minor employees" and a rather large minority of "clerks and civil servants." Destitute persons made up about 8½ per cent of the community.

TABLE XII

OCCUPATIONAL DISTRIBUTION, PROFESSING JEWS, BOHEMIA AND MORAVIA

Occupation	Number
Workers and minor employees	2,999
Clerks and civil servants	2,467
Farmers	261
Agricultural workers	166
Independent businessmen and artisans	906
National administrators of former German properties	716
Professionals	789
Military	184
Housewives	4,343
Children (pre-school)	1,410
Students	1,629
Apprentices	444
Aged and infirm	1,621
Occupation not registered	1,032
Total	18,967

Chapter IV

Postwar Czechoslovakia

Two periods must be distinguished in the history of postwar Czechoslovakia. Before the Communist coup of February 1948 there was a period of slow Sovietization and the extension of Communist control during which democratic appearances were kept up and a certain freedom of criticism was allowed. After February 1948, Czechoslovakia became a police state on the Russian model where no independent criticism or opposition was allowed and the power of the Communist leadership was absolute.

At the end of the war Czechoslovakia was occupied by Russian troops in accordance with the Teheran and Yalta agreements; only a part of western Bohemia, around Plzeň (Pilsen), was for a short time under American occupation. President Beneš returned from exile via Moscow. There, under Russian pressure, an agreement on the postwar government was concluded giving the most important government posts to the Communists and their supporters.

The new government and its program were proclaimed in Košice, a Russian-occupied city in eastern Slovakia. The program provided for the assumption of power locally by self-constituted "National Committees"; for broad autonomy for Slovakia, under a "Slovak National Council" with its own cabinet, called the Council of People's Commissars; for the expropriation and expulsion of all German and Hungarian citizens; for the distribution of all big landed estates among poor peasants; for the nationalization of big industries, middle-sized and small enterprises being left in the hands of private owners; and for a Russian-oriented foreign policy. Four Czech and two Slovak parties (including one Czech and one Slovak Communist party) formed the "National Front of Czechs and Slovaks" and a coalition cabinet under Premier Fierlinger, formally a Social Democrat but in reality a willing tool of Moscow. All other political parties and groups were outlawed.[1]

When the Košice government installed itself in Prague, the country became a "People's Democracy" under Communist leadership and Russian domination. After several months the Russian and American troops departed. To Russia Czechoslovakia had to cede the province of Carpatho-

Russia, now called the Carpatho-Ukraine; it had to place the uranium mines of Jáchymov (Joachimsthal) in western Bohemia completely in Russian hands; and it had to renounce any independent foreign policy. The direction of internal policy was left to the care of Czechoslovak Communists.

Formally, the constitution remained democratic, and there was a certain amount of civil liberty. The first elections, in May 1946, were fairly free. The Communists, polling 40 per cent of votes, proved to be the strongest party and their leader, Klement Gottwald, became Premier. In Slovakia they were defeated, the Slovak Democratic Party winning two-thirds of all the votes; yet the Communist preponderance in the Slovak cabinet was preserved. The new Constituent Assembly unanimously adopted laws calling for nationalization and a Two-Year Plan.

It is important to note that from the very beginning civil and political rights were, even in law, the privilege of citizens "of Czech, Slovak, or other Slavonic nationality" (i. e., ethnic group). Czechoslovak citizens of German ethnic nationality lost their citizenship, their civil rights, their properties, and their right of residence in Czechoslovakia. Many were put into detention or forced labor camps, and almost all were finally expelled from the country. Their properties were either taken over by the state, or distributed among Czech and Slovak settlers colonizing the former German regions. The same thing happened, if somewhat more slowly, to the Hungarians in Slovakia, except that some were allowed to be "re-Slovakized," i. e., to declare themselves ethnic Slovaks.[2] Only in 1948 was the policy changed, after the conclusion of an agreement with Hungary, and Hungarians in Slovakia were allowed to remain and to use their own language.

These measures were applied not only to Nazis and Nazi sympathizers, but to all Czechoslovak Germans. Only those were exempted who could prove that they had taken an active part in the resistance against Germany. Such persons, after overcoming endless obstacles and surviving prolonged investigations, might recover their Czechoslovak citizenship and escape deportation. But their citizenship gave them no political rights, which were still reserved for citizens of Czech, Slovak or other Slavonic nationality. Obstacles easily fell before only one group—the Sudeten German Communists, some of whom, as we shall see, later played a role in Jewish affairs.

Only the political parties forming the "National Front of Czechs and Slovaks" and participating in the government were allowed to conduct political activities. All other parties were prohibited. Only recognized political parties or organizations of an "all-national character," most of them in Communist hands, could publish newspapers or magazines.

The local, district, and provincial ("land") administrations remained in the hands of "National Committees," constituted in the days of liberation and thoroughly infiltrated by Communists. There were no local elections, but the composition of the local bodies was "corrected" in 1946 in accordance with the results of the general election. In some cases in which the bodies elected non-Communist mayors, these mayors were forced to resign after riotous demonstrations. The police, directed by the Communist-dominated Ministry of the Interior, were in Communist hands. Courts of law, however, preserved a certain degree of independence.

Large industry, transportation, power plants, and public utilities were nationalized. A new land reform expropriated large estates and distributed the land among small peasants and landless workers. In addition, all properties of "Germans, Hungarians, traitors, and collaborators," including farms, houses, and furnishings, were confiscated without regard to size. Farms and business enterprises were placed under a "national administration." Whole territories, left empty by the exodus of Czechoslovak Germans, were colonized by Czech and Slovak settlers, including numerous "gold-diggers"—the Czech term for carpetbagger.

Nationalization, the introduction of state planning and regulation, the "national administration of enemy properties"—all this tremendously increased the army of civil servants and public employees. The number of managers and directors, of controllers and supervisors, of chairmen and secretaries, multiplied; there were incessant complaints about overstaffed offices, administrative duplication, incompetence, and endless bureaucratic formalities in the simplest things. Although a shortage of manpower was felt in the factories and on the farms, the percentage of unproductive supervisory personnel increased. A huge new bureaucracy developed, regulating every step in the life of the citizen, who was now completely dependent on the authorities for his job, income, food rations, apartment, permission to travel—in short, for his entire life. Nobody could obtain anything unless he had not only birth, residence, and citizenship certificates, but also certificates of ethnic origin and "national reliability."

Thus throughout this period a profound discrepancy existed between appearance and reality, theory and practice, the letter of the law and its actual enforcement. Czechoslovakia was "independent," but its policies were dictated from Moscow. It was "democratic" but all opposition parties were outlawed. It enjoyed "freedom of press," but only newspapers of the parties participating in the coalition could be published. Elections were free, but their results were disregarded when they went against the Communists. Full equality for all citizens was proclaimed, but only if they were of "Czech, Slovak or other Slavonic nationality."

Yet it was possible—to an extent—to criticize, protest, remonstrate, to demand that the program of the government be adhered to and the letter of the law enforced. There was a limited freedom of information and complaint and a certain regard for foreign opinion. An effort was made not to violate appearances too flagrantly. Because of this we are able, better than in any other country in the Russian sphere, to follow each step in the process of Sovietization, with its attendant effect on the situation of the Jews. Until February 1948 Jews could still publicly complain about the wrongs they suffered. Only after the Communist coup were their communities and periodicals completely regimented and all complaints and criticisms suppressed.

The discrepancy between law and practice was particularly conspicuous in Jewish matters. There was no lack of solemn declarations about the equality of Jews, about their sufferings, about the necessity of their receiving full indemnity and restitution. Several good laws were promulgated at the beginning and advertised the world over. But at the same time the bureaucracy first quietly sabotaged the enforcement of these laws; then official "interpretations" and amendments were made encroaching on Jewish rights; and finally after the February coup the way was clear to revise them entirely so that scarcely anything of the liberal legislation remained.

The fact that the citizen was dependent at every step on some bureaucratic decision, and that it became difficult and increasingly dangerous and finally impossible to have recourse from wrong and unjust decisions, more profoundly influenced the Jewish situation than all the laws. Bureaucrats on the National Committees had the power to interpret all laws in their own fashion. There were many outright antisemites among them. And where there were no antisemites, there were either extreme nationalists, or fanatical Communists, or both. In their eyes the Jew who wanted an apartment, an indemnity, or his lost property, was a foreigner, a German who had cleverly escaped the anti-German measures on the ground of being a Jew, a former capitalist, an "anti-social element," an exploiter. The bureaucrats had a vested interest in nationalizing or placing under national administration as many properties as possible. Wherever Jewish claims and the letter of the law clashed with this interest, they found ways to get round the law, or at least to postpone a decision. Given the infinity of ordinances and regulations and an increasing lack of public control, this was not very difficult. Most citizens were powerless against the decisions of entrenched officials; Jews suffered more than others, as minority groups always do in such situations.

Such was the situation in the transitional period before the Communist coup of February 1948. As there still was a limited freedom of speech and press, and semi-independent political parties and other organizations existed, it is possible to document the situation of the Jewish community at that time in some detail.

The situation changed substantially at the beginning of 1948. At that time resistance against Communist dictatorship and police terror was growing. A few of the non-Communist newspapers and parties began to denounce the crimes and atrocities of the Communist-led police as "gestapism." In several cases the courts acquitted victims of frameups. A Communist conspiracy to assassinate the non-Communist ministers Masaryk, Zenkl, and Drtina was discovered; its organizer, a Communist deputy, was forced to resign from parliament. A Social Democratic Party congress in Brno deposed the pro-Communist wing led by Fierlinger and installed a more democratic leadership. There were prolonged conflicts about the future constitution, which the non-Communist parties wanted to guarantee democratic rights. The approaching general elections were widely expected to end in a substantial loss of votes for the Communist Party.

The Communist Coup

At the end of February 1948 the Communists answered this resistance with their coup d'état. Their Minister of the Interior, Václav Nosek, refused to heed a cabinet decision forbidding him to purge the last remaining non-Communist police officials. When repeated cabinet decisions were ignored, the ministers of the three non-Communist parties presented their resignations and brought the coalition government to an end. President Beneš refused to accept their resignations and tried to reconstruct the cabinet on a democratic basis. Communist Premier Gottwald, however, maintained the rump cabinet in power. Meanwhile the Communists convoked a congress of shop stewards in Prague and organized threatening demonstrations. They formed "Action Committees," extra-legal organs appointed by Communist cells from their members and followers. These action committees took control of every factory, office, and organization in the country, including the headquarters and newspapers of the non-Communist parties. Communist and pro-Communist leaders were put in power everywhere; all independent leaders, officers, and employees were dismissed from their posts and jobs or arrested. Communist factory militias, together with the Communist-led police, patrolled the streets; counter-demonstrations of anti-Communist students were quickly suppressed. The army was paralyzed by the pro-Communist high command. Non-Communist groups, caught unawares, capitulated. President Beneš, sick and helpless, gave in and appointed a new Gottwald cabinet composed almost exclusively of Communists and their creatures. Foreign Minister Jan Masaryk, who consented to participate in the new cabinet, was completely isolated and virtually a prisoner.

A reign of terror followed. All anti-Communists lost their jobs; some were sent to work in mines or on roads; many were arrested; many fled the country. Foreign Minister Jan Masaryk was found dead beneath the windows of his office, having either leaped himself or been pushed by others. Former Minister Drtina's fate was less doubtful; he was thrown bodily out of the window, only to be arrested when he survived the fall. Parliament was purged by its own Action Committee; a new constitution was adopted in the form proposed by the Communists; and new elections were held in May 1948, with only one "Unity List" permitted. The Unity List, which contained a great majority of Communists, was elected in an atmosphere of terror. Those who delivered blank votes—the only possible alternative—were threatened and punished. President Beneš resigned his office in June 1948 and was kept under guard in complete isolation at his country seat until he died on September 3, 1948. The Communist leader Klement Gottwald was elected President, the Communist Antonín Zápotocký becoming Premier. The Social Democratic Party was forced to merge with the Communists; Communist agents displaced the former representatives of the three non-Communist parties in Parliament and in the cabinet.

A full Communist dictatorship was now established. All industrial and commercial enterprises of any importance were nationalized and most of the remaining small businessmen were forced into liquidation by economic pressure. A Five-Year Plan followed the original Two-Year one. It called for a large increase in the output of the heavy industries and a speedy integration of the economy into the Russian orbit. The postwar labor gains in wages, social security, etc., were liquidated and the Russian system of exploitation and speed-up introduced. The forced merger of all village economic organizations into "unified cooperatives," and numerous expropriations of agricultural enterprises for non-delivery of quotas or "political unreliability," prepared the way for the collectivization of agriculture. The state administration, the professions, and all economic and cultural life were radically purged of anti-Communists or non-Communists, and later of "unreliable" Communists suspected of being infected with Western ideology or Czech or Slovak nationalism. Series of "espionage" and "conspiracy" trials resulted in countless sentences of death or long prison terms for political opponents. "Corrective labor" camps were introduced for "subversive," "unreliable," or "unproductive" elements, and many thousands of citizens were sent away by the mere administrative decision of Communist-dominated National Committees and their police organs. The borders of the country were sealed, all Western citizens arrested or expelled from the country, and the staffs of the foreign legations completely isolated. The foreign ministry, army, and police were "integrated" with analogous organs of the Soviet Union, under the supervision and command of Russian representatives.

In the summer of 1949 a violent campaign was begun against the churches and religious communities which resisted complete control of their activities by the Communist regime. It was directed especially against the Catholic church, the last large organization in the country that was independent of the Communist Party. Bills introduced in Parliament forced all priests and ministers to swear allegiance not only to the Czechoslovak Republic, but also to the "people's democratic" regime—that is, to the Communist rule; state authorities were placed in control of all church affairs, including religious education. When the Catholic church resisted, a movement of pro-Communist priests and laymen, called Catholic Action, was organized, but only a few joined. Finally, in June 1949 the palace of Prague's Archbishop Beran was searched, demonstrations were made against him in the St. Vitus cathedral, and finally the Archbishop was interned in his palace in complete isolation from the world. The papal nuncio was forced to leave the country; excommunication of pro-Communist priests or believers was declared a criminal offense; and the dissemination of uncensored pastoral letters was pronounced treason. In October 1949 parliament enacted a series of laws regulating churches. The Catholic bishops, under tremendous pressure, allowed the priests to take the oath of allegiance, though avoiding it in their own case. This did not stop the persecution. Priests were deposed and arrested, monasteries closed and many Catholics were sent to forced labor camps. A series of spectacular trials was organized. In 1950 abbots of many famous Catholic monasteries and high officials of the archbishop's office were sentenced to long prison terms; at the beginning of 1951 three Slovak bishops, two Roman Catholic bishops, and one Greek Catholic bishop received sentences of life imprisonment. At the beginning of 1951 Archbishop Beran was expelled from his diocese and a pro-Communist parish priest appointed as administrator of the Archbishopric.

Meanwhile the war against heresy within the Communist Party was intensified. Mass re-registration of rank-and-file members and removals from office of "unreliable" Communists were conducted periodically. Leaders of wartime partisan groups and those who had been in exile in Western countries were especially hard hit. Czech or Slovak "nationalism" and "concessions" to Western ideological or cultural influences were the usual accusations.

Chapter V

Restitution: Promise and Fulfilment

Most of the Jewish survivors of war and deportation were completely destitute. Inmates of concentration camps returned with their health broken, their families exterminated, and their properties lost. Many of the returning soldiers of the Czech armies abroad were, except for their decorations, scarcely better off. Those who had preferred Czechoslovakia to the Russified "Carpatho-Ukraine" were empty-handed refugees. Only those returning from the West were in a somewhat better plight.

Under these circumstances restitution of lost properties was of paramount importance. By restitution we understand here, of course, the return of properties not subject to nationalization according to law, i. e., small farms, small businesses and factories, and homes, apartments, furnishings, and personal belongings.

The Original Legislation

As early as October 17, 1941, the Czechoslovak Government-in-Exile declared that transfers of property made under duress and in consequence of "extraordinary political conditions," were not to be considered legal and would not be recognized as such after the liberation. Czechoslovak citizens were asked in radio broadcasts from London to record all such transactions clandestinely and to secure documents bearing on them and the names of witnesses. A similar declaration was collectively made by seventeen Allied governments, including Czechoslovakia, on January 5, 1943.

In a discussion among London Czechoslovaks, the Minister of Finance of the government-in-exile expressed a fear that postwar taxpayers would scarcely be able to support the burden of indemnities for crimes committed by foreigners and by a foreign occupation power. There would be resistance, he said, to such restitution which might take the form of a political movement and program.

On the Jewish side it was argued that there were sufficient sources to provide for restitution and indemnity. Defeated Germany would have to pay, Germans and collaborators would be forced to surrender their plunder, and many Sudeten Germans, even if they had not participated in the expropriations, would be obliged, because of their political crimes, to leave the country without their property.[1]

On August 3, 1944, a constitutional decree of the President (in exile), Concerning the Restitution of the Legal Order, reaffirmed the principle of the invalidity of property transfers made under duress.

After the liberation a decree of the President of the Republic of May 19, 1945, stated:

> All transfers of property and all legal transactions of any kind, whether relating to moveable or immoveable, private or public properties, are null and void, if concluded after September 29, 1938, under duress of foreign occupation or national, political, or racial persecution.[2]

The succeeding paragraph promised that detailed provisions for the realization of restitution claims would be made in future statutes.

On December 19, 1945, the presidential decree Concerning the Restitution of the Legal Order was confirmed, with slight changes, by the Provisional National Assembly, and published as Statute No. 12/1946.[3]

The enactment of two special statutes followed. One governed procedures to void court decisions handed down under the occupation and based on laws that conflicted with the provisions or principles of the Czechoslovak constitution.[4] The second voided unconstitutional decisions made by administrative agencies.[5] Both these statutes were limited to Bohemia and Moravia and did not apply to Slovakia.[6]

A definitive Law of Restitution was promulgated on May 16, 1946.[7] It repeated the provision annulling all property transfers made under duress, but added a qualification: the transfer was *not void* if the person to whom the property was transferred was "nationally reliable" and if he could prove that the transfer had been made either for an appropriate payment, or at the instance of the original owner, or chiefly in his interest.

If the original owner was "nationally unreliable," his claim was to be assumed by the state. Among persons considered "nationally unreliable," the law included

> persons of German or Hungarian nationality, except those who can prove that they had remained faithful to the Czechoslovak Republic, had never committed any acts against the Czech or Slovak nation, and had either taken active part in the struggle for liberation or had suffered under Nazi or fascist terror (par. 5, 1, no. 1 and 2).

And also persons

> who abetted Germanization or Magyarization on the territory of the Czechoslovak Republic, *or* behaved in a hostile way to Czechoslovak Republic, *or* to the Czech or Slovak nation, *or* condoned such activities in persons administering their property or enterprise (par. 5, 1, no. 3).

Claims could be made either for the restitution of the actual physical property, or for a money indemnity. Physical restitution, however, was excluded in all cases where it was "against the public interest." What the public interest was would be decided by the Ministry of Justice in agreement with the ministry exercising jurisdiction over such properties, or, in Slovakia, in agreement with the competent People's Commissariat. Courts were bound by this ministerial decision, and had no power to review it. Indemnity was also to replace restitution in cases where the present proprietor "needed the property badly for his family or household and the claimant could live decently without it. . . ."

Payment of indemnities could be postponed for a reasonable period or could be made in instalments. The courts were instructed to seek a voluntary agreement between claimant and possessor in each case. All claims filed more than three years after the promulgation of the law would be deemed inadmissible.

"German" Jews Excluded

The presidential decree of May 19, 1945 also placed all properties of "nationally unreliable" persons under "national administration." As "nationally unreliable," it specified:

1. All persons of German or Hungarian [ethnic] nationality.
2. All persons who had carried on activities directed against the sovereignty, independence, territorial integrity, democratic-republican state form, security, or defense of the Czechoslovak Republic, who had incited or in any way supported such activities, or who had given any aid or comfort to German or Hungarian occupiers. . . .

Paragraph 6 of this decree defines as "persons of German or Hungarian nationality" all those who had declared, in any census after 1929, their adherence to the German or Hungarian [ethnic] nationality, or who had belonged to organizations or political parties in which persons of German or Hungarian nationality were joined together.

The Law of Restitution of May 16, 1946, deprived all Czechoslovak Jewish citizens who had adhered to the German or Hungarian nationality of any rights to restitution. The Decree of May 19, 1945 confiscated whatever restituted or non-restituted property they might have.

Another decree, of August 2, 1945,[8] provided that all persons of "German or Hungarian [ethnic] nationality" were automatically deprived of Czechoslovak citizenship. Only those who could prove that they had remained faithful, etc., etc. (see above), could apply for the preservation of their citizenship. It lay with the Ministry of the Interior to decide, and there was no appeal from its decision.

Thus Czechoslovak Jews who had professed German or Hungarian nationality in the census of 1930—three years before Hitler came to power

—were placed in the same category with "Germans, Hungarians, traitors and collaborators," and in the first months after the liberation were treated accordingly. They had to wear German badges; received "German" food rations (equal to those which the Nazis in their time had decreed for Jews); some of them were interned in detention camps for Germans, and some were selected for deportation to Germany. Many of those who remained outside the camps had to deliver 20 per cent of their wages to the state; pensioners lost their pensions.[9]

Jewish organizations in Czechoslovakia and abroad protested against this treatment. The Czechoslovak Representative Committee of the World Jewish Congress sent a telegram to President Beneš asking him to "exclude all Jews from the group of Nazi traitors" and suggesting that the burden of proof be the government's in cases where national citizenship was at stake. The Chancellery of the President replied that "the solution of this matter has to be found individually and not generally . . . in the framework of existing legislation," and repeated the provisions of the law about the exemption of those who could prove that they had been faithful and had fought for the liberation of Czechoslovakia.[10]

But finally, under pressure of world opinion, the government made some concessions. On September 10, 1946, one and a half years after the liberation, the Ministry of the Interior prohibited the deportation of Czechoslovak Jews to Germany in Sudeten-German transports. And on September 13, it issued a General Ruling on the Treatment of Jews.[11]

The Ruling stated that all persons of Jewish or mixed origin who had lived under the German occupation were to be considered as victims of Nazi or fascist terror within the meaning of the law. Accordingly such persons, even if of German or Hungarian nationality, were to retain their Czechoslovak citizenship, provided that they met the other statutory conditions (loyalty to the Republic, etc.,) and filed applications for renewal of citizenship as required. Their property, except agricultural property, was to be exempt from confiscation.

Even here, the benefits of the law were denied to those who had participated in "Germanization" or "Magyarization." However, the fact that a person had professed German or Hungarian nationality or had talked German or Hungarian or taken part in the social and cultural life of these nationalities was not to be held to constitute a violation of the interests of the Czech or Slovak nation. Persons who had professed Jewish "nationality" were not to be considered Germans or Hungarians unless they again "promoted Germanization." Germanization and Magyarization were defined as "activities for the purpose of promoting German or Hungarian interests, *regardless if prior or subsequent to 1918*," as for instance the establishment of German or Hungarian schools and cultural institutions, and the supporting of such schools, gymnastic organizations, etc.; also, economic or moral support of any "irredentist movement"; or the employment of Germans or Hungarians in leading positions in any enterprise.

Persons of Jewish origin, although of German or Hungarian nationality, would be allowed to emigrate individually, without losing their properties. Jews found guilty of "Germanization" or "Magyarization" were to lose their citizenship and property, but would not be deported with Germans. They could apply for permission to emigrate unless a criminal prosecution was pending against them.

Jews of German or Hungarian nationality and Czechoslovak citizenship who had lived in Allied or neutral countries during the war could not be presumed to be victims of Nazi or fascist terror. They would not be discriminated against only if they satisfied the second condition of the law, that concerning active participation in the struggle for liberation in Czech or Allied armies, or in the service of the Czechoslovak Government-in-Exile.

Persons who had lost a spouse, parent, or child in a concentration camp, or at the hands of Germans anywhere, would not be discriminated against unless they had been disloyal.

This was the height of postwar Czechoslovak liberalism. The *Bulletin* of the Czechoslovak Representative Committee of the World Jewish Congress commented: "This Ruling will be read with satisfaction by those interested in the problems it refers to, both in Czechoslovakia and abroad."[12] However, the Ruling excluded from its benefits a large class of Jews, since only those German- or Hungarian-speaking Jews who had never taken an active part in cultural activities carried on in these languages, had never employed Germans or Hungarians in "leading positions," or having fled abroad had served in the Allied armies, were enabled to preserve their citizenship and right of residence in Czechoslovakia.

In the historic lands the ruling had some beneficial effects. In his report to the Conference of Jewish Religious Communities of Bohemia and Moravia in October 1947, Dr. Wehle stated that "none of those Jews who appealed to us for help" was deported to Germany; the number of those who were deported because they could not appeal for help was probably small.[13] The majority of the 2,000 Jewish survivors of German "nationality" in Bohemia and Moravia had recovered their Czechoslovak citizenship by October 1947. What happened to their properties we shall see later.

But in Slovakia, under Ordinance No. 104/1946 of the Slovak National Council, as amended by Statute No. 64/1946, everybody who had used the German or Hungarian language in his family was considered German or Hungarian. The provision was, according to the Bratislava Jewish weekly *Tribuna*, "aimed exclusively at the Jews." Replying to a complaint, a Slovak member of parliament wrote to a Jew: "If you declared German or Hungarian nationality either in 1930 or in 1940, you are liable to the confiscation of your properties; if you professed Jewish nationality, the language used in the household is decisive."[14]

Throughout the country citizenship was not identical with the enjoyment of political rights. Statute No. 28/1946 declared that only "citizens of Czech, Slovak, or other Slavonic nationality" had the right to vote. Persons who had declared Jewish nationality in 1930 were to be entered in the voting registers only if they now professed Czech, Slovak, or other Slavonic nationality.[15] This law was promulgated before the first, "democratic," postwar election in 1946. It escaped the notice of Jewish organizations abroad that Czechoslovakia disfranchised those of its citizens who considered themselves adherents of the Jewish nationality.

It is also worth reporting that the Law No. 116/1947, concerning the purge of the Reserve Officers Corps, demoted to the ranks all officers or noncommissioned officers who in any census after 1929 had declared German or Hungarian nationality, or who lived in marriage with a wife of such nationality. Exceptions could be made in "special cases" and the Jewish press expressed the hope that Jewish cases would be considered exceptional.[16]

The military authorities were charged with issuing certificates of participation in the struggle for liberation. There were repeated complaints that they "don't respect the law, discriminate against citizens of Jewish origin, and refuse to give the necessary certificates to Jewish inmates of concentration camps."[17] In one case the authorities refused to recognize the claims of a Jewish soldier who had served in the Czech army abroad from September 1940 till August 1945—because "he had left the country voluntarily."[18]

Two examples will illustrate how applications of German-speaking Jews for citizenship were dealt with: Dr. M. Ungerová, a physician, escaped to England during the war. She served voluntarily in a hospital for Czechoslovak soldiers. Immediately after the war, she volunteered to go to the Terezín concentration camp to fight the typhus epidemic there. Later, she applied for Czechoslovak citizenship. The Commission on Internal Security of the National Committee in Prague unanimously decided *not* to recommend her application for the following reasons: Ungerová and her parents were Germans, although of the Jewish faith. She had studied medicine at the German University in Prague. She considered German as her mother tongue, also spoke English and French, but did not know Czech very well. She had no "positive ties" with the Czech nation and had taken a Czechoslovak passport only in order to flee to England.

Dr. Ungerová committed suicide after this decision; the reasons quoted were given in an official statement published after her death. The Commission resolutely denied any antisemitic bias, but declared that "one cannot pass over circumstances caused by the friendly attitude of many Jews towards Germanization. . . ."[19]

Another case: the German wife of a Jew lived with her husband through the occupation. She was repeatedly arrested, underwent many Gestapo interrogations, and was pressed to divorce her Jewish husband. This she steadfastly refused to do, so saving the life of her husband, who would have been immediately deported after the divorce. Their children were finally deported and all the husband's relatives killed. After the liberation, the wife sought exemption from deportation on the ground of having endured racial persecution. The Ministry of the Interior and the Supreme Administrative Court decided that she had not been persecuted, although her husband had. She was deprived of her citizenship and made subject to deportation.[20]

Law and Practice

In an interview with the local Jewish press, the Czechoslovak Consul General in New York, Dr. Kuráž, declared:

> I am able to quote dozens of cases of Jews, right here in the United States, whose properties in Czechoslovakia have been restored, even in their absence. . . .[21] I can quote lists of Jewish properties unapplied for, which were drawn up by the Prague government and sent out in order to find the legal owners. The lists are in the hands of the American Jewish Congress. . . ."[22]

But the lists referred to by Dr. Kuráž were not lists of important properties, but of small personal belongings deposited by deported persons at the Prague Jewish Religious Community. And they were drawn up by this community and not by the government. The mistake was corrected in *Věstník*, the bulletin of the Prague Jewish Religious Community, which declared: "We were asked to state that Dr. Kuráž had in mind the lists published in our *Věstník* and reprinted by the World Jewish Congress in New York."[23] The American press was never informed about what the Consul had "in mind."

About the restitution of the more considerable properties, which were in the hands of "Aryanizers" or of the government, the Jewish press of Czechoslovakia was full of complaints. On April 1, 1947, *Věstník* summarized these in the following words:

> If we ask the statistical question of how much of the seized Jewish properties were restored to surviving Jewish citizens, the astonishing answer is that it does not add up to even 10 per cent of the prewar amount, and that the holders of stolen properties, including state funds, returned a smaller percentage of goods than the Nazi death factories did Jewish lives.[24]

This is only an estimate; statistics are not available. Only those properties still held by the German *Zentralstelle für die Regelung der Judenfrage* (Central Office for the Regulation of the Jewish Question) at the time of liberation were returned in any substantial amount. Also, according to a report of the Prague correspondent of the American Jewish Committee, of the 6,000 Jewish-owned buildings in Prague administered by that German office, 3,000 had been returned by June 1947.[25] One hundred parcels of real estate belonging to the Jewish religious communities were returned.[26] Some of these were seized again, as for example the building of the Jewish Home for the Aged in Prague, which had been taken by the Nazis in 1944, returned to the community by Czechoslovak authorities in 1946, but ordered seized again in 1947 to be used as a home for the nurses of the Vinohrady General Hospital.[27]

Wherever Jews received household furnishings taken from Germans to replace their own, they had to pay for them on the spot; for the restitution of their own properties, they had to wait indefinitely. A plea for Jews to receive extra rations of clothing and shoes because they had not been able to buy such things for years was rejected. The well-known Czech Jewish writer, Pavel Eisner, complained publicly that he had to go around wearing a fifteen-year old coat and nine-year old shoes.[28]

Here are some typical cases of the "restitution" of small business enterprises or houses that were not subject to nationalization: In the town of Žamberk, Bohemia, a Mr. Nettl was the proprietor of a small factory. His two married daughters survived the concentration camp. One of them had given birth to a baby there. She was saved from the gas chamber when her fellow prisoners somehow managed to forge a certificate of her death and then hid her and the baby in the camp. In 1945, the two sisters and the baby came back. They were greeted thus: "Look at the Jewesses! They brought a baby with them. Here you see how they have suffered!" The factory and the family house were still in the hands of the "Aryanizer," who was made the "national administrator" of the properties after liberation. He forbade the women to enter their former home or garden; when the authorities gave them a small apartment on the factory grounds (the administrator keeping the family house), he cut off their water and the telephone. This man had been sentenced to one month in prison for collaborating with the Germans, but had appealed the sentence.[29]

In the town Police nad Metují, Bohemia, a small factory was owned by four brothers named Goldmann. Two perished, one returned from a concentration camp, and one returned from Palestine. The District National Committee in Broumov refused to restore their property because they had been "Germanizers." Though all of the brothers had declared Czech nationality in 1930, they had employed six German clerks in the factory whom they had not fired until 1938, time of the Munich pact.[30]

Two brothers named Gronner owned a hotel and café in Moravská Ostrava, Moravia. In 1939 they fled to Rumania, where they survived underground. Their wives and children were killed by the Nazis. When the brothers came back, the local National Committee offered to buy the hotel at a quarter of its value. They refused and insisted on restitution. The National Committee then decided that they were "Germanizers." They had never professed German nationality, they had sent their children to Czech schools—but the authorities found out that the café had had a German bookkeeper and that it had been frequented by German-speaking guests.[31]

In Prostějov, Moravia, a center of the garment industry, twenty owners of small factories applied for restitution. The factories had been seized after the war as "German properties." A long story of bureaucratic resistance and sabotage of the law is told in the Jewish press.[32] One of the reasons given for non-restitution was Germanization; the original Jewish owners had from time to time contributed the equivalent of one or two dollars to public collections for the local German athletic club, and in one case for the German volunteer firemen. They had also contributed to Czech collections, but this was of no consequence.

When some Jewish houseowners in the Prague suburbs of Břevnov and Bubeneč asked for the return of their property, the local authorities denied them certificates of citizenship and national reliability because they had been "Germanizers" before the war. It was discovered that they had subscribed for tickets to the (state-supported) German Theater in Prague under the Czechoslovak Republic.

Under these circumstances, many of the dispossessed preferred not to apply for restitution.

The Unions Intervene

Most claims for restitution died in the National Committees. But in several cases the claimants were insistent and the courts intervened in their favor. Then Communist-led labor unions organized strikes and demonstrations and forced the courts to change their decisions, or the administrative authorities to ignore them.

The most notorious case of this kind is that of a Mr. Beer of Varnsdorf. Varnsdorf, on the northern border of Bohemia, was before the war a German town with a tiny Czech minority. Mr. Beer, the owner of a factory there, had graduated from Czech schools, had in the census of 1930 declared Jewish nationality, and had always supported Czech minority organizations. In his factory he had favored Czech employees. He had spent the war years in England. When he came back, he applied for restitution. The District National Committee decided, after a delay of 15 months, to confiscate the factory, until then under national administration.

The reason given was that Beer was a German. As this was patently untrue, the Land National Committee in Prague voided the decision. Whereupon the District National Committee issued a new ruling, confiscating the factory because Beer was a "Germanizer." And for good measure it was declared that the owner had not volunteered for the Czech army in England (Beer was 64 years old when the war started).

Beer complained to the court, and the court issued a temporary order permitting him to take possession of the factory pending a final decision. The labor unions then declared a general strike over the whole district. They demanded the immediate confiscation of all Beer's properties, the expulsion of him and his lawyer from the district, and the demotion of the judge who had issued the order. There were demonstrations, during which antisemitic slogans were shouted and some Jews—and incidentally some Slovak workers—were insulted. Beer, his lawyer, and the judge were threatened, the former finally being taken into "protective custody" by the police. He was soon released, but in the meantime the court reversed its decision and the workers returned, with a band playing, to the factory, which remained confiscated.

This incident led to wide public discussion. The non-Communist parties in Varnsdorf, which had voted against the confiscation, demanded an investigation. President Beneš received a Jewish delegation and declared that the law must be enforced without discrimination. A parliamentary commission was sent to Varnsdorf to investigate the behavior of the police.

But the Communist Party and the Central Council of the unions declared their solidarity with the strike. The Chairman of the Central Union Council—and today's President—Antonín Zápotocký, wrote in the Communist newspaper *Rudé Právo*:

> One cannot say that the judge, who returned the factory to Beer, acted against the law. He only dogmatically accepted the old juridicial views . . . because the interest of a private owner was nearer to his heart than the public interest. This old juridicial view is in contradiction with the modern view—therefore we had a strike in Varnsdorf.

And the Central Union Council, answering a complaint of the Jewish Religious Communities, adopted a resolution which said:

> The declaration of the Jewish communities is based on a wrong principle. It does not defend the interests of the citizens of Jewish faith, it defends the private interests of a capitalist. Should the Jewish communities continue this way, they would commit the gravest error possible. We ask the citizens of Jewish religion to decide whether they agree

> when their representatives lead them into the ranks of the enemies of united labor.

The statement of the unions ended with a declaration that the unions always were and are against racial discrimination.

The Jewish communities replied that they were neither against the unions nor for the capitalists, but that they had to protest against anti-Jewish discrimination. Two hundred and fifty employees of Jewish institutions, themselves union members, endorsed this point of view in a meeting called by their shop stewards. The final result was a resolution by a parliamentary committee, adopted against Communist votes, that such things should not happen again. The factory remained confiscated.[33]

In the comments of the Jewish press it was stressed that Varnsdorf was by no means unique. "In Slovakia, people will tell you how many Varnsdorfs there were recently," *Věstník* wrote matter-of-factly.

One such instance was the Weltson leather factory in Bratislava. The factory had been "Aryanized" under the Slovak puppet government. After the war the incumbent made an agreement with the legal owner, and the court restored the factory. But the Slovak People's Commissariat for Industry refused to remove the national administration, maintaining that the factory was essential to the operation of the nationalized Bat'a Shoe Factories. When the administration of the Bat'a Works declared that this was not true, the Commissariat declared that the factory could not be returned because the workers were against it. The owner offered a declaration by the shop stewards saying that the workers agreed to restitution. Whereupon the unions dispatched an official to the factory to "poll" the workers. The roll was called (secret balloting being denied), and when 29 of the 75 workers had declared themselves opposed to restitution, against 27 voting for restitution, the union official arbitrarily stopped the roll call. It had been decided, "according to the will of the working masses," that there would be no restitution.[34]

In Mohelnice, Moravia, the procedure was somewhat different in that the workers of the shop in question could not be brought to declare themselves against restitution, whereupon a vote was taken and a protest strike organized in another factory in the neighborhood.[35]

It is characteristic that in both these cases the workers were forced to protest against restitution by their own organizations. They would seem to have found out already that their lot scarcely improved with the taking over of the factories by the state. However, the bureaucracy of course had a vested interest in nationalization.

In all these cases the favorite pretext for confiscation of properties not subject to nationalization was "Germanization." But in other cases, it was charged that the former owner had ill-treated his employees and was an "antisocial element." This reason was used in the case of the department stores. The unions, by striking, forced their illegal nationalization.

The best known case is that of a Mr. Anders, owner of the ARA department stores. Anders, a Jew, returned after the war as an American citizen and claimed his property. When a court ordered restitution, the unions struck, declaring that Anders was "antisocial." The strike was settled when restitution was put off to the end of 1947. But then new legislation later on nationalized all department stores.

A correspondent of the American Jewish Committee in Prague remarked that "the authorities treated this case very carefully so as not to hurt the Jews." Anders did not ask the Jewish community for help and the community decided, according to the correspondent, "to withdraw its attention from the case."[36]

In all these controversies, the primary motive of the strike organizers seems to have been a desire to extend the scope of nationalization and to expropriate "foreign elements," rather than outright antisemitism; but they were ready to play upon antisemitic feelings whenever it suited their purpose. On the other hand, the non-Communist parties fought the illegal expropriations, not so much to defend the principle of equality of Jews, but mainly because they feared precedents that might be used against Gentile property owners.

Restitution Laws Revised

The situation remained as described up to the middle of 1947: the restitution laws remained on the statute books, but the authorities found a thousand excuses to disallow claims, and wherever courts tried to enforce the law union pressure was brought to bear to prevent it. Thereafter attempts were made to revise the legislation. The first important step was taken in a devious way, in the Law on the Currency Liquidation Fund. The Law of Restitution of 1946 provided that Jewish properties whose legal owners died or disappeared without heirs were to be used for the benefit of Jewish communities. The enactment of a special statute governing the procedure for this had been promised. Instead, when the bill on the Currency Liquidation Fund was discussed in the cabinet, an amendment was suddenly proposed and adopted which gave all heirless properties to this Fund. The Council of Jewish Religious Communities protested. It pointed out that this paragraph was put into the law without hearings and without consultations with the ministries concerned; that it disavowed a legal promise; that in the peace treaties Czechoslovakia had required Hungary and Rumania to restore Jewish heirless properties to Jewish communities; and that it was the first Western European country to expropriate such properties for the benefit of the state.

All protests and representations were in vain. On July 2, 1947, the law was adopted by parliament in the form proposed by the cabinet. A meaningless resolution was appended, asking the government to "take into consideration the social and cultural needs of the Jewish communities."[37] The law still required the signature of President Beneš, and new representations were made by the Jewish communities to him and by a secretary of the World Jewish Congress to Foreign Minister Jan Masaryk. The result was a declaration that "appropriate steps will be taken to harmonize the enforcement of the law with obligations which Czechoslovakia undertook in international agreements."[38] This promised very little, for Czechoslovakia had required former enemy countries to restore Jewish heirless properties, but had not accepted such obligations for itself.

A special case involving heirless property was the so-called "Terezín substance." These were funds and properties, taken by the Nazis from murdered Jews, which had been found in the camp at Terezín after the war. The government, though never recognizing these funds as a collective Jewish property, paid out of them, in the years 1945-1947, certain subsidies to the Jewish religious communities. From this source the communities received, up to the end of 1947, 60 million crowns ($1,200,000 according to the official rate of exchange, and a quarter of that amount according to the illegal rate). Subsidies ceased to be paid at the end of 1947, probably as a result of the previously mentioned Law on the Currency Liquidation Fund.

Two years later, on February 6, 1949, Emil Ungar, the new Communist-appointed President of the Council of Jewish Religious Communities in Bohemia and Moravia, explained the stoppage of the payment of the subsidies thus:

> This subsidy . . . was in fact a gift from the state because the money in this fund had lost its value by inflation. . . . The fact that these fictive values were partly redeemed in the new currency, constituted an inflationary force which the government could no longer tolerate. . . . The fictive character of this resource was soon proved when the State Control Board stopped further payments from the Terezín substance. There is no doubt that we can not and will not count on further payments from this source.[39]

In this way, the remainder of the funds appropriated by the Nazis was now reappropriated by the Czechoslovak government.

The Jewish community, however, scored one small success. The Communist Finance Minister introduced a bill substantially increasing the inheritance tax. This increase applied to all estates which were not formally transferred to their heirs before December 31, 1946. Since in the case of Jews deceased during the war, often in unknown places of deportation and extermination, the transfer of their estates was a lengthy and complicated procedure, the provision struck particularly at Jewish heirs. After many representations, the bill was finally changed in such a way that the increased tax applied to estates of persons who died after November 12, 1947.[40]

But no amount of protests could alter the practice of the Ministry of Finance in enforcing payment of the *Reichsfluchtsteuer*, the special confiscatory emigration tax introduced by the Nazis in occupied Czechoslovakia as well as in Germany. The Supreme Administrative Court of the Republic decided that this tax was not discriminatory, did not conflict with the principles of the Czechoslovak constitution, and had to be paid.[41] In a circular of November 23, 1946, the Ministry of Finance instructed the internal revenue offices to insist on the payment of the tax, at least by all persons who had not returned to the country after the war.[42]

There were also cases where internal revenue offices assessed taxes for the years 1939-41 against persons returned from concentration camps or exile. When these citizens objected, their appeal was dismissed because of failure to file on time. One such decision was finally voided by the Supreme Administrative Court, but only after two years of litigation.[43]

In the meantime a campaign for the wholesale revision of the restitution laws had been started in Slovakia. There, Jewish properties, especially land, had been distributed among Slovaks rather than among Germans. The vested interests opposing restitution were accordingly stronger.[44]

According to Jewish sources, 90 per cent of the Jewish farms in Slovakia remained illegally confiscated after the liberation.[45] Among the expropriated Jews were men who had been killed in battle fighting for Czechoslovakia, soldiers who came back with many decorations, and people who had died in concentration camps.[46]

The decree of December 19, 1945, Concerning the Restitution of the Legal Order (No. 12/1946), did not apply to Slovakia. The cabinet was instructed to extend it to Slovakia in proper time, but never did.[47] The Law of Restitution of May 16, 1946, did apply to the country as a whole. But in Slovakia it was impossible to file claims against the state, as the Czechoslovak Republic was not considered to be the legal heir of the defunct Slovak puppet government.

Claims against private persons were given short shrift by the Slovak People's Commissariat of Justice. In August 1946 it issued a circular to the courts stating that the Law of Restitution could not be enforced as yet, since there were no proper regulations governing enforcement. Soon afterwards another circular informed the courts that they should not go ahead too quickly in adjudicating claims of restitution, since an amendment to the law was being proposed. Courts were instructed not to consider restitution claims during the period of the summer vacations.[48] A judge apologized to the defendant in a restitution case: "We have to trouble you only because of this unhappy restitution law."[49] This expressed a rather typical attitude.

Both Slovak parties, the Communists and the anti-Communist Democrats, outdid each other in campaigning for revision of the Law of Restitution. The Democratic newspaper *Čas* wrote that "the letter of the law cannot be applied thoroughly" because "20,000 Slovak peasants had received Jewish lands, had partly paid for them, and it would be a great social and financial wrong to take them away from them."[50] The United Association of Slovak Peasants, under Communist leadership, demanded the suspension of all restitution proceedings until the law was revised. Two revision bills were introduced in parliament: one by the Democratic deputy Kvet'ko, another by the Communist leader Falt'an.[51] They were almost identical, and the Agricultural Committee of the chamber consolidated them into one.[52]

Finally the Resettlement Office and the National Rehabilitation Fund submitted a comprehensive bill revising all legislation concerning restitution, agricultural and otherwise, for the whole country.

On February 20, 1948, on the eve of the Communist coup, the Jewish organizations declared in a memorandum to the government that this bill "means a complete reversal of the principle of restitution, which had been solemnly accepted by the government of the Czechoslovak Republic."[53] The Jewish press attacked it in very sharp terms.[54]

But after the coup complaints and protests ceased. In Slovakia, immediately after the installation of the new, Communist-dominated, Slovak cabinet, the chief of its Department of Justice, Dr. L. Victory, ordered the courts to cancel all cases involving the restitution of land holdings to Jews. The Communist newspaper *Pravda* welcomed the order, declaring that it would give legal and material security to Slovak smallholders now claiming former Jewish lands as their own.[55]

Soon afterwards a revised law of restitution was adopted for the entire republic by the purged parliament on April 7, 1948. It provided that landed properties which had been distributed (by German or collaborationist authorities) among smallholders were not subject to restitution. A smallholder was defined as a person who would, after surrender of all illegally acquired property, own less than 16 hectares (about 38 acres) of land. The original owner was to receive government lands from the state in the amount of the (nominal) fee paid to the state by the usurper when he took possession. A claimant could sue the new owner for the difference between this amount and the normal price. This was the procedure where land was still in the hands of the original usurper. But if the claim was against a person who had obtained the disputed property after the war, the original owner had to content himself with the nominal indemnity in the form of government bonds; he had no further claims at all.

Industrial and other business property nationalized after the war would not be restored, even if such property was not otherwise subject to nationalization according to the law. Here again, the owner was to receive only an indemnity in the form of government bonds.

When and how these bonds would be issued and redeemed, the cabinet would decree later.

Restitution was denied in all cases where it was "against the public interest." What the public interest was would be decided by the Land National Committees of Bohemia and Moravia-Silesia, and by the Council of People's Commissars in Slovakia. Their decisions would be binding on the courts. Everyone claiming restitution had first to prove his "national reliability." (This requirement had previously been restricted to "dubious cases.")

Restitution in kind could not be claimed for persons whose whereabouts were not known, or for heirs of the third class.[56] All voluntary agreements concerning restitution were valid only if approved by the National Rehabilitation Fund. All restitution claims were null and void if not filed within three months after the promulgation of the new law, i. e., on or before July 27, 1948.[57]

The effect of this law is obvious. Hardly any restitution in kind was to be made because the usurped properties had either been nationalized, or were in the hands of smallholders, or had been seized for the benefit of Czech or Slovak "patriots." Other claims to restitution in kind would be frustrated by invoking the provisions about "the public interest," the "national reliability" of the former owners, persons of unknown whereabouts, or heirs of the third class. If any claims still remained, the statute of limitations would dispose of them.

Such claims to indemnification as were allowed, in addition to representing only a fraction of the value of the usurped properties, would have to wait upon the issuance and redemption of government bonds at some future and uncertain date.

Of special interest was the provision making irrevocable the nationalization of Jewish properties that would not have been subject to nationalization in the hands of their original owners. A Jew lost his small workshop because, after its expropriation by the Nazis, it had been consolidated under the republic with other small shops into a large enterprise. If the owner had not been Jewish, he would not ordinarily have been deprived of his shop under the Nazis in the first place, nor again in 1948 when it would not have been subject to nationalization. This provision clearly penalized citizens who were Jewish.

After February 1948, criticisms of restitution laws and proceedings disappeared from the Jewish press. The weekly *Tribuna* in Bratislava, which had led a vigorous campaign against Slovak "Aryanizers" on economic and moral grounds, now stammered something about "very complicated conditions" and "the interest of the Slovak common man in the solution of this question." It suddenly discovered that Slovak Jews had never wanted their landed properties back anyhow and had always been eager to leave them in the hands of "smallholders" for a partial indemnity.[58] As for the Prague *Věstník*, the restitution problem vanished completely from its pages. To demand restitution of Jewish properties became virtual treason.

The issue of restitution was never taken up again under the Communist dictatorship. The provisions concerning indemnities were not enforced, and a new wave of nationalization swallowed up the remaining small enterprises and properties. Jews permitted to emigrate were allowed to take with them only a bare minimum of personal belongings. Only Jews who were Communist and pro-Communist leaders and officials were able to keep homes, furnishings, and articles of personal comfort which they had retrieved (or acquired) after the end of the war.

Subsequently the properties of Jewish communal and welfare institutions were also nationalized, the buildings and funds of dissolved religious communities being "voluntarily donated" to state or communal authorities, as we shall see in later chapters.

The final result is plain. A minor part of the Nazi-expropriated Jewish properties remained in the hands of Czech and Slovak usurpers or their legal successors; the major part was re-expropriated by the Communist state collectively, or by its high officials individually. Destitution rather than restitution was the lot of most of the Jewish survivors of Nazism.

Chapter VI

Relief, Training, and Rehabilitation

In the first years after liberation the Jewish communities and international Jewish relief agencies gave assistance to thousands of Jews in Czechoslovakia, native as well as transient. The latter were mostly Polish Jews passing through the country on their way to the American zone of Germany. In the ensuing years, 1946 and 1947, the economic situation of the local Jews "improved considerably," according to the reports of the Joint Distribution Committee. "The small Jewish community in the country has made a considerable effort toward self-sufficiency and has achieved a considerable success on the road to rehabilitation."[1] This was probably due to the fact that (1) numbers of middle-class Jews were able to find employment in the public administration or in nationalized industries as officials, managers, and clerks of various kinds; and (2) small industries and commerce had not yet been nationalized, which permitted some Jews to make a living in private enterprise. No figures are available about the degree of the absorption of the Jewish population in different branches of the economy. From scattered data it would seem that assimilated Czech Jews tended to concentrate in the nationalized industries, professions, and civil service; whereas Slovak Jews and the Carpatho-Russian newcomers to the historic lands tried to establish themselves in private business. The year 1947, just before the Communist coup, seems to have been the best one in the postwar history of the Jewish communities.

After the Communist coup the situation deteriorated. Hope of restitution now definitely faded and small industry and commerce were being swiftly nationalized. In the middle of 1948, the JDC reported that "the rapid nationalization of industry following the change in the government has displaced a large number of Jewish businessmen who had been the main support of their communities, and it would seem that JDC will have to assume greater responsibility for the remaining group than it has had to in the past."[2]

In June 1948, about 4,000 persons were still receiving cash relief from the JDC. About 800 of these were transients, leaving some 3,200 native recipients of relief, or not quite 10 percent of the entire Jewish community. In addition, the JDC maintained a kitchen, distributing food to 250 persons, supported 4 children's homes and one kindergarten, and sent 600 children away for the summer. It also gave substantial aid to the Jewish Hospital in Bratislava, to a tuberculosis sanatorium in the Tatra mountains, to 4 homes for the aged, as well as to 2 homes for young men.[3]

The relief program had already been reduced to a minimum and the emphasis was now shifted to "reconstruction activities." With the financial support of the JDC, two credit institutions were established by the Jewish committees, the Obroda in Prague, and the Pomocná Pokladnica in Bratislava. Their task was to make loans to Jewish artisans and small businessmen. According to data obtained from the JDC, there were 700 loan recipients in 1946, 4,000 in 1947,[4] and 640 in 1948. The sudden jump in 1947 is explained by the fact that family members were counted with the recipients in that year. Still, the decline from 1947 to 1948 was real, if not as great as the inflated figure for 1947 would suggest. The *JDC Review* reported:

> Because of the economic policy of the government aimed at the gradual liquidation of the so-called intermediary activities, the loan kassas in both the Czech lands and Slovakia have noted a decrease in the number of applications.[5]

Another report of the same time[6] said that the lending activities of the Obroda in Prague were decreasing, mainly due to increased emigration, lack of raw materials, and the uncertain attitude of the government toward private ownership of small business. In this report is found some information about the extent of the loans that were made. In the second quarter of 1948, the institution in Bratislava issued loans in the amount of 1,209,000 crowns ($24,000 according to the official rate of exchange), an inconsiderable sum even under modest Czechoslovak circumstances.

In this period all credit institutions were being nationalized, but the JDC was semiofficially informed that those it supported would receive special consideration. It was emphasized, however, that such special treatment was possible only because these institutions were of a temporary character.

Jewish producers' cooperatives, also supported by the JDC, had 300 members in 1946, 190 members in 1947, and 250 members in 1948. In the last year, some of their members were non-Jewish "specialists."

JDC statistics for 1947[7] gave the number of cooperatives as 4 (with 190 members). Later reports spoke of 3 cooperatives, 2 of them textile shops in Bratislava and Rimavská Sobota, Slovakia, and the third a carpentering cooperative in Bratislava. In the summer of 1948, the textile cooperatives in Slovakia were able to work at capacity because of the JDC's having purchased their yarn for them.[8]

Training courses in industry were conducted by the Organization for

Rehabilitation through Training (ORT) with the support of the JDC. The number of trainees, though it differed in the different ORT and JDC reports, was in any case not considerable. An ORT report said that 170 trainees were graduated after the first examination from these courses, which were begun in 1947. The same report said that there were 6 training centers offering 11 courses to 292 students at the end of 1947.[9] JDC statistics "as of the end of 1947," showed 6 centers offering 9 courses to 178 students.[10] A third report in November 1947 gave 6 centers offering 9 courses to 166 students.[11] In June 1948 it was reported that there were 7 centers offering 10 courses to 131 students.[12] One hundred and thirty-six of the 166 students reported on in November 1947, and 107 of the 131 students of June 1948, were trained in needle trades, the rest being listed as "others" in 1947, and in "mechanical hand trades" in 1948. The last available report of the JDC lists 2 centers with 70 students at the end of 1948. Czechoslovak sources speak of 116 trainees in the workshops of the Czechoslovak ORT.[13] They mention one typewriter repair and 2 toy and leatherware shops, in addition to a shop for shirtmaking.

The JDC statistics for 1947 also listed vocational and training units organized by other organizations than the ORT. It was explained that these figures included "*hachscharoth, kibbutzim* and some industrial training." In Czechoslovakia there were, according to the statistics, 17 such units with 675 members.[14]

Of the several hundred persons who were trained in the three years of planned vocational training, the majority were members of *kibbutzim* and other prospective emigrants. It is safe to say that neither the small cooperative movement nor the training courses played any considerable role in the economic rehabilitation of the community. Whatever was achieved in this field was achieved with the help of international Jewish relief organizations. The government neither interfered with these activities nor supported them.

This tolerance ceased with the Communist coup. First, the new leadership imposed by the Communists on the Jewish religious communities substantially reduced welfare activities. Later, the activities of the international Jewish relief organizations in Czechoslovakia were ended by government decree, and the Jewish welfare institutions that had been founded with their help were "nationalized."

Revealing details about the curtailment of the number and activities of the community welfare institutions were contained in a report by Dr. Emil Ungar, Communist-appointed President of the Council of Jewish Religious Communities in Bohemia and Moravia, to a meeting of the Council on February 6, 1949, one year after the Communist coup.[15]

Dr. Ungar described the catastrophic financial situation of the communities. He stated that in the years 1945-1947, the Council had had two main sources of income, from "the Terezín substance"[16] and from the American Jewish Joint Distribution Committee. After 1947, subsidies provided from the "Terezín substance" ended with the latter's seizure by the government. According to Czechoslovak law, still in force after the Communist coup, religious communities of every denomination were entitled to government subsidies for their religious as well as relief and rehabilitation activities. When the state budget appropriations for 1949 were being prepared, the Council submitted its budget to the Ministries of Education, Social Welfare, and Public Health. This budget, "very carefully prepared and much lower than in former years," was nevertheless returned to the communities with a demand that personnel expenses be cut in half. "New community budgets are now being prepared," Dr. Ungar reported, but "in consequence of the situation which developed in the fall of 1948, the state budget for 1949 could not take our needs into consideration."

Having lost its subsidies from the Terezín funds as well as state donations, the Council had to finance its needs from "accumulated reserves." That meant, Dr. Unger made clear, that minor communities had to be consolidated, and that the Council as well as individual communities had to contract loans and to sell their properties.

Dr. Ungar strongly criticized the old leadership of the communities for having squandered funds on indiscriminate welfare activities, for having spent too much for relief "without any unified plan for the productivization of Jewish labor." The old Council, he said, "was supporting reactionary, capitalist tendencies under the pretext of cultural and social welfare activities." Its having assisted transient Jewish emigrants from the other satellite countries was a special target of his criticism, but his criticism extended to "unproductive" welfare activities generally. These were now substantially reduced; however, the "unified plan for the productivization of Jewish labor" was never heard of again.

A new blow to Jewish rehabilitation activities came in January 1950, when the Czechoslovak government ordered the American Jewish Joint Distribution Committee to close its offices by the end of the month. The JDC spent, according to some estimates, $6,000,000 for Jewish relief in Czechoslovakia;[17] Dr. Ungar acknowledged, in his above-quoted report, that it contributed, in the years 1945-1947, about $1,000,000 to the welfare activities of the Council alone.

Nevertheless, it was ordered to wind up its affairs in two weeks. Its Prague director, Henry Levy, was requested to leave Czechoslovakia together with all foreign members of his staff. The 32 Czechoslovak citizens on the staff were dismissed. The remaining funds, about $400,000, were taken over by the Czechoslovak National Bank, which agreed to distribute their equivalent in Czechoslovak currency among Jewish institutions under control of Communist-dominated associations of religious communities.[18]

At the same time, Jewish welfare institutions were being "nationalized," i. e., they were placed under government control and lost their specifically Jewish character. Such was the fate, on January 1, 1950, of the model Jewish hospital in Bratislava, which had been equipped with American aid.[19] The nationalization of other Jewish institutions followed.

The ban placed on activities of foreign welfare organizations and the "nationalization" of domestic welfare institutions were officially explained by assertions that Jews, being equal citizens of the republic, should be taken care of by the general social security and public health agencies; they needed no welfare institutions of their own.

Meanwhile, the Jewish "surplus population," which could not be absorbed into the new economy, was being slowly reduced by emigration.[20]

Chapter VII

Antisemitism

In August 1946 the Czechoslovak Institute of Public Opinion conducted a survey of the degree of prejudice entertained against members of different religious communities.[1] The question, put by the investigators to a cross-section of the population, was: "Do you distrust adherents of any specific religious denomination?"

Of those queried, 15.9 per cent admitted to "distrusting" Jews; 7.4 per cent distrusted Catholics; 1.3 per cent, Protestants; 8.2 per cent, atheists; while 67.2 per cent declared that they had no prejudices against members of any religious community.

In the age group 18-29, the percentage of persons admittedly distrusting Jews was markedly higher—20.2. In the occupational groups, the highest percentage of anti-Jewish feeling was found among self-employed professionals (20.3), followed by workers (16.6). The lower middle class professed distrust of Jews in 14.5 per cent of all cases, the upper middle class in 13.1 per cent; strangely enough, the smallest percentage of distrust was found among peasants—11.9.

There is no doubt that antisemitism was much more prevalent than the poll indicated. People sometimes do not like to admit their antisemitic prejudices even to themselves; even less were they inclined to admit them to a semiofficial institution in a country where such prejudices were officially discouraged and described as a weapon of fascism and counterrevolution. And the question, put as it was on the religious plane, missed all persons whose antisemitic feelings have, in their opinion, nothing to do with religion.

Therefore, all that we can reliably conclude from the survey is that at least 16 per cent, and in all likelihood many more, of the population were conscious of entertaining antisemitic prejudice.

Antisemitic attitudes were expressed in popular reactions ranging from remarks to riots; in the behavior of officialdom, especially of its lower strata, toward Jewish citizens; and even in the well-meaning statements of those who advised Jews on how to behave so as not to provoke the wrath of the population. Prejudice often showed through the mask of official benevolence worn by high officials and Communist leaders. In off-the-record speeches and remarks, they often aired feelings that strangely contrasted with their official statements; in the period before the Communist coup, the Jewish press was able to note such remarks and to protest against them.

Rationalizations

What had changed were the rationalizations. There was no more talk about "racial inferiority." That sort of thing had been thoroughly discredited by the Nazis, in whose eyes Czechs and Slovaks were inferior races too. There was also, at least in public, little said about the Jews having sinned against God and crucified Christ. Such would be "religious intolerance," which the laic state discouraged.[2] But the aforementioned poll and some incidents in Slovakia show that this feeling still existed, especially among devout Catholics.

Jews, nevertheless, were "guilty," first of all, of "Germanization" and "Magyarization." This crime they had not expiated by their sufferings under the Nazis. From Beneš down to the last small official, antisemitism was "explained," if not condoned, by the fact that the Jews "had supported German schools, books, and cultural institutions," "had spoken German [or Hungarian] in a provocative way," or had hired German employees. This argument was considered valid even if proofs for it had to be sought many years back in the days of Austrian rule. Grandchildren returning from the Nazi death camps still had to expiate the fact that under Emperor Franz Joseph their grandparents had been obliged to go to German or Hungarian schools. This argument was used both by the Communists and by their nationalist opponents, as a few examples will indicate.

In 1947 the office of the President of the Slovak National Council organized a campaign against "Magyarizing," meaning the "provocative" use of the Hungarian language. Three categories of persons were officially designated as special targets for the campaign: Jews, Gypsies, and emigrants returning to the country.[3]

Assimilated Czech and Slovak Jews did not escape the accusation of Germanization. They were suspected of having adopted the Czech or Slovak language for purely opportunistic reasons. The Slovak press often used the term "Neo-Slovak" as a synonym for Jews.[4] Jews who changed their German names for Czech names after the liberation were, in dealings with the authorities or when applying for a job, often asked their former names and the religion of their parents.[5]

Another rationalization, again used both by Communists and non-Communists, was of social character: the Jews are, or were, "capitalists," "exploiters." A milder version of this had almost an official status. *Občanská Výchova*, an official organ on civic education, carried an article, supposed to serve as directive for school teachers, which declared:

When capitalism penetrated our country from the West, there were Jewish capitalists among the foreigners. From the well-known Jew Basevi, who financed the armies of Wallenstein, through the intendants of custom duties and founders of distilleries, a direct way leads to the founders of the textile enterprises. Their very names bear witness to the fact that the capitalists were of foreign, non-Czech origin.[6]

Pedagogical practice is illustrated by the following quotation from a teacher's lecture in a primary school:

The Jews lived in Palestine but the Romans threw them out. They are black-marketeers and we don't like them. But we don't expel them because we are democrats. In Nazi concentration camps, there were both Jews and Christians, but there were more Christians than Jews.[7]

A report in a local Communist newspaper on a meeting of the workers of the nationalized textile factory, Gschwandt, in Hořice, said:

Workers, clerks, and members of the new management met in all their numbers in order to prove their enthusiasm at this time when the enterprise has definitely got rid of its Jewish, and later German, exploiters.[8]

Usually, the imputations of "Germanization" and exploitation went hand in hand; Jews were not only "exploiters," but "foreign elements" and "Germanizers." They were not only Germans or Hungarians, but helped Germans and Magyars to exploit the people. This explained, and to a certain degree excused, popular antisemitism in the eyes of people who would strongly resent being described as antisemites. Let us quote two statements out of hundreds made by high officials.

President Beneš declared in an interview with the Jewish Telegraphic Agency in August 1945:

. . . Anti-Jewish feelings in Slovakia come from the fact that the political, cultural, and economic level is not yet as high as in Bohemia. . . . There was also antisemitism in Bohemia, but this was because the Jews in Bohemia were representatives of Germanization in the days when Bohemia was a part of Austria. There was hatred against the Jews only because Jews of that generation appeared to be willing tools of the Germans. . . .[9]

Taking his cue from the President, the Czechoslovak Ambassador in Washington, Colonel V. S. Hurban, explained the riots in Slovakia to the American public as follows:

The second accusation . . . is the alleged antisemitism in Slovakia. It was acknowledged, in a certain degree, frankly and honestly by President Beneš. But this antisemitism is not based on racial grounds. The Jews in Slovakia during the Hungarian regime were the privileged class who served the Magyar oppressors to oppress the people and to exploit them

> mercilessly. . . . In Slovakia the Jews living with the Slovaks were nationally Magyars even after the establishment of Czechoslovak independence. It cannot be forgotten easily by the population.[10]

The Chairman of the National Committee in Topolčany, Slovakia, put this same idea more simply. He declared on August 8, 1945, six weeks before the pogrom that shook this town:

> The Jews—with rare exceptions—did not treat the Slovak people well. They did not respect our language, babbled Hungarian and German, declared themselves Germans or Magyars; they were the greatest exploiters of the Slovak people, whose blood they sucked like leeches.[11]

All these arguments were invoked, as we have seen, to prevent the restitution of Jewish properties.

Jews were also said to have suffered too little during the war. They "lived in emigration in comfort"; they joined the resistance "at the very last moment"; they "served in offices rather than at the front." One must pity those who have been in concentration camps; still, it was not as bad as they would like to make it seem because "so many" survived. And anyway, the Czechs were sent to concentration camps because they really fought against the Germans, but Jews were there "for no reason." The Association of Former Prisoners sought to divide its members into three categories: those who were imprisoned because they had actively fought against the Nazis; those who were arrested because of their suspected democratic views; and those who were simply victims of racial persecution. This project was not realized, but some communities, erecting monuments to victims of the Nazis in their towns, put on them first, in alphabetical order, all murdered "Aryan" citizens, and then, again in alphabetical order, all the Jewish names.[12]

But the main source of antisemitic sentiment in postwar Czechoslovakia was the problem of restitution. In Slovakia, under the Tiso regime, Jewish properties had been distributed mainly among Slovaks; this was one of the reasons antisemitism there was more violent than in the historic lands. In Bohemia and Moravia, the first to profit by the expropriations were Germans; but then after the war these properties came into the hands of Czechs, who were either private persons or "national administrators." In addition, many Czechs moved into Jewish apartments or volunteered to "hide" Jewish belongings. When the owners or their heirs appeared after the war and claimed their property, clashes occured; people who were asked to return Jewish valuables in their custody complained bitterly, sometimes openly in newspapers.[13]

The controversy over the extent of nationalization and postwar confiscation evoked still more antisemitic feelings. The people of postwar Czechoslovakia were told that all means of production belonged to the state and that the state was a "state of Czechs and Slovaks." To those who held this view, every restitution claim seemed an attempt to rob the Czech and Slovak nation of its rightful property. Private claims had, in their eyes, to yield to the "public interest"; "foreigners" had no right to encroach upon the collective rights of Czechs and Slovaks. The bureaucracy, with its vested interest in nationalization, knew how to use such feelings.

Antisemitism was also used by the anti-Communists. Here, the main weapon was propaganda about the "tremendous" influence of Jews in the Communist Party and government. Even before the Communist coup, these complaints were never aired in the press; it was too dangerous publicly to attack Communist leaders with such arguments. But there was much talk, *sotto voce*, about the "Jewish Communists."

Communist Attitude Before the Coup

Antisemitic feelings were often expressed in letters, signed and unsigned, to the editors of newspapers and magazines. Here are some typical instances of letters printed in the pro-Communist magazine *Kulturní Politika*, in connection with a complaint by a Mr. Weiss, a Czech film worker, against a Communist writer accused of protecting a well-known antisemitic film director. One reader wrote:

> The Jew Weiss, protected by you, was sitting abroad in security; he cries for his mother, but he calmly left her to the Nazis and saved himself. . . .

Another letter, from a worker, said:

> For the Czechs, there is drudgery, and for the Jews, jobs as bank directors, just like before Munich; these are the jobs they miss, especially the bank embezzlers. Don't you remember the scandals at the time of the First Republic? This is not a racial question. The Jews can live like other Czechs do. But they should not try to take jobs that nobody has invited them to fill, and should wait until we forget their Germanizing. They should try to earn money in other ways than by smart business.

Still another reader, a student, wrote:

> I think, Mr. Weiss, that even if you have good will, neither you nor your children will become good Czechs.[14]

The above mentioned discussion in the *Kulturní Politika* provoked the magazine to comment editorially:

> There are facts which nobody can explain away: a great percentage of Jews considered themselves German and, as had already been said many a time, really supported Germandom, its theaters, schools, and its expansion in our lands. . . . But there were also, even under the Austro-Hungarian monarchy, Jews who consciously assimilated themselves to the Czech nation and considered themselves Czechs. . . . The year 1918 and the foundation of Czechoslovakia thus found the Jewish population divided: some considered themselves Czechs, others Germans.

> Obviously, those Jews who considered themselves Germans (and who, if Hitler had not been an antisemite, would certainly have become furious Nazis) must not be surprised if the Czech people consider them German and do not want them in their midst. Those who feel themselves to be German and want to speak German should go to Germany or Austria. As for those who are national Jews with a capital J*) let them go where they can build a Jewish state. . . . But those who have proved they are Czechs, their love for this country and its people, their loyalty to our state, let them fuse with the people and share in our reconstruction and in our people's life; if they wage with us the common fight against the remnants of fascism and nazism, if they build socialism, they will liquidate the Jewish problem forever. . . . If great artists, as for instance Bezruč, attack Jewish exploiters violently, we shall never suppress their words or work; we are only of the opinion that the period of Nazi occupation, when Jews were made responsible for all the evils ever committed by capitalism and its German-fascist exponents, was not the proper time to solve the internal problem of the Czech nation's relations to the Jews.

This remained, with small modifications, the attitude of the Communists up to 1951.

When, in April 1947, Jewish organizations and the Antifascist League called a special public meeting in Prague against antisemitism, the Communist magazine *Tvorba* commented:

> It is not correct to help the antisemitism of a few individuals by making it appear important in a way it does not deserve, and to organize manifestations against it.[15]

Although antisemitism was officially outlawed, revealing antisemitic slips occurred in the speeches of Communist leaders. The Minister of Information, Václav Kopecký, a prominent Communist leader well known for violent speeches against fascist antisemites, addressed a public meeting in Teplice shortly after the Varnsdorf affair.[16] Teplice, in former Sudeten-German territory, is not far from Varnsdorf. Kopecký discussed, among other things, the Jews from Carpatho-Russia who had settled in this region, declaring that "these bearded Solomons," this "Jewish scum,"[17] had joined the resistance only at the last moment and had no right to special advantages that would wrong decent Czechs.

The Teplice branch of the Association of Former Prisoners adopted a resolution protesting against these utterances, and the Prague Social Democratic newspaper, *Právo Lidu*, joined in their protest.[18] The Communist

*) In the Czech language the initial letter of names of nations are capitalized, whereas the initial letter of the names of religions are not. Thus *Žid* (Jew) describes a man of Jewish nationality, *žid* a man of the Jewish faith.

paper, *Rudé Právo*, replied that Kopecký's words had been misquoted and falsified. According to the Communist organ:

> Comrade Kopecký did no more than take an objective view of the burning question of the immigrants from the Carpatho-Ukraine, many of whom settle, without any right, in our frontier districts, trying to obtain economically advantageous positions.[19]

One year later, after the Communist coup, the Social Democratic newspaper, now taken over by the pro-Communist Fierlinger group, was forced to apologize to Kopecký.[20] But there is little doubt that Kopecký, known for his temperament and violent language, had really used the quoted expressions. The accusation that Carpatho-Russian Jewish soldiers had joined the Czech army at the last moment was never retracted. Jewish and other papers, discussing this charge, accumulated evidence showing that many Carpatho-Russian Jews had fought in the army from the beginning,[21] and that those who had joined later had been detained in concentration camps up to that time.

The Communist Deputy Kapoun, speaking in May 1947 in Brno at a meeting of former participants in the resistance movement, declared:

> The restitution of properties to Jews is a difficult thing. The Jews Germanized; then they ran away for racial reasons; and now they or their sons are coming back as soldiers of our armies abroad. But we cannot trust their patriotism. The pot in which food once spoiled stinks even when it has been thoroughly scoured.[22]

The Communist poet Vítězslav Nezval, the head of the film department in the Ministry of Information, protected the film director Cimbura, who had made antisemitic films under the Nazis. The Jewish press complained about antisemitic passages in the film *Nikola Šuhaj*, which was shown in Czechoslovakia but prohibited in Yugoslavia as antisemitic after a protest by Jewish organizations.[23]

Antisemitic Incidents and Riots

There were, so far as is known, no open antisemitic riots in the historic lands after the war. However, a number of acts of vandalism were committed against synagogues and Jewish cemeteries. On September 25, 1945, the synagogue in Ústí nad Labem (Aussig), in former German territory, was demolished by unknown persons.[24] The Nazis had destroyed many Jewish cemeteries and sold the tombstones to private people. In one case, a Czech national administrator in Mariánské Lázně (Marienbad), after acquiring a German stonemason's shop after the liberation, continued to take tombstones away from the cemetery.[25] On April 17, 1947, Mr. Fuchs of the Prague Religious Community complained that "the streets of Czech towns are still paved with Jewish gravestones."[26] Several Jewish cemeteries were devastated after the liberation.[27] In Roudnice, a Jewish body was exhumed by unknown persons, who removed its gold teeth.[28] At the end of 1947, the Association of Jewish Religious Communities published a list of 31 places in which Jewish cemeteries had been desecrated after the war.[29]

It is impossible to say in how many cases antisemitism was the motive of these acts of vandalism. It seems that at least in some cases they were committed as common crimes, without any antisemitic intent.

Following Jewish complaints, the Ministry of the Interior directed National Committees to punish such acts; the *Bulletin* of the Ministry of Information reprinted Jewish comments;[30] and the Ministry of Education instructed teachers to warn their pupils.[31] Several youthful delinquents were sentenced to short prison terms and placed on probation,[32] as was the national administrator of the stonemason's shop in Mariánské Lázně.[33]

However, such incidents occurred again and again. For example, the Jewish cemetery in Bánovce, Slovakia, was destroyed by "unknown vandals" in June 1948. Thirty or forty tombstones were damaged before the police began an investigation.[34]

In Slovakia there were serious antisemitic riots. Immediately after the war 15 Jews, returning from the concentration camp in Snina, were killed in the village of Svinná, near Humenné in eastern Slovakia. A wave of attacks against Jews followed. It reached its climax in a pogrom in the town of Velké Topolčany on September 24, 1945.

A Jewish doctor had been helping to vaccinate local children against typhus. The riots started when several mothers began to shout that he had injected poison, that Jews were poisoning Christian children. A mob gathered. The doctor was attacked with knives, all Jewish apartments and offices were demolished, and Jews were beaten with iron bars and other instruments. Soldiers and police took part in the pogrom. One Jew was wounded by a hand grenade that exploded at his feet. The riots lasted six hours. The police did not intervene, except to arrest fleeing Jews. Many of the victims were former inmates of concentration camps. There were 49 persons injured.[35]

People from Topolčany went to the neighboring villages and the riots spread. In Žabokreky two Jews, former Slovak partisans, were severely beaten. Several soldiers took part in the excesses, and the police refused to intervene, some of them even helping to spread anti-Jewish rumors. Similar incidents occurred in Chinorany, Krasno nad Nitrou, and Nedanovce.

Several members of the National Committee in Topolčany and in the nearby villages were former members of the Hlinka Guards; some of them had agitated for the expropriation of Jewish-owned land.

The Prague government condemned the riots severely; so did the chairman of the Slovak National Council and the newspapers of both Slovak parties, the Communists and the Democrats.

A thorough investigation followed by punishment of the guilty persons was promised. Eighteen months later, in April 1947, Mr. Fuchs complained in a public meeting in Prague that the perpetrators of the Svinná murders and of the Topolčany riots had not yet been punished.[36]

A year after the Topolčany pogrom, in August 1946, new riots occurred in Bratislava, the capital of Slovakia, and in a number of Slovak towns. The occasion was a Congress of the Association of Partisans, a Communist-dominated organization, which attempted by public demonstrations to impose Communist demands on the Slovak National Council. The Communists insisted that "reactionary elements" used this opportunity to compromise the partisans by antisemitic excesses.

Yet the riots had been openly prepared. *Věstník* said: "Every child in Slovakia knew that there would be antisemitic riots at the Partisans' Congress."Antisemites agitated in trains, in railway stations, and in taverns. Illegal leaflets were distributed throughout the country. The District Committee of Partisans in the town of Dunajská Streda sent out a notice about the organization of riots that ended with these words: "And when your job is done, boys, we will drink your health." It is evident that the Slovak police and the organizers of the Congress had been forewarned, but if they took any measures to protect Jews, they were scarcely adequate.

For four days, August 2-5, Jewish citizens in Bratislava were baited and attacked in the streets, several apartments were demolished by the mob, the Jewish Public Canteen was twice pillaged, and several people were injured. In Komárno, Jewish shops were stoned and a Jewish house demolished by a hand grenade. In Nové Zámky, a café was attacked and 7 Jews injured. In Žilina, there were general riots and 15 people were wounded.[37]

On August 6, the official Slovak Press Agency stated that reports concerning rioting by partisans were absolutely unfounded. The partisans took no part in any riots, and attempts by reactionary elements to disturb the dignity of the Partisan Congress had been nipped in the bud. But on the same day the Bratislava correspondent of the Prague Czechoslovak Press Agency, also an official service, described some anti-Jewish "incidents" and added that "some organs of the public security did not act against the attackers with sufficient energy and did not effectively protect the victims."

Again an energetic investigation was promised. Its first result was a communique from the Prague Ministry of the Interior of August 20, stating that several former members of the Hlinka Guards were among the attackers, but that the main instigators were–Hungarians. Proof of this was the bad Slovak of the illegal antisemitic leaflets and the Hungarian manufacture of the hand grenade thrown in Komárno. . . .

Minor riots continued to take place in Slovakia even in 1947. In the town of Bardejov, on June 6, 1947, a man attacked a Jew in a public square and beat him severely. The local police arrested the culprit, but released him after several minutes. Whereupon he returned to the square and attacked another Jew. Several persons joined in the free-for-all; two Jews were badly wounded and two others slightly injured. Before the police appeared again, the attackers disappeared.[38]

Rioting did not end with the Communist seizure of power. Nor did the benevolence frequently shown by the police to rioters, though the police machine was now entirely in Communist hands. In August 1948 new anti-Jewish riots occurred in Bratislava. Their course followed the old familiar pattern. A detailed description is quoted from the Bratislava weekly *Tribuna*:

> On August 20, at about 9:30 A. M., the wife of a Bratislava businessman stopped at a fruit stand in front of the building of the vegetable market and bought some apples. There was no one else there at the time. She asked the saleslady to hold her package for her, she would come back to get it after she had finished her other shopping. When she came back, several women were standing in line before the stand. The saleslady first served the woman next in line, and then proceeded to deliver to the businessman's wife the apples she had previously bought. At this moment Emilie Prášilová, the wife of an official of the Czechoslovak Broadcasting Office, attacked the saleswoman, complaining that "she waits on those stinking Jewesses first. . . ." The Jewish woman at whom these insults were aimed protested against such words, and when Prášilová attacked her directly, she began to shout: "You Gardist, you SS-woman, we don't live in 1942 any more, the time when you could treat Jews like that has passed." Prášilová then hit her and both women started to fight and pull each other's hair. The other women incited Prášilová and somebody shouted: "A Jewess is beating a pregnant woman!" The Jewish woman then noticed that Prášilová was pregnant, and although Prášilová did not stop striking her, she retreated. A policeman appeared and took both women to the police station where they made their depositions and were told that the affair would be handled by a police court.
>
> But in the meantime a crowd had assembled in front of the police station, and when the women were released the Jewess was attacked and beaten. She retreated into the station house and asked for protection. The police captain phoned for the state police. After 20 minutes, 4 men appeared and posted themselves in front of the building, but did nothing to disperse the crowd which, though numbering no more than 100 persons at that time, increased every minute. Later, a major of the state

police appeared and called for police reinforcements; but he too did not try to disperse the crowd. The threatened Jewess was put in a car and transported to the Regional Office of the State Police, were she was declared under arrest, although she had two small children, one 3 years old and another only 11 months, waiting for her at home. She was first released two days later, on August 22. Prášilová, who started the whole trouble and was the cause of the riot and demonstration, was not arrested because of her pregnant condition.

Meanwhile, the excited crowd attacked two other Jewish women. One was recognized by the Jewish star on her necklace; she was beaten and injured so badly that she needed medical treatment for 10 to 14 days. She was rescued by an officer of the state police, who took her away from the crowd into the vegetable market building and posted policemen in front of her on the staircase. But suddenly an unidentified man of about 50, in civilian clothes, appeared, whispered something to the policeman, and they let him pass to the staircase where he began to beat the woman. Afterwards, some people tried to explain away this incident by saying that he was the poor woman's husband. . . .

The third victim was a Bratislava woman who, hearing the antisemitic shouting and slogans, said that this was like fascist times; the crowd proved her correct by beating her up cruelly. She was saved by the police, who took her into protective custody. She was released soon after, but arrested the next day when a "witness" declared that she was the cause of all the disturbance. She was supposed to have said: "All Christians should be put into concentration camps." This woman, who had to take her 6-months-old baby with her to prison, was only released on August 24.

But to return to the vegetable market where the number of the rioters steadily increased; as nobody interfered with them, they shouted their antisemitic and subversive slogans the whole day. Several civilian employees of the Ministry of the Interior tried to disperse the crowd, some of them conducting themselves bravely, but the crowd was already too big and could not be dispersed without the intervention of uniformed police.

In the evening the rioters sounded the old familiar cry: "To the Jewish quarter!" It was 8 o'clock when the crowd advanced across the Stalin Square to the Jewish Street, to the Jewish Home for the Aged, to the Home for Jewish Orphans, to the offices of Jewish institutions on Markovič Street, and to the Jewish Hospital. Some people warned these institutions by telephone and they were able to close their doors and to inform the security agencies—as if the latter did not already know what was going on.

In the meantime the crowd was marching; volunteers pointed out the windows of apartments in which Jewish families lived. . . . Stones flew, the Jewish Canteen was demolished, and even the Jewish Hospital was attacked. Such heroic deeds were seen before under the so-called

Slovak Independent State. But the German and Tisoist predecessors of today's fascist demonstrators at least spared the hospital. Our present rioters outdid them in this respect.

The rioters continued until 10:15 P. M. This was an hour and a half after the cry "To the Jewish quarter" was raised. And all this happened in the center of Bratislava, on the most frequented streets. In any case the rioters were able to finish their work and to disperse, satisfied that what they had done was neither unlawful nor culpable, as no one made a serious effort to interfere with them.

So the next day, August 22, they attempted new riots. At 10 A. M. they appeared again, several hundreds of them, in front of the vegetable market. But meanwhile the police had received new orders, and the crowd was dispersed in ten minutes by a force much smaller than the one that had stood by the day before.[39]

According to a United Press report from Prague,[40] Bratislava police officers refused to comment on this incident. "A report has been sent to Prague," a police spokesman said. "No one in Bratislava has any right to make any other report." In the Ministry of the Interior in Prague, no one present was authorized to discuss the matter. But reports about the "incidents" leaked out and were telegraphed abroad.[41]

Forty-one rioters were arrested. They were sentenced, not by a court, but by a "special commission of the state police," to prison or forced labor terms; according to a Reuters report from Prague,[42] to forced labor terms from one month to two years; according to an Associated Press report,[43] three persons received 4 years in prison, thirty-eight persons lesser terms. Several police officials were demoted, according to the *Tribuna*. The Jewish Telegraphic Agency reported (from Prague) that even the Bratislava police chief was replaced but nothing was known about this in Bratislava one week later.[44]

Communist Attitude After the Coup

The Communist coup of February 1948 was accompanied by a barrage of declarations stating that now, after the liquidation of "reactionary elements," antisemitism had been definitively defeated and the Jews liberated. In an interview with the Jewish Telegraphic Agency immediately after the seizure of power, Minister Kopecký declared:

> What has happened now in Czechoslovakia also means the defeat of the fascist-minded, antisemitic elements. The new regime wishes to respect even more the religious, civic, and social rights of Jews.[45]

The notion that only anti-Communists, all of whom were now being liquidated, were antisemitic, was repeated in hundreds of statements, resolutions, and greetings adopted by the Jewish organizations under the new leadership of Communist action committees. They thanked the Government, the Communist Party, and its leader Gottwald, for their benevolence toward Jews.

Antisemitism was formally forbidden in the new constitution unanimously adopted by the Constituent Assembly. Under the First Republic, incitement to violence against religious, racial, or national minorities had been forbidden by the Law for the Defense of the Republic. Now antisemitic propaganda was also outlawed by the constitution. In the section on civil rights there is this paragraph:

1. Utterances and activities aiming to endanger the integrity and unity of the state, its constitution, the republican state form, or the institutions of people's democracy, are subject to punishment.
2. Abuse of civil rights and liberties for such purposes is not permitted. Especially is it forbidden to disseminate any form of Nazism and fascism, racial and religious intolerance, and national chauvinism.[46]

The first part of the paragraph abolishes all the civil rights and liberties of those whose "utterances and activities aim at endangering" the institutions of People's Democracy, i.e., all those who are in opposition to the Communist regime. The ban against antisemitism in the second part is thus ingeniously linked with the most undemocratic features of the new government.

The attitude of the Communist Party toward the Jews was interpreted in an article, written for the Jewish press just before the post-coup "elections," by the well-known Communist writer of German-Jewish origin, Paul Reimann:

> When Jewish citizens ask themselves where their home is, they . . . can have only one answer: the Czechoslovak People's Democracy is the home of all its Jewish citizens who have positive ties with the people, who want to work for a new future and to build a new socialist system. . . .
>
> It is a fact, however, that among the Jews as well as among the rest of the population, a tiny minority exists which does not approve of the new conditions. It cannot be overlooked that under the old conditions, a certain kind of Jew was educated in the capitalist spirit and formed a part of the former ruling class. These people did not learn even under Hitler what force they should rely upon, because they entertained the hope that, after the expulsion of the Germans, the old capitalist conditions would reappear and their former capitalist properties would be returned to them. These people don't want to understand that the Jews have to thank the Soviet Union and the fight of the Czechoslovak people for their salvation; they look over the frontiers to the West and hope that American imperialists will help them to recover their former properties. Among these people we find the speculators, black-mar-

> keteers, traitors and other odious creatures who are the shame of all Jewry. . . . The Jewish population must use the elections to settle accounts with this group of subversive Jews and show them up for only a tiny minority, who are condemned by the rest of the Jewish population.[47]

According to this official view, there are two kinds of Jews: good Jews, who are loyal to the new regime and work for it; bad Jews, who either claim restitution of their property, or look to the West and sympathize with Western democracy. They breed speculators, black-marketeers, traitors and other odious creatures, and the regime will "settle accounts" with them.

The Law for the Protection of the Republic, as amended in 1948 after the Communist coup, prohibited any manifestations of or propaganda for racial and religious hatred. Its provisions were adopted and strengthened in the new penal code that came in force after August 1, 1950.[48] Support of or propaganda for fascism, Nazism, and religious or racial hatred now incurred the penalty of prison terms from one to five years; if the offense was committed in the press, a motion picture, a broadcast, etc., the penalty was ten to twenty-five years in jail; threats against the members of such groups, or public incitement against a nationality, language or race, were penalized by imprisonment for as much as two years.

Again, propaganda or incitement against races or nationalities was linked with opposition to the government. Nevertheless, though charges of fascism were liberally used against all opponents of the regime, and scores of public trials of such opponents were conducted, nothing was heard about the enforcement of the specific provisions against racial or religious hatred. Although the general press and the few remaining Jewish publications never reported any such prosecutions, it cannot, of course, be excluded that there were some unpublicized cases. But this is most unlikely. Political or semipolitical trials serve, in Communist countries, an "educational" function; publicity is usually their main purpose. If the authorities had decided that antisemitism was a danger, it would not only have tried the culprits, but would have publicized the trials as well.

Antisemitism, of course, was not done away with by the threat of criminal prosecution. It was only driven partly underground. Reports of antisemitic incidents diminished considerably after 1948. This was probably due in part to censorship, for the press would not now report incidents tending to discredit the regime and Western observers were almost completely excluded from large parts of the country. But major antisemitic disturbances could not escape notice even under these circumstances. It can therefore be safely assumed that in 1949 and 1950 there were no major riots like those that took place in Bratislava in 1948. Information about a few minor incidents leaked out, as for instance the stories of desecrations of Jewish cemeteries reported in one of the last issues of the Bratislava Jewish weekly *Tribuna*, from the Slovak towns of Trenčianské Teplice, Skalica, and others. Generally it can be said that in the first three years after the Communist coup, antisemitism survived and spread under the surface until it became, in 1951, the official policy of the Communist party and government.

Chapter VIII

Jewish Communal Life: the Postwar Revival

During and after the war, Jewish life centered around the Jewish religious communities. Under the Germans, these communities had been the only Jewish organizations allowed, and their jurisdiction was extended to all Jews, believing or otherwise, and to all aspects of Jewish life. They were converted into organs of the state and placed under the supervision of the security police and its *Zentralstelle für die Regelung der Judenfrage*. At the same time they were centralized. First, the Prague community was assigned the duty of supervising all other communities in Bohemia and Moravia; later, all these communities were abolished and the Prague community was transformed into the Jewish Council of Elders for the whole Protectorate.

After the war, a special "National Committee for the Liquidation of the Council of Jewish Elders" was established and the Council's properties were placed under a national administration. At the same time, a "Preparatory Committee" for the revival of the Prague religious community was constituted. In the end, the Czechoslovak Ministry of Education authorized the Prague community, whose first chairman was Arnošt Frischer, the Jewish member of the London Czechoslovak State Council, to supersede the Council of Elders.

The Prague community emerged with powers and responsibilities far exceeding those of the prewar religious communities. In addition to the reorganization of religious life, it undertook the performance of many tasks in the field of economic rehabilitation and social welfare. And, as chief representative of the Jews, religious and non-religious, it was charged with the defense of Jewish interests in all walks of life.

It had also to help wherever it could to revive Jewish communities outside the capital, and to build up their central organizations. This work progressed rather quickly. In September 1945, four months after the liberation, there were already 50 reconstituted Jewish religious communities in Bohemia, Moravia, and Silesia, and 79 in Slovakia.[1]

Later, in 1947, the government officially recognized most of the revived Jewish communities and redistributed the districts of the defunct communities among them. In Bohemia, 130 of the prewar communities were officially abolished because "they had lost the majority of their members and had no financial means to fulfil their legal obligations." Their districts were distributed among 32 revived communities, many of which now had jurisdiction over several counties.[2] In Moravia, 31 communities were abolished and 13 revived.[3] In Silesia (with some adjoining districts of Moravia), 5 communities were abolished and 6 were revived.[4]

At a congress held in Prague on September 1-2, 1945, a Council of Jewish Religious Communities in Bohemia and Moravia (Rada Židovských Náboženských Obcí v Čechách a na Moravě-RŽNO) came into being. Arnošt Frischer, resigning from the chairmanship of the Prague community, became president of the Council, and Kurt Wehle became its secretary.[5]

An analogous but separate central organization was constituted for Slovakia under the name, "Central Association of Jewish Religious Communities" (Ústredný Sväz Židovských Náboženských Obcí na Slovensku-USŽNO). Its president was Emanuel Frieder, its secretary Vojtech Winterstein.

Only much later, in 1947, was a committee to coordinate the activities of the two central organizations established. Its decisions were binding only if ratified by both organizations.[6] Usually, the organizations acted separately, but along parallel lines.

The activities of the revived religious communities were described in a program published by the so-called "Unity List" before the elections in the Prague community in 1947. The program lists the following tasks: to deepen religious life and to develop religious institutions in the spirit of Jewish traditions, preserving the customs of all Jewish cults and rites represented in the community; to support the development of Jewish cultural life and to organize religious education; to fight for the civic equality and social rehabilitation of the Jews; to help the victims of Nazi persecution by relief and training, and to promote their reinstatement in economic life; to help those Jews who want to emigrate to Palestine; to aid Jews in transit through Czechoslovakia; to fight against Nazism, fascism, and antisemitism.[7]

Thus the communities were at once religious, cultural, social welfare, and defense organizations. Rehabilitation and defense, however, already described in the chapters on restitution and antisemitism, were the heart of their activities.

The Jewish religious communities were granted equal recognition with those of other denominations, and religious services and customs were observed without hindrance. In 1948, the principle of freedom of conscience and religion was reaffirmed in the new constitution, with the qualification that this freedom "cannot be a reason for objecting to the fulfilment of legally required civic duties." Also, the right of every citizen to perform functions "related to his religion or lack of it" was guaranteed, with the qualifying clause that such performance "must conform with public order and good morality, and must not be abused for non-religious purposes."[8]

Complaints of encroachments on these rights were first heard in 1948. The action committees that usurped control over the Jewish religious communities after the Communist coup ordered the Orthodox synagogue in Prague to restrict religious services to one hour in the morning and one hour in the evening, and to close for the rest of the day.[9] A complaint against this order was made by the Agudath Israel to the Czechoslovak Embassy in London, and was investigated by the Ministry of Education in Prague.[10] Several local authorities in Slovakia (in Prešov, Lučenec and elsewhere) decided to forbid the ritual slaughter of cattle, but the central authorities restored this right to the communities after the matter was brought to their attention.[11]

Although the official policy of the Jewish religious communities was one of tolerance of all Jewish cults, rites, and customs, there were some clashes of opinion between orthodox newcomers from Carpatho-Russia and latitudinarian Western Jews. Carpatho-Russian Jews sometimes reproached their Bohemian brothers for their "laxity," while Bohemian Jews sometimes criticized orthodox customs as being "backward" and "superstitious." Little of these controversies were aired publicly, but some complaints appeared in the press, accompanied by admonitions to mutual respect, understanding, and tolerance.

Many members of the postwar communities were Jews who had renounced their Jewish faith. According to statistics already cited in Chapter III, they constituted a third of the Jews who returned to Bohemia and Moravia (excluding the Carpatho-Russian newcomers), and one-fifth of the Slovak community. The data for Bohemia-Moravia are from 1948, those for Slovakia from 1946; those who had renounced Judaism under duress, in order to save their lives, had already had ample time to revert to their faith. Apparently there was no major revival of Jewish faith among the non-religious Jews.

Even among those who professed the Jewish religion, a lack of knowledge was felt, especially among the young. From the very first, Jewish communities tried to provide religious education for the young people attending Czech and Slovak schools. Many difficulties were involved, owing to the small number of Jewish children. Thus, in Prague, 117 Jewish elementary school pupils attended no less than 47 different schools.[12] Nevertheless, elementary religious instruction was provided, even in the smaller towns. In Prešov, Slovakia, for instance, Jewish children from local Slovak schools, divided into three grades, had two hours of religious instruction daily. After 1947, the highest grade also received instruction in Hebrew and Jewish history.[13] But in general, the state of religious education was considered unsatisfactory. In December 1947, when the Central Association of Jewish Religious Communities in Slovakia began to publish a monthly for Jewish children, the president of the Association, Emanuel Frieder, wrote in an introductory statement:

> Because of the paucity of pupils and the lack of teachers, our youth in many towns get no religious and Jewish education, or only a very skimpy one. . . . It may be that this magazine will be the only place where your children will hear something about Jewry and the Jewish religion.[14]

The new magazine had therefore to publish elementary religious matter: explanations of the meaning of Jewish holidays, Biblical stories, etc. Even *Věstník*, published by the religious communities in Bohemia and Moravia, often carried material of this kind, although of course on a higher level.

Before the anti-Zionist turn in the Communist line in 1948, much of the energy of the communities was devoted to providing information about and propaganda for the Jewish community in Palestine. Many lectures about Israel and about Palestinian problems were held throughout the country. The speakers were often guests from Palestine. Instructions in Hebrew and the education of future settlers were important activities. Connections were maintained with Czechoslovak *kibbutzim* in Israel.[15] A Society for Cultural Relations with Palestine was founded in Prague under official auspices.[16] In several places, Hebrew theatrical performances were given by local groups. In June 1947, members of Hashomir Hatzair performed a Palestinian drama in Košice in Slovakia; the report stressed that it was the first attempt of this kind in the country.[17] In November 1947, a small Jewish theatre, "Ohel," was founded in Prague; it planned to play "partly in Hebrew" and promised to perform "several modern Palestinian plays."[18] Much of the educational work among the youth was conducted in summer camps organized by the Association of Jewish Students[19] and by the Hashomer Hatzair.[20]

Two B'nai B'rith lodges, "Bohemia" and "Praga" were reconstituted, after some difficulties with the authorities, in 1946.[21] The Zionist sport club Makabi renewed its activities in 1947.[22] A Circle of Czechoslovak Legionnaires (veterans) of Jewish Origin was organized at the end of 1947.[23]

Postwar Jewish literature in Czechoslovakia consisted mainly of several books of memoirs, in Czech, by Jewish survivors of the concentration camps. Most notable among them is Emil Utitz' psychological study of life in the Terezín ghetto.[24] A collection of documents about the deportation and extermination of Jews in Slovakia was prepared by the Association of Jewish Religious Communities in Slovakia. One book was published on the legal aspect of postwar restitution.[25]

Several Jewish periodicals were published. The Bulletin of the Prague Religious Community, *Věstník náboženské obce židovské v Praze*, which resumed publication in 1945, first as a monthly, then as a fortnightly, also became the official organ of the Council of Jewish Religious Communities in Bohemia and Moravia. Until 1948 it carried a great deal of information on all aspects of Jewish life. It had 5,000 readers in 1947.[26] At the end of 1947, the Circle of Czechoslovak Legionnaires of Jewish Origin began to publish, at approximately monthly intervals, a bulletin called *Informační Zprávy*. In Bratislava, the weekly *Tribuna*, which belonged to the Association of Racial Persecutees, described itself as an "Independent Weekly for Politics, Culture, and Economy," and defended Jewish interests. The Central Association of Jewish Religious Communities in Slovakia began publishing, at the end of 1947, the monthly magazine *Halapid*, for Jewish children; it contained religious articles and information on Jewish history and on Palestine. *Cesta* (*Haderech*) in Bratislava was the organ of the Hashomer Hatzair. *Věstník* and *Informační Zprávy* were written in Czech, the other periodicals mentioned in Slovak.

Zionism and Assimilation

For quite some time adherents of different tendencies—Zionists, assimilationists, orthodox Jews—collaborated fairly harmoniously in the communities. This fact was often acknowledged on all sides. Mr. Fuchs, leader of the "Czech Jews" (assimilationists), stressed in his report to the conference of his faction in January 1948 that Zionists and "Czech Jews," formerly at odds, had joined hands under the Nazis. We became friends, declared Fuchs, although neither tendency renounced its convictions, and this cooperation has lasted until the present.[27]

In the period immediately after the war, the Zionists became the most powerful faction in the communities; the presidents and secretaries of both central organizations as well as of the Prague community were from their ranks. There were many reasons for this: wartime sufferings and postwar disappointments strengthened a specifically Jewish consciousness; the Palestine problem appeared near a solution; German and Hungarian assimilationists were completely eliminated; and the Zionists, who had been the only Jewish faction officially represented in the State Council of the government-in-exile, were somewhat favored by the first postwar administration.

The first and only postwar congress of Czechoslovak Zionists took place in Luhačovice, on the Moravian-Slovak border, in July 1946. Two delegates of the Jewish Agency, representatives of the Joint Distribution Committee and the World Jewish Congress, and official delegations from both Associations of Jewish Religious Communities were among the guests. Most of the traditional leaders of the movement had perished during the war; new people, many of them quite young, took their places.

The political composition of the congress had changed. In prewar times, the Mizrachi and the General Zionists had been strongest, while socialist groups had been in the minority. Now, non-socialists and socialists were of about the same strength, the strongest groups being the Mizrachi on the right and Hashomer Hatzair on the left. The General Zionists and Mapai were substantially weakened. Achduth Avodah emerged as a new socialist group. The Hashomer Hatzair proposed a "united socialist front"; but only the Achduth Avodah accepted. The negotiations with the Mapai ended in failure because the latter insisted on parity with the Hashomer Hatzair and refused to accept Achduth Avodah as a partner. The congress adopted several political declarations and protest resolutions and laid the basis for the Central Zionist Association of Czechoslovakia, with headquarters in Bratislava.[28]

A conference of the Zionist leadership with delegates from the provinces took place in Karlovy Vary (Karlsbad) in August 1947, after an international Zionist meeting. Thirty-two delegates represented all parts of Czechoslovakia, and it was decided to convoke a new congress in the following year. Delegates from the historic lands demanded an intensification of work in Bohemia and Moravia, which were in their opinion neglected by the Bratislava leadership, and it was decided to strengthen the organization in this area.

The major controversial issue of the session was the Revisionists' demand that they be permitted to take part as an organized faction in the Zionist movement of Czechoslovakia, and to have a representative with consultative voice on the Executive Committee of the Association. According to a report in the organ of the Hashomer Hatzair, "all the speakers condemned the plague of terror in our nation and stressed that it is time to stop talking and to begin to act." The conference, according to this report, voiced a strong protest "against terrorist bands which break discipline and murder and rob Englishmen and Arabs as well as Jews without any reproaches of conscience." Only the Revisionists tried to prevent the adoption of a resolution against terrorism, although they dissociated themselves from the terrorist acts.

The representative of Hashomer Hatzair denounced the Czechoslovak Revisionists as disruptors of the Zionist movement. The Mizrachi, General Zionists, and a part of the Mapai voted for recognition of the Revisionist faction; another part of the Mapai, the Hashomer Hatzair, and Achduth Avodah voted against it. The Revisionist proposals were rejected by the close vote of 17 to 15. It was decided to accept Revisionists only as individuals and provided they kept the discipline of the movement, and to refuse them representation on the executive committee, all this being subject to final decision by the next congress.[29]

The Hashomer Hatzair was one of the most active Zionist groups. In prewar times it had had organizations in Slovakia; not until 1938, however, were groups founded in Prague, Brno, and Moravská Ostrava. During the occupation the movement influenced, according to its own estimate, about ten per cent of the Jewish youth.[30] But after the war the organization claimed to have groups "in all the large towns" and to be "the strongest youth movement among Czechoslovak Jews."[31] It maintained many summer camps, conducted extensive educational activities, and organized public demonstrations at which the members sometimes paraded in uniform.[32] It issued a monthly (*Cesta*) and a mimeographed bulletin.

In the political field, it cooperated closely with the Communists and with the pro-Communist Fierlinger group of the Czech Social Democrats. At the Hashomer Hatzair conference in Rájecké Teplice, Slovakia, in May 1948, Fierlinger was one of the main speakers.[33] After the Communist coup the group issued, together with Achduth Avodah, enthusiastic manifestos in favor of the new regime, took part under the name of the "Socialist League for Palestine" in Communist May Day parades,[34] and mobilized its members as volunteers for Communist labor brigades.[35]

It changed its policy from advocacy of a binational state in Palestine to one of defending Israel and fighting for a socialist Palestine that would associate itself with Russia and with the People's Democracies. It was strongly opposed to Revisionism and terrorist methods.

The assimilated ("Czech") Jews, although possessing a long prewar tradition, were slow to reorganize formally after the liberation. Their representatives at first took part in the work of the Jewish religious communities on an individual basis. Before the elections in the Prague community in 1947, they received representation on the unity list; a group of Czech Jews issued a manifesto in support of the list, in which they named their adherents among the candidates.[36]

In January 1948 the old Association of Czech Jews (*Svaz Čechů židů*), which the Nazis had banned in 1939, at last reconstituted itself at a conference in Prague and issued the following statement:

> Recently, a Jewish state was established in Palestine by a decision of the United Nations. Conscious of the persecution of Jews . . . we welcome this decision.
>
> But the establishment of the Jewish state in Palestine is for us an opportunity to declare once more that our home is here, on Czech soil and among the Czech people. . . .
>
> We believe that the whole civilized world will help to guarantee the security of the Jewish state, but Jews should understand that . . . Zionism outside of Palestine has now lost its raison d'être. . . . We want all Jews in our country to live a full Czech life. Those of us who profess the religion of our forefathers will find here understanding of their religious needs. The guiding principle must be religious tolerance, respect for the other man's convictions, and understanding of a millenial Jewish

existence lived in common with the Czech nation.[37]

In his report to the Conference, Fuchs stressed the fact that people who did not adhere to the Jewish faith were nevertheless welcome in the organization.[38]

A new element was introduced into the Bohemian-Moravian communities by the influx of orthodox Jews from Carpatho-Russia. These so-called "optants" constituted about one-third of the postwar Jewish population in Bohemia and Moravia, almost a quarter of the Prague community, and an absolute majority in many communities in former Sudeten-German territory. Their adjustment to the new milieu was considered to be a major problem of postwar Jewish life. Oldtimers and new settlers were frequently appealed to for the exercise of mutual tolerance, proving that there were some difficulties.[39] In the aforementioned conference, Fuchs declared that Czech Jews were tolerant, but "demand tolerance from the other side too." Their religious customs, he stressed, were the result of centuries of evolution, and anyone wishing to live there must take this into account. Nobody had the right to force his religious convictions upon others.[40]

It is difficult to estimate the relative numerical strength of the various Jewish groups. The only opportunity was afforded by the elections of the Jewish religious communities in 1947. These elections were conducted according to a democratic election law; but in most cases unity lists, agreed upon among the different groups, were elected without opposition. In 46 communities in Bohemia and Moravia, unity lists solely were presented; only in 6 communities, including 5 in former Sudeten-German territory, did real elections take place. The Jewish press maintained that the communities elected the "best men" without regard to party; it stressed that a Zionist majority had elected a non-Zionist chairman in Brno and that in several Sudeten places oldtimers became chairmen, although newcomers were in the majority.[41]

In Prague, two lists were presented to the voters: the unity list backed by Zionists, Hashomer Hatzair, Agudath Israel, the Mizrachi, and the Czech Jews, as well as a Committee of Carpatho-Russian Optants;[42] and an opposition list headed by one Přemysl Kurt Heller.

The opposition group claimed the merit of having forced the election, which they believed the men in power in the community had tried to prevent. It declared that the leadership of the community lacked energy in defending Jewish restitution and rehabilitation interests. It demanded more energetic action for restitution and the integration of Jews into socialist reconstruction.[43]

The majority replied that the leaders of the opposition were adventurers. It charged that Heller had been a member of the Czechoslovak church, only rejoining the Jewish community shortly before the election. The Communist newspaper *Rudé Právo* announced that Heller "had sneaked into the Communist Party after the liberation, and had been expelled later on for lack of discipline and subversiveness."[44]

In general, the Czech, especially the Communist, press supported the unity list. The organ of the Jewish community *Věstník*, declared: "As a matter of course, the list includes representatives of leftist tendencies from the Czech Jewish as well as from the Zionist camp."[45]

The unity list received 2,774 votes, the opposition, 314; in accordance with the principle of proportional representation, 33 unity candidates and 3 oppositionists were elected to the representation of the Community.[46] Among the 33 unity members, 16 were Zionists, 17 non-Zionists.[47] Among the non-Zionists, 12 were candidates recommended by the Czech Jews.[48] Karel Stein, a Zionist, was elected chairman; among the three vice chairmen, two were Czech Jews.

After the elections in individual communities, a conference of their delegates elected, on October 26-28, 1947, a new Council of the RŽNO.[49] Of its 18 members, 6 were Zionists, 6 Czech Jews, and 6 members of groups from the East.[50]

Frischer, the Zionist leader, was re-elected president and Fuchs, the leader of the Czech Jews, vice-president. Kurt Wehle, a Zionist, remained secretary.

One of the main controversies at the conference turned upon the proposal to affiliate with the World Jewish Congress. The Zionists and a part of the "Eastern group" were for joining, Agudath remained neutral, and the Czech Jews vigorously opposed affiliation. A final decision was postponed and a commission was appointed to study the conditions of affiliation.[51] In January the commission reported to the new Council, and it was decided that the RŽNO would join the WJC on two conditions; first, that this would involve no change in friendly relations with other Jewish organizations abroad; and second, that the WJC would deal with Czechoslovak questions only when the RŽNO agreed. This decision was adopted by Zionist votes only, Agudath and the Czech Jews abstaining.[52]

Such was the situation at the time of the Communist coup. Jewish religious communities had developed broad defense and welfare activities in which all Jewish groups participated. Among these groups, the Zionists were strongest, but the Czech Jews were beginning to press their program of assimilation. All Jewish groups professed loyalty to the regime; in all of them there were pro-Communist wings or factions. The leadership of the communities, however, was in the hands of men who, though loyal to the ruling regime, aimed at defending specifically Jewish interests.

Chapter IX

Jewish Communal Life: Regimentation and Decline

The Communist coup in February 1948 brought in its train a coup in the Jewish organizations; like all other organizations in Czechoslovakia these were taken over by Communist-dominated action committees.

On February 24, employees of all Jewish organizations were ordered by a Congress of Shop Stewards organized by the Communists to take part in a general strike. At a meeting of the employees, the Secretary of the Central Council of Unions, Evžen Erban, was the main speaker. After speeches by two pro-Communist employees, "those present manifested their agreement" with the demands of the Congress, aiming at the transfer of all power to the Communists.[1] There was no recorded vote. Remembering the stand these employees had taken against the Central Council of Unions in the Varnsdorf affair, there are reasons to doubt the authenticity of the agreement.

On February 27, 1948, an Action Committee for the Council of Jewish Religious Communities was formed. It was not elected by anybody, but appointed by the District Action Committee of the National Front in Prague. "We were granted the same power as the action committees constituted in all enterprises, offices, organizations, and institutions," says its first manifesto.[2] Its chairman was Laura Šimková, an employee of the Cadre Commission in the headquarters of the Communist Party; vice chairman was Alexander Knapp, an employee of the RŽNO. Of the other eight original members, only two, from the Czech Jewish group, were members of the representation of the Prague community.

First, the action committee purged the elected organs and offices of the communities. RŽNO and the Prague community were ordered "to present lists of the members of their elected bodies and to take care that among the members are only persons who can guarantee . . . that they will support the constructive program of our new government." A special decision asked the Prague community immediately to expel Přemysl Kurt Heller, leader of the opposition list of 1947 and a man who had been purged from the Communist Party.[3]

On March 2, the action committee appeared before a new meeting of the employees of Jewish organizations.[4] A delegate from the Central Council of Unions, described by *Věstník* as Comrade Schwarz, spoke about the tasks of the action committee:

> In the action committee there will be people from different political parties, but only those who give us guarantees that they will defend people's democracy, that they will support the government. Consider the action committee as a revolutionary organ which will really introduce order. We ask the leaders and elected representatives of the communities when the action committee makes decisions not to oppose their enforcement, because these decisions will be supported, if necessary, by the Central Action Committee of the National Front.

At the same time, Schwarz assured the meeting that there would be no persecution, and people of all parties would be welcome if they obeyed and supported the new regime.

Fuchs, the committee's leader, declared in a long and embarrassed speech:

> We Jews have the duty not only to speak but also to act. . . . It may be that there are people among us who have not yet overcome certain prejudices and certain points of view. But whoever thinks clearly and deeply must understand what we are going through. Everybody who does not stand clearly in the progressive camp, who does not support this camp with all his power, supports reaction. And we know that reaction in the end always turns against the Jews. . . . Maybe it is easier for me to speak to you than for anybody else. You know my views about the fusion of Jews with the Czech nation. I am an assimilationist and I am in favor of a complete fusion with the Czech nation. It is a historical necessity. If we want to fulfil this necessity, we have to feel and think in the same way as the nation does. . . .

After this, Alexander Knapp repeated that the action committee considered itself a "control organ"; no decision could be taken without its consent, and whenever it found persons "who acted in public life in the interests of domestic or foreign reaction," they would be purged. But people who had committed errors would have the opportunity to renounce and correct them. Among the main tasks of the community, Knapp listed the improvement of labor morale, the fight against black-marketeers, and last but not least, the support of the Soviet Union in its "fight for world peace." All speakers stressed the need to reeducate the Jews in a "socialist spirit."

On March 10, the elected Council of Jewish Religious Communities was summoned to an extraordinary meeting and informed about personnel changes recommended by the action committee.[5] The president, Arnošt Frischer, was not present; the secretary, Kurt Wehle, had fled abroad. Laura Šimková, although not a member of the Council, was the main speaker. She announced that the action committee considered the leadership of the Council politically intolerable and therefore had made some changes. Instead of Wehle, it had appointed Knapp secretary of the Council. It also had changed the composition of the representation of the Prague Community: Heller was expelled and four additional members were allowed to resign "voluntarily"; the action committee would decide who would take their place. "Comrade" Pfeffer had taken over the Department for Foreign Affairs and measures had been taken to adapt *Věstník* to the spirit of the National Front.

Then it was announced that Julius Lederer, an old man living in retirement and a veteran of the Czech Jewish movement, had been summoned to the meeting to be appointed president of the Council. Lederer sought to excuse himself on the ground of his age; his excuses were overruled.

In the discussion, two representatives of the orthodox Jews protested against the exclusion of Rabbi Hanuš Rezek from the Prague representation. Alexander Knapp declared: "Decisions of the action committee about the composition of elected bodies cannot be changed."

A Zionist complained that there was only one Zionist, having only a consultative voice, on the action committee, "although the majority of Zionists are of honest socialist convictions." Knapp replied that the Council had no right to discuss the composition of the action committee, which is "a revolutionary organ, constituted in a revolutionary way."

On March 23 the action committee again revised the composition of the organs of the Council.[6] Julius Lederer ceased to be president and became one of the two honorary chairmen, the other being the well-known German Communist writer Egon Erwin Kisch.[7] Emil Ungar, a pro-Communist high official of the Ministry of Health, became president; Fuchs remained as first vice president; Edmund Schwarz, of the Ministry of the Interior, became second vice president; new members included Laura Šimková of the Cadre Commission of the Communist Party, and Bedřich Fertig, chairman of the Action Committee for the Jewish Community in Brno.[8]

In the Prague community, Karel Stein, the elected chairman and a Zionist, remained in office, but not for long. In June he resigned and was replaced by Arnošt Polák.[9]

Regimentation in Slovakia

In Slovakia, things went more slowly. For support inside the communities the Communists could not rely to such an extent upon Slovak assimilationists, who were much weaker than their Czech counterparts. The Slovak communities were much more in the hands of Zionist and strongly religious groups. Inside the Zionist movement the new regime found support in the Socialist League for Palestine, a coalition of Hashomer Hatzair and Achduth Avodah corresponding to the Mapam in Israel. In February, shortly before the coup, a conference of the League demanded "a thorough democratization of Jewish public life, and above all of Jewish public institutions." That demand, later wrote the organ of Hashomer Hatzair, would have attracted little attention in normal times, but soon afterwards the February revolutionary offensive for the purge of Czechoslovak public life gave it an extraordinary importance. The Socialist League now resolved to press the issue; at a session of the Political Commission of the Central Zionist Organization in March, it demanded "adequate" representation in the leadership of the Central Association of Jewish Religious Communities in Slovakia, and the exclusion of Revisionists from the Zionist movement. The majority objected to the first demand, pointing out that Hashomer Hatzair, as a Marxist tendency, took a negative attitude toward religion. The delegates of Hashomer protested in the most energetic way against this reasoning, and the Commission finally decided to consider their demand "in due course."

In August, Hashomer Hatzair aired the issue publicly. In an article in *Cesta*,[10] it reviewed the negotiations and declared that it rejected any attempt to identify Jewry with the Jewish religion. The religious communities had not only religious, but also cultural and social tasks. They had always been dominated by rabbis and rich Jews; their present leadership was the fruit of a compromise between orthodox and neologist (reform) tendencies, but today this difference had ceased to be important. Now the main question was Zionism or assimilation; here, the majority of Slovak Jewry had decided for Zionism, and now "progressive" tendencies inside the Zionist movement had to get adequate representation in the religious communities.

The article complained that religious education was being forced upon children in the orphan homes of the communities, and categorically demanded for Slovak Jewry an elected representation which would, by its spirit and composition, conform to the wishes of Slovak Jews.

In another article in the same issue dealing with the elections to the new Zionist Congress, *Cesta* complained:

> There is a whispering campaign to the effect that Hashomer Hatzair, which is ideologically close to the Communist Party, abuses its influence to denounce and discredit the bourgeois factions before the action committees. Even at a session of the Zionist Executive, an off-the-record accusation was made that the Hashomer Hatzair attacks and denounces Mizrachists, so jeopardizing their freedom and existence.

Cesta's answer to these accusations was:

> We have never hidden our socialist convictions and our ideological kinship with Communism. . . . We will always take the initiative to bring about an alliance of the Zionist movement with progressive and democratic forces. . . . Whenever Hashomer Hatzair published some political

> declaration, even if the Mizrachi was not mentioned, Mizrachists cried that it was aimed at discrediting them politically, that Hashomer was torpedoing the coalition, etc. . . . They refused to vote even on personnel questions, declaring that they were being pressed unduly by the Hashomer Hatzair. . . . We had to defend ourselves against this dirty propaganda and we will continue to fight against it in the future. . . .[11]

Shortly before, *Cesta* had launched a violent attack against those Zionists, including several prominent leaders, who were about to leave the country for America or South Africa. It wrote in an editorial statement:

> They are leaving with the declaration . . . that they will remain good Zionists. Few of them will have the courage and the frankness to admit that, by this emigration, they lose forever the moral right to call themselves Zionists. . . . Zionists who go to America are of no value to us. We must attack them in no uncertain terms, we must openly call them deserters, although they, at every solemn opportunity, shamelessly mouth big words about the Jewish state. . . .

The article implied that these people were afraid to go to Palestine to fight and suffer. It concluded:

> This is not so much a political question—although the matter also has a political side—as a human and moral one. We have the impression that this *aliyah* via America was not fully understood by our Zionist public opinion. A public discussion of this problem is needed to bring clarity and order into our ranks.[12]

In the same issue, another article attacked Jewish students who hesitated to go to Palestine immediately or wanted to go to America:

> What were the arguments of these youth groups? We don't want to deal with those whose world turns around money. . . . They always gravitated toward America. Against this stain on our nation, one has to use not arguments but fists. And it is a tragedy that it will not be the educational fist of their own nation, but, we are sorry to say, the fist of other peoples. The irresistible offensive of people's democracies throughout the world will liquidate this kind of youth in all the nations.[13]

However, the reluctant support given the Communists by the assimilated Jews in the historic lands, and the more enthusiastic support given them by left-wing elements of the Mapam in Slovakia, were by no means decisive. Judging from detailed descriptions of the events in Prague and from articles in *Cesta,* it is quite clear that Communist domination was essentially imposed on the communities from the outside, by decree, by decisions of party-appointed "revolutionary organs" against which no resistance was tolerated. Wherever some timid objections were voiced, they were met by threats and outright coercion. Those elected representatives who were not removed in the purge had to cooperate because they could not do otherwise.

One must bear in mind that whatever was said and done by the Jewish communities after their *Gleichschaltung* did not represent the authentic will of their membership, but rather the will of the Communist Party, imposed from without.

At first glance, it seems that the regimentation of the Jewish communities, at least in Bohemia and Moravia, brought about the complete victory of the assimilationists. The best-known Zionist leaders in the historic lands were eliminated and Czech Jews put in their places. The action committees appealed to Jews in the name of Czech national solidarity: when the Czech nation "became pro-Communist," the Jews, as part and parcel of it, had to become pro-Communist too.

But things were not so simple. The traditional leaders of the Czech Jews soon found themselves transferred to less important positions. The most controversial question for Zionists and assimilationists—affiliation with the World Jewish Congress—was decided against the Czech Jews by the action committees. Not only was the decision to join the WJC not reversed, but no further discussion was allowed. RŽNO joined the WJC and sent to its world conference a delegation composed of three reliable pro-Communists: Mrs. Šimková, Dr. Ungar, and Dr. Fertig.[14]

Period of Friendliness to Israel

Since Russia at that time, for reasons of foreign policy, supported the Jewish state, the Czechoslovak government and Jewish communities had to follow her lead. Nevertheless, *pro domo sua*, among Jews remaining in Czechoslovakia, Zionism had to be discouraged and total assimilation enforced as the only patriotic attitude.

The Czechoslovak government supported the partition of Palestine the moment that Russia did. It was among the first governments to recognize the State of Israel. It extended recognition on May 18, 1948, and on May 21, Yehud Ueberall was appointed the first Israel diplomatic representative to Prague.[15] When on July 28, he presented his credentials to President Gottwald, the friendship uniting the two countries was emphasized in speeches and press comments.[16] On June 1, Deputy Premier Fierlinger, the leader of pro-Communist Social Democrats, speaking at a congress of Zionist youth in Rájecké Teplice in Slovakia, expressed a hope that the economic and political ties between both countries would be very close.[17]

In May 1948, normal postal communications between Czechoslovakia and Israel were resumed.[18] In June, the Israel Minister of Communications, David Remez, came to Prague to negotiate an agreement on the air service between Czechoslovakia and Israel, and described the result as "very satisfactory."[19] Zvi Nadav, another official in the Israeli Ministry of Communications, arrived in Prague to continue the talks soon after.[20] Later, an Israeli purchasing mission arrived[21] and purchased, according to official reports, sugar, potatoes and other foods to the value of $1,000,000. Trade relations developed normally. The Czechoslovak government promised to allow free emigration of Zionists to Israel. Cultural relations between the two countries were also established, and a Society of Czechoslovak-Israel Friendship was founded in Prague under official aspices. Karl Kreibich, a Sudeten-German Communist leader (not a Jew) was elected its chairman. The official declarations of the government and of the society were full of goodwill for the new Jewish state.

The friendly attitude of the Czechoslovak government toward Israel was also expressed in the much discussed deliveries of weapons to Israel. The American press carried many reports of Czechoslovak deliveries of machine guns, artillery, and other arms, including even fighter planes,[22] and at the end of July 1948 it was reported that the United States government had protested in Prague against such dealings.[23] Nor were official Israel authorities the only consignees. According to another report, "many of the guns on the illegal Irgun ship Altalena were of Czech make."[24] All these stories, although officially denied or ignored, were widely advertised by the Communists in their propaganda among the Jews abroad. They sought to show that through Czechoslovakia Russia was supporting the Jews of Israel in their war against the Arabs.[25]

Less publicized were reports of deliveries of Czechoslovak arms to the Arabs. These were officially denied by the Prague Foreign Ministry and by the head of the Czechoslovak National Bank in January 1948.[26] But the rumors persisted. In February, some reports said that the Arab League, after discussing the purchase of Czech arms, had postponed a decision.[27] On February 25, Riad-es-Solh, the Premier of Lebanon, declared in Cairo: "Russia voted with you on the Palestine question, but where do you think we are getting our arms? From Czechoslovakia. And who is Czechoslovakia but Russia herself?"[28] Scattered reports seem to confirm this claim. On March 19, a shipment of Czechoslovak rifles and machine guns for the Palestinian Arab army arrived at the small Lebanese port of Djounish in a large schooner from Genoa.[29] In April, a Syrian government official declared that 8,000 rifles and 6,000,000 rounds of ammunition had been lost en route from Czechoslovakia to Syria in a recent explosion aboard a ship in Bari, Italy; this was said to be the second shipment from Czechoslovakia of arms of a total value of $2,085,000. Both shipments were consigned to the Syrian army.[30]

It seems more likely that Czechoslovakia was delivering arms to both sides in the Palestinian war, though the Jews, being better organized and having more money to buy, probably received more than the Arabs.

Friendly diplomatic and commercial relations with the State of Israel did not change the basic attitude of the Czechoslovak regime toward Zionism and Jewish nationalism. In almost all official declarations, praise of Israel was followed by words to the effect that those Jews who remained in the country would have to assimilate completely.

Minister Kopecký declared in an interview:

> This is a historical moment which has no equal in human history. Only now is the Jewish nation being born, because it is finally acquiring all the conditions of national existence as defined by Stalin. . . . Jews have to choose between total assimilation or joining their nation in helping to build up Palestine.[31]

On April 30, 1948, *Věstník* carried an editorial, written by the Communist writer Louis Fuernberg, which said:

> The terrible fate of Jews under the capitalist system bred in them the psychosis of persecution. This is understandable wherever capitalism is in power, but nonsensical where its power has been broken. We know that we have to use patience and careful understanding. But we will fight resolutely against those backward Jewish circles which want to use the foolishness of the youth, especially the Jewish youth, for adventurous purposes. We believe that the place of the Jewish youth is with the youth of our state. . . . Our youth needs no substitutes, no false romanticism or delusions. We will fight against the nonsensical propaganda which leads its victims into errors, suffering, and jeopardy. . . .[32]

On May 14, 1948, *Věstník* carried on its first page an interview with Professor Arnošt Kolman, a Czech Communist who had spent most of his life teaching in Soviet universities and who had now been appointed to the Charles University in Prague.[33]

Kolman announced that he had been invited to lecture at the Hebrew University in Jerusalem and that he wanted to go there when the fighting ended. He declared that the Jews in Palestine had done wonderful things in the economic as well as in the cultural field, and that they deserved their own state. He added that "a hand soaked in oil" was committing crimes in Palestine, as well as in Greece, China, Indonesia, India.

But when asked if he favored Zionism, this was his answer:

> Not at all. I think that the Zionists make four fundamental errors. First, they see a solution of the Jewish question in the Jewish colonization of Palestine, without taking into account that a large section of the Jews have grown roots in the milieu in which they live and a long time ago already lost their national feelings and national culture. For them, such a solution is artificial, alien, and forced. Second, the Zionists maintain the illusion that it is possible to transform present colonial Palestine into an independent country with the help or support of imperialist powers. Third, they do not understand that the solution of the Jewish question does not signify mere national liberation, and cannot be accomplished as such; in reality it signifies solely social liberation. And fourth, the Zionists do not understand that the Palestine question is an Arab as well as a Jewish problem, and can be solved only by the cooperation of

Arabs and Jews, not only at the top by agreements between politicians, but primarily by the cooperation of the toiling masses of both peoples.

The reporter then asked: What future do you see for the Jews, and especially for Jewish youth, in Czechoslovakia?

I think the answer is clear enough. In our country, antisemitism as a mass phenomenon does not exist. Although there is—especially in Slovakia—still a residue of antisemitism, it cannot hinder the career of an able and honest man or influence his social position. Jewish youth has the best of chances in our people's democracy. It is not necessary to look for better luck in Palestine where against their will they will become . . . tools in the hands of predatory imperialists, and where they will work for exploiters, even in the *kibbutzim* with their pseudo-communist organization.

As can be seen, support of Israel always, even at that time, went hand in hand with active anti-Zionist propaganda inside the country.

Turn Against Zionism

Like the pro-Israel policy, the turn away from Israel originated in Moscow. It was announced by the now well-known anti-Zionist article by Ilya Ehrenburg in *Pravda* on September 21, 1948; this was quickly followed by the dissolution of the Jewish Antifascist Committee in Russia, the arrest of Yiddish writers, the extinction of the Jewish press, and by a violent campaign against Zionism and "Jewish nationalism." The campaign was soon extended to the satellite countries; Zionist organizations were dissolved, Zionists were removed from all posts of influence, and many of them were arrested. Zionism was declared to be an instrument of Western imperialism and was violently denounced first in Hungary and Rumania, and then in Poland and Bulgaria.

In Czechoslovakia where the Jewish communities were comparatively small and Zionism played no significant role in the life of the country, the turn first took less violent forms. Diplomatic relations with Israel remained formally correct[34] and press attacks against the Israeli government were largely confined to the regimented Jewish press. Emigration to Israel was still tolerated, although it was officially discouraged and met with increasing administrative difficulties. Zionist leaders were removed from positions of leadership in the communities, coercion was used against them, and some were arrested on charges of illegal dealings in foreign exchange in connection with their handling of Zionist funds. However, Zionist organizations were allowed to die a natural death by the emigration of their membership rather than being dissolved by government decree. As late as August 1950, the secretary of the Jewish community in Prague assured a foreign visitor that there were still Zionist organizations which were holding meetings freely.[35] Nothing more, however, is known about their activities, which were never mentioned in the press. In an interview with another foreign visitor, the Chief Rabbi, Gustav Sicher, explained that "the 4,000 Jews who live in Prague are in general neither profoundly religious nor Zionist."[36]

The ideological campaign against Israel developed in stages. First, it was necessary to explain that the previous friendly attitude toward Israel had been genuine, but that the Jewish bourgeoisie and social democracy were betraying the new Jewish nation. The first to speak up thus in Czechoslovakia after Ehrenburg's article was Karl Kreibich, president of the Society of Czechoslovak-Israel Friendship. He wrote in *Věstník* in November 19, 1948:

> We founded the Association of Czechoslovak-Israel Friendship not only because of our sympathies for this young state and the valiant fighters and builders who want to construct a really independent and democratic state of the two nations living there, but also because such an Israel will be a tremendously valuable contribution to the cause of peace, freedom, and democracy, and to the cause of friendship among the nations of the world. . . .
>
> Today, however, Israel is not and cannot yet be such a state. Anglo-American capital is too powerful in the whole Palestinian economy; Jewish capital is so strongly tied to this foreign capital that the Jewish bourgeoisie is, in this situation, only a political agent of Wall Street or of London. In the fight against capitalism and imperialism, for state independence and people's democracy, petty-bourgeois nationalism (Zionism) and social democracy are no more reliable than bourgeois nationalism and social democracy in other countries. This was shown by their negative attitude to the common front with the Communists against reaction in the electoral campaign. . . .
>
> This all had to be said in order to avoid illusions about the present situation in Israel, which some people already like to consider as a people's democracy, even one with the germs of socialism; such erroneous inferences are sometimes drawn from the existence of agricultural cooperatives, the *kibbutzim*, which some likened to *kolkhozes* or even "communes." We do have Jewish *kolkhozes* and a Jewish socialist agriculture, not in Palestine but in Birobidjan. . . . There, in the USSR, of course, they have neither "their own" nor foreign capitalists; there they can build socialism in peace. The democratic and socialist workers in Israel will still have to fight and labor in the face of many difficulties before people's democracy and real independence are achieved and made secure.[37]

After the Israeli elections in January 1949, the tone sharpened. Israel was now definitely considered a bourgeois state dependent on American imperialism, and the "toiling masses," it was stated, could change it only by "taking the government into their own hands." This was expressed in the following comment by *Věstník* on the Israel elections:

> Driven by their class interest the Israel capitalists are now leading their state into the camp of the reactionary, capitalist, war-mongering forces, into the camp of those who caused the Palestinian war in order

to promote their oil and strategic interests; who destroyed the lives and well-being of many thousands of the best sons of the Jewish population in Palestine; who, by their disastrous activities, had always brought the Jews only misery, suffering and catastrophe. No bourgeoisie ever respected the real interest of its own nation, and we cannot expect a historical evolution in Israel different from that of other capitalist countries. . . .

From the point of view of international politics, the electoral results and the whole development in Israel up to now mean, in our opinion, that Israel has passed from the power sphere of Great Britain into that of the United States, both politically and economically. It is easy to understand the consequences American "aid" to Israel is bound to have. The examples of far richer, greater and stronger countries, such as France, Italy, Great Britain, Belgium, etc., show us the disastrous effects of Marshallization, which leads only to servitude, unemployment, and virtual loss of state sovereignty.

The fate of the young state of Israel is now in the hands of the bourgeoisie, and the toiling masses which secured the existence of the new state by their heroic struggle do not direct this state; but we do not doubt that they will finally take the government into their own hands and win for their nation real freedom, peace, and general welfare.[38]

In March 1949 it was already "well known" to the *Věstník* that Israel was a state ruled by capitalist exploiters:

Israel, as is well known, is a capitalist state where the workers are exploited by the bourgeoisie. The fact that enterprises officially owned by the labor union Histadrut form an important sector of Israel's capitalist economy does not change this basic condition. In Solel Boneh, the giant firm owned by the Histadrut, the worker is exploited as in any other capitalist plant; he has to fight for higher wages and has no influence on the management.[39]

In *Věstník,* the Israel Communist Party was described as the only group fighting for labor, peace, and the liberation of Israel from the imperialist yoke.

The weekly *Tribuna* in Bratislava, though loyal to the Communist government, timidly betrayed some pro-Zionist sympathies; it ceased publication in the spring of 1949.[40]

In the organizational field, the first step after the turn was the disaffiliation of the Czechoslovak communities from the World Jewish Congress. The Czechoslovak Jews had, as we have seen, joined the WJC after the Communist coup, evidently on orders from above. They resigned from it, again on orders from above, as did analogous Jewish organizations in Poland and Bulgaria. The pretext was the non-participation of the WJC in the Communist-sponsored World Congress for Peace in Paris. The last precarious organizational ties of the Czechoslovak Jewish community with Jewish groups beyond the Iron Curtain were thus destroyed.

Meanwhile, prominent Zionist leaders were either arrested or left the country. In September 1948, Oskar Krasňanský, president of the Zionist Organization of Czechoslovakia, was arrested in Bratislava.[41] Hanuš Rezek, the Zionist deputy chief rabbi of Prague, was allowed to leave the country; flying to Israel, he perished in an air accident in Greece.[42] In January 1949 the police arrested Leo Rosenthal, the head of the branch of the Jewish Agency in Bratislava; Emanuel Frieder, chairman of the Association of Jewish Religious Communities in Slovakia; and an unnamed official of the Ministry of Social Welfare.[43] Many unconfirmed reports about further arrests followed,[44] and some of those arrested were later released. In March 1949, an Associated Press report from Prague said that three Slovak Jewish officials of the American Jewish Joint Distribution Committee and another of the Jewish National Fund had been released at Bratislava after having been imprisoned and questioned for more than a month; the charges against them were not announced.[45]

The chief purpose of these arrests, concentrated mainly in Slovakia where Zionism was comparatively strong, seems to have been to hasten the dissolution of Zionist influence, to discourage any notions of resistance, and perhaps to lay hands on Zionist funds.

Later on, when a new agreement with Israel allowed for further emigration, the Zionist problem inside the country seemed to have been solved by the exodus. The chief object of the government's dislike now became the foreign Jewish organizations in Czechoslovakia. The expulsion of the Joint Distribution Committee in January 1950 left the offices of the Jewish Agency in Prague and Bratislava as the sole remaining organizations with outside connections. In the fall of 1950, when the government refused to grant further exit visas in any substantial numbers, the Jewish Agency decided to close these offices.[46]

Jewish Communities in Communist Hands

Before the Communist coup, the energies of the Jewish religious communities had for the most part been devoted to the fight for restitution, equal rights, and against antisemitism. Now, at the very moment when all rights of restitution were virtually being abolished, they suddenly abandoned their efforts in this direction. And antisemitism in Czechoslovakia, except for some "survivals" among "fascists" opposed to the new regime, had to be considered nonexistent. Instead of complaints against cases of injustice and discrimination, the Jewish press was suddenly filled with expressions of gratitude.

Employees of Jewish institutions "enthusiastically" joined the labor brigades to clean the streets.[47] The rabbis issued a declaration in which they asked all faithful Jews to support the government of Klement Gottwald, adding that "to pray for the government is the command of our forefathers, and social justice, which is the aim of the government, is also the leading idea of our holy Torah and of God's prophets."[48] RŽNO joined, on the "advice" of the Central Action Committee of the National Front, the Association for Soviet-Czechoslovak Friendship;[49] it also joined a Czechoslovak-Greek Society and asked the Jews to collect funds for Greek children sent to Czechoslovakia by the Greek insurgents.[50]

Before the elections in May 1948, the religious communities and their central associations published declarations in which they asked all Jews to vote for the government and denounced as traitors all those who would make use of their legal right to protest by a blank ballot.[51] The new officers of the communities wrote articles about the exemplary way the Jewish question had been solved in Russia and the satellite countries, including East Germany. *Věstník* was full of articles celebrating Lenin, Stalin, Gottwald, the Russian Revolution, the Red Army, and the Czechoslovak Communist Party. The history of Czechoslovakia and of the Czechoslovak Jews was revised to accord with the Communist line. The hundredth anniversary of the birth of Thomas G. Masaryk, founder of modern Czechoslovakia and a famous fighter for Jewish rights, was celebrated by a *Věstník* editorial declaring that Masaryk supported the Austrian monarchy at a time when "only Stalin had clearly formulated the demand for Czech independence"; that his anti-Marxist philosophy brought Masaryk "into the anti-labor camp of the reactionary bourgeoisie"; that Masaryk "shed the workers' blood"; and that his humanitarian ideals only masked the dictatorship of big business.[52]

"Peace" became the chief concern of the Communist-controlled Jewish organizations. As early as February 1949, Emil Ungar, president of the Council of Jewish Religious Communities, stressed in a report to the Council that the participation in the fight for peace was the most important way to increase the authority of the organization.[53]

Subsequently the Council supported all Communist peace drives. In May 1950 it signed a peace appeal by all non-Catholic church groups in Czechoslovakia, admonishing Jews at the same time that no one should fail to sign the Stockholm petition.[54] After the Korean war broke out, it dispatched a telegram to Jacob Malik, then president of the Security Council of the United Nations, protesting against "the inhuman bombing of peaceful cities, the murdering of women and children, the scorched-earth policy in Korea," and calling for the "evacuation of the interventionist armies" of the United Nations.[55] Similar proclamations were issued during the Second Congress of the Partisans of Peace in Warsaw in November 1950.[56]

Antisemitism was still attacked, but all antisemites seemed to have moved to America, England, and Western Europe. Dr. Ungar wrote an article suggesting that the Nazi murderers had been in the service not only of German but also of foreign imperialists.

> The majority of the Jews fell victim to their tormentors, who wanted, in the service of their own and foreign imperialists, to secure their rule

over the world in order to prevent the fall of capitalism and the victorious march of socialism.[57]

A report in *Věstník*, never corrected, announced that Mrs. Roosevelt had resigned as American delegate to the United Nations in order to protest against American anti-Jewish policy on the Palestinian question.[58] Similar biased and nonsensical "dispatches" about American Palestinian policy abounded. In April 1948, *Věstník* reported:

> While preparing a new Munich for the Jews, the government of the United States wants to extend the Marshall Plan to the Arab countries. In its last session the Political Committee of the Arab League discussed the American offer to extend the Marshall Plan to Arab countries. The Secretary General of the Arab League, Azzam Pasha, who went to America after the session, informed the member states that the loan will be granted on condition that the Arab states fight against the Communists with greater energy and that they collaborate with the Western powers more closely in the military as well as in the political field.[59]

False reports about the United States' "antisemitic" foreign policy were matched by reports about the conditions in which American Jews were supposed to live. An article by Arnošt Lustig, new leader of the Jewish students, summarized the situation of Jews in America—and in Russia—in these words:

> The Jew in America was blind for a long time. He allowed himself to be deceived by the delusion of eventual liberty. Only the Fords and the last depression opened his eyes. Antisemitism, as another and not the last form of competition, cuts the ground from under his feet. They close his schools, they exclude him from better jobs, from hotels, associations, meeting places, etc. The Jew in America is not free, he cannot free himself as long as his whole society is not liberated. . . .
>
> But the Soviet Union! A tremendous example of the cooperation of sixty nations! Complete extirpation of religious or any other prejudices! And in what a way! Soviet Society is free from the very possibilities and conditions from which even an attempt at discrimination might grow. . . .[60]

An article called "Is There Antisemitism in America?" by V. Štamberger, said:

> In the United States, there are about 5,000,000 Jews, mostly workers, little tailors, and artisans. Only a few are really rich and influential in public life because it is not so easy for a Jew in America to achieve anything. Everywhere he meets with what is called "the cold pogrom," which is the American phase for the economic and social boycott of Jews. Antisemitism has deep roots in the broad masses of the Anglo-Saxon population in America. . . .
>
> It is worth noting that the center of antisemitic propaganda in America is the State of Michigan with its giant automobile industry, whose fre-

quent strikes Henry Ford fought so sharply. The depression beginning in 1929 hit the auto industry with full strength. The anger and the bitterness of the unemployed and underpaid workers were diverted from the capitalists, who had caused this catastrophe, to the Jews. The Jews had to become—just as in Germany later on—scapegoats for the capitalists. We see here clearly that modern antisemitism is a necessary consequence of the capitalist system. . . .

Jews and Negroes are excluded from almost all American universities and colleges. . . . For this reason many American Jews went to European universities; after the war, however, this way was closed. Anti-Jewish attitudes are especially strong in medical schools. Although there is a shortage of 20,000 doctors, Jews are usually not accepted as medical students. This happens with the knowledge and support of the government, which gives financial subsidies to these schools.

In Germany race discrimination also started with the exclusion of Jews from the universities; it ended with gas chambers in Oswiecim. We don't know what we must still expect in the United States. . . .[61]

Decline of Jewish Life

Under the new regime and the Communist-imposed leadership, all remaining Jewish organizations became tools of the government. They were not able to defend Jewish interests against the authorities or hostile elements inside the country. They were not allowed to make any decisions of their own. Their attitude to specific Jewish questions was governed by the party line, which in turn was dictated by political expediency.

We have seen that after the war, the Jewish religious communities became centers for all Jews and defended the rights and interests of Jews beyond the purely religious, cultural, and social welfare spheres. But their activities began gradually to be restricted from the very moment of the Communist coup.

One important reason for this decline of communal activities was emigration. A great part of the community emigrated to Israel when the agreement of 1949 made it possible. This weakened Jewish communal life more than the number of emigrants would seem to warrant, for it was just those most closely identified with Judaism—Zionists, religious people, and the orthodox Jews from Carpatho-Russia—who were most strongly represented among the emigrants.

But, if the decline of communal life was in some degree due to emigration, emigration also was due in some degree to the decline of Jewish communal life. Many more Jews decided to leave the country in 1949 than would have left before the Communist coup. Ardent Zionists would have gone under any conditions; but many of the others, who had hoped to start a new life in Czechoslovakia in the first postwar years, abandoned this hope, in part for lack of economic opportunity, in part for lack of general freedom. Many were disappointed in their hope of establishing a free and active communal life, important to those who had lost their families, relatives, and friends. And the liquidation of Jewish organizations, official pronouncements against "Jewish nationalism" and Jewish "separate interests," the slow suffocation of the Jewish communities, could not but reinforce the lurking fear of possible antisemitic outbreaks or government measures in the future.

In any case, curtailment of communal activities began before the great wave of emigration of 1949-50. With the loss of payments from the "Terezín substance," the refusal of government subsidies for the year 1949, and the expropriation of their more wealthy members, the communities were in dire financial straits. However, restriction of communal activities had not only a financial, but political and ideological reasons as well. The old leadership had considered the defense of Jewish interests its primary task, albeit within the framework of the "people's democracy." The new leadership's chief purpose was to transmit the Communist line to the Jewish population. This was expressed cautiously but distinctly in the programmatic address of the new president of the Council, Emil Ungar, at a conference of the Jewish religious communities in Prague on February 6, 1949:

> One cannot disregard the political side of the Council's activities. . . . Compared with pre-February conditions, the political line of the Council is now crystal clear; our *Věstník* has to serve it in the field of propaganda, and the whole social, cultural, and administrative apparatus serves it in the field of material interests. . . . As long as the Jewish problem is not solved . . . it remains the task of the Council to warn Jews against the dangers of national ambiguity as well as against the dangers of pseudo-patriotism, which in reality is equivalent to chauvinist nationalism and threatens to lead Jews into the camp of the reaction. . . . Our activities and functions will therefore . . . differ (qualitatively) from the policies of the religious communities as they were understood in the past. Any limited consideration of narrow, particularist communal interests is out of the question; one has to consider the problems of the communities and the Jewish population as part and parcel of all contemporary social problems. It is clear that we can expect a solution of our problems and difficulties only from the complete victory of the truly democratic and progressive forces. . . . We have to exert all our powers, and use all our connections with foreign countries, toward this end.[62]

In November 1950 a message by Emil Ungar, read at another conference of Jewish religious communities in Bohemia and Moravia, summed up the present tasks of the communities in one sentence: "Our religious communities must devote themselves exclusively to their religious, educational, and social welfare tasks, and must endeavor to free our coreligionists of the vestiges of an obsolete ideology."[63]

Nationalization of most of the Jewish welfare institutions left the communities with three old-age homes in Prague, Brno, and Poděbrady; one hostel for young men and one for young women in Prague; and in addition they provided cash payments to sick members. This was the extent of their social welfare work. What remained of their religious and educational functions, to which the jurisdiction of the communities was now confined?

Regimentation of Churches

On November 1, 1949, after a prolonged struggle with the Catholic church, two new laws governing church-state relations went into effect. Their major provisions called for payment by the state to clergymen of their basic salaries; payment of bonuses for meritorious work, educational grants for further study and pensions. The state assumed the financial administration of all churches, charities, institutions, and other properties of religious communities. Only clergymen swearing allegiance to the Communist state were permitted to perform their duties. All churches and religious communities were required to submit an inventory of their goods and holdings within three months. They were also required to submit budgetary estimates before receiving their grants. Violations of the law were punishable by fines and imprisonment up to six months.

A special Ministry for Church Affairs was founded to supervise all religious activities, confirm the appointments of all clergymen and church boards, direct the education of clergy, and introduce compulsory courses for the civil indoctrination of future clergymen.

On December 7, Parliament adopted another law, according to which church weddings were not to be recognized after January 1, 1950, only civil marriages being considered valid. Religious ceremonies might be performed after the conclusion of the civil marriage, but if not preceded by a civil marriage they were a punishable offense. Keeping of vital statistics was transferred from the religious to the civil authorities.

The new church laws meant the complete submission of organized religion to the Communist state. The clergy's pay was now increased, but in compensation the state virtually confiscated the churches' property and charitable institutions. And, as we shall see, state subsidies for religious communities were not increased but decreased after the adoption of the laws, even in the case of communities offering no resistance to the government.

The Catholic church conducted a long struggle against the church laws, attacking them as a means to destroy the autonomy of the church. It maintained that state control of seminaries could only mean the introduction of antireligious ideologies into religious education. Catholic priests declared themselves ready to reaffirm their oath of allegiance to the Czechoslovak Republic, but refused to swear an oath of loyalty to the particular regime in power.

During the controversy, the Prague Archbishop, Joseph Beran, was confined to his palace, dissemination of pastoral letters without special permission from the police was prohibited, and many priests were arrested. The Communists founded a pro-government Catholic organization, but only a minority of Catholic priests and laymen joined it.

After the adoption of the laws, Catholic bishops allowed priests to take the loyalty oath, though still refusing to take it themselves. For a while the tension was relieved and the government granted a "little amnesty" to Catholics accused of minor offenses committed during the church-state struggle. But the fight soon flared up again when executive orders issued to enforce the new law placed all religious publications,religious education, and all activities of religious bodies under strict government control.

The struggle continued throughout 1950. Treason trials were organized against the archbishop's aides, against abbots of monasteries, and finally against two Roman Catholic bishops and one Greek Catholic bishop. They were given long prison terms. In the meantime, the Communist-supervised seminaries began turning out new, indoctrinated priests, who were consecrated by a Catholic bishop who had capitulated and sworn the oath of loyalty to the regime. Pro-regime priests were appointed to church offices wherever there was a vacancy.

The Jewish religious communities took no part in this struggle. There was only one report saying that "several Jewish communities in Slovakia, together with some Protestant groups," raised objections against the church laws before their enactment.[64] The central organization of Jewish religious communities both in the historic lands and in Slovakia welcomed the church laws as "guaranteeing religious equality" and "securing the financial basis of religious life." The Prague Council sent a delegation, consisting of its president, Emil Ungar, and the deputy chief rabbi, Emil Davidovic, to the gallery of Parliament when the laws were adopted.[65] The Central Association of Jewish Religious Communities in Slovakia published a declaration which said:

> We Slovaks of the Jewish faith welcome the adoption of these laws, not only out of a sense of civic and patriotic duty, but with enthusiasm, because they guarantee us the development of religious life and material security for the church (*sic*).[66]

The Chief Rabbi of Prague, Gustav Sicher, was administered the oath of allegiance by Premier Antonín Zápotocký on March 20, 1950.[67]

Expectations that the state would completely finance the communities and pay the salaries of religious personnel did not materialize. Communist reports on the subject were always equivocal. E. Kohn, secretary of the Prague Council, declared in an interview in August 1950:

> Under capitalism, the communities were maintained by the individual Jewish communities, but now the state maintains and supports all Jewish

> institutions. The communities send in to the Jewish Committee [the Council of Jewish Religious Communities] a budget of their requirements for the coming year. These are agreed upon and the government provides the necessary finances.[68]

But shortly afterwards, Chief Rabbi Sicher was quoted as stating the following to a delegate to the international student congress in Prague:

> At present, Dr. Sicher is paid and the synagogues are maintained out of the funds which accrue to the Jewish *Kehilla* from their property. In the future, when the communal property is nationalized, money for both these purposes will be provided by the state.[69]

In November 1950, Dr. Ungar explained the true state of things in his message to the conference of religious communities in Prague:

> The state has . . . solved our financial problems in that it will help us provide for those expenses which we will not be able to pay from our own income. Even though our budget was not fully approved . . . because our state-planned and responsible economy could not permit it, we are looking to the future *almost* without worries, being almost financially secure. . . .[70]

In the discussion it was stressed that it was a misinterpretation of the church laws to believe, as some communities did, that the taxing of members for the maintenance of religious institutions would be discontinued; quite the contrary, payment of the religious tax was "more than a duty." One delegate announced that his community, which was composed mostly of factory workers and numbered 240 members, including children and paupers, had already collected 27,000 crowns in religious taxes.

Thus it seems that communal taxes, contributions by members, and "income from communal property" were still, as before, the primary sources of income, and that even the salaries of rabbis were paid from these sources so long as funds existed. After exhausting these funds, the communities could apply for grants from the state, but had to expect a radical revision of their requests. "Under capitalism" too the state had contributed to clergymen's salaries and had subsidized communal activities; the only difference now was the desperate financial situation of the communal organizations and their members.

Income "from communal property" largely came from selling these properties, including real estate and synagogue buildings. In many cases, communal properties were not even sold but simply "donated" to municipal authorities and in some cases to other pro-government churches.

Liquidation of the Communities

The number of religious communities diminished substantially. After the war, 51 of the 217 existing before the war had been reconstituted in the historic lands. In September 1950, E. Kohn of the Prague Council made the rather dubious claim, in an interview reported in the London

Jewish Chronicle, that there were still 48 of them in Bohemia and Moravia.[71] Only 19 "still existing" communities were represented at a conference in Karlovy Vary (Karlsbad) in June of that year;[72] no data on the number of communities or present representatives were given at the December conference. The report on the conference in Karlovy Vary had spoken very concretely about 32 communities which had been liquidated,[73] whose properties, worth more than a million dollars, had been given, without consultation of the Jewish Council in Prague, to local municipal authorities of local non-Jewish welfare institutions. On June 29, 1952, the remaining Jewish communities in the "historic lands" were "consolidated" into nine at a conference in Prague. They were located in Prague, Plzeň, Karlovy Vary, Liberec and Ústí nad Labem in Bohemia, and Brno, Olomouc, Ostrava and Kyjov in Moravia-Silesia. These were administrative units; synagogues still existed in a few other places, and district rabbis performed religious services and ceremonies, traveling from place to place through rather extensive territories.

The Council of Jewish Religious Communities was not mentioned at the conference, and the *Věstník*, which had called itself the organ of the Council as well as of the Prague community up to January 1952, changed its subtitle to that of "organ of Jewish religious communities in Czechoslovakia" after that date. At the same time, it began to appear only once instead of twice a month and reduced its size to eight small pages.

Reports coming from Czechoslovakia, mostly through Vienna and West Germany and based on accounts of foreign visitors or refugees, spoke of numerous cases of liquidation of synagogues. In March 1949 it was reported that twenty-two former synagogues had been turned into movie houses and dancing schools.[74] In December, a special dispatch from Vienna announced that 33 synagogues had been "confiscated" and converted into dance halls, clubs, and libraries "during the past week."[75] In April 1950, synagogues of the old Moravian Jewish communities in Mikulov, Ivančice, and Valašské Meziříčí were demolished because the decayed buildings were a public hazard.[76] In May 1950 it was reported that two synagogues in small towns near Prague had been seized and sold, the money being retained by the state authorities.[77] In November 1949, *Věstník*, quoting from *Český Zápas*, organ of the government-favored "Czechoslovak church," published a Christian meditation to be read in synagogues that had been transformed into houses of prayer for the Czechoslovak church.[78] An explanatory note said that "many a synagogue which served as a spiritual refuge for our fathers and grandfathers was taken over by the Czechoslovak church" because nobody was left to take care of it. "After appropriate changes, they will be again consecrated to the service of God," wrote *Věstník*, adding that the meditations showed that the synagogues were now in good hands.

As for the Jewish cemeteries, delegates to the conference of religious communities in November 1950 complained that "many of them are still in the wretched state in which the survivors of the concentration camps had found them after the liberation, although some of them have great historical value."[79]

A shortage of trained rabbis was felt in what communities remained. Rabbi Sicher of Prague emigrated from Czechoslovakia in 1939; he returned to Prague from Israel in 1947 and remained at his post only because there was no one to take his place.[80] When the rabbi of Bánská Bystrica, Dr. Aron Schönfeld, died at the age of seventy, *Věstník* remarked that he had been the last rabbi in Slovakia to have possessed an academic education.[81] Reports in the Jewish press abroad cited places where women, in the absence of rabbis, were obliged to preach in synagogues and officiate at weddings.[82]

In all of the historic lands there were three *shochetim*, in Prague, Karlovy Vary (Karlsbad), and Liberec (Reichenberg).[83] In Prague there was a *mikvah* and one kosher restaurant. Analogous institutions existed, without doubt, in Slovakia.

Jews were allowed to celebrate religious holidays on condition that they made up the lost time. This was confirmed by an announcement in *Věstník* on the eve of the high holidays in 1950.[84] Again, the interview with Rabbi Sicher throws more light on the matter. He said:

> If one desires to keep the sabbath, this is possible, although it may involve a little effort, as Saturday work would have to be compensated for by heavier work of a different type on Sunday.[85]

Under these circumstances, Jewish religious life began to decline, though all reports agree that there was no direct government interference with religious services. In one of its last issues, the *Tribuna* of Bratislava reported that it was increasingly difficult to gather a quorum for religious services, not only in small places, but also in the great synagogues in Prague, Brno, and Bratislava.[86]

When the aforementioned delegate to the international student congress in Prague visited the famous Old-New Synagogue on a Saturday morning in the fall of 1950, he found about 25 men there and "a number" of women. He was told that this synagogue was open on Saturday and weekdays; a second synagogue, in the Jerusalemská street, on Friday nights and Saturday mornings only; a third, at the Jewish Home for the Aged, only on Friday nights. There were actually 35 synagogues in Prague, the report continued, but attendance did not warrant opening more than three; the number of worshippers at each did not normally exceed 50. However, it was anticipated that all would be filled during the high holidays.[87]

Rabbi Sicher explained to the same visitor that nothing was done in the way of Jewish education "because there is no demand." And in fact, religious education was now reduced to occasional lessons given by local rabbis to Jewish pupils of public schools, and to frequent articles in

Věstník explaining the meaning of Jewish holidays and traditions. From time to time, the Prague community arranged social gatherings, where lectures on political as well as cultural topics were combined with recitations, concert performances, etc. The communities outside of Prague gathered occasionally to commemorate the victims of the exterminations or to consecrate memorial plaques to them.

The Jewish Museum was one of the outstanding cultural institutions in Prague. At the end of 1950, the Communist press throughout the world announced that the first state Jewish museum in Central Europe had been opened in Czechoslovakia;[88] the impression was given that this was a new institution.

As a matter of fact, the Prague Jewish community had possessed a valuable museum even before the war. During the war the Nazis added to it Jewish books, manuscripts, and religious and art objects seized in Germany and Central and Southeastern Europe. This made the Prague Museum a unique treasury of Jewish history and art. After the war the Museum became the property of the Prague Jewish community and was administered with pious care; several catalogues and other publications were published,[89] and others were in preparation.

But after the February coup, the Communists decided that even this cultural institution should be placed in the service of official propaganda. In an article in *Věstník*, the Communist writer Louis Fuernberg demanded a complete reorganization of the museum. In his opinion, it seemed to be attempting to preserve "the least vital and most superficial" traits of Jewish history. To be sure, it possessed objects of historical and artistic value, but "a contemporary Jewish museum must not only be a museum of history and art, especially if it is located in Prague"; it must "become a museum of the official [sic] political, economic, and cultural history of the Jewish nation." It must "show the situation of the Jews in feudal and capitalist society, and antisemitism as a phenomenon of social reaction." It must "show the situation of Jews where they live as free and equal citizens of their countries: in the Socialist Soviet Union and in the new people's democracies. This and only this can be the task of a Jewish Museum," Fuernberg declared.[90]

At the end of 1949 the Museum was taken in hand by the government. The reason officially given was that "the 4,000 Jews of Prague could not afford to maintain it." An appeal to the government to permit the transfer of a few religious objects to Israel failed.[91] In 1951, the Museum was completely reformed. According to a report printed in *Věstník* of May 1, 1952, it had formerly presented only a record of Jewish religious life and customs. Now, it was reorganized "in harmony with scientific knowledge of our time, i.e., historical materialism," and made another instrument of Communist propaganda.

At the end of 1950, the state of Jewish communal life in Czechoslovakia was as follows: the religious communities, the only officially sanctioned Jewish organizations, still existed and there was no direct governmental interference with religious services. However, the communities had been weakened by the emigration of a great part of their members; impoverished by the expropriation of much of their assets and the cutting-off of their sources of income; forbidden to engage in many of their former activities; and forced to follow the decisions of the party in power in the political, social, and cultural fields. Jewish religious and cultural life was rapidly disintegrating under the omnipresent pressure of totalitarian dictatorship.

Chapter X

Emigration

In the period before the Communist coup the official policy of the government permitted the emigration of those Jews who wished to leave the country, and encouraged the assimilation of those who wished to remain. There were still hopes that at least a part of the Nazi-expropriated properties would be restored; private enterprise, though sharply limited, offered a measure of economic opportunity; and some survivors were able to find jobs in the administration or with nationalized industries. Laws against racial hatred seemed to give a degree of protection against the danger of antisemitism, and Jewish communal life was being revived. In this period Jews were able to decide more or less freely if they wished to stay or leave.

In this first period there was a great difference in attitude between the Jews of the historic lands and those of Slovakia. Most of the Jews in the historic lands decided to remain in the country; the majority of the Slovak Jews wished to emigrate. This is made clear in the report of the Anglo-American Committee of Inquiry Regarding the Problems of European Jewry and Palestine, the delegates of which visited Czechoslovakia in February 1946. About Bohemia, Moravia, and Silesia, it stated that

> the Council of Jewish Communties were confident that in due course Jews would take their place in the life of the Republic and that as intelligent and diligent people they would be a useful and valuable element in the community.

But the situation in Slovakia was different.

> There are many, particularly in Slovakia, who wish to emigrate. Zionism was always strong there and it is estimated that at the present time 60 per cent of the Jews wish to leave. This number is likely to diminish if and when the restitution of property enables them to become established.[1]

In general, the Committee of Inquiry concluded that antisemitism "was likely to diminish"; if this were accompanied by the restitution of property, it could be expected that a considerable number, including many who had professed a desire to emigrate, would decide "to remain in the country in which they were so deeply rooted."

There were reports from the Jewish side which indicated a higher estimate of the percentage of Slovak Jews wishing to emigrate. Max Gottschalk reported to the American Jewish Committee in April 1946 that 60 per cent of the Slovak Jews wished to go to Palestine, 15 per cent to the United States, and that the rest were old, sick, or baptized Jews.[2]

Nevertheless, the number of emigrants in the first postwar years was not very high. According to a report by Arnošt Frischer to the European Zionist Conference in Karlovy Vary in August 1947, about 2,500 Czechoslovak Jews had emigrated to Palestine up to that time, and another 2,500 had gone to Palestine by way of other countries.[3] Palestinian statistics for that time list 770 immigrants from Czechoslovakia in 1946 and 2,064 in 1947.[4] These statistics, however, are incomplete, for a great part of the immigrants (a majority in 1946) were not classified as to country of origin.

The situation markedly changed in 1948 with the Communist seizure of power. All hope ended for restitution and an independent economic existence, for democratic rights and an autonomous communal life. In May, the establishment of Israel opened the door to mass immigration.

The Communist pro-Israel line was still in force and emigration was, for several months, openly favored by the government. In July, the Israeli Minister in Prague, Yehud Avriel-Ueberall, revealed that 250 emigrants were being flown each month to Israel on regular Czechoslovak planes; he hoped to increase the number to 600-700 a month by September. Several twin-engine C-47 transport planes were to be bought by Israel to supplement the existing Czechoslovak air service.[5] At about the same time Julius Levine, Joint Distribution Committee director in Prague, declared in New York that the number of emigrants from Czechoslovakia to the United States, Israel, and other countries had reached the rate of 500 per month and would probably increase in the fall.[6] In April, Daniel Okali, head of the Slovak Department of the Interior, had promised Vojtech Winterstein, secretary general of the Association of Racial Persecutees in Slovakia, to issue one to two thousand passports to emigrants from Czechoslovakia to Palestine.[7] Also, Jews from other Eastern European countries used Czechoslovakia as a transit station. In August, 2,500 such transients were aided by the JDC in Prague.[8]

Yet the actual number of Czechoslovak emigrants in 1948 fell short of expectations. The main reason was that the Czechoslovak authorities did not cooperate to the degree that had been expected. Issuance of passports, exit permits, and other papers was delayed, and after the anti-Zionist turn at the end of 1948, Zionist emigration activities were hampered by police measures. Israel statistics report only 2,558 immigrants born in Czechoslovakia for the year 1948.[9] The number of emigrants from Czechoslovakia was probably greater, first, because some of them were still in transit at the end of 1948; second, because many pretended to be going to Israel, but then went to other countries once past the Iron Curtain; and third, because there was an increasing illegal emigration to Austria and Western Germany. According to the *Aufbau*, 500 Jews left Czechoslovakia for Israel, and 3,000 for other countries, in 1948.[10]

Exodus of 1949

The great exodus came in 1949. Israeli statistics for that year report 15,689 immigrants born in Czechoslovakia.[11] The Committee transported 14,299 emigrants from Czechoslovakia to Israel; it estimated the total number of those who left Czechoslovakia legally at 15,500.

The exodus came about as the result of an agreement concluded between the Czechoslovak government and the Israel minister in Prague, Yehud Avriel-Ueberall. The *Aufbau* reported in a dispatch from Prague:

> The exodus . . . is much more difficult than the exodus from Mizraim [Egypt]. Yehud Avriel-Ueberall, the Israeli Minister to Prague and Budapest, is an exceedingly clever negotiator but he has not the miraculous powers of Moses. And as a matter of fact the arts that impressed the Pharaoh would not move the Czechoslovak government. No miracles except an impressive amount of dollars would succeed here, and it is this kind of argument which made it possible to win this contribution of Czechoslovakia to the existence of the Jewish state and to obtain permission for the emigration of 20,000 Jews.[12]

The agreement provided for a maximum of 20,000 exit permits. Originally, emigration was supposed to end in four months. But only 1,500 persons were able to leave in January, and 1,000 in February, so that it was soon evident the four months were inadequate. The cut-off date was postponed several times, first to May 15, then to September, and finally to the end of the year.

As long as the agreement was in force, emigration was fairly free. Government regulations forbade the emigration of all medical personnel (physicians, pharmacists, dentists, nurses, etc.), engineers, and other technicians, except those who could produce a certificate from their place of employment showing that they were not needed; youths of military age; and of course politically suspect persons. For the rest, the main obstacles were financial.

Emigrants had to pay for their passports. At first, a passport to Israel could be obtained for 3,000 crowns, and collective passports were issued for whole groups of emigrants to Israel. But in the middle of May the Ministry of the Interior announced that no further collective passports would be issued and that the special rate for passports to Israel was abolished. Thereafter, a passport cost 50,000 crowns ($1,000 according to the official rate of exchange) and more.

The emigrants had also to pay many taxes and duties, and the regulations were enforced in such a way that, according to a report from Prague in the *Aufbau*, "the time when one had to pay only a Reich-emigration tax (under the Nazis) looked almost idyllic in comparison." In the opinion of the *Aufbau*, this "put a highly efficient brake on emigration"; a report from Prague maintained that only wealthy people could emigrate.

Emigrants could take along their personal belongings, including furniture for one room, but no refrigerators or machines (a dressmaker could take a sewing machine). Permits to take out such goods were handled by the Ministry of Finance; the procedure for obtaining them was complicated and full of bureaucratic chicanery.[13]

Under these circumstances the decision to emigrate was not an easy one to make. A correspondent of the American Jewish Committee described the considerations influencing such a decision:

> The growing pressure of the party; the increasing costs of living; the uncertain future of the Czechoslovak currency and economy in general; reduced wages; full prisons and labor camps; compulsory "volunteer brigades" for the mines (intellectuals in particular are being sent to the mines for periods of 4-6 months); compulsory Marxist "schooling" lasting at least a fortnight in special centers and including final examinations (civil servants and employees of nationalized industry must attend frequent party and union meetings—the average is 5 meetings a week); celebrations and demonstrations in which all employees are forced to participate under threat of losing their jobs and where they must hear dull speeches on Marxism, Soviet Russia, the Communist Party and the Five-Year Plan—all this is an unbearable burden for Jews and non-Jews alike.
>
> There *is* an antisemitic movement in the central organ of the Communist Party and it is considered that the Jewish intellectuals will not keep their influence for long. They will be replaced gradually by factory workers as soon as the latter finish a special schooling program organized for them. Workers who are chosen have the possibility of graduating from special schools within several months to become judges, army officers, lawyers, etc. faithful to the idea of "popular" democracy. These workers will replace the earlier generation of intellectuals who, although they are reliable party members, think far too much, and incidentally are sometimes Jews. Thus, an unfailing popular gesture will be made by quietly removing Jews from party posts, and simultaneously a new generation of workers will assume the power. No doubt the workers will be more reliable than any Communist intellectual who might become a traitor to the Communist idea and escape abroad, as actually happened in several cases. Of course, there were also Jews among these escapees.
>
> The development of the new antisemitic atmosphere is a great disappointment to the average Jew, who hoped to be able to live in peace after his return home from the concentration camps or from army service. One way to solve the problem is emigration. . . .
>
> Most Jews did not wish to stay in Czechoslovakia because they feared that in the event of war or of any change of government, the Jews will have hard days again. They feared also that they might be hindered in

> their fight for existence in the future. They feared the general development in Central Europe. In case of war, they would not like to be Russian soldiers; many Jews had already had this experience. Naturally, the same reasons that influence the life of every normal thinking citizen behind the Iron Curtain also contributed to the decision to emigrate.[14]

The Prague correspondent of the *Aufbau* described the reasons for emigration in similar but more guarded terms.

> Emigration offers a way out of a dilemma which could acquire dangerous proportions in the future. There is no doubt that the forces which are fighting—although rather hopelessly today—against Communism in Czechoslovakia show antisemitic tendencies which they try to rationalize . . . by saying that the Jews are "guilty" of Communism. On the other hand, the methods of dictatorship of the proletariat are not liked even by the Jewish left, not to speak of moderate socialists or middle-class Zionists. The prospect of a free development in their own country is therefore, in spite of all economic difficulties, doubly tempting.[15]

And the reasons for remaining? One report went as follows:

> If we try to classify those Jews who remained in Czechoslovakia, we find chiefly:
>
> 1. The optimists who believe that the present situation will be changed easily, either by an international agreement or by war (which will be won by the United States within a few weeks). Czechoslovakia will be liberated and separated from the "popular" democracies and Russia.
>
> 2. Those who would like to emigrate, but not to Israel. There is quite a number of such persons who have no possibility of emigrating except to Israel, where they do not want to go because they know the difficulties too well. They would have to start all over again after four years and give up [their present] comparative comfort.
>
> 3. Faithful Communists who try their best to believe that everything is fine in the Czechoslovakia of today.
>
> 4. Persons who are not allowed to leave the country because of legal proceedings, because they hold important positions, physicians, etc.[16]

All reports agree that the sums needed for obtaining passports, exit visas, etc., the long procedures, the impossibility of taking out more than nominal amounts of money, were grave deterrents to emigration. And in general there was, especially among older people, a feeling of weariness, hopelessness, and resignation which great suffering and the loss of relatives and friends had engendered.

No wonder that under these circumstances many people hesitated. When the Israel legation announced that applications for visas would be accepted only until March 15, 1949, there was "a kind of panic."[17] Having in mind how difficult it now was for Jews in other Eastern European countries to emigrate, the Czechoslovak Jews hurried to file their applications in time. But when the cut-off date was repeatedly postponed, many Jews began to hesitate again, especially as the costs of emigration increased with the abolition of collective passports and stricter regulations about the transfer of properties. These circumstances help to explain why, according to press reports, 20,000 Jews applied for passports, whereas only about 15,000 left the country for Israel in 1949. Other reports spoke of 10,000 Jews as still wishing to emigrate. The estimate might be exaggerated for it included those who applied for papers "just in case," without having made up their minds. But it may also be that many of those who were still hesitating in 1949 would have liked to emigrate in 1950, when the mass purges began.

But then it was too late. The government considered mass emigration as over and done with; in individual cases, it was still possible, but very difficult. The number of Jews transported from Czechoslovakia to Israel by the Joint Distribution Committee dropped to 169 for the entire year of 1950. When in July 1950 the Jewish Agency issued a circular asking those Jews who had registered for emigration in 1949 and had not been able to emigrate to fill out questionnaires to expedite the handling of their cases, the Ministry of Labor and Social Welfare answered with a public statement summarizing the government's policy as follows:

> The Czechoslovak Republic is, as is well known, not interested in supporting emigration, since a planned economy and socialist construction offer all able-bodied citizens, irrespective of nationality, race, or religion, an opportunity to take part in economic reconstruction. As for invalids or the aged, our social insurance and relief institutions provide a satisfactory living to all citizens without discrimination. Thus there are no material reasons for anybody to emigrate from Czechoslovakia.
>
> In individual cases, however, if all legal conditions are fulfilled, the Czechoslovak government allows all citizens without exception to emigrate. Like other citizens, the members of Jewish religious communities can apply for permission to emigrate in the prescribed way, and no action or intervention by the Jewish Agency is necessary. . . . The Jewish Agency's circular was issued without the Ministry's consent and its contents do not accord with the aim of the Czechoslovak government.[18]

Soon after this, the Jewish Agency was obliged to close its offices in Czechoslovakia.[19]

Asked whether there were any restrictions on Jews wishing to leave for Israel, the secretary of the Council of Jewish Religious Communities in Bohemia and Moravia answered:

> The laws of Czechoslovakia do not differentiate between Jew and non-Jew. As there is a shortage of labor there is a restriction on emigration, but anyone who has near relatives living outside Czechoslovakia

> is permitted to leave, except doctors because of the great shortage in the medical profession.[20]

Rabbi Gustav Sicher answered a similar question as follows:

> Today the position of the Jew who wishes to emigrate is exactly like that of the non-Jew—it is difficult unless one has retired from work.[21]

There was also some illegal Jewish emigration from Czechoslovakia. It is difficult to ascertain how many Jews there were among the 30-40,000 Czechoslovak refugees who left the country after the Communist coup. Scattered data seem to point to the fact that the percentage was considerable. A Jewish Telegraphic Agency report from Munich announced in January 1949 that "some 400 Jews, including a number of complete family units," arrived in the American zones of Germany and Austria "during the latter part of December 1948." This was stated by officials of the International Refugee Organization who were queried following statements by Bavarian authorities that the rate of Czechoslovak Jews arriving in Bavaria "was increasing daily."[22] In 1948 control of Czechoslovakian borders was not yet perfect and the agreement on legal emigration with Israel had not yet come into force. The number of illegal emigrants seems to have decreased in 1949, but increased again in 1950 when legal emigration became difficult to the point of impossible. In May 1950, the Jewish Community in Vienna announced that "in the last few weeks," 465 Jewish refugees have arrived from Czechoslovakia.[23] In both cases, it is impossible to say how many among the Jews arriving from Czechoslovakia were Czechoslovak Jews, and how many were en route from other satellite countries.

The Transients

Before February 1948, Czechoslovakia had generously allowed transient Jewish emigrants (most of them from Poland, and then later from Hungary) to cross the borders and wait on Czechoslovak soil until such time as they could go on. This changed after the Communist coup. As we have seen, the new leadership of the Jewish communities criticized the old for "excessive" relief activities—support of transient refugees was one of the main targets of this criticism. Czechoslovak authorities soon ceased to issue transit visas to emigrants from other "people's democracies" that prohibited or limited Jewish emigration. When Rumania, for instance, began to place obstacles in the way of Jewish emigrants in 1948, the Czechoslovak government stopped issuing transit visas to them and cancelled visas already issued by its consuls in Rumania.[24]

In Bratislava, however, which is situated at a point where the borders of Czechoslovakia, Austria, and Hungary meet, illegal crossing of the frontier by Hungarian Jews fleeing to Austria was more or less tolerated up to the spring of 1949. Thousands of Hungarian Jews passed this way, receiving every possible help from the Jews in Bratislava. In May 1949, after an intervention by the Hungarian government, Czechoslovak authorities stopped a transport and threatened to return the refugees to Hungary; in the end most of the persons in the transport were allowed to pass. But further emigration via Bratislava was now prohibited. Posters placed on Bratislava's streets announced that all illegal entrants from Hungary would be punished and returned. Czechoslovak Jews were prohibited from inviting their Hungarian relatives to come to Slovakia. The Jewish community in Bratislava had to declare that it would stop intervening with Czechoslovak authorities in behalf of the refugees; nor might it give them any material help. The border guard was reinforced. In July 1949 it was announced that 30 Hungarian Jewish refugees had been arrested by Czechoslovak guards while trying to cross the border; they were immediately tried and sentenced to six months' imprisonment in Czechoslovakia, after which they would be deported back to Hungary. At that time some 100 Jewish refugees were being held by Czechoslovak authorities for the same offense and faced return to Hungary.[25]

As statistics concerning legal emigration are inexact, to a certain degree even contradictory, and as there are no statistics concerning illegal emigration, it is very difficult to estimate accurately the number of Jews remaining in Czechoslovakia at the end of 1950. Estimates for the summer of 1950 varied between 14,000 and 18,000. Leon Shapiro, in his statistics on world Jewish population, gives a figure of 17,000 as of July 1950. E. Kohn, the secretary of the Prague Council, told a foreign visitor in the summer of 1950 that there were 11,500 Jews in Bohemia and Moravia and "about 10,000" in Slovakia[27]—evidently an exaggerated estimate. Chief Rabbi Gustav Sicher told another visitor at about the same time that "the total Jewish population at present is estimated at 14,000, of whom 4,000 are in Prague."[28] In the second half of 1950 legal emigration virtually ceased and illegal emigration was but a trickle, so that these estimates hold for the end of the year.

It is safe to say that from two-thirds to three-quarters of the Jewish survivors of the war left Czechoslovakia. The fourteen to eighteen thousand Jews were all that was left of a Jewish community numbering 360,000 persons in prewar times.

Chapter XI

The Purge

In 1951, one could hardly speak of a Jewish community in Czechoslovakia. Zionism and any activities which could be described as countenancing "Jewish nationalism" were prohibited; only a few courageous believers were still worshipping in public under the surveillance of Communist-dominated "religious communities."

There was no Jewish communal life, but there were still a few Jews. They formed only a negligible percentage—about 1½ pro mille—of the total population. They were ethnically assimilated, considered themselves Czechs or Slovaks, and were either members or voluntary and involuntary followers of the Communist Party. Most of them were Jewish only in their (as the Nazis used to call it) "racial origin." It would seem that there was no "Jewish problem," except for the natural claim of Jewish citizens to equality before the law.

The events of 1951 proved that complete assimilation to the ethnic majority and to the new social order did not protect individuals of Jewish descent from antisemitism. The liquidation of Jewish communal life was followed by a thorough purge of Jews from all positions in public life, and by a new wave of antisemitic agitation which held people of Jewish origin to be members of a "suspect group," convenient scapegoats for the failures of the totalitarian regime.[1]

In Soviet Russia, the mass purges in 1948 began to acquire a distinctly antisemitic character when Yiddish-speaking Communist writers were accused of treason and liquidated because of alleged "Jewish nationalism," and when thousands of Jewish officials and intellectuals were removed from their posts for "cosmopolitanism," which was said to be "alien" to the Russian character and subversive of Soviet patriotism. In the satellite countries the campaign against Zionism, "Jewish nationalism," and "cosmopolitanism" got rid of independent Jewish organizations, but spared the Jewish Communists. But during 1950-51 the purge of the Communist parties took an antisemitic turn. Czechoslovakia, the satellite country with the smallest and most assimilated Jewish minority, was the first to purge its Jewish Communists; subsequent events in Rumania, Hungary, Poland, and Russia itself showed that the operation was inspired from Moscow.

Purge of "Titoists"

A general purge of unreliable Communist leaders was begun in all the satellite countries in 1948, the year of the defection of Tito's Yugoslavia. This general purge started later in Czechoslovakia than in the neighboring countries, and only after prompting from the outside.

In September 1949, a spectacular treason trial took place in Budapest, Hungary. Laszlo Rajk, a former Minister of the Interior and Minister of Foreign Affairs, and a member of the Hungarian Politburo, was accused of conspiring to overthrow the Hungarian government and being a spy for America, England, and Titoist Yugoslavia. Rajk had prevented prosecution of the instigators of the postwar pogroms in Miskolc and Kunmadaras, and so it was expected that he would be accused, among other things, of abetting antisemitism. But this charge was the only one missing from the endless list of his alleged crimes. On the contrary, Rajk was accused of plotting together with "counterrevolutionary Zionism." Three of his co-defendents, Tibor Szonyi, Andras Szalai, and Paul Justus, were Jews. Szallai "confessed" that he had been a member of a "Trotskyite-Zionist group"; Szonyi "admitted" that he had spied, "together with Zionist agents," for the American intelligence service in Switzerland during the war. And Rajk himself was accused of having helped to smuggle "Zionist imperialist agents" out of Hungary into Israel. Thus the allegation of a "world-wide Zionist conspiracy" was already fully developed in this Hungarian show trial.[2]

Some of the Budapest defendants were made to "confess" that a widespread and well-organized Titoist conspiracy in the service of "Western imperialism" also existed in Czechoslovakia. The Czechoslovak authorities seemed to know nothing about this sinister plot. But the hint from Moscow via Budapest, doubtless supported by behind-the-scenes pressure, was enough.[3] Soon afterwards, a purge of Communists in Czechoslovakia was begun.

Its first victims were a number of high officials in the Ministries of Foreign Affairs, Foreign Trade, and Information. Most of these were of Jewish origin: Evžen Klinger, head of the Press Division in the Ministry of Foreign Affairs; Dr. Oskar Kosta (Kohn), deputy chief of the Press Division in the Ministry of Information; Stanislav Budin (Benzion Batz), former head of the Anglo-American desk in the same ministry and later foreign editor of the newspaper *Lidové Noviny;* Evžen Loebl, Deputy Minister of Foreign Trade; Milan Rejman, head of the Office of the Premier. Although most of the victims were Jews, this fact was not publicized and the antisemitic character of this first purge was not evident at that time.[4]

This quiet purge was soon overshadowed by the public demotion and subsequent arrest of two more prominent non-Jewish Communist leaders.

They were: Vilém Nový, editor of the chief organ of the Communist Party, *Rudé Právo*, and chairman of the Foreign Affairs Committee of the National Assembly; and Vlado Clementis, Minister of Foreign Affairs. Nový was accused of being an agent of the Western powers and member of a spy ring organized by the American citizens Noel and Herman Field.[5] Clementis, charged first with a nationalist deviation, was later arrested as a Western spy.[6]

All the men so far mentioned had spent the war years in Western countries and some of them were known to have opposed the Nazi-Soviet pact of 1939. They were accused of Czech or Slovak nationalism and of Titoist deviations. Many of them were known as old friends of President Klement Gottwald. It was generally assumed that their removal was a preliminary to removing Gottwald. The purge was apparently conducted, at this stage, by the boss of the party machine, Secretary General Rudolf Slánský.

The Purge Turns Its Direction

The situation changed dramatically in October 1950, when the party demoted and the police arrested Otto Šling, member of the Central Committee of the Communist Party and its regional secretary in Brno, the capital of Moravia. When a session of the Central Committee was convened in Prague on February 21, 1951, the purge entered a new stage. Clementis was now in jail, and at the meeting it was announced that he had confessed to spying for the Western imperialists. But his case was treated as a second-class affair. The real sensation of the February Central Committee meeting was the sudden "discovery" of another, much more dangerous, "plot," this time not in government offices but in the headquarters of the Communist Party, right among the close collaborators of Secretary General Slánský.

It is one of the most important duties of party secretaries to supervise party cadres and conduct their purges. Therefore it was considered highly significant that Slánský, although secretary general and present at the meeting, was neither allowed to report on the purge in his own apparatus nor elected to the three-men commission which investigated the plot. He was not yet accused of active participation in the conspiracy; on the contrary, it was announced that the conspirators—his aides—had used his prolonged illness in 1950 to further their intrigues. But the list of "conspirators" as well as charges left little doubt that his apparatus was being disrupted. And the antisemitic implications of the purge were now for the first time clearly indicated.

The chief defendants were Otto Šling and his friend Marie Švermová, deputy secretary general of the party in charge of the organizational section of the headquarters. Other demoted and arrested "conspirators" were: Vítězslav Fuchs, regional secretary in the mine district of Moravská Ostrava; Hanuš Lomský (Lieben), regional secretary in Plzeň, the seat of the Škoda Armanent Works; Růžena Dubová, the organizational secretary in Brno; Ervín Polák, Deputy Minister of the Interior; and Major General Bedřich Reicin, head of army intelligence. With the exception of Švermová, all the persons named were Jews. Several of them were party secretaries in districts where workers' resistance against increased exploitation had been greatest and where occasional wildcat strikes and acts of sabotage had occurred; the removal of local party bosses of Jewish origin was obviously an attempt to offer suitable scapegoats. As to Polák and Rejcin, they were commissars of the party machine in the Ministry of the Interior and in the army and their demotion served a similar purpose.

The demoted leaders were all accused of sabotaging party directives, in some cases by "willfully exaggerating" party policies, in order to compromise the party in the eyes of the masses; of having been corrupted by expropriated capitalists; of having suppressed "workers' democracy," ignored "criticism and self-criticism," and introduced "dictatorial methods." Thus they had to take the blame for party policies which provoked opposition and revolt. Not the party and the government, but willful distorters of its policies, acting in the interest of expropriated capitalists and foreign imperialists, were guilty of the prevailing misery and oppression.

Šling was accused of (and confessed) being an Anglo-American agent. He had allegedly placed his agents in the central party headquarters, and with the help of Švermová had sent others out as instructors and secretaries to the districts. The conspirators were waiting for the right moment to overthrow the party leadership and government—by an extraordinary party conference, packed with delegates appointed by the agents of the conspiracy in the provinces. This charge was patently absurd, but it made clear what the purge meant: the disruption of the party apparatus headed by Slánský, and its subordination to the government which Gottwald led.[7]

The reporter on the plot was the Minister of Information, Václav Kopecký, known for his antisemitic speeches of 1947. Without using the word Jew—at least in the official published text of his report—he was able, by innuendo and implication, to appeal to anti-Jewish prejudice. In presenting the accusation againt Šling he reminded his audience that Šling was born of a "German manufacturer's family." But as all "Aryan" Germans of bourgeois origin had been deported, everybody understood that he meant a German-Jewish family. He "revealed" that Šling had had, in his young years, a love affair with "the wife of the coal magnate Petschek," and everybody understood again: the name of the Petscheks, who had owned coal mines in northern Bohemia, was used in the Czech political vocabulary in the same way as the name of Rothchild in Western Europe, as the archetype of the capitalist Jew. Šling's treason was described as the consequence not of his Czech nationalism but of his "cosmopolitanism" and bourgeois origin. The Jewish names of the other conspirators did the rest.[8]

Demotion of Slansky

For a while, Rudolf Slánský was allowed to keep his office and to denounce the other "cosmopolitan traitors." But on September 6, a new meeting of the Central Committee was called, Slánský was removed from his party office, and President Klement Gottwald took over the leadership of the party machine, now thoroughly reorganized.[9] In his report to the meeting Gottwald accused Slánský of "serious mistakes in cadre policies" which made it possible for the Šling group to take over important posts in the party apparatus, police, and army. Slánský's chief crime was now said to have been his attempt to erect a second, parallel center of power. "From where is the country ruled?" Gottwald was quoted as asking. "From the Castle (Czechoslovak White House or from the Powder Tower?" (seat of the party headquarters). This statement fitted into the popular antisemitic legend that the real power was in the hands of Jews who directed the government from behind the scenes.[10]

Šlánský meekly confessed his errors and was appointed a vice premier and head of a shadow office for the coordination of planning. But not for long.

On November 28, 1951, *Rudé Právo* published the following laconic statement:

> At the recommendation of the Premier of the Cabinet, the President of the Republic dismissed Rudolf Slánský from membership in the cabinet and from the office of Vice Premier. At the same time, Rudolf Slánský resigned his seat in parliament. As the investigation of subversive conspiratorial groups has revealed hitherto unknown facts convicting Rudolf Slánský of active subversive activities, he was arrested pending investigation.[11]

On December 6, Gottwald reported to a new meeting of the Central Committee:

> Three months ago—he said—we had no convincing proofs that Rudolf Slánský himself was a direct enemy of the party and state. . . .
>
> After his September demotion, Gottwald complained—Slánský had worked inefficiently and tried to transfer his closest collaborators into his new office, with the intention of transforming this office into an independent center behind the back of the Premier. . . .

These vague accusations did not prove treason. So Gottwald, evidently embarrassed by the meagerness of his charges, added:

> New, hitherto unknown facts were revealed. These new revelations

> convicted Slánský as a direct, active, and, one can say, leading participant in the anti-party and anti-state conspiracy whose liquidation was begun a year ago by the arrest of the traitor and spy Šling. . . . We received irrefutable proofs that the espionage service of the Western imperialists was organizing and preparing Slánský's escape to the West.

Nothing more was said about the "irrefutable proofs." Gottwald felt constrained to add that "everybody will understand that details cannot yet be published." Evidently, there were no details; in order to get them *post facto*, Gottwald called on all party officials and members to help the investigation by reporting everything of a suspicious nature that they had observed about Slánský's former activities to the Central Committee. This was an invitation to wholesale denunciation, to a general witchhunt against "cosmopolitan traitors."[12]

Liquidation of Jewish Communists

The fall of Slánský precipitated a great purge in which hundreds and perhaps thousands of Communist leaders, officials, army and police officers, diplomats, economic administrators, and managers were removed and, in most cases, expelled from the party and arrested. Not all the victims were Jews; but the purge of Jews was so thorough and complete that there can be no doubt of its constituting a principal feature of the campaign.

Only two of the new victims of the purge could be considered near associates of Rudolf Slánský. They were Jarmila Taussigová, member of the central control commission of the Communist Party and its regional secretary in Karlovy Vary (Karlsbad), and Richard Slánský, former ambassador and high official in the Ministry of Foreign Affairs. Jarmila Taussigová, described as a participant in Slánský's plot, was denounced and expelled with him; Richard Slánský was Rudolf's brother. The rest of the Jewish victims of the subsequent purge had nothing in common with the secretary general, except for their membership in the Communist Party and their Jewish "racial origin."

Among them were: Ludvík Frejka (Freund), chief economic adviser to President Gottwald and one of the authors of the Czechoslovak Five-Year Plan;[13] Rudolf Margolius, Deputy Minister of Foreign Trade;[14] Josef Goldman, Deputy Chief of the State Planning Office;[15] Gustav Bareš (Breitenfeld), one of the six deputy secretaries of the Central Committee of the Communist Party of Czechoslovakia, chief of party propaganda and editor of the party theoretical organ *Tvorba*;[16] Bedřich Geminder, head of the foreign division in the party headquarters and former representative of the Czechoslovak Communist Party in the Cominform, Czech editor of the Cominform organ *For a Lasting Peace, for People's Democracy*;[17] Koloman Moško (Moškovič), one of the four secretaries of the Communist Party in Slovakia;[18] Zikmund Stein, for thirty years a trusted party lawyer and counsel for the Soviet Embassy, later chief legal adviser of the government.[19]

Especially systematic (and easy to follow from abroad) was the purge of the Czech diplomatic service. Artur London, Deputy Minister of Foreign Affairs and head of the Personnel Department of the Foreign Ministry, was removed in 1949 and arrested in April 1951; Vavro Hajdu, head of the Ministry's West European Office, was demoted at the same time;[20] Rudolf Bystrický (Weichherz), ambassador to London, was recalled at the beginning of 1951;[21] F. C. Weisskopf, a German-language Communist writer, former first secretary of the Czechoslovak embassy in Washington, later ambassador to Sweden and to Communist China, was recalled from Peking in February 1952;[22] Eduard Goldstuecker, Czechoslovak Minister to Israel, was transferred from Tel Aviv to Stockholm, but never arrived in Sweden and disappeared;[23] Alexander Kunosi, minister to Argentina, was recalled in July 1951 and arrested in February 1952;[24] Otto Fischl, Czech minister in Berlin, was recalled and disappeared in October 1951;[25] Arnošt Tauber, Czechoslovak minister in Berne and member of the European Economic Commission of the United Nations, was recalled at the end of 1951 and never returned to his post;[26] Jan Vinař (Wiener), the first secretary of the Czechoslovak embassy in Washington, was recalled in the fall of 1951.[26a]

Some minor diplomatic officials of Jewish origin escaped arrest by ignoring their recall to Prague and asking for asylum in democratic countries. Among them were Adolf Stern, an official of the Czechoslovak legation in Montevideo, Uruguay,[27] and Karel Stern, member of the Czechoslovak commercial mission in Berne.[28] Other Czech diplomatic officers abroad sought asylum before the purge started; among them were Egon Hostovský, a Czech novelist and former chargé d'affaires in Oslo, Norway.[29]

Dismissals from the highest party and state posts had to be publicly announced, and the disappearance of diplomatic officers was easily noted; but the purge of the domestic economic apparatus could be for the most part concealed, and only the names of some of its victims became known abroad. Thus it was learned that Dr. Robitschek, manager of the nationalized alcohol industry, had been arrested and sent to the Kladno coal mines;[30] that three Jewish directors of armament works had been arrested in Plzeň;[31] and that many Jewish managers had been removed from their posts.

Most of the victims were members of the Communist Party, many of them (Slánský, Geminder, Weisskopf, London, Zikmund Stein) of long standing. None was a Zionist and most had never had any connection with the Zionist movement. The majority had always considered themselves to be Czechs or Slovaks; some (Frejka, Geminder, Weisskopf) were of

German-Jewish descent, but had identified themselves with the Czech nation after the war. None of them showed any interest in Jewish religious or communal life; their only connection with Judaism was their Jewish birth.

The few genuine Zionists still remaining in the country after the exodus of 1949-1950 were rounded up in December 1951. According to a Swiss report, Buechler of the Hashomer Hatzair, Stern of the Mizrachi, and Varga of the General Zionists were among those arrested.[32] According to another report, the well-known leader of the wartime Jewish guerillas in Slovakia, Dov Weiss (who had emigrated to Israel after the war, there joined the Mapam and subsequently returned to Czechoslovakia), was also arrested on charges of espionage.[33]

But these local leaders of former Zionist groups were too insignificant to give color to the official charges of a grandiose Zionist plot. Probably for this reason the Czechoslovak authorities eagerly used their opportunity to arrest a leading Israel citizen and member of the Knesset on the charge of carrying on a "Zionist conspiracy."

He was Mordecai Oren, leader of the pro-Communist wing of Israel's Mapam party. Oren was one of the closest followers of the Communist line and took part in many Communist-sponsored peace conferences. In December 1951, he attended the meeting of the Communist-dominated World Federation of Trade Unions in East Berlin. There he declared that Israel soldiers would never fight against the Soviet Union.

On his way home, he went to Prague on undisclosed business. According to some reports, he wanted to investigate "rumors" about antisemitic tendencies after the fall of Slánský; other sources said that he tried to get information about the arrest of his cousin, Simon Ohrenstein, also an Israeli citizen and a former assistant to Israel's commercial attaché in Prague. He was last seen on December 31, 1951, when he told a member of Israel's legation that he was leaving for Vienna and Zürich that night. He never arrived in Vienna, and for almost three months nothing was known about his fate. His disappearance caused heated discussions in Israel and repeated diplomatic inquiries. Finally, on March 23, 1952, the Czechoslovak government informed Israel that it had arrested Oren on charges of unspecified "crimes against state security."[34] Israel diplomatic representatives were not allowed to see him, and a French pro-Communist lawyer who tried to intervene in his favor was rebuked.[35]

Soon after the arrest of Slánský the Communists began a violent campaign, identifying "cosmopolitans" with "Zionists" and implying that people of Jewish origin, "without roots in the country," were apt to become traitors and spies. The first attack appeared in the magazine *Tvorba*, a party magazine whose articles were considered Communist propaganda directives. On December 13, a week after the meeting of the Central Committee which ratified Slánský's arrest, *Tvorba* wrote:

In recent times many cosmopolitan elements, who later became agents of American-English aggressors, came from the ranks of conscious Zionists, who have no roots in our nation. The Jewish state of Israel is today in the hands of bourgeois Jewish nationalists who have sold themselves to American imperialists. They are using this state as their instrument in the fight against the national liberation movement in the colonies, and the Zionist movement as an agency for organizing disruptive, subversive, and hostile activities against the U.S.S.R. and people's democracies.[36]

On December 18, Premier Antonín Zápotocký addressed the Presidium of the National Front of Czechs and Slovaks. Speaking of "traitors" who had "sneaked into the party," he made the following statement:

We did not punish anybody for his political or religious opinions. But we do and will punish everyone who conspires against the republic. . . . And we will tolerate no interference in our internal affairs from outside, be it from Washington or London, Rome or Jerusalem.[37]

The official report noted that cheers interrupted the Premier's speech at this point. The mentioning of Jerusalem, absurd on its face as Israel certainly has never tried to interfere in Czechoslovakia's internal affairs, was evidently understood as an allusion to Slánský and his Jewish co-defendants. To make it clearer, Zápotocký reminded his audience that "reactionaries" had attempted to return nationalized factories to "Jewish and other capitalists" and cited the case of the Beer factory in Varnsdorf in the year 1947.[38] Singling out Jewish capitalists in connection with the accusations against Slánský and Šling, who were charged with trying to restore capitalism, Zápotocký again evoked the specter of a Jewish conspiracy, which was supposed to have been carried on, after the liquidation of Jewish capitalists, by their agents in the Communist party.

Campaign Against Jews

Zápotocký's hints were eagerly taken up by the Communist press, which now spelled out what Zápotocký left unsaid.

On January 17, 1952, the newspaper *Lidové Noviny* published a long article by Vladimír Klapka, "Zionism, the Agency of Western Imperialists."

Followers of Zionism—Klapka wrote—can also be found outside Israel. They are dispersed over all the countries of the world. Their activities are not limited to organizing emigration to Israel. Their task is the propagandizing of imperialist ideology, and carrying on secret, subversive work against the cause of socialism. This is the great danger from the Zionist agency of imperialism, extending far beyond the borders of the State of Israel.[39]

On January 23, 1952, *Pravda*, the central organ of the Communist Party of Slovakia, wrote:

> Zionism is the ideology of the Jewish bourgeois state, the ideology of Jewish bourgeois nationalism, by which the Jewish nationalistic bourgeoisie, in the pay of American imperialism, is endeavoring to influence our citizens of Jewish descent. It is in the service of the class enemy that the Zionists have wormed their way into the Communist parties in order to disrupt and undermine them from within. Certain members of our party, too, have come under the influence of Zionism. They have succumbed to the ideology of cosmopolitanism and Jewish bourgeois nationalism, and do not judge events from the viewpoint of the working class, of the struggle for socialism.[40]

Seemingly, these attacks were aimed only at Zionists. But the passage about "our citizens of Jewish descent," allegedly influenced by Zionism, and about those who "wormed their way into the Communist parties in order to disrupt and undermine them from within," were in reality attacking not Zionists but Communists of Jewish origin. Everybody knew that the talk about Zionist influence in the Czechoslovak Communist Party was absurd. The charges made sense only when the words "Zionist" and "cosmopolitan" were understood as pseudonyms for "Jew."

Several days later the Communist Slovak newspaper *L'ud* published an article, "Against Cosmopolitanism," by Roman Kaliský, which revised the official position on antisemitism. It started with a general characterization of cosmopolitanism, which is worth quoting because it shows how popular passions were whipped up against the "cosmopolitans":

> What is cosmopolitanism? It is a fruit of decadent Greek philosophy, of cynicism and stoicism. It is a view considering the entire world as the individual's fatherland and denying any duties and obligations toward one's home, one's native land. This morbid philosophy went through various stages and forms of development; today it is the main ideological weapon of imperialism, especially of American imperialism. It beguiles the nations into renouncing their freedom and independence, their way of life, their culture and tradition, for some kind of world community, naturally under the rule of dollar imperialism. The aim of the cosmopolitans is to subject the nations to the rule of Wall Street on the pretext that people should no longer be divided according to nationalities, such a division having become obsolete. It is only natural that such a philosophy should attract people of capitalist origin and outlook; a capitalist always prefers his class interests to those of his nation, and considers dollars and profits more attractive than fatherland and socialism. That's why the cosmopolitans idolize so-called Western culture and the power of the dollar. The capitalist remnants in the city and village and the members of the bourgeois intelligentsia are cosmopolitans simply because they understand that they cannot recapture their lost

positions, their rule over the toiling masses, in the framework of Slovakia or Czechoslovakia, where a counterrevolution by domestic forces is impossible. They expect their salvation from America and dream of some world state in which the world bourgeoisie would rule the toiling masses of the earth. This is their world citizenship, the world rule of the moneybag, of capitalist enterprise and speculation, and of shady exchange deals.

Having thus established the bourgeois, counterrevolutionary character of the "cosmopolitans" and their subservience to dollar imperialism, the author recommends his remedy, a radical purge:

Our people cannot trust men who are infected by the ideology of cosmopolitanism. They cannot tolerate them in offices in the economic or political field; they must take measures insuring against their possible treason. How can we expect such a man to stand up in a crisis? . . . Such a man sees no reason for defending the fatherland, for suffering and sacrificing for it. He who has no fatherland will not suffer or die for it. He is apt to betray it, to ally himself with the enemy.

Who were these servants of capitalism, these men without a fatherland, who could not be tolerated in any responsible position and had to be purged preventively?

This danger threatens from cosmopolitanism in general, as well as from its derivative, Jewish bourgeois nationalism. Zionism is the official ideology of the Jewish bourgeoisie and of the bourgeois Jewish State of Israel. Zionism brought Israel into the service of American imperialism, and is trying to recruit Jews all over the world to serve this imperialism.

In fighting Zionism and cosmopolitanism, the author remarks, one has always to stress the class aspect. You fight a cosmopolitan because he is a cosmopolitan and a capitalist because he is a capitalist, he adds piously, and not because he is a Jew. But after this saving clause the author proceeds to justify Slovak postwar antisemitism as the expression of a "healthy class instinct":

Here we can learn from our workingmen who, led by their healthy class instinct, always found the right orientation in the so-called Jewish question. They have always lived in peace with poor and working Jews, but have always hated the Jewish capitalists because these capitalists exploited and ground down the masses. Antisemitism, extolled under the fascist era, was always foreign to the great majority of the Slovak toiling masses. . . . But the same Slovak people were upset and angry when they saw, after the liberation, how Jewish as well as non-Jewish capitalists attempted to recapture their lost economic positions; they had the right attitude when they saw Jewish capitalists migrating to Palestine, taking with them great wealth.

But very often the little man was intimidated by being told that his protest was influenced by antisemitism, fascism, and God knows what. Unfortunately, we did not always understand the difference between real antisemitism and the healthy voice of criticism, the healthy voice of the working masses. It is true that at that time and up to the recent events, the hidden enemies of our nation and of socialism were able to organize sabotage from high places in which they were entrenched; their primary concern was to suppress, in all such cases, the voice of popular criticism and to protect the enemies of people's democracy. Now we can fight against cosmopolitanism and Zionism consistently and to the very end.

We must not underestimate the danger of cosmopolitanism and Zionism in our country. We must unmask their representatives and render them harmless, and fill leading positions with new men, genuine Slovak and Czech patriots.[41]

In this way, Slovak postwar antisemitic agitation, which had led to bloody riots and outright murders,[42] was represented as the expression of a sound class instinct; those Communists who protested against antisemitic excesses were identified with "hidden enemies" and "saboteurs" who were now at last removed by the purge following Slánský's fall. The way was open to a "consistent," last-ditch fight against "Zionists and cosmopolitans."

On March 2, 1952, Václav Kopecký, Minister of Information and member of the Czechoslovak Politburo, explained in Prague what this fight meant:

We know that one of the main weapons of American ideological warfare is cosmopolitanism, which destroys the ties to fatherland and people and inoculates its adherents with degenerate views of world citizenship. . . . We know that cosmopolitanism is just such a product of the cynical aggressive war ideology of American imperialism as fascism, Hitlerism and Nazism, and must therefore be exterminated forever. . . .

We cannot and must not underestimate the danger of the cosmopolitan tendencies that the enemy is trying to use. The case of the abominable traitors Slánský, Šling, Reicin, London, Kopold, Loebl, etc. has shown how the treacherous agents of Western imperialism also tried to work in our ranks in a Titoist way, using cosmopolitanism in its Trotskyite-Zionist form. Yes! That's why we must destroy cosmopolitanism, this ideological ogre, serving American war barbarism.[43]

All the "abominable traitors" enumerated by Kopecký were Jews. The compound adjective "Trotskyite-Zionist," known already from the Rajk trial in Hungary, was evidently used to accentuate the traitorous as well as the Jewish character of the "conspiracy." And Kopecký used, for the first time, the ominous word "exterminate."

The purge of Jews from all positions of influence was almost complete. Most of the purged officials had been arrested or had disappeared into slave labor camps. Reports from Slovakia announced that "alien" and "bourgeois" elements, among them the remaining Jews, were being deported en masse from Bratislava and other cities. The totalitarian Communist regime in Czechoslovakia had arrived at its "final solution" of the Jewish question: the total elimination of the Jewish minority.

Chapter XII

The Trial

The purge and the anti-Jewish campaign described in Chapter XI set the stage for the final coup: the great antisemitic show-trial against Rudolf Slánský and thirteen co-defendants.

Twenty-five years of experience have taught the free world why and how such trials are arranged. They are well-prepared propaganda shows, whose purpose is not only to sentence and execute a group of defendants, considered to be potentially dangerous or simply suitable scapegoats for the crimes and shortcomings of the regime. The trials also single out a certain broader group, doomed to extermination, as a "breeding-ground of deviations" and "counter-revolutionary crimes"; their purpose is to mobilize public opinion and the organs of the totalitarian power to "watchfulness," hatred, and merciless fight against the strata of the population considered "infected" or "suspect."

Everything in the show serves this purpose: Defendants for a public trial are carefully selected from among thousands of victims available in the jails; they have to be "representative" of the group doomed to liquidation. They are made to confess by long isolation, endless examinations without sleep and rest, threats to their families, and direct torture, until their will power is completely broken. The accusations and confessions are carefully coordinated to prove the political point of the trial. The defense lawyers, selected by the security organs, not only refrain from any efficient defense but admit that their clients were hideous criminals, pleading only, *sotto voce*, the existence of mitigating circumstances. The prosecutors lambast the defendants in a language calculated to arouse a maximum of hatred; the carefully selected public in the courtroom, as well as the press, the public meetings, and all kinds of Communist-dominated organizations outside, serve as a chorus which shouts, in a terrible crescendo, for capital punishment. Finally, the court pronounces the verdict and sentence decided in advance by the Politburo. Most defendants are executed; a few are sometimes spared in order to appear as witnesses in future trials or to disappear without trace in totalitarian dungeons.

This is what happened in the trial against the engineers of the Donets coal basin in 1928, which was followed by the mass liquidation of non-

Communist technicians in industry; in the trial against Ramzin and other famous scientists in 1930, which introduced a purge of "bourgeois specialists"; in the trial against Menshevik leaders in 1931, which was followed by the liquidation of former members of Socialist parties and groups; in the famous Moscow trials against the old Bolshevik guard and against the marshals of the Red Army during 1936-38, when the Great Purge swallowed up several million people. After World War II the same performance was repeated in the satellite countries; the trials of Traicho Kostov in Bulgaria, Cardinal Josef Mindszenty and Laszlo Rajk in Hungary, Koci Xoxe in Albania, and Catholic priests in Poland and Czechoslovakia were only the most conspicuous of hundreds of such instances.

There is little doubt that the trial of Slánský *et al.*, in which the Czechoslovak purge culminated, not only followed the Soviet pattern but was also prepared under the direct supervision of Soviet "experts." We have seen how vague the criminal charges against Slánský were even at the moment when he was arrested, and how the "Zionist" and "Jewish" aspect was injected into the accusations only in the last stage of the anti-Slánský campaign. The Czechoslovak Communist leaders, President Klement Gottwald and Premier Antonín Zápotocký, could not have been unaware that open anti-Semitic policies would do great damage to the prestige of the Czech Communist regime. Somewhat reluctantly, they finally proferred the fantastic criminal charges against their former comrades and competitors for power in the party. It was only too evident that they were acting under direct and energetic prompting from Moscow.[1] The trial of Slánský was a Prague trial in name only. Its character, purpose, method, and behind-the-scene direction were those of a true "Moscow trial."

The Indictment

On November 20, 1952, the official Czechoslovak Press Bureau (ČTK) published a terse communiqué, beginning with the following words:

> This morning a panel of the State Court in Prague began the trial against the leaders of the subversive conspirational center whose head was Rudolf Slánský.
>
> The court is trying Trotskyite-Titoist Zionists, bourgeois-nationalist traitors and enemies of the Czechoslovak people, of People's Democracy and of Socialism. . .[2]

Thus in the very first sentence Zionism was stressed as one of the main characteristics of the entire "subversive" group and put on the same level as Trotskyism, Titoism, bourgeois nationalism, treason, and counter-revolution.

The same day, *Rudé Právo*, the central organ of the Communist Party of Czechoslovakia, published the full text of the indictment.[3]

There were fourteen defendants: Rudolf Slánský, former Secretary General of the Communist Party and before his arrest Vice Premier of the Czechoslovak cabinet; Bedřich Geminder, former head of the Foreign Department in the Secretariat of the Communist Party; Ludvík Frejka, former head of the Economic Division of the Chancellery of the President; Josef Frank, former Deputy Secretary General of the Communist Party; Vladimír Clementis, former Minister of Foreign Affairs; Bedřich Reicin, former Deputy Minister of National Defense; Karel Šváb, former Deputy Minister of State Security; Artur London, former Deputy Minister of Foreign Affairs; Vavro Hajdů, former Deputy Minister of Foreign Affairs; Evžen Löbl, former Deputy Minister of Foreign Trade; Rudolf Margolius, former Deputy Minister of Foreign Trade; Otto Fischl, former Deputy Minister of Finance; Otto Šling, former District Secretary of the Communist Party in Brno, the capital of Moravia; and André Simone, former foreign editor of *Rudé Právo*.

Of the fourteen defendants, eleven were Jews; only three, Vladimír Clementis, Josef Frank, and Karel Šváb were not Jewish. For the final indicting formula, the words "of Jewish origin" (*židovského původu*) were added to the name and date of birth of each Jewish defendant, while Šváb and Frank were described simply as "Czechs," and Clementis as "Slovak." This was an event without precedent in the annals of Czechoslovak justice. The defendants could not be described as of Jewish religion because all of them had renounced that religion many years before; nor had they ever belonged to the Jewish "ethnic nationality," considering themselves either Czechs or Slovaks.[4] The words "of Jewish origin" could mean only "racial origin"; the division of defendants into Czechs and Slovaks on the one hand, and persons "of Jewish origin" on the other hand, implied that a Jew could not be a Czech or a Slovak. The antisemitic intent of this distinction was more than obvious.

To stress the point, the indictment mentioned in another context that the original name of the defendant Ludvík Frejka was Ludvig Freund, and that of André Simone was Otto Katz. A similar practice was observed in mentioning the adopted names or pseudonyms of co-conspirators who were not defendants in the trial. Where the adopted name did not sound Jewish the original Jewish name was usually added in parentheses.

The indictment also stressed the defendants' "social origin." The Jewish defendants were described variously as "son of a manufacturer," "son of a merchant," or simply "of bourgeois origin."[5] Clementis was also introduced as a man "of bourgeois origin," while Frank and Šváb were presented as originating from "workers' families."

As a matter of fact, all the Jewish defendants, being Communist leaders of long standing, had renounced not only the Jewish religion but also all ties with the Jewish community decades before. Not one of them was a

Zionist. Two or three may have belonged to Zionist-influenced youth or boy scout organizations before the age of eighteen; and some, of course, had Zionists among their relatives. The only man whose record of participation in Jewish organizations went beyond his early youth—but not beyond his application for membership in the Communist Party—was Otto Fischl. He had belonged, before he joined the Communist Party, to the Association of Czech Jews (Svaz Čechů-židů), a strongly assimilationist and strongly anti-Zionist organization. All the defendants had been bitter opponents of the Jewish religion, Zionism, and Jewish nationalism throughout their adult lives. Indeed, most of them had been more strongly opposed to Jewish aspirations than their non-Jewish colleagues. They had been fighting with excessive zeal for the expropriation of Jewish capitalists, and some—like Otto Fischl—were known as the greatest tormentors of prospective emigrants to Israel. Their description as Zionists was a patent fraud. It could and did serve only one purpose: to denounce them as Jews, as participants in world-wide "Jewish conspiracy," and to imply that every Jew, however anti-Zionist he might be, was a secret partner in the "Zionist plot."

The text of the indictment leaves no doubt that this was the purpose of the trial. Following the enumeration of the defendants, the document sums up their crimes as follows:

> As Trotskyite-Titoist Zionists, bourgeois nationalist traitors, and enemies of the Czechoslovak people, of People's Democracy, and of Socialism, they formed, in the service of American imperialists and following the directives of hostile Western counter-intelligence outfits, a subversive conspirational center; subverted the regime of the People's Democracy, sabotaged the socialist construction, damaged national economy, organized espionage activities, weakened the unity of the Czechoslovak people and the defence of the Republic, in order to destroy the firm alliance and friendship with the Soviet Union, to liquidate the People's Democratic order, to introduce capitalism, to drag our Republic back into the camp of imperialism and to destroy its sovereignty and independence.

After this summary introduction, the indictment proceeds to specifics. The American, British, and French imperialists, it says, had begun, even before Munich, to recruit agents into their services. During the war they strengthened their recruiting activities among Czech refugees in order to secure the return of Czechoslovakia into the imperialist camp after the war. One of these imperialist agencies was headed by President Beneš and the leaders of the Czechoslovak non-Communist parties. The second one, held in reserve, was composed of agents working inside the Communist Party. Before and during the war, the British Trust Fund, a relief organization—but according to the indictment, "in reality an espionage outfit"—

recruited spies, first in Cracow, Poland, where many Czechs fled from the Protectorate, and later in London. As a proof of the sinister purposes of these activities, the indictment quotes the following passage from a report by a former Czech consul in Cracow:

> To my question as to how people should be selected for transport to England, Field[6] answered:
> 1. They should be left-oriented politically.
> 2. Or they must be Jews.

In this manner, the indictment concludes, Löbl, Šling, Frejka, Hajdů, Simone, and "other Trotskyites, Zionists, and traitors" were recruited for the imperialist counter-intelligence.

To head this "criminal gang," the imperialist selected Rudolf Slánský, an "old agent of the bourgeoisie" and "abject traitor." The selection was not accidental. Slánský was the "son of a rich merchant," who "sneaked into" the Communist Party, but remained always a "servant of the capitalists." To drive home the point that Slánský was predestined by his origin to become a traitor and spy, the indictment quotes what "the outstanding American spy" and "representative of international Zionism" Geiringer-Granwille (*sic*) allegedly told the witness Josef Vondráček:

> I have—said Granwille—a close espionage liaison, among others, with "Rudla" Slánský, the Secretary of the Communist Party of Czechoslovakia. This is our most solid asset because he is the most intelligent Jew I know, and an exceedingly talented and patient man. He knows how to wait, therefore he is very useful for the realization of our long-term plans. And our plans are not for today or tomorrow.

The same Vondráček is quoted as having heard the "Czechoslovak capitalist" Pachner say:

> Rudla [i.e., Slánský] is in the right place in the Communist Party. He comes from an old Jewish family, has wonderful connections in the Czech party, and extensive knowledge. He is the great hope of the Jews in the Communist Party.

Having thus "established" that Slánský was a Jewish agent of the Western powers, the indictment enumerates his crimes: Slánský collaborated—before the war—with President Beneš; his name was included in a list of persons to be evacuated to England when the Nazis occupied Prague in 1939; he went to Moscow instead but collaborated there with the Czechoslovak military attaché, General Heliodor Pika; when he was sent in 1944 to Slovakia as a commissar to lead the anti-Nazi uprising in Bánská Bystrica, he allied himself with Slovak nationalists and was guilty of the death of his colleague Jan Šverma, who froze to death during the retreat of the insurgents into the mountains.

It should be pointed out that Slánský's collaboration with Beneš in the late thirties was in accord with the Communist "popular front" line at that time; that it was only natural that, being a member of the Czechoslovak parliament, he should be included in the list of persons to be saved from the Nazis; that collaboration with a Czech military attaché in Moscow during the war fell into the framework of Russian wartime policies; that, at the time of the Slovak uprising, collaboration with nationalist insurgents was also in harmony with the party line, and that Šverma went much further in concessions to nationalist sentiments than Slánský—if Slánský really allowed Šverma to die unaided in the snow, he was probably following Moscow orders rather than his private wishes.

The indictment then describes the return of wartime Communist refugees to postwar Czechoslovakia, cites the names of several Jewish defendants who returned at that time, and quotes the following passage from the testimony of Clementis during the pretrial examination:

> All these venal individuals . . . among them hypocrites with the membership card of the party like Šling, Löbl, Polák, Moško, Frejka, and others, invaded the territory of liberated Czechoslovakia like locusts in order to work there in the interests of Western imperialists.

It is almost superfluous to point out that all the "locusts" enumerated by name were Jews. . . .

The indictment then goes on to describe how Slánský placed "his men" in all the important positions in postwar Czechoslovakia, relying on "various hostile groups and organizations, like Trotskyites, Zionists, bourgeois nationalists, Freemasons, fake partisans, etc." Among the co-conspirators named in this connection Jewish names abound as they do among the names of the defendants. Where their names are evidently Jewish, no explanation is necessary. Where they sound Czech, the original name is revealed. The following paragraph of the indictment is characteristic:

> In other important industrial districts . . . leading secretaries and workers in the party apparatus [were] people like Vítězslav Fuchs, Mikuláš Landa (Landau), Hanuš Lomský, whose real name was Gabriel Lieben, Ervín Polák, Koloman Moško, whose real name was Moškovič, and other similar Zionist and adventurous elements.

Again, not a single one of the enumerated "conspirators" was a Zionist, but all of them were Jews.

After describing the alleged espionage connections of the defendants, who were active in the Czech diplomatic service, with foreign diplomats, like the American ambassador Laurence A. Steinhardt, the British diplomat Gladwin Jebb, and the French ambassador Maurice Dejean, as well as with foreign correspondents Maurice Hindus, David Schönbrunn, Alexander Werth, and Paul Willert, the indictment implicates the Israel diplomatic service in these words:

> American spies, hiding behind Israel diplomatic passports, like former

> Israel Minister to Czechoslovakia Ehud Avriel (Überall) and legation staff members Felix and Ben Schalom, maintained espionage links with Bedřich Geminder and Otto Fischl.

The next section of the indictment describes the alleged economic sabotage conducted "in order to undermine the socialist order and to restore capitalism." The defendants are charged with intentional errors in planning, with willfully neglecting the development of heavy industry, with organizing artificial shortages of raw materials, with importing unnecessary products in order to make the country dependent on the West, with exporting bread and meat in times of famine, and with giving away billions of Czechoslovak crowns to foreign capitalists under the pretext of restitution.

In this section, the antisemitic tone is especially strong. Löbl, Margolius, and Fischl are accused of selling out Czechoslovak interests in concluding a trade agreement with Israel. Israel ambassador Überall is charged with having been the initiator of an "Überall plan" to sell Czechoslovak export goods in Western countries through Jewish intermediaries, who allegedly enriched themselves at the Czech people's expense. In the hands of Otto Fischl the restitution law became "an instrument for the cynical robbing of the Czechoslovak state by the capitalists." The indictment quotes one Oskar Langer, described as "a former employee of the Central Committee of the Communist Party of Slovakia" and at the same time as an "important Zionist," as having testified in a pretrial examination:

> Immediately after my return to Czechoslovakia, I saw the leader of the Zionist movement, Dr. Winterstein, who had . . . contact with the American ambassador in Prague. Winterstein was generally known as a sly and zealous Zionist and enemy of People's Democracy. . . . Several weeks later, Winterstein invited me to his apartment and during a conversation about Zionist and Jewish problems in general he told me that in these matters I should always deal with Rudolf Slánský, who has a considerable understanding of them. He told me also that a restitution law was being prepared . . . and Slánský told him that he would support it. He explained that the law will serve to concentrate all Jewish property in Zionist hands. . . . Thus the Zionists wanted—with the direct help of Slánský—to restore and even increase their economic power and prepare positions for the overthrow of the People's Democratic order in Czechoslovakia.

Thus the restitution law which, as we saw in Chapter V, was never properly enforced and soon even formally liquidated, was described as a diabolical, Jewish-inspired conspiracy to expropriate the Czech people and to overthrow the Communist government.

The rest of this section is filled with charges that Jewish capitalists, with the help of the defendants, exported "immense values" abroad and earned "fabulous sums" in representing Czechoslovak nationalized industries in the West.

A special section of the indictment is devoted to Zionist organizations, "these reliable agencies of American imperialism." Here appears a fantastic story about a secret conference which allegedly took place in Washington in 1947. The participants, President Harry S. Truman, Secretary of State Dean Acheson, former Secretary of the Treasury Henry Morgenthau, Jr., and the Israel statesmen Ben Gurion and Moshe Sharett, are supposed to have agreed on a Morgenthau plan "according to which American support for Israel was promised in exchange for the use of Zionist organizations for espionage and subversion in the People's Democracies." The authority for this absurd story, reminiscent of the infamous *Protocols of the Elders of Zion*, was the witness Šimon Ohrenstein, an obscure businessman who had for a while been connected with the Israel legation in Prague.

The indictment then gives the following characterization of the State of Israel and its government:

> The lackey of American imperialism Ben Gurion is guilty of the terrible economic conditions in which the working people in Israel live; he abolished the democratic rights of the people and especially of the Arab population, suffering under cruel national discrimination. Ben Gurion's government transformed Israel into American property . . . and fully supports the plans of American warmongers, who are making Israel a staging area for an attack against the USSR.

Americans, the indictment continues, were using Israel diplomats as their spies; together with the conspiratorial center, directed by Slánský, these diplomats had organized a series of sabotage actions which had inflicted heavy damage on Czechoslovakia.

> Under the protection of the conspirators, the American Jewish organization Joint organized extensive hostile activities against Czechoslovakia, consisting of espionage, sabotage, dark currency deals, black-market operations, and smuggling.

Here for the first time appears the name of the American Jewish Joint Distribution Committee which was later charged, in Moscow, with having organized the murder of Soviet statesmen by their Jewish doctors.

Nor was the charge of medical assassination absent from the Prague indictment. In the pretrial examination Slánský was made to confess that he had prepared the murder of President Klement Gottwald by assigning him a doctor who, by deliberate malpractice, "worked to shorten his life, i.e., to hasten his death." But in the Prague version of the Moscow charges the doctor was not a Jew. He was a Freemason, a Dr. Haškovec. True to their Nazi models, the organizers of the Prague trial accused Freemasons of being tools of the "Jewish conspiracy."

Thus the indictment combined all the hideous features of the Moscow trials with all the traditional antisemitic stereotypes. Accusations of espionage, sabotage, murder, fraud, and treason were set into a framework of a grandiose world-wide Jewish conspiracy. Jews were accused of infiltrating every institution, of striving for absolute power, of performing surreptitious and illicit economic operations, of attempts to enrich themselves at the expenses of the working people, of fraud and duplicity, of infamous murder plots, reminiscent of Middle Age charges of the poisoning of the patients by Jewish-hired doctors.

The Trial Proceedings

The trial proceedings were conducted in the same spirit in which the indictment was written. The defendants, all of whom had spent a long time—some of them several years—in detention and complete isolation, competed with each other in confessing the most heinous crimes according to the prosecutor's specifications. None of them denied anything, none tried to minimize his guilt or to plead mitigating circumstances. All of them described themselves as most abject criminals; in flat, unemotional voices they repeated their learned lessons.

Except for the "confessions" of the defendants proper and the "co-conspirators," who were brought before the court as witnesses from jail, there was hardly any other evidence. A few "voluntary" witnesses could say no more than that they had always "suspected" the defendants' criminal activities; the "documentary evidence" that was produced related only to details that were in themselves irrelevant and acquired sinister significance only by the defendants' confessions.[7] The "evidence" was never disputed and the defense lawyers did not ask a single question throughout the proceedings.

The trial was "public" but no correspondents from countries outside the Soviet orbit were admitted. The proceedings were broadcast but in a peculiar way. There was no direct transmission from the courtroom. Rather, selected parts of the testimonies were transcribed and broadcast; the rest of the proceedings was "summarized" by the announcer. *Rudé Právo* reported the proceedings in a similar way: alleged verbatim quotations were interpolated by "summaries" of the rest of the proceedings. If anything "went wrong," if some defendant "got out of hand" for a while, the world never knew about it. The galleries in the courtroom were packed with reliable "workers' delegations" and security agents.[8]

The testimony of Rudolf Slánský began by his pleading guilty to the charges of espionage, treason, sabotage, and military treason. The prosecutor followed up by asking how it was possible that the defendant, a member of the Communist Party for thirty years, had become a traitor.

Slánský answered:

> I came into the workers' movement as a man of bourgeois origin. My father was a wealthy village merchant. The milieu in which I grew up influenced my personal qualities and my character. I joined the Communist Party in 1921. I joined it with various petty-bourgeois views which I never got rid of. That was the reason why I never became a real Communist, never behaved like one, never fulfilled honorably the duties that followed from my membership in the Communist Party.[9]

Therefore, Slánský continued, he had to become an opportunist, a Trotskyite, a hypocrite who deceived the party, a coward who betrayed his comrades to the police, and finally a traitor, murderer, and spy.

Thus, Slánský's "crimes" were derived from his origin; this pattern was then repeated in the testimony of all Jewish defendants. But while, in the case of Slánský, the stress was on his social origin and the Jewishness was just hinted at (everybody knew and the indictment had expressly said that he was of Jewish origin), in the case of other defendants the proceedings were more outspoken.

The first point *Rudé Právo* made about the testimony of Bedřich Geminder was that he testified in "broken Czech." Asked his ethnic nationality, Geminder answered that he was Czech. The following conversation was then quoted verbatim in *Rudé Právo*:

> *The Judge:* Do you speak Czech well?
> *The Defendant:* Yes.
> *The Judge:* Do you want an interpreter?
> *The Defendant:* No.
> *The Judge:* Do you understand the questions and will you answer in the Czech language?
> *The Defendant:* Yes.[10]

Geminder was born in a German-speaking Jewish family and had attended German schools, but he understood and spoke Czech fairly well, although with a German accent. The scene described above was played in order to attract attention to his "alien," Jewish origin.

Immediately afterwards, Geminder was asked why he had joined Slánský's conspiracy. He answered:

> I had always been close to Slánský in the past. He knew my cosmopolitan, Zionist background, my ties with the West, and the fact that I always followed my personal, careerist interests. He expected that I would be a good partner for him. . . .
>
> Being good friends, we kept no secrets from each other. Slánský knew that I came from a Jewish bourgeois merchant family, that I had had a carefree youth and had never had to fight for my livelihood, and he also knew that my education was one that isolated me from the life of the workers and tied me to the bourgeoisie. He even knew that I was

connected with the Western world through my brother Zikmund Geminder, who is a dentist in Santiago de Chile, and that I corresponded with him. In 1912, as a high school student, I joined a Zionist youth organization in which I remained for several years. Connections I acquired as its member tied me to a petty-bourgeois cosmopolitan milieu, hostile to the workers' movement and the Communist Party.

The Prosecutor: What was your attitude toward the Czechoslovak working people?

The Defendant: I never identified myself with the interests of the Czechoslovak people. Their national interests remained alien to me. . . . After finishing my studies, I lived in a petty-bourgeois, cosmopolitan, Zionist milieu, where one spoke German, and that's why I did not master the Czech language.

The Prosecutor: And you never learned to speak Czech well, even after 1946, when you came back to Czechoslovakia and acquired a responsible position in the Party?

The Defendant: That's right.

The Prosecutor: And which language do you speak well?

The Defendant: German.

The Prosecutor: Do you really speak German well?

The Defendant: I have not spoken German for a long time but I know the German language.

The Prosecutor: Do you speak German as well as Czech?

The Defendant: Yes.

The Prosecutor: That means that you speak no language decently. A typical cosmopolitan!

The Defendant: Yes.[11]

Thus Geminder was made to confess that he knew neither Czech, which he might have spoken imperfectly, nor his German mother tongue. All this was to fortify the stereotype of an alien, bourgeois, careerist Jew, whose "Zionism" was proved by his membership in a youth organization forty years before when he had been eleven years old, and whose "ties with West" were established by the existence of a brother who was a dentist in Chile!

The defendant André Simone, "whose real name was Otto Katz," answered the question how he became a traitor as follows:

I am the son of a manufacturer, educated in the spirit of bourgeois ideology. The working class was always alien to me. Therefore, I always moved in circles close to my heart, among traitors of the working people, Trotskyites, right-wing Social Democrats, and Jewish bourgeois nationalists.

The Judge: You considered a worker an inferior being, didn't you?

The Defendant: Yes. For thirty years I defended bourgeois ideology and broke the unity of the working class and of the workers' movement in various capitalist countries. . . .[12]

The defendant Rudolf Margolius testified:

My subversive and hostile activity is the consequence of my hatred toward the revolutionary efforts of the working class and toward the Communist Party. I was educated in this hatred from my childhood. I was born in a Jewish capitalist family. My father was a partner in a large textile business and a member of the Jewish Masonic Lodge Hor. My mother was a member of the Zionist organization WIZO. Most of my relatives were active Zionists. I was educated in the Zionist spirit.... I joined the Communist Party in 1945. At that time, I not only disagreed with its program but was its enemy. I just wanted to secure myself an advantageous position. I took advantage of the fact that hostile elements which penetrated the apparatus of the Communist Party supported the infiltration of bourgeois, and especially Jewish-bourgeois elements, into the Party and into positions in the government and economic apparatus.[13]

The same logic was again applied in the following exchange between the judge and the defendant Otto Fischl:

Judge: Explain why you had such a hostile attitude toward the People's Democracy of Czechoslovakia.

The Defendant: I could not possibly have any but a hostile attitude.

Judge: Why?

The Defendant: I am a Jewish bourgeois nationalist.[14]

Similarly, Otto Šling testified that he had grown up in a bourgeois milieu, that in 1923 [when eleven years old] he had joined the boy scout organization Blau-Weiss, which educated the Jewish youth in the Zionist spirit; hence, after 1924 when he joined the Communist Youth, he had remained an enemy of the party.[15] Bedřich Reicin had been educated "in a bourgeois and religious spirit" in the Jewish Zionist boy scout organization Techelet Levana before joining the Communist Youth in 1926.[16] His "Zionist past" was limited to the period before he was fifteen; yet, according to his confession, he remained imbued with Jewish bourgeois nationalism all his life, including, again according to his confession, a period when he had worked for the Gestapo.

The antisemitic content of the trial was by no means exhausted by the characterization of the men in the dock. In addition to the eleven Jewish defendants, many other Jews were named as co-conspirators. Some of them were dragged from jail into the courtroom to join in the confessions. Many were just mentioned by the defendants and witnesses. As the total number of Jewish officials in Czechoslovakia was rather small and evidently considered insufficient, scores of Jewish businessmen abroad who used to function as importers from, or exporters to, Czechoslovakia, were dragged in to create the impression of a massive Jewish infiltration. Jewish names appear on every page, in every paragraph of the testimony. Where the names are not obviously Jewish, either the former, more Jewish names of the individuals concerned are added, or they are described as "Zionists," "cosmopolitans," "Jewish bourgeois," "Jewish nationalists," and in some cases, simply as Jews.

The one point the prosecutor made and all the defendants admitted was that they had placed Jewish "conspirators" in all positions of influence. Even the non-Jewish defendants Frank, Šváb, and Clementis confessed to having supported this "Zionist infiltration," their only excuse being that the Jew Slánský, who knew about their former crimes and deviations, blackmailed them into doing it.

Slánský's confession contained a special paragraph dealing with the "criminal activities of Zionist organizations" in which he said:

> As I did among other bourgeois nationalists, I found support among the Zionists, whose hostile activities were also aimed at the liquidation of People's Democracy in Czechoslovakia. I filled important sectors of the government, economic, and Party apparatuses with Zionists and protected them. These Zionists placed other Zionists in those sectors, and through them I maintained contact with Zionist organizations.[17]

Slánský then named Geminder, Frejka, Šling, Löbl, Margolius, Hajdů, London, "and many other Zionists" as "direct agents of the big bourgeoisie from which they originated and to which they were linked by common class interest." As none of those mentioned was really a Zionist, it was once more made clear that "Zionist" simply stood for "Jew."

Clementis testified that

> After 1945, Slánský appointed to high positions . . . his partners, the men who had sold themselves to the West: the millionaire Otto Šling, Vilém Nový, who has been unmasked as a Western agent, the cosmopolitan Vítězslav Fuchs, Mikuláš Landa, Lomský-Lieben, Kolman, Moškovič, Ervín Polák, and as the head of the foreign department in the Party headquarters, the cosmopolitan Bedřich Geminder.[18]

He described how these agents of Slánský "infiltrated" the foreign ministry and tried to remove some "faithful"—and by the way, non-Jewish—servants of the regime. His testimony was then confirmed by London and Hajdů, his former deputies, and by Frank, who told the court that Slánský took into the Cadre Commission of the Party headquarters "his people such as Hájek-Karpeles, Jančík-Jung, and others," and how Slánský appointed to high offices "the cosmopolitan" Geminder, "the Jewish bourgeois nationalist, lawyer, swindler, and active Zionist" Fischl, the "English spy" Šling, the "Gestapo agent" Reicin, etc.[19]

Löbl, who had been Deputy Minister of Foreign Trade

> testified how he built up a network of business representatives abroad composed of enemies of the People's Democracy, who received high salaries and commissions, but deserted after February [1948] and used the money they had earned to fight the Republic.[20]

Again, a series of Jewish names follows this charge. Other foreign Jews are named as recipients of "unlawful" payments for their nationalized properties, and still others as illicit exporters of great values to Israel. Margolius and Fischl repeat and amplify the charges.

Frejka, Löbl, Margolius, Fischl confessed that they committed, under orders from Slánský, all kinds of economic crimes. They "sabotaged" the Five Year Plan and invested funds in unprofitable enterprises. They "wrecked" heavy industry and built up light industry in order to make Czechoslovakia dependent on the Western capitalists to whom its products were sold. The Überall-Avriel plan, so called after the Israel minister to Prague, was devised in order that the profits of Czechoslovak industry might accrue to Israel and western Jewish capitalists. The "dollar offensive," an export drive to earn needed foreign currency, was described as a plan to enrich Jewish capitalists abroad.

The confessions were full of evident absurdities, but nobody seemed to care. Whatever the Jewish defendants did was sabotage. When they built up light industry, it was in order to make the Republic dependent on the West. When they bought investment goods for heavy industry abroad, it was to dissipate the reserves of foreign currency. When they tried to earn foreign currency by export, the plan was to enrich Jewish importers abroad. When they exported food, it was to starve the native population. When they imported food, it was because they wanted to increase Czechoslovakia's indebtedness to the West. Even the import of herrings from Norway and Holland was a diabolical conspiracy. Löbl confessed that he tried to get Czechoslovakia foreign credits in order to create financial dependence on the United States, and that he got UNNRA aid for Czechoslovakia in order to spread illusions about American selflessness and to penetrate the country with Anglo-American spies.

If planned economy resulted in a mess, it was the Jewish defendants' fault. If rationing had to be reintroduced, it was the consequence of their sabotage. If there was no bread, no meat, no electricity, they were to blame. Thus all the failures of the regime were ascribed to the Jewish conspiracy. A hundred times the trial raised the question: Who is guilty? A hundred times the answer was: the Jewish conspirators.

This Jewish "plot" was by no means limited to Czechoslovakia. It was, according to the confessions, a world-wide conspiracy, conceived and directed by American Jewish capitalists and Israel statesmen.

Its origin was described by the witness Šimon Ohrenstein, according to a summary of his testimony in *Rudé Právo*, as follows:

> He spoke in detail about a conference in Washington in which, among others, Truman and Acheson took part, and which preceded the founding of the State of Israel. The witness said: "At that conference, it was agreed that the United States and its satellites would support the plan of

the creation of the State of Israel, under the condition that Israel would transfer all its military bases to America. It was agreed that American would grant Israel financial aid in the form of a $100,000,000 loan. There were four conditions for American support. The first was that Haifa was to be built up as a naval base and ceded in the case of a war between the USA and USSR, along with other ports, to the USA. The second point was that the Israel general staff was to be under the American command. The third was that Israel was to become a member of the American-dominated Middle Eastern bloc. The fourth condition was that Israel was, up to the time of war, to be ostensibly neutral in order to enable the Zionist leaders to direct espionage and sabotage actions in the Soviet Union and the countries of People's Democracy from their headquarters in Israel. This Morgenthau-Acheson Plan was known only to a few reliable people.

Judge: Was this plan put into effect?

The Witness: Yes. Ben Gurion issued detailed directives to Zionist organizations to conduct espionage and subversive activities in the countries of People's Democracy. In Czechoslovakia we were directed by Überall-Avriel, the Israel minister to Prague. Avriel selected Prague as the center for our hostile activities . . . because he had intimate connections with Rudolf Slánský, who supported our hostile Zionist activities from his office of Secretary General of the Communist Party.[21]

The witness Mordecai Oren, a left-wing Mapam leader who was described in the Prague radio broadcast as "a small man, the type of an international gangster," was introduced in *Rudé Právo* as follows:

This active international Zionist leader and member of various Zionist organizations, was, as a prominent member of the Zionist headquarters, a professional spy. He was an agent of the British espionage service and carried out its orders in the many countries he visited under the guise of journalist activities. After 1945, he had his headquarters in the countries of People's Democracy where, disguised as a defender of peace and a friend of the Soviet Union, he tried to induce persons in high position in the government and political parties to collaborate with the Zionists and their imperialist paymasters.[22]

Oren testified that the Yugoslav leader of Jewish origin, Moshe Pijade, told him that Slánský was a Titoist and traitor, and that the Israel minister Überall-Avriel had confirmed it. He added that the British minister Herbert Morrison had told him that the British Labor deputy Konni Zilliacus was an imperialist spy who had connections with traitors in Czechoslovakia. As Slánský had confessed that he had connections with Zilliacus, this was considered another "proof" that both took part in the Zionist-Titoist conspiracy.

André Simone added other piquant details:

Before 1939, he [Simone] had had close relations with the Jewish nationalist and French Minister of Colonies, Georges Mandel, who had his own espionage network. . . . In the United States, after 1937, Simone collaborated with the American warmonger L. Fisher, and after 1939 with the Jewish nationalist, Supreme Court Justice Frankfurter.[23]

According to Simone, Mandel recruited him into the French espionage service and thus, says Simone, "I became the agent of the representative of Jewish big capitalists, Georges Mandel." Later, Simone testified, he collaborated with the "British intelligence agents" Paul Willert and Noel Coward, and finally, in New York, he made an agreement with "the agent of American intelligence, the Jewish nationalist Schönbrunn."

Judge: What do you know about Schönbrunn?

The Defendant: I know that he is the son of a Jewish capitalist who emigrated to America before World War I. During 1946 and 1947 he was in the services of the American outfit News Agency,[24] which is an organ of American Jewish big business. Among its financiers is the warmonger Bernard Baruch, author of the plan for the monopolization of atomic energy by the United States. This agency is one of the important connecting links between American Zionists and Jewish nationalists on the one hand, and American imperialism on the other.[25]

It is interesting to note how Schönbrunn, according to Simone, won him for American espionage:

> Schönbrunn emphasized that the United States was conducting the same policy that Mandel had conducted, and one that, if he were still alive, Mandel would wholeheartedly back. Mandel had rendered splendid services to capitalist Jewry. Schönbrunn said: "It is the duty of every Jew to support the Americans, even if he does not agree with every detail of their policy."[26]

André Simone spun his fantastic story further, implicating as "spies" the journalists Alexander Werth, Maurice Hindus, and others. He ended his testimony with this unprecedented appeal:

> I was a writer. There is a beautiful saying to the effect that a writer is an engineer of human souls. What kind of engineer was I who poisoned these souls? Such an engineer belongs on the gallows. The only service I can still render is to serve as a warning to those, who *because of their origin* [*author's ital.*], their character, and qualities are in danger of going the same diabolic way I went. The more severe my punishment, the more efficient will be the warning.[27]

The court granted Simone's wish. He ended at the gallows.

How was it possible that a conspiracy so widespread was not discovered? That question was raised and "answered" in the trial. The answer was given partly in the depositions of the non-Jewish defendants, Josef Frank and Karel Šváb, partly in the confession of Slánský himself.

Josef Frank testified that he had been ordered, in 1930, to distribute illegal antimilitaristic leaflets among the soldiers of the garrison of Olomouc. When he was arrested he betrayed his comrades to the police and testified against the soldiers involved. During the war he was a *Kapo* in the Buchenwald concentration camp in Germany; in this capacity he beat and tortured his co-prisoners and, when working in the camp office, he manipulated the lists of victims to be sent to extermination so that some Russians were put on the list instead of his friends. After the war his name appeared on an allied list of war criminals. Slánský knew about it but kept silent when Frank decided to collaborate in his plot and to put his "Zionist" friends into high office.[28]

Karel Šváb similarly confessed that he had robbed and tortured co-prisoners in the concentration camp of Sachsenhausen. Again, Slánský allegedly blackmailed him into joining the "conspiratorial center." Later, Šváb became Deputy Minister of State Security; in this function he covered up the conspirators' criminal activities, suppressed evidence against them, and warned them whenever they were threatened with discovery. Describing the protection of "Zionist subversive activities," Šváb told the court:

> We covered up the hostile activities of the Zionist organizations in Czechoslovakia on which Slánský relied, because he was himself a Jewish bourgeois nationalist and because the Zionist organizations were the most reliable imperialist agencies and gave Slánský the best opportunity to maintain connections with the imperialist West.

The report in *Rudé Právo* adds:

> The prosecutor then presents documents proving that reports of hostile activities of Zionist organizations were sabotaged by Slánský, Šváb, Plaček, Taussigová, and others,[29] and that Slánský told the conspirators to argue that the revelations about the activities of Zionist organizations were antisemitic.[30]

The use of the antisemitic argument was more extensively described in Slánský's own confession:

> We conducted a vast campaign against antisemitism. The state of Israel was popularized in the press with no indication that it is a bourgeois state and an advance base of American imperialists in the Near East. I protected Zionists by attacking those who criticized their activities. Such men were denounced as antisemites and even prosecuted, persecuted, and expelled from the party. Thus I created an atmosphere in which people were afraid to oppose Zionists and their organizations and to interfere with them.[31]

In this way, combatting antisemitism was branded as a crime and proof of a conspiracy with the traitors and spies.

The Prosecutor's Summation

In his summation the prosecutor, Josef Urválek, devoted a special section to the "Zionist" and Jewish aspect of the trial. He said:

> I must deal in detail with the so-called Zionist movement. That's be-

cause the defendants include eleven alumni of Zionist organizations who entered the service of American imperialism. And also, because the trial shows to all Communist and workers' parties the danger of Zionism as an agency of American imperialism. Zionist organizations have always been linked with world capitalism by a thousand ties. As such they have always been a dangerous enemy of the liberation struggle of the working class. . . .

. . . The Zionist agents in Slánský's conspiratorial center served, by their criminal activities, the efforts of American imperialism to dominate the world and to unleash a new war; they did not serve the interests of the working people of Israel. Their cosmopolitism and their Jewish bourgeois nationalism are indeed only two sides of the same coin, minted in Wall Street. . . .

Socialist construction and the elimination of capitalist interests are absolutely opposed to their [Zionist] class interests. The Zionist movement is not a system of ideas, it is not even a fallacious ideology. The Zionist movement consists of the Zionist organizations in America, plus the ruling clique of the State of Israel, plus the Zionist capitalists all over the world, linked by the intimate ties of their factories, companies, and business deals with American imperialists.

The testimony of the American spy, the Zionist Ohrenstein, reveals that this connection is directly based upon a secret treaty between Truman, Acheson, and the Israel Premier Ben Gurion, that the result of this treaty is the Morgenthau-Acheson Plan. . . . The representative of Israel accepted the obligation to support completely the American drive for world domination—with the help of Zionist organizations not only in the United States but all over the world. . . .

The criminals in the dock have shamelessly abused the Czechoslovak people's traditional abhorrence of antisemitism. . . . This abhorrence was abused by various Jewish hucksters, manufacturers, and bourgeois elements in order to infiltrate the Communist Party, to suppress any kind of criticism, and to hide their faces, the faces of obstinate class enemies, behind the suffering of Jews under Nazi rule.

This speech was made on November 26, 1952, when the unfavorable reaction of Western public opinion to the antisemitic campaign was already known in Prague, and the prosecutor considered it prudent to inject a saving clause for the use of fellow-travelers abroad. Before continuing his antisemitic diatribe, he paused to say:

Our people know very well that our Party will never renounce its proletarian internationalism. . .

But this lip-service to internationalism did not continue even to the end of this sentence, which concluded with this evocation of the oldest anti-Jewish stereotypes:

. . . but that, in this trial, we are trying subversive criminals, international Zionist hucksters, operating on a large scale, the agents of Western imperialism.

The summation continued:

> It is self-evident and logical that Slánský put only Zionists into high positions in the most important sectors of economy and of the Party apparatus, that he received the diplomatic representatives of the State of Israel, that he supported the building and maintaining of Zionist organizations, that he protected their criminal activities, connected with emigration, which cost the Republic 3,900,000,000 crowns. That was because Slánský himself was, by his very nature, a Zionist. . .

The only "nature" by which Slánský could have been connected with Zionism was the fact that he was born a Jew. That did not prevent Urválek from calling him, in the next paragraph, a "Zionist-Trotskyite":

> Slánský, himself a Zionist-Trotskyite, a servant of the bourgeoisie under the First Republic, and a lackey of the imperialists in his further evolution, gathered around him people of the same ilk, men who he knew were the same kind of enemies as himself, who he knew were ready to follow his orders and to realize his counter-revolutionary plans. He found such people . . . among Zionists, Trotskyites, bourgeois nationalists, collaborators, and other enemies of the Czechoslovak people. For whom else could he rely on? . . . .[32]

The Sentence

On November 27, the State Court sentenced eleven defendants, among them eight Jews, to death by hanging. Three defendants, Artur London, Vavro Hajdů, and Evžen Löbl were sentenced to prison for life. Refusing to commute the sentences of the first eleven defendants, the court found that they were "such enemies of the working people that it was necessary to remove them from human society." As for London and Hajdů, the court considered the fact that they had no leading position in the conspiracy and had obeyed orders received from two sources, from Slánský and Clementis, to be mitigating circumstance. Löbl was spared the death sentence because, having been arrested as the first of the conspirators in December 1949, he had "made a spontaneous confession and considerably contributed to the unmasking of other participants."

All the defendants accepted their sentences and "voluntarily" renounced every right of appeal.[33] They renounced even the right to ask President Gottwald for clemency. According to a terse communiqué, those sentenced to death were hanged in the early hours of December 3, 1952.

The Trial Propaganda

A few words must be said about the atmosphere the trial created. From the very first day of the trial, resolutions denouncing the "traitors" and asking that they suffer the ultimate punishment were adopted in factories, offices, and public meetings and published in the newspapers. Every day *Rudé Právo* printed an editorial discussing different aspects of the "crimes" and calling for the defendants' death. On November 24 the editorial was devoted to the "Zionist" aspect of the trial; its tone is evident from the following sample:

> Who are these Zionists? What is their real face, now that the trial has torn their mask away?
>
> The Zionists are the representatives of the reactionary bourgeois-nationalist Jewish movement, which from its beginnings has been ferociously hostile to the cause of the people and progress. Under the pretext of Jewish "national interests" they defend their capitalist class interests, their huckstering and profiteering policies, hostile to the entire international working class. In the interests of this selfish and blood-sucking class policy they organize themselves in international Zionist organizations and serve as the most faithful lackeys of American imperialism.
>
> That's why the Zionist gang became the best support of the subversive conspiratorial center in our country, that's why the arch-criminal Slánský turned for help to Zionist organizations and Zionists, the sworn enemies of the people and of Socialism.
>
> The present trial reveals their degenerate face in all its nakedness. One's very soul is shaken in revulsion when one sees these cold, unfeeling creatures, making shabby deals in everything sacred, cynically betraying everything and everyone who trusts them. With the deepest contempt we recoil from these arch-criminals, the Geminders, Goldmans, Šlings, Simones, Frejkas, Londons, and others, led by Slánský. They have never felt the feelings of the common people, they have not come from their ranks, they have come from a bourgeois, profiteering and manufacturing milieu, they have always hated the workingman. And among these alien elements, among this scum with a dark past, Judas Slánský found his supporters, because they were close to his heart, they were his people and he was their man. With these elements he tried to infiltrate the Party, disintegrate it, and make it a willing tool of his Titoist lust.[34]

The adjectives "huckstering," "profiteering," "blood sucking," "alien," as well as the phrase "scum with a dark past" were calculated to revive the most insidious anti-Jewish stereotypes.

The courtroom "impressions" of Communist reporters followed the same path. Read, for example, the following description of Slánský, printed in *Rudé Právo* under the title "Judas":

> The door leading into the spacious courtroom in the Pankrac prison opens. Flanked by two prison guards, the first defendant in the trial of the subversive conspiratorial center enters. This is the man who has long ago lost any likeness to a human being, whose very name fills millions of Czechs and Slovaks with just wrath, Rudolf Slánský.
>
> Under the red hair, cowardly, sly eyes shift around in a mask of wrinkles. He walks slowly, sits down on the defendants' bench, and for a moment appears depressed. It is just a new mask he has put on to cover his Judas-like face. Like a snake squashed under the boot and unable to free himself, he answers the first questions readily . . . Without excite-

> ment, in a strangely and repulsively calm voice, he begins to talk about the immense crimes which enable him alone to commit more evil deeds than hundreds of the worst criminals. Here begins the last act of the terrible chain of events in which a treacherous scum endangered the existence of all our people, the future of our Fatherland, the lives of our men, women, and children.
>
> At this moment, all hypocritical masks fall—the time has come to pay the bill. Facing the people, facing its wrath, here stands the Trotskyite-Titoist-Zionist criminal, the old obstinate agent of international imperialism, the inveterate enemy of the people, of the Communist Party, and of the Soviet Union, the cowardly and mad pretender to the role of a Czechoslovak Tito, Rudolf Slánský.
>
> He chose and recruited as helpers men like himself, men with a dark past. . . . He organized a gang composed of most abject individuals, traitors without any loyalty to our people and its aspirations, men whose only light is the glow of the Golden Calf, of the Almighty Dollar. These were his supporters—a gang of cosmopolitans, Trotskyite-Titoist-Zionists, bourgeois nationalists, enemies of the Soviet Union, of Socialism, of Peace. He placed these scoundrels in the most important positions in the Party, in the country's economy, in the Army and in the Police, in the Foreign Service. . . .[35]

On November 28, after the sentence had been passed, *Rudé Právo* published the following lines over the signature of the famous Czech Communist writer Ivan Olbracht.[36]

> Before our eyes and ears a trial is being conducted which has no precedent in the history of the Czechoslovak Republic. The State Court is trying eleven typical cosmopolitans, men without honor, without character, without fatherland, without any friendly ties to the Czech and Slovak nation and their people, predatory, merciless individuals who care only for power, for their career, for business, and of course, for money, money, money. We hear the awful Czech they speak and the majority of them, even when they talk Czech, betray that it is not their mother tongue. And these eleven are joined by three seemingly different but in reality equally cosmopolitan faces, those of Clementis, Frank, and Šváb. The last two, I am sorry to say, are of proletarian origin, they are men who have betrayed their proletarian past and deserted the ranks of their former comrades in arms. All the others are children of bourgeois, mostly very rich capitalists, manufacturers, and businessmen. And all of them without exception have sold themselves to Western imperialists, all of them are spies. . . . No, these are no human beings. . . .[37]

The atmosphere of terror was such that the nearest relatives of the defendants were forced to sign letters asking the court for the execution of their husbands and fathers. The letters were read in open court and printed in *Rudé Právo*. Thus the French-born wife of defendant Artur London wrote to the President of the State Court:

> After the arrest of my husband I assumed, on the basis of my knowledge of his life and activities, that he had been a victim of traitors who wanted to cover their treasonable activities with his name.
>
> Up to the last moment, November 20 of this year, I hoped that the errors he might have committed were reparable, that he would answer for them to the Party and to the People's Court, and that after due punishment, he would be allowed to return to the Communist family. After the publication of the indictment my hopes collapsed, my husband was not a victim but a traitor, a traitor to his Party, to his Fatherland. A traitor has lived with me and my family—we are all Communists. Under the occupation, my father used to say: "I am proud that my children are in prison because they are faithful to the Communist Party. I would rather see them dead than traitors." And now I see the father of my three children indicted as a traitor in a People's Court! I have had the sad duty to tell my two older children what happened. They promised me that they would behave like Communists all their life.
>
> As a Communist and as a mother I am happy that the treacherous gang was unmasked and destroyed. I can only join all honest people in demanding a just punishment for the traitors.[38]

And Tomáš Frejka, son of the defendant Ludvík Frejka, wrote:

> I demand that my father be given the severest punishment—the penalty of death. I see now that this creature that cannot be called a human being because he does not possess a bit of feeling or human dignity has been my greatest and most wicked enemy.
>
> I promise, wherever I may work in the future, that I shall always work as a dedicated Communist; I know that my hatred of all our enemies, those who have tried to destroy our increasingly rich and joyful life, and especially of my father, will always inspire me in my work for the Communist future of our people.
>
> I demand that this letter be transmitted to my father, and, if possible, that I be given opportunity to repeat to him personally what I have just said.[39]

Two weeks after the sentence, a dispatch from Prague reported that Tomáš Frejka, who was about eighteen years old, had committed suicide.

Immediately after the start of the trial, a wave of suicides swept the Jewish communities. E. Kohn, the secretary of the Jewish community in Prague, and his wife were among the first victims. The official explanation, telegraphed to the *Daily Worker* in New York, was that Kohn had discovered that he had cancer. The suicide of his wife was not explained, and other reports of suicides were suppressed. An Associated Press report from Vienna listed among the suicides Rudolf Bystrický, former Czechoslovak ambassador to London, and Tibor Kovac, a former Jewish Communist leader in Bratislava.[40]

The trial constituted one great appeal for antisemitism. It must be said, however, that as far as can be judged from reports which have penetrated the Iron Curtain, the response of the Czech people was negligible. It was probably stronger in Slovakia. In Bratislava, in the very first days of the trial, Jewish homes bore chalked inscriptions such as "Down with capitalist Jews!," "Jews live here," or simply, "Jews."[41]

From the Western part of the country it was reported that a kosher restaurant in Prague had been closed, that Jewish pedestrians had been attacked in the street, and Jewish women chased from the queues in front of stores.[42]

One detailed report of anti-Jewish incidents reached the National Committee for a Free Europe in New York. It describes events in Podmokly, Bohemia, near the German border:

> The Café Sport at the corner of Teplická and Divišova street in Podmokly, which used to be the center of the Jewish population of the town, is now completely empty. In mid-December, the local young Communists provoked an antisemitic incident there, attacking persons of Jewish origin with insults and threats. In Café National (Národní kavárna), situated at the Main Square near the local headquarters of the Communist Party, anti-Semitic incidents occured shortly after the Slánský trial. Several Communists insulted citizens of Jewish origin with remarks such as: "They have committed such crimes and they still dare to come to the café!," "Throw them out," etc. In mid-December, antisemitic inscriptions appeared on the walls. One such inscription, near the railway station read: "The Jews want to sell out the People's Democratic Republic to the West." Under the Děčín castle, on the wall over the Elbe river waterfront, another inscription read: "Down with the Jews! Let them go to Palestine!" In several cases, Communist agents have beaten Jewish citizens in the street.[43]

It is characteristic that the incidents described were by no means spontaneous outbreaks of the population, but actions of Communist "activists."

Recent Developments

The Prague trial was watched with horror and revulsion throughout the free world. A wave of protests began in America, Western Europe, and Israel. In some cases, even Communists and fellow-travelers expressed their skepticism, and there was a series of defections from pro-Communist ranks.

By the middle of December 1952, the repercussions must have been known in Prague, for the ruling circles started to look for a formula that would allow the regime to continue the purge and hate-campaign inside the country but provide an alibi for foreign consumption. The formula was found in the phrase: This is anti-Zionism, but not antisemitism. Previously, the words "Zionists" and "Jews" had been used interchangeably.

Now, the difference was stressed, at least in statements meant for foreign consumption.

At a Communist Party conference on December 16, President Klement Gottwald, who had kept remarkably silent throughout the trial, held a speech conspicuous for its apologetic tone and for its evidence of sensitivity to foreign protests. About the Zionist and Jewish problems, Gottwald had the following to say:

> This conference is meeting in the midst of the heightened attention of our friends and the furious barking of our enemies. We are reminded of the echo of the February events and the events after February [1948]. Then, too, our foreign enemies, as if by word of command, let loose a howling and did not calm down for a long time. In fact they never quite calmed down at all. And now they are fuming with fury again and hurling fire and brimstone upon our Republic and our Party. Why are the imperialist and reactionary gentlemen of all shades again getting so angry with us? Simply because we have unmasked and rendered harmless the antistate conspiracy headed by their agent Slánský. . . .
>
> . . . In the course of the investigations and during the trial a new channel through which treason and espionage was penetrating into the Communist Party was discovered. This is Zionism. Why? Simply because after the establishment of the State of Israel and its acceptance of American domination, all Zionist organizations became branches of the American espionage service. They represented an ideal instrument for the penetration of the workers' movement and the recruitment of agents inside the Communist parties.
>
> The Zionist organizations and their American bosses disgracefully abused the suffering of the Jews under Hitler and the other fascists. It can even be said that they tried to make capital out of the ashes of Oswiecim and Majdanek.
>
> Normally a former banker, industrialist, estate owner, or kulak would find it difficult to become a member of the Communist Party and he would never reach a leading position. Yet with people of Jewish origin and Zionist coloration the class origin was often overlooked. In this they were helped by our innate opposition to antisemitism and, after the Second World War, by our respect for the suffering to which the Jews had been exposed.
>
> Before the war the danger was not so great, but after the war, when the Zionist organizations and the Zionist became agents of American imperialism, the situation changed fundamentally. Today Zionism is a dangerous and cunning enemy. Does that mean that a person of Jewish origin is identical with a Zionist? No. The decisive factor is the class origin of the individual, his attitude toward his native country, his devotion to, and work for, socialism. Similarly the fight against Zionism has nothing in common with antisemitism. Antisemitism is a brand of barbarous racialism, such as is today being fostered by the American

supermen or the Hitlerite *Übermenschen* toward the Negroes and the colonial nations. Anti-Zionism is a form of defense against American espionage and against an agency of diversionism and sabotage. Thus anti-Zionism and antisemitism are as different as Heaven and Hell. . . .[44]

Gottwald's declaration did not change the impact of the antisemitic campaign. In Czechoslovakia nobody could be deceived by the pretense of "mere anti-Zionism," since everybody knew that the defendants in the Prague trial and 90 per cent of other victims were not Zionists but simply Jews. The campaign increased in violence after the arrest of the doctors in the Kremlin, who were accused of having murdered Soviet leaders Zhdanov and Shcherbakov on the orders of the American Jewish Joint Distribution Committee.[45] Now it was more than evident that the Prague trial was not a private undertaking of Czechoslovak Communist leaders, but part of a systematic antisemitic campaign directed from the Kremlin.

This campaign was connected with the intraparty struggle in the Soviet Union. The "doctors' plot" and the hints about "negligence" of Soviet security organs were evidently aimed at the liquidation of Lavrenti P. Beria, the powerful chief of the Soviet secret police. In due time, the doctors would have "confessed" that Beria had hired them to commit murder. It seems probable that Stalin himself directed that intrigue. The liquidation of people like Slánský, Geminder, of persons connected with Noel Field, of emigrants who had been serving the Soviet apparatuses in the West during the war, was an attack on Beria agents abroad. His power machine had been destroyed at the periphery of the Soviet empire before it was attacked at its center. Conducting the anti-Slánský and anti-Jewish campaign, Gottwald was probably acting on direct orders from Stalin.

But in the middle of this operation, on March 5, 1953, Stalin died. Klement Gottwald returned from his funeral, accompanied by Soviet doctors, and died a few days later, on March 19. On April 4, Moscow officially declared that the "doctors' plot" was a frame-up, that the evidence was falsified, that the confessions were extorted, and shortly afterward, the Soviet press admitted that the plot had been used to "inflame national enmity" and "sow the seeds of racial prejudice."[46]

At the time of this writing (April 1953), nothing was known of the repercussions of this sudden turn in Czechoslovakia. So far there had been no admission that the Slánský trial, too, was a frame-up; no Jewish prisoners had been released, and no antisemitic excesses punished. Quite the contrary; on April 16, Václav David, the Foreign Minister of Czechoslovakia, told the Political Committee of the General Assembly of the United Nations that Slánský and other Jewish leaders had been executed because they were criminals, and that Zionism was a tool of American espionage, sabotage, and subversion.[47] On April 21 the Slovak Communist newspaper *Pravda* of Bratislava repeated the antisemitic and anti-Zionist charges made at the Prague trial and declared that "Zionist-Trotskyite traitors" were particularly dangerous because they were situated at the very heart of the Communist Party.[48] Even after the Moscow reversal, the anti-Zionist and antisemitic campaign in Czechoslovakia was continuing unabated.

Whatever gestures the regime might make, nothing could repair the damage wrought not only by the Prague trial and the openly antisemitic campaign of the last few months, but also by the systematic destruction of Jewish life pursued for many years. The most that could be hoped for was that some remnants of the Jewish population might be saved, if the regime should again permit emigration. The Jewish communities and Jewish life in Czechoslovakia, as well as the tradition of tolerance and cooperation between the Jews and non-Jews, had been damaged beyond repair during the five years of totalitarian dictatorship. The Communist regime in Czechoslovakia had completely destroyed Jewish life in that country.

Notes

CHAPTER I

1. Moravia and Czechoslovak Silesia were consolidated into one "Moravian-Silesian land" or province in the mid-twenties.

2. Hereinafter, the terms "Israelites" or "Jews," if not qualified otherwise, mean persons of the Jewish *faith*.

3. We can only approximately estimate the number of baptized or non-professing Jews in prewar times. According to the statistics of the Association of Jewish Religious Communities, published after the war, there were, on March 15, 1939, 118,310 "racial" Jews in Bohemia and Moravia, of which 14,350 did not belong to the Jewish religious community. Assuming that the same proportion held for 1930, we obtain a figure of about 16,000 baptized or non-professing Jews in Bohemia and Moravia at that time. The number of such Jews in Slovakia and Carpatho-Russia is not known, but it must have been much smaller.

4. The Czechoslovak census did not distinguish between Czechs and Slovaks, including both in the Czechoslovak "nationality" or ethnic group. With some allowance for Slovak students in Prague and Brno, and for Czech officials and police in Slovakia, one could generally say that the "Czechoslovaks" in Bohemia and Moravia were Czechs, and in Slovakia, Slovaks.

5. This "Russian nationality" includes the Slavonic population of Carpatho-Russia and eastern Slovakia. A long and bitter fight raged as to whether these people were to be considered Russians or Ukrainians. The Czech pre-Munich administration considered them Russian, although it had to make concessions to the Ukrainian language in schools. The province was officially called Carpatho-Russia. In the short interval between Munich and March 1939, an autonomous Ukrainian administration existed within the post-Munich Czechoslovak "Second Republic." In 1939 the area was annexed by Hungary, in 1945 by the Soviet Union. The Soviet administration considers the population Ukrainian and the province, now called "Carpatho-Ukraine," makes part of the Ukrainian Soviet Republic.

6. Data for 1928-1930 are taken from *Die Juden in der Tschechoslovakei*, an unpublished manuscript by Dr. Bruno Blau; for 1931-1933, from the same writer's "Bafelkerung-bavegung bay yidn in tschekhoslovakye," in *Yidishe Ekonomik*, Wilno 1939, p. 177. Dr. Blau's data were computed from published and unpublished reports of the State Bureau of Statistics in Prague.

CHAPTER II

1. Blau, *op. cit.*, Appendix.
2. *Věstník náboženské obce židovské* (Bulletin of the Jewish Religious Community of Prague) IX/23, Prague 1947, p. 330.
3. *Věstník, loc. cit.*
4. Blau, *loc. cit.*
5. *Věstník, loc. cit.*
6. *Věstník*, IX/24, p. 344; see also *Věstník* IX/5, p. 58, where the number of survivors is given as 256.
7. A total of 140,000 Jews were deported to Terezín, the difference being accounted for by Jews from Germany, Austria, France, Holland, Denmark, etc. *Věstník* IX/24, p. 344.
8. The precise number is 4,900, according to a report from the Prague community, dated August 15, 1946, in the archives of the Yiddish Scientific Institute (YIVO) in New York.
9. Since Slovakia was a "Catholic state" and did not use a racist criterion, the census counted "persons of the Jewish faith." But there was also a count made of persons of "Jewish nationality," who numbered 29,928, or 1.11 per cent of the entire population and 34.2 per cent of all Slovak Jews. The decline from 54 per cent of Jews declaring Jewish nationality in 1930 can be explained by fear of reprisals.
10. Blau, *op. cit.*, p. 203.
11. *Počet Židov na Slovensku ku dňu 12.XII. 1940 a 1. IX.1942 [Number of Jews in Slovakia as of December 12, 1940 and September 1, 1942]*, and *Židia na Slovensku v rokoch 1940-1944 [Jews in Slovakia in the Years 1940-1944]*, both in the possession of YIVO.
12. See the report of Juraj Slávik, Minister of the Interior in the government-in-exile, to the Czechoslovak State Council in London, February 1943.
13. *Bericht über die jüdischen Arbeitslager und Zentren*, Bratislava 1943, *and Židovské pracovné tábory a strediska*, Bratislava 1944, in the files of YIVO.
14. "Statistique de la population juive d'Europe après la guerre: République Tchécoslovaque," in *Union O.S.E., Bulletin d'Information*, no. 5, July 1946, p. 30.
15. See *American Jewish Year Book*, 1942-43 (Vol. 44), p. 254.
16. There were 600 Jewish participants according to *Věstník* IX/10, p. 137; the number seems to be exaggerated, but cannot be verified.
17. *Věstník*, IX/9, p. 120.
18. *Ibid.*, IX/8, p. 101, IX/10, p. 137
19. *Věstník* IX/10, p. 137. Russian orders give the patronymic as well as first and last names and we frequently find a Bedřich Solomonovich X. or a Václav Davidovich Y.
20. *Věstník* IX/24, p. 343.
21. *Ibid.*, IX/10, p. 137.

CHAPTER III

1. *Věstník*, X/32-33, p. 356.
2. *Cesta (Haderech)*, November 1946, p. 10.
3. *Věstník*, X/11, p. 124.
4. Report of October 14, 1947, in the files of the American Jewish Committee.
5. We are comparing postwar percentages for Bohemia-Moravia with prewar percentages for the whole of Czechoslovakia. It is possible to do this because about 45 per cent of the postwar Bohemian-Moravian Jews were newcomers from Carpatho-Russia.

CHAPTER IV

1. Two other small parties were allowed to exist in Slovakia, one of them connected with the Czech Social Democracy, another a Communist front organization. Both remained without influence.

2. Nothing was said in the first postwar decrees about persons of "Jewish nationality." How the laws were applied to them will be described in a later chapter.

CHAPTER V

1. Angelo Goldstein: "Obnova právního řádu a sociální problém restituce," in the *Bulletin* of the Czech Representative Committee, affiliated with the World Jewish Congress, New York, No. 12, 1944, pp. 5-7.

2. Dekret presidenta republiky o neplatnosti některých právně-majetkových jednání z doby nesvobody a národní správě majetkových hodnot Němcu, Mad'aru, zrádcu a kolaborantu. Czech text reprinted in part in the *Bulletin* of the Czech Representative Committee, No. 17, pp. V-Va.

3. Ústavní dekret presidenta republiky ze dne 3. srpna 1944 o obnovení právního pořádku ve znění zákona z 19. prosince 1945, č. 12/1946.

4. Law of April 9, 1946, No. 74/1946.

5. Executive Order of April 30, 1946, No. 110/1946.

6. See Paul Reiner, "Report of the Newest Legislation in Czechoslovakia," *Bulletin* of the Czech Representative Committee, No. 20, October 1946, p. 9.

7. Zákon o neplatnosti některých majetkoprávních jednání z doby nesvobody a o nárocích z této neplatnosti a z jiných zásahu do majetku, ze 16. května 1946, č. 128/1946. Czech text reprinted in the *Bulletin* of the Czech Representative Committee, No. 19, July 1946, pp. 8-11; an interpretation by Dr. Bedřich Fried is given in the same publication on pp. 5-7.

8. Dekret presidenta republiky ze dne 2. srpna 1945 o úpravě československého státního občanství osob národnosti německé a mad'arské. Reprinted in the *Bulletin*, l.c., No. 17, December-November 1945, pp. IV-IVa.

9. See the report of Dr. Wehle to the delegates of the Jewish Religious Communities in Bohemia and Moravia, October 26-28, 1947, reprinted in *Věstník* IX/23, p. 327.

10. *Bulletin* of the Czech Representative Committee, No. 9, July 1946, p. 1.

11. *Věstník* IX/23, p. 327. An interpretation by Paul Reiner was made in the *Bulletin*, No. 20, October 1945, pp. 15-17.

12. *Bulletin* of the Czech Representative Committee, No. 20, October 1946, p. 16.

13. In connection with an interview with the Minister of Interior, Václav Nosek, on February 20, 1947, the Czechoslovak press reported that 2,000 Jews had volunteered for emigration to Germany. The Communist newspaper *Rudé Právo* even spoke —probably wishfully—of 20,000 such cases. According to Dr. Wehle, in *Věstník* IX/6 p. 78, the truth of the matter was that the UNNRA tried to organize the emigration of Czechoslovak citizens of German nationality who had escaped being deported, but wished to leave the country voluntarily. There were 800 persons interested in this action, 150 of whom were of Jewish origin. Many of the latter had German spouses and did not know the Czech language.

14. Egon Gold, in *Tribuna*, Bratislava, I/13, p. 3.

15. Cf. *Věstník* X/3, p. 30, and Wehle, *Věstník* IX/23, p. 327.

16. *Věstník* IX/17, p. 255.

17. See the complaint of the Slovak Association of Racial Persecutees, in *Tribuna* II/2, p. 2.

18. *Věstník* X/3, p. 63.

19. *Ibid.*, IX/9, pp. 121-122.

20. *Ibid.*, X/5, p. 51.

21. Here follows the case of Rabbi Leitner from Mariánsk Lázně (Marienbad).

22. *Der Aufbau*, New York, March 21, 1947, p. 19.

23. *Věstník* IX/16, p. 237.
24. *Ibid.*, IX/7, pp. 93-94.
25. Report dated June 17, 1947, in the files of the American Jewish Committee.
26. *Věstník*, IX/20, p. 294. The report does not say what percentage of the lost properties these 100 represented.
27. *Ibid.*, IX/15, p. 90.
28. *Ibid.*, IX/4, p. 39 and IX/7, p. 93.
29. Michal Mareš in *Dnešek*, Prague, July 7, 1947. Mareš, a Gentile who exposed many crimes and atrocities committed by the Communist police, was arrested, condemned to a long prison term, and killed in jail after the Communist coup.
30. *Věstník*, X/6, pp. 57-58.
31. *Ibid.*, IX/24, pp. 341-342.
32. *Ibid.*, IX/5, pp. 61-62.
33. *Svobodné Slovo*, March 6, 11 and 21, 1947; *Svobodné Noviny*, March 7 and 11, 1947; *Národní Osvobození*, March 14, 1947; *Lidová Demokracie*, March 13, 1947; *Právo Lidu*, March 9 and 20, 1947; *Práce*, March 6, 15, 18, 20, and 22, 1947; *Věstník* IX/6, pp. 69-72, 76, IX/7, pp. 85, 95, IX/14, p. 205.
34. *Věstník* IX/11, p. 153.
35. *Ibid.*
36. Report dated June 17, 1947, in the files of the American Jewish Committee.
37. *Věstník* IX/13, p. 181; IX/14, pp. 197-199; IX/15, pp. 213-214.
38. *Ibid.*, IX/16, p. 233.
39. *Ibid.*, XI/11, pp.121-122.
40. *Ibid.*, IX/15, p. 214, and IX/21, p. 370.
41. *Ibid.*, IX/8, pp. 106-108 and IX/15, pp. 213-214.
42. *Ibid.*, IX/9, p. 126.
43. *Ibid.*, IX/25, p. 358.
44. *Ibid.*, IX/29, p. 369.
45. Cf. the interview of Vojtech Winterstein, Secretary of the Association of Jewish Religious Communities in Slovakia, with President Beneš on March 20. 1947, in *Věstník* IX/7, p. 85.
46. Egon Gold, in *Tribuna* I/13, p. 3.
47. *Tribuna*, II/1, pp. 3-4.
48. Circular No. 33.806/47; cf. *Tribuna* I/23, p. 3, and I/27, p. 2.
49. *Tribuna*, II/7, p. 1.
50. *Cas*, Bratislava, December 11, 1947 (quoted in *Tribuna*, I/31, p. 2).
51. *Tribuna*, I/29, p. 3.
52. *Ibid.*, II/4, p. 3.
53. *Věstník* X/8, p. 81. See also report, dated February 19, 1948, in the files of the American Jewish Committee.
54. *Věstník* IX/26, p. 368; *Tribuna* I/29, p. 3 and II/4, p. 3.
55. Reported by the Jewish Telegraphic Agency, March 7, 1948.
56. Heirs of the first class are direct descendants; heirs of the second class are descendants of the parents of the deceased, i.e., brothers and sisters; descendants of the deceased's grandparents (uncles, aunts, and first cousins) are third-class heirs.
57. *Tribuna* II/13, p. 2, II/15, p. 2, II/21, p. 2.
58. Egon Gold, in *Tribuna* II/13, p. 2.

CHAPTER VI

1. *JDC Review* VI, 8-9, November-December 1948, p. 83.
2. *Ibid.*, IV, 5, August 1948, p. 55.
3. *Ibid.*, IV, 8-9, November-December 1948, p. 83.
4. This figure was also given in the *JDC Review*, IV, 4, June 1948, p. 48.
5. *Ibid.*, IV, 5, August 1948, p. 55.

6. *Ibid., IV*, 8-9, November-December 1948, pp. 78-79.
7. *Ibid.*, IV, 4, June 1948, p. 48.
8. *Ibid.*, IV, 5, August 1948, p. 55, IV, 8-9, November-December 1948, p. 83.
9. *ORT Bulletin* 1, December 1947, p. 9.
10. *JDC Review* IV, 5, August 1948, p. 60.
11. *ORT Bulletin* 2, March 1948, p. 8.
12. *Ibid.*, II, 1, September 1948, p. 11.
13. *Věstník* XI/7, p. 75.
14. *JDC Review* IV, 5, August 1948, p. 60.
15. *Věstník* XI/11, p. 121-122.
16. For the "Terezín substance" and its liquidation, see chap. V above.
17. *Jewish Morning Journal*, New York, March 13, 1949.
18. Jewish Telegraphic Agency, January 13 and February 14, 1950; *New York Times*, February 13, 1950.
19. Jewish Telegraphic Agency, October 27, 1949. The decree concerning the nationalization of hospitals in Slovakia was issued in October 1949 and became effective on January 1, 1950.
20. See chap. X.

CHAPTER VII

1. Described in David Bernstein's report to the American Jewish Committee, April 15, 1947, and in *Věstník* IX/4, p. 42. The method of sampling and interviewing was not revealed. Another, more thorough, survey was being prepared by the Institute, in cooperation with Mr. Fuchs in Prague and with advice from the AJC, for 1948. The last report from Prague said that it would have to be postponed until after the general elections of May 1948. Nothing has been heard about it since.
2. "Religious intolerance" did occasionally show itself. The Protestant family magazine, *Českobratrská rodina* (Prague), wrote on September 15, 1945: "A nation which was more than decimated are the Jews. Readers of the Bible who followed their history and their prophets will not be too astonished by this. The nation that received a perfect moral law, that heard the first message of God from the prophets, that was punished many times for its lack of faith and disobedience, until it lost its home and government—this nation definitely rejected the Lord and gave itself up to avarice, idolatry of money, and cunning. . . . They became a curse and were stricken by fate because they had rejected the Savior and hardened their hearts. . . . Ing. Frischer announced that only 7,208 Jews survived in Czech lands. They had to suffer their punishment, but one does not see that this has helped them to recognize themselves for what they are." Cf. *Věstník* VIII/1, p. 4.
3. *Tribuna*, I/23, p. 2.
4. *Ibid.*, I/33, p. 1.
5. *Věstník* IX/13, p. 185.
6. Quoted in *Věstník* IX/27, p. 402.
7. As reported by a non-Jewish pupil. *Věstník* X/7, p. 86.
8. "We Are Weaving for the Soviet Union," in *Pochodeň*, the newspaper of the Communist Party for the District of Hradec Králové, Sept. 5, 1945. See *Věstník* VII/3, p. 20.
9. Jewish Telegraphic Agency, August 10, 1945.
10. *Washington Post*, September 26, 1945.
11. Quoted in *Věstnik* VII/3, p. 20.
12. In the town of Nové Město nad Metují, Bohemia (*Věstník*, IX/25, p. 357).
13. Typical of this is an article by Božena Pátková, in the magazine *Kveten*. She complains bitterly that the heir of one "Mr. Aron," a Jew who perished in the gas chamber, had the effrontery to ask back furnishings that had been "kindly hidden away" by a gentile family. See *Věstník* IX/21, p. 307.

14. Quoted in *Věstník* VIII/2, pp. 14-15.
15. Quoted in *Věstník* IX/9, p. 121.
16. See chap. V.
17. He used, in a Czech speech, the Russian word "svoloch."
18. *Právo Lidu*, March 25-26, 1947.
19. *Rudé Právo*, March 27, 1947.
20. *Právo Lidu*, March 11, 1948.
21. This was confirmed by the Minister of National Defense and former Commander of the Czech Eastern Army, General Ludvík Svoboda, at the Congress of War Veterans, July 5, 1947. But this part of the speech was printed only in the army newspaper, and omitted in the rest of the press. Cf. *Věstník* IX/15, p. 217.
22. *Věstník*, IX/11, p. 153.
23. *Ibid.*, IX/7, p. 95; IX/8, p. 102; X/5, p. 52.
24. *Ibid.*, IX/4, p. 37.
25. *Ibid.*, X/2, p. 14.
26. *Ibid.*, IX/9, p. 120.
27. *Ibid.*, IX/21, p. 309.
28. *Ibid.*, IX/23. p. 332.
29. *Ibid.*, X/4, p. 37.
30. *Ibid.*, X/10, p. 113.
31. *Ibid.*, X/16, p. 118. Quoted from the Bulletin of the Ministry, March 31, 1948.
32. *Ibid.*, X/7, p. 77, X/15, p. 173.
33. *Ibid.*, X/2, p. 14.
34. Jewish Telegraphic Agency, June 27, 1948.
35. *Věstník* VII/3, p. 20. The Jewish Telegraphic Agency's dispatch gave the number of injured as 68.
36. *Věstník* IX/9, pp. 119-120.
37. See the detailed description in *Věstník* VIII/9, p. 74.
38. *Tribuna* I/25, p. 2; *Věstník* IX/14, p. 206.
39. *Tribuna* II/35, August 27, 1948, pp. 2, 4.
40. United Press dispatch from Prague, August 22, 1948; see *New York Times*, August 23, 1948.
41. United Press, Prague, August 22; Jewish Telegraphic Agency, Prague, August 23; Reuters, Prague, August 23; Associated Press, Prague, August 25, 1948.
42. *New York Times*, August 24, 1948.
43. See *New York Post*, August 25, 1948.
44. Jewish Telegraphic Agency, August 24, 1948; cf. *Tribuna* II/35, August 27, 1948.
45. *Věstník* X/11, p. 117.
46. Paragraph 37 of the new constitution.
47. *Věstník* X/21, pp. 241-242.
48. The paragraphs of the new penal code (Statute No. 86/1950) concerning racial hatred (articles 83, 116-119, 125) were quoted in *Věstník* XII/35, p. 398.
49. *Tribuna* III/42, October 23, 1949.
50. A typical instance is the testimony of Erwin Schulhof, a Czechoslovak socialist who spent six years in Buchenwald and Oswiecim. In Vienna, on his way to Israel, Schulhof declared that many positions in the Czechoslovak government were now occupied by men who formerly collaborated with the Nazis. He said that life in Communist-controlled Czechoslovakia has become "intolerable," and members of the group in which he came reported "mounting antisemitism in Czechoslovakia and increasing hostility toward the state of Israel." See report of Overseas News Agency from Vienna, March 30, 1949.

CHAPTER VIII

1. *Věstník* VII/2, p. 14; *Bulletin* of the Czech Representative Committee, No. 18, pp. 11-13.

2. Decree of the Land National Committee for Bohemia in Prague, May 30, 1947, No. I-3c-2100/4-1947.
3. Decree of the Land National Committee for Moravia-Silesia in Brno, November 11, 1947, No. 28629/47-V/30.
4. Decree of the Land National Committee for Moravia-Silesia, Branch Office in Moravská Ostrava, October 20, 1947, No. V/6-6889/10.
5. *Věstník* VII/3, p. 23.
6. See its by-laws in *Věstník* IX/9, p. 126.
7. *Věstník* IX/5, p. 58.
8. The Czechoslovak Constitution, Articles 16-18; see also the Religious News Service, April 19, 1948.
9. Jewish Telegraphic Agency, March 17, 1948; see also New York *Post*, March 19, 1948.
10. *Ibid.*, April 4, 1948.
11. *Ibid.*, January 20, 1948.
12. *Cesta* (*Haderech*), Bratislava, December 1947, p. 6.
13. *Halapid, Piešťany*, No. 7, p. 4, March 1948.
14. *Ibid.*, No. 1, p. 1, December 1947.
15. The Czechoslovak Hashomer Hatzair had three *kibbutzim* in Palestine in 1946 (*Cesta*, November 1946, p. 11); a fourth one was founded in 1947 (*ibid.*, September 1947, p. 4-5).
16. *Věstník* IX/19, p. 227.
17. *Cesta*, June 1947.
18. *Věstník* IX/25, p. 356.
19. *Ibid.*, IX/11, p. 159.
20. *Cesta*, November 1946.
21. *Bulletin* of the Czech Representative Committee, No. 21, p. 11, and report from Prague, dated January 23, 1947, in the files of the American Jewish Committee.
22. *Věstník* X/4, p. 41.
23. "*Informační zprávy Kruhu čsl. legionářu židovského puvodu*," Litoměřice, Vol. I, No. 1, November-December 1947.
24. Emil Utitz, *Psychologie života v terezínském koncentračním táboře*, Prague 1947; Mirko Tuma, *Ghetto našich dnu*, Prague 1946; Ota Kraus and Erich Schoen, *Továrna na smrt*, Prague 1946.
25. Viktor Knapp and Tomáš Bermann, *Restituční zákon*, Prague 1947.
26. *Věstník* X/2, p. 13.
27. *Ibid.*, IX/5, pp. 47-48.
28. *Věstník* VIII/8, p. 70; *Cesta*, July-August 1946, pp. 10-11.
29. *Věstník* IX/17, p. 253; *Cesta*, September 1947, pp 9-10.
30. Rafi Friedl, in *Cesta*, March 1948, p. 14.
31. *Věstník* IX/9, p. 125.
32. A parade of this kind in Prague is described in *Cesta*, June 1947.
33. *Tribuna*, II/21, p. 5.
34. *Ibid.*, II/17, p. 5; *Cesta*, May 1948.
35. *Cesta*, June 1948.
36. *Věstník* IX/5, p. 58.
37. *Ibid.*, X/4, pp 35-36.
38. *Ibid.*, X/5, pp. 47-48.
39. See the report of Kurt Wehle to the delegates of the Jewish Religious Communities, October 26-28, 1947, *Věstník* IX/23, p. 326.
40. *Věstník*, X/5, pp. 47-48.
41. *Ibid.*, IX/18, p. 262.
42. *Ibid.*, IX/6, pp. 76-78.
43. See letter to the editor in *Právo Lidu*, March 2, 1947.
44. *Rudé Právo*, March 8, 1947.
45. *Věstník* IX/5, p. 57.
46. *Ibid.*, IX/7, p. 87.

47. Report of April 13, 1947, in the files of the American Jewish Committee.
48. Ascertained by comparing endorsements of candidates by the Czech Jews (*Věstník* IX/6, p. 76) with the list elected, *Věstník* IX/7, p. 87.
49. *Věstník* IX/22, p. 315.
50. Report of November 2, 1947, in the files of the American Jewish Committee.
51. *Ibid.*
52. Report of January 28, 1948, in the files of the American Jewish Committee.

CHAPTER IX

1. *Věstník* X/10, p. 110.
2. *Ibid.*, p. 108.
3. *Ibid.*, p. 109.
4. *Ibid.*, X/11, pp. 117 ff.
5. *Ibid.*, X/12, pp. 134 ff.
6. *Ibid.*, X/14, p. 154.
7. He died soon after, on March 31, 1948.
8. This action committee had been appointed, like the one in Prague, by the Brno District Committee of the National Front. *Věstník* X/12, p. 138.
9. *Věstník* X/26, p. 311, and X/27, p. 319. The first name of Polák was given once as Bedřich, once as Arnošt—he did not appear to be very well known in the community at that time. *Věstník* did not say who elected or appointed him, confining itself to: Dr. Stein resigned, the new chairman *is* Mr. Polák. Arnošt Polák was a director of a state bank; later, in November 1948, he was appointed Czech representative to the International Bank for Reconstruction in Washington. He died in Prague after being recalled in May 1950 (see *Věstník* XII/21, p. 241).
10. "Slovenské Židovstvo a jeho ustanovizne," in *Cesta,* August 1946, pp. 4-5.
11. "Pred vol'bami do Cionistického sjazdu," in *Cesta,* August 1946, pp. 5-6.
12. Editorial statement, "Alija cez Ameriku," in *Cesta,* June 1948, p. 3.
13. A. Pressburger, "Israel volá svoju mládež," in *Cesta,* June 1948, pp. 6-7.
14. See *Věstník* X/27, p. 323, and the report of April 22, 1948 in the files of the American Jewish Committee.
15. Jewish Telegraphic Agency, May 18 and 21, 1948.
16. *Ibid.*, July 28, 1948.
17. *Ibid.*, June 1, 1948.
18. *Ibid.*, May 24, 1948.
19. *Ibid.*, July 12, 1948.
20. *Ibid.*, July 21, 1948.
21. *Ibid.*, August 1, 1948.
22. For a summary report of the deliveries, see *New York Times,* July 17, 1948.
23. *New York Times,* September 1, 1948.
24. Reported by Kenneth Bilby from Tel Aviv in the *New York Herald Tribune,* August 4, 1948.
25. See, e.g., the article "Bipartisan Gang-Up on Israel," by Moses Miller, in *Jewish Life,* Vol. II, No. 12 (24), New York, October 1948, p. 19.
26. Jewish Telegraphic Agency, January 12, 1948; *New York Times,* January 29, 1948.
27. *New York Times,* February 15, 1948.
28. Reported by Parker La Moore from Cairo in the *New York World-Telegram,* February 25, 1948.
29. *New York Herald Tribune,* March 19, 1948.
30. *New York Times,* April 14, 1948.
31. *Věstník* X/6, p. 59, and X/8, p. 83.
32. *Ibid.*, X/18, pp. 205-206.
33. *Ibid.*, X/20, p. 229. Kolman was later recalled to Russia after criticizing some prominent Czech Communist leaders.

34. In May 1949 the Israel Foreign Minister Moshe Sharett visited Prague and conferred with the Czechoslovak Foreign Minister Vlado Clementis, (Jewish Telegraphic Agency, May 20, 1949.) At the same time, Czechoslovakia announced the appointment of Edward Goldstücker, a Czech Communist of Jewish origin, as Czechoslovak Minister to Israel (*ibid.*, May 21, 1949). Goldstücker arrived in Israel in January 1950 (*ibid.*, January 4, 1950). Dr. Yehud Ueberall (Avriel), the first Israeli Minister to Prague, was later transferred to Bucharest and replaced by Dr. Shmuel Eliashiv, former head of the East European department in the Israeli Foreign Office (*Věstník* XII/16, p. 185). A new trade agreement was signed in Prague in March 1950 (Jewish Telegraphic Agency, March 22, 1950).

35. The foreign visitor was Councillor A. Wolffe, Grand President of the Grand Order of the Sons of Jacob, and an account of the interview was published in the *Jewish Chronicle,* London, September 1, 1950.

36. This was reported by "a delegate to the recent international student congress in Prague" in the *Jewish Chronicle,* London, September 29, 1950.

37. *Věstník* X/47, p. 515.

38. *Ibid.*, XI/5, p. 50.

39. *Ibid.*, XI/11, p. 128.

40. This was reported in the *Jewish Chronicle,* London, May 12, 1950. The last issues of *Tribuna* obtained by subscribers in this country were of March 1950. They carried no explanation about the causes of the discontinuation of the periodical.

41. Jewish Telegraphic Agency, September 9 and October 1, 1948.

42. *Ibid.*, December 24, 1948.

43. *New York Herald Tribune*, January 23, 1949; *New Yorké Listy*, January 25, 1949.

44. Drew Pearson reported in his broadcast of February 13, 1949, that 68 Zionists had been arrested in Czechoslovakia on charges of spying for the United States (see also the Jewish Telegraphic Agency, February 15, 1949); this report, however, was not confirmed.

45. *New York Herald Tribune,* March 28, 1949.

46. See the interview with Itzchak Raphael, head of the Immigration Department of the Jewish Agency, in the *Jewish Chronicle,* London, October 6, 1950, and in the *Jewish Morning Journal*, New York, October 12, 1950.

47. *Tribuna* II/15, p. 6, and II/16, p. 1. With unconscious irony, the newspaper wrote: "Jews had the opportunity to compare their present labor with the forced labor under the Nazis. They could compare and they did compare."

48. *Věstník* X/13, p. 123.

49. *Ibid.*, X/16, p. 185.

50. *Ibid.*, X/20, p. 233.

51. *Ibid.*, X/21, p. 242; *Tribuna* II/22, p. 1.

52. *Věstník* XII/10, p. 109-110.

53. *Ibid.*, XII/11, p. 122.

54. *Ibid.*, XII/21, p. 230.

55. *Ibid.*, XII/35, p. 401.

56. *Ibid.*, XII/47, p. 542.

57. *Ibid.*, X/19, p. 217.

58. *Ibid.*, X/15, p. 173.

59. *Ibid.*, X/14, p. 155.

60. *Ibid.*, X/20, p. 234.

61. *Ibid.*, X/25, pp. 300-301.

62. *Ibid.*, XI/11, p. 122.

63. *Ibid.*, XII/49, p. 569.

64. *Neue Zürcher Zeitung*, Zürich, November 15, 1949.

65. *Věstník* XI/42, p. 474.

66. *Ibid.*, XI/45, p. 505.

67. *Ibid.*, XII/12, p. 138.

68. *Jewish Chronicle*, London, September 1, 1950.

69. *Ibid.*, September 29, 1950.
70. *Věstník* XII/49, p. 569.
71. See n. 35 above.
72. Report from Vienna in the *Jewish Morning Journal*, July 2, 1950.
73. Another report in the same newspaper on August 26, 1950, spoke of 29 "recently liquidated communities."
74. *Jewish Morning Journal*, New York, March 13, 1949.
75. *Ibid.*, December 28, 1949.
76. *Ibid.*, May 2, 1950.
77. *Aufbau*, New York, May 19, 1950.
78. *Věstník* XI/47, p. 532.
79. *Ibid.*, XII/49, p. 570.
80. *Jewish Chronicle*, London, September 29, 1950.
81. *Věstník* XI/7, p. 77.
82. *Jewish Morning Journal*, New York, April 24, 1950.
83. *Jewish Chronicle*, London, September 1, 1950.
84. *Věstník* XII/35, p. 407.
85. See n. 36 above.
86. *Tribuna*, Bratislava, IV/1-2, p. 1.
87. See n. 36 above.
88. *Morgen Freiheit*, New York, September 11, 1950.
89. Cf. Hana Volavková's *The Jewish Museum in Prague: a Guide to the Collections*, Prague 1948, and *The Synagogue Treasures of Bohemia and Moravia*, Prague 1949.
90. *Věstník*, X/21, p. 250.
91. *Jewish Morning Journal*, New York, December 21, 1949; *Aufbau*, New York, May 19, 1950.

CHAPTER X

1. *Report of the Anglo-American Committee of Inquiry regarding the Problems of European Jewry and Palestine*, London 1946, Appendix II, pp. 52-53 (American edition, Washington 1946, pp. 60-61). See also the *American Jewish Year Book*, 1946-1947, (Vol. 48), p. 358.
2. In the files of the American Jewish Committee.
3. *Věstník*, IX/16, p. 229.
4. Sidney Liskofsky, "Immigration Statistics, Israel," in the *American Jewish Year Book*, 1950 (Vol. 51), p. 408.
5. Jewish Telegraphic Agency, July 19, 1948.
6. *Ibid.*, August 30, 1948.
7. *Ibid.*, April 16, 1948. Okali was later arrested in the purge of 1950.
8. *Ibid.*, August 30, 1948.
9. Dov Tibbon, "Immigration Statistics, Israel," in the *American Jewish Year Book*, 1951 (Vol. 52), p. 399.
10. *Aufbau*, New York, March 28, 1949.
11. Dov Tibbon, *op. cit.*
12. *Aufbau, loc. cit.*
13. Emigration procedures are described in *Aufbau, loc. cit.*, and in two detailed reports, of June and July 1949, in the files of the American Jewish Committee.
14. Report of June 26, 1949, in the files of the American Jewish Committee.
15. *Aufbau, loc. cit.*
16. Report of June 26, 1949, in the files of the American Jewish Committee.
17. *Ibid.*
18. *Věstník* XII/34, p. 385.
19. See n. 46, chap. IX, above.

20. See n. 35, chap. IX, above.
21. See n. 36, chap. IX, above.
22. Jewish Telegraphic Agency, January 5, 1949.
23. *Jewish Morning Journal,* New York, May 9, 1950.
24. Jewish Telegraphic Agency, February 26, 1948.
25. *Ibid.,* July 12, 1949.
26. *American Jewish Year Book,* 1951 (Vol. 52), p. 196.
27. See n. 35, chap. IX, above.
28. See n. 36, chap. IX, above.

CHAPTER XI

1. See, among others: Peter Meyer, "Czechoslovakia Purges a Purger," *The New Leader,* New York, December 24, 1951, pp. 4-6; Al Findley, "The Case of Rudolph Slansky: Stalinist Anti-Semitism in Czechoslovakia," *Labor Action,* New York, January 14, 1952, p. 6; G. E. R. Gedye, "Czech Communism—A Tottering Cause," *The Progressive,* Madison, Wis., February 1952, pp. 11-13; Max Nomad, "The Case of Rudolph Slansky," *Jewish Frontier,* New York, February 1952, pp. 19-21;"Lépuration en Tchécoslovaquie et l'antisemitisme," *Bulletin de l'association d'études et d'informations politiques internationales* (*B.E.I.P.I.*), Paris, Vol. IV, No. 61, February 1952, supplement, pp. 6-7; Peter Meyer, "Jews Are Scapegoats in Czech Red Purge," *New York Post,* March 21, 1952; "Czechoslovakia: Short History of the Purge—The Jewish Victims—The Anti-Semitic Campaign—Oren Arrested in Prague,"*Jews Behind the Iron Curtain,* Library of Jewish Information, The American Jewish Committee, New York, No. 7, April 1952, pp. 3-8; P. K. and V. V., "Cistky v Komunistické Straně Československa" (Purges in the Communist Party of Czechoslovakia), *Research and Publications Service, Czechoslovak Section, National Committee for a Free Europe,* New York, 32 pp. (mimeographed), June 1952; "List of Members of the Czechoslovak Communist Party, Victims of Purges Since 1948," *Information and Publication Service, National Committee for a Free Europe,* New York, n. d.; Peter Meyer, "The Jewish Purge in the Satellite Countries," *Commentary,* New York, September 1952, pp. 212-218.

2. For reports on the role of Zionists in the Rajk trial see *New York Times,* September 20, 1949 and *Jewish Telegraphic Agency* dispatch, September 21, 1949. A detailed report about Rajk's activities and fall in our study on Jews in Hungary.

3. For the repercussions of the Rajk trial in Czechoslovakia, see *New York Times,* September 17, 1949.

4. For a comprehensive report on the demotion and arrest of Klinger, Kosta and Loebl, see *Christian Science Monitor,* Boston, January 4, 1950. Loebl's arrest was reported in the *Jewish Chronicle,* London, on December 12, 1949. All these arrests were later acknowledged in the Czechoslovak Communist press. The explanation of the arrest of Milan Rejman was given in a report by Ladislav Kopríva to a meeting of the Central Committee of the Communist Party of Czechoslovakia on February 25, 1950.

5. Noel Field, his wife Herta, his adopted daughter, Erica, and his brother, Herman, all suspected of having worked for the Soviet military intelligence, disappeared behind the Iron Curtain in 1949 and 1950. Noel Field was mentioned as an American spy in the Rajk trial in Hungary. Nový's connection with him was first hinted at by Ladislav Kopríva in the report mentioned in note 4. A year later, Václav Kopecký mentioned Field again (*Rudé Právo,* February 25, 1951). For a comprehensive report on the Field case, see Craig Thompson, "What Has Stalin Done with Noel Field," *The Saturday Evening Post,* New York, December 15, pp. 17-19, 83-84.

6. Clementis resigned from his post as Minister of Foreign Affairs on March 14, 1950, was condemned as a "nationalist" at a party congress in Slovakia in April 1950, and was arrested shortly before the February 1951 meeting of the Central Committee

of the Communist Party. Reports about his disappearance, sent abroad before the official announcement, led to the arrest of the American correspondent, William N. Oatis.

7. Sling's demotion was first announced in a report from Vienna, published in the *New York Times*, October 20, 1950. His arrest was officially admitted in *Rudé Právo*, November 14, 1950, which published a detailed report about his "plot" on February 27, 1951.

8. Kopecký's report on the Sling-Svermová conspiracy was published in *Rudé Právo*, February 27, 1951.

9. Communique on Slánský's removal in *Rudé Právo*, September 7, and *New York Times*, September 8, 1951.

10. Gottwald's speech on Slánský's deviations, delivered before the September 1951 session of the Central Committee, was not published in the party press but reproduced in a circular sent to party organizations. It is quoted in "Cistky v Komunistické Strane Ceskoslovenska," published by the National Committee for a Free Europe, New York, June 1952, pp. 16-17

11. *Rudé Právo*, November 28, 1951.

12. *Ibid.*, December 8, 1951, *New York Times*, December 8, 1951.

13. *New York Times*, January 27, 1952. Freund was later denounced by Zápotocký as a dangerous saboteur. (*New York Times*, June 8, 1952).

14. *Ibid.*, January 30, 1952.

15. Reported by the Czechoslovak Section of the National Committee for a Free Europe, New York.

16. Bareš-Breitenfeld's demotion was first announced by the *Neue Zürcher Zeitung*, Zürich, January 19, 1952. At about the same time his name disappeared from the masthead of the magazine *Tvorba*. *Tvorba* ceased publication on the orders of the Central Committee on February 14, 1952.

17. Geminder's name disappeared from the masthead of the Cominform's *For a Lasting Peace, for People's Democracy* in January 1952. A Czech refugee reported that Geminder was transferred to the Czechoslovak short-wave broadcasting station in November 1951, disappearing from there a few days after the fall of Slánský (*Zpráva o Ceskoslovensku* [Report on Czechoslovakia], Research and Publication Service, Czechoslovak R.I.C., National Committee for a Free Europe, vol. III, no. 1, January 1952, pp. 11-12).

18. *New York Times*, June 5, 1952.

19. *Ibid.*, July 15, 1952.

20. *Neue Zürcher Zeitung*, March 5, 1952, *New York Times*, April 6, 1952.

21. *New York Times*, April 6, 1952.

22. Weisskopf's demotion was reported in the *New York Times*, March 2, 1952, and in the *Neue Zürcher Zeitung*, March 5, 1952; his —otherwise unconfirmed— arrest in the *New York Times*, June 26, 1952. It is worth mentioning that Weisskopf, when he was first secretary of the Czechoslovak embassy in Washington, denied in a press conference reports on antisemitic trends in Czechoslovakia (see *New York Times*, March 5, 1949).

23. List of Members of the Czechoslovak Communist Party, Victims of Purges since 1948, National Committee for a Free Europe, New York, p. 3.

24. *Zpráva o Ceskoslovensku* (Report on Czechoslovakia), National Committee for a Free Europe, New York, vol. III, No. 4, April 1952, pp. 10-11.

25. *Israelitisches Wochenblatt*, Zürich, May 18, 1951; *Jewish Daily Forward*, New York, May 21, 1951.

26. *New York Times*, March 4, 1952.

26a. *New York World-Telegram and Sun*, May 22, 1952.

27. *New York Times*, March 18, 1952

28. *Neue Zürcher Zeitung*, February 18, 1952. Karel Stern declared that he had joined the Communists after the war because he believed that they would end antisemitism. The systematic hunt of all leading Communists of Jewish origin destroyed this expectation.

29. *New York Times*, September 6, 1949.
30. *Israelitisches Wochenblatt*, Zürich, December 7, 1951.
31. *Ibid.*, January 11, 1952.
32. *Ibid.*, See also *Jewish Morning Journal*, New York, May 22, 1952, for the arrest of Dr. Wilhelm Buechler, accused of being a "Trotskyite Zionist."
33. *Neue Zürcher Zeitung*, March 11, 1952.
34. *New York Times*, February 2, March 24, May 23, June 16, 1952; *Jewish Chronicle*, London, February 29, March 28, 1952.
35. *Jewish Morning Journal*, New York, May 20, 1952.
36. *Tvorba*, Prague, December 13, 1951.
37. *Rudé Právo*, December 19, and *New York Times*, December 20, 1951, *Jewish Life*, New York, February 1952, p. 20, quoted the passage on religious equality, but omitted the references to "Jerusalem" and "Jewish and other capitalists."
38. See Chapter V of our study.
39. *Lidové Noviny*, Prague, January 17, 1952.
40. *Pravda*, Bratislava, January 23, 1952; the article was quoted on Radio Bratislava the same day. See also Jewish Telegraphic Agency dispatch February 21, 1952.
41. *L'ud*, Bratislava, January 26, 1952.
42. See Chapter VII of our study.
43. *Rudé Právo*, March 4, 1952; see also *Ost-Probleme*, Frankfurt, March 29, 1952, p. 396.

CHAPTER XII

1. There is an interesting piece of circumstantial evidence for the opinion that the original text of the Prague indictment was either written in Russian or existed in Russian translation before the trial. The trial against Slánský began and the indictment was published in Prague on November 20, 1952. On November 21, *For a Lasting Peace, for a People's Democracy*, the English-language organ of the Cominform appearing in Bucharest, printed a five-column-long summary of the indictment, with many direct quotations from its text. The dispatch was dated "Prague, November 20, by telegraph from our own correspondent." But the first name of one co-conspirator, Hanuš Lomský, was repeatedly spelled Ganus. The sound and letter "H" exists in Czech as well as in Rumanian and English, but not in Russian, where it is transcribed as "G." The "dispatch from Prague" evidently used the Russian text of the indictment.
2. *Rudé Právo*, November 21, 1952, p. 1.
3. *Ibid.*, pp. 3-6. All our quotations from the indictment are taken from this official publication.
4. Some of them, like Frejka and Geminder, were from German-speaking Jewish families and had attended German schools. Before World War II they had considered themselves ethnic Germans. After the war, they declared themselves ethnic Czechs.
5. The only exception was Ludvík Frejka, the son of a doctor.
6. The reference is to Herman Field, brother of Noel Field, who was at that time working for an United States relief organization in Cracow. See Chapter XI, note 5.
7. Such as, for instance, the fact that Slánský was on the list of people to be saved from the Nazis in 1939.
8. There are three sources for information concerning what happened in the courtroom. The broadcasts of the Czechoslovak radio were monitored, transcribed, and translated by American listening posts. A detailed report was published in *Rudé Právo*. And "verbatim minutes" were published—after thorough editing—in book form in Prague in February 1953. All three versions were equally unreliable as to what really happened at the trial because all three versions had been edited according to

the Communist regime's needs. But all three are equally "authentic" in the sense that they all equally reflect what the regime wanted the people to believe, what it wanted to achieve by the show trial. At the time of this writing only the first two versions (the broadcasts and *Rudé Právo*) were available in the United States. There are some slight differences between them. In order to eliminate possible errors in transmission or hasty translation at the listening post, we are here using—with a few exceptions—the version published in *Rudě Právo*.

9. *Rudé Právo,* November 21, 1952, p. 2.
10. *Ibid*., November 22, 1952, p. 2.
11. *Ibid.*
12. *Ibid*., November 23, 1952, p. 4.
13. *Ibid*., November 25, 1952, p. 3.
14. This quotation is taken from the Prague radio broadcast as recorded by the listening post. In *Rudé Právo,* November 25, 1952, p. 4, it is reproduced in a slightly abbreviated form. To the first question, reproduced in the text, Fischl answers: "I am of petty bourgeois origin, son of a merchant and a Jewish bourgeois nationalist."
15. *Rudé Právo,* November 26, 1952, p. 2.
16. *Ibid*., p. 4.
17. *Ibid*., November 21, 1952, p. 3.
18. *Ibid*., November 22, 1952, p. 4.
19. *Ibid*., November 24, 1952, p. 5.
20. *Ibid*., November 25, 1952, p. 2.
21. *Ibid*., November 26, 1952, p. 6.
22. *Ibid*., November 22, 1952, p. 2.
23. *Ibid*., November 23, 1952, p. 4.
24. The reference is to the Overseas News Agency in New York.
25. *Rudé Právo,* November 23, 1952, p. 4.
26. This passage is quoted from the Prague radio broadcast.
27. *Rudé Právo,* November 23, 1952, p. 5.
28. *Ibid*., November 24, 1952, p. 5.
29. Štěpán Plaček, a Communist of Jewish origin, was a high official in the Ministry of the Interior. Jarmila Taussigová was a member of the Communist Party Central Control Commission.
30. *Rudé Právo,* November 26, 1952, p. 4.
31. *Ibid*., November 21, 1952, p. 3.
32. *Ibid*., November 27, 1952, pp. 3-4.
33. *Ibid*., p. 1.
34. *Ibid*., November 24, 1952, p. 1
35. *Ibid*., November 22, 1952, p. 5.
36. There are good reasons to doubt that Olbracht really wrote this article. He had been sick for years and it was common knowledge that his articles were written by Ladislav Štoll, who soon after the trial became Minister of Universities and Higher Education. Olbracht, who was of half-Jewish origin, died a few weeks later.
37. *Rudé Právo,* November 28, 1952, p. 2.
38. *Ibid*., November 24, 1952, p. 7.
39. *Ibid*., November 25, 1952, p. 5.
40. *New York Herald Tribune,* November 26, 1952.
41. *Jewish Chronicle,* London, November 28, 1952.
42. *Neue Zürcher Zeitung,* Zürich, December 28, 1952.
43. *Zpráva o Československu,* vol. IV, no. 1, January 1952, p. 17.
44. Radio Prague broadcast, December 16, 1952.
45. *Pravda,* Moscow, January 13, 1953.
46. *Pravda,* April 6, and *Izvestia,* April 9, 1953.
47. *The New York Times,* April 17, 1953.
48. Associated Press report from Vienna, April 24, 1953.

II. Poland

BY

BERNARD D. WEINRYB

CHAPTER I

Political and Social Background

In Poland today there are some 35-to 40,000 Jews, almost one-half being concentrated in Silesia. These are all that remain of a prewar Jewish community that totalled over three and one-third million.

Jews have lived in Poland probably as far back as the tenth century. Poland for many centuries lacked an indigenous middle class, and Polish Jewry, a great mass of poverty-stricken craftsmen, middlemen and innkeepers, with a small group of rich merchants and toll and tax farmers supplied its place. Within their own community they succeeded in building up a strong organization with regional and central bodies that fostered the development of Jewish life, religion, learning, and charity, conducted important economic, social and political activities, and represented and defended Polish Jewry. For the most part the Jews were protected by the kings, hated and abused by the clergy, townspeople and the great mass of peasantry, and despised but often also protected and employed as middlemen by the nobility.

With the partitioning and disappearance of Poland in 1795, Polish Jewry passed under the rule of three separate political and economic systems. The greatest number were concentrated in the Russian section of Poland, where their initiative and enterprise played an important part in the development of commerce and the building up of such industrial centers as Lodz, Bialystok, and Warsaw. In Galicia, an economically backward region, about a million Jews lived in poverty; nevertheless they enjoyed a great many political rights. In the part of Poland annexed by Prussia there lived a small but economically influential Jewish community.

Poland was reborn out of the First World War. In January 1919 the first Sejm (Diet) was elected; right and left were almost evenly represented, with the center holding the balance. The right comprised the National Democrats (ND), representing the Polish middle class, and two smaller groups: the National Christian Party, composed of big landowners and industrialists; and Christian Democrats, dominated by the Catholic Church. These were all conservative, nationalistic, and very often antisemitic, the ND having already sponsored anti-Jewish boycotts before the war.

The bulk of the center was composed of the Peasant Party (Piast), which represented the more affluent peasants. To the left belonged first of all the Polish Socialist Party (PPS), which had been founded in 1892 and combined nationalist with socialist tendencies; and also the National Workers Party (NPR); the Populist Party, representing the poorer peasants (later merged with the Piast); and a few Communists. The constitution promulgated by this Sejm in 1921 was generally democratic and provided for equal rights for all minorities. In the next Sejm (1922), again, neither left nor right enjoyed a majority, though the former had lost heavily. The political situation was unstable, with center and right-of-center regimes succeeding each other.

In May 1926 came Marshal Pilsudski's *coup d'état* which, though at first supported by the left, soon led to the placing of military men in important state positions ("Colonels' Regime"), attempts to destroy the existing parties, formation of the "Non-party Bloc of Co-operation with the Government," and ultimately to suppression of the center and left and the establishment of a semidictatorial government.[1] After the death of Pilsudski the Non-party Bloc was dissolved because of internal differences, but the Colonels' Regime continued to rule. In 1937 "the Camp of National Unity" (OZON–Obóz Zjednoczenia Narodowego) was formed; it attempted to rally the nation around the army, nationalism and Catholicism, and soon became the chief supporter of the regime.

Almost all of these regimes were motivated by nationalistic Polish sentiments; they attempted to suppress or discriminate against large non-Polish minority groups.

On June 28, 1919, the representatives of the new Polish state signed, rather reluctantly, a treaty with the Allied and Associated Powers; this treaty, in addition to guaranteeing the civil and political equality of the minorities and safeguarding their rights as citizens, proclaimed the right of minorities to use their own languages both in private and public, and to establish their own schools and charitable, religious, and social institutions. Although the substance of these provisions was embodied in the constitution of 1921, Poland considered this treaty forced upon her, never fully implemented it, and renounced it entirely in 1934.

The very inauguration of Poland's independence had been marred by pogroms and mob outrages against Jews (Kielce, Lvov, Vilna). Later, during the Polish-Russian war, Jews were often accused of helping the enemy and were sometimes shot.

The constitution of March 17, 1921, though affirming the equal rights of minorities, required the enactment of special legislation to give force to these constitutional rights. The government did not introduce into the Sejm any bill calling for abolition of old repressive laws conflicting with the new constitution. Local authorities and courts acted on the assumption that the constitution promised equality but had not introduced it. Some restrictions dating back to Czarist times were still in force: Jews were forbidden by local authorities to acquire land, were forced to pay special taxes for the care of their sick, etc.

Position of Jewish Minority

The treaty concerning minorities provided that all persons "habitually resident" within the boundaries of Poland should automatically become citizens. Polish authorities, however, using the French text of the treaty, interpreted the expression *domicilié* to mean those whose names were entered in population registers. Since in the course of the war many documents had been destroyed, thousands of Jews were unable to prove their eligibility for citizenship. Time and again Jewish representatives drew the attention of the authorities to this, but to no avail. Only in 1926, after the so-called Polish-Jewish rapprochement (intended by the government for "foreign consumption"[2]), was the acquisition of citizenship facilitated by instructions from the government to local administrative authorities. It took an additional five years of negotiations to abolish, in 1931, the restrictions dating from Czarist times.[3] In practice, however, discrimination still continued.

There was no equality in the civil service; hardly any Jews were given government or municipal posts. In Galicia, where Jewish civil servants had been employed by the Austrian government, they were gradually dismissed on one pretext or another. At one time the Sejm even considered establishing an official *numerus clausus* for Jewish students in institutions of higher education, but was prevented from doing so by pressure from France. Universities and professional schools, however, introduced their own *numerus clausus* in medicine, engineering, and certain other professions. At the same time, increasing government control of economic life resulted in a great deal of discrimination against Jews. With the introduction of monopolies for match and tobacco production and the sale of salt, for instance, most Jews were eliminated from these fields.

In 1920 promulgation of the Sunday Rest Law caused serious economic hardships to Jews; their stores and workshops, which were closed on Saturday, had thus to be idle two days of the week. Liquor licenses were issued mainly to non-Jews. The law forbidding Jewish ritual slaughtering (Shehita) passed on April 17, 1936 deprived large numbers of Jews of their livelihood, as did the law for the regulation of the cattle and meat trade enacted in 1938.

Excesses against Jews were organized by the National Democratic Party and its offshoot, the NARA (Anti-Jewish National Radical Camp). There was boycotting and picketing of Jewish businesses and shops. In some of the universities and professional schools "ghetto benches" were introduced, while in the bar association and other professional and economic groups "Aryan paragraphs" were introduced or considered. Demands for increased migration of the rural population into towns and cities so as to lessen the Jewish hold on commerce were voiced, and proposals were made for nationalization of some types of industry.

The influence of Nazi Germany's anti-Jewish propaganda, the deepening economic crisis, and the success of the anti-Semitic propaganda of the opposition parties, brought about, after Pilsudski's death in 1935, a change in the heretofore relatively tolerant attitude of the Colonels' Regime. In his statement of June 4, 1936, Premier Skladkowski emphasized that although nobody should suffer violence in Poland, the economic struggle against Jews was justified. Later in the year Colonel Beck, the Polish Foreign Minister, and other Polish representatives at the League of Nations at Geneva, emphasized Poland's interest in finding places for Jewish emigration. The Premier, in answer to an interpellation, stated: "The government of the Republic agrees . . . that one of the most effective means of solving the Jewish question in Poland is a substantial reduction of the number of Jews through emigration. . . ."[4]

Some cabinet members sponsored bills depriving Jews of the right to vote, barring them from civil service, and restricting their admission to the professions. This policy culminated in a flood of local and unofficial restrictions against Jews; in the toleration in 1937 of pogroms in a number of towns (Minsk-Mazowiecki, Czestochowa, Brest), of which the one in the town of Przytyk represented the most gruesome example; in boycotting activities tolerated by the government; and in the official policy of "evacuation" of the Jews from Poland, which led to the sending in 1938 of a mission to Madagascar to explore the possibilities of Jewish settlement there. In the same year special laws were enacted withdrawing Polish citizenship from Jews resident abroad. Such was the setting in which the Jews of Poland attempted to build a life for themselves between the wars.

Poland after the First World War, had, according to the census of 1921, a Jewish population of 2,854,364, which constituted 10.5 per cent of the entire population. Ten years later, at the second census of 1931, there were 3,113,900 Jews in Poland, or 9.8 per cent of the population. Eight years later, in 1939, the number of Jews was estimated to be 3,351,000, out of a total population of 35,393,000, or 9.7 per cent. The number of Jews increased by more than a quarter of a million in the decade ending in 1931, and by 238,000 in the subsequent 8 years. This amounts to an average yearly growth of 0.9 per cent. There is, however, a difference between the first decade and the subsequent years. In the 1920's—particularly in the first half—before the quota system was instituted by the United States, much more emigration took place than in the 1930's. In the years 1921-1930

Jewish emigrants from Poland numbered 292,200, or more than one per cent yearly of the Jewish population, whereas in the years 1931-1938 only 117,138 left Poland,[5] or 0.45 annually. In fact, the Jewish birth rate declined during the interwar years.[6]

TABLE I
JEWISH RATE OF INCREASE, POLAND, 1929, 1936

	Birth rate[a]		Death rate[a]		Net increase[a]	
	Jews	Non-Jews	Jews	Non-Jews	Jews	Non-Jews
1929	20.0	31.1	10.3	17.7	9.7	13.4
1936	19.3	28.1	10.1	15.6	9.2	12.5

[a]Per 1,000 of population.

Although the death rate was somewhat higher among non-Jews, their natural increase was greater; this, together with the larger ratio of Jewish emigration,[7] resulted in a constant drop in the ratio of Jews in the country (from 10.5 per cent in 1921 to 9.7 per cent in 1939).

Still more pronounced was the drop of the Jewish ratio in the town and city population. Here the main reason was the larger influx of non-Jews into cities and towns and the inclusion of suburbs and nearby villages in town areas. This process, which began at the end of the nineteenth century in Eastern Europe, was accelerated after the First World War. In 1931, more than three-quarters of the Jews in Poland lived in cities and towns constituting 27.3 per cent of the entire urban population (towns with 20,000 inhabitants and more). But this percentage was much smaller than the 31.6 per cent of a decade earlier.

The drop in the Jewish ratio in the city population in the 1930's must have been still greater. The deteriorating situation of the village drove many to the cities; the government's deliberate policy of "nationalizing" commerce swelled this tide; and antisemites by boycott and violence attempted to reduce the number of Jews engaged in urban occupations.

More than one-third of the Jewish population in 1931 lived on income derived from commerce (it had been two-fifths in 1921), and more than two-fifths on income derived from industry and handicrafts.

Of the 392,892 Jewish salaried workers and wage earners in 1931, almost two-thirds (65.6 per cent) were manual workers; about one-quarter (23.5 per cent) white-collar workers and professionals; 5.2 per cent were employed in domestic service; and 5.7 per cent as home workers.[9]

Jewish participation in trade began to decline first proportionally, and then later also in absolute numbers. The ratio of Jews among the gainfully employed in trade fell, between 1921 and 1937, from 61.8 per cent to 59 per cent in 1931, and to 52.7 per cent in 1937.

TABLE II

JEWISH POPULATION ACCORDING TO SOURCE OF INCOME, 1931[8]

Occupation	Number (in thousands)	Per cent
Agriculture	125.1	4.0
Industry and handicrafts	1,313.3	42.5
Commerce and insurance	1,140.5	36.6
Transport and communications	139.4	4.5
Liberal professions and religion	193.0	6.2
Domestic service	22.5	0.7
Unemployed	146.3	4.7
Others	33.8	0.8
TOTAL	3,113.9	100.0

The wage earners were divided by occupation as follows:

TABLE III

JEWISH WAGE EARNERS, ACCORDING TO OCCUPATION, 1931

Agriculture, fisheries	0.2%
Industry and handicrafts	62.0
Commerce and insurance	17.3
Transport and communications	2.0
Public service and religion	4.3
Education and medicine	6.8
Domestic service	5.2
Unknown	2.2

In Warsaw there was also a drop in the absolute number of Jews employed in commerce. Whereas the number of non-Jews engaged in commerce and insurance rose between 1921 and 1931 by some 27,973 persons (from 86,360 to 114,333), the number of Jews gainfully employed in this field fell by nearly 9,000 (from 129,251 to 120,705).[10] The percentage of Jews engaged in commerce in Warsaw fell from 41.6 to 34.2 per cent.

Statistics on the classification of enterprises in 1933 show that in Warsaw the percentage of Jewish enterprises fell, between 1921 and 1933, from 73 to 53.9, and the absolute number by some 38 per cent;[11] in the provinces of Polesie and Volhynia the ratio of Jewish enterprises fell from 93.8 and 92 per cent respectively, to 75.9 and 73.6 per cent respectively, and the absolute number of Jewish proprietors fell by 7.4 per cent in Polesie and 16 per cent of Volhynia. At the same time the number of non-Jewish proprietors had risen by about 40 per cent in Warsaw, 450 per cent in Polesie, and 350 per cent in Volhynia.[12] Incomplete data from other regions show a similar trend.

Along with this decline in Jewish proprietorship there was a growing reluctance to employ Jews in industry and handicrafts. Even in factories owned by Jews it was difficult for Jewish labor to obtain jobs. Non-Jewish factory workers were hesitant about admitting Jews into their midst. There were even instances of workers in a Jewish factory striking in protest against the hiring of Jewish workers.[13]

Jewish participation in the crafts was considerable, in some of which they played a very important role. Eighty per cent of the tailors, 40 per cent of the shoemakers, 25 per cent of the butchers and bakers, and 75 per cent of the barbers in Poland were Jews. However, increasing competition from non-Jews, legal restrictions, and the deteriorating economic situation of the peasantry, the principal customers for the clothing, footwear and similar articles produced by the artisans, greatly reduced opportunities in the handicrafts.

By January 1929 there were 78,499 registered Jewish artisans[14] constituting 51.9 per cent of all registered artisans in all except western Poland (Poznań), where only a few Jews lived. There were, however, some 30-40,000 or more Jewish artisans who did not register.[15] We find them a few years later, when the period of registration was drawing to a close, in danger of losing their right to work because of their inability to fulfill all the legal demands for registration.

The Industrial Law of 1927 made the training of apprentices dependent on the extent of the dwelling facilities possessed by the artisan, and on an officially signed agreement between master and apprentice. In the years of crisis and declining income, the housing conditions of many artisans worsened and they were both unable and unwilling to undertake the obligations connected with training apprentices. At any rate available figures show that only a negligible number of apprentices were to be found in Jewish artisans' workshops.

The number of Jewish students at Polish universities and other professional schools decreased from 9,130 in 1922-23 to 4,113 in 1938-39.[16] Trade and handicrafts were unable to absorb the 40-50,000 Jewish youths reaching the age of 16 each year and seeking jobs. Emigration, except for the first postwar years, absorbed only a part of this natural growth. In the years 1926-1938, an average of about 16-17,000 Jews emigrated annually, a considerable part of whom consisted of older people going to join their children overseas (the immigration laws generally made the admittance of such people easier).

What occupations did the new generation and those eliminated from the professions and trade turn to? Great numbers were certainly unemployed; others, however, tried to make their way in other sections of the economy. Of the Jews gainfully employed at the time of the census of 1921, 36.6 per cent were employed in industry and handicrafts; a decade later there were 45.3 per cent so occupied. In the two main cities, Warsaw and Lodz, this percentage rose from 36.6 and 44.1 respectively in 1921, to 46.8 and 55.8 respectively in 1931. From 1931 to the outbreak of the war in September 1939, this trend would seem to have increased.

Not that industry and handicrafts were generally expanding and increasing their absorptive capacity. On the contrary, the index of industrial production fell from 100 in 1928 to 82 in 1930, to 66 in 1935, and rose again to 85 in 1937. But Jews in Poland, like people generally in times of economic distress, sought the lowest-paid jobs, or organized new kinds of production. Some new small industries were developed and Jews tried to find work in these, for the most part as unskilled laborers or in smaller establishments where there were no organized groups of workers to keep Jews out, and where a lowering of wages or a lengthening of working hours was possible. Similarly, homework, with its attendant evils, was expanded in some branches. Jewish organizations such as the American Jewish Joint Distribution Committee (JDC), Reconstruction Fund, the Organization for Rehabilitation Through Training (ORT), and the like, organized cooperatives and workshops where the unemployed could rapidly learn a new trade and find employment.

To be sure, there were also wealthy Jewish merchants, industrialists and bankers in Poland. Jewish firms played an important role in the metal and textile industries, in the export of sugar, textiles, timber, and metal products—although in the last prewar years some were taken over by government agencies or government-sponsored cartels. The owners of these large Jewish firms, however, together with their Jewish employees, comprised only a small fraction of the Jewish population in Poland. Of the 45,044 industrial enterprises in Jewish hands which hired labor in 1931, less than one per cent were large; 25.1 per cent were middle-sized; and 74.2 per cent were small. Only 6.7 per cent of the Jewish urban population belonged to the employer class; the rest were independent craftsmen and merchants without hired help (55.5 per cent) and workers.[17]

Only a very small percentage of the Jewish population belonged to the wealthy or the middle classes; the bulk were either poor lower-middle-class people or still poorer proletarians.[18]

Chapter II

The Jewish Community Between the Wars

Jews in Poland led an active and extensive communal life, although circumstances and the policy of the Polish government in the years between the wars hampered its full development. There existed in Poland the tradition of an autonomous Jewish *kehillah*, or community, which for a number of centuries had not only local but also central bodies, the *Vaadim*, or Regional and Four-Land Councils. In the nineteenth century, when the Csarist government dissolved the Jewish communities (1822), they were replaced by synagogue councils officially supposed to attend to synagogue and religious matters only, but which in fact became a substitute for the *kehillah*.

The law of 1919 concerning the Jewish communities, which dealt with the former Russian Congress Poland only, provided for a national association of communities under the administration of a Religious Council. The Minorities Treaty guaranteed the right of the minorities to use their own languages both in private and in public, and to establish their own schools and institutions. Article 10 of the treaty authorized the Jewish communities to appoint local educational committees for the distribution of the public funds to be allocated to Jewish schools. Article 11 provided that Jews should not be compelled to violate their sabbath. The rights of minorities were, as we know, also guaranteed in the Polish constitution of March 17, 1921. The leaders of the Jewish secular groups in Poland at that time envisaged a broad system of autonomous Jewish communities maintained by funds from the government's treasury. They pressed for new elections to the community councils, to be held throughout the new Polish state.

The communal elections of 1924, however, embraced only Galicia and Congress Poland, and the jurisdiction of the communities was restricted to purely religious matters. The new statute governing the Jewish communities promulgated in 1927 gave the local communities a somewhat wider scope of activity: maintenance of synagogues, the rabbinate, ritual baths (*mikvah*) and cemeteries; supervision of Jewish butchers; administration of Jewish schools and charitable institutions. A Central Council composed of 34 lay members and 17 rabbis was also provided for; its activity was limited to religious matters. Membership in the community was compulsory. The community had the right to levy its own taxes, in addition to collecting fees for ritual slaughter and burial. The state authorities assisted the *kehillah* in the collection of these taxes. The rabbi in each community was *ex officio* one of the eight members of the board. Larger communities had a council and a board. The election ordinance issued by the Minister of Education and Religion provided for direct, equal, secret and proportional elections to the boards and councils of the *kehillah*. All male Jews over the age of 25 had the right to vote; candidates for office were required to be not less than 30 years of age.

The religious groups were on the whole content with the religious character assigned the communities by the government. Some even hoped to dominate the *kehilloth* by taking advantage of the provision (Article 20 of the communal election statute) giving the government power to deprive non-observing Jews of the right to vote. The more secular groups regarded this as an attempt to narrow the community's field of activity and to discard national autonomy. They were opposed to the purely religious character of the Central Council provided for by statute. Instead an attempt was made to set up a voluntary Central Council for Jewish Affairs; the parties, however, failed to agree upon a common program.

The autonomy of the Jewish community also suffered interference in other respects. The government, because of its extensive supervisory rights, was able to confine the *kehilloth* largely to religious functions and to favor the orthodox and conservative groups at the expense of the progressive. Community councils were frequently dissolved by the authorities and replaced by commissioners, who were kept in office for many years.

At the same time the government contributed very little toward the support of Jewish religious functions. In the years 1927/28–1938/39 the allotment to the Jewish community amounted to 0.79 per cent and 0.89 per cent of the whole allotment for religious activities. In other words, the grant to the Jews was about twelve times smaller than the percentage of the Jews in the total population.[1]

The nature of the activities of the *kehilloth* may be gathered from an analysis of their budgets. There are figures available for 599 *kehilloth* embracing, in 1931, about 82.5 per cent of the entire Jewish population. In these communities the distribution of expenditures in 1929 was as shown in Table IV.[2]

The smaller the community, the smaller the percentage spent on education, health and social welfare, and the larger the percentage for religious purposes.

The *kehilloth*, especially the larger ones having a council as well as a board, were also vehicles of democratic expression for the Jewish population. There, the representatives of Jewish parties and groups could advance their programs and seek to influence Jewish public opinion. Externally, the *kehilloth* also served to some extent as representative bodies

TABLE IV

DISTRIBUTION OF EXPENDITURES, KEHILLOTH, 1929

Activity	Per cent
Religious functions	29.7
Social welfare	17.5
Education	9.4
Public health	4.7
Investment	7.2
Palestine	0.4
Taxes	0.5
Debts and interest	11.2
Administration	14.1
Other expenses	5.3
TOTAL	100.0

of the Jewish local population. They did not, however, become generally representative of Polish Jewry because, as we have mentioned, the Central Council provided for in the statute never materialized.

To a certain extent the Association of Jewish Representatives in the Sejm and the Club of Jewish Deputies in the Senate served as a central Jewish organization. But the effectiveness of the Jewish representatives in Parliament, and of Jewish community life in general, was greatly reduced by the division of the Jewish population into multiple parties and groupings. Not until the last prewar years were attempts made to unite around a minimum program. Mounting antisemitic pressure brought most of the parties and organizations into a common "Temporary Representation." The calling of a general Jewish congress based on democratic elections to create a nation-wide Jewish representation was also considered.

Jewish Parties

To begin with, there was the orthodox Agudath Israel (organized in 1916), which was more a religious organization than a political party. It claimed to represent that majority of Polish Jews which was religious and followed tradition. The Agudah in Poland emphasized the religious factor in Jewish life and this attitude dominated its political actions. It waged a bitter struggle to preserve the purely religious character of the *kehilloth*. In politics, however, the Agudah was not always guided by purely religious motives. In its struggle with other Jewish parties the Agudah was at times guided by the Polish government's promises and split the Jewish front. It broke with the Club of Jewish Deputies to join the Non-party Bloc organized by the Colonels' Regime. At first bitterly anti-Zionist, the Agudah became pro-Palestinian in the last prewar years as economic and political pressure mounted, and Palestine came to absorb the majority of Polish Jewish emigrants.

The Zionist movement in Poland was a part of the World Zionist Organization. Following the First World War Polish Jewry became the backbone of the movement. From the very beginning of Poland's independence, the Zionists were of the opinion that, living in concentrated groups with its own way of life, Polish Jewry needed national Jewish rights, or national autonomy. Their activity embraced, therefore, the political struggle for civil and national rights, the fight against antisemitism, the maintenance of Jewish autonomous institutions, the fostering of Hebrew, and the diffusion of Hebrew culture. They also struggled for influence in the *kehillah*, and sought to strengthen the economic and political position of the Jews. They regarded the *kehillah* as the key institution of Jewish national autonomy.

The General Zionists, both conservative and progressive, were well organized and influential; they voiced the overwhelming sentiment in favor of Palestine and spoke for the Jewish middle class. In most national and local elections they commanded a considerable number of votes, sometimes even a majority of the Jewish vote.

The Mizrachi, or religious Zionists, may be placed between the Agudah and the Zionists. They emphasized Jewish religious values and traditional life in their organizations and school system, and at the same time were strongly Zionist. In communal and political matters the Mizrachi usually collaborated with other nationalistic Jewish groups.

The Labor Zionists were divided into four groups: Poale Zion and Zeire Zion (which merged later on), Hitachduth, and the Left Poale Zion. They were made up for the most part of white-collar workers, some manual workers and intelligentsia, and a number of the middle-class youth. They combined Zionism with socialism, and attracted most of the youth preparing for imigration to Palestine. In the 1930's most of these groups were united into the Palestine Labor League. In national elections the Labor Zionists could seldom elect a deputy, but in the local city and Jewish community councils they often had considerable influence.

In the 1930's the Revisionist group made its appearance; its greatest strength was drawn from the younger generation. In Poland it advocated the "evacuation" of Jews.

Of the labor groups, the largest and most influential was the Jewish Socialist Party, or Bund, which controlled most of the Jewish trade unions. It was made up of Jewish workers, manual and white collar, and later also of some artisans and members of the lower middle class.

Strongly anti-Communist and anti-Zionist, the Bund called for national cultural autonomy for Jews, although it attempted to refrain from "kindling national consciousness where it might lead to chauvinism and obscure class consciousness."[3] It recognized Yiddish as the national language of the Jewish masses and demanded special autonomous institutions for fostering Jewish culture and education. The Bund, however, recognized the national interest of Jews only in Eastern Europe, and not the world over. In Poland after the First World War the Bund built mainly upon the Jewish proletariat, and rejected the Jewish middle class. In 1929, however, it organized a union of Jewish (petty-bourgeois) artisans and home workers which reached 12,000 members. In the 1930's, it closely associated itself with the interests of the Jewish lower middle class, voicing protests against inequalities and discrimination. Its influence increased, and in some city council elections just before the Second World War it polled a majority of the Jewish votes, and also won a considerable representation in Jewish community councils.

The Assimilationists, though not strictly a party, were for a time an influential group; they regarded themselves—and all the Jews of Poland—as Poles of the Jewish faith, denying the existence of a Jewish nation. Their numbers were drawn largely from the intelligentsia and well-to-do. With the rise of national and Zionist sentiments among Jews, their influence declined.

The Jewish Communists were not a strictly *Jewish* party. Like Communism generally, they rejected any thought of there being such a thing as a Jewish nationality and opposed Zionism. But the necessity of working among Yiddish-speaking masses obliged them to adopt some sort of temporary positive attitude toward Yiddish and its culture. This attitude was no different from the one formulated by the Russian Bolshevik Chemerinsky at the Congress of the Jewish Sections of the Communist Party of the Soviet Union in 1926, who laid down that Jewish autonomous institutions fulfill the role of a "service apparatus" for furthering the socialist process. "Any consideration of the Yiddish language, the [Jewish] school, etc., as an independent factor, rather than as an organization serving socialism, will become Yiddishism and nationalism."[4] This, of course, was taboo.

Jews were also active in some of the general parties and organizations. Some even held leading positions in the Polish Workers Party. In such cases, however, they neither represented particular Jewish interests nor advocated special Jewish programs.

All these Jewish parties, with the exception of the Assimilationists, Communists and partly of the orthodox Agudath Israel desired full national status for the Jews in Poland and fostered Jewish cultural life.

Some indication of the strength of the different groups may be gathered from the results of the 1934 municipal elections in Poland. At that time, 374,398 Jews participated in the elections. They elected 1,603 Jewish councilmen, of whom 43 per cent belonged to the Zionist group; 18 per cent to Agudath Israel; 20.6 per cent to other traditional middle-class groups; 10.2 per cent to socialist groups; and 8.2 per cent to Assimilationist groups. In the latter part of the 1930's, with the further impoverishment of the Jews and the growth of antisemitism, the Socialist Bund gained a great deal of strength. In the municipal elections of 1938-39, they won a considerable part of the Jewish vote, in some places even a majority.

Jewish Culture, Education and Social Service

These parties, each in its own field, supported and fostered Jewish culture and education. Nearly every one put out a Jewish newspaper and other periodicals. They were usually also instrumental in publishing books and pamphlets in Yiddish or Hebrew, some also in Polish, and in supporting other Jewish cultural activities. Jewish schools in Poland were either directly or indirectly organized and supported by the Jewish parties.

Under the Minorities Treaty signed by Poland in 1919, minorities were entitled to equal treatment in all state and municipal schools. In towns and districts in which a considerable proportion of the population belonged to a minority, the government was obliged to insure the children of that minority the possibility of receiving instruction in their mother tongue in the primary schools; and also to see to it that educational, religious, and charitable institutions (including secondary and trade schools) of minority groups received an "equitable"–interpreted to mean "proportional"–share of the state and municipal funds. A special article (10) dealt with the Jewish minority. "Educational committees appointed locally by the Jewish communities in Poland shall, subject to the general control of the state, provide for the distribution of the proportional share of public funds allocated to Jewish schools and for the organization and management of these schools."

In practice, few of these obligations were fulfilled, at least insofar as Jews were concerned. Ukrainian, Ukrainian-Polish, and German schools were founded, "but not a single Hebrew or Yiddish school was established by the government,"[5] although in most towns, and in cities both large and small, Jews constituted more than 25 per cent of the population. Even the small subsidies granted by some municipalities to Hebrew or Yiddish schools were later withdrawn for the most part. The one thing the government did was to open special primary schools which did not have the Saturday session usual in Poland. The curriculum of these schools was the same as that of other primary schools, the only differences being that some of the teachers were Jewish and a few hours a week were devoted to Jewish religious instruction. In 1934, however, the government began to discontinue this type of school, transferring its children to the regular primary schools.

State control of schooling, the introduction of compulsory education, demands for changes in the curriculum and for qualified teachers, combined with growing secularist tendencies, resulted in the diminution of the importance of the age-old *cheder*. Jews were thus faced with the task of maintaining schools of their own. Antisemitic discrimination encountered by Jews seeking admission to state institutions was an added stimulus to the founding of Jewish schools. Subsidies granted to Jewish schools were small, and in the 1930's were often either reduced or withdrawn.

The Agudath Israel had its Horeb schools for boys and Beth Yakob schools for girls. Its educational system was based on a reformed and modernized *cheder* that sought to meet the demands of the authorities for a minimum of secular studies. It was deemed to be equivalent to the state schools and its pupils were thus freed from attendance at the general primary school. In 1937 the Agudah's educational system, with all its affiliates, comprised 818 institutions attended by 109,000 pupils.

The Mizrachi movement in 1927 centralized its educational system in the Yabneh organization. It strove to synthesize the Zionist ideals of building up a Jewish Palestine and reviving Hebrew with the perpetuation of Jewish religious traditions. Emphasis was divided between religious studies and modern Hebrew and Jewish history. Secular subjects were taught both in order to meet the requirements of the authorities and to raise a generation familiar with its own environment. According to available figures the Yabneh system in 1933 comprised 134 institutions with 14,461 pupils.

The Tarbuth system of Hebrew schools was associated with the Zionist movement. Hebrew was regarded as more than a simple language of instruction, being considered rather as the cornerstone of a new life and culture. All subjects were taught in Hebrew. In 1934-35 the Tarbuth network included 72 kindergartens, 183 primary schools, 9 secondary schools, 1 agricultural, and 4 evening schools. The student population was 44,780.

One manifestation of an awakening Jewish national consciousness in Poland between the wars was the large number of people (87.8 per cent) who gave Yiddish or Hebrew as their mother tongue in the census of 1931 (this was a way of declaring one's Jewish nationality indirectly, since this census asked no direct question about nationality); whereas in 1921 only 74.2 per cent of Poland's Jews registered as being of the Jewish nationality.[6] Since Yiddish was the language of the masses, and for the most part supported by Jewish socialist groups, the Yiddish school soon came to be termed the "socialist school." The Central Yiddish School Organization (CYSZO), founded in 1921, had its principal supporter in the Bund. The curriculum of the Yiddish school was secularist and humanist in tendency; the Yiddish language and socialist doctrine were its cornerstones. In addition to general subjects, Yiddish literature and Jewish history were taught.

Hebrew was taught in about half of these schools; there was no uniform policy with regard to teaching of this subject. During the school year 1934-35, the Central Yiddish School Organization maintained 176 institutions (pre-school, elementary, secondary, and evening), with a total enrollment of 15,486.

The Hebrew-Polish bilingual system, consisting mainly of secondary schools, was, if not officially affiliated, at any rate connected with Zionism. Both teachers and students were imbued with the Zionist ideology. In 1927, the system embraced 122 institutions with 25,283 pupils.

There were three institutions of higher learning: the Institute of Judaism (Machon Lemadaey Hayahaduth) in Warsaw for the training of rabbis and teachers, which was Zionist in outlook; the Yiddish Scientific Institute (YIVO) in Vilna, an outgrowth of the Yiddishist movement, although Zionists participated in its work; and the Yeshiva Chachmey Lublin, a strictly orthodox institution whose ideology was akin to the Agudah's.

Some Jewish communities, notably Warsaw,[7] maintained primary schools, Talmud Torahs, kindergartens, etc. In most of the day schools the language of instruction for the general subjects was Polish, and for the Jewish subjects Hebrew or Yiddish. In 1934-35 there were 58 such community schools with 10,300 pupils.

Elementary religious education in Poland, as in former centuries, was the business of the individual parents or of some local group. A picture of the situation of the *chedarim* can be obtained from an inquiry made in the summer of 1934. Replies were received from 210 towns. In 158 towns there were 720 *chedarim*, of which 598 (83 per cent) were privately conducted. The private *cheder*, being the property of a single teacher, was generally small, with 15 to 20 pupils. The *chedarim* under the auspices of an organization or community had a larger number of pupils (50-60). In 78 places for which information was available, 33-56.7 per cent of the boys of school age (7-14) attended *cheder*.

Most of the vocational education available to Jews was conducted and supported by a few such agencies as the JDC, ORT, the Jewish Colonization Association (JCA), and WUZET[8] (in Galicia).Some other schools and a few Yeshivoth also gave vocational courses. In the 1930's the Agudath Israel established a few vocational schools. In Vilna a technical high school (Technicum) was founded which achieved a high standard. Generally, however, vocational education did not play a large role in the life of Polish Jewry. Statistical data from the JDC show 183 institutions with 16,235 students as of January 1938. Since these figures included apprentices to private masters living in the so-called children's homes, trade information bureaus, and similar institutions, the actual number of students in vocational schools and courses would amount to some 10-11,000. This includes both regular trade schools and short courses ranging from one to twelve months.[9]

The diversity of schools makes it well-nigh impossible to obtain clear figures on the total number of Jewish educational institutions in Poland. The JDC, counting affiliated schools only, found (in 1936) 180,181 pupils attending 1,465 Jewish institutions. Kazdan, adding 40,000 pupils in *chedarim* and *kehillah* schools, found 3,045 institutions with 232,428 pupils.[10] According to government figures, in 1934-35 and 1936-37 there were 468,309 Jewish children attending primary, high and vocational schools. This would mean that over one-half of the Jewish school population received a Jewish education, some 22 per cent in all-day Jewish schools and the rest in supplementary schools. In 1934-35 Polish Jewry spent 26,000,000 zlotys[11] on education, or almost one-half of an estimated 60,000,000 zlotys spent by Jews in Poland annually for communal purposes.[12]

Among other institutions mention should be made of the TOZ, or Society for the Protection of Jewish Health, which maintained about 120 institutions and clinics during the 1930's.

In the field of relief there were numerous organizations ministering to the sick, poor, transients, and the like. In most cities and towns there was one or more of the following organizations: Bikur Holim, Tomche Aniyim, Hachnassath Kalah. Almost every house of prayer in the larger cities and towns had its own relief fund or organization. In addition, there were central societies. In Warsaw, for instance, the organization Beth Lechem distributed food packages among the needy. The Rescue Committee furnished small traders and craftsmen with small loans, to be repaid at the borrower's convenience.

For economic assistance there were free-loan societies (Gmilath Ches-ed), numbering 826 in 1938, with a central office in Warsaw; and Jewish credit cooperatives. In 1924 the JDC in conjunction with the Jewish Colonization Association established the American Joint Reconstruction Foundation for the purpose of granting loans to cooperatives. In the fifteen years before the Second World War, as much as $3,000,000 was granted to the Polish Jewish cooperatives. In 1939 there were in Poland over 700 Jewish cooperative peoples' banks and societies with a membership of over 100,000.

Jewish labor numbered more than a quarter of a million in 1931 and kept increasing during the 1930's. In 1921, the first Trade Union Council was elected. In the same year the Jewish trade unions federated with the Polish, controlled by PPS. The Jewish unions retained a great deal of autonomy and acted almost as an independent section. By 1937, there were 72,000 organized Jewish workers. At the time of the Trade Union Congress in 1939 there were already 98,810. During 1934-39 there was a Central Jewish Trade Union Council comprising manual and white-collar workers. Aligned with the Right Poale Zion, this organization had a membership of 16,830 in July, 1939.

In the 1921 census, people were asked about their nationality as well as their religion. In the next census, in 1931, the question about nationality was replaced by one about one's mother tongue. This last question, however, was interpreted by the Jews themselves as a sort of declaration of nationality, an indication of national consciousness. This national consciousness had increased in the ten years between 1921 and 1931, as we can see from the following figures:

TABLE V

NATIONALITY AND RELIGION OF JEWS, 1921, 1931

Year	Jews by Religion	Jews by Nationality (1921) Jews by Mother Tongue (1931)	Per cent in relation to religion
1921	2,845,364	2,110,448	74.2
1931	3,113,933	2,732,573	87.8

Of the 87.8 per cent of the Jewish population who gave either Yiddish or Hebrew as their mother tongue, the greater number 2,489,034 (79.9 per cent) listed Yiddish, and only 243,539 (7.9 per cent) listed Hebrew.[13]

These figures, as well as revealing a highly developed sense of national consciousness among the Jews of Poland, suggest the scope of Jewish cultural activities in both Yiddish and Hebrew.

Yiddish and Hebrew culture were developed mainly by conscious group effort; the Yiddish language, however, was the spontaneous expression of the masses. At the same time, Jewish cultural efforts were also promoted in the Polish language.

The language pattern revealed in the 1931 census was reflected in the flourishing Jewish press of Poland. In the 1930's there were 30 Yiddish dailies and 5 Polish-language Jewish dailies. There were 112 Yiddish weeklies, 4 Hebrew weeklies, and 14 Polish Jewish weeklies. Of other periodicals, there were 137 in Yiddish, 24 in Hebrew and 55 in Polish.[14]

On the whole, the Yiddish daily press, which represented all sections of Jewish political opinion, was in the best tradition of the Western European press. Besides coverage of general and Jewish news, most Yiddish newspapers devoted a good deal of space to education, science, literature, theater, and the arts. Fiction was also published in the daily press. The periodicals (over 350 weeklies, biweeklies, monthlies, and quarterlies, in all languages) reflected the variegated cultural life of Polish Jewry; they were devoted to politics, economic and social questions, literature, the arts, science, and education.

During a period of acute economic depression (1930-34), an average of 430 books were published annually in Yiddish and Hebrew (the highest for this period was 526 in 1930; the lowest 338 in 1932); of these, about two-thirds were in Yiddish and the rest in Hebrew. About 80 per cent of the Yiddish books fell into the categories of belles-lettres and popular non-fiction of an educational kind. About 7 per cent were devoted to science and research, and the rest were textbooks. Hebrew publications, because of the special nature of their audience, consisted of about 15 per cent textbooks, the rest being popular non-fiction, belles lettres, etc.[15]

Jewish literary and journalistic activity in Poland had its center in the Union of Jewish Writers and Journalists in Warsaw, which served not only as a trade union in the economic sense but also as a vehicle for the social and political expressions of the Jewish literati of Poland.

The Jewish theater was another example of Jewish creativity in Poland between the wars. Attempts to maintain a Hebrew theater in Poland were unsuccessful, but the Yiddish theater on the whole flourished. Most famous were the Vilna Troupe, formed during the German occupation in the First World War in Vilna; VIKT (*Varshaver yidisher kunst teyater*—Warsaw Yiddish Art Theater), organized in the early twenties; and *Yung Teyater* (Young Theater), founded at the end of the twenties. These theaters enjoyed a national and even an international renown. In 1936, there was a total of 15 Yiddish theaters in Poland; they played everything from serious classical pieces to musical comedies and reviews.

Chapter III

War and Occupation

The Nazis attacked Poland on September 1, 1939, and swept the Polish army before them. When, on September 17, 1939, Soviet forces began to occupy eastern Poland, Polish military resistance had virtually ceased. A demarcation line between Russia and Germany was settled by the German-Soviet Boundary and Friendship Treaty of September 28, 1939.[1] To Russia went the eastern and southeastern provinces, comprising 77,606 square miles with a population of about 13 million; while Germany received the western and central Polish provinces, comprising 72,864 square miles with a population of about 22 million. In this region were located most of the large Polish cities, industrial centers, and the coal mines of Upper Silesia.

The western regions, including the former German provinces of Pomerania and Posen, and the Polish industrial centers of Lodz and Polish Upper Silesia, with a population of about 10 million, were incorporated into the Greater German Reich. The Polish central provinces, with a population of about 12 million, were organized as the Government General with its seat in Cracow. It was planned that the area annexed to the Reich should in the course of time be cleared of Poles and settled with Germans, while the Government General was to remain "the home of the Poles." With the invasion of Russia, eastern Galicia was incorporated into the Government General.

In the German-occupied regions lived more than 2,000,000 Jews: 650,000 (20 per cent of all Polish Jews) were in the incorporated areas, and about 1,400,000 in the Government General (42 per cent). This left about 1,-200,000-1,250,000 and more in the Russian-occupied areas (38 per cent).[2] To the latter some 300,000 should be added who came in as refugees. These 300,000, as well as some 68,000 Jewish officers and enlisted men of the Polish army from the western area who were either killed or taken prisoner by the Germans and removed to Germany,[3] should be deducted from the Jewish population in German-occupied Poland; and also some 20-25,000 Jews who in the first weeks fled to neighboring countries (Rumania, Hungary, the Baltic states). Finally, some 30-50,000[4] Jews died in the few weeks of the war in German air raids against Polish towns and cities and against fleeing refugees. Thus it would appear that about 1,550,000-1,600,000 Jews remained in the German-occupied parts.[5]

From the beginning, conditions for these Jews under Nazi domination were such as to make their survival questionable, although definite plans for their annihilation were apparently not worked out until later. In his speech in the Reichstag on January 30, 1939, Hitler threatened that in case of war "the result will be . . . the annihilation of the Jewish race in Europe."[6] This threat he largely made good. It is possible to distinguish three stages in German policy toward Jews in Poland:

1. The first months of occupation, marked by anti-Jewish decrees and regulations, looting of Jewish property, pogroms, shootings, burnings, rape, etc. Violence, though encouraged from above, was more or less unorganized, or only locally organized.

2. The ghetto period, ending with the outbreak of the German-Russian war (1940-41).

3. The period of planned extermination. This began in mid-1941 in eastern, previously Soviet-occupied, Poland, and six months later in the western areas of Poland occupied by the Germans in 1939.

The description given by an eyewitness who lived in Warsaw during the winter of 1939-40 is characteristic of the first period.

> In the first three months of the occupation, the looting usually stopped short of the furniture. Later, however, the Nazis went systematically from house to house and laid hands on whatever they could find. . . .
>
> One of the commonest forms of Nazi brutality was to keep Jews standing for hours half-naked in the bitter cold, and then to compel them to sing and finally to dig their own graves. Sometimes they were all shot together in a batch. At other times the executions took place singly, each of the victims having first to bury his predecessor.[7]

Forced labor and the organization of labor camps were begun in the early days of the occupation. At first Jews were picked up on the streets or indoors and sent to work for a certain period, some being murdered afterwards. Later the community councils were obliged to provide the necessary number of workers. Generally, Jewish forced labor was divided between labor gangs which worked near their domiciles, usually for a short time, and labor camps to which the conscript was sent for years and where he did the hardest work under inhuman conditions and discipline. By the summer of 1941 there existed in the Government General 85 Jewish labor camps with at least 80,000 Jewish workers.[8]

In the spring of 1940 the building of a ghetto wall was begun in Warsaw. In July, Jews arriving in Warsaw and Warsaw Jews changing their abode were forbidden to settle outside this wall. Finally on October 16, 1940, the ghetto was established. On November 15, 1940 the ghetto was closed, and Jewish, Polish, and German police were placed on guard at each of the eleven entrances.

In Lodz a ghetto was set up in February 1940; in Radom, in November 1940; in Cracow, in March 1941; in Kielce, in April 1941, etc.[9]

With the sealing of the ghettos the situation of Jews deteriorated rapidly. Terrible overcrowding,[10] unsanitary conditions, and lack of food were immediately the rule. Officially, rations for Poles were half those of Germans, and for Jews half those of Poles. With the deterioration of the food situation in 1941 owing to the Russian campaign, Jews in Warsaw received three to five ounces of inferior bread daily. Other food items were distributed quite irregularly and were very frequently spoiled. In terms of calories the food ration amounted to 1,350 per day.

Overcrowding, malnutrition, and disease decimated the Jewish population of the ghettos. A Swiss who came to the ghetto in February 1942 paints this picture of its streets:

> In the gutters and on sidewalks the dead lie around, naked and emaciated; next to them sit or stand the living who, not unlike the dead, are starved and of a sickly gray color. One sees women and children apathetically sitting before the doorways on the side streets. They regard us with neither hatred nor pleading; their indifference grates on my nerves more than the most violent accusation.
>
> On the main street, however, the crowd hastens aimlessly along . . . as though driven with whips. Despite the intense February cold, almost all the windows and doors are open, which does not matter, for there is no fuel and the window glass is still broken in many places as a result of the war. One sees mothers with small children either lying nearby or on their laps. I do not know whether they are already dead or whether their mothers are awaiting their deaths. Suddenly there is a movement in the group standing around; a female corpse has been carried out and placed on the sidewalk. . . . I can see men, women and children walk around the corpse, like beasts. In a flash the corpse lies naked in the gutter. Gone are the shawl and the shirt which the woman had still worn. . . . Here corpses are thrown from the windows . . . pushed into the gutter, if they are in the way. People stare blankly as bodies are loaded like dead dogs onto a cart. Each one must recken that perhaps tomorrow he himself will lie in the gutter.[11]

Professor Ludwik Hirschfeld, one of the sanitary officials of the ghetto, testified at the trial of the Warsaw Nazi governor, Fischer, that "if the Jews of the Warsaw ghetto had not been deported to Treblinka and murdered there, they would have died out in eight years."[12]

The labor camps also resulted in a high mortality. Hard labor was accompanied by beatings and torture, disease and malnutrition.[13]

To all these deaths from "natural" causes must be added the hundreds who were shot or otherwise killed daily—the Jewish population in Poland dwindled rapidly.

The Polish eastern provinces seized by the Red Army in 1939, had been incorporated into the Ukrainian and White Russian Republics. Their

Ukrainization and White-Russification led to a great deal of discrimination against Jews. The life of these provinces was gradually Sovietized; Jews lost their means of livelihood, and Jewish institutions were closed. During the process of incorporation a series of deportations to Russia took place in which Jews were included. Jews were sent to forced labor camps and settlements in faraway parts of northern and Asiatic Russia; some 250-300,000 Jews were deported in this way. A further 120-150,000 Jews fled at the beginning of the Nazi-Soviet war. But most of the Polish Jews who resided in or had fled to the Russian-occupied eastern provinces came under Nazi rule after the outbreak of the Nazi-Soviet war in June 1941. About 1,000,000 to 1,100,000 Jews were present in these territories at the time of Nazi occupation. In eastern Galicia, which was placed under the administration of the General Government, there were at the time of the German occupation about 500,000 Jews.[14]

The third stage in the Nazi treatment of the Jews, that of wholesale extermination, began with the outbreak of the Nazi-Soviet war on June 22, 1941. Most of the almost three million Polish and approximately one million other Jews brought to Poland from elsewhere, were killed in the death camps of Auschwitz, Treblinka, Maidanek, Chelmno, Belzec, Sobibór; the rest were worked to death, starved, or murdered in other camps and in ghettos. At the time of the liberation there were some 50,000 or so survivors.[15]

Chapter IV

"People's Democratic" Poland

The new Poland which arose after the Second World War was very different from the Poland of before the war. Geographically, it has been shifted westward; politically, eastward. These two facts shaped the destiny of Poland.

The eastern provinces, comprising some 69,866 square miles with a prewar population of about 12 millions, were lost to Russia. In the west and northwest, Poland acquired Silesia, two-thirds of East Prussia and Pomerania, and a small part of eastern Brandenburg from Germany—a territory of 39,986 square miles having before the war 8½ to 9 million inhabitants.[1] Most of this region, which comprises about one-third of the present area of Poland (125,000 square miles), was highly industrialized, whereas the eastern provinces were mainly an agricultural region.

This westward shift of the Polish frontiers resulted from the decision reached at the Yalta Conference in February 1945 that "the eastern frontier of Poland should follow the Curzon Line, with digressions from it in some regions of three to five miles," and that Poland should receive "substantial accessions of territory in the North and West," leaving the "final delineation" of the western frontier for "the peace conference." Later in 1945, at the conference in Potsdam, the general boundaries of the territories which Poland was to receive in the west and north were worked out.[2]

The Yalta decision came as a result of Russian demands for the eastern parts of Poland, which were populated by a majority of non-Poles, mainly Ukrainians (about 5 million),[3] White Russians (about 1½ millions), and Jews.

After Nazi Germany invaded Russia, the USSR and the Polish government-in-exile signed the agreement of July 30, 1941, according to which "the government of the USSR recognizes the Soviet-German treaties of 1939 concerning territorial changes in Poland as having lost their validity."[4] This formula was a compromise between Soviet Russia's refusal to recognize the Polish-Russian border as that of pre-September 1939, and Polish insistence that it should. This compromise, brought about by British pressure, did not prevent Russia from continuing to claim all or parts of eastern Poland.

As early as August 3, 1941, *Izvestiya* stated that the agreement did not mean a return to the pre-September frontiers, and that the problem could be solved in the future by "good will and wise statesmanship." In the fall of 1941, only a short time after the signing of the Polish-Russian agreement, Stalin mentioned in one of his speeches that Russia's aim was to restore the frontiers of June 21, 1941.[5] Shortly after Pearl Harbor, in a conversation with Eden, Stalin indicated that "he wanted a Soviet-Polish boundary based on the Curzon Line," and proposed "the transfer of East Prussia to Poland."[6] Thereafter, Russia systematically pressed Poland and the Allies to recognize the Curzon Line and her right to eastern Poland. Soviet demands with regard to eastern Poland were presented to the conference of the three foreign ministers in Moscow (October 1943), and some promise appears to have been made to Russia at the conference in Teheran (November 28-December 1, 1943). England and America, with reluctance, agreed in principle to the Curzon line.[7]

At the Yalta Conference Molotov and Stalin demanded as frontier the Curzon Line, "with a digression from it in some regions of 5-8 kilometers in favor of Poland"; and a western frontier for Poland "from the town of Stettin . . . to the South along the river Oder and still farther along the river Neisse." America and Great Britain wanted a somewhat smaller extension of Poland to the west to avoid having to remove too many Germans. Churchill said that "it would be a pity to stuff the Polish goose so full of German food that it gets indigestion."[8] Stalin ceased insisting that the Polish western frontier be delineated.

The decision at Yalta was therefore in agreement with the Russian stand in connection with the Polish eastern frontier, while with regard to the western frontier it was recognized "that Poland must receive substantial accessions in territory in the North and West," leaving the frontier to be settled at the peace conference after "the opinion of the new Polish Provisional Government of National Unity should be sought in due course as to the extent of these accessions." This was reiterated in Potsdam in the middle of 1945. Although it was reaffirmed that "the final delineation of the western frontier of Poland should await the peace settlement," the powers agreed that these territories "shall be under the administration of the Polish State."[9] But dissension between East and West prevented negotiation of a peace and establishment of officially recognized Polish frontiers.[10] Nevertheless, Soviet Russia, in her treaty with Poland of August 17, 1945, fixed the latter's western borders and recognized its acquisitions from Germany.

The Polish government-in-exile, whose demand that the International Red Cross investigate the murder of 10,000 Polish officers in the forest of Katyn caused Soviet Russia to sever diplomatic relations with it in April 1943, was always opposed to the cession of the eastern regions to Russia, as were all Polish parties from the extreme right to the Socialists. Only the Peasant Party changed its attitude, in October 1944, following Mikolajczyk's visit to Moscow. Most of the underground groups in Poland, including the Socialist underground, were also against cession. At the time of liberation, the Socialist underground organization[11] was about to launch a fight against the small Polish Communist underground group supporting the Soviet position.

Before the war the Polish Communist Party had been dissolved as a result of the purges of the late 1930's. After Germany's attack on Russia, a Communist underground was organized by local Communists and emissaries from Russia. This group, organized by Boleslaw Bierut and Wladyslaw Gomulka, took the name of the Polish Workers Party (PPR-Polska Partya Robotnicza).

Another group supporting the Soviet stand on the frontier question and generally sympathetic toward Russia was a splinter organization of the Polish Socialists, constituted in Cracow in 1942 under the leadership of Edward Osubka-Morawski and Stanislaw Szwalbe. This group was later to become the officially recognized Polish Socialist Party in Poland.[12] At the same time a Polish pro-Soviet group consisting of Communists and others, with the former Socialist Wanda Wasilewska as its head, was formed in Russia at the end of 1941. From this group there later evolved the Union of Polish Patriots and the Kosciuszko Division, the Polish military formation organized in Russia after General Anders' Polish army was evacuated to the Middle East. The Union maintained that Poland should abandon the eastern territories and concentrate on winning back "old Polish lands in the west."[13]

At the beginning of 1944 a pro-Soviet Council of National Liberation was formed in Poland;[14] in May 1944 it sent representatives to Moscow to make contact with the Union of Polish Patriots. Shortly thereafter (July 1944), these groups formed, in Russian-occupied Lublin, the Polish Committee of National Liberation, with Edward Osuba-Morawski, a leader of the pro-Soviet Socialist faction, at its head. Among the members of the committee we find a number of Communists, and also such non-Communists as Emil Sommerstein, a Zionist, and Jan Michal Grabecki, a former antisemite and organizer of "Polish Aryans." They, like other non-Communists at that time, apparently believed that "we can do business with Stalin and still maintain our domestic freedom of action."[15]

On December 31, 1944, the Lublin Committee of National Liberation announced itself as the provisional government of Poland; on January 5, 1945, it was recognized as such by Russia and entered liberated Warsaw thirteen days later.

The situation in Yalta was, as Stettinius later explained, difficult because, at the time of the conference, Poland was in Russian hands. "It was not a question of what Great Britain and the United States would permit Russia to do in Poland, but what the two countries could persuade the Soviet Union to accept."[16] The United States and Great Britain refused to recognize the provisional government in Poland, but agreed to its *reorganization*. This was achieved, in form if not in fact, by the addition of a number of members to the Lublin Committee. In July 1945 a Provisional Government of National Unity was constituted and recognized by the USSR, Great Britain, and the United States.

This coalition ministry comprised 6 ministers from the Polish Socialist Party (PPS), 6 from the Polish Workers Party (PPR), 2 from the Democratic Party (PD), 2 from the Communist-sponsored Peasant Party (SL), one non-party member, the Minister of Defense, and 6 from the Polish Peasant Party (PSL) headed by Mikolajczyk, who held the posts of Minister of Agriculture and Second Vice-Premier. In actual fact the Communists controlled more than six ministries, since a number of others were completely dominated by Communist vice-ministers or personnel.

Toward Communist Domination

The Communists constituted a well-organized and aggressive group supported by Soviet Russia and by the presence of the Red Army in Poland, but with only a small following among the Polish population.[17] Traditional anti-Russian and anti-Communist Polish sentiments, plus the loss of eastern Poland, including such historical centers as Vilna and Lvov to Russia, certainly did not help to make Communism and Russian domination more palatable. Moreover, Red Army soldiers raped and looted, and Russian authorities stripped Polish factories of their equipment to send to Russia. According to one observer, "the Russian Army took more Polish farm stock than did the Germans. The trouble with the 1945-46 grain planting was that the Russians had taken so large a proportion of the Polish seed grain."[18]

The small Democratic Party, mostly made up of intelligentsia, and the government-sponsored Peasant Party, were dominated or influenced by the Communists. The Socialists were divided, as we have seen. At the time of liberation, a number of former Socialist leaders tried to reconstruct a Social Democratic party. Some of these were promptly arrested and the Provisional Government refused to allow the formation of a new party. Socialists had to content themselves with the pro-Communist Workers Party of Polish Socialists (PRPS), which had split off from the PPS. This group soon gained an influence in the elections to the Workers' Councils exceeding that of the Communists. At the first postwar Trade Union Congress held in November 1945, the Socialists controlled about 60 per cent of the delegates, and a Socialist became Secretary General of the Central Committee of Trade Unions.

The PRPS soon began to demand a greater voice in the government affairs; it was dissatisfied with the fact that the more important ministries were held by Communists.[19] While right-wing Socialists negotiated with the Peasant Party about joining in a coalition, and some even left the party, the leaders of the PRPS, with representatives of the Communists, went to Moscow, where apparently the Socialists were promised more seats in the government.[20] The "United Front Agreement" declared that the two parties—the Socialist Party and the Workers Party—were "separate and independent and equal political organisms" which would "mutually respect the organizational structure of each." It provided for cooperation in the elections and for combating rightist elements within the Socialist Party.[21]

Mikolajczyk's Peasant Party (PSL), based on the pre-war Peasant Party, was newly constituted in 1945. The membership also included a large number of small businessmen and intelligentsia. It was by no means prepared to submit to Communist policies and dictation.

The war left much of Poland in ruins. Horses and cattle were scarce, farm machinery was greatly depleted, the forests were stripped, and the transportation and communication systems pillaged and destroyed. Schools and government buildings, churches and private houses, had all suffered severe damage. "Ninety-six per cent of the buildings of the capital city of Warsaw were wrecked";[22] many other cities and towns were in ruins.

There was also a food shortage. Planting suffered from lack of seed, and at harvest time (1945) there were not enough workers to gather in the crops. Poland had to maintain relations with the West and to comply, at least outwardly, with the demands for a democratic government, for it needed UNRRA supplies, which proved a vital factor in rebuilding the country. She also needed machines and tools which could be obtained only from the West.

Being in a minority and working in an environment traditionally hostile to Soviet Russia, the Polish Communists sought at least the tolerance of the mass of the population and the peasantry, as a preliminary to their destroying all opposition and gaining complete control of the country.[23] Their first step was taken even before the liberation of the whole country. On September 6, 1944, the Lublin Committee of National Liberation announced a land reform decree, in accordance with which land holdings over 50 hectares (120 acres) were to be taken from their owners and divided among peasant families in 5-hectare (12.4 acres) holdings.

A further step was the referendum of June 30, 1946, which sought approval for the abolition of the Senate, land reform, nationalization, and maintenance of the new western frontier. "The government bloc wanted to gain the support of the people for its policy of accepting Russia's adjustment of Polish territory, both in the East and in the West, and it desired experience in conducting a successful election."[24] The electoral committees at the different levels were determined by the respective national councils, which were predominantly Communist or Socialist. Members of electoral committees who did not belong to the government bloc were either arrested by the Communist-controlled security police or otherwise hindered from participation in the committees. Mikolajczyk and his Polish Peasant Party charged serious irregularities in the counting of the ballots.[25] A United States note of August 19, 1946, said "that the methods used in tabulating the ballots and reporting the vote have given rise to charges of serious irregularities including removal of ballot boxes from polling places."[26] With the practice thus gained in "arranging" elections, the government set the long-deferred general elections for a Constituent Diet for January 19, 1947.

Long before the elections, the PPR and PRPS pressed for a government bloc with a single list, which would of course have been Communist-dominated. They suggested that Mikolajczyk's PSL receive about 20 per cent of the seats. The latter demanded 75 per cent of the mandates on the ground that over 70 per cent of Poland was agricultural. These negotiations had collapsed prior to the referendum. As the elections neared, intimidation of the PSL increased. In some electoral districts it was forbidden to enter its candidates; in others it met with different obstacles; all over the country officials of the PSL were arrested and even murdered.

In July and August of 1946 the Christian Labor Party (SP) was made subservient to the government bloc. Great Britain and the United States protested several times (August 19, November 22, 1946; January 9, 1947) against irregularities in the elections.[27]

The government bloc gained a large majority; the Polish Peasant Party won only 28 seats out of 444. After the Diet met in February 1947 Boleslaw Bierut (PPR) was elected President and Jozef Cyrankiewicz (PPS) became Premier. The cabinet was made up of 7 members from the PPS; 5 from PPR; 6 from the bloc-supported Peasant Party (SL); 3 from the Democratic Party (SD); and 2 from the Christian Labor Party (SP), with one member, the Minister of Defense, a non-party man.

The elections assured the Communist-led government bloc a great majority. It was now free to consolidate its power and impose its will on the population. Officially, the Constituent Diet declared that "it will continue to uphold such fundamental civil rights as: equality before the law, liberty of person, life and property, freedom of conscience, of worship, of scientific research, of press, speech, association, assembly, inviolability of the home, etc."[28] But in practice the secret police laid hands on most suspects and waves of arrests followed the elections. The Constituent Diet itself soon became an institution of no real importance.

The newly elected Diet, by an act (February 19, 1947) amending certain articles of the 1921 constitution, created a new body that continued the Presidium of the KRN, the Council of State acting under the direction of the President of the Republic. This body ruled by decree; the Sejm approved its decrees or passed into law the bills it submitted.

The elections also broke the back of the legal opposition, the Polish Peasant Party. Its left wing, which advocated submission to the government, took control after Mikolajczyk fled from Poland in October 1947. Thereafter, the PSL was forced to unite with the government-controlled Peasant Party (SL) to form the "United Peasant Party" at the end of November 1949.

The Communists set about eliminating their most important opponents, the Socialists, by pressing for unification. On May 1, 1947, Wladyslaw Gomulka, at that time Secretary General of the PPR, declared that the two parties were "on the road to complete unity."[29] At first the Socialist Party, in congress at Wroclaw in December 1947, did not support a merger. But on March 17, 1948, apparently as a result of pressure from Moscow,[30] the Socialist leader Cyrankiewicz declared that his party was prepared to unite with the Communists. Whereupon the Communists demanded that the Socialists purge their rightist elements before entering into partnership. Some Socialist leaders had in the meantime been brought to trial, and others were expelled during the purges or recanted their opposition. On December 15-21, 1948, the United Polish Workers Party (PZPR) was constituted. Eight of its eleven Politburo members were Communists. The government was reorganized; whereas the Communists had previously held 33 out of the 60 more important governmental posts, now they held 53 out of 74.

In the summer of 1948, at the second session of the Cominform, it was "taught that a people's democracy could not halt at any but the final stage of its destruction of the capitalistic elements and . . . that the socialist transformation could not be limited to the towns . . . the Soviet Union is our model."[31] This antinationalist turn marked the second stage in the development of the peoples' democracies" and terminated the phase which had followed the disbanding of the Comintern. But in nationalistic Poland, with some of the Communists themselves being apparently "more Polish than Communist," the new turn led to a crisis. Wladyslaw Gomulka, Secretary General of the PPR, Vice-Premier and Minister for the Regained Territories, defended nationalistic views at the meeting of the Cominform. He also criticized the Cominform's condemnation of Tito. At the same time, at the plenum of the PPR in Poland on June 3, 1948, he held that the Polish Workers Party should follow an independent course. Gomulka, a veteran leader of the anti-German underground and builder of the PPR, was not alone in his heretical notions of a Polish national Communism. In the Central Committee seven members, mostly former underground fighters, supported him. He and his group refused to recant despite the demands of the Politburo. If one can believe the charges made later against Gomulka, he hoped that "the nationalistic Polish Communism in which he believed would acquire such a strong base that it could not be overturned except by direct intervention of the Soviet Union."[32]

But after about two months' time Gomulka did recant, at the plenum of the party in Warsaw (August 31-September 3, 1948). Later he was removed from the secretaryship of the party and had to resign his ministerial posts; however, in comparison with "heretics" in other satellite countries, he was let off lightly.[33]

The party plenum in the summer of 1948 heralded the intensification of the Sovietization of Poland. Hilary Minc and Jacob Berman demanded a fight against capitalism, the gradual elimination of the richer peasantry by taxation, and Sovietization of cultural life. The "mild revolution" of the first postwar years was called rightist and nationalistic, while the cultural policy was accused of having been confused ideologically and insufficiently aware of the achievements of the Soviet Union. During the unification of the PPR with the PPS and after, large-scale purges of "opportunistic" and nationalistic elements took place.[34] Jacob Berman wrote:

> The essential task, that of laying the foundation of socialism in Poland, can be carried out only in close alliance and cooperation with the Soviet Union. . . . Any tendency to weaken cooperation with the Soviet Union is directed against the very foundation of the People's Democracy. . . . Anyone who imagines that the people's democratic state can be formed merely as a self-sufficient body, on a national scale, isolated from the class struggle on an international scale . . . will inevitably sink into the slough of nationalism and treachery.[35]

Soviet Russia was said to have been "impatient over the slow progress of rural collectivization" in Poland,[36] the plan for the period 1949-1951 having called for the collectivization of only one per cent of the land yearly. The tempo of collectivization seems to have been speeded up subsequently,[37] and the new Six-Year Plan "calls for an attempt at collectivization."

The appointment of the Soviet Marshal Konstantin Rokosovsky as Commander-in-Chief of the Polish army, Minister of National Defense, and member of the Polish Politburo, meant the conversion of Poland into a Russian military base and the complete subordination of its army to Russian purposes and control. By the middle of 1950 about 300 Polish officers of high rank had been retired or purged and many of their places taken by Russians.

Ties with the West were progressively cut. At the end of 1949 the government stopped the work of such organizations as the International Committee of the Red Cross, the American Remittances to Europe,

C.A.R.E. and the Joint Distribution Committee. In March 1950 Poland withdrew from the International Bank of Reconstruction and Development and the International Monetary Fund, complaining that these agencies were "a submissive instrument of the United States."[38] A month later Poland left the FAO. In June 1950 she quit (together with Czechoslovakia and Hungary) the International Labor Organization.

The beginning of 1950 saw the opening of a systematic attack upon the Catholic church in Poland, which was always regarded not only as a religious but also as a national institution. In March 1950 a law for the nationalization of most of the church lands was enacted. An agreement between the government and the episcopate was concluded in April 1950; although not all the points of the agreement have been published,[39] the church seems to have made many concessions and the agreement appears to have more or less ended the autonomy of the Roman Catholic church in Poland.

Communist regimentation became ever harsher under the regime of the United Polish Workers Party.[40] Purges of untrustworthy elements continued unabated. According to President Bierut in a speech before the Politburo at the beginning of May 1950, "the party was purged so rapidly and so thoroughly that inadequate replacements were found for ousted members. . . . Over one-half, and in the lower levels almost two-thirds, of the total number of political workers in the entire party apparatus are new men."[41] Nevertheless, at the meeting of the Central Committee of the party held in the second week of May 1950, "deviationists from the orthodox Leninist Stalinism" were "unmasked" and many later purged.

CHAPTER V

The Jewish Survivors

In the summer of 1944, with the advance of the Soviet Army and the Polish Kosciuszko Division into Poland, the remnants of Polish Jewry slowly emerged from hiding. In Lublin 50 Jews were found. In the whole area liberated at that time (about one-third of Poland), 8,000 Jews were listed by the end of the year.[1]

In some of the camps, too, a number of Jews remained alive, despite the last-minute executions ordered by Himmler. Auschwitz was evacuated by the Germans on January 17, 1945—ten days before liberation. They took with them 58,000 inmates, of whom 5,000 Jews were able to escape.[2] Although the last inmates of Chelmno were burned alive just before the arrival of the Red Army, a few Jews did survive. In a number of camps the Nazis were too pressed for time to finish their murderous work. In one camp near Toruń 2,000 Jewish women were found.[3] Camp Hasag, in Czestochowa, contained 3,758 Jews at the time of liberation (January 17, 1945), of whom 1,518 were from Czestochowa itself.[4] In Lodz there were some 870 surviving Jews. Thousands of additional Jews came out of the camps located within Germany.[5] About 15,000 Jews—Polish and foreign—escaped death in a number of labor camps in Lower Silesia. Another group of survivors, apparently a smaller one, comprised those who had been in hiding, or those who had fought as partisans.

Thousands of Jews went through the German occupation masquerading as Poles, on the strength of forged Polish documents. The Relief Council for the Jews, established by an underground representative of the Polish government-in-exile in 1943, as well as Jewish organizations (Jewish National Committee, Coordination Committee, Bund, and others),[6] helped both with money and documents. Still earlier, in Cracow, the Polish Socialist organization (with the active participation of Josef Cyrankiewicz and others) tried to help Jewish Socialists by providing them with documents and shelter. The Socialists were the most active participants. Among other things they succeeded in perfecting the art of falsifying documents[7] to enable Jews to survive. Others found a way to obtain documents and shelter for themselves or for friends upon payment of large sums of money.

Among those who survived several groups were represented. There were the active members of the Jewish underground and other movements who, immediately following liberation, put off their Polish disguise and resumed their true identity. Among the rest two opposing tendencies could be discerned. Most of the Jews disguised as Poles were, naturally, individuals who spoke fluent Polish and whose appearance either resembled or had been made to resemble that of Poles. Such persons were culturally at ease in a Polish environment, and for reasons of safety learned to participate in Polish and Catholic customs and practices. In the course of time they became accustomed to their role and were generally taken for genuine Poles. Living in disguise among non-Jews, they gained a clear insight into the deep-rooted antisemitism of the Polish population.

For one group this awareness of existing antisemitism, coupled with the fact that they had witnessed the liquidation of Polish Jewry, drove them to resume their Jewishness. For others this awareness had a contrary effect. They preferred to retain their new, non-Jewish, identity[8] as a sort of insurance. Others were afraid of losing the jobs or positions which they held under assumed, non-Jewish names.

> I am living as a Polish woman [writes a Jewess from Cracow in a private letter] under the assumed name of ———. I am reluctant to [reveal my real name] because the Germans have imbued the minds of the people with deep hatred against us and have inculcated the opinion that we have no right at all to exist.[9]

There were also the children whom Poles had hidden away for a price, or who had been raised as Poles in monasteries and orphanages.

> Polish families bring Jewish children to Jewish organizations and report how they sheltered the children. There are also cases of Catholic priests informing Jewish organizations of groups of Jewish children who had been hidden in monasteries.[10]

Some of these children—those whose parents had been killed or whose foster parents had moved away with them and could not be traced—continued to live as Poles.

It is of course difficult to gain a clear idea of the number of disguised Jewish survivors, just as the general number of survivors in Poland itself is hard to determine. At the end of November 1945 it was reported "that 20,000 Jews still retain forged identification papers bearing non-Jewish names."[11] Other estimates gave the number as "a few thousand."

The Jewish Central Committee, organized in Lublin in August 1944, conducted a registration of all surviving Jews. By the middle of June 1945 there were 55,509 Jews registered in Poland, 5,446 Polish Jews in camps in Germany, and 13,000 Jews in the Polish army (73,955). According to Friedman, more than 20,000 should be deducted from this number because of double registration, or because the registrants were Jews returned from

Russia. On the other hand, a few thousand Jews possessing "Aryan" credentials did not register. This makes, in round figures, more than 50,000 Jews—among them 5,000 children—who remained alive in Poland.[12] Others, however, put the number of survivors at more than 100,000.[13] The Central Jewish Committee placed their number, as of January 1946, at 86,060. This figure was, however, challenged as being too high.[14]

Another numerically important group of survivors was the Polish Jews who, having escaped to the Russian-occupied areas, later fled or were deported to the interior of Russia. With them also survived a number of former Polish Jews living in Russian-occupied (1939) eastern Poland who were deported or fled to Russia after the outbreak of the Nazi-Soviet war in June 1941. On September 9 and 22, 1944, the Polish Committee of National Liberation concluded agreements with the Soviet Republics of White Russia, Lithuania, and the Ukraine for the voluntary evacuation from their territories of Poles and Jews who were Polish citizens before September 17, 1939; White Russians, Lithuanians, and Ukrainians in Poland were to be sent back to their countries. A similar agreement was concluded on July 6, 1945, between Poland and the Russian Soviet Federated Republic that permitted Poles and Polish Jews to renounce their Soviet citizenship and to return to Poland. Such persons had until November 20, 1945, to apply for change of nationality; the transfer had to be completed by December 31, 1945, which date was later extended to June 15, 1946.[15] The number of Jewish repatriates to Poland by October 1946 reached 130,000[16] or more, and by the end of the year, about 170,000.[17] Smaller groups of Polish Jews were repatriated in 1947 and 1948; their number amounted to a few thousand. Also, more than a thousand Jews were repatriated from Rumania, most of them refugees who had fled Poland in 1939-40.

Composition of the Surviving Group

Before the war in Poland there were among the Jewish population 109 women to every 100 men. Under the occupation the percentage of women increased, because of the large number of men who fled before the approaching German armies, mobilization of the male population at the outbreak of the war, taking of the men by the Nazis for forced labor, etc. In the later period of the occupation, among certain groups of the population the sex ratio was 196 women to 100 men. The extermination of women took place toward the end of the occupation. Hence, after the war we find a completely reversed sex ratio among the surviving Jewish population: 84.2 women to every 100 men.[18]

Among the repatriates from Russia there was a similar predominance of men over women.[19] This was the result of the fact that a considerable part of the repatriates comprised former male refugees from western Poland who had fled from the Nazis, leaving the rest of the family at home.

Also, thousands of young men from eastern Poland had been drafted into the Red Army and labor battalions in the years 1939-1941, and thus were beyond the reach of the Nazis when the invasion of Russia began. It may also be that mortality among the labor camp inmates in Siberia, Kazakhstan, and other Russian regions was higher among women than among men.

The age structures of both groups (the Jewish survivors in Poland and the Polish Jewish survivors in Russia) were also abnormal, but here the difference between Nazi Poland and Russia was tremendous. The percentage of older men among the survivors in Russia was less than normal, both because of their smaller ratio among the Polish refugees in Russia, and their smaller chances of survival under the difficult conditions in Russia. Still smaller was the ratio of older men among the survivors in Nazi-occupied Poland. In Lodz, for instance, the ratio of men over 55 years of age and older was 2.1 per cent against 10.4 per cent in 1931. In Lower Silesia there were, among a Jewish population of 16,000 as of December 1, 1945, only 70 people of 55 years of age and older, or 0.4 per cent.[20]

Even smaller is the proportion of surviving children. The Nazis made a special point of exterminating Jewish children. Not only were they included in the general "evacuations" to death camps, but there were also special "actions" against children, and in the camps themselves they were among the first to be sent to the gas chambers. In general only people able to perform hard work were kept alive for any time, and they made up the bulk of the survivors.

If we take the 2,500 Jews who were rescued from the camp in Bielawa, we find among them only 19 children, of 10-14 years (0.8 per cent), and no one over 50 years.[21] Outside the camps as well, few children and older people survived. In Lublin, for instance, among 1,000 surviving Jews there were only 10 children.[22]

However, as a result of the influx of Jews from Russia the whole age structure of the surviving Polish Jewry changed, although the number of males still remained higher than that of females. Taking the Passover 1947

TABLE VI

AGE GROUPS OF JEWS IN POLAND, 1947[23]

Age Group	Number	Per cent
0-14	17,236	19.5
15-19	4,187	4.8
20-49	57,574	65.2
50-64	7,301	8.3
65 and over	1,972	2.2
Total	88,270	100.0

matzoth registration, we find there were, at that time, 51.7 per cent males and 48.3 per cent females. Table VI, above, shows age divisions.

Also of interest is the occupational structure of each group. By July 1, 1945, there were in Lodz 20,438 Jews, over one -half of whom were former inmates of concentration camps. About 45 per cent were people without any vocation—young people who had been in school at the time of the outbreak of the war; 29 per cent were artisans; 6.5 per cent had been in trade and small industry; 7.1 per cent were civil servants and white-collar workers; 4.5 per cent were workers; 5.5 professionals; and 2.4 per cent school children.[24] In its appeal to world Jewry for material help toward repatriation, the Committee of Polish Jews in the USSR pointed out that the "majority of Polish Jews temporarily residing in the Soviet Union . . . are skilled professionals—physicians, engineers, lawyers, intellectuals, teachers, clerks, artisans, merchants, prominent literary men and social leaders. Many are workers from the heavy industries."[25]

There were also other differences between the survivors in Poland and the repatriates. Not only older people, but also the Jewish intelligentsia, communal workers, and religious Jews failed to survive in the camps. The Germans made a point of exterminating these groups. Their percentage among the survivors was minimal. On the other hand, the stream of refugees flowing toward eastern Poland before and after the Russian occupation of September 17, 1939, had included a large percentage of these elements. It was believed that the intelligentsia—writers, journalists, communal leaders, and the like—were in greater danger from the Nazis than other persons. A great many of these refugees later returned to Poland as repatriates.

This postwar Jewish population of Poland never achieved stability. Because of the coming and going, the number of the Jewish population fluctuated. Repatriates from the camps and later from Soviet Russia swelled the numbers of the Jewish community—in May 1946 it reached 130,000 or more—at the same time that multitudes were streaming westward to Czechoslovakia, Germany, Austria, and Italy in the hope of being able to journey farther.

Condition and State of Mind of the Survivors

The Jews who survived in the camps or who climbed out from the dugouts were emaciated, sick, and in rags. In Warsaw, which was liberated on January 16, 1945, we find conditions described thus:

> Of the few who now crawled out of the bunkers many were sick. . . . The filthy human skeletons, miraculous testimony to the obstinacy of life, moved in the streets like shadows. . . .
>
> Jews began to arrive from camps, still in their striped prison garb; from villages and forests; from partisan groups in Lithuania; and some from Russia, with military travel permits. . . .[26]

Those who returned from the camps in Germany, mostly "women between 15 and 30 years of age, [are in] "a horrible condition. . . . They are exhausted, starved and are half naked, or in rags. Almost all of them are sick."[27] In Czestochowa immediately following liberation "almost everyone was sick with tuberculosis." In Lodz one-third were tubercular.[28] Survivors were ragged and hungry. The help given them was terribly inadequate.[29]

> Jews besieged the Jewish Committee, crying, shouting, complaining, begging for a suit of clothes, a crust of bread, a place to sleep. The Committee had very limited resources and was not in a position to satisfy even the elementary needs of the unfortunate.[30]

In Bialystok at the beginning of 1946, most Jews were still living in dire want, dressed in old coarse jackets, old military coats and shoes.[31] In the Lodz repatriation center:

> Among the homeless Jews . . . I met Jews who lived all their lives in Lodz and whose homes and workshops had not been destroyed but were occupied by Poles. The Jewish owners were not allowed to enter their houses. I also met some who have recovered their homes and workshops by legal action, but who have left them again upon receipt of threatening letters.[32]

Most of these people were alone: men without wives, wives without husbands, parents without children, children without parents. Their first impulse had been to "go home," to see what remained. But such homecomings were usually sore disappointments. Seldom were traces of a living relative to be found. Most Jewish synagogues, schools, and other buildings had been razed. Even the cemeteries were deserted; tombstones had been removed and cattle were grazing on the graves.

Nor did returning Jews receive a pleasant reception from their non-Jewish neighbors. In Warsaw, whence most of the Poles had been moved after the uprising of August 1944, "sharp conflicts broke out between Poles and Jews over apartments and bunkers. The Poles found the few buildings that remained standing occupied by Jews who, having been in the city, were first comers and had taken possession of the better quarters."[33] In other places some Poles asked, "Still alive?" "Didn't the Nazis kill you?" "Still so many Jews?" Others threatened to finish the work of the Nazis. Such Jewish stores, houses, and businesses that remained were in the hands of non-Jews who resented and fought, legally and illegally, against returning them. "Commerce was carried on exclusively by Poles. . . . The black market and the black bourse were exclusively reserved to the Poles."[34] In some places homes were returned to the Jewish owners; elsewhere Jews were either afraid to insist on their return, or got no assistance from the authorities. A considerable amount of goods and merchandise had been abandoned by Jews taken for deportation, or had been left with non-Jewish neighbors. "But until now nothing has been done to make possible the return of even a portion of the loot to the remaining Jews. The Jews see with their own eyes their stolen property and are helpless to do anything about it."[35]

A Polish Jewess, interviewed in Istanbul after the war, said: "We Jews of Poland have never been coddled by our neighbors and we knew they did not love us. But never until the years of horror did we realize how deep is their hatred."[36] According to some observers, a great many survivors believed "that 50 and maybe fully 75 per cent of the Jewish sacrifices in Poland could be laid to the account of Poles."[37]

The sentiments of a survivor are depicted in a letter by a soldier of the Polish army:

> Instead of longing for home, I am in dread of the moment when I shall have to return. Reason says that there is no hope, and only the heart is still longing. Indeed, what is there to hope for after I have seen no more than a mere handful of Jews in towns where thousands of Jews used to live. What can I hope for after having seen Maidanek and similar places?[38]

Those of the repatriates from Russia who had some hopes about their homecoming were as disappointed as the survivors in Poland and in the Nazi camps. The repatriates, too, had bitter memories—of deportations, forced labor camps, the NKVD and the Communist order generally in Soviet Russia; they did not want to remain in the "seventeenth Soviet republic." They came back to Poland only in the hope that it would be easier to emigrate from it than from the Soviet Union. The characterization of Polish Jewry as "sitting on their valises" was no exaggeration.

Zionist sentiments predominated among the repatriates. A number of forces strengthened both nationalist and the Zionist tendencies. It was natural in a time of great calamity for a group to close ranks and become more conscious of internal ties. Forced confinement in the ghettos brought the Jews into close physical contact with each other, and the practice of collective responsibility applied by the Nazis probably intensified ties. Then again, the destruction of Polish Jewry by the Nazis while their neighbors looked on indifferently led Jews to repudiate "universal" ideas and all notions of a common struggle with non-Jews for a better future. It led to a reluctance to participate in a non-Jewish society and culture.

> We, the crucified people, do not bring . . . before the half and wholly fascist world our word of pain . . . because the shameless "humanitarian" mob is unable to feel the depth of our sufferings. Every cynical sigh of sympathy would only desecrate the holy shadows of our martyrs.[39]

At the same time, the vanished Jewish world acquired a halo of holiness and inspired romantic yearnings. There was a return to the Jewish past. A similar change, perhaps on a smaller scale, was to be noted among the repatriates from Russia.

The ideas of Zionism and a Jewish Palestine were not new to the survivors. In the ghetto and in the camp the hope for a Jewish Palestine after the war helped many to keep alive;[40] for tens of thousands who went to their deaths it was "the last hope." It was also the watchword for a great part of the resistance movement.

To be sure, not everybody in postwar Poland became a Zionist or a nationalist. There were the Jewish Communists who still preached universal assimilation under socialism and who regarded Jewish culture only as a tool in the fight for social revolution. There were also the Bundists, or at least the Bundist leadership,[41] who were anti-Zionist and, in part, opposed to emigration. However, both the Communists and the Bund were represented in the delegation of the Central Jewish Committee to the Anglo-American Commission of Inquiry which demanded, "in the name of the entire Jewish population," free immigration to Palestine.

Religious Jews were imbued with the same sentiments. The girls in "Beth Jacob" Kibbutz maintained that they were in Lodz only temporarily, their goal being Palestine. The rabbi of Lodz said:

> It is a bitter Galuth. . . . The majority of the Jews want to go to Palestine. In the meantime they sit in Lodz.

Another member of the religious community was more hopeful of the future of the Jews in Poland; a third emphasized that they needed only one thing, visas to leave.[42] The masses of the Jews—most of the adults, Zionist and non-Zionist alike—turned out in a demonstration in Lodz before the Anglo-American Committee of Inquiry, demanding: "Let us go. Open the doors of Palestine."

Chapter VI

Antisemitism

The Nazis systematically incited Poles to rob Jews of their possessions. Later, when the stage of extermination was reached, Poles were paid for helping to expose disguised Jews; the death penalty was imposed upon those Poles who aided Jews. All this, combined with the incessant Nazi antisemitic propaganda, intensified anti-Jewish feelings. The fascist youth and some of the underground formations cooperated with the Nazis in their anti-Jewish policies. Other reactionary groups sympathized with the Nazis' work of extermination. Hoodlums and similar elements were glad to stage pogroms so as to enrich themselves, and to make a business of blackmailing disguised Jews. Many Poles also aided the Germans because of a desire to eliminate Jews from Polish life. Many of the Jews who escaped from the ghettos and labor or death camps were given up to the Nazis by Poles. Some Polish inmates of death camps even came to the conclusion "that although horrible things are going on in the camps, at least the Jewish problem [in Poland] is being solved."[1] People became accustomed during the years of Nazi occupation to robbing and killing Jews.

To be sure, there were also Poles who thought and acted differently. Some cases are known of intellectuals who, in opposition to the Germans, ceased being antisemitic. There were also Poles—for the most part from labor groups—who aided Jews to hide and to organize their resistance. There existed also a Relief Council for the Jews maintained by the underground arm of the Polish government-in-exile. But these elements were few.

On the first day of the Polish uprising in Warsaw, the military prison, containing many Jews and slave workers, was captured. Instead of freeing them, the Polish military command formed them into labor gangs and sent them to dig trenches at the front line.

> I must confess that the attitude of the military command in the uprising toward these most unfortunate of the unfortunate Jews was far from proper, even considering the difficult times. They were formed into labor brigades and immediately sent into the front lines to dig trenches under the artillery fire of the enemy. Toughs and hoodlums taunted and tormented them. . . .

Some lawless underworld elements joined the uprising. They often took it upon themselves to seize Aryan-looking Jews as German agents or spies. Even the average Pole showed hostility toward the Jews. Often our people were not allowed to enter the defense shelters. Foreign Jews were sometimes regarded with suspicion as *Volksdeutsche*. We had to find special shelters for Jews and provide them with food, money and other necessities. The courtyard committees would refuse Jews ration cards from the commissaries or the public kitchens. We found ourselves constantly appealing to the authorities to win decent treatment for them. . . .

The *Monitor Polski*, the official government gazette, published a communiqué abrogating the laws which the Germans had introduced during the occupation. They forgot to nullify the Nuremberg laws against Jews. We promptly complained, and the government promised to correct the omission. A long time passed and many petitions were necessary before there was any action. And even then instead of being printed in the space customarily reserved for such communiqués, the notice was tucked away in an inconspicuous corner.

The government agreed to ask the military to permit representatives of the Council for Aid to Jews to appear at investigations into accusations of spying and sabotage. It took a long time to arrange this, and in the meantime many innocent people perished. When the Council finally managed to establish a special office to which Jews could bring their complaints, the uprising was in its last stages.[2]

As the Red Army neared Poland, there were many instances of Jews being massacred by Poles. There were the NSZ groups,[3] "cleaning up" before the war was over. There were also two cases in which Jewish partisan groups were killed by Poles, allegedly under orders from the Polish government in London.[4] Many either killed or turned over to the Nazis the Jews they had been hiding, fearing that after liberation these Jews might demand the return of their money and goods.

Stores and market stalls had passed into the hands of Poles. Such Jewish houses as had not been destroyed were occupied by Poles. Furniture, silver and clothing left by evacuated Jews were in possession of Poles, many of whom held in trust from their former Jewish friends, employers, business associates, and fellow workers a variety of items ranging from precious stones and money to clothing and other commodities. Some of these people feared Jews returning to claim their property. Some feared they might have to vacate apartments or houses, lose their businesses, or be forced to compete with "shrewd" Jews. And then there were those who had delivered Jews into the hands of Nazis, or who had even murdered Jews themselves—these simply feared for their own lives. When, in 1946, whole trainloads of Jewish repatriates from Soviet Russia began to arrive, these fears and animosities increased.

Polish nationalism had grown much stronger during the war. This was a natural reaction to the occupation and the humiliations suffered at the hands of the two occupying powers, German and Russian. The Soviet Union, Poland's adversary throughout the interwar years, had annexed about one-half of the Polish lands, including such historic cities as Lvov and Vilna. This was felt very strongly despite the acquisition of the western territories from Germany. What the people saw was Russian armies overwhelming Poland, deporting Poles to the interior of Russia, disarming the Polish underground army, dismantling and removing factories, looting and raping. And this against a background of ruins, hunger, sickness and poverty.

In this situation the Poles had perforce to accept a Communist or pro-Communist government which did as Moscow bade. This government also included some Jews, and seemed tolerant of Jews. Were "not then all Jews Communists and all Communists Jews?" This formula was also a political weapon that could be turned against the government. Antisemitism became an expression of Polish nationalist defiance. It served as a weapon in the struggle for power, and furnished justification for acts of robbery and murder.

The Roman Catholic church also aided, more or less openly, the growth of antisemitism. In Poland the Catholic church had always been nationalist and reactionary. The Catholic press had been openly antisemitic, and dignitaries of the church had labeled Jews freethinkers and Bolsheviks, called them a bad influence upon Christians, etc. Cardinal Hlond had even advocated economic boycott in 1936: "One does well," he wrote in a pastoral letter, "to prefer his own kind in commercial dealings and to avoid Jewish stores and Jewish stalls in the markets," adding that it was not permissible "to demolish Jewish businesses."[5] During the war some monasteries and religious orphanages, as well as individual priests, hid and helped to rescue Jewish children. But the church as such, and most of the Catholic churchmen, were "neutral."

After the war the church opposed the new regime, even though the latter's land reform spared the church lands which are reported to consist of 1,900 estates comprising two million acres. According to Dr. David Kahane, former Chief Jewish Chaplain of the Polish army, "the Catholic clergy in Poland has been backing fascist bands which engage in antisemitic activities and has done nothing to check the antisemitism which is widespread throughout the country."[6] In a church in Leczyca (near Lodz) the police found an exhibit, arranged by the clergy, showing a painting of four bearded Jews draining blood from the body of a Christian boy; a casket near the altar containing the skeleton of a boy bore an inscription saying that the child was murdered by Jews in 1639.

The fact that antisemitism in Poland was part of the political struggle against the government seems to have been another reason why the church preferred to remain silent,[7] or when forced by circumstances to condemn violence, limited itself to a few general strictures against murder; even this mild reproof was neutralized by its being emphasized that Jews, by their support of the government, brought down upon themselves the wrath of the people.

At the beginning of 1946, August Cardinal Hlond, the Catholic Primate of Poland, in a conversation with a Jewish delegation in Poznań[8] had condemned antisemitic terrorism. But later he refused a request by the Jewish Army Chaplain and Jewish community representatives that he issue a pastoral letter officially condemning antisemitism. A conference of Roman Catholic bishops held in Czestochowa in May 1946 rejected a similar suggestion from the League to Combat Racism. It was only after the pogrom in Kielce, when Polish government authorities challenged the church for its failure to combat antisemitism, and the American Ambassador urged the Primate to make a statement to the press, that the Cardinal issued such a statement.[9] He regarded the pogrom as a "painful" event caused by political rather than racial animosities, and "blamed Jews in the government for creating animosities" leading to such events.

> The fact that this condition [friendship between Jews and Poles] is deteriorating is to a great degree due to the Jews who today occupy leading positions in Poland's government and endeavor to introduce a governmental structure that a majority of the Poles do not wish. . . . In their fatal battle of weapons on the fighting political front in Poland it is to be regretted that some Jews lose their lives, but a disproportionately larger number of Poles also lose their lives.[10]

A similar answer was given by the Bishop of Lublin to Jewish representatives:

> The causes are much deeper. They are rooted in the general hatred of the Jews as a result of their active participation in the present political life of the country . . . the Germans wanted to exterminate the Jewish nation because the Jews spread communism.

He even added that the question as to whether or not Jews use blood for their rituals has not yet been clarified.[11] In Cracow a clergyman was barred from the performance of his duties by high church authorities when he declared that "Kielce proves the existence of an organized group of criminals who deliberately pursue a certain objective," and appealed to parents and teachers to do everything to avoid the repetition of such incidents.[12] Only Bishop Kubina of Czestochowa issued a statement condemning the Kielce pogrom.

Other groups, too, used the Jews as a stick with which to beat the regime. Thus the Socialist deputy Zulawski, who broke with his party because of its cooperation with the PPR, in criticizing the government in the Sejm maintained that "the Jews in Poland today are a privileged element." He, like the church dignitaries, blamed Jews for occupying high positions in the government; the growth of antisemitism he called "a reaction to Jewish behavior."[13]

Nor was the government camp free from antisemitic sentiments and tendencies.[14] The PPR emerged from the occupation none too large numerically. Its policy at first was to admit all and sundry to membership, antisemites included. Also, there were the new "converts"—opportunists, office holders, and office seekers; these were as tainted with antisemitism as the population generally.

In this class of converts to the PPR belonged the chiefs of police and of the militia in Kielce, who were arrested after the pogrom. The chief of police in Tarnów was among the instigators of a blood libel. This same individual had in July 1945 arranged the expulsion of the few Jews left in Rzeszów, at which time he shot a Jewish girl. Among the new members of the PPR were also the engineers who stopped trains outside of stations in order to give rioters a chance to rob and kill Jews, and the conductors who in many such cases showed them where the Jews were. In Wroclaw, during a pro-government election demonstration, the people shouted: "Long live democracy—but without the Jews."[15]

The evacuation of the Germans from the western territories and the loss of the non-Polish populations of the eastern territories for the first time gave Poland ethnic homogeneity. For the first time in Polish history a "Poland for Poles only" came within the realm of possibility. Not only the nationalistic adversaries of the government but also Communists responded to these tendencies. It appeared that only the remnants of Polish Jewry were "disturbing" Polish ethnic unity.

All this led to a sharp increase in antisemitism after liberation. Antisemites whispered that each Jewish repatriate from the camps received 30,000 zloty and that Jewish children were receiving milk denied to non-Jewish children. Rumor spread that many Jews were being brought in from Russia; that they were going to control Polish life, etc. At the time of the referendum in Lodz, a leaflet was issued which "warned that the government planned to send 60,000 Jews to Lodz who would take over all industries there," adding that this was only the first step in giving Jews control of the country's economy. It ended by "demanding the removal of all Jews from Poland."[16] Hatred against Jews was preached by the reactionary underground and similar elements. The blood accusation was revived and in some places served as an excuse to start pogroms.

Boycotting of Jewish stores, if and when they were opened, was practised. Even in Lower Silesia, where both Poles and Jews were newcomers and where, at least at first, antisemitism's hold was weak, instances of boycott occurred. Thus, when Polish peasants from the Galician Beskid mountains were settled in a village in Silesia, their membership in the PPR did not deter them from boycotting Jewish stores.[17]

Government offices were not free of antisemitism.

> The local Polish civilian administration was in many cases hostile to the returning Jews and . . . outspokenly antisemitic. Those of the repatriated Jews who have no relatives to give them shelter, must sleep on park benches or in the streets.[18]

Hidden in the woods were the remnants of the Polish Home Army, the NSZ detachment, and other groups; they attacked trains, houses in the cities, individuals in the streets, and under cover of darkness murdered Jews and government officials. In the months following the liberation of Poland, and even during 1946, when the government was still weak, these bands were strong. In different parts of the country near Kielce and Bialystok, the "boys of the woods" were to a certain extent a shadow government.

Pogroms

Immediately after liberation a wave of violence began, largely initiated by the outlawed NSZ formations. In March 1945 alone, 150 Jews were killed. In Klementów, Czestochowa and other localities Jews were notified that if they did not leave they would be killed. In Klementów those Jews who remained were actually killed. In Kazimierz, the first Jews to return were killed and the synagogue was destroyed. In Lublin terrorists invaded a hospital ward, killing and wounding a number of Jews. In other towns Jews were kidnapped and killed.[19]

The wave of terror rose again in the second half of 1945. In Cracow a pogrom occurred in August 1945, during which a synagogue was attacked and set on fire, two Jews were killed and many injured; among the attackers were soldiers of the Polish Army. In another place a house in which Jews lived was blown up together with its inhabitants. Pogroms, shootings in the dark, and similar attacks became frequent in other cities and towns.[20] According to the figures of the Jewish Central Committee in Poland, during 1945, 350 Jews were killed.[21] Nor did attacks upon Jews abate in the first months of 1946; by April 1946 it was estimated that over 800 Jews had been killed.[22]

The most gruesome pogrom was that of Kielce on July 4, 1946. It would seem to have been well organized. A Polish boy was coached to say that he had been caught by Jews, imprisoned in a cellar, and maltreated. He was also told to say that in the same cellar he saw the bodies of other children. Militiamen searched the house and found the whole story false; at the same time they confiscated the few guns with which these Jews, who were members of a *kibbutz*, were armed. The mob, with the participation of the militiamen, fell upon the Jewish community house and 41 Jews were killed. While the pogrom was in progress, four militiamen took three Jews from another house into the woods and shot two.

The pogrom in Kielce seems to have been a part of a larger scheme, for at the same time in Czestochowa an individual—who later turned out not to be a Jew—was accused of having killed a Christian child; and in Radom and Ostrowiec, too, pogroms were attempted. There were a number of assaults on Jews in trains, 33 Jews being murdered in about one week.[23] These and similar attacks were not limited to any one region. Even in Silesia and Pomerania, where the Poles themselves were newcomers, assault and murder were frequent occurrences.

Following the Kielce pogrom the government tried and executed the murderers and attacked the main hideouts of the underground; but antisemitism continued to flourish.

In some factories workers organized a sit-down strike in protest against the execution of the pogromists. Attacks on Jews were renewed in different places and on trains and buses. The blood libel reappeared in different places. Anti-Jewish demonstrations occurred in Cracow and in Lodz.[24] Political demonstrations by the opposition during the elections of January 1947 were accompanied by anti-Jewish slogans; demonstrations of the government camp also betrayed anti-Jewish leanings.

Only in 1947, when the government consolidated its power and used strong measures against the underground, was order restored. Attacks upon Jews became rare. "The superficial calm . . . was a result of strong police measures rather than of a genuine change of mind on the part of broad segments of the population."[25]

Chapter VII

Exodus

The Anglo-American Committee of Inquiry which visited Poland on February 7-13, 1946 listed the antisemitism of the Poles and the Zionism of the Jews as the chief reasons for the desire of Jews to emigrate.

> The desire must be intensely strong to pick up the threads of life again elsewhere—where opportunities appear more favorable, where he will not be surrounded by a population inclined to resent his presence and where he will not be perpetually reminded of past events. . . . Political Zionism with its demands for the creation of a Jewish state is strong among the Jewish survivors. Accounts of life in Palestine . . . [are] rendered doubly attractive by contrast with ordeals they have endured . . . without propaganda or personal influence there are . . . sufficient reasons for Jews to wish to leave Poland and go to a country where they can be assured of sympathy and help.[1]

Dr. Sommerstein, when head of the Jewish Central Committee in Poland, declared as early as January 1945 that because of antisemitism most of the Polish Jews wanted to emigrate, particularly to Palestine.[2]

But Palestine was closed. The British Mandatory Government was granting so few certificates that only a minute portion of postwar European Jewry could be provided with entry visas to Palestine. The possibilities of immigration into America were likewise slight.[3] Proceeding toward Palestine or the United States meant, to Polish Jews, getting out of Poland and moving westward in the hope of later finding a way to continue their journey. Rumors that it was easier to reach Palestine from the camps, the fear that Poland might close her frontiers, and the threat of pogroms, contributed to the flight westward.

The emigration of Jews from Poland began even before the whole country had been liberated. In the Lublin region in the summer of 1944, some Zionist youth leaders began to organize the emigration of *chalutzim* and other elements. The first steps were taken toward planning the subsequently famous *bricha,* or underground railroad for illegal emigrants. In the immediate postwar period millions were on the move. Slave workers of the Nazis, expellees, and others whom the war had cast up in foreign countries were moving homeward. Frontiers had not yet been stabilized. This situation enabled thousands of Jews from Poland to masquerade as

Rumanians, Greeks, etc. Some also moved in the wake of army detachments. The movement was toward Rumania. From there the route led through Hungary, Yugoslavia, and Austria to Italy.

By the fall of 1945 the camps in Italy were crowded and national boundaries more stabilized; passing the borders became difficult if not impossible. But then another exodus was already under way, to the camps in Germany and Austria. The increasing number of attacks upon Jews, and the hope of admittance to Palestine aroused by President Truman's demand for 100,000 additional certificates, served to accelerate emigration.

After August and particularly in October 1945, large numbers of Jews from Poland began arriving in Berlin and in the German camps. Other Jews were making their way to the Austrian camps. Jews from Poland (and Hungary) reached Munich and such Bavarian refugee camps as Landsberg, Feldafing, and Föhrenwald. By January 1946 it was estimated that "more than 25,000 Jews have left Poland since its liberation."[4]

The American authorities were at first startled by the influx of refugees. Soon, however, word came from higher authorities that the refugees were to be looked after, and that "those who reach the American sector of Berlin will be regarded as persons displaced by enemy action."[5]

The British military authorities apparently attempted to stem the tide so as to prevent the refugees from becoming potential immigrants to Palestine. They at first refused them passage through the British zone, but later consented to let a special train go through on condition that American military authorities guaranteed that the refugees would be admitted into the American zone.[6] Upon reaching the camps in Germany and Austria, the refugees were taken care of by the American military authorities, UNRRA, and the JDC.

This migration went on for months in 1946. At that time repatriation from Russia was in full swing, and apparently only a few of these Jews wanted to remain in Poland. According to officials of the Jewish Central Committee in Poland, "the vast majority of the repatriates want to go to Palestine or America. Many try to leave Poland illegally, crossing into Germany or Czechoslovakia."[7] The number of arrivals in the camps of the American zone rose from "about 1,500 weekly to as many as 4,000."[8]

In the main the exodus was organized. Begun by local leaders of Zionist youth and chalutz organizations, mostly from elements which had been active in the underground during the Nazi occupation, the organization of the *bricha* was greatly improved in the fall of 1945 when Palestinian representatives reached Europe. The few Palestinian representatives in Poland served rather as a guiding spirit, while the actual work—organizing the groups, bringing the refugees to the frontiers, crossing them over in the dead of night, running the transient houses, arranging for transportation through Czechoslovakia to the camps in Germany and Austria—was accomplished by the local leadership with no, or only very inadequate, funds.

Outsiders who saw only the continual arrival of refugee transports at the camps bringing in not only the ragged and starving individuals but also the young and healthy, regarded the *bricha* as a large-scale undertaking. This apparently led Lieutenant General Sir Frederick Morgan, chief of UNRRA's operations in Germany, to look upon the exodus as a conspiracy, a "well-organized positive plan to get [the Jews] out of Europe." He doubted the "monotonous story about pogroms," asserting that the Jews arriving from Poland were "well dressed and fed, rosy-cheeked, and have plenty of money. They certainly do not look like persecuted people."[9] A different opinion was expressed by Judge Rifkind, advisor on Jewish Affairs to General McNarney. He maintained that the reason for the flight of the Jews from Poland was the "attitude of intense hostility" shown by the native population toward those returning to their homes in Poland. "Out of those I questioned the proverbial 99 and 44/100 per cent are leaving Poland under a sense of compulsion—genuine or imagined. The predominant factor for the flight from Poland is fear. Jews fleeing out of Poland are, or believe they are, fleeing for their lives."[10]

Meanwhile the sheer numbers involved forced organizations and other authorities to take cognizance of the exodus. Certain attempts were made to legalize it. The American authorities in Warsaw issued a number of transit permits entitling the bearers to proceed through the American zone of Germany to France. The Central Jewish Committee opened an "emigration department" to assist legal emigration. The HIAS began its operations in Poland in February 1946.[11]

However, few were able to emigrate legally from Poland. Only those with wealthy relatives abroad or who managed to secure entrance visas to the United States on their own could hope to do so. The vast majority went by the usual underground route.[12]

The pogrom on July 4, 1946, in Kielce, and the increasing number of attacks on Jews, spurred on the exodus. Panic seized the Jews. Thousands now began to leave daily. At the meeting of the Central Jewish Committee held in Warsaw after the pogrom, almost all of the delegates emphasized that the Jews were in danger. Only the representative from Silesia was optimistic about the fate of Jews in his region. But even many Silesian Jews left their fields sown, their cattle in the stables, their houses and stores, and made their way toward the camps in Germany and Austria. From Stettin, where about 26,000 Jewish repatriates had been settled, over 20,000 fled during July and August, some crossing the border immediately after their arrival from Russia.[13] In 1946 about 150,000 left Poland.[14]

The Polish government, as well as the Jewish Central Committee in Poland, at first tried to stem the tide of emigrants. But their efforts met with little success and they desisted. In August 1946 the exodus ceased to be illegal in Poland.

Difficulties arose when Czechoslovakia temporarily closed the border at the end of September and the Russians imposed a ban on crossing into the eastern part of Austria. The exodus began to fall off in October 1946, almost coming to a standstill at the beginning of December.[15] It revived again at the beginning of 1947, out of fear that the election campaign would cause new anti-Jewish violence and the Polish frontiers were going to be closed.[16] The Polish government had originally sanctioned emigration for only one month. This period was later extended. But in February 1947, the borders were closed. A little later the government even held the Zionist leaders responsible for illegal emigration.[17] This fact, plus the restoration of order in the country, resulted in a certain settling down. Some Jews began to establish themselves in Poland, although "many Polish Jews are waiting for the opportunity to leave the country," and "Jews are still leaving the country at the rate of 300 a month." The same correspondent wrote that

> privately [Jewish leaders] state that Poland's endemic antisemitism plus harrowing memories of the war years and shattered economies will drive all but 10,000 of Poland's remaining 90,000 Jews out of the country by the end of 1948. These 10,000 . . . will be composed almost equally of the die-hard Leftists, bound ideologically to the new conditions here, and the deeply orthodox, mostly aged persons, whose roots are too deep in Poland to be transplanted anywhere else. For the 80,000 others Palestine is still the main hope.[18]

A small, mostly legal, emigration of about 600 a month continued throughout 1947, with some Jews, grown tired of waiting in the camps, trickling back to Poland. In October-November 1947 there was again an increase in the number of departures, involving mainly people of the Hakhsharah *kibbutzim*. With this most of the illegal emigration ended.[19] On March 31, 1948, which date was later prolonged for three months, the granting of passports to countries outside of Palestine was to be made "conditional upon the presentation of a written promise of a visa"—this meant a virtual end to any possibilities of emigration.

While many of the Jews who remained in Poland found a way of being absorbed into the economy of the country, the vast majority hoped to be able to depart eventually, for the most part to Palestine.[20] When, with the founding of the State of Israel and the Polish government's granting of visas to Zionists and those having close relatives in Israel,[21] such an opportunity arose, a considerable number of Jews registered for emigration and left Poland.

CHAPTER VIII

The Government and the Jewish Minority

The postwar Polish government's policies with regard to the Jewish question show a number of contradictory trends. On the one hand, we find innumerable expressions of sympathy for the Jews, and declarations affirming their equal status with non-Jews. We witness efforts to make this equality a reality and to offer assistance—including financial aid—in the reconstruction of Jewish life. On the other hand, a clear reluctance is observable to abrogate Nazi anti-Jewish laws, to institute a procedure for the restitution of Jewish property, and to combat antisemitism. There is also a clearly defined tendency to promulgate, in general terms, laws aimed specifically at the Jews. Formally, the government opposed antisemitism; actually, it stressed Polish ethnic unity with all its anti-Jewish implications.

When the Committee of National Liberation was founded a special point was made of emphasizing its ideas in connection with the Jews.

The manifesto of July 22, 1944, of the Committee of National Liberation not only guaranteed "the restoration of all democratic liberties, the equality of all citizens, regardless of race, creed, or nationality," but also affirmed that "the Jews who had been subjected to inhuman tortures by the occupant are guaranteed full rehabilitation and legal as well as actual equality of rights."[1]

The Provisional Government formed on December 31, 1944, stressed, in a declaration by the Prime Minister Osubka-Morawski, that "our government must supply Jews with work and considers it necessary to create conditions under which Jews could devote themselves to productive work." The declaration pointed out that the Jews in Poland would enjoy equality not only in law, but also in fact, and that they were deserving of special attention from the government.[2]

Upon different occasions high government officers voiced their positive attitude toward the Jews. When Dr. Sommerstein left for the World Zionist Conference in London, in July, 1945, Premier Osubka-Morakski sent him a document, to be presented to the Conference, giving assurances that the Polish government: (1) fights racism and antisemitism; (2) is for the absolute equality of the Jews; (3) will help the reconstruction of Jewish life in Poland; (4) will enable the Jews to receive relief coming from abroad; and (5) "the government of National Unity will not restrict but support the efforts of individuals and organizations for the voluntary emigration of Jewish people from Poland."[3] Foreign Minister Vincenty Rzymovski declared in New York in the fall of 1945 that the Polish government sincerely desired that "a Jew should feel himself in Poland an equal in his citizen rights to a Christian." It was repeatedly stated that the purpose of the government's policy was two-fold: to create conditions which will enable Jews to live in Poland; and at the same time to avoid placing obstacles before those who wished to emigrate.[4]

The Committee of National Liberation included, as did the subsequent governments, a number of Jews. In the Committee itself Emil Sommerstein headed the Department of War Supplies, and Boleslaw Drobner the Department of Press Affairs. Later Hilary Minc came in as head of the Economic Division. In later governments he served as Minister of Industry and Vice-Prime Minister. A number of Jewish vice-ministers, including Jacob Berman, were to be found in the Polish cabinets. Jews were also apparently admitted to a variety of government offices, except where local antisemites interfered. Persons with Jewish names, however, had difficulty in obtaining government positions, or they were advised to change their names.

The Provisional Government permitted Jewish representatives to have a voice in some matters in which Jews were concerned. For example, it allowed the organization of the Jews in Poland to be represented in the commission investigating the crimes committed by Germans in Auschwitz.[5]

The government and municipalities gave Jewish organizations and institutions financial support. Upon its foundation, the Central Jewish Committee received from the government 30 million zloty and some clothing. Later, additional sums were given to the Jewish Central Committee for the support of its work (by February 1946 it had received 90 million zloty), as well as raw materials for Jewish cooperatives. Municipalities frequently granted varying amounts to Jewish institutions. The JDC and other Jewish foreign agencies were given the same status as other foreign voluntary agencies; this exempted them from customs duties and gave them free railroad transportation for their imports and warehouse facilities at reduced cost. The government also contributed 10 million zloty ($25,000) toward the erection of a monument in memory of the martyrs of the Warsaw ghetto.[6]

If the higher branches of the government seemed generally untainted by antisemitism, this was far from being the case in the lower offices and in the local government; nor, as we have seen, was the dominant Polish Workers Party free from it. Police officers, soldiers, and other government officials were often to be found among the instigators of racial hatred and pogroms.

The small group of German Jews who remained in the regained territories were not regarded as Germans, but were granted the same property rights as Polish nationals. Jewish repatriates from Russia were given farms, houses and furniture in the regained territories equally with non-Jewish repatriates, or were provided with jobs in industry.

On the other hand, the repeal of the law forbidding ritual slaughter was postponed for years, although sporadic permission was given to slaughter animals in accordance with the Jewish ritual.[7] Recognition of Jewish schools was withheld and the granting of subsidies delayed on the real or pretended ground that their curricula were not adapted to those of the government schools.

In general, the government gave free rein to Jewish communal development, permitting all prewar Jewish parties except the Revisionists to renew their activities, and lent a supporting hand to Jewish cultural and economic institutions. In matters affecting other sections of the population, however, such as the problem of the restitution of Jewish property, antisemitism, and migration, the government was careful to avoid giving offense or seeming to favor Jews.

Emigration and Palestine

From the first, high officials asserted that the Provisional government would not hinder emigration and that it supported the Jewish demand for a national home. Thus in April 1945 the Polish government's delegate in France stated that "his government was viewing sympathetically the Jewish national work of reconstruction in Palestine in which so many Jews of Polish origin were cooperating." Similarly, Polish Ambassador Lange in the United States asserted that the Polish government was ready to help those Jews who wanted to emigrate—it "supports the request of the Jewish people for a national home in Palestine."[8]

As early as January 1945 Premier Osubka-Morawski declared that Jewish emigration would not be impeded. Later, in his letter to Dr. Sommerstein, he declared that the government was in sympathy with Jewish national aspirations in Palestine, and in a statement before the Polish National Council he reaffirmed this attitude. "While Poland needed the hands and brains of every citizen"—he declared—"the government would not stand in the way of Jews who desired to emigrate to Palestine and realize their national aspirations."[9] In June 1946, when Jews were holding protest meetings in Poland against British actions in Palestine, the Prime Minister assured a delegation from the Central Committee of Polish Jews that "Polish democratic opinion has full understanding of the right of the Jewish nation for the establishment of the Jewish national home." At a protest meeting of Warsaw Jews, Vice-Minister Bienkowski stressed the sympathy of the Polish people for the idea of Jewish renaissance in Palestine. To the representation of the Palestine Federation of Jewish Labor (Histadruth) in 1946, and to Meier Yaari, leader of the Hashomer Hatzair at the time of his visit to Warsaw in January 1947, President Bierut expressed the opinion that the Jews, like all nations of the world, are entitled to their own state, and promised to support their demands.[10]

In practice, as we know, except for some slight interruptions, the government permitted both legal and "illegal" emigration up to 1947. Later, when the frontiers were closed (February 1947) and restrictions on migration were imposed (1948), emigration to Palestine was considered a special case; Jewish leaders "were promised that no restriction will be placed on emigration to Palestine when the Jewish state to be established there is ready to permit the entry of Polish immigrants."[11] Passports were later granted to Zionists and others for emigration to Israel.

In the United Nations Organization, Polish representatives (together with Soviet Russia) throughout 1947 supported the resolution on the partition of Palestine and foundation of a Jewish state. In Poland itself the government permitted, or at any rate did not obstruct, until later, such activities as the collecting of money for the Jewish National Fund, the Jewish Foundation Fund, and, during the Arab-Israel war, for the Haganah.[12] If a report from the Jewish Telegraphic Agency may be credited, it appears that Polish military headquarters facilitated the discharge of Jewish officers of the Polish Army who wished to go to Palestine to join in the fight for a Jewish homeland.[13]

Antisemitism

The government in postwar Poland was, from the first, opposed to antisemitism, which it labeled reactionary and fascistic. It was declared that "the Polish government made the fight against antisemitism part of its program."[14] But this meant that antisemitism was a political issue; charges of antisemitism brought against the opposition were principally a means to discredit the latter abroad.

> Antisemitic propaganda, assaults on Jews [stated the Polish Consul in New York, Jan Galewicz (himself a Jew)] these are but two of the vile and criminal methods applied by the Polish reactionary Fascist groups. They follow exactly the same pattern in their attacks on Poles, on democrats, labor leaders, Socialists, members of the peasant parties or Communists. . . . The government is waging a ruthless and uncompromising and determined battle against these reactionary groups.[15]

In 1946 an organization was founded with government sponsorship for the purpose of fighting antisemitism; it was called the League to Combat Racism. The League, in which people prominent in politics, science and letters were active, began to publish a periodical, *Prawo Czlowieka* (*Human Rights*), and a number of pamphlets against antisemitism.

This identification of antisemitism exclusively with reaction led to its legal condemnation (in the decree of September 16, 1945, as amended on June 13, 1946) in general terms only, as one of many types of subversive activity, rather than to the issuance of a decree especially directed against antisemitism, as had been demanded and promised.[16] An editorial in the *Bulletin* of the Polish Embassy in Washington, D. C., stated for the benefit of foreign opinion:

> The Polish legislator has been forced to deal with numerous problems other than antisemitic propaganda. Repeated assaults, murders and even pogroms have rendered it necessary to define in legal terms a number of factual situations, of crimes against individuals or groups, on ground of nationality, creed or race. Accordingly, as the law now stands, incitement to and approval of nationalist, religious or racial strife (Art. 30) and offenses against groups or individuals on such grounds (Art. 31) are subject to penalties of up to five years' imprisonment. All criminal acts resulting in death or severe physical injury, or constituting a threat to public peace and safety, assume an extraordinary legal character if and when they are directed against groups or individuals on grounds of nationality, creed or race; in such instances they entail a penalty of no less than three years in prison, life imprisonment, or death (Art. 32). . . . And finally the decree holds all persons responsible who, disregarding their civic duties, fail to act with a view to preventing such crimes.
>
> The Polish decree uses the general terms of nationalist, religious and racial strife, but considering the particular conditions prevailing in our country the decree is in fact mainly directed against antisemitic transgressions. There are practically no national, racial or religious minorities in Poland today, except the few Jewish survivors.[17]

But in fact, the Jews in Poland itself were dissatisfied with the lack of such a special decree against antisemitism and the leniency with which it was suppressed. This dissatisfaction was clearly expressed after the pogrom in Kielce in July 1946. At a meeting of the CJC following the pogrom, the government was criticized "for not issuing a decree proclaiming antisemitism a crime against the state." It was maintained that the existing law against racial discrimination was ineffective and that "it was necessary to declare that anti-Jewish instigations were criminal."[18] Dr. Adolph Berman introduced a motion in the Polish National Council calling for a special law against antisemitism. Some non-Jewish deputies also introduced such a motion. The Jewish deputies in the council conferred with the Minister of Justice on the draft of a law to suppress antisemitic propaganda, but no action was taken.[19]

The government at first thought to eliminate anti-Jewish tendencies by means of a program of re-education;[20] it treated anti-Jewish transgressions rather leniently, and tolerated the existence of antisemitism in the bureaucracy. Following the Kielce pogrom a somewhat firmer line was taken. Nine defendants were sentenced to death; commutation of the sentences was refused.[21] Another trial ended with nine persons receiving varying prison terms; four police and militia officials were accused of failing to act promptly so as to avoid clashes, two of them being sentenced to prison terms.[22] Later in the same year a Polish soldier was sentenced to eight years in prison for attempting to provoke anti-Jewish excesses. At the beginning of 1949 a Warsaw court sentenced a Pole to three years for insulting a Jew.[23]

As a result of the Kielce pogrom the government also granted permission to the Jewish communities to organize their own defense, providing them with arms for that purpose; an earlier request by Jewish representatives for such permission had been refused.[24]

Restitution

Almost all Jewish property in Poland that had not been destroyed or removed to Germany was found in the hands of non-Jews. Some of these had acquired such property from their Jewish friends in order to save it from the Nazis. But in the majority of cases the non-Jewish owners of this property had either come by it through Nazi confiscation and resale, or by some other illegal means.

In the first months following liberation when Jews were returning to their former places of domicile, only a few Poles made voluntary restitution of Jewish property. An additional few were forced to do so by local Polish authorities. For the most part, however, restitution met with strong opposition and contributed to the growth of antisemitism. The Committee of National Liberation, in its manifesto published on August 15, 1944, promised that "the property stolen from individual citizens—peasants, merchants, craftsmen, small or medium industrialists, institutions, churches—will be returned to the legal owners." The enactment of a restitution law took about eight months.

The law of May 6, 1945 (amended on July 23, 1945 and March 3, 1946),[25] dealt with property which had passed to a third owner to avoid loss by war or occupation; or had been confiscated by the occupation authorities; or had been abandoned by persons taking flight. The law voided all agreements involving such property concluded with the occupation authorities, or with organizations and persons acting on their behalf; it voided all agreements entered into for the sole purpose of saving the property from loss, as well as all subsequent acquisitions of such properties. The purchaser of such property was a *mala fide* possessor and had no right to claim reimbursement of his investment, even if the value of the property had increased under his care. Abandoned properties were to be returned, upon request, to the original owner, regardless of the present status of their possession. If the owner's whereabouts were unknown, his heirs might demand restitution.

To administer such properties until claimed by the owners or their heirs, a special government Office of Deserted and Abandoned Properties was created; all such properties had to be registered with and given over to this office, which cared for them until claimed by the rightful owner or his heirs. Property in which the state had a special interest, or which had been acquired by the state through the agrarian reform law and law for the nationalization of industry (January 3, 1946), was not returnable.

The law made no provision for voluntary transfers, which could be voided only by regular legal procedure—a long-drawn-out affair. Nor did the law provide for the return of apartments and stores rented by Jews.

There is little information available on the actual course of restitution in Poland. We know of a number of cases in which Jewish property was returned, and also of cases in which it was not, the courts either putting off a decision or rendering an adverse judgment. There are also cases in which the Office for Abandoned Properties refused to make restitution. Property confiscated from Jews during the German occupation was apparently withheld in many cases. Premier Osubka-Morawski avoided replying to a direct question as to why the government did not act to return Jewish property by asserting "that the government treats all repatriates alike."[26]

According to some observers, though the government did not deny the right of Jews to recovery of their property, it was only in exceptional cases that they actually got anything back. "There is no mention of restitution of everything. . . . He would become a rich man—a capitalist—greater than the new Polish economic policy admits. Jewish survivors are asking for their factories, but not getting them. Those who do receive them back are the rare exceptions."[27]

But as antisemitism mounted, attacks upon Jews increased, and the tide of exodus swelled, the law of restitution lost virtually all real efficacy. In many cases in which Jews had received (or should have received) back their properties, threats by antisemites, and even actual murders, forced them to give them up. Other Jews were afraid to begin proceedings to reclaim their property.

For those Polish Jews or their descendants living abroad, the end of 1947 had been fixed as the deadline for filing claims for recovery of property. This period was subsequently extended another year. Such claims, however, necessitated a lengthy court procedure; if successfully concluded, the obstructive procrastinations of the office administering the properties had then to be endured. Not many Jews living abroad effected recovery.

Even more complicated is the matter of properties belonging to Jewish communities and other foundations and organizations. Under Nazi rule properties belonging to Jewish communities, foundations, and organizations had been confiscated or turned over to non-Jews. Following libertion they came under the jurisdiction of the Office of Abandoned Properties, which allowed former Jewish community buildings, including synagogues, to continue to be used for all sorts of foreign purposes. Thus, in Cracow, one synagogue was used as a firehouse, another for storing theatrical material. In other localities, too, Jewish community buildings were occupied by non-Jewish organizations.[28]

For a long time the government did not recognize either the Central Jewish Committee or the Association of the Jewish Religious Communities as the successor of the prewar Jewish community. Thus they were deprived of their right to claim the properties of the old communities. The government would apparently consider the return of such communal property only where a successor community had been founded.[29] Nor did the stipulation in the law of restitution permitting the Office of Abandoned Properties to give some properties over to organizations of groups which had been persecuted by the Nazis, prove of any avail.

> One might have assumed that immediately after the Jewish Committees and Religious Societies had been constituted, the question of the properties of the former Jewish communities and many charitable organizations would have been regulated by legislation. We must regretfully state that this matter, so vital to us, has so far not been settled. Moreover, the decree concerning abandoned and deserted property even provided that juridical persons, especially educational and charitable groups of a section of the population particularly persecuted by the occupant, may receive from the main Office for the Administration of Abandoned Property some such property for administration and use. Yet until today, despite all their endeavors, neither the Jewish Committee nor the Religious Societies have been able to acquire any property which had previously belonged to the Jewish community or other Jewish institutions. What other groups of Poland's population were more persecuted by the occupant than the Jews? . . . Why then in this case did the manifesto of the Polish Committee of National Liberation and the provisions of the law remain a dead letter?[30]

Jewish representatives asked time and again that the restoration of communal property, or of a particular building (*e. g.*, of the Jewish theater in Lodz), be facilitated. Although in June 1947 Premier Cyrankiewicz assured a Jewish delegation "that Jewish institutions will have no difficulty in recovering buildings and other property," the problem was still being discussed when, about a year later, Jewish organizations asked for the "issuance of a law placing in Jewish custody property left by Jewish communities wiped out during the Nazi occupation."[31] Negotiations with the government offices resulted only in the issuance of an order for the return of Jewish tombstones that had been used to pave streets.[32] In 1947 and 1948 a few buildings and synagogues in Praga and Warsaw were returned to the Jewish community.

Chapter IX

Economic Adjustment

The Jewish population of postwar Poland was almost continually in flux. There were arrivals from the camps and from Russia, departures for the West, and a constant movement within Poland itself. It is therefore extremely difficult to estimate their numbers. Following liberation, the number of Jews was placed at 50,000. By June 1945 the number of Jews in Poland was said to be 55,509; in addition, there were 13,000 Jews in the Polish army.[1] By January 1946, the Jewish population was estimated at 86,060. By the middle of 1946 it was thought to have reached 120-150,000. However, the accelerated exodus following the Kielce pogrom reduced the figure considerably, and in the spring of 1947, 88,270 people registered for Passover matzoth. It is estimated that there were in addition some 8-10,000 Jews who did not register. By March 1948 the Jewish population was officially fixed at 94,000, of whom 44,000 lived in Lower Silesia. The JDC estimated the number of Jews in Poland at the end of 1947 as 105,000; at the end of 1948, 88,000; and at the end of 1949, 75,000.[2]

The Jews of postwar Poland were concentrated in a limited number of localities; the centers of Jewish concentration were not always the same as those of prewar days. Warsaw, for instance, had a few thousand Jews, whereas 20,438 were registered in Lodz as of July 1945. Cracow too became, for a time at least, a new Jewish center.

There were two main reasons to account for concentration in these particular cities: they had suffered scarcely any damage, making it easier to find accommodations; and they were securer places than the smaller towns in the event of pogroms.

About one-half of the Jewish population in Poland was concentrated in the new western provinces. About 30,000 Jewish repatriates came to western Pomerania, especially Stettin, in the summer of 1946. For economic and political reasons the concentration of Jews in this area was shortlived; by the end of the year only 4,000 Jews were left.[3] Silesia became a more important center.

Lower Silesia comprises over 10,000 square miles and includes the capital city of Wroclaw (Breslau). It is a region with a well-developed agriculture, broad stretches of woodland, important coal mines, nickel, lead and copper deposits, and is also an important center of the textile and chemical industries. Before the war its inhabitants numbered 3,250,000, with about 50,000 Jews. In the course of the Nazi persecutions most of the Jews either emigrated or were deported.

At the beginning of May 1945, when the Red Army was approaching Silesia, there were about 15,000 Jews alive in its concentration and labor camps. SS men and camp commanders beat a hasty retreat, and in violation of Himmler's orders these Jews were not done away with. Some of the civilian population also fled, leaving behind their houses, furniture, clothes, shops and food supplies. Before liberation, Jews in the camp "Sportsschule," in Reichenbach, organized a Committee of Former Prisoners which undertook to provide the inmates with clothing, food, and shelter. After liberation a Jewish militia was formed to guard factories, shops, and other property against attacks by bands of former Nazi soldiers and police. At the same time the newly formed Jewish committee was busy providing the sick and emaciated camp inmates with medical help and food.

Meanwhile, most of the Jewish camp inmates who were not from Poland returned to their own countries. Many Polish Jews also tried to return to their own cities and towns, only to find homes, families, and friends all gone. Some then decided to return to Silesia. In this way about 6-7,000 Jews settled in Reichenbach, Bielawa, Petrolesie (Peterswaldau), Ludwigsdorf, Walbrzych, Geiszczpusta (Wueste Giesdorf). Reichenbach, unlike Wroclaw, had escaped damage; for a while it was the largest center of the new Jewish settlement in Lower Silesia. Here, on June 17, 1945, was held the first convention of the Jewish Committee in Lower Silesia. Egit, chairman of the committee and himself a former camp inmate, became the promoter of "a Palestine (or Birobidjan) in Silesia."

The Conference, and the District Jewish Committee established by it, took steps to popularize the idea of the resettlement in Silesia of other Jews from Poland, as well as of the Jewish repatriates from Russia. They addressed themselves to the Central Jewish Committee in Poland, to the organizational committee of the Polish Jews in Soviet Russia, and sent a delegation to the Polish government in Warsaw suggesting the creation of a settlement of 20,000 Jewish repatriates in Silesia.

The general repatriation movement was, as has been noted, directed toward the newly acquired western regions, where homes, fields, and factories were to be had. Jewish repatriates, too, were sent in the same direction, and for the same reasons. This also spared the government problems of restitution and indemnification; by giving Jews abandoned German properties it escaped any obligation to recover Jewish property from Poles. Eventually Jewish repatriates were even forced to proceed directly to Silesia; only later were they able to leave it and go on to other parts of Poland.

In the first months after the conference held in June 1945, the Jewish population was steadily enlarged, first by new arrivals from central Poland and by Polish Jews returning from the concentration camps in Germany, and later by repatriates. By mid-1946, the repatriation movement had passed its peak. Altogether, 85,212 Jewish repatriates, or over one-half of all Jewish repatriates from Soviet Russia, reached Silesia.[4]

The exodus before and after the Kielce pogrom of July 1946 removed about half the Jews from Silesia. The remaining 40-50,000 constituted about one-half of the entire Jewish population in Poland.

Economic Situation

Everywhere in Poland after the war transport was crippled, houses demolished, agricultural machinery destroyed, animals and cattle killed; there was a shortage of everything, food, clothing, tools, machinery. Even in 1946 agricultural production was less than one-half of what it had been in the prewar years. According to the Polish Minister of Welfare, "although the whole population of Poland is living in misery, the Jewish people are in exceptionally difficult conditions. They have lost everything."[5] The JDC representative reported that of the 80,000 Jews in Poland, 70,000 needed assistance.[6]

In 1945 and even in the first half of 1946 Jews in Poland were plagued by hunger and disease.[7] The little that the different political movements could provide served as a basis for attracting new members. "The various movements among Jews exist to a significant degree thanks to the fact that they maintain their members, give them bed and board, bread, a dish of soup, and clothing."[8]

In 1945 UNRRA began bringing in food, agricultural machinery, fertilizers, and clothing. But at first this was hardly sufficient to supply the needs of the population. Among Jewish organizations, the JDC began sending none too large quantities of food and clothing as early as the last months of 1944. But these things had then to be sent from Teheran, later also from Sweden and South Africa, and did not arrive in Poland until the summer of 1945, when it was found that some things were missing. According to a JDC report, by October 24, 1945, a total of $197,554 in supplies had been shipped. The American and World Jewish Congresses sent some clothing and vitamin tablets.[9]

None of this, however, amounted to much, and relief from abroad did not become a factor in Jewish rehabilitation in Poland until the beginning of 1946, when the JDC began to make larger allocations for immediate needs.[10] Until then Polish Jews had to rely mainly on the little which the Jewish Committees could afford to give them.

Nor were occupational opportunities promising. The middle-class occupations of the Jews had been taken over by non-Jews. In the antisemitic atmosphere which reigned in Poland it was often either impossible or dangerous for Jews to appear in the market to compete with the new Polish peddlers and shopkeepers. And even if they had, Jews would have been boycotted.[11] No better was the situation of the Jewish craftsmen. Lack of raw materials made it virtually impossible to reopen a shop. The prewar Industrial Law making the conduct of a workshop dependent upon registration and prolonged training at a recognized master's shop, was still in force in postwar Poland. Most of the Jewish survivors had lost their registration cards during the occupation; younger people had been unable to receive regular training.

Communist domination of Poland scarcely favored private enterprise. Agricultural reform, nationalization of larger industrial enterprises, partial payment in kind to workers (up to 1949), a planned economy— all this spelled insecurity and limited opportunities for the individual businessman and artisan.

Businessmen were also obliged to pay higher rents, even for their apartments, amounting to some fifty times the rent paid by a worker or state employee. These were further augmented as Communist control tightened after 1948. The government tax law of October 25, 1948, changed the progressive tax system into one based on "the source of income"; this raised the taxes on income from private enterprise by 25 per cent and also imposed a series of special taxes. A special authority was appointed empowered to scrutinize all transactions at any time. This authority, plus the new tax system, elminated many businessmen and small producers.[12]

If we take the situation in Lodz, the largest Jewish center, at the middle of 1945 as an indication, we find that almost half the Jews (mainly those who had been in school when the Second World War started) lacked any occupation. The occupational structure of the rest of Lodz Jewry was as follows:

TABLE VII

OCCUPATIONAL STRUCTURE OF JEWS IN LODZ, 1945

Occupation	Number	Per cent
Artisans	6,087	52.2
Commerce and small manufacturers	1,386	12.0
Civil service and white-collar workers	1,535	13.1
Workers	963	8.2
Professionals	1,183	10.0
Students	520	4.5
TOTAL	11,674	100.0

The occupational structure of the 136,579 repatriates up to the middle of 1946 was not too dissimilar from that of the Lodz Jews.

TABLE VIII
OCCUPATIONS OF REPATRIATES[13]
(Male, aged 14-55)

Occupation	Per cent
Artisans	50.9
Commerce and manufacturing	6.2
Civil service and white-collar workers	10.5
Workers	14.2
Agriculturists	1.1

In Silesia, at the end of 1945, no more than 13.3 per cent of the Jews were employed. At that time the pace of the "rehabilitation of Jewish communities and the reconstruction of the lives of thousands of Jews [in Poland] was still maddeningly slow."[14] Only a few thousand Jews bearing Polish names held administrative, managerial, and sales positions in Lodz and a few other places.

Even in the following year Jews in Poland made small progress toward establishing themselves. Repatriation from Russia, on the one hand, and exodus to the West, on the other, absorbed most of the energies of the population. What was needed were soup kitchens, homes for repatriates, and relief both in money and kind.

Poland as a whole made a comparatively speedy recovery. UNRRA in 1945 and 1946 brought into Poland food, grain, medical supplies, farm and industrial machinery, livestock, trucks, etc., to the value of over $480 millions; this relief was a potent factor in Poland's recovery. Another important factor was the acquisition of the factories, homes, fields, and livestock of the western territories from which the Germans had been expelled. The government itself, by means of nationalization, acquired substantial capital. Polish coal, augmented by the mines of Silesia, zinc, soda, chemicals, timber, and agricultural products began slowly to be exported again; exports reached a considerable volume by the beginning of 1947.

The Three-Year Plan, drawn up in the fall of 1946, contemplated a more highly industrialized economy than prewar Poland had possessed. According to Wladyslaw Gomulka, at the beginning of 1948 capital goods production was 74 per cent higher than before the war, while consumer goods output was up 2.9 per cent. Agricultural produce was still below the prewar level.[15]

When the Three-Year Plan was completed in 1949, Poland had considerable achievements to show. According to official figures, total production had more than doubled since 1946, while agricultural production rose by 70 per cent. "Per capita production has risen 112-115 per cent compared with prewar"; per capita consumption of agricultural products surpassed that of 1946: wheat, 231 per cent; meat and fats, 131 per cent; woolens, 119 per cent.[16] Although these official figures undoubtedly exaggerate, and the adoption of the Soviet practice of restricting data to percentages makes an accurate assessment difficult, the achievements do seem to have been considerable.

Naturally, the improved situation had its effect on the Jewish population in both the private and the nationalized sectors of the economy.

> Almost unbelievable is the extent to which this group, penniless, homeless, and physically run-down only a year or two ago, has succeeded in rooting itself in the economic life. There are today no Jews in Poland who do not make a living. They are all settled—some in their former occupations as traders and middlemen, and some in varied types of labor. . . . There is no anxiety about bread; they have it, even though it is not too plentiful.[17]

According to Dr. Sommerstein's statement in London in August 1945, about "225 small [private] workshops have been started, employing some 3,000 workers." Jewish craftsmen worked to fill individual orders, or for non-Jewish stores.[18] Shortages, black markets and abnormal conditions made commerce in part a matter of obtaining small quantities of supplies, sometimes illegally. "Jews bring goods from Silesia [to Lodz], or buy a few meters of cloth illegally from the nationalized mills, or import through different channels some small quantities of goods from abroad."[19] Some people even gained the impression that "all are trading and speculating."[20] Some Jews became partners in non-Jewish stores; others opened stores for themselves but "concealed their name and appearance."[21] In Silesia, where antisemitism was weaker, Jews kept stores openly. With the stabilization of the country the number of Jews in Poland engaged in business rose considerably.

The cooperative field seemed from the outset more promising, for here the individual artisan was not only freed from the difficulties of securing premises, raw materials, and tools, but was also supported by the government, the Central Jewish Committee, JDC, and other organizations. The government as a rule supported cooperatives by tax concessions and other means. "Cooperatives have been reorganized by the present government and closely linked to the state."[22] Jewish cooperatives were helped by assignments of raw material from government factories and in other ways. The Rehabilitation Department of the Central Jewish Committee organized and financed cooperatives of Jewish workers and artisans.

The JDC helped with initial investments, some machinery, and later by arranging for the procurement of raw materials. It supplied most of the capital (by 1948, 213 million zlotys out of 326) for the Bank of Rehabilitation (Bank dla Produktywizacyi Zydow), which advanced loans to cooperatives and individuals.

The increase in the number of Jewish cooperatives was remarkable. On January 1, 1946, there were 13; a year later, 124. At the end of 1947 there were 203.[23] In general, the cooperative movement had a great measure of success, although shortages of machinery, tools, working capital, and raw materials hampered its development, while a "resulting lack of rationalized and mechanized methods of production has caused a low output per person."[24] Yet according to computations of the shoemaking and leather goods cooperatives, members were earning (1947-1948) 15-25,000 zlotys monthly; clothing cooperatives reported 9-16,000 zlotys monthly; and metal and woodworking cooperatives 8-12,000 zlotys per month. In Dzierzonów's bakery cooperative in 1947 a skilled worker earned 30,000 zlotys, an unskilled worker 15,000. In a tailoring cooperative in Liegnitz (Legnica), a qualified worker earned some 40,000 zlotys. The average wage of factory workers at the end of 1948 was 8-15,000 zlotys per month.[25]

The cooperatives were concentrated in the tailoring, shoemaking and other traditional Jewish crafts. Of 164 Jewish producer cooperatives in March 1947, about one-third, employing almost one-half of all the membership of the cooperatives, were in tailoring. Shoe and bootmaking and leather goods came second with some 20 per cent of the membership.[26]

The Economic Center (Centrala Gospodarcza "Solidarnośc" [Solidarity] of the cooperatives, in existence from the beginning of 1946, concentrated on purchase of raw materials and sale of finished goods; it received 100 million zlotys from the JDC. At the end of 1947, 155 cooperatives (or three-quarters of the total) were members of the Economic Center.

At the end of 1948 there were 220 Jewish producers' cooperatives having 9,000 members and constituting about 20 per cent of all producers' cooperatives in the country. The cooperatives operated retail outlets in the principal cities of the country. Some cooperatives grew into large factories. "Zgoda" in Wroclaw and "Einikeit" in Liegnitz were large tailoring shops employing several hundred workers each. In Lower Silesia the Economic Center took over some plants and set them up as cooperatives.

But even in its heyday (end of 1948) the cooperative movement embraced no more than 8,000 or 9,000 members. The great limitation was always lack of raw materials and working capital. Thus, in January 1947 the productive capacity of the cooperatives was five to six times higher than the actual production.[27] Lack of capital even prevented full utilization of a government offer (1947) to supply raw materials in the amount of 250 million zlotys.

Another obstacle to the development of the cooperatives was the Jewish exodus of the first postwar years. "In the last two months [summer of 1946] the membership [of a carpenter cooperative in Lodz] changed several times. . . . Not a week passed but some of the members went away."[28]

Thus only some 15-16 per cent of the gainfully employed were associated with the cooperatives. A considerable part of the remainder had to undergo a course of training or retraining in order to find work in the growing number of nationalized enterprises. The traditional economic forms of Jewish existence in Poland seemed doomed. Jews had perforce to find a place for themselves in the new order, with its emphasis on manual labor and "productivization." From the very first the Central Jewish Committee had stressed "productivization," and had made every effort to get Jews employed in government factories. The Committee set up a department whose principal tasks were to: (a) obtain employment for Jews in government enterprises; (b) establish cooperative workshops; (c) provide assistance in establishing private workshops; and (d) arrange for vocational training for the youth. Although this department devoted a great deal of attention to the cooperatives, it emphasized both retraining (and training) and placement in government enterprises.

The Polish government, too, set up a special department in the Presidium of the Council of Ministers for the "productivization" of Jews. Its tasks were outlined largely as finding employment for Jews in existing factories, furnishing cooperatives of artisans and workers with tools, and bringing idle factories into operation.

In the middle of 1946 ORT began to give courses in vocational training. Later it opened technical schools for training cutters, metal workers, and farmers. By the end of 1948 some 70 schools, with 2,000 students, were in existence.

These efforts, plus the fact that some repatriates had acquired certain skills while in Russia, made it possible for Jews to find jobs in factories, particularly in Silesia. In these years Polish factories needed workers; the government was augmenting production in accordance with the Three-Year Plan and industrial labor grew by some 25 per cent, reaching 3,600,000.[29]

In Silesia, 1,000 Jews began to work as miners. Soon inexperience and the unaccustomed nature of the labor caused many to quit. Of the 600 who remained, only a few dozen were employed underground; the rest worked at the surface. Their meager earnings had to be supplemented by the JDC to keep them at their jobs.

More successful was the penetration into the metal and textile industries, which were employing several thousand Jews by the summer of 1947.[30]

Relatively large numbers of Jews found employment in the government administration, in the expanding nationalized sector of the economy, and in the administration of Jewish institutions. According to certain information, about one-sixth of all gainfully employed Jews worked for Jewish institutions. Administrative costs of the Central Jewish Committee and its affiliates ran (in 1947) to 24 per cent of all expenses. At the beginning of 1948 it was decided to reduce personnel by 40 per cent.[31]

According to official information (apparently none too exact) from the Economic Rehabilitation Department of the Central Jewish Committee, in February-March 1947, 13 per cent of all gainfully employed Jews were working for government or communal organizations. They were principally employed in: industry (39 per cent); artisan work (22 per cent); professions (5 per cent); trade (3 per cent); agriculture (2 per cent).[32]

The Jewish occupational structure had thus changed to a certain extent. Jews were employed in industry to a greater degree than in the prewar years, although the percentage of individual artisans was still high and constituted, together with those in producer cooperatives, over one-third of the gainfully employed. On the other hand, the percentage of those engaged in commerce had sunk to about one-tenth, with a few, however, occupying managerial and sales positions in the government sector. In the cooperatives, too, the percentage of administrative and commercial employees seems to have been high.[33]

The diverse methods of calculating and classifying data make it difficult to gain a clear notion of the changes in occupational distribution. One thing, however, seems clear, namely, that the ratio of gainfully employed was rising constantly with the consolidation of the country and improvement of the economic situation. While in the spring of 1947 the ratio of gainfully employed[34] amounted to only 30 per cent—a very low one, taking into account the comparatively small percentage of children and old men in the Polish Jewish population[35]—this ratio rose to 36 per cent in the spring of 1948,[36] and 42.2 per cent[37] at the end of 1948. Insofar as the different classifications permit of comparison, it would seem that the main increase was in commerce, the number therein employed more than doubling. The number employed in the civil service and professions increased about one-third, while those employed in industry, including producers' cooperatives and artisans, increased by a smaller ratio. It is also impossible to gain a clear notion of how many Jews actually worked in factories, as the figure for the end of 1948 includes cooperatives and private artisans. If we take the figure of 5,070 members of cooperatives as of January 1948 and add to it the 5,000 individual artisans of 1947, we find that at the end of 1948 industry employed some 7,000 Jews, or only a little more than in

1947. The ratio of those employed in industry proper thus constituted at the end of 1948 some 19 per cent of the gainfully employed Jews.

TABLE IX

OCCUPATIONAL DISTRIBUTION, 1947, 1948[38]

Spring, 1947			End of 1948		
Occupation	Number	Per-cent	Occupation	Number	Per-cent
Industry	6,100	23	Industry	17,080	46
Individual artisans	5,000	19	Commerce	4,380	11
Producer cooperatives	4,200	16	Transportation and communications	523	1
Commerce	2,000	8	Civil service	6,879	19
Government and city employees	3,500	13	Education and culture	1,842	5
Social Work	3,600	13	Health and social work	3,540	10
Professions	1,500	6	Agriculture	677	2
Agriculture	650	2	Others	2,033	6
Total	26,550	100		36,954	100

It is scarcely possible, because of the varying methods of classification, to make any exact comparisons with prewar conditions. But the figures do indicate that the occupational structure of the Jews in Poland underwent some change, for the most part in conformity with the general changes in the country. The percentage of those employed in industry rose, whereas the ratio of those in agriculture declined considerably. A considerable decline is to be noted in commerce and in transportation, and a tremendous rise in civil service and social work.

The percentage of service occupations as a group (commerce, white collar, civil service, and professions) did not change markedly from before the war. In 1947 this group comprised 40 per cent (plus some members of cooperatives who should be counted in this group), and in 1948, 45 per cent; before the war it had amounted to some 43 per cent. Changes occurred only within the group itself: commerce declined considerably, whereas government and institutional employment (civil service and social work) increased greatly. Analysis of the group of secondary occupations (industry and handicrafts) would show the same to be true of that group. Over all, it increased only by a few per cent.[39] But there were shifts within the group: individual artisans, and even artisans associated in cooperatives, constituted a smaller percentage than before the war, while factory work took on added importance. And in factory work itself it was no longer the smaller enterprises which employed Jews, but the larger state factories. On the other hand, the branches in which Jews were employed in the factories did not differ greatly from those of prewar times: textiles, clothing, etc. seem to have been predominant, although Jews were also employed in metallurgy, and a few hundred in mining.[40]

In line with the tendency in Poland generally, in Lower Silesia the percentage of gainfully employed kept rising. From 17.8 per cent at the end of 1946, it reached some 30 per cent a year later, and 39 per cent in 1948.[41] The number of Jews working in cooperatives rose from 120 at the end of 1945 to 1,673 a year later, and 3,000 in 1948. The rise in agriculture was small, which meant a decline of the ratio of agriculture in the occupational structure. Factory work rose somewhat, but heavy industry and mining seem not to have accounted for more than 12.6 per cent. On the other hand, the greatest increase was shown in employment in institutions (probably Jewish, including teaching) which amounted to 22 per cent at the end of 1946.

There is no reliable information on the Jewish occupational and economic situation after 1948.[42] Conditions, however, seem to have deteriorated in the first half of 1950, when the government began to deny raw materials and the like to independent entrepreneurs. As this pressure increased, independent craftsmen, businessmen, and small industrialists apparently began to emigrate.[43] Thus their numbers must have considerably decreased. The monetary reform of October 1950 undoubtedly effected a further reduction in the number of such people. The law introduced a new zloty at the official exchange rate of four zlotys to a dollar (previously it had been 400 zlotys). Prices were to be reduced to 3 per cent of the former value, and the cash assets of cooperatives, state enterprises, and institutions, as well as workers' savings, were exchanged at the rate of 3 new zloty for 100 of the old. Money held by private individuals and private enterprises was exchanged at the rate of one new zloty for 100 of the old. Thus the real value of money in the hands of private persons and entrepreneurs was reduced by two-thirds. This affected shopkeepers, artisans, and owners of small industrial enterprises, whose elimination from the Polish economy was admittedly one purpose of the reform. From Lodz we hear that 400 Jewish workers formerly employed in private enterprises whose owners had emigrated, and a number of individual artisans who had given up their shops, were taken into cooperatives.[44]

On the other hand cooperatives almost doubled their membership. By November 1949 the total number employed in some 190 producer cooperatives was about 16,500. Some cooperatives, in accordance with the government's demands, seem to have burgeoned into large-scale enterprises employing hundreds of Jewish and non-Jewish workers. In this way the number of non-Jewish workers in Jewish cooperatives increased a great deal, amounting by the end of 1949 to more than one-fourth. At that time the Jewish cooperative center was dissolved and merged with the Polish workers' cooperatives.

The percentage of Jews gainfully employed seems to have risen, although there were still some Jewish unemployed.[45] There were apparently large numbers of Jews who still needed support. In July-August 1949, when negotiations were already going on about the government's taking over the Jewish old-age and children's homes and similar institutions, the CJC maintained that a "hard core" would still remain not provided for by the government's social insurance laws. This comprised widows, old people, invalids, etc., for whose maintenance they at that time demanded the continuance of JDC relief. The CJC estimated their number at 18,333 (4,599 men, 4,673 women, and 9,061 children). If we accept this number, it would mean that something between one-fourth and one-fifth of the Jewish population was still unable to support itself or to be supported by their families.

Chapter X

Community Life

The Jewish survivors in Poland immediately after liberation, and later the repatriates from Soviet Russia, manifested a profound interest and immense energy in reconstructing Jewish life, restoring Jewish cultural and social institutions, and creating forms of Jewish self-expression.

> Along with the mass of Jews smuggling through to Germany, with the stream leaving for Palestine, along with the alluring dream of an American visa, go the formation of tens of Jewish producers' cooperatives . . . the foundation of trade courses, opening of schools, children's homes, the establishment of newspapers, periodicals, theaters. . . .[1]

Actually, Jewish literary and artistic creativity had not ceased entirely during the ghetto period, nor even in the camps and partisan underground. The Jewish Historical Institute possesses a collection of paintings and sculptures done in the Warsaw ghetto. In 1944 the Jewish National Committee in Warsaw illegally issued a small anthology of verse written during the Nazi years.[2] In the death and labor camps, literary activity, and even special gatherings for the purpose of reading new poems, were a frequent phenomenon despite the danger of discovery and severe punishment by the Nazis. The famous "Song of the Partisans" and a number of other songs were composed in the partisan groups.[3] But for the most part, of course, there was little possibility or opportunity for creative work during that period.

Afterwards, it was as though all the survivors felt an obligation to fulfil an unwritten pledge to revive the life which had been destroyed by the Nazis. The opinion expressed by some of those who remained, that Jewish life in Poland would be possible only if they had an active community and cultural life—only if they continued the "chain of the generations"—was apparently more than a mere phrase. This revival developed in spite of the general nationalist atmosphere of Poland, with its emphasis on homogeneity and hostility to all minorities.

> Jews were afraid to speak Yiddish in public. One day I was walking with —— conversing in Yiddish. Someone stopped us with a curt insult, and we answered him sharply. At his complaint a policeman led us to the local police commissariat. There we were loftily told that it was "inad-

visable" for Jews to provoke Poles by speaking Yiddish on the public streets.[4]

> In Poland . . . Jews no longer speak Yiddish and many find it expedient to disguise their Jewish-sounding names.[5]

This cautious attitude was a reaction to the growing antisemitism. But this same antisemitism, and the sense of isolation in an unfriendly environment, led to a more stubborn determination on the part of the survivors to develop their own institutions and culture. The fact remains that no country of Europe, even Rumania, Hungary, and France, with their larger Jewish populations, could match the activity and achievements of the 80-90,000 Polish Jews.

> One of the clear signs of Jewish political activity is the number of daily gatherings. The impression created by the mass of announcements at street corners is that there are in Poland not a few tens of thousands, but hundreds of thousands of Jews. Crowds attended the gatherings. . . . And the cultural life, the strong tradition of Polish Jews, survived and retained its sweep and achievements. It may even have grown stronger since the limitations imposed by the authorities disappeared. There exist schools, libraries, and publication houses, and there is a fine press. The Jewish world is filled with plans. . . .[6]

This cultural revival was accomplished in spite of the exodus both of the general Jewish population and of teachers, cultural workers, writers,[7] and rabbis.

Communal Organizations

Postwar Polish Jewry evolved two main communal organizations. The Central Committee for Polish Jews was founded in November 1944, shortly after the liberation of Lublin. It had branches in every district (district committees); and almost every town had a Jewish committee, organized in the same way as the central body, which administered such Jewish institutions as schools, cooperatives, and the like.

The other organization, the Union of Religious Communities, was also founded soon after liberation, to fill the need for a religious body. The government treated both the Central Committee and the Union of Religious Communities as representative bodies of the Jewish population, though they were not officially recognized as such. Following the liberation of Warsaw, the Central Jewish Committee in Lublin announced that among its tasks was "the reconstruction of Jewish community councils as centers of cultural, economic, and religious activity."[8] In the first months the chief problems were the feeding of the Jewish survivors and the caring for surviving children, the majority of whom were orphans and in poor health. Relief work thus was, for the time being, the main task. At first, the CJC distributed what little relief was given it by the government, and tried to increase the food ration for former camp inmates. The local committees opened soup kitchens; those people who had their own cooking facilities were given food. The Committee also sought to distribute clothing sent from abroad. Children's homes, sanatoria, and schools were opened in which undernourished and sick children were cared for. The Committee also began to reclaim Jewish children from Polish families and institutions with whom they had found shelter during the occupation.

In economic affairs, the CJC first concentrated on finding employment for the survivors in government enterprises and municipal and social institutions; hand in hand with this went efforts to organize cooperatives and to provide them with loans, and to establish private artisan shops.[9] The statistical and information divisions were engaged in compiling lists of surviving Jews, this information being used in the search for survivors and their relatives. The CJC also undertook to collect what remained of Jewish libraries. A central library was established which by the middle of 1945 had the modest sum of 3,300 volumes. The Historical Department, created only a short time after the organization of the Committee, undertook to collect material on the Nazis' persecution of the Jews. Up to July-August 1945 the CJC had spent 57 million zlotys (or some $142,000), most of which was donated to it by the government, the rest being a loan.

Almost one-half (47.3 per cent) of these expenditures went for direct relief in different forms, and an additional 17.7 per cent for the care of children. Add to this the amounts spent on repairing children's homes, lodgings, etc., and we find that almost three-quarters (73.7 per cent) was spent on relief. This left 14 per cent for rehabilitation, and only 1.8 per cent for cultural and religious purposes. At the beginning of 1946, when the JDC started to expand its operations in the country and covered about 80 per cent of the budget of the CJC, the rehabilitation and cultural activities of the Committee also expanded considerably, although it now faced the new problem of the repatriates from Russia.

By February 1946 the School Department of the CJC was founded. An effort was made to unify curricula, find buildings for schools, and prepare materials for holidays and other occasions. Yiddish and Hebrew pamphlets were issued, and a children's supplement was added to *Dos Naye Lebn.*

In 1946 the Department of Social Welfare gave a great deal of help to the incoming repatriates.

> In the period of mass repatriation, 35 houses with 7,435 beds were established for the repatriated; 38 people's kitchens distributing 25,000 meals daily were organized; 91,349 persons received relief in the form of food, and 60,000 got clothing. Money allowances amounting to 36 million zloty [$90,000] were distributed among 25,694 persons. Night shelters accommodated 28,850 repatriates. The Department of Social

Welfare established eight homes for invalids and the aged. During the first six months of 1946, it provided 123,849 persons with food relief, distributed clothing to 78,056 persons and money allowances in the amount of 25,586,724 zloty [about $83,969].[10]

With increased funds from the JDC, and the stabilization of the situation of the Jews in Poland, the activities of the CJC and its district and local divisions branched out to embrace cooperatives, a bank for rehabilitation, schools and children's homes, publications, lectures, and theatrical performances. The CJC, together with its branches, became the largest single employer of Jews and the principal force in Jewish communal life. This concentration of most of the relief work in the hands of the CJC gave it great power and prestige in Jewish life, and up to 1950 it acted as the representative body of Polish Jewry.

Religious organizations were also founded shortly after the liberation. Religious Jewry had probably suffered most under the Nazis, because of particularly harsh treatment and because their way of life made it more difficult for them to hide and masquerade as Poles. "In all of liberated Poland there hardly remained one rabbi. It is impossible to get a prayer book."[11]

The repatriates included a comparatively large number of religious Jews. Most of them had been forced to work Saturdays and holidays in the Russian labor camps, had very seldom been able to pray publicly, and had had to wear non-Jewish attire. Back in Poland most of these religious Jews found it impossible to resume completely their traditional mode of life, although some were again wearing long beards and caftans.

In postwar Poland, despite (or because of) decreased numbers and the diminished role of religion, communal religious organizations had an added importance. It was impossible for a private individual to obtain a prayer shawl, a *mezuzah*, phylacteries or a prayer book outside of the congregation, or to provide for such ritual functions as circumcision, burial, etc. For some years after the war, observance of such holidays as the New Year and Passover became something of a public affair, with thousands of Jews—among them members of the militia and armed forces—participating in the synagogue services and at public *Seders*. All of which lent added importance to the religious organization, which, in accordance with prewar usage, called itself the *kehillah*.

At this point it encountered the opposition of the CJC, which tried to limit the *kehillah's* functions to purely religious matters. A memorandum is said to have been submitted to the government pointing out that the *kehillah* meant "reaction." The government announced in a circular of the Minister of Public Administration (February 1945) that no revival of the old *kehillah* on the basis of the law of 1927 (compulsory adherence with right of taxation) was contemplated. Free Jewish associations, however, were permitted. The central body was called the Union of Religious Communities. Thus the postwar *kehillah* was a free association of people for the fulfilment of their religious needs.

In 1945, when the Union was created, it embraced the 39 communities then in existence and the Chief Rabbinate. By the beginning of 1946 there were 45 organized communities, with 12 rabbis, maintaining 33 kosher kitchens, 25 schools, an orphanage, a home for the aged, and other institutions. The duties of the reconstructed *kehillah* and of the Union included equipping kosher kitchens, founding rabbinates, opening prayer houses and ritual baths (*mikvah*), providing for religious slaughterers, caring for cemeteries, establishing religious schools, and furnishing relief. It is claimed that by the spring of 1947 about 50,000 Jews were members of the religious communities, the number of the latter amounting in 1948 to 86.

The budgets of the religious communities and of the Union were covered for the most part by the JDC. However, the subsidies allotted to the Union were much smaller than those allotted to the CJC. This situation created ill feeling and a sense of grievance in the Union, adding to the resentment caused by other things. The Jewish Communists, seeking to dominate the Jewish community, in 1946[12] began to talk of unification of the CJC and the Union. Protracted negotiations were carried on through most of 1947. In the end, under pressure, an agreement with the CJC was reached, the Union of Religious Communities joining it in June 1948. The Union, however, retained its sovereignty in all religious and related matters, its own educational system, and its own budget.

Both organizations were soon to be transformed by the impending Communist dictatorship. Jewish members of the PPR in the CJC called a conference in October 1948 for the purpose of reorganizing the Committees:

> . . . Because of changing conditions in the country [the Committees have to] make corresponding changes in their composition and structure so as to be able to do their job as centralized organs, harmonizing and controlling the ramified mass organizations. Democratization of the Jewish Committees—by sending to them as delegates representatives of all Jewish public organizations, factory cooperatives, cultural institutions, etc., who will participate in the Committees alongside of delegates from political groups—will be the first step in this direction.[13]

More plainly, this meant Communist domination of the Committees, and their "organic union with the new conditions in Poland." The main tasks of the Committees were no longer to be found in the Jewish but in the general sphere, according to the words of J. Lazebnik, the General Secretary, at a plenary meeting on May 16, 1949:

> Matters of national importance are now the subject of the work of the Committees: for example, efforts to maintain international peace, to complete economic plans ahead of time, to eliminate waste in produc-

tion, the problems of cooperatives, educational matters involving children's homes, boarding schools, people's clubs, reading rooms.[14]

The Religious Communities were now officially recognized by the government, but as "Congregations of the Mosaic Religion." The word "Jewish" was avoided apparently in order to stress their divorce from anything smacking of "Jewish nationalism."[15] Their activities were limited for the most part to religious matters.

Jewish Political Parties

Both the Central Jewish Committee and the Union of Religious Communities were run by a combination of all the Jewish political parties and groupings. Participating in the Union of Religious Communities were the Agudath Israel, the Mizrachi, and General Zionists; and on the Board of the Central Committee almost all the existing Jewish political divisions, including the Partisans, were represented.

Before the war the Jewish Communists had had no real interest in Jewish communal life; now the role of this group was decisive. Until 1948 they were content to work for a (Communist-dominated) "united front" –such then was the line. Although strongly anti-Zionist, they sought a minimum program insofar as Jewish communal matters were concerned. They countenanced the need of those with relatives abroad to emigrate, and accepted the emigration of those who could obtain certificates to Palestine; but the rest they thought should unpack the valises they always had ready and remain in Poland. With respect to Jewish education, they were ready to accept a little more Hebrew; but Yiddish must be the language of instruction. Both in their Yiddishism and in their opposition to emigration they were supported by the Bund–which in postwar Poland was a remnant of a remnant, many of the surviving leadership having emigrated immediately after liberation to escape the Russians. At the time of the eighth conference in Wroclaw in February 1947, they had 30 organizations with a total membership of 2,000.[16]

Like the Bund of prewar times, they regarded antisemitism and the Jewish problem as a part of the general class struggle. For them, the fate of the Jewish population was connected with "the victory of liberal socialism." Consequently they opposed any "nationalistic approach to the problem," and especially a nationalistic Jewish approach. Realizing that under the influence of the Jewish tragedy Jewish nationalism had increased and penetrated even into "circles educated in the socialist spirit," they attempted to "resist this nationalistic wave."[17] They favored close cooperation with the Polish Socialist Party (PPS). The Bund made none of the PPR's gestures toward support of Zionism. But with the foundation of the State of Israel it underwent an (apparently forced) metamorphosis, being pressed by the PPR to unite with it. At any rate, the official organ of the Bund in Poland came out in sympathy with the Jewish fighters against the Arab invasion, branding the Arabs as tools of English imperialism. It also upheld the Jewish state.

The Zionists were the strongest group in Poland. Their attention fixed on Palestine, they virtually abandoned their prewar struggle for minority and national rights. The Zionists had little hope of the Jewish minority—the only one in Poland—surviving there as Jews. Thus they favored emigration, helped to organize it, and talked of the "exodus" of Jews from Poland. Only the Left Poale Zion were at first reluctant to participate in these activities, fearing that the emigration of the Jews placed the Polish government (which they supported) in a bad light abroad.

The fact that the Communist PPR, backed by Soviet Russia, was the dominating force in the country, gave the Jewish PPR members, though in the minority, a dictatorial position.

> In Jewish life the Jewish section of the Communist Party has usurped first place. . . . The workers of the various Committees are nominated from above. Nobody from the Jewish group empowered them to represent them and to speak in their name. These are commissars who live by means of the power from above. Around them assemble various groups. It is more convenient. It pays. One is nearer to the higher-ups. . . .[18]

Their discipline, and the consistency with which they pursued their objectives, also helped them to dominate the CJC.

Zionists of all shades constituted a majority in the CJC, but were in practice none too active in it. Their attention was concentrated on the exodus. Meanwhile, the PPR entrenched itself in the principal Jewish communal institutions and filled the leading positions in the district and local committees with their own people.

The PPR, by loudly calling for unity, on the one hand; by threatening to leave the CJC unless its demands were met, on the other; and by joining with the Bund and fellow-traveling Partisans, often forced the Zionists to compromise. In this way the Zionists were made to agree to an official proclamation against emigration.[19] At the end of 1946 the CJC clashed with both the Zionist and the religious groups. The Youth Aliyah had planned to transfer 2,000 children to France and from there to Palestine. The Union of Jewish Religious Congregations wanted to send 150 children to England. The CJC declined to participate in either enterprise, on the ground that emigration of the few children left would endanger the growth of the Jewish population. The Conference of the Jewish Committees held in Warsaw in March 1947 among other things dramatized the friction between the groups, particularly between the Zionists and non-Zionists.

Discords such as these increased the suspicion of Communist dominance, and the desire to reconstruct the CJC on a different basis. The Zionist and religious groups were of the opinion that the CJC should either be elected in a democratic way, or reorganized on the pattern of the prewar *kehilloth*. Ichud, the central organization of all Zionist groups, adopted a resolution, at the national conference held in Wroclaw on November 10-11, 1946, demanding that "democratic elections to the Jewish Committees be held in the shortest time." The Zionists hoped that "if the elections are conducted in such a way that the whole population will be free to express its will, then the Jewish Committees will represent all the vital forces within the Jewish population. They will express its wishes and national aspirations."[20] The Right Poale Zion voiced similar ideas,[21] as did groups not represented in the CJC. Under this pressure the CJC in 1947 decided to hold elections. But they were never held. Instead, the leadership of CJC was enlarged to include economic institutions, most of which were under Communist control. In this way the Communists gained even more power in the CJC, which they now completely dominated.

Jewish Schools and Publications

Soon after liberation the question of schooling arose. Because of a heightened Jewish consciousness and because of the antisemitic atmosphere in the general Polish school, Jewish parents wanted a Jewish school for their children. Prewar differences again asserted themselves. While the Bund and Jewish Communists favored a school in which all the subjects would be taught in Yiddish, the Zionists, especially the Labor Zionists, advocated the use of Hebrew. Other Jews wished to revive the traditional religious education provided by the cheder and yeshivah.

Having spent their early years in hiding in non-Jewish homes and institutions, in the woods, or in the Soviet Union, a great many of the children knew no Yiddish. They were polyglot, speaking Polish, Russian, Ukrainian, and even some Asiatic tongues. Moreover, the Zionists, regarding emigration as the only course for Polish Jewry, wanted to prepare their children for Palestine.

The first Yiddish school to be opened in Lublin after the liberation had 50 pupils, no textbooks, and untrained teachers. Following the liberation of the rest of Poland in the spring of 1945, other schools, with a variety of curricula, were opened in different places. In Lublin, Cracow, and Bialystok there were Jewish schools with 450 children. In Lodz a Jewish school with 300 children opened in October 1945.[22] Hebrew schools in Lodz, Bytom and Walbrzych were founded on the initiative of teachers. Religious Jews provided their children with their own type of instruction.

All these different kinds of schools encountered the same difficulties: a polyglot student body, insufficient school buildings, equipment, and textbooks, as well as a dearth of qualified teachers. The Yiddish schools, for example, were obliged to employ many who knew scarcely any Yiddish and spoke Polish among themselves. They also frequently taught in Polish instead of Yiddish.

At the beginning of 1946 there were eight schools with 603 children; of these only two schools used Yiddish as the language of instruction. Four elementary schools and one high school (in Cracow) used Polish as the language of instruction; and one elementary school used Hebrew.[23] These difficulties were not entirely overcome by the summer of 1947, although the first-grade pupils, having grown up in liberated Poland, spoke fluent Yiddish. In Warsaw and Cracow, knowledge of Yiddish was so poor that Polish was the principal language of instruction.

The situation of the Hebrew schools was considerably better. Repatriation from Soviet Russia returned a number of former Tarbuth teachers who knew Hebrew well enough to teach all subjects in that language. However, another difficulty arose—the instability of the teaching staff. Emigrating Hebrew teachers often left their classes in the middle of the school year.

At the beginning of 1946 a conference of the CJC decided to establish a network of Jewish schools in which the language of instruction would be Yiddish. The curriculum of the state public school was adopted as a basis, its scope being extended to include Yiddish language and literature, Hebrew, and Jewish history. In the second grade the teaching of Polish was begun, and in the fourth grade, of Hebrew. All subjects (up to 1949) were taught in Yiddish, except for Polish geography and history which were taught in Polish. When the first normal school year (1946-47) began, there were 28 schools with 106 teachers and 2,236 pupils. Of these schools three were conducted in Polish and one (in Bialystok) in Hebrew. The next school year (1947-48) saw 33 Jewish schools in session with 179 teachers and 2,847 children.[24]

The CJC, led by Jewish members of the Polish Workers Party, sought to gain a monopoly of the Jewish school. Its schools were more "democratic" (i.e., pro-Communist) and secular in emphasis than Jewish. Even Yiddish was not always maintained as the language of instruction. The Zionist and religious groups, who wanted a school conducted in Hebrew with a strongly Jewish (or religious) content, could not accept the CJC school. They therefore retained their own schools, and in June 1946 established their Office for Education and Culture in Lodz. In the following months this office established a number of new institutions. By August 1946 it had 15 institutions with 3,000 children and 100 teachers. Emigration caused some of the schools to close. When conditions grew more stable after the end of the exodus, new schools were again opened. In 1947 there were 14 schools (6 in Silesia) in existence with over 1,000 pupils. These were full-time general schools in which Hebrew studies (with a Labor Zionist emphasis) were woven into the general curriculum. Since all the children did not speak Hebrew fluently, general subjects were often taught in Polish.[25]

The religious school system comprised a number of schools connected with the Agudah children's homes; religious all-day schools; and Talmud Torahs and *chedarim* offering Jewish studies to supplement those of the general school. The Beth Yakob opened up girls' homes (Lodz), and there were attempts to start a Yeshivah. This system was sustained principally by the Union of Religious Communities. In 1947 this organization established a seminary for rabbis in which 15 students were enrolled.

In addition, the ORT conducted a number of vocational schools and courses, while WIZO offered courses in Hebrew, English, dressmaking, corsetmaking, etc. Schools and educational institutions supported by the JDC in 1946 were as follows:

TABLE X

JEWISH EDUCATION IN POLAND, 1946[26]

	Number of Institutions	Number of Students
Children's homes (boarding schools)	15	969
Day care schools	66	4,398
Elementary schools of the CJC (Yiddish, 3 Polish, 1 Hebrew)	35	2,734
Hebrew schools	11	905
Talmud Torahs	36	1,200
Vocational schools	11	365
Vocational and language courses	59	1,290
Educational centers	40	8,500
Seminaries	5	270
TOTAL	278	20,631

According to official figures (which are not entirely exact), the total enrollment in Jewish elementary schools in 1947-48 was 4,752. The Yiddish schools of the CJC had 2,735 children; the Hebrew schools 917; and the religious schools 1,100. Among the Yiddish schools was a high school in Wroclaw which had been opened in September 1946. In April 1947 a Jewish music school was founded; in 1948 a Jewish ballet school was opened in Wroclaw.[27] During the year a number of schools were closed, so that the next year (1948-49) saw 22 schools (including 2 high schools) in operation with 3,129 pupils; one music school with 73 pupils; and 12 afternoon courses attended by 174 pupils.

Beginning with the year 1949-50, the Yiddish schools were provided for in the government budgets. Still earlier the Minister of Education had demanded that all other schools should make their curricula conform to that of the CJC. This of course threatened the Hebrew schools. Of the 11 existing Hebrew schools, 5 were closed by local authorities for technical reasons (1948); a few were reopened upon the intervention of the central authorities. But the process of liquidating the Hebrew schools went on. In 1949, only 4 Hebrew schools with 850 pupils were left.

The ORT began its training activities in liberated Poland about the middle of 1946. By 1947 it was running 47 vocational training courses with 80 instructors and 1,070 students.[28] Most of the courses were short, only 6 of them being as long as one year. Over one-half of the occupations taught had to do with tailoring; courses were also offered in leather-working, electrotechnics, and mechanics. In 1948 ORT added new classes in typewriter repairing, typesetting (in Warsaw and Lodz), and a linotypist class in Warsaw.They also organized three secondary trade schools in Wroclaw, Walbrzych and Lodz.[29] In the following year this trend toward industrial courses became even more pronounced. All in all, 1,555 students attended ORT's courses in 1949.[30]

All these schools and educational institutions were maintained by Jewish organizations, with most of the money coming from the JDC. Efforts to secure financial assistance from the government proved unavailing; the Ministry of Education demanded a uniform curriculum as a prerequisite for such support. After 1947 such a uniform curriculum was introduced in the schools of the CJC. This curriculum corresponded to that of the state schools, with the addition of Yiddish, Hebrew, Jewish history, etc.

In August 1948 the Minister of Education gave notice that the government was preparing to take over the Yiddish schools; he requested all other Jewish schools to adapt their curricula to that of the CJC.[31] In the school year 1949-50, Yiddish schools were taken over by the government. Hebrew schools, with their different curriculum, were forced to close.

Like the schools, most of the Jewish publications were divided along ideological lines. Every party, every group, sought to publish its own organ, often even two—one in Yiddish and one in Polish. The Jewish section of the PPR issued *Di Folksshtime* (a translation of the name of the PPR's principal periodical, *Glos Ludu*); and the Bund put out *Di Folkstsaytung* in Yiddish and *Glos Bundu* in Polish; the Zionists (Ichud) issued *Opinia:* the Right Poale Zion, *Unzer Wort* and *Nasze Slowo;* Hitachdut, *Dos Fraye Vort; Befrayung*, Left Poale Zion, *Przevlom;* Hashomer Hatzair, *Mosty*.

The first Jewish periodical to be published in postwar Poland, in the fall of 1945, was the organ of the CJC, *Dos Naye Lebn*. It remained the official organ of the CJC until discontinued in October 1950. In 1947 the CJC also started to publish a monthly for the youth called *Oyfgang*, which in 1950 was made bilingual (Yiddish and Polish). The District Committees of the CJC had their own publications. Of the latter, *Nidershlezye*, published in Lower Silesia from 1946 on, became an important periodical.

In 1946 the Yiddish writers began a monthly literary review, *Yidishe Shriftn*, the organ of the Association of Jewish Writers and Journalists. It is estimated that by 1948 there were about thirty Jewish periodical publications (in Yiddish and in Polish).

Books were published by a house called "Dos Naye Lebn" (later "Unzer Buch") which was connected with the CJC. In 1948 "Unzer Buch" published eight books, and in 1949, ten. A Jewish publication house, "Nidershlezye," existed in Wroclaw.

Beginning after liberation with a dramatic group in Lodz and in Bialystok, the Jewish theater developed rapidly. A conference of Jewish actors in March 1947 was able to note many achievements, for which the Union of Jewish Actors was largely responsible. Two regular Yiddish theaters in Lodz and Wroclaw offered periodic performances. There were also a number of dramatic groups in different places performing from time to time.

Jewish choirs, libraries, reading circles, and cultural clubs also sprang up. According to information from Poland, in 1947 there existed 6 libraries, 42 reading rooms, and 23 clubs; in 1948, 31 cultural clubs, 26 dramatic groups, 3 "people's universities," 12 choral groups, and 13 libraries with 2,300 readers and 16,500 books.[32] A Jewish Art Society was established with about 60 Jewish artist-members in 1948.[33] In 1947 a Jewish Society for Culture was founded; a year later it had 4,000 members, and by the beginning of 1949, 49 branches with 10,000 members. It made arrangements for lectures, managed libraries and reading rooms, organized evening classes, theatrical groups, choirs, and orchestras.[34] In 1948 *We Survived*, the first Yiddish movie, was produced.

A few surviving Jewish historians and writers conceived the idea of collecting materials on German atrocities and presenting them as an indictment. Thus in 1944 a Historical Commission came into being which soon became the Central Jewish Historical Commission, associated with the CJC. The Commission broadened its scope to include the collecting of materials on modern Jewish history in Poland generally. In 1948 the Commission was transformed into the Jewish Historical Institute, which publishes a quarterly, *Bleter far Geshichte*, and also *Yedies*. The Institute opened a Museum of Jewish Martyrdom in Warsaw in 1948.

Chapter XI

Communist Policy and Practice

The transformation of Poland from a "people's democracy" into an outright Communist dictatorship had deep repercussions on the Jewish community. Not only did the changing socio-economic order affect the daily life of individual Jews, but also the Jewish Communists (and fellow travelers) began to remake Jewish communal life in the Soviet image. Indeed, the very existence of Polish Jewry as a group was rendered problematic.

The position of the Jewish Communists of the PPR vis-à-vis the Jewish community resembled that of the PPR vis-à-vis Poland as a whole. Like the Polish Communists, they were a minority within their own people, whom they strove to dominate and regiment and make conform to the Soviet pattern. Like the Polish Workers Party generally, the Jewish members of the PPR pursued the general line of giving support to (in their case Jewish) nationalism and national unity, only then to turn around, once their position was secure, and eliminate their erstwhile confederates in the "united front." They, too, knew the value of foreign relief in the first years after liberation—Jewish organizations abroad contributed more than 30 million dollars for the relief of Polish Jews, the JDC alone providing 21 million.

The general policies applicable to the Jewish population were laid down by the ruling bodies of the whole PPR; there was very close liaison between party officials and the PPR factions in Jewish organizations.[1] Again like the Polish Communists, Jewish Communists in the "people's democratic" period fell into two groups: those who took at face value Communist espousal of (Jewish) nationalism; and the more knowing, who remained prepared for a reversion to the policy of class struggle and "socialist assimilation" when Soviet Russia so decreed. When that reversion took place, some Jewish Communists were found guilty (at a conference of the PPR's Jewish section in November 1948, following the party plenary session of the previous August 31-September 3) of having evidenced "the characteristic Jewish nuance of the general right-nationalist deviation apparent in the party leadership."[2] What this jargon means is that, as Gomulka had been accused of Polish nationalism, so there were Jewish Communists guilty of Jewish nationalism.

Even though, for reasons of expediency, in the first three or four postwar years the practice of the Jewish Communists was generally directed toward maintaining the Jewish community, building up Jewish institutions, and "cooperating" with other Jewish groups in ideology most of them remained assimilationist, as indeed Leninist doctrine required them to. This may be illustrated by analyzing a few major points:

Jewish Culture. During the years of "people's democracy," before the Sovietization of the country, Jewish Communists in Poland asserted time and again that they were fighting for the reconstruction of a Jewish culture in Poland. But what was their concept of Jewish culture at that time? We may take the words of M. Mirski, a leading Communist and editor of *Dos Naye Lebn*, as representative. For him, modern Jewish culture was chiefly the product of the Russian Revolution, its value lying in its "progressive" (i.e., Communist) content.

> The October revolution (1917) brought a fundamental change in the modern cultural movement. . . . For the first time in the history of the Jewish people its culture was freed socially and nationally. It became the culture of a people that has equal national rights. . . . From that historic date begins the creation of modern Jewish culture, including the new Hebrew literature. . . . The most important instrument of our culture is Yiddish, the language of our people. We, however, do not separate language from content. Only the progressive content creates the relation to language.[3]

Jewish Institutions. When the Jewish Communists were boasting of their achievements in building new institutions, and claiming that without the PPR the Jewish Committees would not be able to exist,[4] a controversy arose in connection with a central Jewish students' organization. At a conference of Jewish students held in Warsaw in January 1947, such an organization was proposed by Zionist and nationally minded students, while the leftist groups of the Central Jewish Committee opposed it. This opposition stemmed, among other things, from the desire to keep Jewish youth within the youth sections of the CJC, and the fear that a central students' organization might be dominated by the Zionists. In formulating their opposition to such an organization, however, they expressed the view that separate Jewish institutions were the result of discrimination and antisemitism only, and disregarded their positive character and their role in Jewish political and social life. To a criticism in the Poale Zion press that "it is queer and incomprehensible . . . to endeavor to prevent the creation of a central organization of Jewish students in Poland,"[5] the CJC's organ published an entire article, written by a Communist, which stated:

> Before the war the danger of *numerus clausus* and *numerus nullus* hung constantly over the heads of Jewish students. . . . Why did the Jewish

> students create an organization of their own before the war? . . . Regardless of his political affiliation the Jewish student was persecuted—for the one reason that he was a Jew. But what purpose can a separate Jewish student organization serve today, when Jews enjoy all rights, when they are admitted everywhere, and when a Jewish student can be a member of "Bratnia Pomoc" [fraternal Polish students' organization]? Should it be done only in order to emphasize that the Jews do not want to belong to the general students' organizations, but prefer to have one of their own?[6]

Jewish Nationalism. Not very different was the Communist attitude toward Jewish nationalism. The internationalist tradition of socialism as reinterpreted for Communism by Marx, Lenin, and Stalin, forbade Jewish Communists to advocate Jewish nationalism. But, for opportunist reasons, they did not *oppose* it in public, and themselves employed a resounding nationalist phraseology. (They recanted this "nationalist deviation" in the second half of 1948.) On numerous occasions, when certain achievements were being reviewed, their importance from the Jewish national point of view was always emphasized. "The national importance of our settlement [in Silesia]," "the national creativity of our culture," were insisted on, and also the essential importance of all phases of the past millenium in the continuity and tradition of Jewish culture.[7] They placed Jewish patriotism on a par with Polish patriotism. Thus, the CJC emphasized that the Jewish school "does a great deal to provide the Jewish child with an education aimed at raising up a type of pupil who will be a keen Jew and a faithful citizen of the new Poland—a patriot both of his people and of Poland."[8] This nationalist note was even stronger in the Communists' call for Jewish national unity.

Unity. The slogan of "unity" was a general one in the "people's democracy" of Poland. In the Jewish community this "unity" was supposed to have found expression in the Communist-controlled Jewish Committees and other organizations—the PPR was claimed to have been the promoter of this Jewish national unity, beginning with the antifascist committees of the occupation period. This unity was extended to embrace Jewish people the world over, all of whom were bound together by the Jewish catastrophe. A declaration by Hirsh Smolar,[9] one of the leaders of the Jewish PPR and in 1949 chairman of the CJC, is representative of this attitude:

> Jewish brethren, with warm hearts and outstretched hands, come to help us, to ease our heavy task of building Jewish life on Polish soil. We here do not ask any of our visitors about the color of their party cards, or about their ideological affiliations. . . . The keen interest among us in all that occurs in Jewish life the world over is a result of the deep conviction of all Jews in Poland that never has the fate of one Jewish community been so closely connected with that of all other Jewish communities

as it is today. It is a conviction which derives from our own personal experience of suffering. . . . We regard the Jewish Committees in Poland, headed by the Central Committee, as a form representing and expressing the trend of unity within the Jewish community in Poland.[10]

On three of these four basic points—Jewish culture, institutions, and nationalism—the Jewish Communists held essentially negative views from which it was but a short step back to their basic compulsory assimilationism. On the fourth point of unity alone, did they seem to take a positive attitude toward Jewish nationalism. This, however, was merely a tactic to achieve dominance, and was later summarily abandoned. After the turnabout in 1948 they accused themselves of having promoted national cultural autonomy, deferred to the influence of "reactionary nationalist parties," encouraged a positive attitude toward the past and its traditions; of having advanced the idea of Jewish unity (Klal Yisrael) over and above every party affiliation. Cultural work had meant "abstract Judaism and abstract culture which effaces the differences between the progressive [Communist] . . . elements of our cultural heritage and the nationalist ones."[11]

Communism Supreme

The events of the summer of 1948, in connection with Tito's condemnation by the Cominform and the open appearance of the Gomulka faction in Poland, changed the country from a "peoples' democracy" into a "socialist state." The PPR, following Moscow, turned toward the left. It declared war on private capitalism—at that time only 24 per cent of the gainfully employed in Poland were in nationalized enterprises—and Polish nationalism. The Sovietization of cultural life was called for and the achievements of Soviet Russia and Marxism-Leninism lauded. Polish Communism, until then masquerading under the quasi-neutral name of Polish Workers Party, began to point out its connection with the Russian Communist Party and its direct descent from the prewar Polish Communist Party (PKP),[12] whose traditions it intended to follow. These policies were reaffirmed at the unity congress of the PPR and PPS, held at the end of 1948, when the necessity of strengthening socialist labor competition and fulfilling the Three- and Six-Year Plans were also stressed. "The fight for complete elimination of opportunism, nationalism and social democracy" was in full swing.[13]

The Jewish PPR members immediately followed suit. On August 4-5, 1948, a meeting of the PPR faction in the CJC was held. Here Zachariasz "analyzed the situation of the Jewish population in the light of the last historic plenary session of the Central Committee [of the PPR]."[14] In the following months similar sessions of Jewish Communists connected with various Jewish institutions were held, at which the new party line was laid down.

Like the party generally, the Jewish Communists espoused class struggle, antinationalism, the supremacy of Soviet Russia, and the tradition of the prewar PKP. This involved adoption of the PKP's views on the Jewish question: full equality for Jews, opposition to antisemitism, denial of Jewish nationalism and of the necessity for Jewish institutions and communal life. The connection between the new line of the Jewish PPR and the PKP was pointed out by Zachariasz at a meeting of Jewish PPR activists in Lodz on August 19, 1948. According to him, their ideological traditions were derived from the Russian Communist Party "and the PKP, which were internationalist and uncompromisingly . . . against every kind of national-cultural autonomy advocated by the Bund and other Jewish petit-bourgeois parties, in favor of an international party of all workers—such was the struggle for Marxism-Leninism in the Jewish milieu."[15] Seeking to interpret most of the problems in the Jewish community in the light of the class struggle, he found that the next tasks were to "strengthen the propaganda for the USSR, bastion and shield of the independence of our country; also to strengthen the fight against nationalism, against the elements thwarting the class struggle, which are to be found in the cooperatives and in many other organizations. . . ."

At that time the Communist attitude toward the state of Israel was still in part a positive one, so that Zachariasz considered it to be one of their tasks "to strengthen aid to Israel." But this, too, was soon changed, in Poland and in all the satellite countries, when an article by Ilya Ehrenburg, appearing in the Russian *Pravda* (September 23, 1948), declared that Israel was no solution to the Jewish question, which solution was only to be found in the Communist order of the Soviet Union. It was reprinted in the *Folksshtime* on October 8, 1948; this organ in the same issue called "political diversionists" those Zionists who minimized the importance of Poland as against Israel. Two weeks later the same Mirski who five months earlier had maintained that there was not a single Jew or democrat in the world who had not rejoiced at the news of the establishment of the Jewish state, now found that Zionism "spreads the reactionary theories of emigration," masquerades as a national liberation movement, and had "emerged in Poland not as an internal Polish force, but as a foreign one. . . . The false appearance of Zionism as an alleged national freedom movement attracted mistaken individuals both from the Jewish and the Polish society, and reached even the workers' camp."

> [But] it did not take long for Zionism to emerge in Palestine, where it was parading as an alleged national patriotic element, in its true form—that of a reactionary political movement which sells out the national interests of the Jewish people and is ready to exchange the [UN] reso-

> lution of November 29, 1947, concerning an independent Jewish state, for a ghetto. Zionism will not create the independent democratic Jewish state. The Jewish state will be created by the democratic forces in the country in the struggle against imperialism and against the present Zionist coalition in Israel.[16]

The Jewish counterpart of the general party's August-September plenary session, at which deviations were recanted, was a conference of Jewish Communists at the beginning of November 1948. The resolutions adopted were filled with "criticism and self-criticism."

> Although our party rightly evaluated the character and role of Jewish nationalism—Zionism and Bundism—we did not sufficiently oppose the Zionist-nationalist ideology, which is foreign to us. This ideology was, and has remained, in contradiction with the Marxist-Leninist theory of the national problem and national tendencies among the Jewish masses in the whole world. Submission to the pressure of Zionist nationalism led some comrades into the characteristic Jewish nuance of the general right-nationalist deviation apparent in the leadership of the party. This deviation became clearly observable:
>
> 1. In the identification of the fight for national liberation of the masses of Israel with the ideology of Zionism.
>
> 2. In the evaluation of petit-bourgeois utopian chalutzism as one of the forces leading to the establishment of the State of Israel. This led to insufficient evaluation of the most decisive factor; the role of the peoples' democracies led by the USSR. This tendency is false for another reason, namely, because it created illusions to the effect that the national problem can be solved through a pseudo-constructive chalutzism and not through the development of the national freedom movement on the basis of Marxist-Leninist teachings on the class struggle.
>
> 3. In the false notion that the Jewish settlements in the countries of people's democracy and socialism constitute the *hinterland* for the state of Israel.
>
> 4. In the . . . failure sufficiently to evaluate the role of the PPR as the main force and initiator of the ghetto uprising.
>
> 5. In the inadequate manner of combatting the nationalist attitude, in the insistence that the transference of the Jewish schools to the state would mean their liquidation. . . . In the half-hearted struggle against the destructive activity of the Zionist parties in the Jewish schools; in the failure to teach . . . adherence to the fatherland of the people's democracy, the spirit of internationalism, and love for the great USSR.

The resolution went on to state that the same deviations on the "cultural front" which the August plenary session found in Poland, existed in the Jewish community, too. In literature, the theater, and the work of the Historical Institute there was an opportunistic accommodation to nationalist ideology "and a failure to make use of the only creative method—dialectical materialism." Inadequate opposition was offered to the nationalist idealization of the past, nor was sufficient recognition given to "the blossoming of Jewish culture in the USSR." The press had not taken a firm stand against nationalism and the exodus from Poland, nor did it lay enough stress on "the problem of nationalism and education of the Jewish population in a patriotic [Polish] spirit."

A further sin was "the inadequate opposition" offered to "the false Bundist-Zionist evaluation of the role of the Jewish committees as organs of national-cultural autonomy for the Jewish population."[17]

A few pages back we considered the pre-dictatorship Communist position on Jewish culture, institutions, nationalism and unity, when negative assimilationism was for the most part in abeyance. Now we not only find it in the forefront, but joined with a distinctly inimical attitude toward everything Jewish.

Jewish Culture. The new policy (which was only the old one revived) was clearly expressed at a conference of the Jewish Cultural Society on October 14-16, 1949. In his opening address, Smolar, after praising the government, emphasized that the tasks of Jewish culture were to build a socialist Poland in conformity with the Lenin-Stalinist ideology:

> We want, through our cultural activity, to bring the Jewish worker into the front line of the builders of socialist Poland. . . . The Lenin-Stalinist idea has illuminated our path, inspiring us with courage and faith. It will give us strength to carry out our great task. . . .[18]

He rejected any Jewish "cultural particularism," any "abstract Judaism" or "abstract culturism."

Slavish adherence to the new antinationalist line imposed by Moscow on the satellite countries led to such contradictory nonsense as: "National peculiarity . . . means moral degradation . . . means cosmopolitan self-abasement before His Majesty the Dollar, and national treason. On the other hand, the more closely we bind ourselves to the new Polish culture . . . the more we shall learn of the great Soviet Russian culture, which means to deepen the content of our culture, broadening its national form." The ideological basis of Jewish cultural work, as formulated by Mirski, meant in reality not only the negation of any Jewish content, but also an active combating of any expression of Jewishness. He pointed out in a philosophical disquisition based on Marx, Lenin, and Stalin, that culture is essentially class culture—culture in capitalist countries like America is degenerate, as is Jewish culture everywhere in capitalist countries, including Israel.

> Concentration of Jews [in Israel] is not decisive for the national character of the culture. . . . The Jewish worker in Israel does not yet have his state, his fatherland. . . . How is it then possible to build in Israel? How is it possible to build a culture, a "national" culture, upon a dying capitalism? Comrade Stalin has shown in his work of genius . . . that this is impossible.

National culture is an impossibility save in socialist countries, where culture is socialist in content and national in form. . . .

The practical conclusions are:

1. Realization, in the environment of the Jewish working population, of the ideological functions of the dictatorship of the proletariat.

2. To acknowledge as a model . . . the cultural revolution and the socialist cultural achievements of the great USSR. . . .

5. To strengthen, in the sphere of Jewish cultural creativity, the struggle against Jewish nationalism and against Zionism as an ideology of the Jewish bourgeoisie, who are traitors to the nation. . . .

8. Socialist [labor] competition should be emphasized as a cultural factor of high rank.

9. Our cultural heritage should be analyzed and from it should be extracted the progressive portions of the Polish, Russian, and other peoples, the progressive phases of the Haskalah; classic Yiddish literature should be more widely enjoyed and, above all, we should trust in the revolutionary cultural elements of the progressive antifascist cultural movement, led by the Communist Party in Poland.

10. Of first importance in cultural work should be the internationalist education of the Jewish worker. A fight should be waged against every national limitation, and against nationalism generally. . . .

13. The whole cultural effort should be filled . . . with the struggle for peace. . . . Our cultural reconstruction is the torch which lights our way toward world peace and toward socialism in Poland.[19]

This theme of national self-negation runs through all the reports read at the conference of the Jewish Cultural Society.

Yiddish literature, too, must take part in "the great struggle of humanity against forces of reaction." The Jewish theater must be based "on the Soviet stage"; Jewish historiography should "attack ideologically the old historical problems"; the transference of the school system to the state "insures the proper [Communist] shaping of their ideological character."[20] "The principal problem," said Zachariasz, who called the tune for the Jewish Communists, "of the cultural workers, writers, teachers, journalists, and the [Jewish] press is—the fight against our own Jewish nationalism."[21]

Jewish Institutions. From this it is not difficult to guess the attitude toward Jewish institutions. "Separatism" is reaction and smacks of the ghetto. Jewish institutions are vestiges of a reactionary and outmoded "national-cultural autonomy." Jewish cultural activity must "cooperate systematically and closely with the cultural movement of the Polish worker"; the Jewish theater "is an organic part of the Polish theater." "There is, and can be, no specifically Jewish approach to the problems of the Jewish population. Such an approach is inherent in Jewish nationalism."[22]

Jewish Nationalism. This is not only treason, but "antisemitism in reverse," i.e., "anti-Gentilism." "What is antisemitism? It is anti-Jewish nationalism. What is Jewish nationalism? It is anti-Gentilism, anti-Polonism."

The Zionists and Bundists who demand a fight against antisemitism do so in order to cover up their own nationalism. Jewish nationalism is charged with impeding the "incorporation of Jews into Polish life, wanting to turn Jewish institutions into separatist, autonomous affairs, as an anti-Polish base for their ideological influences."[23]

Unity. Since the emphasis was now on class struggle, it naturally followed that there was no such thing as a united Jewish people the world over. The cultural conference of October 1949 decided to "liquidate entirely all traces of . . . the Klal Yisrael concept in our organization." The notion of Jewish universality is merely a means of minimizing "the special character of the Jews in the peoples' democracies and in the socialist countries"; "it is an expression of the expansionism of American imperialism, of its desire to influence, through the American Jewish bourgeoisie, the Jewish masses in different countries. There is no Jewish universality as regards content, but only as regards form. The political and economic interests of the Jewish masses and their national fate are bound up with the fate of the struggle of the workers in a given country."[24] In place of the unity of all Jews, and the common heritage of the Jewish people, there is now only unity with the Poles, with the Polish soil, with the Polish socialist motherland.

Jewish education, Jewish culture, "work in the Jewish milieu,"[25] now became a means to an end—the end being to abolish any sign of Jewish particularity and to rear good Polish Communist patriots who would fulfil production quotas and follow without question the teachings of Marx-Lenin-Stalin as interpreted by the party leaders.

Chapter XII

Regimentation and Dissolution of the Jewish Community

The "initiative" of the Jewish Communists may have had some part in the dissolution of Jewish community life, but that of the party and government was of course decisive; the latter in turn followed closely the line set by the party. The campaign against the Bund, which subsequently led to its dissolution, was launched in the Polish organ of the Communist Party, *Glos Ludu*, in the middle of 1947. When the state took over the Yiddish schools and Jewish welfare and other institutions in 1949-50, this was heralded by the Jewish Communists as the most important event in Jewish history. But a close scrutiny of the facts indicates that leading Jewish Communists had at first been either not in full agreement with these acts; or, while wanting government support for the institutions, they had also desired to retain some control over them. Similarly, they were anxious to retain the support of the JDC, even when the government was about to ask the JDC to withdraw from Poland. When in 1948 the Jewish Telegraphic Agency issued a statement that Jews in Poland would need no further assistance after 1949, the CJC denied it, insisting that "more assistance is needed for constructive purposes, for the development of Jewish culture, the school system, social agencies, care of children . . ." and that it would "still take a long time" before Polish Jews could stand on their own feet.[1] Again in the fall of 1949, a few weeks before the government announced that JDC relief was no longer needed, the Communist leadership of the CJC requested the JDC to continue to support 18,329 individuals.

The outright liquidation of Jewish institutions and parties in Poland after 1949, or their amalgamation with and absorption by non-Jewish ones, would seem to have been part of a scheme by the Communist party (PZPR) and the government to solve the Jewish problem. A plan was drawn up by a special government commission headed by Franciszek Mazur,[2] a member of the Politburo of the United Polish Workers Party (PZPR). This "Commission for the Solution of the Jewish Problem," after making a study, decided that the Jewish problem "must be radically solved by 1950."[3] At the government level the special office for Jewish productivization and the Jewish offices in the Ministries of Foreign Affairs and Interior were closed. In the Jewish community, the process of the dissolution of Jewish institutions went by the euphemism of "unification."

Schools. First to undergo "unification" were the Jewish schools. The CJC had sought support for its Yiddish schools both from local municipalities and the central government. In April 1948 the Ministry of Education declared its readiness to take over nine or ten of the larger schools. The CJC sought a certain autonomy for its Jewish schools within the state's educational structure—"Jewish separatism" was not yet taboo. This request was flatly refused by the Minister of Education in August 1948 on the ground that the "government executive power must be uniform."[4] He was prepared instead to approve the appointment of a government inspector who would also serve as a liaison officer with the CJC. At that time the government thought of nationalizing all the existing Yiddish schools except the very small ones. "In conclusion, the Minister suggested that all the other Jewish schools [meaning the Hebrew schools] which are not included in the network of the Jewish Central Committee should make their program conform to that of the schools of the CJC in Poland, so that the Jewish school system would be uniform."[5]

The Hebrew schools had been under attack by the Jewish Communists for a long time. They were allegedly the cause of "disunion" among the Jews, by virtue of their nationalist attitude.[6] By 1949 only four Hebrew schools with 850 pupils were left, and these were gradually closed.

It took about a year, following the above-mentioned declaration by the government, for the CJC schools to be taken into the state budget (at the beginning of the 1949-50 school year). It was apparently found necessary to bring the Jewish schools into line with the government system. According to Lozowski, the government-appointed inspector of the Yiddish schools, he found deficiencies "in the ideological content of the studies," and "little attention has been paid to fostering a patriotic spirit and establishing ties with the Polish soil." At a conference of teachers held at the beginning of March 1949, the same Lozowski, as well as Zachariasz, demanded a reform not only of ideology but also of the subjects and the language of instruction. The use of the Polish language was to be extended to include all except Jewish subjects, beginning with the sixth grade.[7] Russian was to be introduced in the sixth grade. Hebrew was to be taught as a dead language only. The spirit of the schools had to be Communist and Polish. These were the schools' objectives:

1. Raise up active builders of and fighters for the new socialist order. Connect our school system more closely with the economic and political life of the country. Deepen the interest of Jewish children in Polish culture and literature.

2. Develop in the pupils a feeling of indestructible friendship and warm love for the country of victorious socialism—the USSR.

3. Develop in the pupils a sense of solidarity with the movement of liberation of the workers' class in capitalist countries.

4. Imbue the pupils with the heroic spirit of the Jewish masses struggling in Israel for an independent democratic state.

5. Educate the pupils in the history of the heroic struggles of Jews at all times against their oppressors, and particularly in the spirit of the heroes of the Warsaw ghetto uprising and of Jewish progressive culture of all periods.[8]

Before long, item 4 was dropped, Zionism and the state of Israel passing out of Communist favor. The raising up of patriots of Socialist Poland filled with "love" for Soviet Russia remained the basic goal. The Jewish schools were now eligible for inclusion in the government school system. Officially, they ceased to be Jewish or Yiddish schools, and became "state schools with Yiddish as the language of instruction."[9]

The nationalization of the elementary schools was the first step toward taking over other Jewish institutions. In the beginning of 1950 the ORT schools were taken over by the state. ORT, having severed its connections with the World Union, remained for a while in a sort of consultative capacity. By that time nationalization of Jewish institutions was in full swing.

Social Welfare Institutions. In the second half of 1949, when the Polish government was severing its contacts with the West and ousting foreign agencies from Poland, the JDC was dismissed. The Polish government said it was prepared to take care of Jewish welfare and other institutions in the government budget, and indicated that the JDC should leave. Both the JDC and the leadership of the CJC seem to have been unprepared for such a step. The latter, unlike the government, did not consider that "the specialized character of JDC relief has become superfluous." It informed the JDC that even if the government took over all Jewish institutions, there would still remain over 18,000 persons (about one-quarter of the Jewish population) not provided for under the existing laws of social insurance. The JDC applied to the government for permission to continue its work. It was refused and the JDC was forced to leave. At the beginning of 1950 such Jewish institutions as old-age homes, children's homes, as well as the Jewish theater, were nationalized and provided for in the government budget.

Other Jewish Institutions. A number of other Jewish institutions were either already being absorbed, or about to be. "The presidium [of the Cultural Society] drew attention to the absolute necessity of closer relations with the Polish organizations of mass culture so as to include our cultural units in the general network of cultural institutions. . . ." This began with the Jewish library in Szczecin, and by February 1950, about ten Jewish libraries had been merged with the general libraries.[10]

The Jewish Writers Association was dissolved in 1950 "since the Polish Writers Association admits Jewish writers. . . . There are no ideological barriers dividing Jewish from non-Jewish writers."[11] In May 1950 the Jewish *landsmanshaften* with their lending facilities "became superfluous" because of the "improved situation of the Jews in Poland"; they were dissolved and their funds turned over to the Jewish Historical Institute.[12]

Jewish youth organizations had been under fire from Jewish Communists who wanted, first to "unite" them,[13] and then later to merge them with the Polish organization. The Ministry of Education in 1948 instructed all Jewish schools to organize scout groups as part of the general scout organization. In the same year the Bund's youth organization, SKIF, was absorbed into the general scout organization. In the middle of 1949 the coordination committee of Zionist youth in Lodz was dissolved.

Cooperatives. The Jewish cooperatives of the postwar years were private enterprises owned and directed by their members, who were paid for their work and received a share in the profits. Many members regarded the cooperatives as their own property and were loath to admit new members. There were also instances in which members were opposed to mechanization[14] because they did not want to become a "hand" in a large factory. A great many of the cooperative members, as well as the JDC which supported them, favored small cooperatives with a membership of not much more than 100. The Polish government, however, with its state-planned economy, preferred large, factory-like cooperatives. The PPR activists in the Jewish cooperatives tried to limit the distribution of profits among members[15] so as to leave larger sums for expansion. The Jewish cooperative center, "Solidarność," under the directorship of the Communist Zalicki, tried to carry out the government's wishes. One step toward centralization of the cooperative movement was the law of May 21, 1948, which created a central union of cooperatives (CZS) to which all cooperative centers had to belong. Although the Jewish center, "Solidarność," comprised cooperatives of various trades, it was left as one unit associated with and controlled by the central union of cooperatives. Only 5 Jewish agricultural cooperatives and 17 service cooperatives affiliated with non-Jewish centers.

The new law gave "Solidarność" considerable power over the cooperatives. In practice, it meant that the Jewish Communists running "Solidarność" would have it pretty much their own way. But this situation was short-lived. In December 1949, "Solidarność" was united with the Polish central workers' cooperatives PRACA and thus ceased to exist as a Jewish organization.

Parties. From 1947, as in the other peoples' democracies, the process of forcing the Socialists to "unite" with the Communists had been going on in Poland; it culminated in the Unification Congress of December 1948 at which the PZPR was created.

In the Jewish sphere similar tactics were used against the Socialist Bund. Jewish Communists constantly attacked the Bund for its international affiliations.[16] During the first months of 1948 the Bund withdrew from the Coordinating Committee of the Bundist organizations abroad and from the Committee of Socialist Parties in London (as did the PPS). In the spring of 1948, at a joint meeting of Bund and PPR representatives, "unification" was decided upon. In May 1948 the first joint meeting of activists of the Jewish PPR and Bund was held in Wroclaw. Zachariasz criticized the Bund's past and demanded "a psychological preparation" for organic unity.[17] Committees were soon established to bring about the merger.

On October 23-24, 1948, a plenary session was held in Lodz of the Central Committee of the Bund together with delegates from 16 districts. A resolution was adopted calling for organic unity of the workers in Poland within the framework of one revolutionary party. "Right-reformist" tendencies were condemned, and separatism and the theory of national-cultural autonomy rejected.

Final dissolution of the Bund came at a conference held on January 16, 1949, in Wroclaw, when many of the former leaders were refused admittance to the Communist Party.

Liquidation of the Bund called forth a pronouncement from Soviet Russia. The organ of the Jewish Antifascist Committee, *Einikeit*, which did not usually have much space for Jewish matters, devoted almost one-quarter of an issue to the Bund. The approaching liquidation in Poland was hailed with satisfaction.

> The glorious materialization of the Lenin-Stalin national policy in the USSR finally undermined the none-too-sure ground of the Bund. What a fine figure was now cut by "the only representatives of the Jewish workers," the preachers of "national-cultural autonomy," against the background of the actual, full equality which the Jewish workers achieved in the USSR after the great socialist October revolution.[18]

There followed a condemnation of the Bund for nationalism and anti-Sovietism.

It did not take long to make the other Jewish parties disappear. In October 1949 a representative of Mapam (Wasser) could still appear at the Jewish Cultural Conference, dominated and run by the Jewish Communists, and call for the patterning of Jewish culture in Poland after that of Israel. At that time, however, the fate of the Jewish parties in Poland, including that of Mapam, was already sealed. Mapai closed down in October. In November 1949 the offices of the Agudath Israel, Jewish National Fund, and Jewish Foundation Fund (Keren Hayesod) in Lodz, Warsaw, Cracow, and Wroclaw were closed;[19] the Polish government appointed government administrators to dispose of their remaining funds. At the end of the month Mizrachi decided to disband. Ichud (General Zionists) held its last conference in Lodz at the end of December, at which time Mapam also went out of existence.

Central Bodies. With the nationalization of the schools and welfare institutions in 1949, and the stopping of the JDC's relief work, most of the functions of the Central Jewish Committee passed into the hands of the government. The days of the CJC were numbered. Already at the beginning of 1949 representation in the Committees, which had been on a party basis, was changed to give a representation by institution (cooperatives, etc.). This meant their complete domination by the Communists, who ran most of these organizations. For some time Dr. Adolph Berman, a Left Poale Zionist, retained the chairmanship of the CJC, but he was soon forced to make way for the Communist Smolar.

In a meeting on November 18, 1949, the new "tasks" of the CJC were outlined. These were of a vague social and cultural nature having to do with the Jewish schools, theater, etc. From an executive body the CJC became an advisory body serving the government in matters concerning Jews. But the very existence of the CJC was abhorrent to the Communists. In March 1950, at a meeting of the CJC, the Jewish Communist leader, Zachariasz, pointed to the overlapping activities of the CJC and Jewish Cultural Society.[20] Eight months later, in October 1950, a conference of Jewish organizations was held at which the representative of the PZPR proposed the merger of the CJC with the Cultural Society in a "Central Social Union of the Jews in Poland." This was the end of the Central Jewish Committee. The conference itself was held "under the banner of the struggle against Jewish nationalism in whatever shade and shape." At this conference it was decided to merge *Dos Naye Lebn* with the official Yiddish organ of the PZPR party, *Folksshtime;* in this way the organ of the CJC was liquidated, together with the CJC itself.

The Union of Jewish Religious Congregations was neither taken over by the government nor "unified organically" with CJC as the latter had wanted, probably because the dissolution of the CJC had already been decided on. But in September 1949 the Ministry of Public Administration imposed limitations on some of the activities of the religious congregations, restricted their contact with Jewish organizations abroad to obtaining an opinion on strictly religious matters from the Chief Rabbi in Israel, and changed their name to the Union of Congregations of the Mosaic Faith.[21] Thus "Jewish" with its "nationalist" connotations was avoided.

The process of nationalizing Jewish schools and welfare institutions did not go forward with perfect smoothness. Elimination of non-Communist elements from the organizations appears to have considerably lessened their effectiveness.[22] There are indications that in some places teachers either protested or left their posts. In the old-age home in Lodz, for instance, inmates protested its transfer "to Gentiles, which endangers the Jewish character of the home." Among kindergarten teachers in Szczecin and elsewhere there was "open agitation" against being obliged to apply for transfer of the schools to the state. In Silesia, a number of teachers and pupils left the schools. The secretary of the CJC complained that "a certain portion of the educators and officials in our institutions was untrustworthy. . . . Besides openly hostile elements, there have been, up to now, antisocial elements who . . . prevented the transfer of our institutions to the state."[23]

Despite such opposition practically the entire structure of Jewish Communal life was destroyed. Gone were the Jewish Committees, the Jewish parties with their periodicals and publications. Jewish associations such as the Union of Jewish Writers, or of theatrical people, had also disappeared. The *landsmanshaften*, which had served as a link with Jewry in other countries, were closed. Connections with the World Jewish Congress, or with any Jewish organization abroad, were severed. Gone were the Jewish youth organizations. The Jewish cooperatives were lost to sight in the sea of Polish workers in which they had been dissolved.

Gone also were the two Jewish deputies supposed to have represented the Jewish population. In the elections of January 1947, PPR and PPS had included one deputy each (Zack from Poale Zion and Shuldenfrei from the Bund) in the united list. By 1948-49 they had both been forced out; Zack, after having been abroad, was charged with a misdemeanor, and Shuldenfrei was expelled from the Bund in the course of its dissolution.

Hebrew schools were closed; Yiddish schools, and the entire network of Jewish welfare institutions, were removed from the control of the Jewish community. It is true that the latter institutions are now supported by state funds (though not completely, judging by repeated reports in the Yiddish press in 1950 of Jewish social and parents' commissions charged with raising funds for schools, etc.). But this is nothing against the fact that they are no longer *Jewish* institutions, that, indeed, an anti-Jewish spirit has been introduced into them. Moreover, as is to be expected, some of these institutions are now being liquidated, and in other instances personnel have been fired. In March 1950 it was reported that "in Lodz there is the problem of concentrating old people from smaller places in one large old-age home"; it was stated that "too many people" were employed in the Jewish institutions, making it difficult to transfer the latter to the state.[24]

All that remained was a steadily declining number of impotent religious congregations in which even the word "Jewish" (because of its "nationalist" connotations) is officially taboo, and whose rabbis are "persuaded" (like the Catholic clergy) to make "peace appeals" and the like; a Jewish Historical Institute rapidly being *gleichgeschaltet;*[25] and a Social-Cultural Union whose task is "to induce the Jewish working population to become socially active in the broadest sense, to participate in the historic struggle of reconstruction of socialist society in Poland, in the struggle to strengthen our motherland."[26]

A few periodicals in Yiddish remained, taking their cue from the official *Folksshtime;* the only thing "Jewish" about them is the language in which they are printed. What they print is chiefly translations of the general Polish press, which in turn is an echo of the Russian newspapers. They are full of praise of the government, of Soviet Russia and Marxism-Leninism-Stalinism; calls for increased production; appeals for support of the Communist peace drive; denunciation of "reaction," racism, and "American imperialism." Jewish matters figure in the Jewish periodicals only negatively, when attacks are made against Zionism, "treacherous" Jewish nationalism, Israel and Jewishness, and "Jewish fascists" abroad. Here and there one also finds an article or report on antisemitism in the Anglo-Saxon countries; these convey the impression that the Jews of those countries are on the threshold of extermination by new Hitlers. A similar elimination of all Jewish content is going forward in the Yiddish theater, and the Jewish repertory is criticized for "being Jewish in form."[27]

An effort is also being made to deprive Jewish historical events of their Jewish character. Thus the Jewish ghetto uprising in Warsaw in April 1943 is now celebrated as "one of the most important events in the struggle for freedom, conducted by the most faithful national-dignified sons of the Polish people."[28] To Lazebnik "the decisive role of the Polish Workers Party as the leading force in the uprising of the Warsaw ghetto" is clear.[29] The *leitmotiv* of the commemoration of 1950 was "mobilization of the Jewish and non-Jewish population in the struggle against the war plans of Anglo-Saxon imperialism" and the unmasking of "the antinational and treacherous face of the Jewish nationalist bourgeoisie and its 'socialist' abettors."

Even the Yiddish language, that "national form" which Stalinism allows to express a "socialist content," has been losing ground. The Cultural Society was thinking of beginning to work in Polish as well as Yiddish.[30] From Lodz we hear (at the beginning of 1950) that the cooperative "Lewartowski" has a "general" [Polish] dramatic circle of 30 members, and a "Jewish" [Yiddish] one of 12. The choir of the same cooperative arranged evenings with "mixed Yiddish-Polish-Russian repertories." The wall paper of the cooperative "Osnowa" is written chiefly in Polish; it *also* has articles in Yiddish. In Szczecin the Jewish dramatic group frequently appeared before Polish labor organizations[31] (and must therefore play in Polish).

The Jewish Cultural Society was judged according as it served as "a sharp and efficient weapon in the struggle against nationalism and reaction [and for the] liquidation of all harmful tendencies of separatism and ghettoism [i.e., all Jewish communal life] in our cultural work."[32] The Jewish writer was praised for his contribution to the fight against Jewish nationalism, while Jewish culture should, according to the president of the Cultural Society, "fight against the ghetto and camp complex . . . [which] creates a wall between us and the environment." The conference held in October 1950 at which the Central Jewish Committee and the Jewish Cultural Society were dissolved (or merged), and the Social Cultural Union was established, was part of the struggle by Jewish Communists against every aspect of "the Jewish environment." This struggle was inseparable from the context of the emigration of Jews from Poland during 1948-50.

CHAPTER XIII

Emigration and Israel

Although the Polish government more or less openly permitted Jews to emigrate during the first years, Jewish Communists active in the Jewish community took a negative stand on emigration. This attitude was already evident at the conference of the Jewish PPR group held at the end of 1945. The immediate postwar atmosphere precluded a flat condemnation of any and all attempts to emigrate. The Jewish Communists therefore differentiated between individual departures "in search of relatives and friends outside of Poland, so as to find the moral support they need to go on living," and mass emigration which they regarded as harmful.

> The conference is sharply opposed to the atmosphere of confusion and panic created in the Jewish community by some Zionist elements, who, ready to capitulate to reaction, are organizing illegal emigration. The concentration of despairing Jews without legal status in Munich, Trieste, and Bucharest constitutes a social crime and an adventure which must be prosecuted in the interest of the Polish state and in the vital interest of the deceived masses.[1]

Mass emigration meant, according to the Jewish Communists, capitulation to antisemitism, lack of faith in democracy, interference with the reconstruction of Jewish life in Poland; and it might "spell catastrophe for the emigrés."[2] They had also to accommodate themselves to the prevailing sentiment in favor of Palestine; but they drew a hard and fast line, from the very beginning, between Palestine and Zionism. At the abovementioned conference of the Jewish PPR at the end of December 1945, we hear of a protest against the British White Paper; it was said that "the Jewish settlement in Palestine has a right to develop, even to develop in the direction of statehood." There followed later a passage on Zionism:

> The Zionists hold that Palestine solves the Jewish problem, that all Jewish settlements in the world should revolve around one center, namely, Palestine. This thesis is wrong. . . . Palestine is only a sector, a fragment of the Jewish nation, and not its center.[3]

They forced Zionists in Poland to agree to official proclamations against mass emigration, and they opposed the Hebrew school system, Zionist youth organizations, *hakhsharah kibbutzim*, etc.

Then followed the UN resolution on the partition of Palestine, the foundation of the State of Israel, and the Arab-Israel war. The Eastern bloc supported Israel, and hope ran high in the Jewish population. Mass emigration had in any case been stopped in February 1947, and the Jewish Communists seemed for a time to be swept along by the current—they took part in mass meetings supporting Israel, collections for the Haganah, and the like. The clash between Communists and Zionists seemed to have disappeared, with the former even stealing the limelight from the latter.

But this period was of short duration, ending with the establishment of the Communist dictatorship. The attitude of the Jewish Communists in Poland now rapidly "progressed" from their previous anti-emigrationist and anti-Zionist reservations to an open campaign against Zionism and Israel. At this juncture certain differences between the Jewish Communists and the government and party leadership appeared. The latter were now striving for uniformity, for dissolution of the Jewish minority. But whereas government circles apparently thought that emigration of the less assimilable Jews would hasten this process, the Jewish Communists would seem to have wanted all Polish Jews to remain in Poland.

After the mass exodus of 1946-47, which had been carried out in part with the permission of the government, the borders were closed to emigrants. New passport regulations were introduced as of April 1948, according to which Jews, like all other Poles, needed the promise of a visa from another country before they could apply for a passport. An increased fee was charged for passports. According to information from the JDC, some 160 Jews emigrated from Poland to Australia during the months April-September 1948, and 1,834 were helped to emigrate to Israel in 1948. The Israeli representative received, in the last months of 1948, a promise of 500 (or 800) passports. By December 1948, the government ordered the "Palestine Amt," which was in charge of emigration, to close down; in February 1949 the emigration section of the JDC was also closed.

At that time, however, the government was negotiating with the Zionist organizations in Poland about allowing a certain number of Zionists to emigrate on condition that these organizations would later be dissolved. The leader of the Jewish Communists, Zachariasz, is supposed to have submitted memoranda objecting to such a step.[4] Similar discussions were continued with the Israeli legation during those months, when arrangements were made for a commercial agreement which included provisions for the transfer of some of the Jewish National Fund's money from Poland.[5] New regulations were issued permitting a number of active Zionists and those who had close relatives in Israel (for the most part old people and invalids) to obtain passports.[6] In January-February 1949, 962 Polish Jews received visas for Israel. Later that year acceptance of applications for passports ceased.

The above-mentioned special government Commission for the Solution of the Jewish Problem decided "that by January 1950, all Jewish institutions should be taken over by the state, and that Jews should be accorded the right of free emigration to Israel if they so desired."[7]

On September 1, 1949, the Ministry of Public Administration announced new regulations for obtaining passports. For one year (up to August 31, 1950) Jews could register for emigration to Israel. The applicant had to sign a statement that he was proceeding to Israel to settle there permanently and would give up his Polish citizenship.

Immediately after the announcement by the Ministry of Public Administration of the emigration registration, the Jewish Communist leadership came out strongly against emigration. The same issue of *Dos Naye Lebn* that printed the announcement, declared the place of every working Jew to be in the ranks of builders of the socialist society of Poland.[8] At a meeting of the CJC on November 1, 1949, its secretary, J. Lazebnik, said only Jewish reactionaries advocated emigration.[9] In the Communist-dominated Jewish institutions, Yiddish press, Jewish cooperatives and clubs, and at specially arranged meetings, Polish Zionists were abused and denounced. Emigration was termed reactionary. Strengthen "proletarian internationalism," increase the patriotic attachment of Jews to "the Polish homeland"—this was the only way to combat all shades of Jewish nationalism.[10] All this was accompanied by the most vituperative attacks on Israel and Zionism. Whispered threats were supposed to have been made against Jews who registered for passports.

But the campaign did not stop here. The Communists of the CJC began making difficulties about issuing the registration certificates required for an application for exit papers. They requested large donations to different funds from the applicants, delayed the issuance of certificates, or demanded that applicants come personally to Warsaw. It was reported that they persuaded the authorities to limit the amount of personal belongings an emigrant might take with him, thinking in this way to discourage people from emigrating.[11] Persuasion and pressure was brought to bear on individual Jews by officials of the CJC, and even by non-Jews sent around to Jewish homes. Jewish Communists apparently arranged for the searching and questioning of applicants for permission to emigrate.

By these and other means some applicants were induced to "change their minds." "The Jewish workers," *Dos Naye Lebn* commented editorially, "have now understood that . . . they have every opportunity to resume creative labor . . . and not vegetate in the camp of Ben Gurion." The Yiddish papers printed tens and hundreds of letters from registrants who had decided to remain in Poland. Some merely say that "we will remain in Poland," or "we resign from emigration to the Truman-Israel state." Others say "that they made a mistake in registering, led on by the propaganda of the Zionist organization, etc."[12]

There are indications that the government was unprepared for the large-scale exodus which ensued. About a month after the issuance of the passport regulations, Szlapczynski, the governor of Lower Silesia, in speaking at a conference pointed out that "all who interpret the government's help in facilitating the emigration of Jews as a desire to get rid of them, are indulging in harmful and hostile propaganda against the Polish state."[13] A few weeks later a representative of the Central Committee of the PZPR, speaking in the name of the party, came out against "emigration propaganda" as follows:

> [In] making possible the emigration of those seeking to leave our country, we want at the same time to emphasize that every Jewish worker and working intellectual who participates in the reconstruction of our country has the rights and opportunities of economic, cultural, and social life. All propaganda among the working masses for emigration from our country is harmful and not in the interests of the working Jewish population.[14]

The Ministry of Public Administration itself, on December 7, 1949, issued a communiqué in which, among other things, it is emphasized that "the large majority of Jews do not want to emigrate."

> The Polish government has consented to permit those Polish citizens of Jewish nationality who wish to leave for Israel to do so. The government is facilitating their departure by simplifying and speeding up formalities, and by organizing transportation through the travel office "Orbis."
>
> It is clear that those applying and leaving for Israel are mostly persons ideologically connected with the Zionist movement. The above facts have had a direct influence upon the activities of Jewish political groups and Zionist organizations. It is mostly their active members who are leaving and, as a result, their organizations are in the process of liquidating and concluding their activities.
>
> The large majority of Polish citizens of Jewish nationality appreciate that full equality of rights is being realized in Poland and they do not intend to leave for Israel.[15]

Trybuna Luda, the official organ of the PZPR, published an article on "The Situation in Israel and Emigration Propaganda"[16] which labeled as a falsehood the insinuation that the government was facilitating the emigration of the Jews in order "to get rid of the Jewish population."

> Because the Jews have been drawn into production and have been given an opportunity for cultural development, the experiences of the Jewish masses are undergoing a deep transformation. Sources of Jewish nationalism, in all its shapes and forms, are drying up. The Zionist move-

> ment is rapidly dwindling, and proof of this is in the fact that it had entered the first stages of dissolution. Keeping in step with their determination, active members of the Zionist movement will emigrate. But the Jewish people engaged in production will remain in Poland, joining their fate with that of the non-Jews in Poland. . . .

Thereafter the idea that only "a small percentage of Jews" would emigrate to Israel, while "the great majority of Polish Jews have indicated their desire to stay," was repeated over and over again by Polish officials.[17] All these statements to the contrary notwithstanding, almost all Jews who were eligible registered for emigration. It is safe to assume that, in view of the large number of registrations for exit visas, the government, even if it did not actually institute it, at least gave its blessing to the anti-emigration propaganda of the Jewish Communists.[18]

The announcement of the registration for emigration electrified the Polish Jews. "It is difficult to describe the excitement which this aroused among tens of thousands of Polish Jews."[19] According to a report by a JDC representative to a conference of his organization in Paris in October 1949, "there is a most serious movement among the intelligentsia, who until now showed no interest in emigration to Israel. Thousands of professionals, employees, and those in similar situations decided to apply for passports." Antipathy to the Communist dictatorship and to the communization of Jewish life undoubtedly contributed to this. Moreover, according to foreign correspondents, the appointment of Jews to government posts and offices, or their promotion if already in office, was discontinued. Jews holding office were advised to be inconspicuous when participating in Jewish activities.[20]

Before disbanding, the Zionist organizations called on their members to register for emigration. In the following months, when more severe measures were taken against private enterprise, many small Jewish businesses were liquidated and their owners registered for departure. Among orthodox Jews, too, emigration was heavy. According to Polish statistics, over two-thirds of the emigrés belonged to Zionist parties. The rest were non-party Jews. Many members of cooperatives left, some even forming the nuclei of new cooperatives for Israel. Workers in nationalized industry had difficulty in securing exit permits. Such professionals as physicians and engineers were refused permission to emigrate. By December 15, 1949, some 15,000 Jews had registered, with a similar number registering in the following months.[21] The technical problems of transportation were arranged between the Polish government and the Israeli legation in Warsaw.

The government permitted emigrants to take out about $280 plus some pocket money. Jewelry was limited to two rings and one watch. Personal articles were permitted the emigrants as follows: 1 overcoat, 1 nightshirt, 2 pillows, 2 blankets, a few pairs of shoes, 1 sheet, 5 books.[22] Special trains with sleeping cars and diners, accompanied by representatives of the Israeli Consulate and the Jewish Agency, left Warsaw for Venice and Bari, where the travelers were transfered to a boat, usually an Israeli one. Some transports were later sent through the Polish port of Gdynia, where the emigrants embarked to Israel.

TABLE XI

POLISH JEWS ARRIVING IN ISRAEL

Month	Number	Month	Number
September 1949	157	May 1950	1,212
October	142	June	1,845
November	466	July	2,638
December	680	August	2,406
January 1950	2,059	September	3,355
February	1,868	October	3,599
March	1,784	November	1,892
April	1,161	December	667

Total, 25,931

These figures include the emigrants from Poland who were assisted by the JDC. Some one to two thousand additional Jews left Poland, ostensibly for Israel, but forsook the transports en route and went to other countries. Altogether, about 30,000 Jews have left Poland since the beginning of 1949. Add to this the 8,000 Jews who according to Polish sources registered for emigration but did not emigrate,[23] and we find about 38,000 Jews who apparently intended to emigrate. Some were subsequently forced, either by circumstances or under pressure, to remain. These 38,000 Jews probably comprised the total number who, under existing circumstances, could have hoped to emigrate. The remaining 30-40,000 Jews[24] were made up of Jewish members of the PZPR and their families, widows, old people, invalids and others unable to emigrate (the "hard core"), and some Jewish orphans in the orphanages and children's homes. Polish sources put the number of Jewish PZPR party members at 10,000, making with their families at least 20,000 persons. In the late fall of 1949 the CJC estimated the hard core at 9,272, while the number of orphans and other children in institutions at that time was put at 9,061. None of the "hard core" is likely to emigrate, while children in orphanages are kept in Poland by the government. This leaves a maximum of 10,000 Jews in Poland who were in a position to register for emigration but have so far been unable to leave.

Notes

CHAPTER I

1. Cf. S. Segal, *The New Poland and the Jews,* New York 1938, pp. 41 ff.
2. *Ibid.,* pp. 37 ff.
3. A. Hartglass, "Milchamoth Yehudey Polin al Zuchuyotehem Haezrachioth ve-Haleumiyoth," *Beth Israel Bepolin I,* Jerusalem 1948, pp. 134 ff; Bernard D. Weinryb, *Jewish Emancipation under Attack,* New York 1942, pp. 32-34.
4. *Nasz Przeglad,* January 24, 1939.
5. A. Tartakower, *Nedudey Hayehudim Baolam,* Jerusalem 1947, p. 36.
6. A. Ruppin, *The Jews in the Modern World,* London 1934, pp. 73, 84; *idem., The Jewish Fate and Future,* London 1940, p. 79. Cf. also A. Tartakower, "Zibur Mitnaven," *Sefer Hashanah Leyehudey Polanya,* Cracow 1938, pp. 99-114.
7. Jews made up 43.6 per cent of all emigrants during the years 1926-1935, as against 9.8 per cent of the general population (Tartakower, *op. cit.,* p. 38).
8. *Concise Statistical Yearbook of Poland,* September 1933-June 1941, Glasgow 1941, pp. 10-11.
9. J. Lestchinsky, "Der Yidisher Proletariat in Poyln," *Yivo-Bleter* XV (1940).
10. Segal *op. cit.,* p. 137.
11. The comparison is made between the number of "proprietors" in 1921 and permit holders in 1933; in such a comparison a reasonable margin of error must therefore be expected.
12. All figures from J. Bornstein, "Di Strukur fun Handel in Poyln," *Dos Wirtshaftliche Lebn,* II, July-December 1935 (Warsaw) pp. 9 ff.
13. The textile industry was to a considerable extent in Jewish hands. Even before the First World War it became the usual thing to hire non-Jewish labor as soon as an enterprise was mechanized. In Bialystok this even led to disputes between Jewish and non-Jewish workers. In that city all large textile factories, 85.4 per cent of the middle-sized, and 93.7 of the small were in Jewish hands. But only 20.4 per cent of the workers in the large, 22 per cent in the middle-sized, and 42.7 per cent in the small factories were Jews (Lestchinsky, *op. cit.,* pp. 26-27).
14. The registered Jewish craftsmen were divided as follows: textile and needle trades, 33 per cent; leather, 22.7 per cent; food, 14.9 per cent; metals and electricity, 11.9 per cent; woodwork 7.9 per cent; building, 4.3 per cent. Jewish craftsmen constituted 97.1 per cent of the capmakers; 77.8 per cent of the goldsmiths; 73 per cent of the tanners; 64.8 of the tailors; but only 30.8 per cent of the cabinetmakers and 15 per cent of the builders (Weinryb, *Jewish Vocational Education,* New York 1948, p. 152; B. Olszewicz, *Obraz Polski Dzisiejszej,* Warsaw 1938, p. 103).
15. According to the estimate of the Polish Minister of Commerce, there were in Poland 315,000 artisans of whom 197,802 were registered. The percentage of Jews among the unregistered was probably not lower than their ratio among the registered artisans (cf. Weinryb, *ibid.,* pp. 137 ff, 179).
16. R. Mahler, "Jews in Public Service in Poland, 1918-1939," *Jewish Social Studies* VI (1944), p. 341.
17. Lestchinsky, *op. cit.,* p. 14.
18. The number of applicants for Passover relief may serve as an indication of the situation of the Jewish population. In 1937 they amounted to about 40 per cent of the Jewish population. In Warsaw the percentage was 30; in Lodz, 41; in Vilna, 43; in Lvov, 47; and in smaller communities it was more than 50 (Segal, *op. cit.,* p. 179). It should be mentioned that at the end of the nineteenth century (1898) about 20 per cent of the Jewish population in Tsarist Russia applied for Passover relief (cf. Weinryb in *Sefer Hashanah Liyehudey Amerika,* 1940, p. 335).

CHAPTER II

1. J. Lestschinsky, "Economic Aspects of Jewish Community Organization in Independent Poland," *Jewish Social Studies* IX (1947), p. 334.
2. Lestschinsky, *ibid.*, p. 323.
3. N. A. Buchbinder, *Geshichte fun der Yidisher Arbeter Bavegung in Russland*, Vilna 1931, p. 107.
4. Quoted in Abraham Lewenson, *Haleumiyuth Hayehudith*, Jerusalem 1942, p. 238.
5. N. Eck, "The Educational Institutions of Polish Jewry," *Jewish Social Studies* IX (1947), p. 6.
6. J. Lestschinsky, "Di Shprachen bay Yidn in Umuphengikn Poyln," *Yivo-Bleter* XXII, November-December 1943, p. 152.
7. The Warsaw *kehillah* spent about one-third of its 1938 budget for education (C. S. Kazdan, *Di Geshichte fun Yidishn Shulvezn in Umuphengikn Poyln*, Mexico 1947, pp. 517 ff).
8. Wykształcenie Zawodowe (Vocational Training).
9. All figures from Weinryb, *Jewish Vocational Education*, pp. 144 ff.
10. Kazdan, *op. cit.*, pp. 519, 549, 550.
11. At the time 5.29 zlotys equalled one dollar.
12. Of this, about 15 per cent came from subsidies from abroad (JDC, ORT, JCA, *landsmanshaften*, etc.) and from government sources (Lestschinsky, *op. cit.*, pp. 336 ff).
13. Jacob Lestschinsky, "Di Shprachn bay Yidn in Umuphengikn Poyln," *Yivo-Bleter* XXII, pp. 147-162.
14. Commission on European Cultural Reconstruction. *Tentative List of Jewish Periodicals in Axis Occupied Countries*, New York, Conference on Jewish Relations, 1947, pp. 30 ff.
15. M. Linder, "Dos Yidishe Drukvezn in Poyln in di Yorn 1933-1934," *Yivo-Bleter* X (1936), pp. 303 ff.

CHAPTER III

1. *Nazi-Soviet Relations 1939-1941*, Washington, D. C., U. S. Department of State, 1948, pp. 105 ff.
2. Poland's Jewish population in 1939 amounted to some 3,300,000. At the time of the 1931 census there were in Poland only 3,113,000 Jews (plus 18,000 in the armed forces). According to this census, 632,000 (20 per cent) lived in the incorporated areas, 1,269,000 (41 per cent) in the area of the future Government General, and 1,214,000 (39 per cent) in the regions which Russia was to occupy (Moshe Prager, *Yeveyn Metzulah Hachadash*, Tel Aviv 1941, pp. 24-25; Ph. Seraphim in *Die Burg*, Cracow, October 1940.).
3. Polish military authorities put the number of killed at 32,216 and that of war prisoners at 61,000 (Israel Cohen, *The Jews in the War*, London 1943, p. 67). One may assume that a proportionate part originated from the eastern provinces.
4. Some sources give 60,000 (*Black Book of Polish Jewry*, p. 169; *Hitler's Ten-Year War on the Jews*, 1943, p. 155); but this figure seems to be exaggerated.
5. With the conquest of eastern Galicia in the summer of 1941 and its incorporation in the Government General, some 500,000 additional Jews came under the German occupation.
6. *Voelkischer Beobachter*, February 1, 1939.
7. A. Weiss, *Contemporary Jewish Record*, 1940.
8. "Jewish Forced Labor," *Jewish Affairs* I, No. 8 (March 1942), p. 4.

9. Only in some parts of the incorporated areas (*Zaglebia*) was the establishmen of ghettos delayed until 1943.

10. Cf. A. Melezin, "Demografishe Farheltnishn in di Getos in Poyln in 1939-1945," *Gedank un Lebn* V, (1948).

11. Franz Blaettler, *Warschau 1942*, Zurich (n. d.), pp. 83-84.

12. *Dos Naye Lebn*, III, No. 10 (February 3, 1947), p. 2.

13. Cf. *Die Judenausrottung in Deutschen Lagern*, Geneva 1945, pp. 3-6; N. Blumental, *Obozy* [*Dokumenty i materialy*, Vol. I], Lodz 1946, pp. 296, 300; Trunk "Yidishe Arbetlagern in Warteland," *Bleter far Geshichte*, Vol. I, No. 2 [Warsaw 1948], pp. 134 ff, 158 ff; cf. also, F. Friedman, *Zaglada Żydow Polskich*, p. 12.

14. According to SS General Katzmann, by June 27, 1943, 434,329 Jews had been evacuated and 21,156 Jews concentrated in camps, which makes the number 455,485 (Doc. L-18 [USA 277], *Nazi Germany's War Against the Jews*, III, New York 1947. pp. 23-31). To this one should add the tens of thousands living in disguise, dead of sickness, or killed on the spot (not deported).

15. According to Kermisz (Akcje i Wysiedlenia I, p. LXVIII and *idem.*, *Nasze Slowo* 1946, No. 6-7), 100-120,000 Jews were able to disguise their Jewish identity, both at large as well as in the camps (Auschwitz, Hasag, Czestochowa, Stutthof and others).

CHAPTER IV

1. The census of February 14, 1946, showed a population of 26,622,334 in Poland, including the two million Germans later expelled.

2. James T. Shotwell and Max M. Laserson, *Poland and Russia, 1919-1945*, New York 1945, pp. 98, 110-111.

3. According to the Ukrainians themselves, about 7 million.

4. *New York Times*, July 31, 1941.

5. Jan Ciechanowski, *Defeat in Victory*, New York, 1947, p. 63.

6. Edward R. Stettinius, Jr., *Roosevelt and the Russians*, New York 1949, p. 9.

7. James F. Byrnes, *Speaking Frankly*, New York 1947, p. 29; Jan Ciechanowski, *op. cit.*, pp. 156, 228; Arthur Bliss Lane, *I Saw Poland Betrayed*, New York 1948, pp. 55 ff; Stettinius, *op. cit.*, p. 151.

8. Stettinius, *op. cit.*, pp. 152 ff., 181, 184 ff., 211, 301, 338.

9. Shotwell and Laserson, *op. cit., passim.; Occupation of Germany, Policy and Progress*, Washington, The Department of State, 1947, pp. 74-75.

10. The United States pointed out that the agreement made at Potsdam meant that the area east of the Oder-Neisse line should be "under the administration of the Polish State. . . . However . . . the heads of government did not agree to support at the peace settlement the cession of this particular area" (Byrnes, in his address in Stuttgart, September 6, 1946). Only Soviet Russia recognized the western Polish frontiers, and recently East Germany signed an Oder-Neisse boundary agreement with Poland recognizing the Polish western boundary. The State Department reiterated that the German-Polish frontier cannot be settled either "unilaterally or bilaterally," but "only at the time of the final peace settlement for Germany" (*New York Times*, June 9, 1950).

11. WRN (Wolnośc, Równośc, Niepodteglośc—Freedom, Equality, Independence).

12. *Foreign Affairs*, October 1949, pp. 128 ff.

13. J. B. Schechtman, "The Polish Soviet Exchange of Population," *Journal of Central European Affairs*, IX, pp. 200.

14. Cf. Shotwell and Laserson, *op. cit.*, p. 58. The National Council was created by Boleslaw Bierut, later President of the Polish Republic and formerly chief of the Polish section of the Soviet secret police.

15. *Foreign Affairs*, XXVIII, No. 1, p. 126.

16. Stettinius, *op. cit.*, p. 301; cf. also pp. 156-158, 181, 210, 212 ff., 224 ff., 259, 313, 337, 341.

17. In private conversations "most informed Polish Communists seldom claimed the real adherence of more than 12 per cent of the population, at least through the year 1946" (S. Harrison Thomson, "The New Poland," *Foreign Policy Reports*, December 1, 1949, p. 228).

18. S. Harrison Thomson, *Journal of Central European Affairs*, IX, p. 370.

19. Each party had six ministries, but the Communists held the important posts: Public Security, Recovered Territories, Food Supply, and Trade. The "non-party" Minister of National Defense, General Zymierski, was under the Communist thumb.

20. *Foreign Affairs*, October 1949, pp. 131 ff.

21. *Robotnik*, November 29, 1946.

22. S. Harrison Thomson, "The New Poland," *Foreign Policy Reports*, December 1, 1949, p. 227.

23. Joseph Revai, Hungarian Minister of People's Culture and a leading Communist, made it clear, in a speech to party leaders, that the coalition governments in the satellite countries had been dominated by the Communists and represented a "dictatorship of the proletariat though not in the Soviet form." The Communists, by participating in the government, were able with the support of the Soviet Union to destroy the other parties and attain power. "When we struggled directly and apparently only for a steadfast achievement of bourgeois-democratic tasks, we fought as well for the establishment and assurance of the conditions which made possible the socialistic transformation." This holds for Poland as well. (The speech appeared in *Tasadalmi Szemle*, March-April 1949; an English translation is printed in *Foreign Affairs*, October 1949, pp. 143-152.)

24. Thomson, *op. cit.*, p. 230. This was the explanation of the Polish Premier in a speech in the National Council.

25. Stanislaw Mikolajczyk, The Rape of Poland, New York 1948, p. 164.

26. *New York Herald Tribune*, August 21, 1946.

27. *New York Times*, October 20, August 21, November 23, 1946, January 16, 1947; Mikolajczyk, *op. cit.*, pp. 173-184, 296 ff.

28. *Poland of Today*, II, No. 4, April 1949.

29. See *Foreign Affairs*, October 1949, pp, 139 ff. Later in the summer of 1948, when the Politburo charged Gomulka with nationalist deviations, he was accused of having favored the merger for the purpose of strengthening the nationalist wing in the PPR.

30. The year 1948 marked the destruction of the Socialist Party not only in Poland, but also in Hungary and Czechoslovakia.

31. Quoted in *Foreign Affairs*, October 1949, p. 147.

32. *Ibid.*, p. 140.

33. Gomulka was, at the end of 1949, accused of "distrusting the Soviet Union on the question of Poland's Western frontier" (E. A. Morrow, in the *New York Times*, December 11, 1949).

34. Before unification, 82,000 Socialists and 29,000 Communists had already been purged (Vernon Bartlet, *East of the Iron Curtain*, New York 1950, p. 161).

35. Jacob Berman, "Role of the Soviet Union in Establishing New Democracies," *For a Lasting Peace, for a People's Democracy* [organ of the Information Bureau of the Communist and Workers Parties], Bucharest, March 15, 1949.

36. *Christian Science Monitor*, February 1, 1950.

37. In 1949, 243 cooperative farms were established; in January-March 1950, 484 (according to a lecture by the Polish consul in Tel Aviv, as reported in *Davar*, April 7, 1950).

38. *New York Times*, March 26, 1950.

39. *Ibid.*, May 4, 1950.

40. The three other existing parties—United Peasant, Democratic, and [Christian] Labor—are composed of fellow travelers and similar elements dominated by the Communists.

41. *New York Times*, May 15, 1950.

CHAPTER V

1. These figures should not of course be regarded as exact.
2. Klausner, *Miparshath Hashoa* III-IV, Jerusalem 1947, pp. 57-58.
3. *New York Herald Tribune*, February 26, 1945.
4. J. Pat, *Ash un Fayer*, New York 1946, p. 129; on p. 112 the same author gives a round number of 4,000 Jews surviving in Hasag.
5. According to the Warsaw radio, 10,826 Jews came back to the city of Lodz from German concentration camps (Jewish Telegraphic Agency, August 9, 1945).
6. Bernard Goldstein, *Finf Yor in Varshever geto*, New York, 1947, pp. 373 ff.
7. Tadeusz Seweryn, "Chleb i Krew," *W 3-cia Rocznice Zaglady Ghetta w Krakowie,* Cracow 1946, pp. 164 ff.
8. Zerubavel, *Barg Churban,* Buenos Aires 1946, pp. 32 ff; Shoshkes, *Poyln 1946*, Buenos Aires 1946, pp. 20 ff., 24 ff.
9. The Rescue Committee of the Jewish Agency for Palestine, *Bulletin*, May 1945.
10. Jewish Telegraphic Agency, January 8, 1945.
11. *Ibid.*, November 29, 1945.
12. Friedman, *op. cit.*, pp. 34-35.
13. Cf. Kermisz Akcje i Wysiedlenia I, p. LXVIII and *idem, Nasze Slowo,* 1946 nos. 6-7.
14. L. Shapiro and J. Starr, "Recent Population Data Regarding Jews in Europe," *Jewish Social Studies*, VIII (1946), p. 83.
15. How many Polish Jews remained in Russia is difficult to ascertain. The Committee of Polish Jews in the USSR estimated them at a quarter of a million (Jewish Telegraphic Agency, March 26, 1945), while the delegate of the Polish provisional government in France put their number at 150,000 (*Palcor*, April 16, 1945).
16. J. B. Schechtman, "The Polish Soviet Exchange of Population," *Journal of Central European Affairs*, IX, October 1949, p. 313.
17. *New York Herald Tribune*, December 29, 1946.
18. A. Melezin, *op. cit.*, pp. 98-99.
19. J. Egit, *Tsu a Nay Lebn*, Wroclaw 1947, p. 35.
20. Melezin, *op. cit.*, p. 98; Egit, *op. cit.*, p. 35.
21. Egit, *op. cit.*, p. 35.
22. Jewish Telegraphic Agency, September 6, 1945.
23. Quoted by Leon Shapiro and Boris Sapir, "Jewish Population of the World," *American Jewish Year Book,* Vol. 50, 1949, p. 720. This registration has been contested as none too exact.
24. Report of the Central Jewish Committee, *Dos Naye Lebn,* quoted in *Haboker*, October 21, 1945.
25. Jewish Telegraphic Agency, March 26, 1945.
26. B. Goldstein, *The Stars Bear Witness*, New York 1949, p. 276.
27. According to a statement by the Central Committee of Polish Jews, as reported in Jewish Telegraphic Agency, September 30, 1945.
28. *Haboker*, October 21, 1945.
29. A repatriate from a concentration camp received from the Jewish Committee some bread, 50 zloty (about 25 cents), 4 ounces of sugar, 8 ounces of fat. Some invalids received additional small amounts.
30. Goldstein, *op. cit.*, p. 277.
31. Pat, *op. cit.*, p. 92.
32. S. L. Shneiderman, *Between Fear and Hope*, New York 1949, p. 176.
33. Goldstein, *op. cit.*, p. 276.
34. *Ibid.*, p. 277.
35. From reports of Jews who left Poland for Palestine (*Haaretz*, April 19, 1945, p. 2; September 2, 1945, p. 3.)
36. *Haaretz*, September 7, 1945.
37. Zerubavel, *op. cit.*, p. 131.
38. The Rescue Committee of the Jewish Agency for Palestine, *Bulletin*, May 1945.

39. Leo Finkelstein, *Megillath Poyln*, Buenos Aires 1947, p. 10. It seemed to be a general occurrence for Jewish survivors in Europe to divorce themselves from European civilization and from the non-Jewish world. According to some reports, those who went to their death insisted "on a divorce from non-Jewish culture." They advised: "Do not believe in the civilization of the civilized world . . . concentrate on your religion and your culture. Fill your lives with Jewish content. In this way it is easier to live and better to die." Cf. Y. Pilch, "Hirhurim va-irurim," *Hadoar* XXX, No. 39, October 13, 1950, pp. 1087-1088.

40. Cf. *Bleter far Yidisher Geshichte*, Vol. I, No. 2 (1948) pp. 118, 122.

41. According to some accounts the average Bund member wished to go to Palestine (cf. Zerubavel, *op. cit., Passim*).

42. Pat, *op. cit.*, pp. 63, 68.

CHAPTER VI

1. As related by Josef Cyrankiewicz, Polish Prime Minister, formerly an inmate of Auschwitz (quoted in Michal M. Borwicz, *Organizowanie Wściekłości*, Warsaw 1947, p. 40).

2. Bernard Goldstein, *The Stars Bear Witness*, pp. 243-44.

3. Cf. *A Yid fun Klementov Dertseylt*, Warsaw 1947, pp. 123 ff.

4. The Polish ND Party had a large representation in the Polish National Council of the London government-in-exile. In many cases they were joined by members of other parties and voted against motions made by Jewish representatives. Communications from the Jewish underground in Poland were frequently suppressed by the Ministry of the Interior; a telegram from the Jewish National Committee in Warsaw, dated April 28, 1943, asking for help in the uprising was not given to the Jewish representative, I. Schwarzbart, until May 21, 1943, when the struggle was virtually ended. Incidents of antisemitism in the Polish army abroad were reported several times. Some Jewish volunteers even found themselves forced by antisemitism to leave their formations. They were later court-martialed for desertion (Jewish Telegraphic Agency, April 7, 1946).

5. Quoted in S. Segal, *The New Poland and the Jews*, p. 80.

6. Jewish Telegraphic Agency, December 11, 1946.

7. This seems to have had the approval of Rome. After the Kielce pogrom the unofficial Vatican newsletter, *Ari*, published a Vatican declaration which conforms to the statements of the Polish clergy. This also makes it clear that the reluctance of the clergy to label the pogroms as racial violence resulted from the desire to avoid condemning "the political trends responsible for them."

8. Jewish Telegraphic Agency, January 20, 1946; March 7, 1946.

9. *Ibid.*, July 10, 1946, July 21, 1946, July 24, 1946; *New York Times*, July 14, 1946.

10. *Christian Science Monitor*, July 17, 1946; *New York Herald Tribune*, July 12, 1946.

11. Shneiderman, *op. cit.*, p. 117.

12. Jewish Telegraphic Agency, August 21, 1946, July 30, 1946.

13. *Ibid.*, July 13, 1947, Mikolajczyk and his Peasant Party were accused by government circles of fostering antisemitism. In reply, Mikolajczyk and other opposition groups accused the government of staging the Kielce pogrom, and of inspiring pogroms generally. These they maintained were deliberately arranged to cover up the falsification of the results of the referendum, or in order to discredit the opposition abroad.

14. Survivors related that the "Armja Ludowa" of the PPR did not during the Nazi occupation always admit Jews; in conversations people of this group "consoled" themselves with the fact that in the Soviet Politburo there was only one Jew, Kaganovitch (*Haaretz*, September 7, 1945).

15. Jewish Telegraphic Agency, August 27, 1946; January 19, 1947; *New York*

Times, July 16, 1946; Shneiderman, *op. cit.*, p. 97; Pat, *op. cit.*, pp. 151-152, 89 ff.

16. Jewish Telegraphic Agency, July 10, 1946.

17. Shneiderman, *op. cit.*, pp. 251, 256.

18. As related by an inmate of a concentration camp who returned to the camp after a few weeks in Poland (Jewish Telegraphic Agency, August 17, 1945).

19. Jewish Telegraphic Agency, June 26, 1945; Pat, *op. cit.*, pp. 88 ff, 151 ff; Shneiderman, *op. cit.*, p. 34; Jewish Telegraphic Agency, *Daily News Bulletin*, April 17, 1945.

20. *New York Times*, December 10, 1945; Jewish Telegraphic Agency, December 19, 1945, September 12, 1945, August 21, 1945, August 22, 1945, August 8, 1945.

21. Jewish Telegraphic Agency, January 30, 1946.

22. Jewish Telegraphic Agency, April 1, 1946; *New York Herald Tribune*, July 21, 1946. This figure of 800 represented approximately one per cent of the postwar Jewish population, comparable to a prewar proportion of about 31,000 Jews.

23. Jewish Telegraphic Agency, June 1, 1946.

24. Shneiderman, *op. cit.*, p. 118; Jewish Telegraphic Agency, October 15, 1946, October 21, 1946, November 25, 1946; January 28, 1947, August 15, 1947, October 2, 1947.

25. L. Shapiro in the *American Jewish Year Book* (1948-49), p. 390.

CHAPTER VII

1. Anglo-American Committee of Inquiry, *Report to the U. S. Government and His Majesty's Government in the U.K.*, Washington, D.C., U.S. Government Printing Press, 1946, pp. 57-58.

2. *Hayom Baitonuth Haaretz*, January 16, 1945.

3. In the first postwar year about 2,500 Jews—not only from Poland—were admitted to the U.S. and 10,000 entered Palestine (B.D. Weinryb, "Jews in Central Europe," *Journal of Central European Affairs*, VI [1946], p. 63).

4. H. M. Caiserman, a member of the Canadian Jewish Congress, upon returning from Poland (Jewish Telegraphic Agency, February 7, 1946).

5. Jewish Telegraphic Agency, December 11, 1945; *New York Post*, January 10, 1946.

6. Jewish Telegraphic Agency, December 10, 1945; *New York Times*, December 9, 1945; *Christian Science Monitor*, January 19, 1946.

7. *New York Post*, June 17. 1946.

8. *New York Times*, June 21, 1946, June 27, 1946.

9. *New York Herald-Tribune*, January 12, 1946; Jewish Telegraphic Agency, January 8, 1946, February 1, 1946; *New York Times*, January 6, 1946.

10. *New York Times*, January 4, 1946.

11. Jewish Telegraphic Agency, February 15, 1946, February 27, 1946.

12. According to official information, 8,777 Jews left Poland legally between liberation and the end of 1946; an additional 3,194 emigrated during the next five months. The number of exit visas granted in January-July 1946 amounted to 4,764. A great many of these legal immigrants were orphans and children for whom visas for entry into France, Italy, Belgium, and other countries were secured. (Jewish Telegraphic Agency, August 16, August 26, August 27, September 9, November 29, 1946, June 10, 1947; *New York Times*, August 29, 1946).

13. Jewish Telegraphic Agency, July 23, September 8, 1946, January 5, 1947.

14. At the beginning of 1946 there were over 80,000 Jews in Poland. During 1946 some 150-170,000 Jews were repatriated. In 1947 the number of Jews in Poland was placed at 90,000.

15. Jewish Telegraphic Agency, August 29, September 22, September 30, October 3, October 19, October 22, November 1, December 5, 1946, January 6, 1947; *New York Times*, November 5, 1946.

16. *Christian Science Monitor*, April 7, 1947.

17. Jewish Telegraphic Agency, April 14, 1947.
18. S. Gruson in *New York Times*, April 6, 1947.
19. Jewish Telegraphic Agency, April 8, April 10, April 17, 1947, November 7, 1947; *New York Times*, April 16, 1947, February 18, 1948, March 19, 1948; *New Judea*, July 8, 1947; *New York Herald Tribune*, October 31, 1947.
20. A. Tartakower in *Davar*, November 7, 1947; Mekler in the *Jewish Journal*, December 16, 1947.
21. Jewish Telegraphic Agency, March 3, 1949.

CHAPTER VIII

1. *Poland of Today*, April 1946, p. 3.
2. As reported in the *Day*, January 25, 1945.
3. Reprinted in the *Jewish Observer* (London), August 17, 1945.
4. Jewish Telegraphic Agency, February 15, August 6, November 17, 1946.
5. *Ibid.*, April 11, 1945; November 30, 1945.
6. *Ibid.*, April 9, 1948.
7. *Jewish Morning Journal*, March 15, 1945; Jewish Telegraphic Agency, October 29, 1945.
8. Jewish Telegraphic Agency, April 16, 1945; *New York Times*, June 12, 1946.
9. Jewish Telegraphic Agency, May 5, 1946; *Palcor*, May 15, 1945.
10. *Haaretz*, April 9, 1946; Zerubavel, *op. cit.*, p. 116.
11. S. Gruson, "Poland Would End Jewish Emigration," *New York Times*, February 8, 1948.
12. However, it limited to six the number of exit visas for delegates to the Conference of European Zionist Federations (Jewish Telegraphic Agency, August 19, 1947).
13. Jewish Telegraphic Agency, November 7, 1947, February 16, April 10, July 14, 1948; *New York Times*, April 9, 1948.
14. *Jewish Life in Poland*, July 1, 1947 (issued by the Polish Embassy in Washington, D.C.).
15. "Jews Find a New Life in Poland," *Poland of Today*, April 1946.
16. This would seem to be the decree issued by the Polish National Council after the riots in Cracow. In many statements by government officials both in the country and abroad, this law was represented as a law against antisemitism (Jewish Telegraphic Agency, August 22, August 28, October 10, October 12, October 22, October 23, December 23, 1945).
17. *Poland of Today*, No. 5, May 1947. This is an excerpt from an article in *Przeglad Socjalistyczny* (reprinted in *Jewish Life in Poland*, July 1, 1947).
18. Shneiderman, *op. cit.*, p. 232.
19. Jewish Telegraphic Agency, October 7, November 4, 1946.
20. Statement of Foreign Minister Wincenty Rzymowski in New York in the fall of 1945.
21. Jewish Telegraphic Agency, June 12, 1946; *New York Herald Tribune*, July 15, 1946.
22. *New York Times*, July 16, November 28, 1946; Jewish Telegraphic Agency, July 17, 1946, May 20, 1947. Before the Kielce pogrom the death sentence was also sometimes invoked against pogromists (Jewish Telegraphic Agency, October 11, 1945, May 19, 1946).
23. *Ibid.*, September 30, 1946, January 28, 1949.
24. *Ibid.*, March 13, May 5, August 28, 1946.
25. *Dziennik Ustaw Rzeczypospolity Polskiej*, May 7 and August 30, 1945, April 13, 1946; Jacob Goldberg, "Sprawa Odzyskiwania Mienia w Polsce," *Nasza Trybuna*, November 30, 1945.
26. Jewish Telegraphic Agency, January 18, 1946.
27. D. L. Mekler in the *Jewish Journal*, December 19, 1947.

28. Shneiderman, *op. cit.*, p. 264; Jewish Telegraphic Agency, February 26, 1947.
29. Jewish Telegraphic Agency, October 24, 1945.
30. S. Rogozinski in *Opinia*, No. 2 (1946).
31. Jewish Telegraphic Agency, February 26, March 7, July 1, December 3, 1947, April 4, 1948, May 9, 1948.
32. *Ibid.*, October 16, 1947, April 22, June 7, 1948.
33. *Ibid.*, September 18, 1947, February 13, 1947, February 18, 1948.

CHAPTER IX

1. *Haaretz*, January 18, 1946.
2. *Statistical Abstract of Activities of JDC, 1947*, No. 2 (1948), p. 7; 1948, No. 3 (1949), p. 8; 1949, No. 4 (1950), p. 6.
3. Jewish Telegraphic Agency, January 14, 1947.
4. Egit, *op. cit.*, p. 33.
5. *New York Times*, September 2, 1945.
6. JDC *Weekly Review*, No. 44 (August 24, 1945).
7. Jewish Telegraphic Agency, June 14, 1946.
8. P. Lubianiker, "The Last Polish Jews," *Jewish Frontier*, December 1946, p. 18.
9. JDC *Weekly Review*, Nos. 33, 43, 44, 52; J.T.A., October 5, 1945.
10. JDC *Weekly Review*, Vol. II, No. 4, January 25, 1946; cf. also the *Day*, February 26, 1946.
11. Goldstein, *op. cit.*, p. 277; Shneiderman, *op. cit.*, p. 23 ff.
12. Ann Sue Cardwell in the *Christian Science Monitor*, January 6, 1949.
13. H. Szner, "Oblicze repatriacji ludnosci zydowskiej z ZSRR," *Prawo Czlowieka*, September 15, 1946.
14. According to the report of Mr. Caiserman to the Canadian Jewish Congress on his return from Poland (Jewish Telegraphic Agency, November 28, 1945).
15. "Three Years at Work," *Poland Today*, III, No. 7, July 1948, p. 3.
16. *Poland Today*, V, No. 1, January 1950, pp. 3-4.
17. A. Tartakower in *Davar*, November 7, 1947.
18. Pat, *op. cit.*, pp. 45-46.
19. *Ibid.*, pp. 39-41.
20. Zerubavel, *op. cit.*, p. 59.
21. Shneiderman, *op. cit.*, pp. 269-272.
22. Vera Micheles Dean, "Economic Trends in Eastern Europe," *Foreign Policy Reports*, April 1, 1948, p. 25.
23. JDC *Review*, IV, No. 6-7, September-October 1948, p. 68.
24. *Ibid.*, III, No. 28-29 (November 28, 1947), p. 2-3.
25. *Christian Science Monitor*, January 6, 1949; JDC *Review*, IV, Nos. 6-7, p. 69; *Nidershlezye*, June 25, 1948.
26. JDC *Review*, III, Nos. 21-22, July 18, 1947, p. 21.
27. *Dos Naje Lebn*, April 15, 1947.
28. Shneiderman, *op. cit.*, p. 183.
29. *New York Times*, January 4, 1950.
30. R. Mahler in the *Day*, May 9, 1948.
31. *Dos Naje Lebn*, No. 9, January 31, 1947.
32. Jewish Telegraphic Agency, March 4, 1947.
33. Cf. JDC *Review*, IV, No. 6-7, September-October 1948, p. 68.
34. In official or semiofficial declarations of the Central Jewish Committee, higher percentages were sometimes given (cf. *Dos Naje Lebn*, No. 9, 1947). These, however, were either gross exaggerations or based on inadequate information.
35. The attempt to explain the low percentage of gainfully employed by the fact that about "one-third of the Jewish population of Poland consists of the aged, ill and others unable to work" would seem to be inaccurate (cf. for instance, S. Gruson in *New York Times*, February 3, 1948).

36. 34,000 out of 94,000 (Jewish Telegraphic Agency, April 2, 1948).

37. Spring, 1947: 26,550 gainfully employed out of 88,735; 1948: 36,954 out of 88,257. According to other sources (Jewish Telegraphic Agency, March 4, 1947), 33,000 out of about 100,000 were then gainfully employed.

38. JDC *Review*, III, No. 21-22, p. 25; *Dos Naje Lebn*, December 13, 1948.

39. Compared with the occupational structure of the survivors and repatriates, the ratio of manual workers did not increase; there was, however, a shift from artisanship to factory work.

40. Pro-Communist Jewish leaders in Poland boasted about a "profound" change in the Jewish occupational structure. Thus S. Zachariasz wrote (*Nowe Zycie*, No. 2, January 18, 1947): "The social set-up of Jews has changed in New Poland. We have not only watchmakers, tailors, and shoemakers, but there are already the Jewish worker in heavy industry, the Jewish miner and the Jewish farmer." These statements were uncritically repeated by JDC officials and others. William Bein, JDC director for Poland, echoing Zachariasz some eight months later (Jewish Telegraphic Agency, September 23, 1947), said that "a significant shift in occupations" had occurred, with Jews earning their livelihoods in cooperatives, "in factories, mines, and on farms, in contrast to their former occupations as private merchants and artisans." A thorough analysis shows that the changes were of minor importance, except for the fact that Jews were admitted into government owned factories and the civil service.

41. Computed from figures given by Egit, *op. cit.*, pp. 42, 44, and *Nidershlezye*, No. 8-9 (June 25, 1948).

42. Some indication of the improved situation of the Polish Jews may be found in the fact that the number of recipients of cash relief from the JDC declined from 7,950 in 1946 to 3,600 in 1948 to 1,400 in 1949 (JDC *Statistical Abstracts*).

43. The *Day*, March 11, 1950; J. Bornstein in *Der Weg* (Mexico), June 15, 1950; H. Gurson in *Morning Freiheit*, August 18, 1950.

44. *Folksshtime*, October 20, 1950.

45. *Dos Naje Lebn*, November 25, 1949.

CHAPTER X

1. J. Pat in the *Forward*, April 19, 1946.

2. Z. *Otchlani*. A number of the poems were later reprinted in *Nasza Trybuna* (November 1944) and *Poezja Ghetta*.

3. Cf. Michal M. Borwicz, *Literatura w Obozie*, Warsaw 1945; and *idem.*, *Piesn Ujdzie Cialo* (Warsaw 1947), an anthology of poems written during the Nazi occupation. There appeared after the war poems written during the occupation by Itzhak Katzenelson (*Dos Lid funem Oysgehargetn Yidishn Folk*); M. Gebirtig (*Lech Lecha*) (*Es Brent*); Sz. Szajewicz; and others.

4. Goldstein, *op. cit.*, p. 277.

5. Statement by Isaac L. Asofsky, Executive Director of HIAS, on his return from Poland (Jewish Telegraphic Agency, January 9, 1947).

6. A. Tartakower in *Davar*, July 11, 1947.

7. It is estimated that about seventy Jewish writers left Poland during the years 1946-50. The majority of the original staff of the Jewish Historical Institute are now outside Poland.

8. *The Day*, January 20, 1945.

9. As of mid-1945, 90 loans had been made to cooperatives (2,774,000 zloty); 135 loans to professionals (1,620,000 zloty); 310 loans to private workshops (2,997,300 zloty)—(Report of the Polish Delegation at the European Conference of the World Jewish Congress, August 19-23, 1945).

10. B. Zachariasz, in *Nowe Zycie*, No. 2, January 18, 1947.

11. *Der Poylisher Yid*, No. 28, April 1945, p. 23.

12. H. Mirski, "Vi Lang Vet Ir Pravn Shabes far Zich," *Dos Naye Lebn*, No. 9, March 23, 1946.

13. *Jewish Life in Poland,* December 1948, p. 7.
14. *Ibid.*, October 1949, p. 4.
15. Kahane, *Unzer Veg* (Paris), October 7, 1949.
16. M. Maniewitz, "Der Bund in Poyln," *Unzer Tsayt,* No. 3-4, November-December 1947, p. 154.
17. *Gtos Bundu,* August 1946.
18. Zerubavel, *op. cit.*, p. 85.
19. *Al Hamishmar,* May 5, 1946.
20. H. Parnas in *Opinia,* No. 4, 1947.
21. L. Leneman in *Nasze Stowo,* November 10, 1946.
22. Jewish Telegraphic Agency, October 29, 1945.
23. A. Melezin, "Di Itstike Yidishe Shul in Poyln," *Zukunft* LIII, No. 6, July-August 1948, p. 406.
24 Melezin, *ibid.*, p. 407.
25. *Davar,* February 5, 1947.
26. Compiled from JDC *Review,* III, No. 17, May 9, 1947, p. 3.
27. *Poland Today,* III, No. 6, June 1948, p. 9.
28. *Jewish Life in Poland,* July 1, 1947.
29. *Ibid.*, December 1948.
30. *Ibid.*, September 1949.
31. Jewish Telegraphic Agency, February 27, 1947, August 25, 1948.
32. JDC *Review,* III, No. 17, May 9, 1947; Jewish Telegraphic Agency, April 2, 1948.
33. *Jewish Life in Poland,* December 1948.
34. *Ibid.*, September 1949.

CHAPTER XI

1. The Central Committee of the PPR passed several specific resolutions in connection with Jewish policies. Special sessions of the PPR factions in Jewish institutions were often held with leading officials of the party (*Folksshtime,* January 1, 1948; February 3, 1948).
2. *Folksshtime,* November 12, 1948.
3. "Di Yesoydes fun Unzer Kultur-Shafung," *Yidishe Shriftn,* I, No. 2, December 1946, pp. 6-7.
4. *Folksshtime,* December 1946.
5. *Nasze Slowo,* No. 12 Dec. 13, 1946, No. 3, Feb. 18, 1947.
6. *Dos Naye Lebn,* No. 6 (84), No. 10 (88).
7. *Nidershlezye,* June 25, 1948; *Dos Naye Lebn,* January 31, 1947; D. Sfard in *Yidishe Shriftn,* III, No. 11, January-February 1948, p. 10.
8. Editorial in *Dos Naye Lebn,* No. 21, May 9, 1948.
9. His biography is illuminating. Hirsh Smolar was born in Poland. In 1920 he left it with the Red Army and settled in Russia. There he became, first a Yiddish writer, later a Communist agitator, and in 1936 was sent to Poland. Arrested by the Polish police, he was freed by the Red Army in September 1939, and occupied a post in Bialystok. During the Nazi-Soviet war, he was a member of different Partisan groups; he returned to Moscow after liberation and was sent back to Warsaw. He was active in the CJC, and advanced to become head of the cultural department. In 1949 he was made chairman of the entire organization.
10. *Dos Naye Lebn,* No. 15, 1947.
11. Cf. Dr. Sfard's report in *Baricht fun Land Tsuzamenfur fun der Yidisher-Kultur-Gezelshaft in Poyln,* Warsaw (1950) p. 20 ff.
12. At the July (1948) plenary session of the Central Committee of the PPR, one of its top leaders, Zambrowski, pointed this out, in answer to Gomulka, who maintained that place should be found in a united party for the long tradition of the Polish Socialist Party.

13. General Edward Ochab, first Vice-Minister of National Defense, writing in *Nowe Drogi*, as quoted in the *New York Times*, November 13, 1949.
14. *Folksshtime*, August 13, 1948.
15. *Ibid.*, August 27, 1948.
16. *Ibid.*, October 22, 1948.
17. *Ibid.*, November 12, 1948.
18. *Baricht fun Land Tsuzamenfor fun der Yidisher-Kultur-Gezelshaft in Poyln*, Warsaw 1950, p. 3.
19. *Ibid.*, pp. 27 ff.
20. B. Heler, "Di Yidishe Literatur in Nayem Poyln"; Ida Kaminska, "Der Yidisher Artist Vet Dinen dem Folk in der Zach fun Sotsyalizm"; B. Mark, "Di Yidishe Historishe Visenshaft in Poyln"; L. Lozowski, "Di Yidishe Meluche-Shul un di Yidishe Gezelshaft"; *Baricht fun . . . Yidisher Kultur-Gezelshaft in Poyln*, pp. 43, 44. 45, 46.
21. *Ibid.*, p. 57.
22. J. Lazebnik in *Folksshtime*, November 4, 1950.
23. Zachariasz in his report to the cultural conference, October 1949; Lazebnik at the conference, October 1950 (cf. *Baricht* . . . pp. 57-58); *Dos Naye Lebn*, October 26, 1949; *Folksshtime*, *November* 2, 1950.
24. Zachariasz in *Dos Naje Lebn*, October 26, 1949.
25. The phrase "Jewish milieu" replaced such former phrases as "Jewish population," and "Jewish group."

CHAPTER XII

1. *Jewish Life in Poland*, October 1948, p. 13.
2. Mazur seems to have been a specialist in such "problems." He also negotiated the agreement with the Catholic church of April 14, 1950.
3. A. Berman, in the *Day*, June 2, 1950.
4. Lozowski in *Folksshtime*, No. 35, August 27, 1948.
5. *Jewish Life in Poland*, October 1948; *Folksshtime*, October 27, 1948.
6. *Folksshtime*, October 15, 1948.
7. *Dos Naye Lebn*, March 4, 1949; March 9, 1949.
8. *Ibid.*, March 23, 1949.
9. Lazebnik in *Folksshtime*, November 5, 1950. On a certificate reproduced in *Dos Naye Lebn* (June 23, 1950), the school is called "gruntshul far algemeyer bildung mit der yidisher lernshprach," or "elementary school for general education with Yiddish as the language of instruction."
10. *Unzer Buletin*, No. 1, February 1950, p. 6.
11. *Folksshtime*, June 23, 1950.
12. *Dos Naye Lebn*, May 17, 1950.
13. Cf. Mirski in *Dos Naye Lebn*, No. 67, 1947.
14. Mirski in *Naye Presse* (Paris) January 6, 1950.
15. *Folksshtime*, February 13, 1948
16. Cf. *Folkstseytung*, September 2, 1947; *Folksshtime*, February 6, 1948.
17. *Nidershlezye*, June 25, 1948.
18. No. 112, September 16, 1948; *Dos Naye Lebn*, January 21, 1949.
19. Jewish Telegraphic Agency, November 10, 1949.
20. *Folksshtime*, March 17, 1950.
21. Zwiazek Religijny Wyznania Mojzeszowego.
22. Cf. Smolar in *Unzer Buletin*, No. 1, February 1950, p. 2.
23. Lazebnik in *Dos Naye Lebn*, March 3, 1950.
24. *Dos Naye Lebn*, March 15, 1950.
25. The January-June 1950 issue of *Bleter far Geshichte* features an article by the Russian historian, Sidorov, on Stalin's role in the development of historiography.

26. *Folksshtime,* November 14, 1950.
27. Zachariasz on *Homens Mapole* (*Baricht* . . . , p. 59).
28. Smolar in *Yidishe Shriftn,* V, No. 4 (April 1950).
29. *Dos Naye Lebn,* March 15, 20, 1950.
30. *Unzer Buletin,* No. 2 (March 1950), p. 8.
31. *Ibid.,* No. 1 (February 1950), p. 20; No. 3 (May-June), p. 33; No. 2 (March), p. 24.
32. M. Hurwitch in *Yidishe Shriftn,* No. 10 (October 1950), p. 7.

CHAPTER XIII

1. *Dos Naye Lebn,* November 12, 1945.
2. *Folksshtime,* No. 7, 1946;*Tygodnik Informacyjny* (Szczecin), No. 7, 1947.
3. *Dos Naye Lebn,* November 12, 1945.
4. *Tsionistishe Shtime* (Munich), February 9, 1949.
5. *Haboker,* January 28, 1949, February 17, 1949; *Davar,* January 25, 1949.
6. Jewish Telegraphic Agency, March 3, 1949, March 24, 1949.
7. A. Berman in the *Day,* July 2, 1950.
8. *Dos Naye Lebn,* September 2, 1949.
9. *Ibid.,* November 21, 1949.
10. *Folksshtime,* February 23, March 1, 1950; *Dos Naye Lebn,* March 20, 1950.
11. B. Zilberberg, "Polish Jewry Under Communism," the *Day,* April 16, 1950.
12. *Nidershlezye,* April 19, 1950; *Folksshtime,* September 13, 1950.
13. *Jewish Life in Poland,* No. 10, January 1950.
14. Kazimierz Witaszewski, representative of the Central Committee of the PZPR at the Cultural Conference, October 14, 1949 (*Baricht* . . . , p. 10).
15. *Poland Today,* V, No. 2, February 1950, p. 15.
16. February 1, 1950, republished February 2 in *Rzeczypospolita,* semiofficial government organ (*Jewish Life in Poland,* No. 11, April 1950).
17. The Polish Consul General in Detroit in a statement at the beginning of February 1950 (Detroit *Jewish Chronicle,* February 2, 1950); editorial on Warsaw uprising, *Poland Today,* April 1950; *Jewish Life in Poland,* No. 13, October 1950, p. 1. The PZPR organ, *Trybuna Ludu,* (February 16, 1950) also attacked the "chauvinist-nationalist" state of Israel.
18. In November 1950 permission to take a few hundred children out of an orphanage was refused (*Davar,* November 22, 1950).
19. A. Berman in the *Day,* July 2, 1950.
20. *Christian Science Monitor,* January 1, 1950.
21. According to Dr. Berman, by the summer of 1950 about 25,000–30,000 (counting children) had registered. Others put the number at 40,000, which figure seems to be the more accurate. Up to the end of 1950 about 30,000 Jews left Poland; 8,000 registrants remained.
22. The *Day,* February 7, 1950.
23. *Jewish Life in Poland,* No. 13, October 1950.
24. According to JDC figures (Passover registration), there were in April 1949 about 80,000 Jews, besides a few thousand unregistered (so-called "Aryan") Jews. Dr. Berman estimates that there were only 70,000 Jews in Poland at the time of the beginning of the exodus of the fall of 1949.

III. Polish Jews Under Soviet Rule

BY

BERNARD D. WEINRYB

Chapter I

Soviet Occupation of Eastern Poland

When Germany attacked Poland on September 1, 1939, the Nazis urged Soviet Russia to occupy those Polish areas which according to the Soviet-Nazi pact of August 23, 1939, were designated as the Russian sphere of influence. On September 17, 1939, Russian troops crossed the border; in a few days they had occupied all of eastern Poland. The demarcation line between Germany and Russia was later fixed by the German-Soviet Boundary and Friendship Treaty of September 28, 1939.[1] The Polish eastern and southeastern provinces,[2] comprising 77,606 square miles with a population of about 13,000,000 people,[3] were acquired by Soviet Russia.

The official pretext for the occupation was defense of "the kindred Ukrainian and White Russian peoples"; the provinces were called the Western Ukraine and Western White Russia. Less than a month after the occupation of this region elections to the People's Assembly of the Western Ukraine and Western White Russia were proclaimed. The National Assemblies meeting in Lvov and Bialystok in the latter part of October voted for the incorporation of the two provinces into the Soviet Union. On November 1 and 2, 1939, the Supreme Council of the USSR decreed the incorporation of these provinces into the USSR and their union with the Ukrainian and White Russian Socialist Soviet Republics respectively.[4]

On November 29, 1939 a decree on citizenship declared the following classes of persons in the incorporated territories to be Soviet citizens: (a) all persons living in these territories at the time of their incorporation into Soviet Union (November 1 and 2, 1939); (b) all those later coming from western Poland as a result of population exchanges with Germany, and all those coming from Vilna after its cession to Lithuania. Residents of the eastern Polish provinces not belonging to either of these two categories could acquire citizenship by the regular process of Soviet naturalization.[5]

In the former Polish provinces the Ukrainians and White Russians barely constituted a majority. The Ukrainians had a majority in Volhynia, but comprised only about one-half of the population of eastern Galicia. The 1½ million White Russians in Poland constituted almost one-half of the population in the provinces of Vilna and Polesie, but only 40 per cent in the province of Novogrodek.[6]

To strengthen the local Ukrainian and White Russian elements a number of measures were taken. This included arrest of a part of the Polish intelligentsia as early as October 1939, and deportation in February 1940 of about 100,000 people, consisting mostly of Poles settled in this region in former years, forest employees, members of the police force, etc.[7] In such cities as Bialystok, Grodno and Pinsk, where there were only a small number of White Russians, mayors were appointed from among them.[8] Similar policies were employed in the Western Ukraine. Government offices and the school system were Ukrainized. Polish schools in the Western Ukraine decreased during the first year of Russian rule from 95.4 to 12.9 per cent, while the percentage of Ukrainian schools increased from 0.6 to 80 per cent.[9]

The policies of Ukrainization and White-Russification brought a larger number of Ukrainian and White Russian nationalists and antisemites into office, at least at the lower levels of administration. These local antisemites disguised their antisemitism under the overt slogan of fighting Jewish speculation. At the same time this official nationalist policy barred many Jews from government office. Thus, while the middle-class occupations in which the majority of Jews were employed were eradicated by the new Soviet regime, only a small number of Jews could find employment with the government.

Jewish cultural life and institutions were suppressed and the growth of a new Jewish cultural life was prevented by the official policy of Ukrainization and White-Russification. Local Jewish groups were too weak to do anything about this and Jewish Communists in Russia were either not interested or afraid to intervene.[10]

In the territory of eastern Poland in the winter of 1939-40 were concentrated a great many refugees, most of them Jews, from the Nazi-occupied parts of Poland. Most of the non-Jewish refugees returned to western Poland; most of the Jews (about 300-350,000) remained. They congregated in a few cities where they became a separate community. Hundreds and thousands of ragged, hungry people queued up before offices and welfare organizations, slept outdoors and jammed railway stations. They were a burden to the local people, who sometimes treated them with brutality.[11]

The refugees had relatives and friends on the Nazi side of the border. Everyone was eager to communicate with his own family and eventually to bring them over. A lively traffic over the frontier went on constantly, mainly carried on by non-Jews. This increased the suspicions of the already suspicious Soviet NKVD officials. Jews were accused of spying for the Nazis and mass arrests, investigations, and deportations took place.

The Jewish Community

In the eastern Polish provinces occupied by the Soviets there had been, at the time of the 1931 census, 1,222,000 persons of the Jewish faith. This constituted 10.2 per cent of the total population of 12,012,000.[12] Of these Jews about 80,000 lived in the Vilna area, which was transferred to Lithuania on October 10, 1939. Deducting this number, and allowing for the natural increase since 1931,[13] we find approximately 1,200,000 Jews in eastern Poland at the time of the Russian occupation. Eastern Poland was, except for Bialystok and the oil-producing areas in eastern Galicia, a more agricultural and backward region than the western parts. The village population was mostly Ukrainian and White Russian, with some admixture of Poles. Among the latter were thousands of Polish settlers given land by the Polish government with the intention of Polonizing the region. In the cities and towns the non-Jewish population consisted mainly of Poles and some Ukrainians, White Russians and Russians.

A great part of the urban population was made up of Jews. They were chiefly engaged in supplying the agricultural population with consumer goods, buying and selling agricultural produce, and milling and processing food products. Jews also played a considerable role in the crafts, in the lumber trade, and in the tobacco industry.

Bialystok's textile industry, the second largest in Poland, was chiefly Jewish-owned. Of the 201 enterprises in Bialystok province at the time of the 1931 census, 88.5 per cent were Jewish. Of the employed personnel and workers 74.2 and 25.9 per cent, respectively, were Jews.[14]

In eastern Poland were concentrated a majority of the 125,000 Polish-Jewish farmers. But Jews also made up a large part of the town population of this area. Of the businesses in the cities of Poland, 58.5 per cent were Jewish; of the businesses in the eastern and southern cities, 76 per cent were Jewish. In crafts and industry the percentage of the Jews was 24 in all of Poland, but 53 in eastern Poland.[15] In Pinsk in 1933, 95 per cent of trade was in Jewish hands; in Lutsk, 86 per cent.[16] In the districts of Tarnopol and Stanislav in eastern Galicia, 57.7 per cent of the physicians were Jews; in Lvov 73 per cent of the lawyers were Jews (whereas in Warsaw Jewish lawyers were 53 per cent of the total).

Efforts by the Polish state and by non-Jews to dislodge Jews from commerce and manufacture were not wanting in eastern Poland. The introduction of a state monopoly of the production of tobacco resulted in virtually complete elimination of Jews from this branch; the Polish state's taking over of lumbering ousted many Jews from that industry. Non-Jews opening up stores in towns and cities were able, with the support of the Polish state, to drive Jewish storekeepers out of business.

In eastern Galicia the struggle of the Ukrainians against Polish domination also affected the Jews. The Ukrainians built up a cooperative movement of their own as a result of which hundreds of Jewish storekeepers were eliminated from the villages. In Volhynia and the northeastern provinces, Poles—sometimes also Ukrainians—moved into the towns and opened stores and workshops. The percentage of Jews in these cities and towns began to decline.

In Lvov, the percentage of Jews dropped from 35 in 1921 to 31.9 in 1931; in Brest, from 52.9 to 44.3; in Rovno, from 71.2 to 56; in Pinsk, from 74.6 to 63.4; in Bialystok from 51.6 to 43—all in the decade between 1921 and 1931.

The ratio of Jews employed in trade in Poland as a whole was declining because of the invasion of this field by non-Jews. In eastern Poland this decline was even steeper. An investigation made in 1937 of 91 towns showed a decline from 87.4 per cent in 1932 to 77 per cent. In 11 towns in the Bialystok region the decline was from 92 per cent in 1932 to 64.5 per cent in 1937.[17]

As in Poland generally so in eastern Poland, those eliminated from the middle class had to seek employment lower down on the economic ladder, organize new kinds of enterprises,[18] emigrate, or suffer unemployment. In general, however, the Jews of eastern Poland were in the lower middle class, either as storekeepers, entrepreneurs, or employees of small enterprises.[19]

The communal and cultural life of the Jews of eastern Poland resembled that of the rest of Poland in certain respects, while differing in others. By the statute of 1927, the Jewish community organization (*Kehillah*) enjoyed the same legal status as in the rest of the country. Here, too, there were a variety of Jewish parties, Jewish schools, and a Jewish press.

Jewish activities in eastern and southeastern Poland, however, were more intensive than in other parts of the country. In these regions there was a continuous struggle going on between the Polish and Ukrainian (or White Russian) populations for political and cultural supremacy. This national struggle also influenced Jewish national feelings. Zionism was very strong. Moreover, Jews felt it wiser to be neutral and to use their own language so as not to appear to be siding with either group. Eastern Galicia, before World War I, was an interesting contrast of Polish assimilationist tendencies, extreme orthodoxy, Chassidism, and Jewish nationalism. Before the war there existed a few Hebrew schools. This was also observable in Lvov.

The first Hebrew elementary schools in Poland were opened near Bialystok in 1916, and near Grodno in 1917. Most of the larger towns and cities in the eastern Polish provinces had a Hebrew public school or high school. Of the 162 Hebrew (Tarbuth) elementary schools in 1937-38 in Poland, 145 schools (90 per cent) with 91 per cent of the school population were to be found in these eastern regions (including Vilna and Stanislav).[20] Many Yiddish schools were also to be found in this region. Of the 47 Yiddish kindergartens and 130 elementary schools existing in Poland in the middle of 1921, 16 kindergartens and 44 elementary schools were located in eastern Poland.[21] Of 86 Yiddish (CYSZO) elementary schools in 1934-35, 66 (76.7 per cent) were to be found in the eastern provinces (including Vilna and Stanislav).

Yeshivoth, some well known beyond the boundaries of Poland, were to be found in Mir, Radom, Grodno, Vilna, Baranovichi, Brest, Kremenets, Slonim, Rovno, Lutsk, Kobryn, Korets and other localities. Belonging to the Yeshivah Committee (*Vaad Hayeshivoth*) in Vilna were 78 Yeshivoth with 6,000 students, all in the eastern parts of Poland.[22]

Lvov, Bialystok, Grodno, Rovno had Yiddish dailies. Of the 391 Jewish periodicals (in Yiddish, Polish, Hebrew) appearing in Poland in the pre-war years, 75 (19.2 per cent) were published in eastern Poland outside of Vilna.[23]

The Lvov Jewish community had a library of some 20,000 volumes and a B'nai B'rith library; Bialystok, 2 libraries; Stanislav, Tarnopol, and Przemyśl each had community libraries. Almost every Tarbuth (Hebrew) school had a library.

Soviet Policies

For this middle-class Jewish population possessing its own institutions and an active communal and cultural life, the coming of the Soviet forces to the region was bound to bring many changes.

Jews greeted the Red Army as their savior from the Nazis.[24] The youth hoped that the new order would make it possible for them to study, work, and obtain government employment. Young Jews and some of the intelligentsia saw an opportunity, denied to them under Polish rule, to put their knowledge and education to use. Rising prices, prohibition of private trade, etc., were overlooked.

"It is easy to imagine with what great delight the Jews of Lvov met the Red Army which saved them . . . from the Germans almost at the last moment."[25] Many began to believe that things would no longer be as they had been in Poland, and that the Russians would live and let live. Nor was it felt that the elimination of private enterprise was fatal. The Jewish lower middle class believed it would find employment in the government, police, schools, and cooperatives.

This general feeling of gratitude and relaxation fostered many illusions, particularly among young people. Older Zionists almost immediately looked for ways to escape abroad, whereas *chalutzim* members of *hakhsharah kibbutzim* at first thought they would be able to continue to live and work on a communal basis and prepare themselves for Palestine.

An observer who travelled from Bialystok to Lvov (apparently in November 1939) observed that in the small towns the Jewish working population was happy, despite the lack of food. Occasionally one could even find enthusiasm for the Russian regime. Police duties were carried out by local Jewish youths, mostly former political prisoners. On Saturdays religious Jews wore their traditional attire and walked through the streets to and from the synagogues.[26] Only in the larger places were apathy and fear to be felt.

The initial feeling of sympathy toward Soviet Russia passed rapidly. "The people feel the rope tightening around their neck. . . . There is the feeling in the air that everything that now exists will be no more in the future."[27] One reason for this changed feeling (which we find as early as the beginning of 1940) was the fact that schools of higher education, when reopened, often refused admittance to many Jewish applicants; students had to be children of peasants and workers. But this was only the beginning.

Sovietization started with the nationalization of large landed estates, large real-estate holdings, and industrial and commercial enterprises. In the latter cases, Jews constituted a majority of those affected. Nor was nationalization accomplished in an orderly way. It was not always clear which enterprises were required to be nationalized and which were not. The regulations were often contradictory, and the committees in charge of nationalization frequently exceeded their instructions,[28] without, however, subsequently being called to account. Even court decisions holding certain cases of nationalization illegal were powerless to effect restitution.[29] Owners of industrial enterprises were sometimes employed in their former enterprises, but after a few weeks or months they were dismissed and often jailed and deported to the interior of Russia.[30] Others were forced to leave the big cities to seek refuge in smaller places.

Small stores and artisans' shops were not nationalized—their owners were ruined in other, more leisurely ways. Taxes on private enterprises were high while stores lacked an adequate supply of commodities and artisans' shops of raw materials. Goods, once sold, could rarely be replaced. Prices were fixed at prewar levels, one Russian ruble being made equal in value to one zloty. This enabled the Russians to buy up commodities,[31] while the purchasing power of both currencies was falling. Stores were soon emptied and storekeepers unemployed, unless a man preferred hiding part of his stock and becoming a "speculant." Artisans' shops, too, were rapidly being closed down. According to information from Polish sources in Lvov, in the course of a few months over three-quarters of the existing 8,500 workshops were closed.[32] All those possessing currency received in exchange for their merchandise lost it when the zloty was withdrawn in January 1940. Thus the Jewish middle class was pauperized.

Some former independent artisans could find employment in newly organized cooperatives, but former storekeepers were regarded as "capitalists" and barred from trade unions, or were otherwise discriminated against. Some Jews (preferably Communists but in any case no "bourgeois") were given employment in the Soviet administration, in post offices, railways, cooperatives, and in the militia (police). In every application for work one had to furnish an autobiography which the police would then investigate.[33] There were also other difficulties in the way of securing employment. "Class enemies" or persons suspected of being unfriendly to the new regime received passports with "paragraphs." These paragraphs forbade the holder of the passport to live in a large city, or within a certain distance of the border. They could not leave their place of domicile without a special permit from the Soviet police.[34]

People lived by the sale of their personal belongings or on the earnings of their relatives. Workers had to submit to the lowering of their standard of living, although some who in Polish times had suffered from unemployment were now able, after the first transitional months, to find work. Introduction of Soviet "work norms" meant a lowering of wages, while the prices of food and consumer goods rose. "A weaver in Bialystok earning 250 rubles a month as a Stakhanovite could never lift himself above the level of mere sustenance. Bread was sold at the official price of one ruble a kilogram; meat eight rubles; and butter twenty rubles. Clothing was too expensive for the average worker to buy."[35]

The greater part of the Jewish intelligentsia was deprived of the possibility of earning a living in their own occupations. Lawyers, accountants, etc., naturally lost their positions, while the income of others declined considerably. According to reports, "the average monthly salary of a physcian was 400 to 600 rubles, while a pair of shoes on the 'private market' cost some 1,000 rubles."[36] Only teachers were in a somewhat better position; their services were required in the schools being opened (even a number of refugees found employment), although pay was small and inadequate in a time of rising prices.

Government employment was hard to get for a number of reasons. First of all, there was the obstacle of a middle-class past. There were also cases of denunciation and betrayal by former friends or foes.[37] The policy of Ukrainization and White-Russification, with all its implications, was yet another barrier. This policy meant the official employment of the Ukrainian and White Russian languages, and the Jewish intelligentsia, having been reared in Polish, Jewish and even in the Russian or Galician prewar schools, did not know these languages. But far more than language was involved.

As already noted, many local nationalists and antisemites came into office. They possessed a virtual monopoly on the lower levels of the bureaucracy, and were not without some influence at the higher levels. This group—including at times even known antisemites who had collaborated with the Poles or Nazis against Jews—discriminated against others,[38] and engaged in antisemitic practices. The central authorities and the Russian officials sent to these regions were interested in gaining the sympathy of the local population[39] and overlooked discriminatory practices. Discrimination against a Jew could always be justified by calling him a "speculator," or a former "Polonizer." Only in the so-called "Soviet commerce" was a high percentage of Jews employed.[40]

As we have seen, Soviet policy favored the Ukrainian and White Russian elements. Politically, this meant their domination of the government bureaucracy and representative organs of the region.[41]

The general trend toward Ukrainization and White-Russification was bound to jeopardize the cultural needs and rights of the Jews; the authorities were inclined to forego or limit the rights of the Jewish minority in favor of the majority. In Lvov, for instance, permission to publish a Yiddish periodical was at first refused because "Lvov was to become a Ukrainian city; there is in the meantime no room or time for Yiddish periodicals. Later we shall see."[42] Later, in 1941 a Yiddish daily (*Der Lemberger Shtern*) was published in Lvov.[43]

When Itzik Fefer from Russia exclaimed at a meeting of Yiddish writers in Bialystok,—"Back to the past! We are now celebrating the 800th anniversary of Judah Halevi. Judah the Maccabean and the Hasmoneans are national heroes and revolutionaries,"—some took it as encouragement to Jewish cultural work.[44] Generally, however, Jewish intellectuals and writers from Russia accepted and defended the anti-Jewish policies of government officials.[45] Nor was the general atmosphere at all favorable to the development of a Jewish culture. When a child did attend a Yiddish school, its Communist-organized youth and extracurricular activities worked against the spirit of the school. Children in Yiddish schools encountered a Russification policy intended to make them look down on Yiddish schooling.[46] Yiddish writers and journalists in Poland, scorned by their colleagues from Russia, were expected to atone for their "reactionary" past and to start anew in the Soviet spirit.[47]

Nevertheless, in the beginning signs of activity could be observed alongside those bespeaking decline and stagnation. This activity was an echo of the general revival stimulated by the Soviets, with their youth organizations, reading rooms, propaganda meetings, measures to combat illiteracy, opening of many schools and courses of every kind, and the like. Thus, when a decree about the liquidation of illiteracy led to the opening of a network of schools for adults, Jews learned Yiddish (just as Poles learned Polish and Ukrainians, Ukrainian) and also Russian.[48] To Jewish intellectuals accustomed to Jewish cultural institutions being at best tolerated, but scarcely ever supported by the government, the new possibilities seemed glowing.

In Lvov and Bialystok Jewish actors, mostly refugees from western Poland, organized groups which the government transformed into state theaters. "It sounded high and mighty: the Jewish State Theater. And all the artists received a fixed salary . . . and did not have to worry about technical matters, costumes, sale of tickets, etc. . . . The first performances in the theater [in Lvov] were impressive holiday celebrations for a large and varied Jewish public."[49] A Yiddish hour was presented on the radio.[50] Artists were given rooms in which to exhibit their work, and a club where tea and meals were served—a very important matter in those days. Writers and journalists—Polish, Ukrainian, Jewish—organized a club with sections for every group.

The old Jewish school system with its *chedarim*, Yeshivoth, Hebrew and Yiddish schools, were closed down by the government. Most of them were converted into Yiddish schools supported and maintained by the state. A whole network of elementary and high schools arose. Where there was a shortage of teachers, teachers' seminaries or training courses were opened.[51] Even so, only about one-third of all Jewish children attended Yiddish schools.[52] Attending Yiddish schools were children some of whose parents would have preferred a Polish school for them.[53] The schools themselves were, of course, "imbued with the Soviet spirit."

In political as well as cultural life, officials sent out from Russia began to dominate the scene as early as the summer of 1940. The new director of the Jewish theater in Lvov was one of these. In the field of education Russian regimentation went hand-in-hand with the Ukrainization policy. The director of the Jewish high school in Lvov was removed in the summer of 1940 and a Ukrainian appointed in his place, who later Ukrainized the school. Lvov's other Jewish high school had been Ukrainized earlier. In Kovel the Jewish high-school building was turned over to the Ukrainians. Some Yiddish schools, for the most part high schools, had their language of instruction changed to Ukrainian or Russian.[54] "Teachers were forbidden to urge Jewish children to attend Yiddish schools; and when one of them criticized this order at a teachers' conference, he was described in the press as a Trotskyite, nationalist, and diversionist, and haled before the NKVD."[55] The dissolution of the Yeshivoth and Hebrew schools has already been mentioned. Libraries were also purged, sports clubs disbanded, and other cultural organizations closed.

The Jewish community organization (*Kehillah*) was deprived of its official status; adherence was no longer compulsory for Jews and it could not levy taxes; but it continued to function as a social welfare [56] and religious agency.[57] Jewish religious life was for a time unmolested, except for attacks by *Bebozhnik* (atheists) against Chassidim.[58] According to eyewitness accounts, worship in the synagogues in eastern Galicia was not forbidden; however, high taxes had to be paid for the upkeep of these synagogues.[59] A rabbi from Brest testified that Jewish schools and synagogues were closed on or about October 15, 1939. "As a religious man who, with others, protested against this antireligious action of the Bolsheviks, he was arrested on November 3, 1939," kept in solitary confinement, and after 14 months deported to Russia.[60] Another eyewitness (from Drogobych, eastern Galicia) declared:

> All synagogues in our city were closed with the exception of the Central Synagogue. The supervisor of this synagogue was my father-in-law. . . . He was often, 3-4 times a week, called to the political department of the NKVD where he was forced to listen for hours to different charges against those Jews who continued to frequent the synagogue for prayer. They often threatened to shoot him like a dog . . . unless he informed them of any conversations of a political nature among the worshippers. Putting the matter in this way forced my father-in-law to turn in the keys of the synagogue, as had been expected.[61]

The Jewish youth was forced to join the Communist youth organization (*Komsomol*) and to take part in other Communist organizational and cultural work. In small places where everybody was known to the authorities they simply demanded a declaration of membership in the new groups.[62] *Kibbutzim* were liquidated; some of the *chalutzim* left for Vilna (which had been turned over to Lithuania), or set out for the Rumanian border; others went underground.[63]

Jewish parties, from the orthodox Agudath Israel through the Zionist groupings to the Socialist Bund, disappeared rapidly under the harassment and terrorization of the Communists and their new fellow travelers.[64] Arrests were made first of Bundists and later also of Zionists.[65]

Economic institutions and relief organizations such as loan societies, Jewish cooperative banks, TOZ, ORT, etc., continued to function for the most part. Later, however, these institutions were all closed as a matter of general policy.[66] All that remained of Jewish communal and cultural life was a Sovietized Yiddish school (which, however, underwent a process of amalgamation with the general schools), a Yiddish theater, a small Yiddish press (*Bialystoker Shtern* with a circulation of 5,000; *Lemberger Shtern* which first appeared on June 1, 1941;[67] Yiddish sections or groups in general writers' clubs; and Jewish libraries, or Jewish sections of general libraries purged of their Hebrew and non-Soviet books.

Underground activities were carried on mainly by Zionist youth. People were smuggled across the border to Rumania and Lithuania,[68] secret meetings were held, and Jewish holidays were celebrated. Hebrew-speaking groups, an underground Hebrew library, circles for the study of Jewish history, and new groups of Zionist youth were formed.[69]

A convention of the underground chalutz movement was held in January 1940 in Lvov. It called for a fight against assimilation, and the strengthening of Jewish consciousness. After the conference an energetic underground program was developed; new groups joined, bulletins were published, and an underground press put out. This movement also worked to prevent the conversion of Jewish schools into Ukrainian and Russian institutions, arranged celebrations of Jewish holidays, and commemorated Jewish writers.[70]

Chapter II

Jewish Refugees

Eastern and southeastern Poland had not only its native Jewish population, but also Jewish refugees from western Poland. They had come in two waves: one immediately following the outbreak of war before the Red Army occupied eastern Poland on September 17, 1939; the other after the occupation. It is estimated that about one-quarter of a million Jewish refugees made up the first wave, of whom not more than one-third reached eastern Poland, afterwards occupied by the USSR.

In western Poland the Nazis began to perpetrate anti-Jewish atrocities immediately following occupation. Many Jews fled eastward, their number being swelled by a host of Jews expelled *en masse* by the Nazis. Following the Russian occupation of eastern Poland, the Nazis drove entire Jewish communities over the border. Frida Zerubavel found Malkinia burned and the Jews expelled.[1] An official German Foreign Office memorandum, dated December 5, 1939, refers to the practice "of expelling a few thousand Jews across the Russian border at a quiet place in the woods."[2] "Several thousand Jews whose townships are near the Soviet border were directed by the Nazis to the frontier."[3] A harrowing account of such an expulsion (from Chelm and Hrubieszów) is given in a Jewish Telegraphic Agency dispatch from Geneva dated January 21,1941. The Germans also brought (apparently some time in October 1939) a trainload of 3,000 Jews from Kalisz.

Some German authorities acted in the belief that an agreement with Russia concerning the admittance of Jews from Poland was in effect, or at least they expected the Russians to admit these Jews. At any rate, we learn from the same memorandum by the German State Secretary of the Foreign Office that "lately there have been repeated wrangles on the boundary between Russia and the Government General, into which the army, too, was drawn." The reason for these wrangles was that "the expulsion of Jews into Russian territory, in particular, did not proceed as smoothly as had apparently been expected." The Russians, that is, rounded up Jews expelled by the Germans and were "trying to force the German [commander] to readmit the group."[4] At that time—November-December 1939—the mass expulsions had begun from certain regions in German-occupied Poland. Hordes of Jews, expelled from their homes, streamed to the border and thousands managed to cross to the Russian side.[5]

The German authorities in Poland also made a "legal" attempt to transfer Polish Jews across the Russian border. A confidential protocol, appended to the German-Soviet Boundary and Friendship Treaty of September 28, 1939, provided for transfer of Germans living in the Russian area and a reciprocal transfer of "persons of Ukrainian and White Russian descent" from the German area.[6] In accordance with this protocol, an agreement was signed on November 16, 1939 by Germany and the USSR concerning evacuation of Germans from the Russian-occupied parts of Poland and of Ukrainians and White Russians from the German-occupied areas.[7] A German commission was sent to Russian Poland and a Soviet Commission to German Poland to carry out this agreement. The Nazis then conceived the idea of registering Jews as "Ukrainians of Mosaic religion." A number of Jewish communities–Radom, Piotrków, Czestochowa, etc.–were ordered to register a certain quota of Jews as Ukrainians. Such Jews had to submit a declaration stating that they were Ukrainians; they were promised early transfer to the Soviet side.[8] Those Jews who had the right to be transferred into Soviet-occupied Poland were exempted from the forced labor required of all Jews in Nazi-occupied Poland.[8a] Instructions from the Gestapo specified that these Jewish transferees could not take along any of their property except the clothes they wore. According to information originating in Polish circles, a controversy developed between the Nazi and Soviet authorities over the Nazi prohibition against transferees taking their property along with them. If we are to believe this source, 83,000 Jews were registered for transference to Russia in exchange for 150,000 Germans from Russia.[8b] Either because of this controversy or because the Russian repatriation commission did not accept Jews as Ukrainians or White Russians, no Jews were transferred to Russia on this exchange basis.

Right after the occupation of eastern Poland by the Red Army, the border remained open and the Russians made few difficulties for those crossing the demarcation line. Sometime in the second half of October, however, the border was closed,[9] later to be reopened temporarily at certain points. A dispatch from Paris dated December 29, 1939, announced that "the border was temporarily reopened to permit Jews who wished to do so to enter the Russian area. . . . Thousands of Jews were massing at three points on the border–Przemyśl, Stanislaw-Jaroslaw and Lubaszów-Belz–for entry into Soviet Poland, despite the fact that most of them did not enjoy living under the Soviet regime. Most crowded of the border points was Przemyśl, where the bridge over the San River appears to mark the Soviet-German border. The numbers passing over this bridge are so large that one must stand in line from six to eight hours . . . ."[10]

This was a temporary measure, with most of the other border points remaining closed. By the end of 1939, the Soviet authorities had issued strict orders against crossing the frontier. "Violators will be liable to three years' imprisonment." There was also a prohibition against remaining "in a frontier zone without special permits."[11] There was a great deal of smuggling across the border with the help of local peasants and professional smugglers. According to Prager,[12] during the months of November-December 1939, tens of thousands of Jews crossed the "green border . . . . There were days—or rather nights—in which groups of Jews, numbering a few thousand each, went over the border at one time. This illegal emigration has been estimated at 200,000 Jews." The attitude of the Soviet guards enforcing the prohibition against crossing the border varied. We hear of guards that looked the other way, and of guards that fired on the refugees. Some refugees were driven back; others were arrested and sentenced to varying terms of imprisonment or forced labor.

Many of those arrested were accused of spying. "Arrested in Przemyśl [apparently in November 1939] I was 3 weeks in prison together with 80 people in a cell meant for 6. From Przemyśl they sent me to Kiev, where they accused me of spying . . . for 8 months I was imprisoned in Kiev. In September 1940, I was sentenced to 5 years' imprisonment ."[13] A former resident of Chelm testified to meeting in Novosibirsk "thousands of girls, all minors, who were freed as a result of the amnesty. The majority of them had been sentenced to 5-10 years. Their ages ranged from 11-12 to 19 and higher. Almost all of them were imprisoned for crossing the border and 'spying.' At least 90 per cent were Jewish . . . ."[14]

It is almost impossible to give an exact figure for the number of Polish Jewish refugees in Soviet-occupied Poland. Estimates range from 150,000-200,000[15] to 600,000[16] and more.[17] It would seem, however, that the number was nearer 300,000.

These 300,000 or so Jewish refugees comprised about 20 per cent of the Jewish population of these regions. They were concentrated in a few of the larger cities where their numbers equalled and even exceeded those of the native Jewish population. Bialystok, with a Jewish population of about 40,000, very likely had more than that number of refugees.[18] The same was true of Lvov and other cities.

This at once created a housing problem. "At first they slept in the fields and woods. Later they found temporary shelter in railroad stations, empty freight cars . . . synagogues, school buildings, and the collective quarters of the chalutzim. . . . Here they lived for months, herded together like cattle, hungry and unwashed."[19] In Bialystok "the railway station is filled with refugees. It is their living quarters in these days. Later they were driven from here, too. On bedding lie whole families, the children cry, the grown-ups quarrel. They push each other, sit around on the benches, or stand crowded close together."[20] When, later, deportation made more space available, there were obstacles in the way of refugees acquiring it. Even if one succeeded in finding a room, one needed the approval of the department of housing, which did not give it to people without work. Moreover, the authorities for the most part forbade the renting of rooms to refugees; these were reserved for incoming Soviet officials.[21]

No easier was the food situation. Food prices were constantly rising. Foodstuffs disappeared from the market. "Local people could manage somehow; they knew where one might buy something. They also had money with which to buy. The refugees neither knew where to buy, nor were they able to pay. They suffered from hunger."[22]

The large percentage of intelligentsia and middle-class people among the refugees could hardly find employment at a time when the economy of the region was undergoing radical changes and hundreds of thousands of local Jews had lost their livelihood. However, not all of the refugees remained unemployed. A number of the intellectuals were able to get jobs with the Soviet administration, some even attaining relatively high position;[23] teachers readily found employment in schools;[24] and actors organized theater groups. Some found positions as bookkeepers in cooperatives and government enterprises;[25] others were employed as laborers or were admitted to railway training courses and later employed by the railway.[26] There were also cases of refugees working in small private enterprises or peddling and trading.[27] But all these constituted a small minority.

Efforts by local Jews, Jewish organizations, and Soviet authorities to help the refugees were of little avail.

The kibbutzim sheltered and fed members of refugee kibbutzim, as well as other people. In some places they were more effective than official relief organizations.[28] In Bialystok, Kovel, and Vilna, the JDC organized systematic relief, the Jewish communities and other organizations doing their bit. In Bialystok a Jewish Refugee Committee was organized which supplied food obtained by donation. Later, however, such organizational activity was stopped or taken over by the Soviet authorities. In Bialystok the above-mentioned Jewish Refugee Committee became a general committee "directed by a Russian commissar"; it provided hospital facilities for women in childbirth, wood for fuel, and food for the sick."[29] In Lvov, Kovel, Rovno, Lutsk and Bialystok, the authorities established free kitchens for the refugees. But all this was too little in comparison with the need. "In Bialystok, for the 33,000 refugees officially registered in November 1939, and for hundreds who arrived each day, only one kitchen was used. It was located in a Talmud Torah . . . and the needy had to stand in line for hours in order to get a bowl of watery soup and a piece of black bread."[30]

In the last month of 1939 registration for work in Russia was commenced. Applicants were promised work in their own occupations and a decent living. Pressure was also brought to bear on refugees to make them register. Those who registered were escorted with music and made much of in the press. Their number apparently varied from place to place; while some were eager to register, others were reluctant.[31] Most of the refugees preferred to remain in Lvov and other places rather than be sent into Russia.

Soviet Attitude Toward Refugees

Registrants were well treated at first. But later the promises made them were broken. Everyone, young and old, was assigned to the mines, to cutting timber in the woods, or to digging peat. The work was hard and unfamiliar; pay was small; living conditions primitive.[32] There were cases of registrants being brought to the interior of Russia, deposited in some remote spot, and then left there alone.[33] Refugees began to leave their assigned work, or were released and tried to find employment elsewhere. Others preferred to go back to eastern Poland and even staged demonstrations in the Donets Basin, Minsk, and Vitebsk, demanding permission to return. Some were actually sent back to eastern Poland, others slipped back illegally.[34] The stories told by those who returned discouraged other refugees from volunteering. The bulk of the refugees remained in the larger cities and towns of eastern Poland, an impoverished, ragged group distinct from the local population.

In the atmosphere of rising prices, vanishing commodities, unemployment, and housing shortages, there was a tendency to blame all difficulties on the "strangers," the refugees.[35] The Jewish local population was also none too friendly to the refugees, especially in the cities where large groups were congregated.[36]

For the Soviet authorities the refugees were not only a burden, but also "dangerous." Their interests and connections beyond the frontiers where they had left their families and relatives were enough to make them seem suspicious. The constant passage to and from Nazi-occupied Poland of some of the refugees, their attempts to bring over relatives or to emigrate overseas, were in the xenophobic eyes of the NKVD officials conspiratorial activities. This suspicious attitude was strengthened by the refugees' imperviousness to Soviet propaganda and failure to conform to the Soviet order. In Lvov, for instance, were gathered a number of Jewish refugee writers who in the beginning condemned any of their number who capitulated and began writing poems in the Soviet style.[37] The Jewish writers from Poland were also disgusted by the demand of the Russian-Jewish writers that they "erase everything that they had written before and start anew."[38] Again, those recruited for work in the interior of Russia who returned, either legally or illegally, with their stories about Russia, were regarded by the NKVD as criminals and hunted down and imprisoned.

This atmosphere of suspicion led to a distinction being drawn between local residents and refugees; the latter received much the worse treatment, were deprived of "the right to work,"[39] removed to smaller places, and were ultimately deported.

The Soviet authorities regarded everyone found in the newly incorporated territory as a Soviet citizen, regardless of his provenance. Even those refugees who arrived after the time of incorporation were deemed such. The Jewish refugees were none too happy about their new citizenship. Most of them regarded their stay in the Soviet area as a temporary sojourn, to last either until they could leave for Palestine or America, or until the end of the war. A great many had their immediate families on the German side, and hoped either to bring them over or to be united with them abroad. Thus, a former refugee stated: "Having my family in Poland, I naturally made no endeavor to take out Soviet papers." When called to the NKVD and questioned as to why he did not have Soviet papers, this man answered that he would obtain them after his wife and children had been brought over.[40] Others simply told the NKVD that in exchange for help in bringing over their families they would become Soviet citizens.[41] There were also refugees who disliked Soviet life, for a variety of reasons.

There was another factor which made the refugees hesitate to become Soviet citizens. The Soviet authorities sought to move the refugees out of the big cities and scatter them about in smaller places. The Soviet papers given the refugees generally contained what was known as Paragraph 11, which forbade the holder to live in a large city and in places located within 100 kilometers of the border. Residence was limited to certain places; official permission had to be obtained to move from these places. All this gave the refugee a foretaste of the strict police regime in Russia to which he would have to submit permanently if he became a citizen. Citizenship also meant his immediate leaving of the big center in which most of the refugees were concentrated and moving to a small and unfamiliar place.

The result of all this was that the majority of the refugees refused to take out Soviet papers. Those refugees with positions in cooperatives, hospitals, and other Soviet institutions were discharged upon their refusal to become Soviet citizens.[42]

The Soviet authorities said it was a choice between becoming a Soviet citizen or returning to Nazi-occupied territory.[43] Some refugees reasoned that the Russians would deport them[44] and preferred this—as a temporary situation—to becoming Soviet citizens and being forever confined to Russia. Others, however, were ready to go back to Nazi-occupied Poland.

The reasons for wishing to return to the German zone were the same as those for refusing Soviet citizenship.

> Their motives were varied; family ties played an important part, many refugees returning to their families having been separated since the outbreak of war . . . many sought to leave the new Soviet territories before their borders were as irrevocably and hermetically closed as all the other borders of the Soviet Union.[45]

"Many people did not want [Russian] citizenship because their families remained under German occupation."[46] Another witness attributes this desire to return to unemployment and disappointment with the Soviet order.[47] Yet another witness said that he knew how "the Germans were treating Jews," but "I regarded their presence in Poland as temporary. So I would suffer a year or two, I thought, and later everything would return to normal."[48] Some even hoped that from Nazi-occupied Poland they would be able to smuggle themselves over the frontier, on to Slovakia and even Italy, where the situation of the Jews was better.[49] In this way an indeterminate number of people began registering with the NKVD for return to Nazi-occupied Poland.

Those who registered with the NKVD had to register again with a German commission operating in Soviet-occupied Poland in April-May 1940, in accordance with the Russian-German agreement of April 1940 on exchanges of population.[50] But only a few Jews were admitted by the German commission. According to Gliksman, Jews "used pull and bribery to be able to return to German-occupied territories."[51] Some refugees tried to return to western Poland illegally across the "green frontier." In this way "several thousand Jewish refugees returned . . . to German-occupied territory."[52] Arrests were made by the Soviet police from among those who refused to accept Soviet citizenship and registered for return to the Nazi area. "In Bialystok, Brest, Lvov and other places a hunt was launched for those who did not take out Soviet papers, or wanted to register with the German commission for repatriation. Some of them were arrested immediately upon leaving the building where the commission had its offices."[53]

"In June 1940 the Soviet police in Brest arrested those who registered to return. In jail people were kept under the worst possible conditions [and were] constantly questioned as to their reasons for wanting to return to the Nazi area. . . . They maintained that we wanted to return because we did not like the Soviet order."[54]

Registration became a reason for deportation, with the NKVD gathering "proofs" that the refugees were a hostile and unreliable element. Deportation was the Soviet authorities' answer to a refugee problem they were unable to solve in any humane way.

Chapter III

Deportation

The Jewish refugees in eastern Poland were not the first to be deported from that region to the interior of Russia. Even in the first few weeks, former members of the Polish army living as civilians were called in and sent to concentration camps, from which some of the lower ranks were soon released, but not the commissioned officers.[1] Also a number of Polish social workers, politicians, civil servants, local government officials, professors and priests were arrested in October 1939; some of these were deported subsequently.

Mass deportations started on February 8, 1940; they included Polish civil servants, Polish settlers in the eastern region, forestry employees, and former members of the police force,[2] as well as members of the intelligentsia and of the middle classes (among the latter being some Jews).

A second wave of deportations began in April 1940; it included the families of individuals who had gone abroad, of Polish prisoners of war, of Polish officers and policemen, and in general people belonging to the intelligentsia and wealthier classes, as well as merchants. This time the proportion of Jews was much larger. The southeastern districts and Pinsk in Polesie were the localities particularly affected. During May lesser deportations from the Bialystok, Lida and Grodno districts—involving mainly Jews and Poles—were carried out.

A big new wave of deportations began in June and July; it chiefly involved Jewish refugees concentrated in Lvov and its environs, as well as in Volhynia and Bialystok. A fourth wave began just before the outbreak of the German-Russian war in June 1941. Social workers, intelligentsia, and children were the victims.

Registration for return to Nazi Poland served as the ostensible motive[3] for the deportation of the refugees. In Brest the police arranged a second registration, after the German commission had left, in order to have the names of those who wanted to return.[4] In Lvov, according to some witnesses, the NKVD made special lists of the registrants.[5] Others reported that after the German commission left, the Russian authorities told them that the system of registration was not efficient; they advised the refugees to organize themselves into groups and draw up lists indicating the documents in their possession, their addresses, etc. Later the NKVD and militia (police) used these lists for arresting and deporting the refugees.[6] In some cases they were first held for weeks for questioning in prison and specially arranged camps[7]; in other cases they were immediately put on trains and sent away. "People were rounded up in the streets. An effort was made to clear Bialystok of refugees. Those refugees who had Soviet citizen papers were also forbidden to remain in Bialystok. The others were exiled."[8]

> Four days and four nights the campaign lasted. For its realization all divisions of the NKVD from the whole province [Lvov] were mobilized, party members and higher officials of the Soviet institutions. . . . In the first night committees of three went to homes of which they had a list and took single persons who had come over from the part of Poland occupied by the Nazis. . . . The second night they looked for and took not only single persons, but whole families—husband, wife and children. . . .[9]

It is hard to say how many Jews were deported. Estimates range from 50-70,000[10] to half a million.[11] A semiofficial Polish source[12] puts their number at over 250,000, a figure which seems to be near the truth. Only a small number of these Jewish deportees were citizens of the former eastern Polish areas; the majority were refugees from western Poland whom the NKVD was eager to clear out of the newly acquired regions.

The NKVD began with those who had registered to return to Nazi Poland. But after this there was no differentiation between registered and non-registered. Even those holding positions in Soviet schools and offices were taken away. Deportations continued from bureaucratic inertia even during the first days after the outbreak of the Nazi-Soviet war in June 1941, much to the chagrin of local Soviet officials and Communists who clamored that the railroad cars be used not to deport Jews, but to evacuate themselves.[13]

Deportees were brutally treated. They were rounded up at night, loaded with or without belongings onto large trucks, and brought to the railroad station, where they were packed into unheated freight cars with no sanitary provisions.[14] Some of the weaker ones and children died on the way.

Descriptions of the different deportations by former deportees are almost identical. They travelled for weeks in overcrowded railroad cars, with little or no food.[15] Food brought to the trains by local Jews in White Russia was denied them by the guards.[16] Railroad cars meant for 30-40 persons were made to carry 100-150. People suffocated for lack of air. Some were placed in sealed cars and received no food or water. Some families were allowed to take along a few of their belongings; others were forbidden to do so.[17]

Conditions worsened as they approached their destinations.

> After two weeks I reached Kotlas. We were placed on a boat—there were 8 boats with 1500 on each. One boat bore only Jewish women. Many of them had to be carried on board for they were unable to walk. After 2 weeks we reached Wajkini. During the trip an epidemic of dysentery broke out. Each day 50 dead were thrown into the water. Two physicians, Dr. Bromberg of Pinsk and Dr. Sirots, asked for permission to aid the sick. Their request brought the reply that there was room enough in Russia for graves. Of 1500 people only 550 reached the destination, and the percentage of dead was even higher on the women's boat. We were driven from the shore during a shower and walked in swamps up to our knees. Every few meters somebody fell. . . . The way was strewn with the dead and fainting. . . . So we reached Wajkini.[18]

Deportees from Bialystok sent to the Vologda district were assigned to work in a forest. All two hundred and fifty had to go into the forest, even mothers of infants. "Of two hundred and fifty people, twenty-two perished. When children fell ill because of inadequate food and their mothers requested larger rations, the mothers would be jailed."[19] In Archangel deportees working in the forest had to surrender 20 per cent of their earnings to the NKVD.[20] Some deportees were set to work building roads and canals, or digging in mines.

A few deportees fared better. M. K. from Warsaw, deported from Rovno to Rostov, was sent with his brother, an engineer, "to the Scientific Experimental Sovkhoz 2, nineteen kilometers from Rostov. . . . Seventeen refugees were sent there. They were well received and were quartered in a hotel."[21]

Deportees from eastern Poland were split into three groups.[22] Those taken from prisons and unattached individuals generally were treated as political prisoners and sent to penal camps in northern Russia and Siberia. These camps were working units engaged in lumbering, mining, construction of canals and railroads. Another group was sent to the so-called settlements (*posiolki*). These were isolated places where they worked under supervision of the NKVD. A third group was sent to Kazakhstan, into "free exile" (*wolnoye poseleniye*) in kolkhozes. They were not compelled to work, but no one looked after them and they had scarcely anything to eat.

In most of the penal camps there was the problem of completing the work norm. On this norm was based the ration of food, usually bread and some kind of soup. Only those able to fulfill the work norm received more or less sufficient food. The refugees had to work nights and seven days a week to make up their norm. Insufficient output, inevitable under such circumstances, led to the use of force by the NKVD and the commandants.[23] For minor transgressions people were placed in solitary confinement. On the other hand, there were cases where the deportees went on strike in protest against the hunger regime.[24]

In the "settlements," too, everyone was obliged to work, mostly in forests. In some places the stores had a number of things which the settlers could buy. In others the "settlers" could purchase only the ration of bread, one kilogram for a grownup and half for a child.[25]

The situation of those sent to Kazakhstan, into "free exile," was not much better. The deportees were distributed among the kolkhozes, where they worked in the fields, ploughing and sowing, meanwhile having to live by the sale of their belongings. After the harvest they received a share of grain and potatoes in accordance with their "working days"; but this did not suffice to feed them for more than a part of the next year.[26]

Scurvy, typhoid, tuberculosis, dysentery and malaria decimated the deportees. "Many persons died of heart attacks and tuberculosis, but still a greater number perished as a result of accidents at work. Mortality was particularly high among the children, who suffered from a variety of digestive ailments."[27] A group of refugees sent north, near the Finnish border, lost half its members in six months.[28]

Another deportee tells this story about Forest Station Guzh, not far from Kotlas: "The doctor was 12 kilometers away and you had to walk to him, even though your feet were swollen. Even persons suffering from gangrene or high temperatures had to walk to the doctor. The officials had horses for their own use, but the refugees were not permitted to use them."[29]

Orthodox Jews found even a minimum of observance impossible in the camps. Not only were requests for kosher food ignored, but even on high holy days they were generally denied permission to remain at home to recite their prayers. "Among the refugees [at the forest station near Kotlas] was an elderly Jew, a Chassid. On Yom Kippur he put on his prayer shawl and refused to go to work. The official in charge shouted that he must report for work, but the old man said: 'If I do not go to work you will punish me, and if I do, God will punish me. I would rather that you punish me.' The official became enraged, pulled off the old man's prayer shawl, tore it up, and drove him into the forest."[30]

In a camp in the Vologda District, during the high holy days, orthodox Jews held services after work. The "organizer" of the services, an elderly Jew, was exiled to an unknown destination and was never again heard from.[31]

The situation in the so-called settlements appears to have been somewhat different. Here at times one could observe the Sabbath by hiring a substitute to do one's work. But here, too, "the commissar drove out thirty Jews in the middle of their Rosh Hashanah devotions, threatening them with heavy fines. They returned, however, and continued their prayers. Although some of them were later fined, all the Jews of the place stayed home and prayed on Yom Kippur; the commissar finally gave in, and excused them from working on holidays."[32]

There were also non-Jews in the camps and "settlements," although Jews sometimes constituted 75 per cent and more. There were also Polish deportees and Russian convicts. With some exceptions, relations seem generally to have been friendly.

CHAPTER IV

War and Flight

The German attack of June 22, 1941 found Russia unprepared. Right up to the day on which war broke out trains with freight for Germany were still moving toward the western frontiers. A refugee from Poland who had become a conductor on a Russian freight train stated that "the day the war broke out [he] came with a train to Bialystok just as the city was bombarded. He thought it was British and French planes that were bombing the city, because only the day before he had taken a transport of lumber and corn to the German border."[1] In some places military forces along the frontier had been reduced only a few days before the German attack.

Civilian and military authorities were taken by surprise; they even lacked general orders governing such an eventuality. There was no plan for the evacuation of Soviet offices, their staffs, or the civilian population. In Lida, for instance, no mobilization took place until June 23. German planes meanwhile were dropping their bombs. At first, the mobilized men were told to assemble five kilometers from town; later came an order for each man to take to his heels.

In Lvov, "when the war broke out between Germany and Russia all officials were asked to remain at their posts. There were Soviet officials who fled, but some of them were apprehended on the way and compelled to return. A few days later all Soviet officials were given an opportunity to leave the city."[2]

In Bialystok, when Jewish volunteers reported to the military garrisons, they were deserted. "The Soviet military, together with their wives and children, the entire 'Komsostav' [commanding staff], had fled, leaving everyone behind."[3]

Many cities and towns were already in German hands in the first days; in a little more than a week they had overrun the whole area of what had been eastern Poland. There was no time for a planned evacuation. The authorities usually placed the available trucks and railroad cars at the disposal of Soviet officers, Communists, and workers in factories.

Unorganized flight was the chief recourse of the Jews. Thousands left towns and cities and fled eastward to escape the invading forces. Most, however, were overtaken by the German armies.[4] Refugees, if they got that far, met with difficulties at the former Russian border, sometimes being refused permission to proceed.

The number of Jews who were evacuated or fled to the interior of Russia can only be guessed. Perhaps 10 to 15 per cent of the Jews of what used to be eastern Poland succeeded in escaping the German onslaught. This would mean that about 120-180,000 Jews reached Russia, thus swelling the number of Polish Jews in Russia to about 400-450,000 at the beginning of the Nazi-Soviet war.

Chapter V

Amnesty and Liberation

On June 22, 1941, after the outbreak of the Nazi-Soviet war, the British Foreign Office made endeavors to reconcile the Polish Government-in-Exile—residing since the collapse of France in London—with Soviet Russia. The Polish-Soviet negotiations started on July 7 and led to the signing, on July 30, 1941, of an agreement between the two governments, who undertook to help each other in the war against Nazi Germany. The Soviet government recognized "that the Soviet-German treaties of 1939 relative to territorial changes in Poland had lost their validity," and consented to the formation in Russia of a Polish army.

At that time all of Poland was in the hands of the Nazis so the agreement could at first affect only those Poles who were in Russia as deportees or prisoners. A protocol appended to the agreement promised that "as soon as diplomatic relations are established, the government of the USSR will grant amnesty to all Polish citizens who are at present deprived of their freedom on the territory of the USSR. . . ." A decree of amnesty was issued on August 12, 1941.[1]

This agreement, however, and the decree concerning the release of Polish citizens from prisons, labor camps, or places of compulsory exile, were never carried out in full. Soviet Russia in general followed a policy of keeping hold of as much of eastern Poland as it could. This influenced the whole Soviet attitude toward Poland, and toward the granting of the amnesty. Soviet officials sabotaged the amnesty order and disobeyed directives to furnish food and supplies to the Polish army being formed. To release prisoners often meant loss of a labor force, and camp commanders, anxious to fulfill work quotas, would fail to inform them of the amnesty, or would in some way render their departure impossible. "In some instances local authorities may have desired to secure for themselves virtually unpaid man power. . . . Many camp commanders who have to carry out a production plan do not wish to deprive themselves of workmen without whom the execution of their plan may be impossible."[2]

In this way Polish inmates of labor camps, prisons, and places of exile were released gradually. The liberation of Polish prisoners, decreed in August 1941, was still incomplete in April 1943, when Russian-Polish relations were ruptured. Time and again the Polish ambassadors in Moscow drew the attention of Molotov and the Deputy Commissar for Foreign Affairs, Vishinsky, to this situation. The Polish Foreign Minister and Prime Minister also intervened with the Russian ambassador in London, to little avail. Replies alternated between assurances that the detainees had been liberated and promises to look further into the matter.[3]

In some places, when the Jewish refugees heard about the amnesty, they simply went off to join the Polish army,[4] or headed for southern Asiatic Russia. Later some of those in the labor battalions, hearing of the amnesty, tried to flee south.[5]

Others were liberated after the amnesty apparently without difficulty.[6] Still others reported that "after the amnesty they were transported from Kotlas to Samarkand[7] or Bukhara,"[8] which would mean that the authorities even furnished transportation.

In some places a number were liberated, after which the commander attempted to put off the liberation of the rest.[9] In other places there was a general attempt to postpone liberation. "Our commander did whatever he could to keep us longer. He refused to give us horses and wagons to take us out of the woods. Nothing remained but to continue to work and thus we kept on until October. In the end, those of us who still had strength decided to take a chance and rather march on foot to the railroad station than stay in the settlement for another winter."[10] In another place the deportees went on strike against their detainment. "They tried to persuade us to remain, promising to improve the conditions of work, to give us land and goats. Some remained, but the majority left."[11]

The great majority of released inmates of the camps and settlements streamed south to Uzbekistan, Turkmenistan, Tadzhikistan and Southern Kazakhstan. It was the milder climate, above all, that drew the refugees, who had been suffering from the cold of northern Russia and Siberia. The other attraction was the Polish army being formed and the nearness of the Iranian border—both gave some hope of leaving the country.

Once arrived, the liberated inmates of labor camps and settlements enjoyed a measure of freedom to move about and to organize their own religious and other affairs. In Andizhan, Jewish refugees from Poland freely conducted prayers in the open air[12] on Rosh Hashanah and Yom Kippur. In Dzhambul, "Polish Jews . . . founded a Yeshivah which was attended by more than twenty students. . . . No permission for this school was asked and nobody interfered with its studies."[13] The refugees organized theatrical performances, and lectures. Later, the Union of Polish Patriots opened up a Jewish section which brought in Yiddish books and newspapers and encouraged Jewish cultural work.[14]

But the situation of the Jews was precarious. They lacked funds and clothing, were in bad health, and faced the necessity of finding shelter and food. In the poor southern republics of Central Asia, possibilities of employment were limited. Jews wandered from place to place, for weeks and months. Some settled on farms, which were principally engaged in raising cotton. Wages were low and the work unfamiliar. The flour, cereals or bread which they received as remuneration did not provide even a minimum of nourishment.

Conditions in the towns appear to have been even worse. Hunger and lack of shelter were common. Tuberculosis, malaria, and scurvy were rampant; epidemics of typhoid fever, typhus, and dysentery caused many deaths. "In Bukhara we lived two weeks in the open, until we found a hole in which to lodge."[15] Another reported that after liberation in Samarkand, "it was worse than in exile. After a short time my father and mother died of hunger."[16]

Some took to trading on the market,[17] thus risking persecution for "doing business" illegally. A former resident of Warsaw tells how "they went to work in an Uzbek kolkhoz in Tashlak. . . . Following the birth of their child his wife received supplementary rations, but bread was getting more and more scarce in the kolkhozes. People began eating grass. An epidemic of dysentery broke out and many of the Jewish refugees died. . . . He was employed on a cotton plantation, but after taxes were deducted from his earnings—income tax, war levy, cultural tax and others—he was left with 150-160 rubles a month, enough for two days' subsistence. So he would have to do various kinds of work in the evening. Burying the dead was at that time one of his supplementary occupations. He also made coffins. On other occasions they would collect rags in the streets and make slippers out of them, which they sold in the market place."[18]

In such circumstances, the relief activities organized by the Polish Embassy for Polish citizens were invaluable. Following the visit of Prime Minister Sikorski to Russia in December 1941, came agreements (December 23, 1941) which provided for the appointment of embassy delegates and for a loan of 100 million rubles for relief. The delegates were to register Polish citizens as to their professional qualifications, organize and supervise relief activities, and provide legal protection for Polish citizens. They worked with the help of representatives appointed in provincial centers.[19] The work began in February 1942; in one year, over 800 kindergartens, schools, hostels, feeding centers, and orphanages were organized. In addition, financial assistance, food and clothing—coming mostly from America—were distributed to the needy.[20] These relief activities benefited Polish Jews and non-Jews alike. According to the figures of the Polish Embassy, 104,602 Jews were assisted in this way.

But before long, as Russia's relations with Poland worsened, obstacles began to be placed in the way of this relief work. It was demanded that the delegates refrain from intervening on behalf of Polish citizens; persons of Jewish, Ukrainian and White Russian origin, whom the USSR began to regard as Soviet citizens, were forbidden to receive Polish relief. Soon there followed the arrest of the delegates and staff members, and the closing of the relief offices in July 1942, and of kindergartens and medical centers a month later; the rest of the relief work was taken over by the Russian government at the beginning of 1943.

Chapter VI

Citizenship and Repatriation

The Polish-Russian accord of July 30, 1941, was imperiled at its very inception by the question of who was to possess the eastern Polish areas after the war. During the negotiations of July 1941, Soviet Russia refused to admit officially that the future Polish-Russian border should be that of the 1921 Treaty of Riga (the pre-1939 border). Great Britain, however, pressed Poland to accept the hazy wording of the agreement nullifying the German-Russian treaty of 1939. In their note on the Polish-Russian agreement the British assured the Polish government that Great Britain "does not recognize any territorial changes which have been effected in Poland since August 1939." In America an announcement was made to the press about the agreement which stated that it was in line with the United States policy of non-recognition of territory taken by conquest. Great Britain at the same time made it clear—through the answer given by Eden in the House of Commons—that her declaration "does not involve any guarantee of frontiers."

Soviet Russia stubbornly insisted on its right to eastern Poland. In a speech at the beginning of November 1941, Stalin declared that the Soviets aimed to restore the frontiers of June 21, 1941.[1] In October or at the beginning of November, a Russian interpretation of the Polish-Soviet agreement was enunciated which considered the former Polish region as belonging to Soviet Russia. The war commissar for Kazakhstan at Alma-Ata issued orders that Polish deportees of Ukrainian, White Russian or Jewish origin of military age were to be enrolled in the Russian Army. The commissar "declared that he was acting on instructions from the central authorities who . . . have directed him to treat as citizens of the USSR all citizens of the Republic of Poland of other than Polish origin possessing Soviet passports."[2] The Polish Embassy in Kuibyshev (then the seat of the Russian government) protested against this on November 10, 1941. The reply of the People's Commissariat for Foreign Affairs on December 1 stated that Soviet Russia recognized eastern Poland as part of Soviet Russia.[3] Then ensued an exchange of notes between the Polish Embassy and the Soviet Commissariat for Foreign Affairs. On the Polish side it was claimed that all former inhabitants of eastern Poland were

Polish citizens, while Russia reiterated that its annexation of eastern Poland "was not an occupation but an attachment . . . as the result of the freely expressed will of the population of those districts,"[4] and it was requested that the issuance of Polish passports by Polish authorities should be made only to persons "to whom the competent Soviet authorities raise no objection."[5]

These legalities were designed to stress Russia's claim to eastern Poland. In the meantime the first successes of the winter offensive made Russia's attitude more demanding. On January 17, 1942, Soviet Russia informed the Polish Embassy that she would in the future not consider notes questioning the inclusion of any place in eastern Poland in the USSR. In a declaration of March 1 issued by the Soviet news agency, the Polish government was accused of "disregarding the universally known fact of the reunion of the Ukrainian and White Russian peoples," and advocating partition which "bears witness to an imperialist tendency."[6] A campaign in favor of the "ethnographic rights of Soviet Russia to certain territories"[7] was started in America in February 1942, while Eden, in conversations in Moscow about a treaty with Soviet Russia, was pressed to concede Russian territorial claims in eastern Europe. Only at the last moment did the British yield to American insistence and force the elimination of the territorial clauses from the British-Russian treaty of May 26, 1942.

Finally, on January 16, 1943, a Soviet Russian note stated that all inhabitants of the former Polish regions there residing on November 1-2, 1939, automatically became Soviet citizens. The only exception the USSR was prepared to consider were persons of Polish origin. But since Poland was so distrustful of Soviet Russia's good faith in this matter, this exception would not be allowed.[8] The immediate result was that former Polish citizens, Jews and non-Jews alike, were forced to accept Soviet citizenship,[9] with the exception of persons who had been temporarily resident in eastern Poland at the time of its annexation by the Soviet Union (as Molotov and Stalin explained to the Polish Ambassador in February-March 1943).[10]

Status of Jewish Refugees

The legal status of the Jewish deportees and refugees from Poland thus underwent several transformations. Immediately after the amnesty they were regarded as Polish citizens; a little later (in December 1941) they were generally regarded as Soviet citizens. Again, after March 1943, deportees and refugees from western Poland (who were the majority) were supposed to remain Polish citizens. This last, however, had but little practical consequence, since in April 1943 Soviet Russia broke off relations with the Polish government-in-exile over the question of the massacred

Polish officers whose graves had been found in the Katyn forest near Smolensk.

The question of citizenship vitally influenced the fate of the Polish Jews in Soviet Russia. It had a bearing, as we have seen, on their liberation from the camps and their right to accept relief from the Polish government. Still more important was its effect on the possibility of their joining the Polish army and leaving Russia with it when it was evacuated. According to the military agreement of August 14, 1941, between Poland and Soviet Russia, a Polish army was to be recruited and equipped in Russia to fight against Germany. But when Soviet authorities subsequently placed obstacles in the way of the development of this army, it was agreed—at the United States' suggestion—that first one part and then later the rest should be evacuated from Russia. With the army, the families of soldiers were also evacuated in March, April and August, 1942.

By the end of 1941 the Soviet authorities began regarding Jews (as well as Ukrainians and White Russians) from Poland as Soviet citizens. Once again the refugees were pressed to accept Soviet citizenship. "The NKVD interviewed each of the refugees individually and informed them that they were no longer Polish citizens and must accept Soviet passports. Those refusing to do so were at once arrested."[11]

"Jews from Poland were again forced to take out Soviet passports. Refusal to do so meant a five-year sentence. . . . One was accused of being a British spy in the course of the campaign to force the refugees to accept Soviet passports. As proof it was stated that he was receiving packages from abroad [via Palestine]."[12]

At the same time recruiting boards, in which Soviet and Polish representatives participated, refused to allow Jews to join the Polish army.[13] At the time of the Polish army's evacuation, the Soviet authorities had instructions to allow only those Jews coming originally from western Poland to be evacuated; actually, however, they hindered such Jews as well[14] and limited the number of family members permitted to accompany Jewish soldiers out of Russia.[15] There were also the obstacles of antisemitism on the Polish side. Thus, in Guzar, near Chkdlov, at the recruiting station of the Polish army, "the antisemitism of the Poles was noticeable. Other Jews advised the two to leave but for the moment they refused. . . . But after the Poles attacked and made a pogrom in one tent which housed many Jews, about twenty persons took their blankets and uniforms, which they sold, and left for Dzhambul."[16]

On the other hand, Polish members of the recruiting boards often helped Jews to be accepted into Polish formations, advising them to claim that they were Poles.[17] In other cases Jews had actually to be baptized in order to join up. Others smuggled themselves out with the Polish army.[18] In many cases no difficulties were made either about joining the army or about evacuation.[19]

This claim by the Soviet government on former Polish citizens of course aimed at more than the keeping of a few hundred thousand people in Russia; for by insisting on this the Communists were pressing their claim to eastern Poland.

But with the changing situation in 1943—Russian successes in the war; severance of relations with Poland; winning over of opinion in Great Britain and America to the so-called Curzon Line; its apparent acceptance in Teheran; formation of the Soviet-dominated Union of Polish Patriots[20] —Soviet Russia could afford to relinquish its claims to the citizenship of Poles, the issue of the Polish-Russian boundary no longer being implied in the citizenship question. It stopped differentiating between Jews and ethnic Poles in matters of admission to the new Polish army[21] organized by the Union of Polish Patriots, and later, in matters of repatriation. The Union even had a special Jewish section. By the end of 1943 about 30 per cent of this army was made up of Jews.[22] The Soviet authorities now regarded both Jews and Poles as Soviet citizens, but gave them the right to apply for Polish citizenship. This right was first given to those who served in the new Polish army,[23] and later to those who wished to be repatriated to Poland.

In August 1943 the British and American ambassadors, seeking to repair the Polish-Soviet break, met with Stalin and Molotov in Moscow and made proposals; among other things they anticipated "the granting of permission to the Poles in Russia to apply for Russian or Polish citizenship."[24] Again in January 1944, after the Teheran Conference, Churchill tried to persuade the Polish government-in-exile to agree to the Curzon Line, prolonged through eastern Galicia, as Russia's western boundary. Among other points he mentioned that "all Poles left on the Soviet side of Poland's eastern frontier would be given the right to return to Poland."[25] The United States also broached the idea of a population transfer.[26]

On September 9 and 22, 1944, the Polish Committee of National Liberation concluded agreements with the Ukrainian, White Russian, and Lithuanian Socialist Soviet Republics on the voluntary evacuation of their ethnic groups from Poland and of former Polish citizens from these republics to Poland. "All persons of Polish and Jewish ethnic nationality who were Polish citizens before September 17, 1939, and resided within the territory of the Ukrainian, White Russian, and Lithuanian Soviet Socialist Republics were allowed to opt for Polish citizenship and to be evacuated to Poland."[27] Registration for repatriation was to take place between October 15 and December 1, 1944. Repatriates were permitted to take their families along, and most of their belongings.

On July 6, 1945, a similar agreement was concluded between Poland

and Soviet Russia permitting Poles and Polish Jews who, prior to September 17, 1939, had been Polish citizens to renounce their Soviet citizenship and return to Poland.[28] Such persons could apply for change of citizenship up to November 20, 1945, and transfer was to be completed by December 31, 1945, which date was later extended to June 15, 1946. According to a broadcast by Zygmunt Modzelewski, Polish Ambassador to the USSR, the provisions of this agreement included not only "all Poles and Jews who relocated on the territories of the USSR because of the tragedy of the war," but also "all those who helped to regain the independence of our country, either through military service in the Polish army or through other means."[29] This also made it possible for some who had not been Polish citizens prior to September 1939 to opt for Poland.

Both governments promised to provide food and medical care for the repatriates. The order of repatriation from the USSR was to be as follows: "First, the families of military men; second, peasants and their families; third, specialists and technicians; and fourth, those not included in the previous categories." The first repatriates were to be from the north of the USSR and the European areas; they were to be followed by repatriates from Central Asia and other regions.[30]

In October 1944 the Polish Committee of National Liberation in Lublin set up an office for repatriation, and registration of repatriates was begun. At the end of 1946, with the transfer of one and one-half million Poles and Jews (1,236,941 from the former Polish eastern provinces and 248,198 from other parts of Russia[31]), the wave of repatriation was spent. In 1947 only 10,801 arrived, of whom 7,954 were from the interior of Russia and the remainder from territories beyond the Curzon Line.

The number of Polish repatriates—and registrants—hardly exceeded 50 per cent of all Poles residing beyond the Curzon Line,[32] whereas the percentage of Polish Jews who opted for repatriation and came to Poland was somewhat higher. It is estimated that of the Polish Jews in the USSR about 250,000-300,000 survived. By October 1946 the number of Jewish repatriates reached 130,000.[33] Another source puts their number at the end of 1946 at 170,000.[34] About 20,000 were still awaiting transportation and 5,000 were reported to have been released from camps in Uzbekistan.

A number of Soviet Jews managed to pass as Poles and to be "repatriated," some coming as the husbands, wives, etc., of Polish Jews; others contriving to procure Polish papers. Thousands of Polish Jews were still left in Russia who had not been released from the prison camps after the amnesty, and some of them were among the repatriated in 1947. Other groups came back in 1948 when Polish Jews in Russian prisons and labor camps were released, together with a number of Poles who had been arrested and deported from Poland in 1944-45 following the arrival of the Red Army.[35] These repatriates of 1947 and 1948 were the last to return.

Notes

CHAPTER I

1. *Nazi-Soviet Relations 1939-1941*, Washington, D. C., U. S. Department of State, 1948, pp. 78, 86-87, 90-96, 105 ff.
2. A part of the Vilna province was ceded to Lithuania on October 10, 1939.
3. At the time of the census of 1931 these provinces had a population of 12,012,000. An estimate for 1939 put the number of people at 13,199,000 (*Polish Facts and Figures*, No. 2, New York 1944, pp. 8 ff.).
4. *Izvestiya*, October 28, 29, November 4; *Polish-Soviet Relations, 1918-1943*. Official documents issued by the Polish Embassy in Washington, D. C. (n. d.), pp. 102 ff.
5. *Polish-Soviet Relations*, pp. 104-5.
6. S. J. Parochi, *Minority Affairs in Poland*, 1935, pp. 52-54; Joseph S. Roucek, "Minorities in Poland," *Poland*, ed. by Bernadotte E. Schmitt, Berkeley and Los Angeles 1947, pp. 157, 164.
7. *Polish-Soviet Relations*, pp. 17-18.
8. J. Lestchinsky, *Di Yiden in Soviet Russland*, New York 1943, pp. 367-68.
9. *Shtern* [Kiev], September 21, 1940.
10. Tania Fuchs resigned her position with a Yiddish high school in Lvov when it was changed to a Ukrainian one. When she drew the attention of Jewish writers in Russia to this policy of Ukrainization, their answer was: "We have confidence in the policy of the USSR toward the national minorities. The government knows what it is doing." (T. Fuchs, *A Vanderung ibër okupirte Gebitn*, Buenos Aires 1947. p. 94).
11. Cf. Fuchs, *op. cit.*, p. 52; F. Zerubavel, *Na Venad*, Buenos Aires 1947, pp. 67, 73.
12. *Polish Facts and Figures*, No. 2, New York 1940, p. 11.
13. The general population grew by about 10 per cent up to the beginning of the war, bringing it up to 13,190,000. The increase of the Jewish population was much smaller, for considerable emigration was going on during the 1930's. (Cf. M. Prager, *Yeveyn Metzulah Hechadash*, Tel Aviv, 1941, pp. 23-24, for estimates of the Jewish population in Poland before the war.)
14. J. Lestchinsky, *Yivo Bleter* XV No. 1-2, p. 26.
15. *The Black Book of Polish Jewry*, ed. by J. Apenszlak, New York 1943, p. 256.
16. *Beth Israel BePolin I*, Jerusalem 1948, p. 206.
17. J. Lestchinsky in *Yidishe Ekonomik*, 1937, No. 1, pp. 11-13.
18. Cf. B. D. Weinryb, *Jewish Vocational Education*, New York 1948, pp. 120 ff.
19. Of all gainfully employed Jews in 1931, 55.5 per cent were independent owners of establishments employing no help, and only 6.7 per cent were owners of establishments employing help. Of the Jewish manual workers, 81.5 per cent worked in small shops employing 1 to 5 workers.
20. *Tentative List of Jewish Educational Institutions in Axis-Occupied Countries*, New York, Conference on Jewish Relations 1946, pp. 77-78.
21. H. S. Kazhdan, *Di Geshichte fun Yidishn Shulvezn in Umophengikn Poyln*, Mexico 1947, pp. 66 f; 413.
22. Cf. M. Wischnitzer in *Yivo Bleter* XXXI-XXXII, pp. 27 ff.
23. Commission on European Jewish Cultural Reconstruction, *Tentative List of Jewish Periodicals in Axis-Occupied Countries*, New York, 1947, pp. 30 ff. The items listed in the *List* were not all in existence in the last year before the war.
24. *Al Mashuoth Polin*, Merchavia, 1940, p. 122.
25. Fuchs *op. cit.*, pp. 45 ff.
26. Zerubavel, *op. cit.*, pp. 76-77.
27. *Al Mashuoth Polin*, p. 131.
28. Fuchs (*op. cit.*, pp. 62-64), in describing the nationalization of real estate in

Lvov, tells how a great many committees were employed, each one working according to its own lights. Some confiscated jewelry and money; others took away small houses which were not supposed to have been nationalized; still others simply threw out the occupants and put other people in the houses—all actions contrary to instructions. Another witness describes nationalization of houses put through without regard to regulations. If a Soviet officer took a liking to a certain apartment, the house was nationalized and the owner barred from living in that city. (Testimonial 10,592.—All testimonials in the Library of YIVO if not otherwise indicated.)

29. Testimonial 10,556.

30. Testimonial 10,554.

31. Testimonials 10,584, 10,592.

32. *Documents Relating to the Administration of the Occupied Countries*, No. 5, p. 18.

33. Fuchs, *op. cit.*, p. 53.

34. *Ibid.*, p. 73.

35. David Grodner, "In Soviet Poland and Lithuania," *Contemporary Jewish Record* IV (1941), p. 141.

36. Jerszy G. Gliksman, "Jewish Exiles in Soviet Russia," unpublished manuscript in the files of the American Jewish Committee, p. 12.

37. Fuchs, *op. cit.* p. 73.

38. Testimonial 10,582.

39. Cf. Zerubavel, *op. cit.*, p. 89; Testimonial 15,545.

40. Testimonial 10,588.

41. In the northeastern provinces, where White Russians and Russians constituted about 40-50 per cent of the population, they had 175 (86.5 per cent) of the 200 seats in the National Assembly; the Poles (50 per cent) had 15 seats (7.5 per cent); and the Jews, constituting over 9 per cent of the population, had 12 seats (6 per cent). (Cf. *Izvestiya*, October 29, 1939; *The Eastern Provinces of Poland*, Information Studies, No. 3.) Among the representatives of eastern Galicia to the Ukrainian Supreme Soviet there was not one Jew. (Cf. *Die Judenausrottung in Polen*, Augenzeugen Berichte, Erste Serie, Geneva 1944, p. 43.)

42. Zerubavel, *op. cit.*, pp. 82-83.

43. Fuchs, *op. cit.*, p. 105.

44. Grodner, *op. cit.*, p. 143.

45. A Jewish teacher, brought from Minsk to a Jewish high school in eastern Poland, was questioned by students as to why the building of the Jewish school was turned over to the Ukrainians. He answered: "For generations the Ukrainian people suffered. Today they are the rulers. Therefore they must study in fine institutions." (*Al Mashuoth Polin*, p. 141).

46. Testimonial 10,582.

47. Cf. Grodner, p. 143; Zerubavel, p. 82 ff.; Fuchs, p. 68 ff.

48. Fuchs, *op. cit.*, p. 65.

49. *Ibid.*, p. 60.

50. *Ibid.*, pp. 61ff.

51. *Ibid.*, pp. 65, 89.

52. Published figures (*Oktyabr* [Minsk] September 12, 1940 and *Shtern* [Kiev] September 31, 1940) give the percentage of Jewish children in Yiddish schools as 2.7 for western White Russia and 3.9 per cent for the western Ukraine. This would mean that about 30-35 per cent of the Jewish school children attended Yiddish schools. It is impossible to ascertain if the rest of the Jewish children attended non-Jewish schools because of necessity or preference.

53. Zerubavel, *op. cit.*, p. 81.

54. Testimonial 10,588.

55. Grodner, *op. cit.*, p. 145.

56. Zerubavel (p. 73) tells of assistance given to refugees, distribution of railway tickets, etc.

57. According to Grodner (p. 142), the kehillah was closed down; Gliksman (p. 15), however, reports that they "limited their activities almost entirely to funerals and cemeteries."

58. Jewish Telegraphic Agency, January 10, 1940.

59. Testimonials 10,554, 10,582.

60. Testimonial 10,578.

61. Testimonial 10,579.

62. *Al Mashuoth Polin,* pp. 120, 123, 125.

63. Cf. also Grodner, *op. cit.,* p. 147.

64. Cf. Segalowicz, *Gebrente Trit.* p. 98. One eyewitness relates that "the scum of different nationalities, among them Jewish scum," were made use of as spies (Testimonial 10,554).

65. According to Gliksman (*op. cit.,* pp. 15 ff.), the arrests began "almost immediately after the entry of the Red Army. . . . The Soviet authorities must have been in possession of lists of all prominent men in political and cultural life, for they arrested them within the first few weeks." This may have been true for the particular locality in which the author was at that time. Victor Alter of the Bund was arrested in Kovel a few days after the occupation. Henryk Erlich's arrest also came soon (Grodner, *op. cit.,* p. 146). Others may also have been arrested immediately. But the mass arrests of the leadership started much later. From letters from different places in Volhynia it becomes clear that before 1940 there were few arrests of Zionists (*Al Mashuoth Polin,* pp. 127, 135). In Pinsk Jewish parties were closed only in the spring of 1940.

66. Cf. Grodner, *op. cit.,* pp. 142 ff.

67. According to H. Weinrauch (Vinocur), at that time assistant editor of the *Bialystoker Shtern,* the Communist Party forbade enlargement or increase in the number of copies printed, despite a demand from the readers (*Forward,* April 17, 1948).

68. Zerubavel, *op. cit.,* p. 103, 112; *Al Mashuoth Polin,* p. 129.

69. *Al Mashuoth Polin,* pp. 119, 120, 124, 140.

70. Cf. K. Brodzky in *Unzer Kamf,* New York: Poale Zion Zeire Zion 1941, pp. 101 ff.

CHAPTER II

1. *Op. cit.,* p. 57.

2. *Nazi-Soviet Relations,* p. 128.

3. Jewish Telegraphic Agency dispatch from Paris dated December 18, 1939 (*JTA News VI,* No. 113; cf. also December 19, 1939).

4. *Nazi-Soviet Relations,* p. 128.

5. Cf. Prager, *Yeveyn Metzulah Hachadash,* Tel Aviv 1941, p. 32.

6. *Nazi-Soviet Relations,* p. 106.

7. *Dokumente der Deutschen Politik,* VII, p. 667; *Izvestiya,* November 20, 1939.

8. Prager, *op. cit.,* pp. 35-36.

8a. *Verordnungblatt des General Gouverners der Besetzten Polnischen Gebieten* (Nos. 13-14, Dec. 21, 23, 1939), pp. 232, 246.

8b. *Jewish Telegraphic Agency News,* VI, No. 122; cf. also No. 125.

9. Grodner (*op. cit.,* p. 137) writes that "about the fifteenth of October . . . the borders were suddenly shut tight." In a communication from Vilna written in January 1940, it was stated that the border was open until October 22, 1939, the day of the elections to the Soviets in the occupied region (*Forward,* January 20, 1940).

10. *Jewish Telegraphic Agency News VI,* No. 122.

11. Related in a Jewish Telegraphic Agency dispatch from Copenhagen, January 3, 1940 (*JTA News VI,* No. 124); described also, in part, in a cable to the *Forward,* dated December 30, 1939 (*Forward,* December 31, 1939).

12. *Op. cit.,* p. 32.

13. Testimonial protocol 149/15560; cf. also J. Chaimson in the *Forward*, May 31, 1948. The writer was arrested with others in November 1939 when he tried to cross the border near Biala Podlaska. The Red officer who interrogated him called him a "sly Jew" and accused him of spying. In the prison of Brest he met "thousands of Polish Jews who had also tried to cross the Soviet border illegally." After half a year in prison he was sentenced to a labor camp for 8 years.

14. Testimonial 10,580.

15. *Jewish Affairs*, New York, August 1941.

16. AJDC report of November 23, 1940 states that in 1939 there were 300,000 refugees in Lvov; 120,000 in Rovno and Lutsk; 100,000 in Kovel; 25,000 in Vilna and Kaunas; and 60,000 in Bialystok (*Forward*, November 24, 1940).

17. A. Pechenik, *Yidn un Yidishkeit in Sovyet Russland*, New York 1943, estimates their number at one million.

18. According to Grodner (*op. cit.*, p. 139) in November 1939 there were 33,000 refugees officially registered in Bialystok, and hundreds continued to arrive each day. The JDC report of 60,000 (see n. 16 above) was doubtless an exaggeration.

19. Grodner, *op. cit.*, p. 138.

20. Zerubavel, *op. cit.*, p. 65. The situation of the non-Jewish refugees was no better.

21. Fuchs, *op. cit.*, p. 58.

22. *Ibid.*, p. 57.

23. Tania Fuchs, whose book is often cited in these pages, was placed in charge of adult education in two districts of Lvov.

24. *Al Mashuoth Polin*, p. 134.

25. Testimonials 148/15,561; 10,569.

26. Testimonials 15,551, 15,554; Interview 14 (American Jewish Committee Library).

27. Testimonial 15,564.

28. *Al Mashuoth Polin*, pp. 78, 85; Grodner, *op. cit.*, p. 138.

29. Interview 17 (American Jewish Committee Library). The individual interviewed goes on to tell how the commissar appropriated the funds for his personal use and how the Jewish workers on the committee resigned in protest.

30. Grodner *op. cit.*, p. 139. Testimonial 201/15,551, however, speaks of more than one soup kitchen in Bialystok.

31. According to Gliksman, "only a few thousand people left for work." Some of the testimonials (10,586, 15,554) maintain that many registered. The latter relates that in Brest one had to wait in line for two days to register.

32. Testimonials 10,580; 15,569; cf. also Merestovski in *The Forward*, March 11 and 23, 1940.

33. Testimonial 15,554.

34. Testimonials 10,512, 10,582, 10,588.

35. In Lvov the Ukrainians apparently threatened to carry out pogroms. (Zerubavel, *op. cit.*, p. 83.)

36. Fuchs, *op. cit.*, p. 52 and also Segalowicz, *op. cit.*

37. Fuchs, *op. cit.*, p. 55.

38. Zerubavel, *op. cit.*, p. 82.

39. Grodner, *op. cit.*, p. 139.

40. Testimonial 26/15,564.

41. Testimonial 138/15,564.

42. Testimonials 148/15,561, 10,569; interviews 3, 8 (American Jewish Committee Library).

43. Testimonials 10,560, 15,564. According to a JTA dispatch dated January 4, 1940, from Paris, those refugees who did not wish to become Soviet citizens or to return to the Nazi zone were to be permitted to remain but would be denied the right to work (*JTA News VI*, 126).

44. It may be that this reasoning came only after the fact. Gliksman reports (p. 7) that the mass deportations were "a very important motive for returning to the German zone." This is confirmed in testimonial 10,580.

45. Gliksman, *op. cit.*, p. 7.
46. Testimonial 191/15,554.
47. Testimonial 10,588.
48. Testimonial 10,584.
49. Testimonial 10,560.
50. Cf. Grodner, *op. cit.*, p. 141.
51. *Op. cit.*, p. 7; Testimonial 10,584.
52. Gliksman, *ibid.*
53. Testimonial 10,560.
54. Testimonials 191/15,554; 15,560.

CHAPTER III

1. *Al Mashuoth Polin*, p. 83.
2. *Polish-Soviet Relations 1918-1943*, pp. 18, 20 ff; Testimonial 239/15,543.
3. Testimonial 251.
4. Testimonial 148/15,561.
5. Testimonial 10,572.
6. Testimonial 10,584.
7. Testimonials 138/15,564, 148/15,561.
8. Interview No. 17 (American Jewish Committee Library).
9. Fuchs, *op. cit.*, pp. 80-81; this report is supported by Testimonial 239/15,543.
10. Prager, *op. cit.*, p. 190.
11. Pechenik, *op. cit.*, pp. 59-60.
12. Ciechanowski, *Defeat in Victory*, 1947, pp. 120, 115; Gliksman (p. 20) estimates their number at 300,000; cf. also *Polish-Soviet Relations*, p. 21.
13. Fuchs, *op. cit.*, p. 82/112.
14. *Polish-Soviet Relations*, p. 21; J. Gliksman, *Tell the West*, New York 1948, p. 48.
15. Testimonials 191/15,554; 10,588.
16. Interview No. 8 (American Jewish Committee Library).
17. Testimonials 10,572; 201/15,551; 249/15,544.
18. Testimonial 201/15,551.
19. Interview No. 15 (Ameircan Jewish Committee Library).
20. Interview No. 10 (American Jewish Committee Library).
21. Interview No. 12 (American Jewish Committee Library).
22. Cf. also *Poland*, edited by Bernadotte E. Schmitt, Berkeley and Los Angeles, 1947, p. 445.
23. Testimonial 191/15,554.
24. Testimonials 10,580; 119/15,570.
25. Testimonial 10,588.
26. Testimonial 250/15,545.
27. Interview No. 3 (American Jewish Committee Library).
28. Testimonial 191/15,554.
29. Interview No. 8 (American Jewish Committee Library).
30. Interview No. 8 (American Jewish Committee Library).
31. Interview No. 15 (American Jewish Committee Library); Testimonial 216/-15,548.
32. Testimonial 214/15,549.

CHAPTER IV

1. Interview No. 14 (American Jewish Committee Library).
2. Interview No. 1 (American Jewish Committee Library).

3. Interview No. 14 (American Jewish Committee Library).
4. S. Kot, *Churbn Bialystok*, Buenos Aires 1947, pp. 10 ff; Philip Friedman, *Zaglada Zydow Lwowskich*, Lodz 1945, p. 5; A. Suckever, *Fun Vilner Getto*, Moscow 1946, p. 15.

CHAPTER V

1. *Polish-Soviet Relations*, pp. 107-110.
2. *Ibid.*, p. 112; Ciechanowski, *op. cit.*, p. 67.
3. *Polish-Soviet Relations*, pp. 22 ff., 110-126.
4. Testimonial 191/15,554.
5. Interview No. 2 (American Jewish Committee Library).
6. Interviews 3, 10, 15, 17; Testimonials 201/15,551; 239/15,543, 250/15,545; 10,554.
7. Interview No. 1 (American Jewish Committee Library); Testimonial 214/15,-549.
8. Testimonial 119/15,570.
9. Testimonial 10,560.
10. Testimonial 249/15,544.
11. Testimonial 15,564.
12. Interview No. 5 (American Jewish Committee Library).
13. Interview No. 4 (American Jewish Committee Library).
14. Interview No. 15 (American Jewish Committee Library).
15. Testimonial 201/15,551.
16. Testimonial 214/15,549.
17. Interviews Nos. 7, 15.
18. Interview No. 17.
19. By December 1942 there were 387 such representatives, of whom 297 were Poles, 82 Jews, 8 Ukrainians and White Russians.
20. *Polish-Soviet Relations*, pp. 47 ff; 180 ff.

CHAPTER VI

1. Ciechanowski, *op. cit.*, pp. 40, 63; cf. also pp. 31 ff., 37 ff.
2. *Polish-Soviet Relations*, p. 164.
3. *Ibid.*, p. 165.
4. Note of January 5, 1942 (*Polish-Soviet Relations*, p.168).
5. June 9, 1942 (*ibid.*, p. 169).
6. *Polish-Soviet Relations*, pp. 207-209.
7. Ciechanowski, *op. cit.*, pp. 92 ff.
8. *Ibid.*, p. 171.
9. *Ibid.*, *pp.* 149 ff.
10. *Polish-Soviet Relations*, p. 219.
11. Interview No. 2 (American Jewish Committee Library).
12. Interview No. 15 (American Jewish Committee Library).
13. *Polish-Soviet Relations*, pp. 28 ff; testimonials 10,556, 10,588.
14. Testimonial 10,588.
15. Testimonial 10,569.
16. Interview No. 2 (American Jewish Committee Library).
17. Interview No. 3 (American Jewish Committee Library); testimonial 10,556.
18. Testimonials 191/15,554; 201/15,551.
19. Testimonials 138/15,564, 149/15,560, 201/15,551, 249/15,544, 250/15,545, 10,560.
20. Ciechanowski, pp. 149 ff, 230 ff.
21. As early as February 1943 the pro-Soviet Polish paper *Nowe Widnokregi* (New *Horizons*) appealed for enlistment in a new Russian-sponsored Polish army. In April-May the Polish Kosciuszko Division was formed.

22. *Der Tog* (New York) December 25, 1945.
23. James T. Shotwell and Max Laserson, *Poland and Russia,* New York 1945, p. 61.
24. Arthur Bliss Lane, *I Saw Poland Betrayed,* New York 1948, p. 39.
25. *Ibid.,* p. 56.
26. Ciechanowski, *op. cit.,* p. 342; Lane, *op. cit.,* p. 70.
27. Joseph B. Schechtman, "The Polish-Soviet Exchange of Population," *Journal of Central European Affairs,* IX, October 1941, p. 296.
28. *Izvestiya,* September 14, 26, 1944; July 7, 1945.
29. *Polpress News* (New York) July 18, 1945; Schechtman, *op. cit.,* p. 304.
30. Schechtman, *op. cit.,* p. 303.
31. *Statistical Yearbook of Poland 1947,* p. 29; Schechtman, *op. cit.,* pp. 309 ff.
32. According to Polish estimates based on the 1931 census, there were 4,222,037 Polish-speaking persons in the territories occupied on September 1939 by the Red Army. The number of repatriates together with those who came in the Polish Army did not exceed 2 millions.
33. Schechtman, *op. cit.,* p. 313.
34. *New York Herald Tribune,* December 29, 1946.
35. Jewish Telegraphic Agency, March 17, 1947, August 11, 1948; *Forward,* No. 9, 1948.

IV. Hungary

BY

EUGENE DUSCHINSKY

Chapter I

The Jewish Community Before and During World War II

According to official Hungarian census figures, in 1920 there were 473,355 persons of the Jewish faith (5.9 per cent of the total population) living within the confines of the reduced territory left Hungary by the Treaty of Peace of Trianon. The last census taken prior to the First World War, in 1910, had shown 932,000 persons of the Jewish faith (4.5 per cent of the total population). Thus, one of the results of Hungary's defeat in the war was the loss of almost half its Jewish population to the four neighboring countries of Czechoslovakia, Rumania, Yugoslavia, and Austria. By 1930 the number of professing Jews in Hungary had declined to 444,567, or 5.1 per cent of the population. This loss was due in part to a declining birth rate, and in part to emigration, the latter directly attributable to the antisemitism of the Horthy regime.

In 1940, wartime conditions caused the postponement of the usual decennial census, but estimates worked out under the sponsorship of the Budapest Jewish community put the number of Jews within the territory of prewar Hungary at some 435,000. By this time, however, Hungary had regained, with the help of Nazi Germany, a substantial part of the territories lost to her neighbors as a result of the First World War.

Before the First World War, there had been few cases of Jews being converted, although their number was greater than in other Eastern European countries. Following the short-lived Communist regime of Bela Kun and the subsequent counterrevolutionary and antisemitic period of 1919-20, about 12,000 Jews abandoned their faith. Between 1920 and 1937, the rabbinate of the Budapest Jewish community estimated an average annual conversion of 400, a loss fairly regularly counterbalanced by an average annual conversion of 350 Christians to Judaism. During 1938, however, in the vain hope of escaping the consequences of the first anti-Jewish law, 8,584 Jews adopted Christianity (as reported by the Budapest rabbinate). A small panel of rabbis from Hungary now living in the United States are agreed that the total number of baptized Jews in prewar Hungary (1938) was between 32,000 and 36,000. Subject to the provisions of the various anti-Jewish laws, these "non-Aryans" augmented the number of persons affected by discriminatory legislation after 1938 to some 470,000 within the smaller Hungarian national territory.

According to a census taken by the municipality of Budapest in 1930, 204,371 Jews, or 46 per cent of the total Jewish population, lived in the nation's capital, where they made up 20.3 per cent of the city's population. (Until 1938, official Hungarian statistics provided no information about the Jewish population apart from their number.) By the end of 1935, their number had decreased to 201,069. (None of these figures includes baptized Jews.) According to the same survey, the average percentage of Jews in the general urban population in 1930 was 14.8, in the rural population 2.8. In addition to Budapest, there were two cities each with between 10,000 and 15,000 professing Jewish inhabitants; 24 communities each with around 1,000 Jewish individuals; and 180 communities with fewer than 1,000 Jews. The White Terror and pogroms following the overthrow of the Bela Kun regime set in motion a large movement of provincial Jews to the capital. By 1924 this movement had largely subsided; later, many Jews returned to their small towns and villages.

The official *Hungarian Statistical Review* of April 1938 contained, for the first time in the history of Hungarian statistics, a description of the occupational distribution of the population by religious affiliation for the year 1930 (to prove the existence of an inordinate Jewish "influence"). The total number of individuals engaged in the various occupations, and the percentage of these who were Jews, are shown in Table I.

On April 5, 1938, the *Jüdische Rundschau* (organ of the Zionist Federation of Germany) quoted "from official Hungarian census figures" the data shown in Table II regarding Jewish participation in Hungarian cultural and intellectual occupations.

In 1930, of a Jewish population of 444,567, 189,712 (43.2 per cent) were gainfully employed—an unusually high ratio indeed. Of the latter, 74,728 persons (38.4 per cent) were independent businessmen or practitioners of the liberal professions; 53,146 persons (27.8 per cent) were intellectuals, commercial, industrial and other white-collar employees; while 63,838 persons (33.4 per cent) were workers and helpers. Both tables clearly show Hungarian Jewry's important middle-class role.

Table I, however, by including handicrafts in the category of industry, gives an incorrect impression of the Jewish industrial role. It represents the total number of "industrialists" as being 216,516 (of which 11 per cent, or 23,817, were Jews); but this category included an overwhelming majority of small craftsmen. In fact, in 1930 there were only 3,491 establishments of a really industrial character in Hungary. In this category of industry proper, the same issue of the *Hungarian Statistical Review* (p. 456) states that the percentage of Jewish "industrial executives" (owners,

TABLE I

DISTRIBUTION OF JEWS BY INDUSTRY AND OCCUPATION, 1938

Occupation and Industry	Total Number Gainfully Employed	Number of Jews Gainfully Employed	% of Jews Gainfully Employed
A. *Independent* (*self-employed*):			
Agriculture	700,466	2,802	0.4
Industry	216,516	23,817	11.0
Commerce	83,671	37,970	45.5
Credit, banking	324	223	68.8
Transportation	9,335	1,167	12.5
Public service and liberal professions	19,735	6,749	34.2
Total	1,030,047	72,728	
B. *Employees* (*white collar*):			
Agriculture	5,611	926	16.5
Industry	43,372	14,431	33.3
Commerce	40,398	21,330	52.8
Credit, banking	17,467	6,236	35.7
Transportation	21,124	1,373	6.5
Public service and liberal professions	117,999	8,850	7.5
Total	245,971	53,146	
C. *Laborers, helpers*			
Agriculture	788,681	789	0.1
Industry	633,138	35,522	5.6
Commerce	79,502	24,010	30.2
Credit, banking	3,418	106	3.1
Transportation	80,567	1,611	2.0
Public service and liberal professions	58,078	1,800	3.1
Total	1,643,384	63,838	
Grand Total	2,919,402	189,712	

leaseholders, managing directors) was as follows: iron, steel and metallurgical industries: 46.8; machine construction: 37.2; generation and distribution of electricity: 24.1; stone, earthenware, ceramic, asbestos, and glass industries: 39.3; leather, hair, bristle, feather, linoleum, and rubber industries: 61.5; wood and bone industries: 60.8; textile industry: 62.2; clothing industry: 73.2; paper industry: 65.5; food and liquor industry: 40.1; chemical industry: 62.2; and printing and graphic industries: 69.5.

TABLE II

DISTRIBUTION OF JEWS IN INTELLECTUAL INDUSTRY OR OCCUPATION, 1938

Industry or Occupation	Number of Jews	Percentage of Jews
Arts and literature	119	27.0
Science (unaffiliated)	84	24.7
Journalism	480	31.7
Music	199	28.0
Stage	475	24.1
Chemists and engineers	402	37.5
Printing trades (shopowners)	330	60.7
Lawyers	2,693	49.2
Candidates for the bar	525	34.9
Law employees	924	30.6
Physicians	2,151	54.5
Veterinary surgeons	206	24.0
Total	8,588	

This publication, as part of the same effort to justify the impending anti-Jewish legislation, represented (on p. 462) the percentage of Jewish merchants in the various major branches of commerce as follows: trade in agricultural, cattle, and animals products: 51.3; lumber and mineral products: 57.2; iron and metal products, machines, household articles, etc.: 65.3; wood, leather, rubber, and paper products: 73.9; textile goods and clothing: 79.2; food and liquor: 37.4; chemical and pharmaceutical products: 60.7; grocery trade: 58.9; other commercial branches: 60.8.

These figures must, of course, be suspected of a certain degree of tendentiousness. They very likely include not only industrialists and merchants of the Jewish faith, but also the considerable number of converted Jews (leading Jewish businessmen being most exposed to the pressure to change their religion). However, the leading position of Jews in banking, industry, and commerce was a long-established fact in Hungary, and an official government publication did not need to juggle figures to any serious degree to show it. These statistics convey a rough approximation of the facts about the Jewish economic position in Hungary prior to the impact in 1938 of Nazi German power upon Hungary's internal life.

Jews in Hungarian Life

How did the Jews come to occupy this position in the economic life of an East European agrarian country? The Hungarian "liberal era," beginning in the early 1860's and ending with the defeat in the First World

War, was in reality a precapitalist and predemocratic era. Hungary's semi-feudal system was ruled by a large landowning Magyar aristocracy which, by a compromise concluded in 1867 with the Hapsburgs of Austria, instituted the Austro-Hungarian Dual Monarchy. This Dual Monarchy (symbolized in the person of the Emperor-King of the combined Austrian Empire and Kingdom of Hungary) was a constitutional arrangement by which foreign affairs and national defense were supervised by "joint" Austro-Hungarian ministries in Vienna, under the governance of "delegations" of the Austrian and Hungarian parliaments, while the internal affairs of the two constituent states were solely within the jurisdiction of the separate "national" governments. This "liberal system" was stubbornly—and, as it turned out during the Great War, fatally—illiberal in its attitude toward the numerous minorities of the country, as it was toward the Magyar peasant masses and urban working class. At the same time the ruling aristocracy displayed a consistently liberal and tolerant attitude toward the Jewish population of the country, which it gave broad opportunities to engage in industry and commerce.

During the five or six decades ending with the First World War, the Hungarian aristocracy constituted a highly political group like that of the nobility of England a hundred years before. It was no historical-social relic like the nobility of Italy, or a mere economic interest group, but a tightly-knit caste exercising its political power directly. Its political position was firmly secured by the open ballot, and control over all appointments to the administration. The aristocracy steadfastly refused to share political power with other groups, no matter how many their numbers, or how important their economic role.

But the Magyar aristocracy was no half-Asiatic autocracy of the Tsarist type. Toward the popular masses, especially the peasants, this nobility displayed a harsh and negative conservatism; but it did not share the obscurantist fear and contempt of the average Russian nationalist and boyar for intellectual pre-eminence and liberal middle-class development. Its social conservatism was blended with and balanced by a certain European respect for the educated, productive individual. Its traditionally strong respect for legality caused it to adhere painstakingly to the terms of all the liberal concessions it made.

But unlike the British aristocracy, the Hungarian inflexibly refused to engage in "trade" or industry. And since the peasants and workers lacked the education necessary for engaging in the middle-class occupations, by a process of elimination the Jews were left as the sole social element ready and able to establish and conduct Hungary's industry and commerce. The ruling aristocracy realized the compelling national need for such a development; but since its members were loath to do the job themselves, they willingly acquiesced in its assignment to the Jews. Later, the gradual enlistment of many noblemen by Jewish bankers and industrialists as stockholders and board members made them friends and silent partners of the Hungarian business community.

The explanation of this attitude is to be found in the so-called "Reform Era" of 1820-48, when the aristocratic leadership of Hungary, in its struggle against Austrian oppression, played, at least temporarily, a truly liberal and forward-looking political role. It learned then that only Hungary's industrial, commercial, and legal development would enable her to withstand foreign encroachment. Counts Stephen Szechenyi, Louis Batthiany, and Baron Joseph Eotvos were representatives of this early liberal tendency in the Hungarian ruling class. The first called for the Western political and social orientation of Hungary, as well as her systematic industrialization. The second was executed for his leadership of the democratic revolutionary government in the war of independence of 1848-49; while Baron Eotvos was the father of Hungary's liberal educational system and perhaps the foremost advocate in Eastern Europe of the emancipation of Jews. The favorable atmosphere created by this development was instrumental in opening up to the Jews the field of economic initiative, particularly after the middle of the last century.

Another consideration in this ruling class attitude was of a political nature. In pre-1914 Greater Hungary, a near-perfect numerical balance obtained between the Magyar population and the national minorities (Rumanians, Slovaks, Croats, Serbs.). In this situation, the 900,000 Hungarian-speaking Jews tipped the scales in favor of the Hungarian element. While Greater Hungary lasted, this important "statistical" role played by Hungarian Jewry helped to secure its social and economic position.

The poor and exploited peasants (who in 1930 constituted about 60 per cent of the total population) and industrial workers of Greater Hungary attributed their plight exclusively to the oppressive policies of the landed aristocracy, whose bureaucracy and police held them in subjection. For the peasantry, land distribution was the only way out of their age-old predicament; and it was manifest to all that not Jewish businessmen but the agrarian barons were blocking the realization of this reform. Labor for its part knew full well that its efforts to organize political parties and unions were opposed by the ruling aristocratic element. In general, Jewish employers displayed a more enlightened attitude toward unionism and the social requirements of labor; their liberal attitude, and perhaps also the fact that most of the founders and early leaders of the Hungarian democratic labor movement were Jews, helped to make the Social Democratic Party and trade unions reliable bulwarks against antisemitism throughout the "liberal era" and even into the Horthy regime. It is significant that as late as September 1943, when Hitler was most strongly pressing the Horthy regime to annihilate Hungarian Jewry, the Smallholders Party, representing the broad peasant masses, and the Social Democratic Party, representing labor, were the only groups to stand resolutely with the Hungarian Jews; in a nationwide joint campaign, under the very nose of Hitler, they demanded the abolition of all anti-Jewish legislation and discrimination.

The only competition Hungarian Jews had to face before the First World War was that of a relatively small group of German businessmen of limited position and influence. Not until the advent of the Horthy regime did this group seriously threaten the Jewish middle class. Another potential threat was represented by the impoverished small landowning gentry which, reduced to taking minor positions in the administration and army, looked with growing envy at the affluence of the Jewish middle class. Finally, there was a small Christian Socialist movement sponsored by the Catholic church which was made up mainly of workers in the public services (trainmen, streetcar conductors, etc.); its antisocialist propaganda had subdued but unmistakable antisemitic overtones. However, since the aristocratic rulers of Hungary gave antisemitism no support, these potential threats to the Jewish middle class remained ineffective until the advent of the Horthy regime in 1919.

The Magyars, led and controlled by the landed aristocracy, considered the Hungarian-speaking Jews as members of the "state-forming" Magyar element, and allowed them to work and prosper in commerce, industry, and finance. This, of course, did not mean that there was no poverty among the Jews, especially in the backward eastern areas of Greater Hungary; but it did mean that the predominantly middle-class character of Hungarian Jewry was a firmly established social reality.

The consequence of this tolerance was that the overwhelming majority of Hungarian Jews felt themselves to be members of the Hungarian nation, with every inducement to remain so. They had taken a full share in the development not only of the Hungarian economy, but also of Hungarian culture. In the last four decades of the nineteenth century Jewish scientists, historians, philosophers, lawyers, legislators, writers, dramatists, poets, composers, musicians, and actors played leading roles in the cultural life of the nation. To most of them, this wholehearted participation in Hungarian cultural endeavor seemed entirely compatible with their being Jews. Hungarian Jewry felt little need to embrace Jewish political nationalism, or even a Jewish culture more nationalistic than the established Jewish religious and cultural tradition. Until the advent of Hitler to power, political Zionism, the prophecy of the Hungarian-born Herzl and Nordau, failed to exercise any considerable influence upon Jewish thinking and sentiment in Hungary.

This seems all the more strange in that Hungarian Jewry, as late as the middle of the nineteenth century, still shared all the ideological and cultural characteristics of the Eastern European Jews. But we must bear in mind that Hungary had proved, for at least two generations and up until the end of the First World War, an island of resistance to both of the two great antisemitic currents engulfing Eastern and Central Europe: the semi-Asiatic and feudal antisemitism of Czarist Russia; and the middle-class socio-economic and nationalistic antisemitism of Germany and Austria. On this island the Jews of Hungary lived and progressed, without danger, decline, or even disturbance; it was a life of slight anxieties and barely noticeable transitions which seemed to be sheltered from the uncertainties of history.

Civil Status Between Two Wars

The emancipation of Hungarian Jewry was decreed by parliament on December 22, 1867 (Law XVII of 1867); according to the *Jewish Encyclopedia* (London, 1904), this act "was received with universal satisfaction not only by the Jews, but also by the whole country." In February 1868, at the initiative of the Minister of Education and the Cults, Baron Joseph Eotvos, an assembly or congress of the Jews of Hungary was called to regulate the internal affairs and organization of the community. The General Jewish Congress of Hungary was convened in December 1868, but it failed to produce that unity expected of it by its sponsors, for the orthodox groups refused to enter a unified Jewish community organization. In March 1870, parliament ruled that the principle of religious freedom dictated that Jewish groups were not obliged to submit to regulations by the congress which were contrary to their convictions. On this ground, the orthodox Jews seceded from the congress, and another, smaller group of communities declared themselves neutral between them and the supporters of the Congress. As a result, three separate Jewish religious national organizations were established: the "Congressional (Neologic) Central Office of Hungarian Israelites," the "Autonomous Orthodox Jewish Central Office," and the small "Central Organization of the Status Quo Ante Jewish Communities"; the first embraced the more assimilated industrial, commercial, and intellectual element, concentrated in and around Budapest, while the two latter organizations were strongest in the border areas of the country. The three organizations gradually worked out a system of cooperation for matters of common interest.

The next step was the legal recognition of the Jewish faith by the state. This was done by parliament on May 16, 1896, through passage of the so-called Reception Law (Law XIII of 1896) which "received and established" the Jewish faith as "a legally recognized religion," with a status equal to that of the leading Catholic and Protestant churches, and higher than the status of certain smaller Protestant and Greek Oriental denominations. The privileges of the Jewish communities included the compulsory taxation of members (with state aid in tax collection), the maintenance of theological and general educational institutions, and the right to a proportionate share in state subsidies. The Congressional Jewish Communities of Budapest founded great religious, educational, health, and welfare institutions which were strongly supported by the membership. On October 4, 1877, the Theological Seminary and Teachers Institute of the Congressional organization was opened; it trained most of the rabbis and teachers needed by the Congressional and Status Quo Ante communities. The Orthodox communities continued to train their rabbis and teachers in traditional Yeshivot.

After the First World War, Hungary smarted under the loss of large territories and considerable population blocs (including ethnic Hungarians) to the "upstart" successor states, states which this "thousand-year-old" nation regarded with contempt. Chaotic economic conditions were worsened by the influx of hundreds of thousands of Hungarian refugees from the lost territories. Other harsh features of the Treaty of Trianon and chaotic postwar conditions further increased this mood of despair and bitterness. Since the Jews in Hungary had always been the staunchest partisans of that West which had now inflicted upon Hungary the harshest terms of peace, resentment was immediately directed against them. A relic of the prewar multinational Hungarian state, the Jews were now the only considerable minority to "trouble" the ethnic homogeneity of the country.

Moreover, much of the odium of the abortive Communist dictatorship of Bela Kun attached to the Jews as a group, because of their large representation among the Communist agents recruited from Hungarian prisoners of war and sent to Hungary by the Soviet government. If Bela Kun was Moscow's present to Hungary, the Western powers matched it with their gift of Nicholas Horthy. Horthy's Western-sponsored Regency was the product of backstage political manipulation and on-stage violence. But by setting up the antidemocratic regime of Admiral Horthy as an anti-Hapsburg and anti-Soviet bulwark in Eastern Europe, Paris and London only made sure in 1919 that Hungary would at the decisive moment ally itself not with the democratic West, but with a vengeful Germany.

Around Horthy rallied the three reactionary and antisemitic groups of Hungary: the Swabian *Auslanddeutsche* (ethnic Germans) who at the time wore the mask of Hungarian nationalism; the restless and dissatisfied landless gentry; and sections of the Catholic-sponsored Christian Socialists. The pro-Hapsburg high nobility lost all its political power to this pro-Horthy camp.

The Horthy regime started out in a blaze of pogroms that lasted for two years; these raged especially in the provinces. Most of the leading Communists had escaped to Russia, leaving the Jews, who had overwhelmingly opposed the Communist adventure, as the chief target of the counter-revolution. For two years the life of the average Jew was unsafe in

Hungary, and the number of victims of the "white-gloved murderers" (chiefly army officers) ran into the thousands.

During the regime's first year, a number of administrative measures were taken which resulted in the elimination of the majority of Jewish public servants from the administration, judiciary, and school system. But it soon became clear to General Julius Goemboes, chief political adviser to the Regent, and his German followers that wholesale confiscation of Jewish property and the expulsion of at least the more recently settled groups of Jews were impossible of achievement. In spite of their eagerness thus to "solve the Jewish problem" in Hungary, these Hungarian forerunners of Hitler had to content themselves with a single major infringement on the equal rights of Jews, namely, a *numerus clausus* law restricting the enrollment of Jewish students at universities to the percentage of Jews in the general population. More radical antisemitic measures were prevented by other considerations.

First, large-scale confiscatory measures smacking of Bolshevism in nationalist disguise might have compromised the Horthy regime's anti-Communist reputation abroad. Second, Hungary needed foreign loans which it would not get if there were economic upheavals and disturbed property conditions in the country. Third, they saw themselves confronted by the determined opposition of the rich landed aristocracy to any change in property conditions which might have encouraged a demand for land reform; they had even to fear the possibility of a defensive alliance of the high aristocracy and Jewish middle class against the regime; the combination might have drawn away Western support from the regime. Finally, the urgent need for reviving production so as to satisfy growing consumers' needs also argued against any serious tampering with Hungary's economic order.

All these were arguments on the side of conservatism. The outstanding advocate of the conservative position was Count Stephen Bethlen, a descendant of the Hungarian ruling family of Transylvania, in whose duchy the first decrees of religious toleration had been enacted in the early seventeenth century. Originally a staunch supporter of Horthy and a rival of Goemboes in the Regent's graces, this aristocrat stood for the traditional opposition to land reform on the one hand, and for the preservation of the economic position of the Jews on the other. In 1924 Bethlen succeeded, much to the chagrin of Goemboes' antisemitic faction, in attaining the position of prime minister. During his almost nine years' tenure of office, he gradually altered the regime's tone from one of antisemitic aggressiveness and reactionary mob activism to legalistic economic and social conservatism. After putting a stop to the physical violence used against Jews and socialists, he recognized the Social Democrats and other small democratic political groups as legitimate political parties; obtained substantial League of Nations loans; and sought, with the aid of Jewish industry and commerce, to make Hungary economically self-sufficient.

All that remained of the original anti-Jewish program of the Horthy regime was the policy of keeping Jews out of the public service, and a second and more discreet version of the educational *numerus clausus* law. In practice, however, there was unlimited admission of Jewish students to the three provincial universities; only in the case of Budapest's university and polytechnicum was the law rigidly enforced. Poor Jewish students who failed to obtain admittance to Hungarian universities were sent to study abroad by a special Jewish fund established for this purpose by Dr. Simon Hevesi, chief rabbi of Budapest.

In these nineteen years the Horthy regime thus failed to bring about any lasting legal or constitutional change which would have fundamentally affected the political and civil rights and economic position of the Jews. On the contrary, so far as the civil status of Jews was concerned, the Supreme Court had decided as early as 1924 that the Jews could not be regarded as a separate nationality in Hungary because their mother tongue was Hungarian.

When in 1933 General Goemboes finally succeeded in displacing Count Bethlen as prime minister, it was generally expected that the regime would immediately revive its original antisemitic program. But even Goemboes felt compelled to adhere, at least temporarily, to Bethlen's policy with respect to the Jews. Hungarian Jewry was able, almost miraculously, to preserve its economic substance and social position until the downfall of neighboring Austria in the crucial year of 1938.

Below this surface of seeming stability, however, lay the quicksand of the misery and dissatisfaction of the broad masses, especially the landless peasants, virtually disfranchised by the open and controlled ballot. There was the dangerously xenophobe quality of irredentist Hungarian nationalism. And there were the pro-Nazi *Auslanddeutsche* with their continuing ominous influence on the Horthy regime.

But most of all, perhaps, there was the devastating effect of the relentless defamation of Hungarian Jewry by the press and platform, often by the pulpit, and by every organ of the "patriotic," "revisionist," "Christian" and "race-defending" elements of Hungary. This abuse was somewhat softened during Count Bethlen's tenure, but its poisonous spirit remained. In the mid-1930's the oratory of the mushrooming Nazi parties, the aspersions of the many Nazi publications directly sponsored by the Reich, and the machinations of innumerable German visiting journalists and businessmen kept going the antisemitic agitation which the Horthy regime itself had started. In a year or two, this Nazi campaign was extended to include among its targets the Regent himself and the patriotic anti-Nazi conservative minority of the Bethlen school. In 1938, with Austria under the Nazi heel, Mussolini following Hitler's lead, and the democratic West apparently helpless, Nazi propaganda furiously attacked the Jews of Hungary in preparation for that country's infiltration and subjugation.

At this point, in order to prevent Hitler from openly backing and perhaps putting into power the Nazi movement in Hungary, the Horthy government decided to make its first serious move to appease Hitler. On May 24, 1938, both houses of Parliament, in face of the bitter opposition of the Smallholders and Social Democratic parties and of the conservative followers of Count Bethlen, enacted Hungary's first anti-Jewish law. It was supported in the upper house by representatives of the Catholic and Protestant high clergy. The substance of this first law was the reduction of the employment of Jews by private business firms to 20 per cent of the total staff of each firm. By 1943, some 15,000 Jews were scheduled to lose their livelihood.

A year later, on May 3, 1939, a second and far more drastic anti-Jewish law was adopted by parliament. The Smallholders, Socialist, and Bethlen factions fought the bill with unprecedented bitterness, Count Bethlen arguing to no avail that "if we adopt this bill we shall no longer be the friends but the servants of Germany, and that will be the end, once and for all, of our independence."

The law defined Jews as persons with at least one professing Jewish parent or two professing Jewish grandparents. In the economic domain it provided for the reduction of the original 20 per cent employment quota of the first law to 12 per cent. It barred Jews from "responsible" positions in the press, theater, radio, and cinema. It prohibited the issuance of new trade licenses to Jews or the renewal of old licenses. It barred any further admission of Jews to the legal, medical, engineering, journalistic, theatrical, and motion picture professions, until their share in these professions fell, through death or retirement, below 6 per cent. It authorized the government to expropriate, with compensation, Jewish landed property. Jews could no longer acquire Hungarian citizenship by naturalization, marriage, or adoption. The government could take away the citizenship of Jews naturalized after July 1, 1914; Jews were barred from membership in the upper house of Parliament, despite the Jewish community's right to be represented in it by two rabbis, according to a law sponsored by Premier Bethlen ten years before; the electoral rights of a large class of Jews not born in Hungary or permanently resident before 1868 were cancelled.

Post-Munich Policies

After Munich, the "Vienna awards" returned substantial territories from Czechoslovakia, Rumania, and Yugoslavia to Hungarian sovereignty. In these territories lived some 324,000 Jews, who now became subject to the drastic Hungarian anti-Jewish legislation. The population census on January 1, 1941, showed a total of 725,007 inhabitants of the Jewish faith in the new Greater Hungary (including those Polish, Slovak, and other Jewish refugees who had registered). In addition, the *Hungarian Statistical Review*[1] estimated the number of Christians of Jewish origin at around 100,000 for Greater Hungary. Thus, some 825,000 persons were subject to the anti-Jewish laws. A third anti-Jewish law, enacted on August 8, 1941, prohibited marriage and sexual intercourse between Jews and "Aryans." Finally, the law of 1942, the first and only measure aimed at Jewish property in Hungary, ordered the seizure, against token compensation in government bonds, of all landed property owned by Jews.

However, this anti-Jewish legislation did not mean the total economic ruin of the Jews in Hungary. Large sections of the Jewish population were able to continue in their businesses, professions, and employment; Jewish property and its proceeds remained, in the main, intact and available. These laws represented a calculated compromise: the Nazi mob was thrown the sop of thousands of jobs wrested from individual Jews, while the Jewish collectivity was permitted to exist with its property rights intact against the day of Hitler's defeat. Because of the relative mildness of Hungary's antisemitic legislation, Jews in the neighboring countries, where Nazi extermination was in full swing, looked to Hungary as a haven.

But this situation proved of short duration. The measures taken against Hungarian Jewry failed to appease Hitler. Under constant German pressure Hungary soon felt compelled to work in closest "friendship" with the German Reich (as well as with her old sponsor, fascist Italy); on February 24, 1939, she formally joined the Berlin-Rome Axis by signing the anti-Comintern pact and withdrew from the League of Nations. To counterbalance the disruptive domestic effect of these policies, the government campaigned strenuously against the growing Nazi parties at the successive elections, dissolved the largest of these parties, the Arrow Cross movement, arrested a number of Nazi leaders, and supported the parliamentary system of government. In the field of foreign policy, the only anti-Nazi step was a short-lived rapprochement with Yugoslavia looking toward a defensive alliance; but this soon had to be given up as a result of both German and Italian pressure. At the beginning of World War II, Hungary followed Italy's example and remained neutral. After the fall of France, Hungary, again following Italy's lead declared war not only against the Soviet Union and Great Britain, but also against the United States.

Hungary's first military action in the war was to participate in the German attack on Yugoslavia; this attack was accompanied by massacres of the Serbian and Jewish populations of the Yugoslav-Hungarian border areas. Hungary sent several armies to the Eastern front; her soldiers were notably unenthusiastic.

From the middle of 1942 on, Germany urged upon the government of Hungary the "transfer and transportation of all Jews to the East." *The Black Book on the Martyrdom of Hungarian Jews* by Eugene Levai, published in English in Vienna in 1948, devoted twelve closely printed folio pages to an enumeration and synopsis of the flood of German notes, oral representations, and diplomatic démarches aimed at the one objective of having the Jews deported from Hungary. We quote only one single protocol, read at the Nuremburg trial during the examination of Joachim von Ribbentrop, which describes Hitler's meeting with Horthy on April 17, 1943. On this occasion, reports the protocol,

> The German Chancellor attacked the Kallay Cabinet violently, protesting in vehement terms to the Regent against the lack of interest in the Jewish question displayed by the Hungarian government. . . . Horthy defended himself by saying "he could not slaughter them, [the Jews]," to which Hitler, in the presence of Ribbentrop, replied as follows: "In Poland we settled this problem by very simple means. We shot those Jews not willing to work. Those unable to work we exterminated. The Jews are parasites undeserving of any forbearance, they must be dealt with like tubercular germs. I see no cruelty in this when I consider that innocent animals such as deer or hares are killed by the hundreds of thousands in order to satisfy the hunger of man. Why then should we suffer these Jewish brutes to live, who wish to infest Germany with Bolshevism?" Horthy referred to the fact that Hungary was a constitutional state and that also in the Jewish question he was unable to take any steps whatsoever without the consent of Parliament. To this Hitler made some very disparaging remarks about the parliamentary system, and declared that the gist of the trouble lay in the fact that Hungary had no intention of switching over to the totalitarian system. . . .

In the middle of March 1944, Regent Horthy was ordered by Hitler to visit him "immediately" in Germany. In his absence, at dawn on March 19, German airborne troops occupied all airfields in Hungary and motorized troops swept into the country. By the time Horthy had returned to Budapest, the occupation was complete and the doom of Hungarian Jewry was sealed. Horthy summoned a meeting of the Crown Council, according to whose minutes he declared that one of the chief causes of the occupation was the fact that "Hungary has not yet introduced the steps necessary to settle the Jewish question. We are accused, therefore, of the crime of not having carried out Hitler's wishes, and I am charged with not having permitted the Jews to be massacred. . . ."

General Keresztes-Fischer, the anti-Nazi Minister of the Interior, announced at the meeting that "he would not remain at his post one minute longer," seeing that the Germans had taken charge of the police and the Gestapo was busy rounding up Hungarian democrats. "I will not allow one single Jew to be taken out of town," he declared, thus presenting to all (including the Regent) the alternative of protecting the Jews from the Germans or resigning from office. The Kallay government soon resigned, but Horthy stayed on as the nominal Regent of occupied Hungary; he soon appointed a Quisling cabinet headed by Hungary's ambassador in Berlin, General Sztojay (Stojakovits).

According to the *Black Book,* at that time 231,435 Jews were living in Budapest and 530,554 in the provinces—a total of 761,989 Jews in all of Greater Hungary (the term "Jew" used this time in the sense of the anti-Jewish laws to include converts to Christianity). The difference between this figure and the 825,007 given by the 1941 census is attributable to an estimated loss of 63,000 as a result of persecution between January 1941 and March 1944, when the mass deportations began. Of this 63,000, some 42,000 were missing members of the military labor services in the various military areas; some 17-20,000 were non-Hungarian Jews who had been deported in July 1941, the great majority of whom had met death in the Ukraine at the hands of German and Ukrainian bands assisted by Hungarian gendarmes; and about 1,000 were victims of the Ujvidék pogrom staged in reoccupied Northern Yugoslavia by the Hungarian military.[2]

Nazi Deportations

The following brief summary of the history of the mass deportations of Jews from Hungary is quoted from the deposition made before the Inter-Allied Military Tribunal in Nuremberg by Dr. Rudolf Kastner, lawyer, journalist, and a leader of the Hungarian Zionist movement.[3]

> March 19, 1944. Following the occupation of the country by the Germans, a *Spezialabteilungskommando* arrived in Budapest, whose only task was the liquidation of Hungarian Jewry. It was commanded by Adolf Eichmann, SS *Obersturmbannführer* and chief of Section IV.B of the Central Security Office of the Reich. His immediate collaborators were SS *Obersturmbannführer* Herman Krumey, *Hauptsturmführers* Wisliceny, Hunsche, Novak Dr. Seidl, and later Dannecker and Wrtok. They immediately arrested the Hungarian democratic and antifascist political leaders, and all Jewish personalities of the political, economic and journalistic world, and deported them to Mauthausen. Taking advantage of the four days' interregnum following the German occupation, they placed in charge of the Hungarian Ministry of the Interior the collaborationists Ladislas Endre and Ladislas Baky.
>
> With the help of the Hungarian adminstration, they (a) arrested all Jews arriving in Budapest or about to leave their provincial communities; (b) prohibited the use of the mails and of the telephone by Jews; (c) confiscated for the use of the SS . . . all Jewish public buildings, schools and hospitals.
>
> On March 23, 1944, the Quisling government was installed whose only task (according to statements made to us by Wisliceny in June 1944) consisted in the solution of the Jewish question. . . .

On March 26, 1944, the entire territory of Ruthenia, Upper Hungary and Northern Transylvania was, at the demand of the German High Command, declared a zone of military operations. On April 9, the military authorities started the concentration of the 320,000 Jews of this military zone in ghettos. Immediately thereafter, Ambassador Veesenmayer and a representative of von Sauckel concluded an agreement with Prime Minister Sztojay, whereby Hungary obligated herself to place at the disposal of the Reich 300,000 Jewish laborers, to be selected by a German-Hungarian mixed commission. On the basis of this agreement, at a meeting held at the Ministry of the Interior on April 14, 1944, Endre, Baky, and Eichmann decided to deport *en masse* all of the Jews of Hungary. . . .

April 28, 1944, marks the start of the deportations, with the transfer of 1,500 able-bodied persons to Auschwitz, where they were compelled to write reassuring letters to their families. These messages were brought by SS courier to Budapest, and distributed by the *Judenrat*. Soon, however, the Budapest Jewish Relief Committee received two communications from its counterpart in Bratislava (Pozsony), one of which advised of the restoration to full working capacity of the gas chambers and four crematoria at Auschwitz which for several months had not been functioning, while the second reported that an agreement had been arrived at between the Hungarian, Slovak and German railroad adminstrations providing that 120 trains were to depart from Northern Hungary via Prešov (Eperjes) to Auschwitz. It was clear that this meant deportation convoys. . . .

After consultation with all Jewish organizations, we approached the Germans. In the beginning, these consultations were, on the German side, conducted by Krumey, Wisliceny and Hunsche. Later they were replaced by Eichmann. The negotiations started on April 3. The Germans started out by demanding an indemnity of two million dollars, promising in return that not a single person would be deported. Later Eichmann declared: "I cannot sell the Jews of Hungary, unless to the benefit of Germany. It is necessary that Brand be sent immediately to Istanbul to tell the Jews and the Allies that I am ready to sell a million Hungarian Jews in exchange for merchandise, in the first place transportation material. I either have them taken to Auschwitz or 'put them on cost.' If my generous offer is accepted, I shall release them all. If not, all will be gassed." In the meantime, Wisliceny went from town to town to organize ghettos. The Hungarian police and gendarmerie were everywhere at his disposal. Officially, he acted in the capacity of an "adviser" to the Hungarian government but in reality everything was done under German orders.

May 15, 1944, marked the start of mass and total deportations. On the eve of the departure of the first convoy, all hospitalized, newly born, blind, deaf, mentally diseased and arrested Jews were transferred to the ghettos. Then 80 to 100 persons were placed in every sealed boxcar. At Kassa, the SS took over the convoys from the Hungarian gendarmes, but not before many of the victims were ruthlessly tortured by the latter under the pretext of searching for valuables. Thousands died en route, and many hundreds committed suicide. The Hungarian press and radio failed even to mention these developments. Abroad, the government published denials of "alleged mistreatment" of Jews.

Between June 5 and 6, Eichmann declared to me: "We undertook vis-à-vis the Hungarians that not one single Jew shall return alive." The Pope and the King of Sweden made representations to Horthy. President Roosevelt launched an appeal which closely resembled an ultimatum, urging the Hungarian government to put an end to the brutal persecution of the Jews. As a result, Horthy stopped the deportation of the Jews of Budapest, scheduled for July 5. Since this decision provoked protests on the part of Endre, Baky and the Germans, another 30,000 Jews were soon deported from the Trans-Danubian region. Also the farther environment of Budapest was emptied of Jews. On the order of Horthy, Endre was removed from office. By this time almost all the Jews of Greater Hungary (except for those of Budapest) had been sent out of the country to their death. Nevertheless, Endre (in an unofficial capacity), Baky and the Germans continued to make every effort to have the Jews of Budapest, too, exterminated. At this time, Liberators started bombing Budapest and the railway centers serving the deportation convoys. To prevent a planned Nazi *coup d'etat*, Horthy ordered the army and the gendarmerie, which were still loyal to him, to Budapest. This prevented the deportations from Budapest starting. But Eichmann managed to have 1,700 Budapest Jews, detained at the Kistarcsa camp near Budapest, dispatched toward Auschwitz. At Horthy's order, this convoy was stopped at the frontier and the prisoners were returned to camp. Three days later, Eichmann repeated the same manoeuvre before the Regent could be informed of the fact.

On July 15,1944, the German Ambassador Veesenmayer presented an ultimatum to the foreign minister of Hungary demanding the deportation of the Jews of Budapest. In its answer, dated July 27, the Hungarian government indicated its readiness to transfer these Jews from the capital to the extent justified by requirements of military security, but exclusively to areas within Hungarian territory. Soon the military successes of the Allies reinforced the position of the Hungarian government vis-à-vis the Germans. As a result, the new prime minister, General Lakatos, sent a note to the German government demanding the recall of Eichmann and his staff, the release to the Hungarian authorities of the camps of internment controlled by the Germans, and the liberation of Hungarian politicans and army officers held in captivity in Germany.

On August 25, Veesenmayer informed the Hungarian government that in accordance with instructions he had received from Himmler, satisfaction would be given to these Hungarian demands.

However, on October 15, 1944, a *coup d'état* carried out by the Germans in Hungary put an end to the regime of Horthy, and power passed into the hands of the Arrow Cross Nazi leader Szalasi. On October 17, Eichmann returned to Budapest by airplane and immediately ordered

> the Arrow Cross Party and the police to proceed with the deportation of all Jews in the capital who were concentrated in buildings marked by the yellow Star of David. Some 25,000 persons, mostly women, were forced to march on foot, in rain and snow, without food, the 160 kilometers to the Austrian border. Thousands of them expired en route, and many more died in Austria from exhaustion and dysentery. . . .
>
> On December 8, 1944, the deportations finally ended. They could have ended somewhat earlier, because Himmler had given orders to Eichmann to stop them. However, as he had told Wisliceny, Eichmann refused to carry out this order until he obtained written instructions to this effect, emanating from Himmler in person.
>
> Between November 1944 and February 11, 1945, the murder gangs of the Arrow Cross Party conducted a ceaseless manhunt against the Jews of Budapest, especially against those who had tried to hide under false identities. In the course of the last two months, 10,000 to 15,000 Jews were shot to death on the banks of the Danube, or in the open streets. Many thousands perished in the ghettos of disease, hunger and air attacks.

In these tragic days certain patriotic Hungarian military leaders were secretly planning to arm the Jewish labor battalions and concentrate them around Budapest as a defense force. Negotiations toward this end took place between Generals William Nagy and William Schroeder on one side, and on the other the Committee of Jewish War Veterans, headed by Dr. Bela Fabian, former M.P., with Margrave George Pallavicini serving as liaison. The overnight occupation of Hungary by the Wehrmacht put a stop to this attempt.

The almost 100,000 Jews of Budapest owed their lives to the halting of deportations by Horthy, a step taken following protests by President Roosevelt, supported by the interventions of the Pope and King Gustaf of Sweden.

Neutral Sweden was particularly energetic in saving Jewish lives in Hungary, through the heroic activities of the late Raoul Wallenberg, one of the noblest humanitarians in history. After the Soviet occupation of Budapest, Wallenberg disappeared without a trace.

Under the German occupation 105,453 Jews from Budapest and 512,554 Jews from the provinces lost their lives, or a total of 618,007 (including Christians of Jewish origin) in wartime Greater Hungary.[4] Levai estimated that on December 31, 1945, by which date most of the surviving deported Jews had already returned to Hungary, 96,500 professing Jews were living in Budapest and about 45,000 in the provincial localities. The total number of the surviving population of Jewish faith in reduced postwar Hungary was therefore about 141,500. It will be recalled that the number for 1941 was about 401,000. Nearly two-thirds of the professing Jewish population of lesser Hungary perished, the overwhelming majority between May 15 and December 31, 1944.

CHAPTER II

Liberation

On March 19, 1944, in spite of Hungary's occupation by the Wehrmacht, hope that the bulk of Hungarian Jewry would be preserved seemed justified. The Red Army at this time was already at the Kolomya-Lvov line, eighty miles away from the northeastern frontier of Hungary and within close range of the densely populated Jewish centers of Sighet, Munkacs, Ungvar, and Huszt. An attack against the northeastern Carpathians by armies under the command of Soviet Marshals Malinovski and Tolbuchin in the spring of 1944 might have resulted in the surrender of all Hungarian troops of anti-Nazi sentiment (who might then have fought against the Germans), the capitulation of Regent Horthy, and the saving in the nick of time of the Hungarian Jews.

Instead, for strategic reasons, the Red Army moved against Rumania, on the southeastern side of the Carpathians. King Michael of Rumania concluded an armistice with the Allies and turned his intact armies against the Germans on August 23, 1944. With the help of the Royal Rumanian Army, Malinovski's troops marched through Transylvania, reached the Hungarian Plain, and at the beginning of October 1944 took Szeged on the southeastern frontier, the second largest city of Hungary. In two months the whole of eastern Hungary was captured by the Red Army. After the failure on October 15 of Horthy's abortive attempt at an armistice, a Hungarian government was established in Debrecen in November 1944.

All this, however, came six months too late for the Jews of Hungary. The Russian forces found only those relatively few Hungarian Jews who had been in hiding, or had escaped to Rumania before the Germans, or who were in slave-labor battalions not carried off to German-held territory.

War and strategy are of course seldom influenced by humanitarian considerations. But the utter lack of interest of the Soviet Union in the fate of the Hungarian Jews is sufficiently indicated by the fact that it did not even bother to protest to the Hungarian government the deportations of Jews, leaving such matters entirely to the Western powers, although the Soviet Union considered Hungary its own exclusive field of operations.

In December 1944 the belt of the besiegers around Budapest closed; Pest, on the eastern bank of the Danube, was liberated in January 1945, and Buda, on the western bank, in February, after one of the bloodiest battles of the Second World War. It was not until April 4, 1945, that the whole of Hungary was cleared of Nazi troops. Thirty-five days later the German Army surrendered unconditionally. May 9 saw the liberation of those remnants of Hungarian Jewry who were still alive in the different extermination and labor camps in Germany, Austria, and Poland.

Owing to the chaotic state of the transportation system at the end of the war and the enfeebled condition of most of the deportees, months passed before all the survivors who wished to return were able to do so. During the summer and fall of 1945 a stream of returning or repatriated Jews poured in from every direction. By November 1945 most of the able-bodied survivors had returned to their homes, with the exception of those who had decided not to return at all, or who were kept from returning by the Russian authorities.

The Western Allies (including the Czechoslovak) authorities proved helpful and conscientious in their handling of the survivors' problems. They were treated like free men, given food, clothing, and medical care, and looked after by Jewish chaplains of the American, British, and French forces. They were free to go back to their former homes or to stay where they were. All means of transportation were placed at the disposal of those wishing to be repatriated. All survivors were registered and their names and places of origin published. In many cases, as in Dachau, Gunskirchen, and Belsen, the German population was ordered to do the household work for the sick survivors of the camps. Thousands in ill health were invited by the Swedish government to Sweden to recuperate.

The fate of those whose bondage to the Nazis was ended by the arrival of the Red Army was not so uniformly good. The Red Army's orders as to the treatment of Jews were not clear. Treatment differed according to the interpretation and attitude of the lower grades of officers. The general directives prohibited all discrimination against ethnic groups. This was interpreted by many officers to mean that no distinction was to be made between Jew and Nazi, between yesterday's slave and his slave driver. This became apparent in the very first weeks of the liberation of Hungarian territory. All prisoners were transported to camps in Russia, usually via Rumania. Huge transit camps were established in Szeged, Timisoara, Târgu Jiu, Focsani, and Corbeni. Hundreds of former slave laborers fortunate enough to be liberated by the Rumanian army, reported to Jewish organizations in the Rumanian capital and to representatives of the International Red Cross that those of their comrades taken prisoners by Soviet Russian units had been sent to prisoner-of-war camps in Rumania, preliminary to their being sent to Russia.

Attempts by Jewish organizations in Bucharest to liberate Jews from the Russian camp at Focsani had no result. Jewish prisoners who died in the transit camp of Timisoara were not permitted religious interment by the local rabbinate. In June 1947, Stalin at the personal request of the Hungarian Communist leader Mathias Rakosi, agreed to release 50,000 Hungarian prisoners of war. Among them were a few less than 1,000 Jews. The official bulletin of the Central Board of Hungarian Jews published an interview with four of these released Jewish prisoners. Three of them had been taken prisoner on Hungarian territory in October 1944; it was not until 1947 that they were set free!

Even many women "liberated" by the Red Army units were sent to prisoners' camps in Russia if the officer in command "had no orders." More than two years after the armistice, on May 25, 1947, the Jewish Telegraphic Agency reported the following from Budapest:

> A report that about 10,000 Hungarian Jewish women were rescued by the Red Army from German concentration camps and are now in the Soviet Union, was published here by the [pro-Communist] weekly newspaper *Figyeloe*. The writer of the article, Ethel Faludi, who recently returned from the USSR, says that the women are receiving excellent care and are recuperating from the harsh physical conditions in the Nazi camp. She writes that they are now housed in a camp at Motynski.

Before the publication of this news item no official report had been received from Soviet authorities about these women, nor had any of their relatives received mail from them. The news of their existence came as a complete surprise to Hungarian Jews in 1947.

Up to the present, no official report has been obtained from Soviet authorities on the number and names of the former Hungarian Jewish slave laborers who were taken prisoner by the Red Army.

The Jews of Budapest also suffered as a result of some Soviet officers' interpretation of the "no discrimination" order. Among the thousands of civilians who under the pretext of being requisitioned for public work were carried off first to Gödöllö and Szeged and then to Russia—by way of the chain of Russian camps in Rumania already mentioned—were many Jews.[1]

Jews in Soviet Labor Camps

Before attempting to estimate the number of Hungarian Jewish slave laborers carried off to Russia, we must first estimate how many such slave laborers there were in general. A report by George Gergely on his negotiations, in October 1944, with Horthy's military adviser, Brigadier General Charles Lazar, commander of the Budapest Army Corps, is very valuable here. Horthy then was preparing to bid for an armistice; in his search for reliable anti-Nazi troops he toyed with the idea of arming such Jewish forced laborers as were available. In his report dated October 4, 1944 (ten days before Horthy's armistice proclamation), Gergely wrote:

> Today I went to the Fortress where I was received by Brigadier General of the Guard Charles Lazar. . . . I submitted to him in an envelope a list of 520 slave labor battalions as compiled by the Jewish Veterans Federation. The list contained the number of the battalions and their locations. He opened the envelope in my presence, and after being asked certain questions by him I was compelled to acknowledge that the list was not complete.[2]

The smallest number of men constituting a labor battalion was 250; the largest number, especially after the German occupation, was in the neighborhood of 700. Accordingly, the number of Jews in these 520 labor battalions (and there were admittedly more than 520) could not have been less than 130,000 and was certainly as much as 150,000, of whom 80,000 were in Hungary at the time of the German invasion and 70,000 were outside the country (most of the latter being with the Hungarian army in Russia).

We get the same figures by a reverse method of reckoning. It will be recalled that the total number of Jews in Greater Hungary in 1941 was 725,007; the estimated number of Christians of Jewish origin ("non-Aryans") was 100,000; yielding a total of 825,000 Jews in the sense of the antisemitic laws. Of these the number of Budapest Jews and "non-Aryans" was 246,803.[3] After the last deportation of Jews from the countryside, Lieutenant Colonel Ferenczy of the Gendarmerie, who was in charge of the operation, reported that 434,351 Jews had been deported in 147 trains.[4]

TABLE III

Jews in Hungary, July 1944

Category		No.
Original Number of Jews and Non Aryans		825,007
Deported from Countryside, July 1944	434,351	
In Budapest, not deported as of July 1944	246,803	
Total Accounted For		681,154
Remainder Unaccounted For		143,853

The remainder of 143,853 represents those Jews who were not deported but pressed into the labor battalions. (The figure 143,853 of course includes 20,000 people massacred in Kamenets-Podolski, 1,000 massacred in Ujvidék, and 5,000 who escaped to foreign territories.)[5]

What became of these people?

The number of forced laborers liberated on (Greater) Hungarian territory did not exceed 20,000. The number of those killed in the Ukraine by the Germans before the retreat in early 1943 from Voronyesh was about 10,000.[6] There are no reliable figures available on the number of former slave laborers in the total of 121,500 Jews who had returned to the territory of Greater Hungary from the camps by the end of 1945, but more than 50 per cent of these were women.

The problem of former Jewish slave laborers who were held as prisoners of war in Russia was dealt with at a meeting on October 28, 1946, of the National Association of Hungarian Jews (MAZOT). Max Domonkos, secretary of the Jewish Community of Pest, stated that there were still "approximately 25,000" former Jewish forced laborers of Hungarian nationality (apparently not including those from the formerly annexed territories who were of Rumanian, Czechoslovak, and Yugoslav nationality) in the Soviet Union as prisoners of war. Domonkos added that according to information obtained from official quarters, "part of these prisoners had been assigned, on the basis of work contracts valid for one to two years, to agricultural establishments and factories in the Soviet Union; hence they were under an obligation to stay on until these contracts expired. The official representative organs of Hungarian Jewry obtained additional information to the effect that even forced laborers whose work contracts had already expired were in many cases prevented from returning home because their funds were exhausted."[7]

This figure of 25,000, and the aforementioned 10,000 Hungarian Jewish women held in Russia, indicate that at the end of 1946 there were at least 35,000 Hungarian Jews in Soviet prisoner-of-war camps. *Uj Elet* published the names of all Jewish prisoners as they were released from Russian captivity. Up to August 1949, the number of these, as reported by *Uj Elet*, did not exceed 2,000. The fate of the rest is unknown. In its issue of February, 1953, the *National Jewish Monthly* published an account of an interview held in Paris with Zoltan Klar, former president of the Social Federation of Hungarian Jews. Klar asserted that he possessed documents which proved that 30,000 Hungarian Jews who had been forcibly sent to Russia had never returned; he added that undoubtedly most of them were dead. "When I came home to Budapest in May, 1945 [from the Mauthausen camp]," he declared, "we formed, together with Grand Rabbi, Francis Hevesi, the Social Federation of Hungarian Jews which had as its first object the repatriation of Hungarian Jews. The Federation sent to Gynla Szekfu, the Hungarian Minister in Moscow, the names of several thousand Hungarian Jews who had been sent to Siberia by the Russians. Mr. Szekfu subsequently confirmed that there were 30,000 such victims in Siberian camps. All his attempts to have these people repatriated failed. The Hungarian Communists refused to appropriate any money for this purpose."

Chapter III

The Survivors

More than 60,000 of the Jews who had been crowded into the narrow confines of Budapest's ghetto were rescued after the last attempts of the Nazis to blow it up had failed. There were about 25,000 Jewish survivors in the country who had been sheltered by Christians. There was another group, also numbering about 20-25,000 (the so-called "protected Jews"), who possessed letters of protection issued by the Papal Nuncio and the Swiss, Spanish, Swedish, and El Salvador legations. Most of these "protected Jews" escaped deportation by Szalasi's gangs. About 40,000 survivors of the labor battalions and Nazi camps returned by the end of October 1945. Of course, these groups were not distinctly marked off from each other. There were many escaped slave laborers among those hiding with non-Jews and among the "protected." Many in the ghetto also received letters of protection.

In 1946, a year after liberation, there were, according to the official census, 96,500 adherents of the Jewish religion living in Budapest, and 47,124 in the countryside. (Hungary, by the cession of the territories it had annexed from Czechoslovakia, Rumania, and Yugoslavia, was now reduced to its pre-Second World War dimensions.) A comparison with the figures of 1941 shows the extent of Hungarian Jewry's losses.

TABLE IV

ADHERENTS OF THE JEWISH RELIGION, 1941, 1946

Year	Budapest	Countryside	Total
1941	184,453	216,527	400,980
1946	96,500	47,124	143,624
Loss	87,953	169,403	257,356

There are no statistical data available on Christians of Jewish origin, as all racial laws were abrogated after the war. It is estimated that 30,000 such "non-Aryans" perished.

In Czechoslovakia, Yugoslavia, and Rumania no separate census was taken after the war of the Jewish populations of the territories that had been annexed by Hungary in 1940. Only a rough estimate can be made of the number of survivors of the 324,027 Jews living in those areas before March 19, 1944.

Czechoslovakia. The Carpatho-Ukraine (called Carpatho-Russia by the Czechs), taken from Czechoslovakia by Hungary at the beginning of the war, was annexed by Soviet Russia at the end. After this last annexation, all the surviving 8,500 Jews left the province, most of them going to Czechoslovakia. The number of former slave laborers who came back with the army was around 4,000. Of the Jews of southern Slovakia, about 12,000 survived. Thus the total number of Jewish survivors of Czechoslovak territories seized by Hungary is around 25,000.

Yugoslavia. At least 60 per cent of the estimated surviving Jewish population of Yugoslavia,[1] or about 6,000 people, may have come from the areas ceded to Hungary. The list of re-established Jewish communities in Yugoslavia supports this estimate.

Rumania. About 20,000 of the Jews of northern Transylvania—the part of Rumania ceded to Hungary in 1940—were able to escape to Rumania after the German invasion of Hungary. There, if caught, they were put into detention camps by the Antonescu regime. They were released after Rumania came over to the Allied side on August 23, 1944. The number of those who returned from forced labor and Nazi camps was 45,000. The total number of surviving Jews of northern Transylvania was therefore 65,000.

Thus the number of survivors of the Jewish population of the territories annexed by Hungary in 1940 (not including survivors in Displaced Persons camps who refused to return to their homes and not including former slave laborers in Russian captivity) may be estimated as follows: Czechoslovakia 25,000; Yugoslavia 6,000; Rumania 65,000; total 96,000.

Ninety-six thousand survived of a population numbering 324,027 in 1941. These, plus the 143,624 survivors of the Jewish population of present-day Lesser Hungary, make a total of 239,624 survivors for Greater Hungary from a former population of 725,007 in 1941.

In the Jewish population of postwar Hungary, there were only 7,712 children under the age of 14, or roughly one child to every 20 adults; whereas there were 27,256 Jews over 60 years of age, or every fifth member of the community. Of the Jewish survivors under the age of 16 outside of Budapest, 31 per cent had lost one and 12 per cent both parents. In Budapest, 60 per cent of the surviving Jewish children had lost one or both parents. There were 1,500 female to every 1,000 male survivors in Budapest. The percentage of Jewish widowers in Budapest was 65; of widows, 70.[2]

In 1944, before the deportations, 170,582 of the Jews in the countryside lived in villages and smaller townships, and only 45,945 in provincial towns. In 1946, 39,270 of the 47,124 Jews in the countryside were living in 14 of the larger towns. Thus 6/7ths of the entire postwar Jewish population of Hungary were residents of urban communities.

In the days of persecution the entire Jewish population of Hungary were driven from their homes, except for inhabitants of the eighteen blocks of the ghetto in Budapest. Their houses were pillaged and the rest of their movables "sold by auction" to members of the Nazi party. The assets of Jewish communities were distributed by the Hungarian Nazis among their groups. Synagogues, where not demolished, were used as stables. Only fourteen synagogues survived more or less undamaged.

After the war it proved impossible to revive 474 of the 732 prewar religious congregations, as the number of their surviving members who returned was less than 10. In the capital and in 14 leading cities of the countryside, 35 congregations were functioning with a total membership of 117,500 men, women, and children. The remaining 26,124 Jews, living in villages and small towns, re-established 225 congregations.

Of 732 rabbis, 588 perished. Of the surviving 144, 64 were orthodox (17 in Budapest and 47 in the countryside), and 80 belonged to Congressional and Status Quo groups (44 in Budapest and 36 in the provinces).

The following provincial towns had a Jewish population of over 1000: Miskolcz 2,353; Makó 1,123; Szeged 2,332; Debrecen 4,640; Ujpest 1,096; Nyíregyháza 1,210; total 12,754.

The following table compares the number of Jewish children attending Hungarian schools in 1942/43, the last complete school year preceding the deportations, with the number of Jewish children attending Hungarian schools in the first complete school year after the war, 1946/47.

TABLE V

JEWISH CHILDREN ATTENDING HUNGARIAN SCHOOLS, 1942-43, 1946-47

Type of School	1942-32	1946-47
Elementary	57,931	807
General	—	4,880
"Civic" (lower secondary)	10,436	614
Gymnasium	9,616	2,065
Technical high	372	320
Commercial high	553	155
Total	78,908	8,841

The prewar Jewish community in Hungary maintained the following all-day Jewish schools (Yeshivahs and Talmud Torahs not included): Elementary 175; "Civic" 6; Gymnasia 4; Teachers seminaries 2; total 187.

Immediately after the war every effort was made to reorganize the Jewish school system. Jewish parents were reluctant, especially in the provinces, to send their children to school with non-Jewish children because of the widespread antisemitism among the young. Table VI shows the Jewish schools functioning in 1946-47.

TABLE VI

JEWISH SCHOOLS IN HUNGARY, 1946-47

Type of School	Number	Teachers	Pupils
Gymnasia	3	174	3,495
Technical high	2	54	831
Teachers seminaries	1	52	281
Elementary, general, and "civic"	42	5	35
Total	36	285	4,642

More than half of the Jewish children of the provinces between the ages of 6 and 14, because they were scattered about, had to go to non-Jewish schools.

Table VII shows the distribution, among the chief occupations, of gainfully employed Jews in Budapest at the end of 1945.

The most striking feature of this table is the 51,299 gainfully employed out of a total population of 96,500. Of the 45,201 Jews not employed, 7,451 were children under the age of 14, and 24,001 were people over the age of 60. As a rule there was no more than one dependent, if that many, to every gainfully employed person in the capital, a fact which bespeaks the terrible losses suffered by the Jewish family.

Another important feature is the high percentage of those engaged in commerce or as "independents" in industry—more than 45 per cent of all gainfully employed Jewish persons, as against only 38.4 per cent in 1930 for the entire country. There are no exact statistics available on the occupational distribution of Jews outside Budapest; it is evident, however, that among these the percentage engaged in commerce and in industries of their own was considerably higher.

TABLE VII

DISTRIBUTION OF BUDAPEST JEWS BY INDUSTRY AND OCCUPATION, 1945

Industry or Occupation	Independent	Non-manual employees	Manual employees	Total
Agriculture	165	12	105	282
Industry	8,840	3,940	9,462	22,242
Commerce	9,173	2,300	3,213	14,686
Finance	62	523	26	611
Transport	194	59	161	445
Public service	......	878	851	1,729
Liberal professions	2,949	1,261	......	4,210
Functionaries of institutions	......	932	......	932
Armed forces	......	101	274	375
Unskilled laborers	......	......	692	692
Pensioners	......	1,311	1,658	2,969
Rentiers	417	......	......	417
Domestic servants	......	......	326	326
Other	......	145	277	422
Unknown	......	331	630	961
Total	21,800	11,793	17,675	51,299

Chapter IV

Postwar Reconstruction: The First Period

The Democratic National Provisional Government was established in Debrecen in November 1944 and a National Assembly was called together. The National Assembly consisted of members of the parties forced underground by the Arrow Cross Nazis: Smallholders, National Peasants, Social Democrats, Democrats, and Communists. The Cabinet was presided over by General Bela Miklos, former commander of the Hungarian army, who had surrendered to the Russians. The local instruments of the government were the National Committees, consisting of local representatives of the above-named parties.

Hungary was under occupation. The highest authority was the Allied Control Commission, made up of an American, British, and Russian military commander; the latter—none other than Marshal Voroshilov—being chairman of the commission. All of the country more than 100 kilometers behind the front line (in Austria) was placed under the authority of the Hungarian government, the 100 kilometer zone (i.e., western Hungary) remaining under the military administration of the Red Army of Occupation. The presence of this occupation power was decisive.

The behavior of the Russian troops belied their claim to being liberators. Pillage and rape were the rule everywhere in the country. The amount of property confiscated was enormous. Livestock was carried off to Russia in great caravans; farmers were often afraid to cultivate their land. The transportation system was in ruins, and a rapidly intensifying shortage of food, fuel, and raw materials made itself felt. After the very bad harvest of 1945 the country plunged over the brink of starvation.

It was to Debrecen, seat of the Provisional Government, that the few thousand liberated Jews came. Most of them were former slave laborers, people who had been in hiding, or who had just returned from Rumania. Here they organized the Association of Jews in Hungary. Their president, Eugene Leitner, was invited to become a member of the National Assembly, as a representative of the Civic Democratic Party—an old political party founded by such Jews as William Vazsonyi and representing the lower-middle class and intellectuals.

The Association of Jews in Hungary had no program or orientation with regard to problems of Jewish life; it did not pretend to represent either the Jewish religious denominations or a Jewish national minority. It was merely the spokesman of the Jewish collectivity, advocating the abolition of antisemitic legislation and the restitution of the rights of the liberated Jews. It also established contacts with representatives of international Jewish organizations in Bucharest.

Soon after the liberation of Budapest the Debrecen government sent its first emissary to the city in the person of a commissar of food supply. Hunger was acute in the capital. Such necessities as bread and milk were simply unobtainable. The Jewish population, which had just left the ghetto, suffered most. In the latter part of March 1945, Budapest's mayor approached representatives of the Jewish Burial Society (Chevra Kadisha), urging them to do something about a situation in which fifty people out of every one hundred dying in the capital were Jews. Most to suffer from this famine were children just released from the ghetto. In one single apartment house in what used to be the ghetto, thirty-five Jewish children died of hunger in the first two months after liberation.

These conditions necessitated prompt action by the representatives of American Jewry in Bucharest. Offices of the Joint Distribution Committee and HIAS were established in two western border towns of Rumania, Arad and Timisoara; from there food supplies were sent to Budapest. The surrender of the German forces on May 9, 1945, opened the way for supplies direct from the West.

In the following months more than 85 per cent of the capital's Jewish population was fed in public kitchens established by the JDC. Arrangements for the reception of Jews returning from deportation were organized by the National Jewish Relief Board and the National Board for the Care of Deportees, both Hungarian Jewish organizations serving as distributing agencies for the JDC.

Restitution

Restitution was a vital matter, for the destitute and ragged Jewish survivors found their homes occupied by favorites of the Nazi regime, their property scattered or destroyed, and their stores pillaged, empty, or burnt. The regular answer of the possessors of Jewish property was that it had been taken by the Germans or by the Russians, although it was common knowledge that in the countryside Jewish property had been handed out ("auctioned") among the members of the Arrow Cross Party. In many cases returning Jews had to appeal to the police in order to get back their homes and the remnants of their property. This resulted in the common identification of the police with Jewish interests, in spite of the fact that the police were only too eager to hand over such property to pro-Communist party organizations or to the Commissariat of Abandoned Property.

The Hungarian Nazis had rewarded their adherents with Jewish property. After liberation the occupying forces interned and arrested many of the local Nazi leaders. But as these were almost always identical with the possessors of Jewish goods, it was soon being whispered that the reason for their arrest was not their Nazi actions, but their possession of Jewish property.

The general devastation in Hungary called for a tremendous effort of reconstruction. Private enterprise was encouraged and Jewish merchants were invited to resume their activities as a patriotic duty. Reassurances were given even by Communist and Social Democratic leaders that private enterprise would not be curtailed. Arpad Szakasits (then Deputy Prime Minister and leader of the Social Democratic Party) on October 16, 1945, made the famous statement: "You cannot nationalize ruins."

The zenith of this policy was reached when Mathias Rakosi, the chief Communist leader, publicly upbraided his overzealous tool in the leadership of the Communist-sponsored Peasant Party for advocating the nationalization of industry. Rakosi declared that the government was interested only in one thing, the rehabilitation of the productive capacity of the nation, and he urged industrialists and merchants to carry on without fear.

They did so, in a manner which restored Hungary's economy with a speed and efficiency bordering on the miraculous. On November 26, 1945, Ann O'Hare McCormick reported to the *New York Times* from Budapest:

> That commerce is alive is largely due to the Jews. The Jews comprised one-fourth of the population, and most of the mercantile class in Budapest. . . . Only a minority of Hungarian Jews are Zionists. The majority are loyal Hungarians who desire to remain in their country and help reconstruct it. It is estimated that about 60 per cent are back, and these are the hopeful citizens of Hungary. It is impossible not to admire their courage, energy and patriotism as they clear a little space among the ruins and begin over again. "I see here," said a keen American observer of the prostrate lands of Eastern Europe, "that what this part of the world needs to get going is to resurrect the Jews. They [the Nazis] destroyed the leaven in the lump."

But already in this early period the Communist Party followed a negative policy with respect to the claims of Hungarian Jews. They flatly refused from the beginning to restore Jewish landed properties to their owners. The entire nation approved of the long overdue land reform, which distributed all landed property consisting of more than 100 cadastral yokes (100 acres). Peter Veres, leader of the pro-Communist Peasant Party, was put in charge of land distribution, which was carried out under the slogan of "the land belongs to him who tills it." No Jews were given back their lands, which had been taken from them by the Kallay government under German pressure. The land remained in the hands of those favorites of the former pro-German regimes to whom it had been given in 1941, even if, being smaller than 100 yokes, it was not subject by law to confiscation. Among 2,158 surviving former Jewish landowners, there were 1,552 whose former property was less than 100 yokes.[1]

Countless complaints and representations by Jewish organizations failed to change the situation. The then Deputy Prime Minister, Mathias Rakosi, himself of Jewish descent, reportedly answered the plea of a delegation of former Jewish small landowners for the restitution of their lands, as follows: "Jews do not till their lands. My own father owned two yokes of land, but he never worked them. The land belongs to him who tills it." Jews were put off with the explanation that taking landed property away from their present owners would create antisemitism, and that ultimately Jewish claimants would be compensated with "exchange properties" in other parts of the country. They of course never were.

The Communist Party was equally reluctant to restore homes and apartments to Jews in the cities. On March 25, 1945, in its official organ *Szabad Nép*, it "requested" Jews to show more understanding by sharing their apartments with those living in them already. In the same paper an article was published by Joseph Darvas in which he attacked Jews for "always trying to take the easier road." The shock caused by this was the greater as the same Joseph Darvas soon became a member of the cabinet, in the capacity of Minister of Construction. In most cases, Jewish apartments were occupied by Hungarian Nazis, who had moved into them after Jews were driven into the ghetto under the Sztojay regime. The Communist Party sought to obtain the votes of the rank and file of the *nyilas*, or Hungarian Nazis, by purchasing their adherence with Jewish apartments in the capital, just as it purchased it with Jewish lands in the countryside.

At the end of 1944 the Association of Jews in Hungary had already urged that a government agency with personnel appointed by the government on the recommendation of Jewish representative bodies be placed in charge of the properties of deported Jews. After long deliberation the establishment of the Commissariat of Abandoned Properties was decreed. But the order proved a heavy blow to Jews, by placing under the same management the abandoned properties of deportees and the properties of those Hungarian Nazis who had fled the country with the retreating German army. This lumping together of two widely different categories of properties made the identification and restitution of Jewish possessions even more difficult. The Commissariat had local boards in every city and district in the country; these consisted of members delegated by the political parties. The number of Jewish managers was considerable. But as they had to adhere to a policy of "no discrimination," soon the Commissariat was buying Arrow Cross sympathies with the property of deported Jews.

The abuses and mismanagement of the Commissariat led to its being described by a high government official in parliament as a dunghill.

Jews got back only the empty walls of their stores. They started from scratch, without capital, equipment or stock. Yet within a few months the ruined stores of Budapest were selling to the public again and factories were producing. The volume of production was not enough, either in agriculture or in industry, to meet the requirements of a country pillaged of all its resources, obliged to pay reparations to the Soviet Union, and burdened with the maintenance of the Red Army of Occupation.

The government began issuing paper money and inflation began. Confidence in the currency rapidly dissipated. Farmers refused to sell their produce. Workers' committees in different enterprises organized their own purchasing departments and bartered their manufactures for what they needed. Scarcely any "official" trade was left. Soon all commerce was branded "black market," the Jewish commercial population being held to blame for it.

Community Rehabilitation

The prewar central agencies of the Jewish religious denominations were revived in the form of the Central Board of Jews in Hungary (incorporating the central board of the Status Quo Ante Congregations) and the Central Bureau of Orthodox Jewish Congregations. These central agencies were recognized by the government and empowered to negotiate all problems connected with Jewish restitution. However, the Judenrat installed by the Nazis had also consisted of members of these central agencies; it was natural that they should now be distrusted by the Jewish public. In the past, moreover, they had been made up of members of the so-called Jewish aristocracy elected on the basis of an obsolete electoral system, and it was felt that they did not represent Jewish public opinion and the interests of the Jewish masses. Also, the central agencies were strongly opposed to Zionism. Since the Zionists had gained an unprecedented popular following after the war, the elimination of the old leadership was a foregone conclusion.

The Zionist groups followed the old Herzlian tactics of "conquering the community offices." In the case of the Jewish Community of Pest, the largest in Hungary and perhaps in all of Europe, they forced the resignation of the president, Samuel Stern, and under the temporary presidency of Louis Stoeckler organized a committee to prepare for holding community elections within six months. (At this time, the Zionist leadership, and the Hungarian Jews in general would have refused to believe what later developments so clearly demonstrated, namely, that Stoeckler was in reality a tool of the Communist Party working inside the Jewish community.) The Zionists themselves were represented in the leadership of the community by Albert Geyer, president of the Zionist Organization, and others. Similar changes took place in the leadership of the Orthodox community, where members of the Zionist Mizrachi obtained half of the council seats.

Full rehabilitation of the official status of the Jewish denominations was accomplished in this first period and under the Minister of Religious and Educational Affairs, Count Geza Teleki, a member of the Democratic Party. A Jewish Chaplains' Department was established in the War Ministry. A special cultural attaché was appointed to Palestine by the Ministry of Religious and Educational Affairs. Jewish religious institutions again received the same amount of state subsidies as Christian institutions. Unlike the Christian churches, the central agencies of the Jewish religious denominations were obliged to represent not only the religious interests of the Jewish population, but their claims to economic restitution and political rights as well. As there was no united central agency to represent the whole of Hungarian Jewry, this obligation was undertaken jointly by the Central Board of Jews, the Central Bureau of Orthodox Congregations, and the Zionist Organization. But as the Zionists were also members of the Central Board and of the Orthodox Central Bureau, in fact they were represented twice.

This state of affairs encouraged the organization of the Social Federation of Hungarian Jews, a body consisting of middle-class non-Zionist Jews led by Chief Rabbi Frances Hevesi, son of the late Chief Rabbi Simon Hevesi, Stephen Varannai, president of the National League of Hungarian Lawyers, Zoltan Klar, and Ernest Brody, a member of parliament. The Federation sought to unite Hungarian Jewry on the basis not of a religious but a civil rights program. It organized assistance for the needy and aged, established contact with international Jewish organizations, and fought antisemitism in collaboration with church leaders. The Federation secured Hungarian Jewry's right to hold divine services over the radio equally with other denominations, and was granted permission by the Government to publish a regular Jewish weekly newspaper. It was also to the Union that the government entrusted the distribution of clothing to former Jewish slave laborers.

At the same time the Zionist parties made great advances. Local groups of every shade of Zionist opinion were organized all over the country as well as in the capital. The Mapai, under the leadership of Bela Denes, was the strongest among the non-religious Zionist groups, including in its membership large numbers of small storekeepers and workers. Hashomer Hatzair, or Mapam, under the leadership of A. Grossman, appealed to the Jewish intellectuals disappointed with Communism. Their intellectual center was the "Borochov Circle," consisting of university students, professors, and other intellectuals. The General Zionists, under the leadership of Rabbi F. Herschkovitz, appealed to the members of the middle class. There was also a Revisionist movement, but it was branded "fascist" and opposed by the authorities. Agudath Israel also made notable progress.

Zionist work in this period laid the strongest emphasis on education. Most of the orphanages established by the JDC were under the management of Zionist groups. The Zionist School Union (Tarbuth) established a gymnasium as well as elementary schools with Hebrew as the language of instruction. A very strong movement of adult education was also started, chief emphasis being laid on the teaching of Hebrew and of Palestinian culture. The Zionist organizations encouraged strong youth movements and established agricultural and industrial training camps—Hachsharoth—to prepare their members for settlement in Palestine. Each Zionist group published its magazine, always in the form of pamphlets and under changing names so as to avoid the necessity of licensing.

A noteworthy feature of this early period was the virtual ignoring of Jewish affairs by the Communists. The party seemed intent at this early stage upon employing its Jewish members in general political work, leaving the infiltration of Jewish community life to a later stage.

A picture of Jewish life in Hungary in this period would be incomplete without a description of the vital role played by the American Jewish Joint Distribution Committee (JDC). In this initial period it undoubtedly saved Hungarian Jewry from starvation and set it on its feet. Scores of public kitchens were erected, and more than 80,000 people, almost all the survivors in Budapest, were kept alive during the terrible famine ravaging the capital. At this time Budapest was cut off from the meager supplies existing here and there in the provinces by the almost complete disruption of the transportation system. Jews in the countryside were also dependent on the food supplies and public kitchens of the American organization.

Thousands among the survivors were afflicted with serious diseases so that a large-scale health program had to be undertaken immediately. The Jewish Hospital of Budapest, one of the most important in the country, had suffered very heavy damage from bombing. It was rapidly rebuilt and re-equipped with the help of the JDC. Sanatoria for the convalescent and tubercular were established in the capital and many other places.

The work of the JDC called for a large organization with departments for food, clothing, health, children, and the provinces. Before long the number of persons employed in the administration of the JDC reached 3,000, or 6 per cent of the gainfully employed Jews of Budapest. The total amount of relief sent to Hungary by the JDC in the first postwar year was well over $10,000,000.

The religious and administrative organs and institutions, as well as the Central Boards of both the Congressional and the Orthodox communities, were also subsidized by the JDC. A special feature of the JDC's work in Hungary was the financial support it gave to non-Jewish relief organizations.

The great significance and potential moral effect of the JDC's activities in Hungary awakened the Communists to the need of placing these activities under the supervision of their own party agents. Egged on by the Jewish Section of the Communist Party, Communists in the government insisted on the appointment of commissars to the head office of the JDC to control all its transactions and activities. Their main task was to report regularly on the activities of non-Communist chiefs and employees of departments, and later to see to it that most of the funds and supplies assigned by the JDC to non-Jewish relief should be distributed by organizations approved by the Communists. The JDC was the first Jewish body in Hungary upon which Communist agents were imposed.

In spite of the fact that the Jews of Hungary had little success in regaining their property, their reappearance on the scene was strongly resented by broad strata of the Hungarian population. Later this served as one of the contributing factors to a new wave of antisemitism which was allowed by the Communists to degenerate into a series of anti-Jewish riots and pogroms.

The hostile atmosphere caused thousands of survivors who came back in a vain search for family and home to decide to return to the Displaced Persons camps in Germany and Austria.

Joseph Schwartz, European director of the JDC, after a visit to Hungary, testified as follows before the Anglo-American Committee of Inquiry on Palestine:

> I happened to be in Hungary when Mr. Bevin said he would want the Jews to stay in European countries and help to rebuild their economy. The reaction that I noted among Hungarian Jews was something like this: We have been persecuted; we have been shoved into concentration camps; we have been deported; we have been treated as aliens; even though we were patriotic. Now the time has finally come when we must act and live in our own interest, when we must build something which will mean a future existence for us; when, if we lose, we lose with people whom we understand, with people whom we love.

When asked by Sir John Singleton "If conditions improved in Europe, would not the number of those wishing to emigrate be reduced?" Dr. Schwartz answered:

> The unprecedented catastrophe which happened to European Jewry has left such profound after-effects that it would take a very long time —and much more than the promulgation of laws and decrees—to make Eastern Europe livable for Jews again. These people prefer even an unsettled Palestine to their present homes.[2]

Chapter V

A Losing Struggle

According to the Yalta and armistice agreements, all liberated countries were to hold elections to decide in a democratic manner the lines along which they wished to develop as free nations.

Hungary was the Eastern European country upon which the Communists centered their highest hopes for receiving a mandate from the population for establishment of a Soviet regime. These hopes were based chiefly on the fact that Hungary was the only country of Eastern Europe in which Communism had ever seized power, in 1919. Communist leaders believed that they had the support of the industrial workers. And following the agrarian reform, in the course of which all the great estates were distributed among over half a million landless peasant families, they felt sure of obtaining the support of the peasant population as well. So it was that the only free and democratic postwar election to be held in all of Soviet-controlled Eastern Europe (with the exception of Czechoslovakia) took place in Hungary.

It shows how confident the Hungarian Communists were that, unlike their colleagues in the other satellite states, they did not press for a united list of all parties. They felt that with the Social Democrats they would win the majority of the popular vote. But in the municipal elections in industrial Budapest, held in advance of the general elections, the "Workers' Unity" slate of Communists and Social Democrats, despite the assistance given it by the Red Army, was signally defeated by the democratic Smallholders Party, which received more votes than all the other parties combined.

A month later, at the national elections of November 4, 1945, the Smallholders won 57 per cent of the total vote. After the Budapest defeat, the Social Democrats had refused to run on a common list with the Communists; each of the two parties received 17 per cent of the vote. The rest were divided between the National Peasant and Civic Democratic parties.

Thus the majority of seats in parliament was won by the Smallholders. The presence of the Russian army made it impossible to form a government without the participation of the Communist minority; the Communists immediately took control of the Ministry of the Interior, which had jurisdiction over the all-important police.

The "Jewish question" was no issue in these elections. The only party which betrayed antisemitic tendencies, and which had no Jewish members, was the Communist-sponsored National Peasant Party, which failed in the elections.

Jews were elected on the slates of each of the three major parties. Among the Jews elected on the Smallholder Party's list were Edmund Antl, president of the Kaposvér Jewish congregation, Michael Borsa, and Alfred Offner. There were also a number of baptized Jews, such as Victor Chornoky, son-in-law of Pastor Zoltan Tildy, the Smallholder Party's president. In the leadership of the Social Democratic Party were a large number of Jews and baptized Jews, such as Manuel Buchinger, Paul Justus, Nicholas Kertesz, Stephen Ries, Francis Szeder, and Ladislas Farago.

The relatively large proportion of Jews in the Moscow-trained top leadership of the Communist Party was one of the secondary reasons for that party's unpopularity. It seemed to substantiate the Nazi propaganda's identification of Communism and Jewry. In their bid for popular backing the Communist leaders felt it more and more advisable to compromise with this anti-Jewish mood. Jewish Communists leaned backwards in all matters involving Jews, including even the action taken against antisemitic riots and pogroms.

Hungarian Jewry had been without a licensed press organ of its own since the liberation. Not until after the elections and the entry into office of Prime Minister Zoltan Tildy of the Smallholders was a license granted for the publication of a Jewish weekly, *Uj Elet*. *Uj Elet* proved in this early period to be an outspoken champion of the interests of Hungarian Jewry; it regularly attacked the government's hostile or procrastinating attitude toward questions of Jewish rehabilitation and faithfully tried to represent all major shades of opinion within the community.

Attitudes of the parties making up the government toward the Jewish question differed markedly. As we have mentioned, it was the Communist Party's *Szabad Nép* that published, on March 25, 1945, the first article in the daily press on the Jewish question. In this article by Joseph Darvas the Communist attitude on this question was defined according to the rule that "no one may claim privileges on the basis of former sufferings." In its third issue *Uj Elet* published an interview with Joseph Darvas who, after stating that he had never been an antisemite, declared as follows:

> Noticing the symptoms of the new antisemitism, I felt that I had to say a "sincere word" [the title of his article in *Szabad Nép*] on this matter, a word addressed to all concerned. Thus, among others, I also had to address myself to those elements of Jewry who by their behavior are contributing to the growth of the new antisemitism. In my article

I dealt with those elements who could not and would not learn the lessons of the horrible tragedy, and who wish to go on from where they left off. . . . These elements instead of joining the work of liquidation of the past and of the upbuilding of democracy, a task which *demands* equal *sacrifices* from everybody, are devoting their energies to the rapid advancement, by any means, of their own personal fortunes. They wish to regain, in a few weeks or months, everything they lost. But as we must judge every person . . . by the yardstick of his work for democracy alone, we cannot but employ the same yardstick for the Jews as well. It is therefore impermissible that anybody should claim special treatment for himself on the ground of the sufferings he underwent in the past. . . . Those who want to live and prosper in the easy way, *we have to force back* to productive work. I know very well that black-marketeers and "speculators" are not to be found exclusively among Jews. . . . But I am prepared to judge only by the criterion of the individual's participation in the creation of the new democracy. . . .[1]

The Smallholders in the government, on the other hand, did not regard Jews claiming restitution of their property as pleaders for "special privileges." Under Secretary to the Prime Minister, Father Stephen Balogh, addressing a mass meeting of Jews in the Royal Theatre on November 25, 1945, stated:

The fact that a representative of the Hungarian government, who represents the person of Prime Minister Zoltan Tildy as well, is here with you, is proof of two things: first, that the Hungarian government wholly condemns everything that was done in the past against Hungarian Jewry; and second, that it wishes to demonstrate the democratic Hungarian government's determination to do everything in its power to rehabilitate and indemnify Jewry for the multitude of injuries and injustice to which it was subjected. That is why we abrogated a whole series of decrees, and did our best to reinstate all the rights and privileges of Jews as human beings and citizens of the state. The government has not yet accomplished this task; it knows that it still has many obligations in this field—and it will fulfil these obligations. To a degree, however, the government must ask for patience, not because we lack goodwill but because we lack the material means necessary to bring about full material and moral rehabilitation. . . . It is my conviction that . . . we will rebuild this country much more speedily than expected, and reinstate to every Hungarian—Jew and non-Jew alike— the full possession of the rights and middle-class well-being to which he was accustomed. The Hungarian government does not wish to interfere with the endeavors of any section of Jewry. [This was a reference to the Zionists.] One thing is beyond doubt; the events of the past will never occur again. And if Jews will remain here in the future, they will be treated by every Hungarian as brothers and citizens of equal rank and right.[2]

Revival of Jewish Life

The government realized that Jewish organizations in the West would make their influence felt at the peace conference, and would try to validate Jewish claims to restitution and indemnification, as well as to freedom of assembly, culture, and the right of emigration. The Jews of Hungary were animated by the same expectation. Out of this feeling came an unprecedented upsurge in Jewish public life. The winter of 1945-46 witnessed a vigorous revival of Jewish activities; Talmud Torahs were opened in all cities and in all districts of Budapest. In the Jewish schools providing a general education, Hebrew, replacing the traditional German and the Communist-sponsored Russian, was required to be studied as a modern language. Hebrew elementary schools and two gymnasia were opened under the aegis of the Zionist Tarbuth School Board; all subjects were taught in Hebrew. Yeshivahs were reopened in Hüvösvölgy, Hajduhadház, Szombathely, Bonyhád, Paks, and Makó. The rabbinical seminary of Budapest, which for so many years had trained rabbis for the Congressional denomination, opened again; its student body was made up mostly of those whose studies had been interrupted by the arrival of the Germans. In the first two years after the liberation nineteen rabbis were ordained. However, the number of those registering as new students in the seminary decreased markedly. This was also true of the Jewish Teachers Institute, where the total number of students did not exceed thirty-five.

Religious congregations organized again in all districts of the capital, as well as in a number of provincial towns. The Jewish sports clubs resumed their activities, especially in the capital, where there were the old-established VAC (Fencing and Athletic Club) and the recently organized Zionist club, Hapoel. The Jewish Agricultural Society was also revived and its model farm on the outskirts of Budapest reopened.

To the postwar Jewish schools went 48 per cent of all Jewish children in the country. In the rural districts only Jewish elementary schools were functioning. In the capital, except for the schools of the Orthodox community, the entire system of Jewish education was placed under a new Inspector of Schools, Andrew Gellert, a leading member of the K'lal (General Zionist) group. As a result of thorough instruction in Jewish history and Hebrew language and literature, most of the students became members of Zionist youth groups.

The doors of the universities, partly closed to Jews since the *numerus clausus* established in 1920, were now opened. (This freedom, however, lasted only a short time; in 1948 the Communist requirement of plebeian descent again barred large numbers of Jews from acquiring a higher education.)

In April 1946 the HICEM-HIAS organization opened offices in Budapest. In the absence of legal emigration (owing in part to Hungary's having no diplomatic contacts with other countries and no consulates abroad, and in part to the fact that the Hungarian government could not issue passports without the permission in each and every case of the Russian chairman of the Allied Control Commission), it was principally engaged in bringing members of families scattered around the world into touch with one another. This was all the more important as the Hungarian post office could not yet deliver mail to all countries.

The Hungarian B'nai B'rith Lodge also was established at this time on the initiative of Chief Rabbi Francis Hevesi. It submitted its by-laws to the Hungarian Ministry of the Interior for approval and engaged in important cultural and charitable work. It also took the first steps toward forming a national interfaith Board of Social Reconciliation which was initiated on the non-Jewish side by a foreign ministry official, Elmer Radisich, for more than ten years Hungarian representative at the League of Nations. Representatives of all the churches participated in the Board, as well as prominent teachers, writers, and artists.

On February 5, 1946, R. H. Markham cabled the following dispatch from Budapest to the *Christian Science Monitor*:

> . . . Fortunately, some effort is being made to counteract this [antisemitism]. Lectures are now being given in Budapest recalling the meetings arranged in the United States by the Conference of Christians and Jews. The Reformed Church also is attempting to bring Jews and Christians together at the round table—which is difficult, since some of the leading Jews consider the chief Reformed Bishop antisemitic. A striking illustration of this effort to encourage humaneness and good will was the declaration by a group of distinguished Hungarian writers published a few days ago in the government [?] paper *Magyar Nemzet* urging fairness to the Germans who are now being ejected from Hungary. For publishing this appeal, the government paper on Russian demand was suspended. This was the third suspension during January.

The Jewish Telegraphic Agency reported on May 21, 1946:

> The Council for Social Reconciliation, an organization of Jews and Christians dedicated to healing the breach between the Jewish and non-Jewish community . . . today announced that it will appeal to the Government to abolish all sections of the property restitution decrees which are hindering Jewish economic rehabilitation, it was disclosed here today. According to Dr. Joseph Cavallier, a Catholic leader of the Council, the organization's first fight is against antisemitism, "which has cropped up again." Dr. Cavallier, who risked his own life to hide many Jews during the war, and helped them get out of the country, pointed out that the Council is now attempting to eliminate those sections of the housing and movable property restitution laws which discriminate against returned deportees.

As we shall see, antisemitic riots occurred in the country during this period; the Unitarian Bishop Szentivanyi demanded in parliament an energetic investigation of these riots. His demand resulted in the appointment of an inter-party committee under the chairmanship of the leader of the Communist-dominated National Peasant Party, Peter Veres. Veres was reported in *Uj Elet* (December 5, 1945) as having openly declared at a mass meeting: "Out with the Jews and 'Swabs' [Swabian Germans]!"

Bishop Ladislas Ravasz, at the Council of the Convent of the Hungarian Calvinist Church, moved a resolution which was unanimously passed:

> The Council of the Convent of the Hungarian Reformed Church . . . confesses with deep humility the sin by which it has offended God's Majesty. It has offended God's Majesty by not fulfilling faithfully the prophetic mission received from Him. It failed to warn the people and their superiors when both entered on a path which went against God's laws, and it failed to step bravely forward to defend those who were innocently persecuted. We deem it necessary for the Hungarian nation to arrive at a salutary recognition of its sins under God's judgment and to confess them with repentance. . . . The Council orders penitential services to be held on one Sunday of every year in all congregations of the Hungarian Reformed Church.[3]

Stoeckler and the Communist political forces secretly supporting him went one step further and tried to place the blame for the pogroms that occurred in the summer of 1946 directly on Cardinal Mindszenty. In *Uj Elet* (June 13, 1946) the following article appeared under the heading, "Why, Where Is the Refutation?" ("Hol kesik a cafolat?"):

> In connection with the echoes and voices raised about the Kunmadaras [pogrom], it is worthwhile taking notice of a peculiar statement made by the Cardinal, dealt with by Francis Vasarhelyi in the columns of *Kepes Figyelo* [a left-wing paper]. In this statement the Cardinal, with great understanding, treated the Kunmadaras affair as if it had been provoked by the Jews. Days have passed since the publication of the article dealing with the Cardinal's statement. But to date we have failed to see any refutation. Accordingly, we must assume that the statement was really made. . . . We would like to mention in this connection a lecture given by John Korody-Katona to the Credo Association in the Jozsefvaros district, in which he said among other things: "*We Catholics are sharply opposed to the happenings at Kunmadaras.* We demand just retribution, so that such things may not occur again. But we request the sober majority of Jewry to advocate moderation, within their own circles, against all unjustified violence and encroachment." We admit that when we read this statement we were startled. Where did Jewish "violence and encroachment" show itself? In Ozd, Kunmadaras, or the rest of those places? Were Jews the committers and not the victims of violence? . . . Such words do more harm than good even if well meant. . . .

Uj Elet (July 4, 1946) then published a letter by John Korody-Katona which expressed the position of Mindszenty and the Catholic church on the Jewish question. After mentioning that the Papal Nuncio issued 13,000 letters of protection to persecuted Jews during the Szalasi terror, Korody-Katona went on to say:

> We wish to work for reconciliation. The Cardinal [in a sermon] explained the Ten Commandments with all their unalterable consequences. He did not say a word which would have been in contradiction of the ancient teachings of the Catholic Church and of the spirit of Christian humanity. Still, it was after this sermon that the attack was launched against him, mainly by the party press. The trouble is that many Jews listened to these press attacks and now consider the Cardinal their enemy. This is unjust and mistaken. . . . It would be an important station on the road to reconciliation if both sides—Catholics and Jews—could establish a joint lay committee, possibly consisting of legal experts, which would investigate grievances as they arise. . . . We believe that religious Catholics and religious Jews will understand each other, will eliminate misunderstandings, and will resist the flood of hatred, which is being incited mainly for *political reasons*.

But Stoeckler did not accept this proposal and seek an understanding with the Catholic church; he became instead an increasingly servile tool of the Communists, who in their long-range plans for the penetration and control of religious life, systematically encouraged strife among the different religions.

Communist Infiltration of Jewish Life

The Communist policy of infiltrating Hungarian Jewish life, as well as the life of all the other religious groups, was initiated after the general elections, when the Communists, failing to secure their domination over Hungary by the vote, realized that more direct and effective means were required. In this period the Communist effort to capture Jewish public life from within became manifest; ever growing numbers of Communists began to show an "interest" in Jewish communal life.

Immediately after the elections Ilya Ehrenburg appeared in Budapest, met with the Stoeckler leadership, and lectured before an audience assembled by him. Within a few days of Stoeckler's statement that "surviving Jewry owes its life and liberation to the glorious Red Army and to the Western Powers,"[4] the Soviet writer declared to the correspondent of *Uj Elet*:

> The Jews of Hungary have to realize that they owe their lives *exclusively* to the Red Army, although our army did not fight for the Jews alone, but for every enslaved human being.

Stoeckler stood corrected. Writing a Passover front-page editorial in

Uj Elet, he stated:

> The rescue of our ancestors [in Egypt] was miraculous. But how much more miraculous was the rescue and liberation of Hungarian Jewry from certain death. Our liberator, the glorious Red Army, fought gallantly. We know what struggle and blood sacrifice was demanded by this greatest war in history which was fought for liberty, for the reassertion of human rights, and for our rescue. Our gratitude to each and every son of the Russian nation will last forever![5]

Again, on May 30, 1946, Stoeckler in an editorial exclaimed:

> Hungarian Jewry! Don't forget! You owe your very life to the Red Army! Help it, strengthen it, it is your defender, your liberator, the preserver of your life.

It cannot be accurately ascertained when Stoeckler, a factory owner, became a member of the Communist Party. That he at least enjoyed the trust of the Hungarian Communists and Russian occupation officials as early as February, 1946, or three months after Ilya Ehrenburg's visit, is evident.

At this time an incident occurred that clearly indicated the determination of the Soviet authorities in Hungary to restrict the official spokesmen of Hungarian Jewry to "trustworthy" persons who would defend the regime rather than the cause of the Jews.

The Anglo-American Committee of Inquiry on Palestine was refused permission to enter Hungary, Rumania and Bulgaria. The Jewish Telegraphic Agency reported:

> Replying to a question in the House of Commons yesterday, British Minister of State, Sir Philip Noel-Baker, disclosed that the Soviet government has said that the refusal of its representatives on the Allied Control Commissions in the Balkans to agree to allow the Inquiry Commission to visit those countries was motivated by the fact that the armistice terms in each case forbade religious discrimination. The Control Commissions, the Russians said, make certain that this rule is observed. . . . The Inquiry Commission is leaving Europe without having received virtually any oral testimony concerning the Jews of the Balkan countries, aside from the report by Dr. Ernest Marton, Rumanian Red Cross delegate.[6]

What was the report of the Hungarian-born Dr. Marton, former Zionist member of the Rumanian parliament and editor of the Transylvanian Zionist Hungarian language weekly *Uj Kelet?*

> It is an inevitable development that the Jewish people are in a great mass movement. They return from the concentration camps only to begin a feverish search for their lost relatives. They travel to all parts of their country and find nothing. Everyone has been killed. When they become convinced of this, a great crisis enters their lives. Either they

commit suicide or they flee. They cannot remain in places where once they were happy, but where now they can see in their neighbors murderers of their families. Antisemitism is stronger than at the height of Hitler's power. The first reason for this is the antisemitic education that began in the kindergarten. The results of that education will continue for another generation or two. Second, we are hated because we returned from the dead. They thought of us as dead. They buried us. They were quite satisfied that there were no more Jews, and no more Jewish problem. Our return was a painful surprise for them. They look upon us as ghosts, and no one loves ghosts. Even the politically liberal were unpleasantly surprised, because while they had sympathy for us, at the same time they recognized the advantages of our absence, because our absence solved the Jewish problem. Now we are returning, and though in small numbers, with us return antisemitism and the entire difficult Jewish problem. Third, a large part of the population feels personally cheated and defrauded by our return because now they have to return the Jewish property they had taken. The Nazis saw to it that Jewish property would be as widely distributed as possible so that most people should have a stake in Nazism. Fourth, there is a collective feeling of guilt among these people, which makes them resent us. And fifth, the Jews who returned from the camps are nervous and distraught. They are difficult to live with.

"The Communist Party is reputedly anti-Zionist," Mr. Crossman, M.P., observed. "Do you have anything to say about this?"

Dr. Marton replied that there was no official statement on Palestine, but it was his opinion that the Communists resented Zionism because they felt it siphoned off abilities among the Jews which might otherwise help to build the new social order.

"Because the economic and social grouping of the Jewish people in Europe is more unhealthy than ever before," Dr. Marton went on, "the percentage of Jews in non-productive work is increasing. The returned men and women cannot return to economic life. They need an environment that can substitute for their loss of families and that will give them productive work. That is possible only in Palestine.[7]

Though this statement reflected fundamental Zionist ideology, it was an accurate summary of certain parts of the situation. The Soviet and Communist authorities were unpleasantly surprised to find a Zionist spokesman testifying before the Commission of Inquiry. Dr. Marton was not permitted to return to Rumania after his appearance before the Committee. As soon as it was learned that, in spite of the Soviet ban, the Jews of the satellite countries had been represented before the Committee of Inquiry by Dr. Marton, a Zionist, the Russian chairman of the allied Control Commission experienced a sudden change of heart. Stoeckler and Ladislas Benedek were given permission to go to Vienna, and arrived there on February 26.

> We arrived around midnight in Vienna [said Ladislas Benedek in his report] where we wished immediately to get in touch with the Committee. But as the English cling to the formalities, this was naturally out of the question, and so we showed up at 7 A.M. (an hour the British consider early dawn) at the Hotel Sacher, which is appointed with prewar luxury. We saw that our arrival was not a cause of unanimous joy to the Committee. They had already formed their opinion without having asked suffering Jewry of countries situated to the east of Vienna. They referred to the fact that the Hungarian government did not permit them to enter the country, and that the Russians refused their request for permission to enter. They were very much surprised when we unexpectedly arrived in possession of regular passports and permits. We submitted to them the memorandum of the Central Board, which they received with the remark that they would study it. We had little opportunity for personal expression as the airplane taking the Committee to Cairo left at 8:30 A.M. . . . We feel that our journey and our talk with the Committee were not in vain, either from the point of view of Hungarian Jewry, or from that of Hungary. It was through us that Hungarian Jewry made its problems known to the world, and it was through us that Hungary gave the lie to the belief that it had wished to prevent Jewry from contacting the Committee.[8]

Only during the short-lived pro-Zionist early period of post-war Soviet foreign policy were genuine Hungarian Zionists permitted to attend the World Zionist Congress, the European Conference of the World Jewish Congress at Prague, and a Conference on Jewish Education in Jerusalem.

Antisemitism

Immediately after liberation antisemitism was at its lowest point. The populace took it for granted that Jews, as the chief target of the Hungarian Nazis, would be aided by the victors. Jews returning from the camps and claiming restitution of their property were sufficiently numerous to make their presence felt. The relatively high proportion of Jews in the top leadership of the Hungarian Communist Party and their role in the people's courts and political police, encouraged the identification of Jews with the Soviet power in the minds of the population. As the majority of Jews worked in commercial occupations, they were at the same time charged with black-market dealings. After the elections, in the chaos caused by the inflation, which was chiefly the result of the tremendous volume of reparations taken by the Russians, the Communists sought to shift the blame for economic conditions to the Smallholders in the government and the Jewish mercantile class in the business world. Their agitators incited the population against the black-marketeers with the standard demand that they be hanged. (Joseph Darvas' statement about his knowing that not all black-marketeers and speculators were Jews will be recalled.) Thus on the one hand Jews were identified with Communism and the

Russians, and on the other, they were made answerable for the "black market" (often simply an opprobrious Communist term for private enterprise) and the inflation.

In this period the ancient antisemitic blood libel was also revived. In the whole of Hungarian history we know of only two major cases of this sort: one in the Middle Ages, when Jews were tried and executed in Bazin, and the other in Tisza Eszlár in 1882, when the accused Jews were exonerated.

But in 1946 it was not whispered that Jews were killing Christian children for ritual purposes; the libel went to the effect that Christian children were disappearing and being killed (by Jews) to be made into—sausages! Here the influence of the semi-famine is unmistakable. If we remember the frequent cases of people being spirited off to Russia, the whole campaign acquires a certain perverted logic and expresses the population's resentment against the Russian terrorization and exploitation of Hungary. But since the Communists could not be safely attacked, the Jews were substituted for them.

Later, the blame for the entire anti-Jewish campaign, and for the riots and pogroms resulting from it, was placed by Communist propaganda on "former" fascists, the church, and the Smallholders; but this could not alter the fact that all the riots had occurred in Communist-controlled industrial localities, the most flagrant instance being the Miskolc pogrom, which took place less than two weeks after a speech by Rakosi against black-marketeers and in the wake of a local workers' mass meeting.

In February 1946 the miners of Ozd and Sajószentpéter and the workers of Tótkomlós and Szegvár gave notice to the Jews that if they wished to live, they had better leave the locality within twenty-four hours.[9] In Csanádpalota it was rumored that a local Jewish physician had poisoned children while pretending to vaccinate them. In Debrecen the rumor spread that the head of a child had been found in the cellar of a Jewish leather merchant. It was the talk of the village of Tiszaladány that someone had found a child's fingernail in a sausage bought from a Jewish butcher. A married couple in Mezökovácsháza circulated the story that Jews were kidnapping children and killing them in underground hideouts. The local teacher told her pupils to keep away from Jews, who would cut off their heads.[10]

In Makó, an important Jewish community in southeastern Hungary, a synagogue was set afire and burned to the ground.[11] In the village of Földeák, children were warned by their teachers that Jews capture children, skin them, and cut their heads off. In Sopron, a large city in western Hungary, children were warned against Jews with beards who kidnap Christian boys and girls and eat them. In Mezökovácsháza, this same rumor was spread by a German named Lichtmann. In Debrecen, a man named

Emil Jonas was arrested for spreading such rumors. In Mecsekháza, children were told by a teacher that Jews kill Christian children and grind them into sausage meat.[12]

The *Jewish Morning Journal* in New York reported on April 7, 1946:

> Pro-Nazi elements in Hungary exploit the chaotic situation prevailing in the country as a result of famine and high prices of food. The blame is put, as usual, on the Jews, and the result is an alarmingly increasing antisemitism. The Government is not in a position to control the situation.
>
> Hungarian Nazis daily raid the Jewish quarters of several cities in Hungary, even in cities with large Jewish populations, such as Budapest, Miskolc, Szeged. Last Monday the hooligans attacked the charity kitchen of the Budapest Jewish Community in Bathory Street, took hold of all food provisions and distributed them among themselves.
>
> Hungarian Jews are being made the scapegoat of the inflation that is prevailing in the country, where one American dollar costs twenty million pengos.

The New York *Herald Tribune* published the following United Press dispatch on May 12:

> Mobs incited by Hungarian Nazis and carrying antisemitic placards lynched three workmen in Budapest suburbs yesterday and today. Police fired into a mob in the Pesterzsebet suburb and saved one man from being hanged after he had been wounded gravely. The mobs have been aroused by rumors that Jews were kidnaping Hungarian children and selling their flesh for food. None of the workmen lynched was a Jew, though the mob apparently thought that all were.

Chief Rabbi Hevesi wrote a sharp front-page editorial in *Uj Elet*, under the heading: "No More!"

> A wave of indignation and consternation is spreading over Hungarian Jewry. In several provincial localities organized masses, nay gangs, attack our Jewish brethren, beat and mistreat them, pillage their homes, rob their stores, wreck their furniture and equipment. . . . Was it not enough that over 600,000 innocent brothers of ours were delivered to the German hooligans? . . . How do these gangsters dare, whence do they take the courage to attack with organized brutality those who had suffered beyond endurance, and who returned to their homes to start life anew, and to help rebuild this country with their honest labor?
>
> We demand an answer to this question from the Hungarian government. The government must know what is in the background. . . . The government will perhaps be in the position to explain why these riots could not be prevented, and if they could not be prevented in time, why they could not be punished without delay.

Most of the antisemitic riots were fomented by "little Nazis" who had sought a haven for themselves principally in the up-and-coming Communist Party. As a result, the accusations against the party grew so loud that Rakosi found it necessary to state at a national conference of the party's district secretaries:

> We must keep greater order in our own ranks than hitherto. First of all, we have to act sharply against the most frequent manifestation of fascism, which is antisemitism. It is absolutely intolerable that the most consistently democratic party, the Communist, should be open to the accusation that it tolerates antisemitism. . . . We took sharp measures against those who committed grave mistakes in the course of our "mass actions," and these measures have already resulted in organizational consequences.[13]

As to the nature of these "mass actions," the following statement by Rakosi, quoted by all Hungarian daily papers on February 7, 1946, is illuminating: "There is a place in a democracy for spontaneous acts of the masses, and it is only right that the people should take justice into its own hands when it sees fit."

All political parties issued statements condemning antisemitism. Prime Minister Ferenc Nagy, the Smallholders' leader said:

> The government is determined to defend the peace of the nation, both within and without, against harmful *kulturkampf* and racial hatred. . . .[14]

Arpad Szakasits, Vice Premier, the Social Democratic Party's president, said:

> Let us not deceive ourselves with the belief that with the defeat of the Hitlerite beast, the European atmosphere was henceforth cleared. Seven hundred thousand Hungarian Jews perished; it seems that for some people this is not enough. The flame of antisemitism is flaring up again and again. We must extinguish it, because this was the manner in which Hitlerism began leading to the downfall of all Europe. Antisemitism is the disguise of reaction. We will face it. For us only human beings exist, without any difference of race, religion or nationality.[15]

None of these Smallholder and Social Democratic leaders found it necessary to excuse the attitude of members of his party, or to report "measures" taken against them, because no such charges were leveled against members of their parties.

However, the Ministry of the Interior, which controlled the police, was entirely in the hands of the Communist Party's Laszlo Rajk, whom Jews generally considered an antisemite and several of whose own brothers had been leading members of the Arrow Cross Party. Rajk did not protect pogromists merely out of personal antisemitic conviction; it is most unlikely that he could have been acting in so important a matter without Communist direction. Rajk and his police, instead of fighting antisemitism, chose other employment for themselves. On March 8, 1946, the *Jewish*

Morning Journal published a special cable from London:

> Zionist activities in Hungary lately lost some of their vigor as a result of denunciations and persecutions by Jewish Communists. The [Jewish Section of the CP] in Hungary recently started a campaign of incitement against Zionism and Zionists. They went so far as to denounce Zionism as reactionary and fascist, and Zionists as agents of fascism and reaction. The Hashomer Hatzair (Mapam) group went hand in hand with the Communist informers.

The *Day*, on May 14, published a United Press and Palcor dispatch from Budapest.

> The five Palestinian Halutzim who were arrested on April 9 by the Hungarian political police during a raid on the office of the relief organization "Ezra" in Budapest, were set free on May 10. Ministers Rakosi and Rajk promised a prominent Jew that Jonah Rosenfeld, the chairman of the organization, would also be released from prison in the course of the week. Ministers Rakosi and Rajk declared to Gideon Rafer, correspondent of the JTA, that the government was not opposed to the emigration of Jews from Hungary.

On May 19, the *Jewish Morning Journal* published a special cable from Budapest:

> Under the pretext of searching for Hungarian fascists, 4,000 policemen and 500 detectives raided the Jewish district around Lake Balaton and searched 15,000 Jewish homes; 760 people were arrested. The Communist press is attacking the Jews bitterly, and charges them with hiding fascists.

A different version of these actions by the political police was reported in the *American Hungarian People's Voice* (*Amerikai Magyar Népszava*) by R. Polgar on February 16, 1948:

> By July 1946, inflation had reached its lunatic peak; the worker and official could not buy a piece of bread in the afternoon with the salary he had received in the morning, and rebelliousness was rampant. Something had to be done to appease the general bitterness. The public pillorying of "black-marketeers" was hit upon. As under Nazism, for weeks and months groups of hundreds of Jewish businessmen were driven into the streets to clear the pavement, and also into interment camps and into factories to do the most menial and backbreaking jobs without pay. On one occasion, for instance, a large group of café and restaurant owners and other business people were driven into the large Weiss Manfred foundry in Csepel, a suburb. There the workers, many of whom had been Arrow Cross hooligans eighteen months before, lined up the Jews one by one and after having torn off their clothes, pushed them against the walls of hot Martin ovens, which workers may approach only when dressed in asbestos, then pulled them back again and rolled their scorched bodies in hot tar, beating them all the time with

steel shovels and trampling on them with spiked boots. Two of the victims died directly, and most of the survivors were crippled for life. After release from the hospital, all were interned for "indefinite terms," a good way of keeping their lips sealed.

Such was the Communist Party's interpretation of Darvas' promise that "we will force them to do productive work." These outrages soon turned into pogroms, as every encouragement was given the population by the police to blame their woes on "Jewish blackmarketeers." The first full-scale pogrom took place in the town of Kunmadaras in the latter part of May 1946: A description of it was published a week after in *Uj Elet* (May 30, 1946):

Two of our coreligionists from Kunmadaras visited the editorial office of *Uj Elet* and reported the following in connection with the pogroms:

The Jews returning from deportation were received by a population chagrined to see them again. They did not wish to return to Jews the property stolen from them. Before the deportations there had been 300 Jews living in Kunmadaras, of whom only 100 came back from slave labor service and from deportation to Austria.

The plan of the pogrom was born at a meeting held at the offices of the local trade union board. The Protestant school board issued a warning to the parents that they should not let their children go into the streets unescorted. On the day of the pogrom, at 8 A.M., many women gathered in the market place and shouted impatiently: "When do we begin, it's eight o'clock already." The mob then attacked all Jews who could be found in the market place. The village magistrate ordered the mob to clear the market place. Whereupon, they invaded Jewish homes and started to beat up women, children and old people until they bled. They killed Joseph Rosinger, a poor carter. They killed Francis Kuti, a poor huckster, and pillaged his home. The third victim, Francis Mailander, died from his injuries in the Karczag hospital. Within a few hours a larger detachment of policemen arrived in Kunmadaras under the command of Major Polonyi of Szolnok. Polonyi ordered the mob to disperse, and asked them what was the matter with the Jews. There came an answer from one of the mob: "Nothing. They just kill our children." Polonyi said: "Let all those come forward whose children have disappeared." Nobody came forward. The murderous mob, in the course of the pogrom, answered to women who implored them to spare their lives: "Did you have to come back? Why didn't you stay in Germany? It wasn't the Russians who liberated you, we are going to liberate you, but you won't thank us for it. . . . Now it is the people who deal with justice. This is the real people's court, not the one you have. . . ."Following the arrival of a Budapest police detachment, order in the town was restored completely.

The news of the pogrom reached Budapest immediately. The cabinet resolved to try the culprits at once. In the absence of the Minister of Justice, the Social Democrat S. Ries, his Under Secretary, Zoltan Pfeiffer (Smallholder), gave orders to the State Prosecutor to complete the investigations as rapidly as possible and bring the accused to trial within the week.

In parliament three representatives sharply condemned the pogrom and demanded immediate punishment of the culprits: Stephen Szolnoki, (Smallholder), Victor Drozdy (nonparty), and Francis Szeder (Social Democrat). No Communist representative spoke. Memorial services were held for the martyrs of Kunmadaras in every synagogue in the land. Following a sermon preached by Chief Rabbi Hevesi in the Dohany Street Synagogue of Budapest, the crowd of worshipers improvised a procession of protest which wound its way to parliament. *Uj Elet* reported:

> At a number of places en route, small incidents took place following provocative remarks by fascist onlookers. Apart from these occurrences, the impromptu and spontaneous demonstration passed off soberly and without disturbance. In front of parliament, Under Secretary Father Balogh addressed the gathering. He stated that he appreciated the feelings of righteous indignation that had brought this demonstration before the building of parliament. . . . "The government has decided," Balogh said, "to be on guard so that neither Kunmadaras nor anything like it should recur.[16]

At the same time, however, the captive leadership of the two Central Boards and the Zionist Organization published a statement on the demonstration of May 25 which declared, at the behest of Stoeckler, that it had taken place without their previous approval.

> We have taken the necessary steps with the government in connection with the sad events of Kunmadaras, and the authorities assured us of their complete agreement with our presentations. They immediately restored order, arrested the culprits, and invoked courtmartial proceedings. There was no need whatsoever for a private association, calling itself the "Social League," to disturb, by its irresponsible activities, the measures of the government and the activities undertaken by the official leaders and organs of Jewry in connection with this matter. The official leaders of Hungarian Jewry, having regard to the steps undertaken by the government, had cancelled as unnecessary the meeting convoked by them for May 26.[17]

This was of course a denunciation, by Communist order, of the National Social League of Hungarian Jews and its leader, Rabbi Hevesi. Stoeckler was thus in the position of attacking the rabbi of the congregation of which he himself was lay leader, and in the pages of the newspaper over whose editorial board the Chief Rabbi still presided (but only nominally, as it had been completely under Stoeckler's control since the Ehrenburg visit to Hungary).

The investigation of the Kunmadaras case revealed that the culprits were members of the Communist Party. Zoltan Pfeiffer, then Under Secretary of the Interior, in an article written for the International News Service described the pogrom and the events following it in this manner:

> My conflict with the Communists reached its peak in connection with the Kunmadaras pogrom, the perpetrators of which were members of the Communist Party. How is it that Communists turned pogromists when the party line was so strongly opposed to antisemitism? Simply as a result of their compromise with the Arrow Cross Nazi mob who constitute a substantial part of the Communist Party membership, seeking shelter from the consequences of their earlier crimes. The recruiting of Nazis reached such a degree of brazenness that Communist Party organizers systematically visited the internment camps where the Nazis were detained and promised immediate freedom, full amnesty and even public careers to those who signed an application for Communist Party membership and who pledged blind obedience to orders of the party.
>
> The Kunmadaras case was the work of seven murderers whom I brought before a court-martial within the legal limit of three days. At the trial it was established that all of them were members of the Communist Party. The next thing that happened was that Rakosi and Szakasits addressed a demand to me that I also indict some members of the Smallholders Party. This happened in the lobby of the House of Representatives. My answer was that only murderers can be convicted of murder.
>
> A few hours before the announcement of the sentence [of the court-martial] the political police interfered by suddenly declaring that they had succeeded in arresting the instigators. Since according to the law the latter could no longer be tried by court-martial, the Communists demanded the quashing of all court-martial proceeding and the transfer of the case to a regular court. By these tactics the Communists finally succeeded in saving the culprits from the gallows.

Two of those arrested by the political police as instigators were members of the Smallholders Party. Matters had been so managed by the Communists that neither murderers nor instigators could be tried by court-martial. The Communists in the Ministries of the Interior and of Justice picked a special panel of judges which immediately sentenced the two Smallholders to death as "instigators" of the pogrom, while the actual murderers received only short prison sentences. The case was reviewed by the People's Court of Appeal, which found the two Smallholders innocent of the charge and set them free.[18]

No protest was made by the Communist-dominated Jewish leadership against the leniency shown the pogromists by Communist judges. Instead, a campaign was launched against the National Social League of Hungarian Jews. Stoeckler wrote a front-page editorial in *Uj Elet* three weeks after the Kunmadaras pogrom under the heading, "With Open Vizier," which among other things said:

> In these last days we have heard the warning of the Moscow Radio against the reactionary intrigues being carried on in Hungary, against certain persons who conduct their antidemocratic activities under the protection of the clerical cloth. . . . It is our duty in defending democracy to be on guard among ourselves, to make sure that such persons cannot exist within our ranks. . . . We will not tolerate their disguise of Jewish patriotism . . . even if they are rabbis. Jewry today expects to hear from the pulpit words bringing peace to the soul. We will no longer tolerate members being canvassed for a so-called "holy covenant" [B'nai B'rith] from the pulpit. . . .[19]

At a national convention, Jewish delegates of all opinions save the Communist had stated their dissatisfaction with the way things were going; they attacked the Jewish leadership for its failure to secure a settlement of the most elementary problems of restitution and to wage an effective fight against antisemitism. Nicholas Vida, president of the Regional Center of Jewish Communities in Pécs, demanded that heirless Jewish properties be transferred to a Jewish fund managed by Jews in order to support those Jews wishing to emigrate. Alfred Sussmann, president of the Miskolc community, declared: "Jewry of the provinces demand a new spirit. The overwhelming majority of Jews in the provinces wish to leave the country." Ladislas Frank of Kaposvár (one of the prosecutors in the trial of Ferenc Szalasi) declared: ". . . It is sad that the Hungarian government, in questions of interest to Jews, deviates from the principles of democracy and of the armistice treaty." Edmund Antl, president of the Jewish community of Kaposvár and a member of parliament (Smallholder), stated: "The government is not antisemitic, but is not in a position to carry out its plans owing to the interests of party politics." Theodor Scheiner, president of the Jewish community of Karczag (within ten miles of Kunmadaras) said: "The desire of Jews to emigrate has two sources—the memories of the past and the fear of the future." Emeric Heller, vice president of the Buda community, demanded that all those who worked against the full rehabilitation, moral and economic, of the Jews, be listed as war criminals.[20]

The bitter dissatisfaction of Jews with the failure of restitution, their fear of pogroms and of nationalization, their "fear of the future," resulted in an increasing desire to emigrate from Hungary.

Communist counter-action soon commenced. As early as April 11, one of the most important ideologists of the Communist Party, Minister of Public Welfare Eric Molnar, gave a lecture before the Political Academy of the Communist Party in which he outlined the official party position on the Jewish question. His remarks were aimed chiefly at Zionism. After virtually identifying Jews with capitalism, Molnar said:

> There are two solutions to the Jewish problem in Hungary, a reactionary and a progressive one. The reactionary solution is Zionism. As Jewry has lost its language, inevitably its national culture and religion are in a process of decline. Thus, the cohesion of the Jews as a group was possible only transitorily. Zionism aims at the perpetuation of this artificial procedure which is in opposition to social evolution, even if some Zionists claim to be socialists. Whoever wants socialism must remain here. The progressive solution is the complete social amalgamation of Jews. In the course of democratic development and by the defeat of reactionary forces, antisemitism will cease to exist. The distinctiveness of Jews will also cease to exist. . . .[21]

The strong response of Jews to the appeal of the National Social League necessitated the creation of an organization subservient to the Communists, the National Association of Jews, which was founded on July 8, 1946. The slogan of the new organization was "Jewish unity." It began its membership drive with the open support of the Communist Party. It soon became evident that the Association was intended to help the Jewish Communists in consolidating their control over the representative organs of Jewish public life.

Meanwhile, the antisemitic campaign continued, and riots and pogroms took place on a scale known only during the Nazi era. On July 30, 1946—about ten days after Mathias Rakosi, addressing a mass meeting in Miskolc, demanded the scaffold for black-marketeers—the miners of Diósgyör (about five miles from Miskolc) gathered under Communist leadership to demonstrate against black-marketeers. The demonstration turned into a pogrom. The mob seized three flour mill owners, two of whom were Jews. The third, a non-Jew, was set free at once, while one of the Jews, Jungreisz by name, was killed, and the other, Rejto, was sent to the hospital in a critical condition. The police arrested sixteen demonstrators who were charged with instigating the pogrom. The following day the same mob, numbering some 25,000, again marched through the city demanding the release of the sixteen. They besieged the building of the regional police headquarters, where about 300 fully armed and Communist-commanded policemen were assembled. The mob was admitted to the prison. They freed the instigators of the pogrom, who then told them that a Jewish captain of the police, Farago, had mistreated them during the hearing. The mob found Farago in the basement of the building and beat him to death. All the armed policemen, most of them Communists, looked on as their officer was killed. *Uj Elet* reported:

> There are indications that there had been considerable agitation in the iron works and that the lynchings were not spontaneous. An interparty rally was held at the Diósgyör plant last night, and speakers appealed to the workers to remain calm.[22]

"Inter-party rally" meant a Communist-sponsored meeting which Social Democrats were compelled to attend.

This pogrom, too, was discussed in parliament, but court-martial proceedings were no longer even mentioned. Again a national convention was held by the Jewish communities, which passed a resolution asking the government to establish special armed commands to deal with antisemitic riots. It also urged the authorities to put an end to antisemitic utterances appearing in the press. The Labor Service Veterans Federation distributed posters appealing to the population to help Jews "realize their hopes for security," and urging that perpetrators of antisemitic incidents be punished.

Zoltan Pfeiffer writes:

> The culprits in the Miskolc pogrom could not be brought to justice at all. They were all set free by the Communist police, in spite of their guilt being completely established. This was the only course open to the Communists for the simple reason that it was known all over the country that the pogrom had been prepared and carried out under the influence of a rabble-rousing speech delivered in Miskolc by Rakosi himself, under the leadership of local functionaries of the Communist Party. All this is topped by the fact that hardly a year after the event the chief instigator and participant in the Miskolc pogrom, Francis Dusek, Communist Party secretary of the Diósgyör steel works, entered the parliament of Hungary as a representative of the Communist Party.[23]

Professor Stephen Bibo reported:

> The official position of the decisive elements [Communists] in the government, and the burden of their statements on the case, were that the Miskolc affair was not a Jewish affair, merely the expression of outraged popular sentiment over black-marketeering in general. But even these official statements failed to deny the fact that the Christian offenders were released by the rioters, that indicted Arrow Cross criminals were set free by them, and that only Jews, including a police officer, were killed.[24]

Ferenc Nagy describes these events as follows:

> The demonstration had hardly ended when I was notified. I instantly instructed the Minister of the Interior to make a thorough investigation; in view of the fact that he assumed the murderers were not Communists, a few were quickly arrested. When the workers of Diósgyör learned of the arrests the next day, they told the Communist workers of the district to assemble *en masse* in Miskolc the following afternoon. They came, a bigger crowd than ever, and demanded immediate freedom for the murderers. When the Minister of the Interior asked my advice, I said: "The law must be enforced."
>
> When the local administrator rejected the demands of the mob, it broke into the prison and freed the killers, who complained that during their examination a Jewish police officer had dealt harshly with them.

That was enough. The mob stormed the building, found and lynched the officer and proceeded to the internment camp. Breaking in, it released all the Nazis and Fascists.

The Communist-controlled police, watching impassively while their own officer was killed and the Nazis and Fascists released, did not take a single step to halt the terrorism. This made it clear that the police force was under Communist influence, and did not disagree with the antisemitism of the Communist mob. In response to great public indignation the Minister of the Interior finally assembled several groups of police from different parts of the country, and had the murderers rearrested. A few of the police officials were dismissed and some transferred; but, alas, Justice Minister Ries eventually ordered the murderers freed without trial.[25]

The Jewish Telegraphic Agency reported from Budapest on August 6 that "members of the right-wing Smallholders Party, the largest in Parliament, are demanding the resignation of Minister of the Interior Rajk, and of the [Communist] administrator of Miskolc county, on the grounds that they are responsible for the agitation which resulted in the mob's resorting to lynch law."

All efforts by Jewish leaders to secure punishment of the instigators and culprits were in vain. Rakosi himself made the following statement to a Jewish delegation protesting against the official handling of the Miskolc and Kunmadaras cases: "My hands are tied. I am responsible only to the extent of 17 per cent for the policies of this government," referring to the fact that the Communists had received only 17 per cent of the vote. The Smallholders' satirical paper, *Szabad Száj* ("Free Mouth") printed a cartoon depicting a head and a fist, with this text: "I am only responsible for 17%. . . ."

Antisemitic propaganda, in the meantime, went on unabated. Peter Veres, of the Communist-sponsored National Peasant Party, in a course for teachers held in the Ministry of Culture, according to *Szabad Nép* declared: "The peasant folk of the villages already disliked squires, priests and Jews in their childhood," and he emphasized the word "Jews." *Szabad Nép* stated that the audience "received his words with suspicious applause." In the next session, at a lecture by the liberal Emeric Csecsy, "many participants, impressed by the statements of Peter Veres, tried to justify the new antisemitism of the Hungarian peasant, thus finding ideological and social support for their own antisemitism.[26]

Open pogroms ceased following the introduction on August 1 of the new currency, the forint, which put an end to the frenzy of inflation. The "official" leaders of Jewry appealed in *Uj Elet* to the Jewish public to support the new currency in a way that virtually admitted the Communist charge that Jews were responsible for the inflation. But attacks against the opposition elements in Jewish life continued. Thus *Uj Elet* reported:

> Zionist leaders were arrested when police raided a train carrying Jews fleeing Hungary. They have been cleared by the Budapest court. At the time of the raid it was alleged that among the refugees there were former Nazis who embraced Judaism in order to escape punishment. The court acknowledged that the aim of the arrested Zionists was to facilitate the emigration to Palestine of persons who no longer wished to remain in Hungary and that they had not been aware that Nazis were aboard the emigration train.[27]

These attempts to emigrate were of course illegal. As the Jewish Telegraphic Agency reported from Budapest on August 21:

> Persons wishing to emigrate from Hungary must secure the permission of the Allied Control Commission since, until the peace treaties are signed, the Hungarian government has no authority over emigration, it was stated here officially today. The announcement of policy came in reply to a query from the JTA as to the government's stand on emigration to Palestine and other places. The Control Commission is issuing few permits.

At this time there was a stream of emigrants coming into Hungary from countries where the Communist conquest of power was more advanced. Thousands found their way at night across the borders. Those who came from the Carpatho-Ukraine (by this time incorporated into the Soviet Union as a district of the Ukrainian Socialist Soviet Republic) brought with them the story of nationalization's final ruin of the Jewish economic position and news of the open antisemitism of Ukrainian officialdom. The greatest number came, however, from Rumania. Tens of thousands of Jews living in Bessarabia and Bukovina had been allowed by the Russians to choose between Soviet and Rumanian citizenship. All went to Rumania, which was the first stage of their flight westward; they warned Rumanian and Hungarian Jews that sooner or later their frontiers would be closed as tightly as those of Russia.

The antisemitic riots and pogroms caused thousands of Hungarian Jews to leave their homes again and move back clandestinely to the Western zones of Germany. Among them were many unmarried young people, former deportees who had lost their wives or husbands, and childless couples. Older people, however, and those with more attachments hoped that with the signing of the peace treaties and Hungary's recovery of jurisdiction over emigration, they would be able to emigrate without being exposed to the rigors of life in the Displaced Persons' camps. The leaders of the government—including Rakosi and Rajk—still thought it prudent at this time to assure Jewish public opinion abroad of their readiness to permit Jewish emigration, especially to Palestine.

In the fall of 1946 the main preoccupation of Hungarian political life was with preparing for the signing of the peace treaties. The "official" leaders of Hungarian Jewry appealed to world Jewish opinion to support Hungary's request for just terms of peace. They argued that the Hungarian government had guaranteed the equality of every citizen, promulgated decrees providing certain rights to Jews, notably in the economic field, and placed the blame for antisemitic excesses on the remnants of fascism.

The Hungarian government in its memorandum to the Peace Conference enumerated all the measures it had taken to restore the civic, economic, social, and religious rights of Jews. It pointed out that the restoration of Jews to their former positions largely depended on the economic situation of the country. It admitted that restitution could not be accomplished owing to inflation, heavy reparations burdens, and the difficulties of rebuilding the country; stating that only after the ratification of the peace treaties would Hungary be in a position to decide in what manner to indemnify the Jews.

Regarding the question of postwar antisemitism, the memorandum stated that all riots had taken place in the countryside, at the instigation of fascists, and declared that the government had made every effort to punish the guilty and re-educate those still imbued with the spirit of Nazism.[28]

The Communist Party during this period succeeded in postponing settlement of the major restitution and indemnification claims of Hungarian Jewry until after the signing and ratification of the treaty of peace; it made the Hungarian Jews, as soon as they had got the commercial and industrial life of the country going again, an object of hatred. As we have seen, the propaganda campaign against "profiteers" ended in a nation-wide wave of anti-Jewish violence.

Within the official Jewish community, the Communists won a decisive influence by their control of the unelected temporary head of the Jewish community of Pest and his handful of collaborators.

In official statements, the desire of many Jews to emigrate to Palestine was countenanced; but there were unmistakable signs of the Communists' implacable hostility to Zionism and Jewish emigration.

CHAPTER VI

The Communist Capture of Hungary

The Peace Conference was held at Paris in September 1946 and a treaty was soon ratified. According to the latter, Russia was entitled to maintain troops in Hungary, not as occupation forces, but to guard the Soviet lines of communication through Rumania and Hungary so long as Russia maintained occupation forces in Austria. The Red Army of Occupation merely underwent a change of name; now it was called troops for protecting communications to Austria. Formal peace only brought a tightening of the Soviet hold on Hungary. The Allied Control Commission with its British and American members was dissolved; henceforth the Western Powers had no say in deciding the destinies of the country or in controlling the actions of the Russian troops "maintaining communications to Austria."

Restitution

The Hungarian Communists, as we have seen, showed a marked reluctance to make restitution to Jews of their confiscated property, or to indemnify them for their losses. Because of their strategic position in the coalition government, their attitude generally prevailed. Even the promulgation of a decree regulating the certification of deaths during the war—so that heirs to Nazi-confiscated property might be able to recover—was put off until May 1946, after a long fight had been waged by Jewish organizations.[1] But no time was lost in promulgating a law restricting—as a first step—possible heirs to first cousins or nearer relatives.

In the absence of a general law of restitution, and because of the discord among the political parties making up the coalition, a long series of executive decrees and orders was issued which created even more confusion and, in most cases, further curtailed the rights of Jews.

In reviewing a book published in August 1946 on *Legal Regulations Protecting the Persecutees of Fascism, Uj Elet* wrote:

> It is no fault of the distinguished authors that in most cases the unlucky Jew just escaped from the clutches of death and now deprived of everything—land, home, workshop, etc.—who is trying to find out how to recover his property, must come to the conclusion that there is scarcely any chance of doing so, as the opportunities offered by existing

regulations are practically nil. Many hundreds and thousands of our brothers, when they venture to claim the return of their apartments, stores, etc., are faced with obstructive walls of decrees which are supposed to *protect* them. . . . It is almost an *exception if anybody can get back* his home, land or movable assets. The decrees supposed to protect their rights in reality limit them, even as compared with regulations promulgated during the old "reactionary" times. . . .

Article 27 of the Peace Treaty obligated Hungary to indemnify all persons whose property had been confiscated under Nazism because of their racial origin or religion. Immediately after signing the treaty (so as to secure and accelerate its ratification), the Hungarian government introduced a bill in parliament to "stigmatize the persecution of Hungarian Jewry and mitigate the consequences thereof." The bill was passed unanimously and became law.[2]

The law (1946:XXV) consisted of three articles. In Article I:

1. The National Assembly of Hungary solemnly states that all laws and decrees issued by the defeated system which were dictated by foreign influence and deprived a part of the country's population of their rights on the ground of their Jewish religion or origin, were in contradiction with the eternal ideals of humanity, the moral concepts of the Hungarian people, and the spirit of Hungarian law. . . .

2. Recalling the decrees of the democratic government, which . . . abolished the barbarous regulations and re-established equality of rights, thus providing the legal conditions for indemnification: the National Assembly proclaims the indebtedness and gratefulness of the Hungarian nation to all those who, bravely defying intimidation, unselfishly and self-sacrificingly stood by their persecuted fellow men, thereby not only saving many thousands of human lives from destruction, but also contributing to clearing the reputation of Hungary of its disgrace.

In Article II, the state assigned all property of persons of Jewish religion or origin deceased without heirs to a special Heirless Property Fund. This Fund was for the support of needy persons who had suffered persecution because of their Jewish religion or origin, and for institutions serving the welfare of such persons. The president and vice president of the Fund were to be nominated by the President of the Republic upon the recommendation of the Central Board of Jews and the Orthodox Central Bureau. Two-thirds of the Fund's members were to be designated by these representative bodies of Hungarian Jewry, and one-third by the Prime Minister.

Article III stipulated that no inheritance taxes were to be paid upon property so assigned which did not exceed 20,000 forints ($1,900).[3]

This law left the main grievances of Hungarian Jewry unremedied. It did not restore illegally confiscated Jewish landed property; it said nothing about the recovery of Jewish apartments occupied by others; it left the matter of savings and bank deposits unsolved; and it made no provision for restitution of property sold under duress or confiscated by the state. Moreover, for more than fifteen months no action was taken along the lines laid down in the law. It was only after banks and industry had been nationalized, including those which fell within the category of heirless Jewish property, that officers were appointed to the Fund and a few meager assets, formerly handled by the Commissariat of Abandoned Property, transferred to it. These assets represented only an insignificant portion of all Jewish heirless property in Hungary.

The hopes raised in Hungarian Jewry by this law were not strong. They knew how meaningless even the moral satisfaction given to them by it had become as a result of the atmosphere created by the pogroms at Kunmadaras and Miskolc. *Uj Elet* stated editorially:

> As to the financial part of the law, it only affords a faint hope that we may be in a position to educate our orphans, support our aged, and rebuild our synagogues.[4]

Three years after the promulgation of this law the orphanages and the homes for the aged were still dependent on the American Joint Distribution Committee (JDC).

On November 26, 1947, almost fourteen months after the passing of the law in parliament, a government decree (No. 13,160) on the administration of the Fund and the liquidation of the Commissariat of Abandoned Properties was published in the official gazette. In January 1948 local branches of the Fund were at last set up. But their work was confined to assuming control over the heirless Jewish properties formerly administered by the Commissariat of Abandoned Properties, the latter organization doing its best to obstruct the transfer. It was not easy for representatives of the Fund to ascertain the number and identity of Jewish properties—especially in the case of movables—as these had to be separated from properties abandoned by Nazis. Early in 1948, however, it became clear that little was left. According to a report (by a correspondent of the American Jewish Committee), most of this consisted of real estate: about 150-200 houses in Budapest and about 600-700 small buildings in the countryside.

Antisemitism

Outright pogroms no longer took place. The consternation caused abroad by the Kunmadaras and Miskolc riots had made it advisable to forestall such (in Rakosi's words) "spontaneous acts of the masses." But minor anti-Jewish manifestations continued. On October 30, 1947, *Uj Elet*, which still voiced some genuine Jewish grievances, reported:

> In October—the Social Democratic newspaper *Népszava* writes—antisemitic demonstrations took place in the industrial city of Sarkad,

one of the main centers of the Hungarian sugar industry. A mob led by District Chief Notary [chief administrative officer of a rural district] Ladislas Porkolab, a baker, Michael Monojlovics, and the president of the Sarkad trade association, John Makai, demanded the removal of some Jewish officials of the sugar factory. The mob shouted: "Jews! Hang them! Death to the Jews." Of the 176 Jews deported from Sarkad only 39 had returned. Since 1945, six of them have been arrested under various pretexts by the local authorities. The paper revealed that the district chief notary used to be a member of the anti-Soviet Finnish Legion; the baker was proud to have presented pastries to the dinner parties of Szalasi; the president of the trade association was even sentenced by the People's Court; and another person, John Tulkan, who has taken part in the arrests of Jews *since 1945*, used to be a fascist guard with forced labor units. We find no explanation for these elements being in a position to arrest Jews or anybody else.

A new feature came to be added: the destruction of Jewish cemeteries. In September 1947, the first such instance took place in Kecel, where unknown persons, under cover of darkness, destroyed the Jewish cemetery's ancient tombstones and a recently erected monument to the Jews of Kecel martyred in Auschwitz.[5]

In early November 1947, "unknown persons destroyed the fence of the Jewish cemetery in Dunaharaszti, in the County of Pest, and desecrated the graves."[6]

In the middle of November, the Jewish cemetery of Marcali was desecrated. The culprits could not be found.[7]

Early in February 1948, the synagogue in the working-class district of Zugló in Budapest was raided and Torahs and other religious objects were torn and desecrated. The culprits could not be found.[8]

Antisemitic demonstrations took place at a soccer game in Szolnok, when the local team was beaten by a visiting team from Budapest, many of whose players were Jews. Spectators shouted threats against the Jews. The match was suspended for five minutes until the police restored order. Further matches at Szolnok were prohibited by the Hungarian Football Association pending an investigation of the disturbances. A similar incident had occurred in Budapest several weeks before.[9]

In Pécs several students, acting upon the instigation of one of their instructors, painted antisemitic slogans on walls of buildings. In Orosháza, the municipal council adopted a resolution condemning local Jews for addresses made at the unveiling of a memorial to Jews murdered by Hungarian fascists, charging that the addresses were unfriendly.[10]

The only organized attempt at interfaith understanding, the Board of Social Reconciliation, was doomed to failure. The Board had submitted its by-laws for approval to Ladislas Rajk, the Communist Minister of the Interior. After a delay of more than a year, Rajk refused to approve the

Board's by-laws; without such approval it could have been charged with conspiracy, and so it disbanded.

Another attempt was made to combat antisemitism. Rabbi Eugene Duschinsky, in his capacity as representative of the Orthodox Jewish denomination to the National Council of Adult Education (an advisory body to the Ministry of Religion and Education), together with Andrew Gellert, a representative of the Congressional Jews, made the following motion at the Council's general meeting on March 12, 1947:

> Be it resolved that the fight against antisemitism is one of the tasks of adult education. In order to fulfil this task let the General Meeting instruct all organs of adult education to consider it their duty to engage systematically in the work of enlightenment against antisemitism. Be it resolved that a special committee be appointed to direct and secure the effectiveness of this work, and to establish the necessary channels and methods of work. It would be desirable that this committee consist of the representatives of all churches and political parties who are members of the National Council.[11]

The motion was passed unanimously and the subcommittee was appointed. A Moscow-trained historian, Elizabeth Andics, was appointed chairman. After a few meetings of this committee, however, at the suggestion of its chairman the political and presidential committees of the Council, in contravention of the unanimous resolution of the general meeting, dissolved the committee against prejudice. Two years later the entire Council, representing all churches and political parties, was dissolved, its functions being assumed by a new department, the Ministry of Culture, which was under Joseph Revai, chief Communist propagandist.

Communists in the Jewish Community

The Communists feared a united opposition to their efforts to infiltrate, undermine and rule the different religious groups, one by one. Any cooperation among them for whatever purpose was suspected and opposed as a step in the direction of solidarity against the Communist policy of "divide and rule." In this period, the efforts to subject the Protestant and Jewish smaller denominations to party control were considerably intensified and accelerated, in preparation for the final attack on the powerful Catholic church.

As noted before, the organizational groundwork for the Communist penetration of Jewish life was laid by the foundation of Mazot (Magyar Zsidók Országos Egyesülete). This national association of Hungarian Jews assiduously tried to represent in a favorable light the situation of Jews in the Soviet Union, always with the reminder that Hungarian Jewry owed its life solely to the Red Army. It emphasized that there was no antisemitism in Soviet Russia, and that Jewish cultural life was sponsored and supported by the state. It established, through its president, Louis Stoeckler, a Committee for Hungarian Soviet Jewish Cultural Relations. On February 22, the Association organized a mass meeting which

> coincided with the 29th anniversary of the Red Army. This gave a new opportunity for Hungarian Jewry to express its added gratitude to the liberating Red Army and its mighty leader, Generalissimo Stalin. Dr. Joseph Pasztor, the executive director of Mazot, emphasized: "After God, Hungarian Jewry owes its very life to the glorious Red Army. It bears in grateful rememberance Generalissimo Stalin, who opened the gates of Jewry's prisons."[12]

On April 12 the "Cultural Committee" of the Pest Jewish Community organized a literary matinee, with the purpose of acquainting Hungarian Jewry with Soviet Yiddish literature. Stoeckler in his opening address said:

> This is the first step along the road leading to the establishment of strong relations with the Jews of Soviet Russia. We are determined to build up and develop these contacts.

Bela Vihar, a writer who in this period specialized in translating Soviet Yiddish poetry into Hungarian, said:

> The Constitution of Stalin not only permits the survival of Jewish national customs and culture, but it fosters and assists their development, just as it does the culture of other nationalities. The poetry of Soviet Yiddish authors reveals to us the life of Jews reborn under socialism.[13]

In May 1947, just before the ratification of the peace treaties, all Hungarian papers published a letter by Rakosi requesting Stalin to release Hungarian prisoners of war.

> The Empire which liberated our country from the yoke of fascism did not wait until the peace treaties would make it an obligation to release the Hungarian prisoners of war. Generalissimo Stalin, in answer to a letter by Rakosi, made it known that the release of Hungarian prisoners of war will start this month. Together with the entire Hungarian people we are thankful for this noble gesture by the Soviet Union. The prisoners will come home and become fighters for democracy and antifascism. . . .

But as we have seen, these hopes were disappointed by the small number of former Jewish slave laborers who actually returned from captivity in the Soviet Union. The campaign to persuade Hungarian Jewry about the happy condition of Jews in the Soviet Union went on. Thus, on July 31, Hungarian Jews could read in *Uj Elet* about Gromyko's speech in favor of the independence of Palestine; members of the Moscow Yiddish theater entertaining Jewish kolkhozes; a conference at which *Einikeit* (the Moscow Yiddish paper), the Federation of Yiddish writers in the Soviet Union and the Emes publishing house planned the further development of Soviet Yiddish literature; a Sholem Aleichem memorial evening held by

Jewish students of the Chernovtsy colleges; the achievements of the Jewish engineer Abram Malzev in promoting scientific methods of growing cotton in the Soviet Republic of Uzbekistan; an article on European antisemitism by the president of the Antifascist Committee of Soviet Jews, Itzik Feffer; and a gala performance by the Moscow Symphony Orchestra of Weinberg's *Jewish Rhapsody*. Within two years there was no Yiddish newspapers or theaters, no Antifascist Committee, no news about the whereabouts of Itzik Pfeffer and many other Soviet Jewish writers.

In October a special committee was established in the Central Board of Hungarian Jews for "developing cultural and artistic ties with Soviet Jewry," under the leadership of the Central Board's president, Stoeckler. On October 30, long editorials extolled the merits of the Soviet Union in Hungary's only Jewish weekly. They reminded Hungarian Jews of their debt to the Red Army, and then went on to speak of the Soviet Union's championing of national and racial minorities. "The Soviet Union made sure from the very beginning that the different national, ethnical, racial and religious minorities of the huge empire would enjoy equality and harmony." During the Russian Civil War, they said, it was the Red Army which fought against the pogromists. In 1936, the new Stalin Constitution secured the rights of all religious denominations and declared that incitement against any race or religious denomination was a culpable offense. "The very existence and activity of the Jewish Antifascist Committee, with its pamphlets and books, bear witness to the fact that Soviet Jews have not been cut off from Judaism." Festivities were arranged by the Committee for Developing Cultural Relations with Soviet Jews on the occasion of the thirtieth anniversary of the October revolution.

On January 7, 1948, after the UN decision on the partitioning of Palestine, an article appearing in *Uj Elet* purported to describe a meeting, in America in 1942, between Chaim Weizmann, Itzik PFeffer, and the director of the Moscow Jewish State Theater, Mikhoels.

> The two Soviet emissaries wished to negotiate, among others, with Weizmann. Weizmann, however, wanted to avoid the meeting. Although of Russian origin, Weizmann, under the influence of reactionary propaganda, bore a grudge against Soviet Jewry. Finally, however, the meeting was agreed upon. Weizmann received the two illustrious guests in his apartment at twelve o'clock. The meeting commenced in a chilly atmosphere. . . . Mikhoels took out of his briefcase documents proving the flourishing and highly developed cultural life of Soviet Jewry. Weizmann tensely studied all the pamphlets, pictures and proofs of the effective fight of the Soviet Union against antisemitism. Now he started asking questions. The three Russian Jews sat like brothers around the table. They studied the order of the Soviet Army, issued on the second day following the outbreak of the war, requiring all military authorities in charge of evacuation of civilians to give priority to the most threat-

> ened stratum of the population, the Jews. . . . "The Soviet Union," they explained, "sends its best sons to fight for the freedom of the world and for us." Weizmann's eyes filled with tears. He shook the hands of his guests, and in a tearful voice said: "*Briderlech, chotossi*—brothers, I committed a crime, I was mistaken, forgive me. . . ."[14]

In Weizmann's autobiography there is of course no mention of this outrageous story. Its publication in Eastern Europe was just one of many ruses employed to convert Zionists into supporters of the Soviet Union during the latter's pro-Israel period.

At the same time Communists sought to frighten Jews into subservience by making them believe that any anti-Communist seizure of political power would bring with it pogroms and extermination. Professor Bibo writes:

> The great majority of the stratum of middle-class Jews joining the Communist Party refused to turn Communist; they had even less reason to follow the Communist Party after the different anticapitalist actions; it is only that they considered any regime in Hungary which would restore capitalism would have to be counterrevolutionary, necessarily resulting in antisemitic action. . . .[15]

Communist propaganda tried to identify the Western "imperialist" powers with the Hungarian Nazis (who, fleeing westwards with the German troops, came to be known in the Hungarian press as "the Westerners"), and thus to persuade Jews they had no choice but to pray for the victory of the Soviet Union. Ilya Ehrenburg was quoted as having said:

> American Jewish capitalists support a policy which prepares a new Auschwitz. . . .[16]

In June 1948, less than a month after the United States was the first to recognize the state of Israel, the following proclamation by the Soviet Jewish Antifascist Committee was published in the Hungarian Jewish press:

> The Jewish people, which suffered so much during the war under the horrors of Nazism, view with deep unrest the fury of fascist terror in little Greece. The Jewish people well know that the same Anglo-American reaction which is unleashing wild terror against the Greek democrats is responsible for the hatreds dividing nations, and is also guilty of the blood being shed in the towns and villages of Palestine. In the name of Soviet Jewry we protest against the monarcho-fascist murders. We call all progressive organizations of the world to add their protests to the united struggle of progressive humanity.[17]

This, then, was the Communist strategy with respect to the Jews: first persuade them that they owed their liberation exclusively to the Soviet Union; and then incite the population against the Jews by anti-capitalist slogans, while accusing all non-Communist political forces, national and international, of being reactionary and antisemitic, thereby persuading Jews that their security depended on the perpetuation of Communist power alone. The goal was the complete elimination of non-Communist influences from Jewish life. In the preliminary stages even middle-class and Zionist dupes were welcomed into the Communist ranks. But later the Communist Party was purged of its "class enemies." The number of such Jews expelled from the party could not have been insignificant, as the Council of the Pest Jewish Community found it necessary to modify its constitution so that:

> In the future no person can be a member of the Board of Representatives of the Pest Jewish Congregation against whom a valid resolution of ejection has been passed by any democratic party. This [Stoeckler explained] does not mean that we want to encourage a manhunt, but no enemy of democracy can play a role in the life of the Congregation.[18]

The Hungarian Constitution of 1867 failed to provide for the separation of state and church. The constitution differentiated between the "established" religions and those which were merely "recognized." The "established" churches were represented in the upper house of parliament and had members on all state and municipal school boards. Every person had to belong to a church, unless he formally declared himself an atheist. Churches had the right to tax their members, and, if necessary, these taxes were collected, like all others, by state collectors. But in 1895, with the enactment of the so-called "reception" law, Judaism was "established" and the Jewish denomination was granted all the rights and privileges of the Catholic and Protestant denominations.

The consequence of this was the centering of Jewish life around the religious institutions and organizations of the congregations. Jewry as a collectivity had only a religious and never a political existence. To influence Hungarian Jewish affairs meant to influence the congregations, the traditional and official centers of Jewish life. In the years following the First World War all Jewish affairs continued to be managed by the religious congregations. Their political activities, however, did not demand strict piety on the part of the individuals conducting them. Thus the connection between religion and state led to a gradual secularization of the leadership of the congregations. In the years between the two World Wars the official leadership, in accord with its traditional ideology, continued to oppose Zionism. A policy seeking to fix the status of Hungary's Jews as that of a national minority was considered incompatible with the egalitarian character of the Jewish constitutional position in Hungary. Before the First World War, it would also have been considered detrimental to Hungarian interests, for in the peripheral minority areas the Jewish population was the bearer of the Hungarian language and culture. The encouragement given to the Zionist movement and Jewish nationality after 1920 by the successor states was motivated by the desire of the Czechoslovakian, Rumanian, and Yugoslav governments to decrease the number of Hungarians in their territories: by increasing the number of adherents of the "Jewish nationality" (a legal concept unknown in Austria-Hungary and introduced into Hungary for the first time, under the influence of Nazism, at the census of 1939) they reduced the number of Hungarian nationals and the proportion of such nationals to the total population.

The power vested in the congregation by constitution, law, and custom could not be ignored by the governments of postwar Hungary. The traditional preponderance of the Pest Jewish Community became even more marked after the Second World War, when it comprised 90,000 of a total Jewish population of 140,000. It was evident from the outset that if the legal status of religious denominations was to remain unchanged, those dominating the Pest community would continue to dominate all of Hungarian Jewish life.

In the first period after liberation, before the general elections of November 1945, it was expected that a left-wing government which had introduced so many revolutionary changes in the life of the country would speedily separate church and state. Inside the Jewish community itself, a basically religious organization was not considered able to cope with the problems of a Jewry decimated and ruined by the war. The necessity of rebuilding Jewish life from the ground up also provided an opportunity for introducing fundamental changes in the legal status of the community.

But it soon became apparent that for the time being any separation of church and state was out of the question. The elections clearly showed that the influence of the churches was too strong. This influence was helpful in winning the majority of votes for the Smallholders Party in the first and only free elections; for this reason alone the Smallholders could not think of separating church and state. The Communists, on the other hand, instead of trying to force the issue of separation, embarked upon the roundabout policy of capturing the different churches for themselves by infiltration and political pressure. Only in 1948 did it become evident that the Communist aim was not separation of church and state but submission of the church to the state.

As we have seen, the old leadership of the Congressional Community of Pest and of the Central Board was swept away immediately after the liberation. The driving force behind this were the Zionists, who had gained a large following and constituted virtually the only organized group at the end of the war. In the absence of many deportees, community elections were put off six months and a temporary administration was appointed.

The Zionists did not wish to assume sole responsibility for the solution of the difficult problems of the postwar period. In their search for allies, they hit upon Louis Stoeckler, who was appointed president *pro tempore* of the community. Stoeckler was unknown in Jewish public life until after the occupation of Hungary by Germany when he was appointed a member of the Judenrat.

After the war, Stoeckler became an ally of the Zionists in the temporary leadership. But, as he was not their own representative, he could not expect to be elected president by a Zionist majority. Nor could he rely on the once dominant non-Zionist elements, who would not co-operate with a newcomer brought into Jewish public life by the Nazis. And as the Orthodox group had its own organization, Stoeckler's only chance of perpetuating his power was through the Communists. Accordingly, he immediately surrounded himself with Communist coadjutors, chief of whom was Ladislas Benedek, a gynecologist, who through his family connections with Zoltan Vass, the Communist minister, was appointed director of the Jewish Hospital and physician to the Russian Embassy. Through this association, direct access was secured for Stoeckler to the Soviet rulers of Hungary.

The six months' postponement of the Pest community elections passed, but Stoeckler was still not ready for them. The opposition was too strong. Difficulties arose in compiling the lists of voters; they were not expected to be ready for a year. Within this year, however, as we have seen, the middle-class elements, organized around the National Social League of Hungarian Jews, made great advances inside the community. It gained added strength from the Smallholders' victory in the national elections at the end of 1945.

As we have seen, the demonstration lead by the League's director, Zoltan Klar, from the Dohany Street Synagogue to parliament following a sermon preached by Rabbi Hevesi against the Kunmadaras pogrom, gave Stoeckler his first opportunity openly to disavow and attack the League. The leadership of the League made no secret of the fact that Hungarian Jewry held the government, and above all the Communist-dominated police, responsible for tolerating antisemitic riots and even encouraging them by unbridled anticapitalist propaganda.

Stoeckler, it will be recalled, attacked Rabbi Hevesi, president of the League, for pursuing "antidemocratic activities" under protection of the "clerical cloth";[19] he continued to denounce and intrigue against the rabbi. A heart attack forced the latter to go abroad in October 1946, at which time he was compelled to sign a proclamation to the leaders of the League urging them to shun a struggle within the Jewish community. The League, however, knew under what duress the rabbi had signed the proclamation and were even more determined in their opposition to Stoeckler. Its leaders visited Under Secretary Balogh and asked the government, as the final authority in religious affairs, to fix a date for the community elections. A report of this was published in the daily *Magyar*

Nemzet (January 22, 1947). Stoeckler's group, in a front-page editorial entitled "Wreckers'" burst out against the League, calling its leaders "traitors," and welcomers of foreigners," for having urged the government to see that elections were held in the Jewish community.[20]

The next step on the part of Stoeckler's Communist backers in the government was to inform the United Nations Relief and Rehabilitation Administration (UNRRA) that they desired Hungarian Jewry to be represented on its committee by Stoeckler's Board, instead of by the League.[21] Then Minister of the Interior Rajk refused to approve the by-laws of B'nai B'rith. Immediately after this became known, the Communist Minister of Public Welfare barred a large relief shipment of clothes sent by the American B'nai B'rith to the Hungarian chapter for distribution. The goods were seized and their distribution prevented during a winter of dire need. It was only after a year that the Ministry of Public Welfare permitted the distribution of the shipment by persons designated by Stoeckler and to categories of recipients prescribed by the Minister of Public Welfare. The by-laws of the National Social League were also disapproved. But as this was not yet final, the League's work was not interrupted. It established the "Jewish Oppositional Electoral Party."

As the stubborn resistance of the League could not be broken by these methods, penetration was employed. The Communist Tibor Ferenc, chief prosecutor of the Budapest People's Court, joined the League. In a short time he succeeded by intimidation and intrigue in "persuading" a minority of the League's leaders to come to terms with Stoeckler, who promised them 40 per cent of the seats on the Community's Board of Representatives.[22]

The power of the Communist Ministry of the Interior was also used against the Federation of Former Forced Laborers. It will be recalled that the Federation had raised its voice against the pogromists and put up posters threatening to come out itself against future perpetrators of antisemitic violence. This was followed by a request to the government for permission to bear arms to defend the Jewish communities against attack, if pogroms could not otherwise be prevented. Needless to say, permission was not granted. At the end of 1946 agents of the Ministry of the Interior raided the offices of the Federation, placed seals on its doors, seized its files, and suspended it from further activity.

The Federation remained closed for months. As a result of negotiations with the Communist Party, it was reorganized as the National Antifascist Federation of Forced Laborers. Ladislas Benedek was appointed secretary general. Instead of a program defending the interests of persecutees of Nazism, a new one was proclaimed:

> It is our aim to eliminate all obstacles in the way of the unity of all democratic forces in the country. We will call for the unity of all

people who believe that there is only one difference between man and man: the measure of his self-sacrificing work in the service of democracy.

As soon as the elimination of the middle-class opposition was achieved, Stoeckler turned upon his first allies, the Zionists. On March 11, 1947, the latter sent Stoeckler a letter informing him that they had decided to run as a separate party at the elections.

It is our conviction [they wrote] that the only possibility of establishing solid foundations for the Jewish future is to . . . pursue Jewish objectives in a self-reliant and unconditional manner independent of any non-Jewish point of view or influence [an allusion to the Communists]. . . . Your refusal to listen, and the autocratic stiffness with which you have dealt with our proposals, in contradiction with your constant asseverations of loyalty to the Zionists and to the fundamental postulates of democracy, have frustrated all our efforts.[23]

The rupture of the accord of the Zionists with Stoeckler ended the fiction of unity in the community. Most members of the Social League had refused to follow Tibor Ferenc into Stoeckler's camp; they now saw that an electoral struggle was inevitable and renewed the activities of the Jewish Opposition Party.

Stoeckler and his partisans were careful never to utter a word against Zionism. On the contrary, they claimed to be better Zionists than the Zionists. Max Domonkos stated at one of the campaign meetings:

I declare that we are . . . as good soldiers of Zionism as anybody else. We are not anti-Zionists; on the contrary, we are pro-Zionists; but under no circumstances are we reactionaries.

Ernest Brody, one of the leaders of the Social League who joined the Stoeckler camp, said at the same meeting:

Our adversaries the Zionists want to make the Jewish state a reality. Very good. Everybody wants that. But for that it is not necessary to form a new party, because we want the same thing.

Stephen Foldes, vice president of the Pest community, declared: "We are all the servants of the idea of Zionism."

Domonkos voiced the inevitable threat:

Democracy in Hungary has, among others, a Man with a Hammer [the emblem of the Socialist Party]. This man will crash down his hammer on all those who oppose him.[24]

The hammer soon struck. Two leaders of the Zionist movement, Alexander Nathan, director of the Palestine Office of the Jewish Agency in Budapest, and Francis Jambor, a journalist, were expelled from the country *brevi manu* by the Ministry of the Interior. Before the break, the Zionists had somehow succeeded in getting permission to publish a weekly, "*Zsidó*

Ut ("The Jewish Way"). After two issues the license was withdrawn, because the paper was too outspoken about the events leading up to the pogroms.

At the same time Stoeckler's new "Jewish Unity Party" established a group of its own consisting of Zionists who had left the Zionist Organization. The name of the group was B'achduth L'Eretz Israel (United for Israel).

But neither the infiltration of the Zionist Organization nor use of the "hammer" achieved satisfactory results. More than two years after establishment of the temporary administration of the community, Stoeckler still did not dare risk a vote of the membership. A new pretext for delay was found in the dissolution of parliament and the scheduling of new general elections for the end of August 1947, after which Stoeckler hoped finally to defeat both wings of the opposition.

A new national electoral law was passed depriving many former supporters of the Smallholders of their right to vote. It introduced a system which gave to any federation of parties that received 60 per cent of the popular vote additional (so-called "premium") seats in parliament. The Smallholders Party, after the exiling of Premier Ferenc Nagy and Speaker Bela Varga, was purged. Its left wing, keeping the name of Smallholders, entered an electoral federation with the Communists, Social Democrats, and National Peasant Party. The leaders of the original Smallholders Party were forced into opposition and compelled to form new splinter parties: Father Balogh's Independent Democatic Party, the Democratic People's Party of the Catholic Stephen Barankovits, Zoltan Pfeiffer's Hungarian Independence Party, and the League of Christian Women.

The new electoral law provided that workers living away from their homes receive "blue tickets" enabling them to vote outside of their districts. These "blue tickets" enabled Communist Party members to vote over and over again in different places.

Yet the popular vote remained much what it had been in 1945. The Communist Party received 22 per cent, as against 17 per cent in 1945; the Social Democratic Party polled 14.8 per cent as against 17 per cent in 1945. The rump Smallholders won 15.4 per cent of the popular vote, this, together with the returns of all parties that had been forced to secede from the Smallholders, amounted to more than 51 per cent. But the renegade Smallholders with their 15.4 per cent were members of the "left-wing bloc," and supported the Communists. The left-wing bloc of Communists, Social Democrats, Smallholders, and National Peasants polled 60.8 per cent of the votes. As a result of the premium system, they received 271 seats in parliament, against 140 seats for the opposition, which polled roughly 40 per cent of the popular vote. Even after manipulating the vote and extracting all the benefits of the premium system, the Communists themselves failed to receive more than one-third of the seats in parliament in the general election of August 1947.

But this was only the beginning. The Communists had orders from Moscow to gain absolute control over parliament. Accordingly, they first eliminated Pfeiffer's party by charging its leader with "conspiracy"—all forty-nine of his representatives were deprived of their seats, thereby reducing the opposition's seats to ninty-one. Then came the turn of the Christian Women's League, led by Margaret Schlachta, one of the most determined protectors of Jews under Nazism—its four seats, as well as those of some members of the Catholic Democratic People's Party, were taken away.

The finishing stroke was the submission of the Social Democratic Party, and a campaign was carried out against non-collaborating Social Democrats which resulted in the exile of such well-known leaders as Charles Peyer, Anne Kethly, Anthony Ban, and William Bohm. Over forty members of parliament of the Social Democratic Party, or more than half its representation, among them many Jews, were forced to resign; they were replaced by left-wing Social Democrats under the leadership of Arpad Szakasits, George Marosan, Paul Justus, Stephen Ries, and Alexander Ronai. Eight months after the elections, in April 1948, this left-wing Social Democratic Party was forced to join with the Communists to form the Hungarian Workers Party under the presidency of Mathias Rakosi. As a result, the Hungarian Workers Party controlled 167 seats in Parliament and the opposition was reduced by the purges to less than 70. The Communists could now dispense with their Smallholder and National Peasant allies.

Most Social Democratic sympathizers with Zionism were by now in exile and the Socialist Zionists had no support inside the government. The non-collaborating wing of the Social Democrats had been publicly branded as "reactionary." The stage was now set for the Stoeckler clique to charge with "reactionary tendencies" not only Zionists in general, but also the Socialist Zionists.

Almost immediately after the forced resignation of Ferenc Nagy, the government, under Communist dictation, embarked upon a policy of wholesale nationalization. First came the banks, followed by heavy industry. Finally, in March 1948, all enterprises having in their employ one hundred persons at any time after August 1, 1946, were nationalized, as well as many smaller enterprises. A propaganda campaign was started against private wholesale trade, and state-owned or party-sponsored cooperatives were established all over the country.

These radical changes deprived a considerable part of the Jewish population of their livelihood. Nationalization coincided with the establishment of the State of Israel. The desire to emigrate grew to an unprecedented extent. Jews felt they faced economic extinction in Hungary, and they knew that the gates of the Jewish state would soon be open to them. Under such conditions no anti-Zionist party could expect a majority in the Jewish community elections and the Stoeckler party hastened to hail the birth of Israel in print and at mass meetings.

In the ensuing war in Palestine the Hungarian government, following the Soviet line (aimed at embarrassing Great Britain), supported the Jewish side. It soon gave *de jure* recognition to the State of Israel and sold it some tools and arms.[25] Fund-raising campaigns were launched in all the Jewish communities of Hungary, with considerable success. Thousands of young members of organized Zionist groups and large numbers of sympathizers registered for emigration and volunteered for service with the Haganah.

Internally, however, no mercy was shown to Zionists or Zionism. On March 14, 1948, at the National Convention of the Zionist Organization, Michael Salamon felt compelled to resign as president for the following reason:

> At the start of the electoral campaign we decided that the Zionist camp should enter the electoral contest independently. We emphasized that we would conduct our campaign on the basis of absolute fair play. Today, after the lapse of a few months, I have to state that we feel convinced that the Hungarian Jewish masses are no longer in a position to conduct such a legitimate contest based on principles. It was for this reason that we have decided that the fight must cease.[26]

The leadership of the Zionist organization passed into the hands of Moses Bisseliches, an old Zionist and one-time member of Herzl's circle. It was probably his great age that made him acceptable to Stoeckler as the head of a completely discouraged Zionist organization. The first move of the new Zionist leadership was to surrender to Stoeckler.

The main Zionist promoter of collaboration with Stoeckler at this time was the Mapam and its leader, Alexander Kertesz. This group hoped that thanks to its pro-Sovietism it would at least be tolerated by the Communists. A year later, this same Kertesz was among those convicted and sentenced for "smuggling people" to Israel.

A Committee to Conduct the Elections in the Pest community was appointed, exclusively composed of Stoecklerites. Its chairman was Joseph Szucs, a close relative of Stoeckler's. Szucs found a simple answer to Stoeckler's fear of a strong and determined opposition manifesting itself. He disqualified the opposition's list of candidates for unspecified technical reasons and then published the following official statement:

> The Elections Committee of the Pest Jewish Community announces herewith that as only one *correct* list of candidates has been submitted, the elections scheduled for the 23rd of May, 1948, *will not take place*. . . . The Elections Committee at its meeting on May 19 established the fact that in accordance with the statutes and by-laws, the candidates of the

Joint Bloc of the Jewish Democratic Unity Party and the Election Party of the Hungarian Zionist Organization are elected.[27]

The Jewish community was not even allowed to register a yes or no. Stoeckler and his Communist followers simply did not dare to face the voters, even after elimination of the opposing candidates. So ended the long struggle for democratic elections in the largest single Jewish community of postwar Europe.

At the very first meeting of the newly "elected" representatives of the Pest Jewish Community, Stoeckler declared:

> We have always been steadfast in our resistance to all attempts at reaction, even if based on the alleged interests of our denomination. I may state that I cannot wish for more religious freedom for ourselves than what we already possess. We may spread our culture freely, we may educate our children, live our lives within our own congregations. We cannot make extra demands which would weaken democracy. . . . Our life is secure only so long as there is a people's democracy. Any change would mean the extermination of Hungarian Jewry.[28]

Ladislas Benedek was appointed a member of the Pest Jewish Community Council, *as a representative of the Hungarian Workers Party*. It was the only instance of a general political party delegating a member to represent it in a religious community organization in Hungary.

The commanding position of Stoeckler's Communist group was now firm and unshakable. He himself was president of the Pest Jewish Community, of the Central Board of Hungarian Jews, and of the Jewish Rehabilitation Fund; his was the dominant voice in the Hungarian Committee charged with distribution of JDC supplies; through Ladislas Benedek he controlled the Antifascist Federation of Forced Laborers. He was master of the entire Jewish Congressional school system, including the Rabbinical Seminary and Teachers Institute. His word was final in the Hungarian Jewish Association for Literature, and even in the Jewish Museum; and he presided over the Committee for Sponsoring Relations with Soviet Jewry. He represented Hungarian Jewry in all Jewish international organizations, serving as chief spokesman for the Hungarian Section of the World Jewish Congress at the latter's Montreux Conference in 1948. All his opponents had been silenced, interned, imprisoned, or forced into exile. The regimentation of Hungarian Jewry was complete. With these "elections" the Communist-controlled government secured for itself complete dominance over an entire religious denomination.

Since by this time most Protestant churches had been subjected to strict control through the appointment of hand-picked bishops and lay leaders, the stage was set for the elimination of all genuine religious influence from public life. The churches were being transformed into subservient agencies of the government by gradual infiltration, rather than being driven out of existence entirely.

The new Jewish leadership first introduced itself to world Jewry at the Montreux Conference of the World Jewish Congress in July of 1948. At a previous European conference of the World Jewish Congress, held in Prague in 1947, the Hungarian Section had been represented by its president, Albert Geyer, and by Bela Ungar, both legitimate Zionists at that time. The Prague conference was the first international Jewish gathering at which Communist emissaries attempted to promote the party line. Poland, Bulgaria, Yugoslavia, and Rumania were all represented by full-fledged Communist delegations. But the Hungarian delegation did not vote with the delegations from the other satellite countries. It was therefore decided to change the Hungarian delegation to be sent to Montreux. The Montreux delegation consisted of Stoeckler, Szucs, Benedek, and the "collaborating" Zionists Moses Bisseliches and Salamon Beck. The latter delegates were there to guarantee the trustworthiness of whatever the Stoecklerites had to say; the Hungarian regime realized that the Western Jewish delegates would believe Zionists of long standing much more readily than such Communist newcomers to Jewish affairs as Stoeckler and Benedek. The Zionist leaders played the part allotted to them. Moses Bisseliches, president of the Hungarian Zionist Organization, and the friend and pupil of Theodor Herzl, was required to declare:

> As president of the Hungarian Zionist Organization, whose greetings I herewith convey, may I state that we can do this work of ours undisturbed under the protection of the Hungarian People's Democracy. In our delegation all shades of Jewry are represented. We all agree that our country, Hungary, which has been destroyed by Nazi vandalism, must be reconstructed. We all agree that we are duty bound to help the upbuilding of the Jewish state, and we are therefore united in our gratitude to those countries which without hesitation and calculation have recognized the state of the Jewish people. We are grateful to the Soviet Union, the great friend of the Hungarian and Jewish nation, which saved our lives in the twelfth hour.

In another year Bisseliches was forced to announce the "voluntary" dissolution of the Zionist movement which he had served from its earliest days. At the Montreux Conference, Stoeckler himself made the following statement on June 30, 1948:

> Our presence at this conference demonstrates that we wish to serve the unification of Jewish forces. An all-out struggle of two world philosophies is raging, but we know by experience that progress . . . cannot be stopped. . . . Jewish brethren, do not fall into the mistake of being afraid of radical changes. Think of our martyrs and of your own children, and take cognizance of the fact that a false position cannot mean

security and a life without fear—but that, on the contrary, it may lead only to growing insecurity and . . . perdition.

We in Hungary have gone through all these experiences, and we are already living the life of the free, and our children grow up to be free people . . . we live in a system which is dedicated to eternal effort against war, because the people's democracy is the only guarantee of human dignity and peace.

Chapter VII

Under the Communist Heel

Soon after the forced merger of the Social Democrats with the Communists into the Hungarian Workers Party in April 1948, the government began to prepare to carry further its program of nationalization both in industry and agriculture. Industry was no longer represented in parliament and could offer no opposition. Nationalization of the land, however, would have resulted in an overwhelming agrarian majority at the elections. The Communist program of collectivization had therefore to be kept a secret for the time being; Communist leaders in their electoral campaign expressly denied having any such plans. But after the elections and the elimination of the major opposition parties, when the new Hungarian Workers Party possessed an absolute majority in parliament, the puppet Smallholders and the National Peasants could be dispensed with.

The leader of the National Peasant Party, the antisemitic Peter Veres, resigned as Minister of War, his party's place being taken in the cabinet by the even more antisemitic Joseph Darvas and Francis Erdei, both Communist tools. The next step in the elimination of the peasantry as a political force, and ultimately of the system of small individual holdings, was the removal from office of Zoltan Tildy, the President of the Republic. His son-in-law, Victor Csornoky, was charged with illicit dealings in currency, allegedly to provide funds for Tildy's escape from Hungary. After Csornoky was hanged, Tildy resigned as President of the Republic; he stated in a declaration that he did not disagree with the policies of the government, but that persons associated with him had committed crimes and this made him doubt whether he had the confidence of the nation. Prime Minister Lajos Dinnyes was also forced to resign. Arpad Szakasits, the collaborating head of the Social Democratic Party, became President of the Republic. In order to maintain the appearance of legitimacy, the Smallholder Stephen Dobi (actually a secret Communist of long standing) was appointed Prime Minister. There remained only one group in Parliament which could be considered as representative of the anti-Communist majority of the population, the Catholic Democratic People's Party.

After the elections, Rakosi declared that the most urgent matter facing the government was the settlement of the problem of the relationship between church and state. The Communist leadership knew that in order to eliminate the last trace of organized opposition, it had to crush the Catholic church. This was accomplished during the first three months of 1949, when Cardinal Mindszenty was made to confess various crimes against the state. The Mindszenty case led to the dissolution of the Catholic Democratic People's Party, which had gained the second largest number of ballots, or more than 18 per cent of the popular vote, in 1947. Its elimination in turn enabled the government to dissolve parliament in May 1949 and to hold new "yes-or-no" single-list elections on May 15. The Communists of course obtained an "overwhelming majority" and went on to introduce a new constitution in July 1949 of the Soviet "people's democratic" type.

Nationalization Policies

These political changes opened the gates to radical economic changes of which the Jewish population was the chief victim. Credulous people, misled by government protestations that Hungary would not eliminate all private property, still believed in the possibility of a mixed economy in which at least the medium and small industries would be permitted to remain in private hands. This dream was shattered on March 29, 1948, when the cabinet unexpectedly decreed the nationalization of all industrial and commercial undertakings employing more than 100 people. Neither the National Assembly, nor the leaders of the non-Communist political parties, nor industry itself had known in advance about this measure to collectivize the economy. (In preparation for it, on November 11, 1947, the National Assembly was maneuvered by the Communists into passing a law granting the cabinet power to govern by decree.) At the end of April 1948, the Communist-dominated parliament, faced with the *fait accompli* of the decree, legalized it *ex post facto* in the form of Law No. 108.

The exemption of enterprises employing less than 100 people had little meaning, as Article 12 of the law gave the government final authority to decide what enterprises fell within the purview of the law. Former owners had no right of appeal; there was no independent judicial authority recognized to hear such appeals. The government was the sole judge of its own action. Article 9 declared that the government did not recognize private claims of any nature upon nationalized enterprises.

The manner in which this law was executed was indicated with clarity and courage by Geza Supka in an editorial in the liberal daily *Vilag*. This article, written as early as April 29, 1948, declared that in actual practice even workshops employing three to five workers were being nationalized. On May 5, 1948, a survey published by the same newspaper showed that in a little more than one month after the publication of the decree, seventy-eight per cent of the total of 361,000 industrial workers were working for state-owned and managed industries.

The last remaining group of independent business people, the retail merchants, had now to depend for their supplies on state-owned enterprises and to meet the competition of state and party-owned retail cooperative stores. The latter were granted priorities in supply and lower prices by the state-owned industry. There was an even more formidable obstacle for the private merchants to overcome: the huge mass of workers of state-owned enterprises received only part of their wages in cash, the rest being paid out in the form of certificates for the purchase of commodities exclusively from state-owned cooperative stores. Thus the majority of workers were forced to patronize government retail cooperatives only. State stores had to pay no taxes, while private retailers, selling goods bought from the state-owned factories at prices fixed by the government, had to pay heavy taxes as well.

Pursuant to a decree issued in May 1948, public building activities (roads, public housing, etc.) could be undertaken only by "agencies of the Ministry of Construction."[1] The same month it was announced that special state planning offices would be established to plan for housing, social and cultural institutions, and industrial production.[2]

As for former Hungarian owners of industrial property who had become citizens of foreign countries, the nationalization law provided that their properties were not exempt from confiscation unless the owners furnished documentary proof of their formal release from Hungarian citizenship, or their having acquired their new citizenship on or before August 8, 1931—thus excluding all those Jews who had fled from Nazism. *Vilag* reported on May 5, 1948 that by virtue of a new decree the government was authorized to deprive of Hungarian citizenship all persons who, because of "criminal acts of a political nature" or "for economic reasons," emigrated from Hungary. (In 1951 an "amnesty" was decreed for emigrants returning to Hungary; however they were not exempted from having their properties confiscated.)

In September 1947, special workers' courts had been set up to deal with cases of "usury," meaning violations of price regulations, acts against the interests of public supply, the illicit export of commodities, hoarding of and trade in gold, and silver and foreign currency. On July 23, 1948, it was reported in *Amerikai Magyar Népszava* (New York) that these courts were frequently meting out prison sentences of five to ten years to "economic offenders," most of them Jews. In Budapest, a Jewish jeweler was given a long prison sentence because one ounce of gold was found in his shop. Private trade, the paper reported, was being used by Communist propaganda as the whipping boy for every economic mistake and failure of the administration, and for all the consequences of the policy of economic isolation.

On November 17, 1948, Vincent Nagy in a lecture before the New York Rotary Club declared that 80 per cent of the Hungarian population was living in misery. Industrial workers, representing 15 per cent of the population, had a steady income which, however, did not permit them to eat meat more often than once a week and to buy more than one pair of shoes a year. Five per cent of the population was living in luxury; these were the secretaries, organizers, and office workers of the Communist Party, its representatives in the government, in the proliferating government agencies, and in nationalized industry. Sharing with them in this luxurious living were their "silent partners" in business, black-marketeers, political and economic spies, and some Communist-licensed lawyers who "defended" victims of the police regime.

On December 10, 1948, Leo Lania reported from Budapest to the New York *Aufbau* that even after the last bumper wheat crop, the government was prohibiting the baking of wheat bread and rolls because the wheat surplus had to be delivered to Russia.

As a result of nationalization and its attendant measures, the number of Jews dependent on relief provided by the American JDC grew apace. According to a report by the Institute of Overseas Studies of the Council of Jewish Federations and Welfare Funds (New York), dated March 9, 1949 at the end of 1948, of a total of 143,000 Jewish persons in Hungary, more than 95,000, or two-thirds of the Jewish population, were receiving American Jewish relief in one form or another.

Jewish Education

In order to curtail the traditional rights of the churches, based on law and custom and guaranteed by the constitution of 1867 and the treaty of peace, it was necessary for the Communist regime to impose a servile leadership on the churches; this new leadership would then "voluntarily" resign the churches' rights (to tax their members, maintain their own schools, etc.). The most important of the prerogatives abandoned in this way by the churches was the educational. The Protestants were the first to agree to the nationalization of their elementary and high schools.

In the case of the Jewish community Stoeckler signed a compact with the government renouncing, in the name of the Jewish denomination, its right to maintain its own schools, with the exception of the Rabbinical Seminary and a Jewish gymnasium in Budapest. On December 8, 1948, he reported to a meeting of the Board of Representatives of the Pest Jewish Community, delegates of the Orthodox Central Bureau, and leaders of the Hungarian Zionist Organization.

> I wish to announce that the Jewish denomination signed this Tuesday an agreement regulating the relations between the state and itself. The text of the compact guarantees the most complete freedom of religion. There is no doubt that the equal rights of the Jewish denomination are also guaranteed. The general schools of the Jewish denomination

were nationalized in the same manner as were those of other denominations. No difference of opinion can exist about this, for nobody can demand that, in order to have two or three Jewish schools continue to exist [there were more than thirty], a whole series of schools of other denominations should be permitted to continue, schools where the youth would be taught to be antisemitic. . . . The agreement permits 20 per cent of the students of every school to be exempted from attendance on Saturdays. Our children . . . will have to be scattered among the different municipal and state district schools so that all may observe the sabbath—among non-Jewish children their number would not exceed 20 per cent. (Here Mr. Stoeckler raised his voice [continued the report] and said the following:

It is intolerable that some people should criticize this part of the agreement by interpreting it falsely. Anybody who voices unfounded and malicious criticism only makes trouble for the Jewish community.[3]

Even in the former Jewish schools attendance on the sabbath was made compulsory, as we may see from the above. And since the student body of these schools remained overwhelmingly Jewish, most Jewish pupils were compelled to attend on the sabbath.

In connection with the "most complete freedom of religion" allegedly guaranteed in the compact with the government, Stoeckler neglected to mention the promulgation of a new and unprecedented decree by the Minister of Commerce and the Cooperatives (No. 45.500/1948 K.Sz.M.) regulating business and closing hours of stores and shops.

Section 5 of this decree prescribes that in justified cases exemptions may be granted by the Commercial Directorates from the compulsory hours of business for stores on Saturdays. . . .[4]

This referred only to those still engaged in or working for a private enterprise. Those who worked for nationalized undertakings and were thus employees of the state either worked on Saturdays or lost their jobs.

Under such conditions it was clearly false to state that the Jewish denomination had religious rights equal to those of other denominations. Also, the curricula of the two schools still left to the Jewish community were completely changed in their structure and tendency. The Zionist spirit was banished. Andrew Gellert had to quit his post as school inspector of the community, his place being taken by the Communist psychologist Andrew Jozsef. The Jewish schools were rapidly turned into bulwarks of Marxist-Stalinist indoctrination.

To excuse the sad state of Jewish education, Stoeckler habitually pointed out that religious instruction was "not only available but even compulsory" in all public and nationalized schools. But compulsory religious education in public schools had been the law of the land since 1867. The Communists had simply not got around to repealing the law. This omission, however, was corrected on September 6, 1949, when "compulsory teaching of religion in Hungarian schools was abolished by a decree of Hungary's Presidential Council."[5] On December 15, 1949, a new decree was published announcing that "religious instruction in the two Jewish or in the other denominational schools cannot be compulsory." The dispatch reporting this added that the teaching of Hebrew had already been prohibited.[6]

Uj Elet stated on August 25, 1949, in connection with the promulgation of Hungary's new constitution, that the Jewish denomination "will continue to obtain the state subsidy agreed upon in the compact with the state." On December 12, *The New York Times* reported from Budapest that the total amount of state subsidies to all churches had been decreased from the equivalent of $5,200,000 to that of $3,333,000. On September 8, 1949, Joseph Balazs wrote a despairing article in *Uj Elet* about the financial prospects of the Jewish communal institutions; he pleaded for voluntary contributions—from people hopelessly ruined economically. The article clearly implied that the community's tax powers existed on paper only. The regimentation of the professional staff of the religious community was completed when the employees of the Central Bureau of Hungarian Jews and of the Pest Jewish Community were made to form a professional branch of the Communist Party. On June 15, 1949, at the opening meeting of the new branch, the speaker asserted:

> Budapest Jewry must be permeated with the spirit of the Hungarian Workers Party; they must learn its progressive ideology, and march along the road which leads to the end of class differences and the establishment of socialism.[7]

On September 29, *Uj Elet* reported that "the semiannual period of the Stakhanov competition of the workers of the National Office of Jews and of the Pest Jewish Community has ended . . . with a beneficial effect on the employees' willingness to work." Several rewards were distributed. On December 1, 1949, the paper reported that the employees of these organizations had offered to perform extra work as their contribution to the celebration of the seventieth anniversary of Stalin's birth.

Antisemitism

Throughout all these political changes in the country antisemitic riots and desecrations of cemeteries continued in Paszto[8] and in Kormend.[9] In contrast with the period of Ferenc Nagy's Premiership, when antisemitic occurrences were fought in parliament by Smallholders and other democratic deputies and discussed frankly in *Uj Elet*, now they were mentioned only briefly in the back pages of the Jewish paper, finally ceasing to be published at all.

The strengthened rule of the Communist Party and the elimination of the openly antisemitic Communist Minister of the Interior Ladislas Rajk (on charges of Titoism) further contributed to the popular identification of Jews with Communism. Stoeckler, leader of the official Jewish community, eagerly sought to identify it with Communism; its paper, *Uj Elet*, became one of the many party-controlled organs spreading antidemocratic and anti-American propaganda. The New York Hungarian-language weekly *Az Ember* published a series of articles on conditions in Hungary by an unnamed "special correspondent." One of these articles, dealing with "The Tragic Lot of Surviving Hungarian Jews," stated:

> In 1945, the total number of Jews in Hungary was under 180,000 (including those who did not adhere to the Jewish religion), and yet antisemitism today is raging across the land. This is so in spite of the fact that the overwhelming majority of Jews, nearly 170,000 people, are starving and suffering, and live only in the hope and desire of leaving the country. . . .
>
> They would gladly go anywhere, to America, Palestine, or Canada, but they are simply not permitted to leave. Even if some of them have a chance to obtain a passport, they are unable to pay the ransom demanded for it, which on the average amounts to 5-600,000 forints. . . .
>
> Why this intensification of antisemitism? Simply because of the fact that in the Communist leadership there are people like Rakosi, Gero, Revai, Farkas, Vass, Berei, Vajda, Horvath and a couple of hundred second- and third-rate party exponents who happened to be born Jews. The crucial point, however, is that these people perform their misdeeds not as Jews, but as agents of Moscow. They have nothing in common with Jewry, whom they oppress and maim even more cruelly than the others. In the light of the role of the many leading non-Jewish Communists, this antisemitic attitude is both idiotic and criminal. . . . Without the role of these and some other 10,000 active non-Jewish Communist leaders and protagonists, the 500 Communists of Jewish descent would offer a sad picture indeed, the picture of a handful of nobodies incapable of action. . . . This antisemitism is, therefore, just as unforgivably moronic and sadistic a development as the persecution of Christians in Hungary would be. But for these Jew-baiters no arguments exist. They are, as former Nazis and often as fanatical Communists, simply aching for new pogroms. This time, however, they are determined not to transfer their bloody work to Auschwitz but to carry it out right "*on the spot*." Already they greet each other in the streets of Budapest, not with a "hello" or "good morning," but with the words: "On the spot!"
>
> Democratic Hungarians abroad must make it clear to all concerned that for the conditions prevailing in Hungary only the Communists are responsible, regardless of whether they are Jewish or Christian in origin, and they must enlist all their energy in a democratic effort to check the new antisemitic frenzy. . . .[10]

The presence of Jewish Communists in the government of Hungary to some extent explains the frenzy of the anti-Zionist drive of the Communist leadership which followed the first elections in Israel resulting in the defeat of the pro-Soviet elements there. In the Communist leadership of Yugoslavia, Bulgaria, and Czechoslovakia the number of persons of Jewish origin was much smaller than in Hungary. Non-Jewish Communists in Bulgaria and Czechoslovakia could afford to concede something to the desire of Jews to emigrate to Israel. But the Jewish Communists in Hungary and Rumania felt obliged to prove their loyalty to the party, and so as to escape Moscow's charging them with "bourgeois nationalistic Zionism." It was significant that Tibor Szonyi and Andras Szalai, former leftist Zionist leaders in Hungary who turned Communist, and Minister of the Interior Ladislas Rajk, an official protector of pogromists, were sentenced to death at the same time on the same charges of nationalism. Szonyi and Szalai had to confess that they had been members of "Zionist spy rings"; Rajk himself was charged, of all things, with Zionism!

Attack on Zionism and Israel

The significance of the Rajk trial, held in September 1949, from the point of view of Jewish interest, and in the perspective of the series of anti-Zionist trials that followed in Prague, Moscow, etc., in late 1952, lies in the fact that it was at this trial that an attempt was made by Communist authorities to charge the Zionist movement with collaboration with the American Secret Service. One of the accused, Tibor Szonyi (formerly Hoffman), the leader of the Cadre Department of the Communist Party of Hungary was found guilty of espionage and cruelty, and executed. During his trial Szonyi was asked by the People's Prosecutor:

> Have you been a member of the Zionist movement?
>
> *Szonyi*: As far as I know, Ferenc Vagi and Gyorgy Demeter were members of the Zionist movement. In this connection I know, and I have had personal experience in Switzerland to bear it out, that the Zionist movement generally co-operated very closely with the American Secret Service.
>
> (From *Rajk Laszlo es Tarsai a Nepbirosag Elott*, Budapest, Szikra, 2nd Ed., p. 137)

As a result of the deliberate anti-Zionist tendency of the trial and execution of these people in Hungary, a new wave of attacks against Zionists swept the entire Eastern European satellite area.

Following the UN decision on the partition of Palestine and the proclamation of the State of Israel, thousands of Hungarian Jews escaped to Israel. During this period, ending with the Israeli-Arab armistice, according to reports of the Israeli Ministry of Immigration (published in the Hungarian Tel Aviv daily *Uj Kelet* in February 1949), more than 10,000 Hungarian Jews entered the new state. All Hungarian Jews had to leave "illegally" via the camps. The Jewish Communists during this period of "benevolent indifference" tried to use Zionism for their own purposes. The fight of the Jews in Israel was described by them as an "anti-imperialist" fight, meaning in the jargon of the Cominform a pro-Soviet, anti-British and anti-American fight. On June 8, 1948, Stoeckler, in an address delivered after his "election," said:

> I wish to serve the lofty cause for which our brethren are bleeding in the Holy Land. In the ancient country our youth sacrifice their blood for freedom and democracy, against imperialist intentions and oppression. I, who with unswerving loyalty fight for our Hungarian People's Democracy, want them to know that we all are with them, with all our strength, in this struggle, and that in this we are backed by democratic Hungary and by all democratic nations. This is not a struggle between Zionists and anti-Zionists; this is a bloody struggle between fighters for freedom and oppressors.[11]

In their wish to strengthen the small pro-Soviet Zionist minority, the Jewish Communists published an editorial in *Uj Elet* entitled: "We Want Progressive Zionists at the Head of the Zionist Organization." The editorial said:

> There is no doubt that a struggle is inevitable among the parties in Israel, which range from clerical-religious to Marxist parties, because such a struggle is inescapable in any capitalistic country. . . . In the Hungarian Zionist Organization middle-class elements were in power. . . . In recent times it became evident that the majority of the members of the Zionist Organization belong to the Marxist-Zionist parties. . . . The progressive character of the Zionist Organization can only be maintained under a Marxist-Zionist leadership. The present leaders of the Zionist Organization will have to resign. . . .[12]

The outcome of the elections in Israel brought among other things an abrupt change in the Soviet line on Zionism: from benevolent neutrality it changed to outspoken hostility. In the meantime, the leaders of the left-wing Zionist parties tried to capture the Zionist Organization of Hungary. As a protest against the non-Mapam leaders' continued participation in the leadership of the organization, these left-wing groups, called "Borochov Circle" and "Achduth Haavodah," had their members walk out from the Zionist leadership; by paralyzing the elected leadership they hoped to impose their own views upon the whole federation of Zionists in Hungary. The support given them by Stoeckler's *Uj Elet* shows that they enjoyed the favor of the Communists. At the same time, the pro-American trend indicated by the Israeli elections was sharply attacked. An alleged remark by Henry Morgenthau, that "Palestine may become an essential bulwark against the Soviet Union," was answered by such statements as:

> It is our conviction that American capital has nothing to look for in Israel. The toilers of the State of Israel did not fight for the freedom

of their country and did not drain the swamps in order to become an anti-Soviet drill ground, or a colony of American monopoly capital. The toilers of Israel will never forget Ilya Ehrenburg's words about the freedom of Palestine having also been won at Stalingrad.[13]

Soon open and direct attacks were launched against emigration to Israel and the Zionist Organization as such. Max Domonkos, secretary general of the Pest Jewish Community, wrote a front-page editorial entitled "Let Us See Clearly," which stated:

There is a section of Hungarian Jewry which is living in an unhealthy state of nervous tension. Even at the risk of unpopularity we have to inform those who are misguided by false propaganda . . . that it is a mistake to believe that if somebody's name is on some list or other, this already means that he has a possibility of emigrating, or that a "pre-visa" is an entry ticket to any promised land. . . . Historical progress cannot be stopped. The Hungarian People's Republic never objected to the work of movements which served the realization of the Jewish state, it did not even complain about these movements being directed from abroad. . . . But it is not irrelevant to inquire why the Jewish stratum feeling disappointed here did not depart immediately after liberation, instead of postponing the exercise of this right to the years of prosperity [!]. It is curious that these elements do not want to identify themselves with the new planned social economy, and only now see fit to claim a right that they did not speak about for years. . . . Behind this unhealthy nervous tension there are the machinations of reaction, which wishes to discredit the Hungarian People's Democracy. . . .[14]

A week later, the Communist journalist Andrew Sos wrote:

The State of Israel maintains diplomatic missions and embassies. Its Ambassador presented his credentials to the President of the Hungarian Republic. Henceforth Israel will be represented in Hungary through its legation and consulate. There is no longer any need for parties and movements directed from Israel. These movements have lost their justification. . . . We are, of course, glad that there is a distant country which in case of need may offer refuge, together with the Soviet Union, to Jews persecuted by fascism. We are not living in a world of illusions, and we know that any of the monopoly-capitalistic powers may at any time rekindle the fires of antisemitism within their own territory. We view with alarm the growing influence of capitalists on the national development of Israel, and we fear lest this growing nationalism and influence of monopoly capitalism jeopardize the harmony between Jewish and Arab toilers. . . . We understand that the Zionist leaders living in this country seek to go to Israel. We take it for granted that the leaders of the Hungarian Republic will enable them to do so soon. We are not speaking of them, but of the great masses of Jewry: the Jewish toilers, progressive intellectuals, small storekeepers and small craftsmen. They ought not to fall victim to delusions and get themselves into a state of nervous tension. The Hungarian People's Democracy guarantees the rights of every Hungarian worker. . . . But we must emphasize: the application of social hygiene to Hungarian Jewry is inevitable. A restratification at home must take place, we must create new Jewish producers' cooperatives. Is it right that toiling people should squander away their furniture for passports to the moon? No, and a thousand times no. Let us go along the path fixed by Ilya Ehrenburg. Let us remember that only the people's democracy, marching ahead toward the realization of socialism, can put an end to antisemitism. . . .[15]

Stoeckler himself defined the new line as follows:

Hungarian Jewry rejoices with those in reborn Israel whose struggles have been crowned with success. It will find ways and means for establishing contact with them, as it has done in the case of other countries. But this is an affair between the two states, and it is of paramount importance to Hungarian Jewry that it should be so. Anybody failing to understand this troubles our tranquillity and disregards the position of the great majority of Hungarian Jewry, who wish to devote all their energies to strengthening the socialist order. Hungarian Jewry rejects all attempts at disunity—the Hungarian People's Democracy will take care of any such attempts with a strong hand, no matter from what quarters the provocation may come. . . . We have to clarify our thinking. We want to be understood both by those who doubt our denomination's love of Zion, and by those who would like to identify it with Zionism. It is the duty of the leaders of Hungarian Jewry to heed the views of the democratic Hungarian government even to the minutest detail.[16]

This reveals the difficult position of a "leadership" compelled to act under party orders without being sure what would be demanded of it tomorrow. Stoeckler's clique could not afford to take an openly anti-Zionist stand, lest it alienate the Jewish public. On the other hand, this leadership had to prove to the Communists that its past support of Israel had not been Zionism.

Soon the propaganda attack reached its final stage; in another month Sos spoke as follows:

The Hungarian People's Democracy, which has granted human rights to the Jews and guarantees their freedom from fear, demands nothing of them but that they be good democrats in their own interest and in that of the Hungarian People's Democracy, and that they work for the realization of a new socialist world. . . . The Hungarian People's Democracy demands a clear understanding of the question of Zionism. This clarification has already been achieved in Poland and Rumania. It is no secret that the Bund in Poland was dissolved, and that its best members joined the Workers Party. The Zionist Organization both in Poland and Rumania voluntarily disbanded. The premise for this was the declaration by the Political Bureau of the Rumanian Workers Party that it considered Zionism a form of nationalism and, as such, incompatible with the principles of socialism. It was the party's position that in the State of Israel one may be a good Israeli Socialist or Israeli Communist, but that there is no such thing as a "Socialist-Zionist" or a "Communist-Zionist." This principle was carried into practice in the past few months, when during the revision of the membership of the Hungarian Workers Party all Zionists were excluded, even those professing to be "Socialist-Zionists" or "Communist-Zionists." As to the problem of emigration: this is a question which is subject to settlement by an international agreement between the governments of Hungary and Israel. There are good prospects for such a settlement as not only normal but also friendly diplomatic relations exist between the two states. We must not permit the emigration fever to spread. Irresponsible and unscrupulous agents and profiteers must not be permitted to succeed. Should the emigration of certain strata be permitted, this must take place in a manner which would cause no disturbance to the order of production in the Hungarian People's Democracy.[17]

This was the death knell for the Zionist Organization in Hungary. Five days later, a body called the "Committee for the Liquidation of the Hungarian Zionist Federation" published the following statement:

The National Council of the Hungarian Zionist Federation, at its meeting of March 13, 1949, passed the following unanimous resolution: Since with the establishment of the State of Israel the main objective of the Federation has been attained; and since moreover normal diplomatic relations exist bewteen Hungary and Israel—the National Council has decided to terminate the activities of the Hungarian Zionist Federation. The Federation, its subdivisions and local groups have terminated their activities in accordance with the above resolution. In the name of the Liquidating Committee: Dr. Galos, Secretary General.[18]

Two months later, ten Zionist leaders were arrested for organizing "illegal" emigration to Israel, among them Bela Denes, president of the Mapai, Alexander Kertesz, president of the Mapam, Rabbi J. Frenkel, president of the Mizrachi Organization, and seven others. All but one were sentenced to several years' imprisonment. Frenkel, at a separate trial, was found not guilty and released, but then was immediately interned in a camp. On appeal, three of the defendants were acquitted in December.

It should be noted that the Sos's report that all Zionists were being excluded from the Workers Party did not fully describe the calamity which had befallen Jewish party members. The facts were revealed by John MacCormac in *The New York Times;* he reported on January 9, 1948, that "most of the Jewish members of the Hungarian Workers Party have been excluded by a purge now going on in its ranks." These expulsions in their overwhelming majority were because of the "alien class" background of the Jewish members.

On June 23, 1949, *The New York Times* reported under a Prague date line that at least 200,000 persons had been expelled from the party in the purge following the Rajk case.

The mood of those elements of the Jewish intelligentsia who out of socialist belief had joined the Communist Party, is described in the following excerpt from a letter received from Budapest by a Mr. Tibor Adam and published in the December 25, 1948, issue of the New York weekly *Az Ember*. The letter was brought to him by an emissary from a young Jewish woman, a physician, who had joined the Communist Party in Budapest.

> I must confess that your predictions came true. As soon as you left Hungary I plunged headlong into party work and did my best to serve the "cause." It was in vain. The situation here has completely changed. You just cannot be an intellectual. As you know, both of my parents have university degrees and such an "inheritance" today constitutes the same fatal burden that four Jewish grandparents did in 1944. We are being thrust out of every post. In spite of my having served as party trustee, popular educator, agitator and "village worker," I was suspended as a member, "re-evaluated," and finally sent to an elementary party seminar where I had to rehash "Basic Communism" dozens of times—instead of being permitted to continue my vocation, scientific research. On the day of the review of my party membership, the commission treated me with the utmost contempt and brutality. . . . The result was that they declared me an "alien class" element, on probation as a candidate for party membership, after two years of arduous party work. . . . Since then I have been surrounded with lynx-eyed watchers who are more than eager to trample the likes of us down on the slightest pretext. I still have my job, but I am afraid that at the end of the "probation period" I shall be through, without a position or a livelihood, without the right to a living. . . . I am a socialist today as I have been before, and still I know that my days here are numbered. . . . My parents are leaving soon for Palestine. The fever of emigration has assumed a hysterical character. There at least 60,000 applications for admission to Israel. . . . You know that I am too weak for manual labor. What should I do? What is to become of me? If you cannot help me by some good advice, at least give me a bit of consolation and moral support, because I am at the end of my strength.

On June 30, 1949, the Jewish Telegraphic Agency reported from Tel Aviv that, following the sentencing of the nine Zionist leaders, many new arrests of Zionist representatives took place. The report estimated that at least two hundred Zionists had been arrested in one week and placed in a concentration camp near Budapest. The arrests took place following the escape of a number of Jews who had been subpoenaed as "agents of Zionist fascism." On November 29, 1949, the *Jewish Morning Journal* reported that thirty-six members of the left-wing Hashomer

Hatzair were arrested in Hungary while visiting the graves of two of their leaders said to have been executed several months earlier. It is interesting to note that according to a dispatch from Tel Aviv, the Hungarian section of the Israeli Communist Party resigned from it in protest at the persecution of Zionists in Hungary.[20]

At the end of 1949 even Rumania gave up her opposition to the emigration of Jews to Israel. This placed Hungary, because of the conspicuous role of Jewish Communists in the government leadership, in the position of being the only country which prohibited the emigration of Jews. Shortly thereafter, however, Rumania halted (temporarily) Jewish emigration to Israel, Poland and Czechoslovakia following suit when their emigration agreements with Israel expired.

Israel made a series of representations to the Hungarian government. After long negotiations with local diplomatic representatives of the Israeli government, Hungary finally saw fit, in November 1949, to allow 3,000 persons to go to Israel. This quota embraced two categories: 1,000 persons whose immediate families were already in Israel, provided the latter had left the country legally after January 1, 1948; and 2,000 persons fifty-five years of age and older. The agreement with Israel established priorities for Zionist and religious leaders, with the "right to recommend" candidates granted to the local representatives of Israel; but the final decision on every single case was reserved to the Hungarian authorities. Emigrants were prohibited from taking out of Hungary any funds or property, except for a few specified personal belongings. In May 1950 it was reported in New York that every emigrant had had to pay a fee of $1,000 in person or through his representative into the Hungarian treasury fifteen days prior to his departure. Nevertheless, the report added, within a few days 14,000 persons had petitioned the authorities to be placed on the list of 3,000.[21] But, according to Israeli sources, by the end of June 1951, or over a period of more than eighteen months, only 2,200 persons were permitted to leave Hungary for Israel.

Economic Assistance

In view of the fact that nationalization deprived a very broad section of the Jewish population of their livelihood, and emigration was barred, the only way of solving the economic problem of Hungarian Jews seemed to be the establishment (with American help) of Jewish producers' cooperatives and schools for teaching people new trades. A new Bureau for Retraining and for the Organization of Cooperatives for Hungarian Jewry was established. In the first month of its existence, in February 1949, 889 persons had recourse to the Bureau; of these, 468 wished to be trained in some craft, whereas 421 wanted to work in one of the Bureau's cooperatives.

These cooperatives are described as follows in a report of the Institute on Overseas Studies of the Council of Jewish Federations and Welfare Funds (dated March 9, 1949).

> In December, 1948, there were 12 producers' cooperatives in operation with a membership of over 500, making wearing apparel of all sorts. Two others, one making boxes and the other candy, were organized during December. In addition, there is a textile buying and selling cooperative with 300 members and 5 other cooperatives which are about ready to begin operations. JDC plans envisage the creation of 25 more cooperatives in the next six months, with 50 members each. The average wage for a full-time employee in the cooperatives is between 700 and 800 forints ($60-68) per month, which is about the equivalent of the wage of a skilled worker in a government factory. This wage may be compared with an estimate that 1,350 forints ($115) a month are required to maintain a minimum living standard for four people in Budapest.
>
> The instrument through which the JDC has financed and encouraged the creation of producers' cooperatives is a bank, largely set up with JDC funds, called the Reconstruction Credit Cooperative. It has a total capital of about 14,000,000 forints ($1,000,000) of which nearly 13,000,000 forints have come from the JDC. The government has contributed 600,000 forints. . . . The government has established a special bureau, called Okisz, which regulates the activities of the producers' cooperatives, serves as their agent in obtaining allocations for goods, sells them their raw materials and buys from them the finished goods for resale to government ministries, government retail stores, consumer cooperatives and private retail stores. No producers' cooperative can be established unless Okisz approves. . . .

This, then, was the economic role intended in theory for Hungarian Jewry. In practice, the task of creating livelihoods for the entire mass of economically uprooted Jews in this expensive manner was a manifest impossibility, particularly on the basis of almost exclusive American Jewish voluntary aid. Little more than a year later, as we shall see, the Communists employed an incomparably simpler, inexpensive and final way of solving the problem of the economically and socially "expendable" masses, including the middle-class and politically unreliable Jews. They deported them.

Nor was the JDC destined to be allowed to continue its much-needed aid. Throughout 1949 the JDC was hard put to carry on its life-preserving work under the continuous harassment of local Communists, particularly those of Jewish origin. The peak of this harassment was reached with the arrest in December 1949 of Israel Jacobson, an American who served as director of the JDC office in Hungary. For two weeks Jacobson was held incommunicado by the political police on unspecified charges and subjected to interrogations. He was then released from jail and expelled from Hungary.

One day before the trial of the ten Zionist leaders in Budapest, Stoeckler made a speech to a meeting of the Board of Representatives of his community. He informed his coreligionists that the government was about to stop all financial aid to religious organizations. This bitter pill he coated in the following way:

> We stand on the basis of the principle of free denominations in a free state. The new Hungarian Constitution, to be promulgated in the near future, will loosen still further the ties between the state and the religious denominations. We shall gradually have to become self-supporting.

Of the Pest Jewish Community's estimated budget of 2,000,000 forints for the coming year, Stoeckler said that "we hope to receive 1,200,000 forints from the American JDC." He went on to announce that the Zionist Federation had dissolved itself, and thus Jewish unity was firmly established. One-third of the Board of Representatives, however, were members of the former Zionist Federation; these "will have to recognize in a new statement that they accept our program as binding on them." After reaffirming "our undying gratitude to the mighty Soviet Union and the glorious Red Army," Stoeckler went on to say:

> The leadership of our community devotes much attention to maintaining good relations between Hungarian Jewry and Jewry abroad. We view with alarm the fact that certain Jewish organizations abroad, unrepresentative of the interests of the "little Jew," endanger the interests of their brethren. They join the foes of the peoples' democracies. They are a great danger to us by helping to revive antisemitism. We refuse to maintain any contact with such Jewish organizations, and we shall do everything in our power to warn our Jewish brothers abroad of this danger. The foreign relations of Hungarian Jewry are meant to serve the Hungarian people's democracy. . . .[19]

The economic situation of Hungarian Jews steadily worsened. On the basis of a decree published in September 1949, a nationwide seizure of retail stores was begun in the following month under the direction of the Ministry of Finance. All merchandise, as well as buildings owned by private storekeepers, was expropriated. According to Bela Fabian, a leading member of the Hungarian National Committee in Exile, by the end of 1949, 1,721 retail stores of different kinds had been expropriated without compensation, together with 294 buildings. Of the 1,721 confiscated stores, 1,504 were owned by Jews.

Early in December 1949, the confiscation of other real estate was begun; by the end of the month 491 buildings were expropriated by the state, without compensation. Of these 491 houses, 383 were owned by Jews.

According to the Fabian report, during 1948 and 1949 a total of 687 lawyers were disbarred, of whom 439 were Jews or of Jewish origin. Between

May and December 1949, 310 Communist Party functionaries were purged from the party and from their jobs. The same report states that 209 of the 310 were Jews, and 47 "non-sectarians" of Jewish parentage. In connection with the Rajk trial alone, 38 functionaries were arrested at party headquarters, 8 of whom were severely sentenced; the whereabouts of the rest is unknown.

Propaganda

Meanwhile, the tide of propaganda against "fascist America" rose to new levels of mendacity. On August 25, 1949, *Uj Elet* stated that the situation of American Jews in the Yorkville section of New York had "become untenable as a result of antisemitic unrest." Because of the activities of the Hungarian Arrow Cross and German Nazi underworld in this district, "the Jewish families and merchants are fleeing, one after the other, from the neighborhood. Day after day, posters inciting to pogroms are being pasted on the walls of houses. . . . The authorities do nothing about removing them. . . ."

Quoting the Hungarian-language New York Communist paper *Magyar Jövo, Uj Elet* stated on September 15, 1949, that in an unidentified Jewish neighborhood in New York, an arrow was shot into the home of Charles Faber, a Jew, by the local Ku Klux Klan, because he had rented his apartment to a Negro couple. There are 25,000 Klansmen in New York State, it reported, but the authorities did not care.

On November 17, 1949, the same paper printed a three-column editorial on the offer to Jefferson College of a grant of fifty million dollars, provided it would bar Jews from the student body. The editorial ended with the allegation that even if there were people in America courageous enough to fight the bequest in court, they would be bound to fail because the reactionary Supreme Court couldn't be expected to remedy the situation. The paper never reported that the bequest was rejected by Jefferson College.

Uj Elet wrote on December 22, 1949, (referring to a report attributed to the New York Communist paper *Magyar Jövo*) that the "anti-Negro mass demonstrations in Chicago have assumed an antisemitic character. 'Hitler has not burned enough Jews, let us burn those who survived,' shouted the berserk mob."

On December 22, 1949, *Uj Elet* printed a letter to the editor by one Ladislas Hermann stating that American and British Jewry, under fascistic monopoly capitalism, were threatened with the same fate that befell the Jews of Europe under Nazism. "Auschwitz may easily be duplicated in the West."

A characteristic example of this attempt to make the United States out as the world center of antisemitism and fascism is an editorial printed in

Uj Elet on October 27, 1949, under the headline, "Squaring Accounts with All Manifestations of Fascism.":

> We read in the New York publication *Magyar Jövo* that the progressive Jewish writers, artists and scientists of America held a mass meeting in Town Hall protesting against the Peekskill riots. Henry Wallace sent the following interesting message which was read at the meeting: "Under Hitler, too, antisemitic excesses were initiated under the guise of anti-Communism. . . . In the same manner, the fascist attack at Peekskill at once assumed an antisemitic character. . . ."
>
> Not Wallace alone but also other representatives of the progressive circles of America have already called attention to the fact that certain phenomena of American fascism closely resemble what took place in the first stages of the Hitlerite movement. The fascist attack at Peekskill was in the very image of the attacks which the Storm Troops of Hitler launched against the movements of progressive circles in Germany. However, not only was the attack itself a copy of the Nazi model, but also the fact that the American authorities, like the Germans, sabotaged the entire affair. . . .
>
> Ilya Ehrenburg has called the world's attention to the danger represented by all forms of fascism. By now, every word of his has been borne out by reality. We see that antisemitism in Germany failed to cease with the collapse of Hitlerite Germany—because the occupiers of the Western zones of Germany see to it that Hitler's spirit stays alive. We should never forget that in a modified form Hitler's ideas continue to prevail. Nuremberg and Peekskill, Hitler and Truman, they are all manifestations of the same monopoly capitalism.

While American democracy was thus identified with Nazism, the Jews of Hungary were encouraged to regard East Germany in a favorable light.

A good example of the official Communist attitude in the matter is a front-page editorial printed on October 20, 1949, in *Uj Elet*:

> It is impossible to correct injustice by injustice. *It would be a grave injustice, and the debasement of humanism if we charged the things that occurred in Germany to the German people.* . . . We cannot afford to be unjust, and so we have to acknowledge that in Hitler's Germany, even if they had to suffer most, the Jews were not the only victims. Modern sociology does not recognize guilty nations. There are no guilty nations, only guilty classes and ruling strata. *Those who try to make out and use the German people as the scapegoat, have only one objective: to efface the responsibility of Hitler and of the criminal ruling circles supporting him.*
>
> For this reason *all those who confuse hatred for fascism with hatred for the German people are on a very wrong and dangerous path. . .*
>
> On this ground, we have faith in the new Democratic Eastern Germany in which Generalissimo Stalin, our own saviour, has also put his faith. . .

> *From now on, we are no longer going to speak about hatred for the Germans.* A passion of this kind would lead us dangerously astray. *The German working people are just as good allies of the toilers of the world as any other people.* All the more bitterly are we going to hate all forms of fascism, and with all the greater determination are we going to oppose any generalization branding all Germans as Nazis, and *casting doubt upon the democratic forces which have arisen in the Democratic Republic of Germany.*

Throughout 1949, *Uj Elet* printed not a word about the series of decrees and laws being issued by the government; these determined the economic future of the Jewish community. In fact, the only subject of an economic nature that found its way into the columns of this paper was an appeal to its readers to subscribe to a loan floated in support of Hungary's Five-Year Plan.

Finally, on September 8, 1949, *Uj Elet* implicitly explained its silence on Hungarian Jewry's economic needs by describing the Jewish middle class as an anachronism and vestige of the past:

> The middle classes as such have now terminated their historic role. Whether they like it or not, they are retiring from the scene of history, yielding place to upsurging social classes: the workers and peasants who with fresh strength assume their history-shaping role and who are strong enough to counter the danger of fascism. . . . Let us speak frankly: within the Jewish middle classes, too, there are elements that still fail to see the situation clearly, people who do not understand the call of the times even today. These elements do not want to give up the remains of their middle-class style of life. . . . Today [this middle-class style of life] belongs completely to the past. Today the person who fails to understand this fact is committing a crime against himself, his family and the community. . . . It is clear to us that the required break with the so-called "middle-class style of life" constitutes not only a spiritual problem but also a bread problem to certain strata of Hungarian Jewry. . . . But the paramount truth is that whoever would consider the old economic order and absolute middle-class style of life worthy of preservation, is insisting upon a condition which may lead only to a new Auschwitz and to new mass murders.

Forced Unification of Jewish Community

The last measure taken in 1949 to assure the subjection of the Jews of Hungary was the forced unification of the Congressional (Neologue) and Orthodox Jewish community organizations. There was bitter opposition to the move in both religious camps, particularly among the Orthodox leadership; it took almost half a year before the representatives of the many Jewish organizations and institutions could be made even to commence negotiations. At least, early in January 1950, Stoeckler of the Neologue organization and Samuel Kahan-Frankl of the Orthodox group jointly announced in *Uj Elet* (January 5, 1950) that agreement had been reached on unification. At the same time, on the occasion of the annual meeting of the Jewish community of Pest, Stoeckler declared that "the transformation has been made necessary by the changes that have taken place in the relations between our religious denomination and the state, particularly by the change of the material position of Hungarian Jewry." He added that "the members of our community cannot help the fact that their ability to contribute to the needs of the community has diminished."[22] This meant that if ruined Jewry wished to maintain at least its synagogues, it would need state subventions, the price of which was unification.

At the end of February 1951, the national conference of Hungarian Jews convened and adopted statutes creating a unified Jewish community organization. The surprise of the meeting was the bitter tone in which all Orthodox leaders spoke of the historic role of conservative Jewry, and of the futility of organizational changes which cannot affect the substance of Torah-centered traditional Judaism. The result was that none of the recognized Orthodox leaders obtained a place on the presidium and board of the new organization. Kahan-Frankl, Reiner, Zussmann, and all other prominent Orthodox leaders were replaced by an unknown provincial rabbi, Joseph Czitron of Sopron.

Another consequence of this meeting was the summary dismissal of the Minister of Cults and Education, Julius Ortutay. While addressing the convention, this new Communist, apparently carried away for a moment, declared that "when we say that we stand on the principle of religious freedom and of the freedom of conscience, and that we are the true protagonists of these freedoms, we do not exaggerate or indulge in empty talk but are determined to punish any one attempting to violate these principles."[23] Next day, the Minister was summoned to Rakosi's chambers and discharged from office. His whereabouts are now unknown.

Unification meant more than the merger of two Jewish religious communities. It meant the complete subordination of every Jewish organization, institution, fraternity, and club to the central communal authority, which was completely controlled by the Communists. Groups which neglected or refused to join within a prescribed period of time were dissolved.

By the end of 1949, the irremediable ruin of the overwhelming majority of the Jewish population was manifest. After the government had worked the economic ruin of the Jewish middle class, it was announced that they were a thing of the past, condemned to "retire from the scene of history." What form this "retirement" would take was not yet known.

Chapter VIII

Deportations

In a memorandum submitted to leading Jewish organizations in the United States early in 1948, Bela Fabian, a former member of the Board of the Budapest Jewish community, predicted that the economic uprooting and social ostracism of the middle-class Jewish population of Hungary would inevitably condemn it to ultimate physical elimination by deportation. Fabian predicted that thousands of Social Democratic workers and many Communist Party members suspected of opposing the Soviet stranglehold on Hungarian affairs would share the same fate.

This prophesy came true in the early fall of 1950. The first mass deportations from Hungary coincided with a period of economic crisis brought about by a catastrophic crop failure and increased requisitions of food, fuel, and industrial products for export to the Soviet Union and certain satellite countries. A letter received from Budapest during this period stated:

> The chief reason for the lack of food and fuel is that everything must be sent abroad. Apart from the Soviets' own requisitions . . . the shop-windows in Eastern Germany are full of Hungarian butter and meat products, labeled "Gift of the Soviet Union to the German people". . . . Here the milk is skimmed to a watery substance because its food value must go abroad. We get two decilitres of skimmed milk a day per person and meat is available only to state employees, rationed to twenty decagrammes a week. . . . Clothing is of the poorest quality because the better grades of textiles are exported; but nobody can afford to buy even the cheapest anyway.

In January 1951 even such Hungarian staples as wheat and sugar had to be strictly rationed; *Uj Elet* characteristically commented that "the people are convinced that this measure was taken in their own best interest."[1] A year later, when the rationing of these products was suspended, *Uj Elet* made the same interpretation: "The broad masses know that this was done for them."[2] As late as the end of 1951, Budapest was without fuel and adequate medical supplies; the result was an unprecedented epidemic of influenza and lung diseases.[3] The grave housing shortage completed a truly dismal picture of "socialist achievement." Matters were made even worse by the constant influx of thousands of Soviet emissaries, technicians, and secret agents, all of them demanding comfortably furnished quarters and a high standard of living.

Early Deportations

It was under these circumstances that the first mass deportations from Hungary took place. John MacCormac, correspondent for *The New York Times* in Austria, was the first Western newspaperman to report them.[4] According to his report, the victims of this first wave of deportations came from every walk of life and included peasants, workers, intellectuals, and businessmen. A large part of the 2,000 or so Social Democratic leaders arrested between 1947 and 1950 for resisting the dissolution of their party was included. Subsequent reports confirmed MacCormac's information that a high proportion of the deported businessmen were Jews; also, many of the Social Democratic victims were Jews. A marked "legalistic" feature of these early deportations was the fact that all the victims were taken from prisons or concentration camps in Hungary, having previously been sentenced for political or economic offenses to prison terms exceeding two years, or to internment for indefinite periods. Thus, in a sense, these were people held individually responsible for some crime.

The total number of these deportees cannot be established with any degree of certainty. Estimates vary from 20,000 to 80,000. Nor is there any reliable way of determining the number of Jewish deportees; it is the consensus of all available sources of information that it was extraordinarily high. According to MacCormac, the Soviet Union was reported to have "exchanged" these deportees for Soviet technicians given the double task of helping the satellites to build up their heavy industry, and seeing to it that they did this "strictly in accordance with Russia's interests and wishes"—in other words, Hungarian slaves for Russia were bartered for Russian slave drivers for Hungary.

All available sources of information agree that these deportees were shipped as slave labor to the Soviet Union. Their traces can be followed only to the border stations of Rahovo and Zahony; some private reports indicate that for a short period they were kept in Soviet distribution camps near Uzhorod in the Carpatho-Ukraine, the Hungarian province which the Soviet Union annexed after the war. Their final destinations in the Soviet Union are unknown.

Later Deportations

The second type of mass deportations started in Budapest early in May 1951. The legal basis was provided by a law and two decrees, Nos. 8130 M. F. and 760 B. M., passed by the German-dominated Horthy regime in

1939 and aimed at the Jews. These laws were first applied in 1944 when the Germans occupied Hungary.[5] These mass deportations thus differed from the earlier deportations in two respects.

First, it was officially admitted that not a single one of the new victims had ever been charged with, or sentenced for, any crime or offense. They were condemned simply on the basis of their "alien class origin," for being members of the middle class or aristocracy. Second, the victims received individual orders to ready themselves within a period of from one to three days for expulsion to some eastern rural area of Hungary, in the vicinity of the Hungarian-Soviet border; thus it was implied that any deportation of these people beyond the confines of Hungary was not contemplated.

There were three different grades of expulsion orders, but in practice they amounted to the same thing. Those assigned to the first category were required to surrender for expulsion on the day of the order's presentation, and to relinquish all of their belongings without compensation. The second category got a few days' grace to "liquidate their affairs." Those assigned to the third category were permitted to seek employment as manual laborers within a brief time limit, on pain of expulsion in case of failure. Since in Hungary there was almost no chance for such employment for "class enemies," particularly for unskilled older people, this "privilege" soon turned out to be meaningless; most of the people in this category were deported with the others. As a rule, there was no appeal from an expulsion order, which in most cases was carried out on the spot.

The destination of the deportees was the bleakest region of Hungary, the arid northeastern area along the Soviet border. Tens of thousands of urban people, most of them members of the intelligentsia, went to live in primitive villages and farmsteads; they were crowded into old shacks and stables, under unsanitary conditions, without medical care and adequate nourishment, doing backbreaking slave labor in wheat and rice fields, or constructing roads in the hottest part of the Hungarian countryside. Half of their upkeep was supposed to be supplied by the state, the other half by the locality. In most cases both contributors failed to do their share and the deportees were "on their own."

In the summer of 1951, President Harry S. Truman and Secretary of State Dean Acheson of the United States, Prime Minister Clement Attlee of Great Britain, and other Western statesmen publicly condemned these policies. On July 27, 1951, President Truman declared that "the government of the United States is giving the closest attention to the deportations in Hungary with a view to taking such steps as may appropriately expose this situation to public view and judgment and render the Hungarian government accountable for its infamous conduct. . . ." Following these protests, the deportations from Budapest were halted. But in November the deportations, carried out somewhat less drastically, were resumed. They now took in a number of provincial cities and towns, as well as Budapest; but the method of mass roundups was replaced by that of sending off smaller groups or even single family units. (This second wave of deportations was again suspended during the 1952 spring session of the United Nations General Assembly, probably in order to forestall condemnation of Hungary in that forum. The deportations started up again as soon as the session was over.)

A letter smuggled out of Hungary in February 1952 and published in New York[6] stated that the deportations were continuing on a large scale, although involving smaller groups than before, particularly from the Trans-Danubian region and from cities in eastern Hungary like Miskolcz. This letter also stated that while all earlier expellees had been told their destinations in advance and permitted to reveal this information to their neighbors and friends, after October 1951 not a single deportee knew where he was being taken. The letter further disclosed that expellees were no longer being located in open villages and farmsteads, but without exception were being herded into punitive camps. The report calls these places "hellholes" administered like Soviet MVD camps, describing them as:

1. Isolated prison settlements on the Hortobagy heath. Thousands of deportees work in the new rice fields, knee-deep in water, most of them suffering from malaria, lung diseases, and undernourishment. They are permitted to write letters home, but the letters never arrive.

2. In the punitive camp of Satoraljanjhely, about one thousand deported families have been mixed in with the original five thousand criminals and "politicals."

3. The punitive camp at Jaszfenyszaru has been set aside for deportees over sixty years of age, who must do such things as clean the latrines of the village.

4. At Balmazujvaros, a punitive camp has been established for woment and girls separated from their children.

5. At Cserepes there is a heavily guarded punitive camp for deportees from Budapest.

6. The camp at Hajdunanas was built in a swamp and has caused the death of hundreds of people. Many of the inmates are deported clergymen.

7. Ujfeherto is reported to be the most dreaded of these "social institutions" of Communism in Hungary. It is used primarily for the "treatment" of recalcitrant peasants, the so-called "kulaks." One of the methods applied is the fourteen-hour work day.

The most important revelation of this report, however, is contained in the following passage, which is quoted verbatim:

> What is the end of the road for these people? . . . We are in a position to answer this question on the basis of irrefutable facts. Thousands of physically fit people are being regularly and secretly removed both

from the open villages, farms and kolkhozes and from the closed punitive camps. These large contingents of deportees would simply disappear without a trace if occasionally some decent people among the guards or administrative personnel or railwaymen did not feel obliged to drop an anonymous S.O.S. note addressed to a relative of one of the deportees, stating the basic facts and listing the names of a few of the victims. The long freight trains with sealed doors travel only at night, carrying thousands of people toward Satoraljaujhely-Beregszasz-Radvanszk. Near Radvanszk, under the direction of Russian army engineers a huge distribution camp was recently built by eight thousand workers, into which thirty to thirty-five thousand people may be crowded. This is the Hungarian terminal, but not the end of the tragic trek. Beyond this is the point of no return.

At this camp, mixed medical and administrative commissions classify the victims, just as in the accursed days of Nazism. Just as in Auschwitz, Bergen-Belsen, or Mauthausen, sadistic doctors and terrorists do the selecting. There is this difference, however; here "international commissions" are engaged in the murderous task; they consist of Czech, Rumanian, and Hungarian physicians and representatives of the three Peoples' Democracies'—believe it or not!—Ministries of Public Welfare. . . . The deportees are classified according to their physical condition into five categories. . . . Russian MVD detachments guard the camp and supervise the inmates. In a separate section of the camp built on sloping terrain, inside wire fences charged with electricity, are thousands of political prisoners, all of whom have been "extradited" to the Soviet Union. The fate of all "politicals" is sealed in advance. The rest, if assigned to the three top categories, are sent in successive shipments through Rumanian territory to Russia, for various kinds of labor service. Their first station there is Kiev, then come the Urals and other areas. Lately, however, written messages have been received to the effect that thousands of Hungarians have been sent to military labor service in China.[7]

The nature of these punitive camps and the secrecy surrounding their operations make it probable that they were established with the ultimate purpose of sending their inmates to the Soviet Union. The victims of the first deportations who we know were shipped to the Soviet Union established precedent for this policy. On the other hand, this report is the first evidence so far received of people expelled to the rural areas being sent on into Russia. The report seems more credible in the light of the mass deportation plans recently drawn up by the government of Rumania; these indicate the existence of a Communist master plan to eliminate all opposition elements by deportation to Soviet Russia. Moreover, it is unlikely that the Hungarian and Rumanian countryside, and even the Danube-Black Sea canal construction project, could permanently "absorb" hundreds of thousands of expellees. The only places likely to be able to manage this are the huge forced labor camps of the MVD in the Urals and far north of Siberia; their high death rate requires an unceasing flow of replacements.

Estimates of the number of people deported differ widely. The Hungarian government announced in August 1951 that only 3,785 persons were affected, but the thousands of private communications received in the United States alone, many of them telling about the expulsion of more than one family, indicate the magnitude of the deportations. There were a number of early reports that the government was planning to remove 100,000 people from Budapest alone, or more than 10 per cent of the city's population.

On June 13, 1951, Lord Vansittart stated in the House of Lords:

> I should like to ask whether the Government was aware that some 35,000 people have already been affected and that the target is supposed to be 100,000; that these unfortunate people are being shipped along in cattle trucks, and left for thirty-six hours in a siding. The effect of deporting these people into the countryside, leaving them with people who cannot afford to keep them, means that they will die of starvation. . . .

(On August 1, 1952, Ernest Davies, Parliamentary Under Secretary of State for Foreign Affairs, officially estimated that *at least* 24,000 persons were deported from Budapest during this period.) In December 1951 the Vatican radio put the number of persons deported from Budapest alone at 38,000, among them 14,000 Jews.[8] In January and February 1952, it was estimated that between 50,000 and 70,000 people had been deported. In April 1952, the first report claiming to be based on official Hungarian statistics was smuggled out of Hungary to Graz in western Austria. This report, published in New York in the same month (April 1952), stated that during the course of 1951 alone 73,633 persons were deported.

> After stubbornly maintaining that only a few hundred people were deported to slow death in the misery of backwoods villages, the Hungarian government finally confessed the truth—at least *in camera.* The State Statistical Office submitted a top secret report to the Minister of the Interior on last year's deportations. We were able to look into this report, and are therefore in a position to state that in the course of last year exactly 38,633 persons were deported from Budapest. . . . The total of deportations from provincial localities was given in the round figure of 35,000, which, according to the State Statistical Office, cannot be considered final, since reports from several localities were delayed and could not be added to the total. It is probable, therefore, that the total will exceed the reported round figure.[9]

As an indication of the permanence of the system of deportations, the report then referred to an article by Ernest Gero, Hungary's Minister of Industry and Commerce, published in March 1952 in the Soviet *Pravda* and reprinted in the Hungarian press. In this article the minister admitted that the Hungarian coal, oil, steel, and electrical industries had fallen far behind schedule; he stated that the lack of labor discipline was solely responsible for the failure. Gero announced that the severest measures would be taken against all "shirkers," and concluded with a tirade against the remnants of the bourgeoisie: "people who consider only their own personal advantage must disappear from Hungary." In Hungary this was interpreted quite literally to mean that the middle class would continue to disappear into deportation camps, and that deportation would soon be used as a disciplinary measure against industrial labor as well.

For a time only scattered and sometimes contradictory information reached the free world about the proportion of Jews among the deportees. On July 12, 1951, the Jewish Telegraphic Agency reported from Tel Aviv that some 10,000 Hungarian Jews had been deported up to then. At the end of the summer of 1951, eyewitnesses arriving in Israel stated that about 75 per cent of the deportees were Jews, clearly an exaggerated estimate. In August 1951 the Hungarian National Committee in New York received an underground communication from Hungary that the Jewish share in the deportations that had taken place before the end of July 1951 was around 35 to 40 per cent of the total. As we have seen, in December 1951 the Vatican radio reported that about 36 per cent of the deportees from Budapest were Jews. All of these estimates referred to Budapest alone, there being no information up to then about deportations from provincial localities. Finally, the above-quoted report naming the State Statistical Office of Hungary as its secret source[10] stated that of the 38,633 persons deported during 1951 from Budapest alone, exactly 14,353 Jews, or 37.19 per cent, had been Jewish. This figure pretty closely accords with the earlier estimates received by the Hungarian National Committee and the Vatican radio.

Unfortunately, the April 19, 1952, report said nothing about the proportion of Jews deported from provincial localities (after November 1952 the provincial deportations claimed the majority of victims), or about the new deportations beginning in April 1952. As a result, no reliable figures are available for the deportation of Jews from the provinces and the deportation of Jews from Budapest since the end of 1951. However, an estimate of some seven to eight thousand would not be inaccurate. Such a figure would raise the total number of Hungarian Jews deported by May 15, 1952, to about 25,000.

There were undoubtedly many expropriated capitalists among the Jewish deportees, particularly in the first groups deported from Budapest. As early as June 1951, reports were received in New York stating that most of the industrialists and more substantial businessmen of the capital had been deported.[11] Most of these "fascist reactionaries" were Jews and survivors of the Nazi deportations of seven years before. But there is ample evidence that the great majority of Jewish deportees consisted of lawyers, white-collar workers, Social Democrats, workers, artists, students, Zionists, and the like. Letters received by relatives in the United States tell of a seventeen-year-old Jewish girl taken from her family and deported the day after her graduation from high school, to a remote village where she was working as a woodcutter; of a fourteen-year-old orphan boy taken from the home of his grandfather to an eastern Hungarian kolkhoz; of a Jewish house painter deported with his family because his father was a businessman; of a Jewish bookkeeper deported on the same pretext; and of many such "actions against the class enemy."

Another feature of the Hungarian deportations also recalls the Nazi system. In the fall of 1951 the Hungarian government created a special office for the administration and sale abroad of jewels, gold, silver, antiques, and works of art confiscated from the deportees; this provided the treasury with foreign exchange.[12]

An indication of the effect of deportations upon some of the official Jewish leaders is the suicide of the twin brothers Szucs, first cousins of Stoeckler and members of his administration. Originally bank executives, they had been brought by Stoeckler into Jewish community work. Joseph Szucs was secretary general of the National Representative Federation of Hungarian Israelites, while Geza Szucs headed the governing board of the Joint Distribution Committee in Hungary. On August 11, 1952, after having administered poison to their eighty-year-old aunt, the two men jumped to their deaths from the window of their fifth-floor apartment.[13]

The last news dealing with Hungarian deportations that reached the free world was a report that appeared on January 1, 1953, in a London daily newspaper. Based on a dispatch from Yugoslavia, it asserted that the Jews of Szeged, the second largest city of Hungary, located in the vicinity of the Yugoslav border, had been deported. Those of them who were capable of hard work had been sent to slave labor camps in Russia where they faced slow mass extinction. The rest of the Jewish deportees were reported to have been dispatched to concentration and labor camps in the eastern districts of Hungary adjacent to Russia.[14]

Popular Reaction

The measures were unpopular even among some of the police. These made a point of explaining to deportees that they had to obey orders and that they hoped they would remember the consideration shown them by the police.

When two State Security Police Officers called to take away a couple of old ladies from a flat in the Istvan Körut, in Budapest, the crowd which collected to see them off became so large and insulting that the two police officers had to press the people back with their guns levelled in order to prevent a popular demonstration, for once spontaneous.

In Budapest, on several occasions workers' deportations (including once some Stakhanovites) called at several ministries to protest against the deportation of elderly fellow-workers, who had once belonged to the old professional classes. These deputations were never allowed a hearing. At one steel factory workers staged a demonstration against the deportation of some of their comrades, and the police had to be called in.

Paradoxically, it was the Communist-imposed Jewish leadership that defended the anti-Jewish actions of the Hungarian Communist regime.

On July 15, 1951, the National Representative Federation adopted a resolution protesting against "the slanders spread by the Western press, radio, and the warmongers behind them, with regard to the attitude of our people's democracy toward Hungarian Jewry." After stating that the Jews of Hungary enjoyed full religious freedom and that "nobody discriminates in any way against them," the resolution went on to declare:

> In the course of the current expulsions not a single individual of the Jewish faith has been expelled on the ground that he was a member of our confession. In refutation of the current rumors, we declare that the expellees are either persons who were once very rich wholesale merchants, manufacturers, landowners, or those who, together with the former, had been partners in and profited from the Horthy regime, whose anti-Jewish terrorism is universal knowledge, a regime which had enjoyed their material and moral support. We protest against and reject the slanders spread by the Western powers and their flunkies, even if they be Jews, and will not tolerate their machinations to misrepresent the expulsions as persecutions of Jews. . . . We despise their stupid tricks and clumsy lies, which are bent upon using us, Hungarian Jews, as a means to blacken the name of our fatherland. We tell them that they had better clean their own house if they want to deal with racial discrimination and anti-Jewish persecutions. These slanderers are actually servants and wire-pullers of that fascism which a few years ago exacted a toll of six hundred thousand lives from Hungarian Jewry. We want no part of their "protection," and this rejection refers to the activities of representatives of the State of Israel as well. Hungarian Jewry keeps faith with our people's democracy which, after decades of oppression and persecution, offers them a free and peaceful life.[15]

Only two articles dealing with the deportations appeared in *Uj Elet;* an excerpt from one of them follows:

> . . . No tear will be shed for the Jewish capitalists who, interested only in their profits, have been allies of the slaveholding lords and the flayers of the common people . . . People of this ilk have excluded themselves from the community of our working co-religionists. . . . The people of Hungary have the sovereign right to govern their internal affairs; for-

eigners have no right to interfere. . . . Thousands and tens of thousands of our patriotic co-religionists approve of the decision that the partisans of a fascist or semifascist world, the exploiters and torturers of the people, and the counter-revolutionary rumor-mongers should have no place in the capital of the Hungarian People's Democracy. . . . They approve of the transfer of the homes of the people's enemies to the best workers, officials, engineers, teachers, and artists, who are working for us and devoting all their energies to the commonweal, to a better life, and to our fight for peace. . . . These are historic times, and we admonish our co-religionists to remember who are our friends and who are our enemies. The memory of our six million martyrs obligates all working members of our community to beware of getting involved, even by accident, with the dark forces of fascism. Our place is at the side of the People's Democracy advancing toward socialism, at the side of the partisans of peace.[16]

Anti-Western Propaganda

The chief function of the spokesmen and publications of the captive community organization was to intimidate Hungarian Jewry: directly, by blunt threats against any kind of dissidence; and indirectly, by representing the Western world, particularly the United States, as a fascist and anti-Semitic conspiracy of aggression, whose victory would restore the era of Auschwitz and wipe Jewish life from the face of the earth.

The pages of *Uj Elet* were, of course, filled with reports of antisemitic occurences in Western countries, some of them true, most of them invented. But all antisemitic manifestations were blamed on Europe's "Marshallization": antisemitism was an American export imposed on the otherwise innocent victims of imperialism.[17]

In Korea, *Uj Elet* declared the Americans were systematically using Jews and Negroes as cannon fodder in order to reduce the proportion of these "inferior" races in the population.[18]

Uj Elet expressed great alarm over developments in "Nazi" Western Germany; but for "democratic" Eastern Germany the paper had only praise. It tried to exploit the treatment of war criminals by the American authorities in Germany, particularly of the seven Nazi mass murderers imprisoned and later executed at Landsberg, among them the notorious Ohlendorf and Pohl. In January 1951 the paper predicted that Ohlendorf would soon be pardoned by the Americans and given an important position on the staff of the Atlantic army.[19] Since a totalitarian propaganda organ can never be wrong, the paper reported, after their execution, that both Ohlendorf and Pohl had been pardoned and set free.[20]

A characteristic example of the policy of representing the United States as the world center of "antisemitic fascism" is a four-column front-page article published by *Uj Elet* on March 15, 1951. Its main theme is that a huge antisemitic fund had been collected by a secret super-government in America; American war industry and the criminal underworld, represented by the Du Pont family and Frank Costello, respectively, had contributed to this fund. The objective of the combine was twofold: to launch an aggressive war against the Soviet bloc, and to prepare a war of extermination against the Jews. The Kefauver Senate Crime Investigating Committee, said the article, had publicly revealed that many important American officials and public figures owed their positions to and were in the service of the combine. A number of state governors had been elected with their help. The most notorious among these new "fascist governors" were Gerald L. K. Smith of Missouri and Earl Warren of California. The Du Pont-Costello-Smith triple alliance aimed to make antisemitic fascism the most potent political force in imperialist America. There were many rich Jews in America who supported this reactionary and war-mongering conspiracy not realizing that they would be its first victims. The only fact in this fantasy was that the governor of Missouri was named Smith—*Forrest* Smith, who had nothing in common with the notorious antisemite Gerald L. K. Smith. Later, in a "Glossary of the week," *Uj Elet* quoted the Soviet organ *Trud* as declaring that the situation prevailing in the United States was reminiscent of "the darkest era of German fascism." *Uj Elet* commented that, unfortunately, this was the case. The symptoms of American fascism were dangerously like those of the Hitler era. "Here the FBI, there the Gestapo, here the American Legion, there the SS; here the murder of Negroes, there the murder of Jews; here Hitler, there Truman. . . ."[21]

Israel was portrayed in much the same light. For example, in a series of interviews with former emigrants who had returned from Israel to Hungary, *Uj Elet* commented that "all of these unfortunates are as emaciated as if they had been in Auschwitz"; the water in Israel ruined people's teeth and the climate was murderous; the tent camps were under water and there was no food or medicine for new arrivals; people of "progressive" convictions could not get jobs and workers were paid starvation wages; immigrants were hated, despised, discriminated against, and called "gypsies." All the interviews ended with the declaration that Israel stood revealed as an imperialist country where labor was oppressed.[22]

The Jewish Community

The fiction of a freely functioning Jewish community was maintained, as in the case of the other religious organizations, by the authorities' permitting a limited number of formal religious observances to take place, A few synagogues were open and held services. Rabbis could officiate at weddings (but only civil marriage was legally valid). The Chevrot Kadisha (burial societies) continued to bury their dead in the traditional manner. A cultural section of the unified community organization arranged weekly lectures on innocuous religious themes, with occasional performances of synagogue music. But, as we have seen, all religious institutions (with the sole exception of a seminary for the training of a few rabbis) and Jewish schools had been abolished; the younger generation was completely cut off from all traditional Jewish influence.

The members of the Hungarian rabbinate were compelled to read from the pulpit political and propaganda statements prescribed by the government; but most had resisted the pressure exerted upon them to turn their own religious teachings into the outright preachment of Communism.

In the above-mentioned Report of the Hungarian Research Section of the National Committee for a Free Europe, the author, Robert Major, stated:

> The annual meeting of the National Federation of Hungarian Jews was held in March [1952]. . . . Inasmuch as Hungarian denominations today, in addition to their religious work, can only conduct very restricted cultural activities supervised by the state and the Communist Party, the reports and interpolations at the meeting did *not* touch on the most important problems of Hungarian Jewry.
>
> At the same time that which was said, and that which was ostentatiously left unsaid, reveal much about the present situation of Jews in Hungary, if we supplement this with news from other sources. The president of the State Office of Religion on this occasion threateningly warned Hungarian Jews that "they must support the building of socialism and the peace front directed by the Soviet Union. Today a veritable war rages, and no one may be neutral."
>
> The National Federation is led by agents of the Communists; the sole Jewish paper, *Uj Elet* ("New Life"), aside from printing religious and church news, is a strictly party-line paper. So in this field the Communists are not likely to come up with new demands. The tendency is obviously to fill religious life, and ever-dwindling Jewish cultural life, with positive Communist content—something which the diminishing number of rabbis, Jewish scholars, and lecturers till now have resisted with determination.
>
> The majority of Hungarian Jews are strongly opposed to Communism. So far, 40,000 have reported for emigration to Israel, but of these only a portion are Zionists, the rest simply want to be rid of People's Democracy. That is why, in Hungarian Jewish circles, there is a veritable "emigration fever."

Chapter IX

Purges

On January 17, 1953, the Hungarian government issued a one-sentence official communique stating that the Hungarian Office of State Security had arrested Louis Stoeckler, president of the Budapest Jewish Community, of the unified National Representative Organization of Hungarian Jews, and of the operating branch of the American Joint Distribution Committee (JDC) in Hungary. The communique identified Stoeckler only as "a former industrialist." Significantly, no charge was specified; the communique indicated only that the police had found a considerable sum of dollars and Swiss francs in Stoeckler's home. In Hungary, the technical charge of currency manipulations had often been used as a basis for the arrest of people selected to make "confessions" of a far more consequential political nature.

According to an Associated Press dispatch of January 17 originating from Budapest, the arrest was disclosed forty-eight hours after *Szabad Nep*, the official government daily, had denounced Zionism and declared that the danger from the "hostile undermining activities" sponsored by the JDC was greater in Hungary than it was in the Soviet Union itself, where the JDC was then being charged with having instigated a number of leading physicians to murder prominent Soviet leaders. It will be recalled that on December 29, 1949, Israel Jacobson, director of JDC relief activities in Hungary, had been expelled from Hungary for unspecified deeds that were alleged to constitute "an abuse of the rights of foreigners."[1]

The official press reference to alleged hostile activities of the JDC in Hungary quoted above casts an ominous light upon reports reaching Vienna toward the end of February. These described a major purge of important Communist officials, as well as a number of physicians including Dr. Ladislas Benedek, the official representative of the Communist Party within the Jewish community leadership—actually assigned to supervise Stoeckler's activities for the Party.[2]

About a month later, in March, a special dispatch to *The New York Times* emanating from Vienna[3] clarified the extent and character of this purge. It noted the fact that none of the non-Jews originally listed as victims had been actually purged or harmed in any manner–only Jews had been affected. At the same time, the March report corrected several errors contained in the previous (February) dispatch–notably the statement that Zoltan Vass, the Jewish-born president of the Hungarian National Planning Office had committed suicide. However, later reports established the fact that Vas had been dismissed from his office.

According to this report of March 25 those arrested included Lieut. Gen. Gabor Peter, head of the secret police; Ladislas Benedek, chief physician of the Jewish hospital in Budapest; Stephen Szirmai, chief of Radio Hungary; at least six high officials, generals or colonels, in Gabor Peter's State Security office; Stephen Bálint, chief physician of the hospital of the political police; Stephen Loewi, an eye specialist, and some thirty other unnamed doctors. The report named Lieut. Col. Sabersky of the secret police as a Jew who was said to have committed suicide at the moment of his arrest. It failed to retract the report of February 21 that Gen. Gabor Peter had been executed together with his children and his wife, who had been a secretary in Premier Rakosi's office, merely confirming the fact that Gen. Gabor was missing.

In addition, in a dispatch from Vienna that was received at the United Press office in Paris but probably not forwarded to New York, Mrs. Laszlo Steiner, Stoeckler's secretary, was reported to have arrived at Vienna from Hungary after a daring escape across the Austrian-Hungarian border during which her husband was arrested by Hungarian border guards. Mrs. Steiner was quoted as having furnished the United Press office in Vienna with the following additional data:

Under arrest were: Imre Biro, the former father-in-law of Mathias Rakosi, Communist boss of Hungary; Col. Csapo of the secret political police; Col. Hand, cabinet chief attached to Lt. Gen. Gabor Peter, the head of the secret police; Judge Ladislas Garay, a former army captain and recently a chauffeur in the service at the French legations in Budapest, and Dr. Klimko, a professor of surgery. Erwin Deutsch, an official in the Budapest Communist party headquarters, had committed suicide together with his wife when it became apparent that they were scheduled to be arrested. Mrs. Steiner stated that all these arrests had taken place on January 8, 1953, the same day as those of Stoeckler, Dr. Benedek, and Lt. Gen. Gabor Peter.

Professor Klimko seems to have been the only purge victim identified by name who was neither Jewish nor of Jewish origin.

These facts seemed to indicate that a trial of "Jewish conspirators" was in preparation in Hungary, in order to corroborate, through "confessions" complementing those extorted from the Moscow doctors, the accusations levelled against the JDC. The Associated Press dispatch of February 21 noted that this purge of Jews in Hungary was being carried out under the supervision of a "Soviet purge commission especially dispatched to Budapest for this purpose," a fact which seemed to bear out the existence of such a plan. Hungary was probably chosen as the scene of the purge because it was the only one of the satellite countries where the JDC had continued to be active.

However, on April 4, 1953, the Soviet authorities retracted the charges against the Moscow physicians; consequently at the time of writing (April 1953) no major antisemitic show trial was expected to take place in Hungary. The situation of those purged and arrested, as well as the future of Hungarian policies *vis-a-vis* Jewry in general, remained uncertain. There was no reliable information concerning the status of Jewish community affairs, nor any indication whether the Jewish community would be permitted to function, under what leadership, and to what extent. It was assumed that no government projects would replace the JDC in supplying the vital needs of many thousands of Jews, including a large number of deportees. The prevailing general uncertainty was accentuated early in April when the Communist authorities discovered a new Jewish "medical plot": as reported by the Budapest Communist organ *Szaebad Nep*,[4] a Jewish physician had supposedly obtained party secrets from a high Communist official who was under the influence of drugs as a patient at a Budapest hospital.

The only concrete indication of a possible relaxation of the atmosphere of persecution and intimidation was a hint in the party press than an amnesty might be declared after the May 1 general elections for certain categories of people who had committed "mistakes" against the regime.[5] A similar amnesty had been declared in the Soviet Union a few weeks earlier.

But, in any event, the situation of Hungarian Jewry appeared hopeless. The expulsion of middle-class elements, including large numbers of Jews, from Budapest to rural areas had been resumed. Socially expendable, the Jews could be expected to continue to be the first to suffer unemployment and liquidation even under milder, less hostile conditions.

Notes

CHAPTER I

1. No. 4-5, 1944, p. 96.
2. Eugene Levai, *Black Book*. pp. 469-470.
3. The deposition is contained in Protocol PS 2605, executed by the tribunal; its contents were confirmed before the tribunal by *Hauptsturmführer* Baron von Wisliceny, one of the chief organizers of the deportations.
4. Levai, *op. cit.*, pp. 471-472.

CHAPTER II

1. *See* the report by Rudolph Polgar, a Hungarian Jewish economist, now in the United States, printed in the Hungarian American newspaper *Népszava* (February 16, 1948).
2. Published in Ernest Munkacsi, *Hogyan Tortent?* ["How Did It Happen?"] p. 240.
3. Levai, *op. cit.*, p. 474.
4. *Ibid.*, p. 251.
5. *Ibid.*, p. 474.
6. *Ibid.*, p. 427.
7. *Uj Elet,* October 31, 1946.

CHAPTER III

1. *American Jewish Year Book*, Vol. 50 (1949).
2. These and all subsequent statistics for which sources are not given are drawn from the official *Hungarian Statistical Review*, 1946, supplemented by data from Levai, *op. cit.*, and Munkacsi, *op. cit.*

CHAPTER IV

1. *Uj Elet*, March 6, 1947.
2. Bartley C. Crum, *Behind the Silken Curtain,* New York, 1947, p. 141.

CHAPTER V

1. *Uj Elet*, November 22, 1945.
2. *Ibid.*, November 27, 1945.
3. *Ibid.*, June 5, 1946.
4. *Ibid.*, November 27, 1945.
5. *Ibid.*, April 11, 1946.
6. Jewish Telegraphic Agency, February 28, 1946.
7. Bartley C. Crum, *Behind the Silken Curtain,* New York 1947, pp. 137-139.
8. *Uj Elet,* March 7, 1946.
9. *Ibid.*, March 14, 1946.
10. *Ibid.*, June 5, 1946, quoting from *Szabad Nép*.
11. *Ibid.*
12. *Ibid.*, June 20, 1946.
13. *Ibid.*, March 28, 1946.
14. *Ibid.*, April 4, 1946, p. 3.
15. *Ibid.*

16. *Ibid.*, May 30, 1946.
17 *Ibid.*
18. Ferenc Nagy, *The Struggle Behind the Iron Curtain*, New York 1948, pp. 245-249.
19. *Uj Elet,* June 20, 1946.
20. *Ibid.*, May 9, 1946, pp. 2-4.
21. *Ibid.*, April 11, 1946.
22. Jewish Telegraphic Agency, August 2, 1946.
23. *Loc. cit.*
24. *Valasz* (VIII, 10-11), p. 865.
25. Nagy, *op. cit.*, pp. 245-249.
26. *Uj Elet,* August 29, 1946
27. Jewish Telegraphic Agency, October 11, 1946.
28. *Uj Elet*, September 19, 1946.

CHAPTER VI

1. *Uj Elet,* May 9, 1946.
2. *Ibid.*, October 10, 1946.
3. *Ibid.*, October 3, 1946.
4. *Ibid.*, October 10, 1946.
5. *Ibid.*, September 18, 1947.
6. *Ibid.*, November 6, 1947.
7. *Ibid.*, November 20, 1947.
8. *Ibid.*, February 20, 1948.
9. JTA, November 20, 1947.
10. *Ibid.*, November 24, 1947.
11. *Uj Elet,* March 20, 1947.
12. *Ibid.*, February 27, 1947.
13 *Ibid.*, April 17, 1947.
14. *Ibid.*, January 7, 1948.
15. Bibo Valasz (VIII, 10-11) p. 871.
16. *Uj Elet*, December 11, 1947.
17. *Ibid.*, June 3, 1948.
18. *Ibid.*, October 7, 1948.
19. *Ibid.*, June 20, 1946.
20. *Ibid.*, January 30, 1947.
21. *Ibid.*
22. *Ibid.*, February 27, 1947.
23. *Ibid.*, March 20, 1947.
24. *Ibid.*, June 5, 1947.
25. *Utunk,* June 17, 1948.
26. *Uj Elet,* March 18, 1948.
27. *Ibid.*, May 20, 1948.
28. *Ibid.*, June 5, 1948.

CHAPTER VII

1. *Vilag,* May 15, 1948.
2. *Ibid.*, May 5, 1948.
3. *Uj Elet,* December 9, 1948.
4. *Ibid.*, November 20, 1948.
5. Associated Press, September 6, 1949.

6. JTA, December 15, 1949.
7. *Uj Elet*, June 24, 1949.
8. *Ibid.*, February 19, 1948.
9. *Ibid.*, November 18, 1948.
10. *Az Ember*, September 3, 1949.
11. *Uj Elet*, June 3, 1948.
12. *Ibid.*, December 9, 1948.
13. *Ibid.*, December 2, 1948.
14. *Ibid.*, February 3, 1949.
15. *Ibid.*, February 10, 1949.
16. *Ibid.*, February 17, 1949.
17. *Ibid.*, March 17, 1949.
18. *Ibid.*, March 24, 1949.
19. *Ibid.*, June 17, 1949.
20. JTA, June 27, 1949.
21. *The Day*, May 10, 1950.
22. *Uj Elet*, January 5, 1950.
23. *Ibid.*, February 23, 1950.

CHAPTER VIII

1. *Uj Elet*, January 11, 1951.
2. *Ibid.*, December 6, 1951.
3. *Az Ember*, February 16, 1952.
4. *The New York Times*, December 28, 1950.
5. An extract from Law No. II of 1939 of the Hungarian Government relating to National Defence, follows:

Expulsions as well as putting under police control or into custody.
Clause 15D

1. The Cabinet may order that persons whose stay in a certain town (village) or certain parts of the country gives reason for anxiety from the view-point of public order, public security, or other important State interest, or is harmful for economic reasons, can be expelled from the respective town (village) or parts of the country irrespective of their permanent domicile. These persons may be put under police control or, if necessary, into custody either in their domicile or in any other part of the country.

2. On the basis of the present clause persons put into custody may be compelled to work according to their abilities.

3. If persons expelled, put under police control or into custody are unable to ensure their livelihood from the revenues of their fortune or earnings, and have no relatives in a position to provide for them, they must be provided for by the State; in these cases even those persons who are not put under custody may be compelled to work according to their abilities for provisions granted.

4. Detailed regulations relating to police control and detention will be given in an ordinance issued by the Minister of the Interior in agreement with the Minister of Justice."

5. The following is an extract from Decree No. 8130 M. C. 1939 Section I. Persons whose presence in certain communities or certain parts of the country may endanger public order and security or any other important interest of the State, or whose presence there is harmful for economic reasons, may be restricted by police authorities:

a. by subjecting them to police surveillance at the place of residence, or

b. by prohibiting them from residing at the place of their residence or in certain other parts of the country including the place where the persons enjoy their home and support right, and by placing them under police surveillance, or, if necessary, taking them into police custody at some other place of the country.

Decree No. 760 B. M. of 1939, issued by the Minister of the Interior in implementation of the above-mentioned decrees, calls "police custody" also "internment." There is no provision for a maximum period of custody, although it is provided under paragraph 18 that after six months each case must be reviewed. Persons taken into police custody are to be placed in special internment camps, where, according to paragraph 16, they are forced to work.

6. *Az Ember,* February 16, 1952.
7. *Ibid.*
8. May 1952 Report of the Hungarian Research Service of the National Committee for a Free Europe.
9. *Az Ember,* April 19, 1952.
10. *Ibid.*
11. *Az Ember,* June 23, 1951.
12. *The New York Times,* November 11, 1951.
13. *Ibid.,* August 12, 1951.
14. *Daily Telegraph,* London, January 1, 1953.
15. *Uj Elet,* July 19, 1951.
16. *Ibid.,* June 21, 1951.
17. *Ibid.,* January 11, 1951.
18. *Ibid.,* January 26, 1951.
19. *Ibid.,* January 18, 1951.
20. *Ibid.,* February 8, 1951.
21. *Ibid.,* October 11, 1951.
22. *Ibid.,* January 18, 1951.

CHAPTER IX

1. *The New York Times,* January 18, 1953.
2. Associated Press dispatch, Vienna, February 21, 1953.
3. *Ibid.,* Vienna, March 25, 1953.
4. Jewish Telegraphic Agency, Vienna, April 1, 1953.
5. Associated Press, Budapest, April 12, 1953.

V. Rumania

BY

NICOLAS SYLVAIN

Chapter I

Rumanian Jewry Before the Second World War

About 757,000 persons of the Jewish faith lived in Rumania[1] before the war. The last pre-war census, taken in 1930, shows a Jewish population of 756,930, representing about 4.2 per cent of the total population of the country. It was distributed through the various provinces as indicated in Table 1.[2]

TABLE I

JEWISH POPULATION OF PRE-WAR RUMANIA, ACCORDING TO THE 1930 CENSUS

Region	Jews	% of total pop.
Old Kingdom		
Oltenia } Wallachia	3,523	0.2
Muntenia } Wallachia	94,216	2.3
Moldavia	162,268	6.7
Dobrogea (Dobrudja)	4,031	0.5
Bessarabia	206,958	7.2
Bucovina	93,101	10.9
Transylvania	81,503	2.5
Banat	14,043	1.5
Crishana-Maramuresh	97,287	7.0
Greater Rumania (total)	756,930	4.2

The density of the Jewish population grew from west to east. Roughly 25 per cent of the Jewish population lived in the western part of the country—Transylvania and the adjacent provinces; 35 per cent or so was located in the "Old Kingdom"; the remaining 40 per cent lived in the northeastern and eastern regions—Bucovina and Bessarabia. The heaviest relative concentrations were to be found in Bucovina, where the Jewish population was 10.9 per cent of the total, and in Moldavia, Bessarabia and Crishana-Maramuresh, where it oscillated around 7 per cent.

About one-third of the total Jewish population (31.8 per cent) lived in the countryside, the rest in towns. Jews formed 25 per cent to 35 per cent of the town populations of Moldavia, Bessarabia and Bucovina; in Crishana-Maramuresh the percentage fell to 15 per cent and in Wallachia and Transylvania it varied between 8 per cent and 10 per cent.[3]

The Rumanian "Principalities" (Wallachia and Moldavia) are the nuclei of twentieth-century Rumania. They were dominated throughout the Middle Ages and up to 1878 by the Ottoman Empire. The hinterland of a backward empire, cut off from the main currents of Western, Central European, and even Russian civilization and trade, the Rumanian provinces vegetated for centuries under the Turkish yoke. The Rumanian peasant population toiled as serfs on the large estates of Greek-Turkish "boyards," who were the upper class of the provinces. This region first began to play a part in European trade and to come under European influence after 1829, when the Treaty of Adrianople established freedom of shipping on the Danube and the right of the Rumanian provinces to trade freely with all countries. After a brief occupation by Russia (1828-34), the Principalities united under Prince Ion Cuza and were granted autonomy under Turkish suzerainty in 1859. They became independent after the Russo-Turkish war and the Treaty of Berlin (1878). At the same time, Rumania was enlarged by the addition of Northern Dobrudja, taken from Bulgaria. In 1881, Rumania became the "Kingdom of Rumania" under King Carol I, a descendant of the poorest branch of the German princely family of Hohenzollern-Sigmaringen.

The buoyant capitalist development of Central Europe was slow to affect Rumania, the latter's industrial development proceeding very slowly at the beginning of the twentieth century. In 1913 the Second Balkan War added Southern Dobrudja to Rumania. After a period of prosperous neutrality (1914-16), the Old Kingdom entered the First World War on the side of the Allies. The peace treaties increased its area from 53,489 square miles to 122,282 square miles, so that the new Greater Rumania had a population of over 16,000,000, as against 7,500,000 before the war. Chief among the newly acquired areas were Transylvania, formerly held by Hungary; Bessarabia, taken from Russia; and Bucovina, formerly under Austrian rule.

Many Rumanian historians have contended that the Jews first "invaded" the Old Kingdom in the second half of the nineteenth century. But there is documentary evidence to prove that Jews were living in these regions long before this time. They were already established in Wallachia and Moldavia in the fifteenth and sixteenth centuries. In fact, the first massacre of Jews in Bucharest is recorded at the end of the sixteenth century. In the nineteenth century three groups of Jews could be distinguished in the "historical structure" of the Jewish population. The first group consisted of Jews who had lived in the Principalities for centuries; these were called *Pamanteni*, i.e., "natives." The second group were descendants of the Jewish merchants called into the country by certain boyards and granted special charters (in Rumanian *hrisov*, hence their designation as *Hrisovelitzi*—"chartered" by the latter). And, finally, there were the new settlers, mainly immigrants from the East.

The Jews of Wallachia and Moldavia were confined to a geographical and social ghetto and were largely deprived of civil rights; they were the special target of the hatred, envy, and distrust of peasantry.

The country's first legal code, the *Regulamentul Organic* ("Organic Regulations"), granted during the Russian occupation of the Principalities (1828-1834), dealt harshly with the Jews, classing them as "foreigners." The first constitution of the United Principalities, adopted in 1866, specified that "only foreigners of the Christian rite may attain the status of Rumanians." The Treaty of Berlin stipulated that the sovereignty of the new state was to be contingent upon the admission of the Jews to full civil and political rights. Rumania, however, circumvented this obligation; the Rumanian constitution of 1879, though it apparently repudiated the 1866 provision limiting naturalization to "foreigners of the Christian rite," stipulated that "noncitizens might be naturalized only by vote of both houses of the legislature," except in the case of veterans. Of course, only a handful of Jews were naturalized under these provisions.

The census of 1899, which showed a Jewish population of 266,652 in the Old Kingdom, broke down this figure into Rumanians—i.e., naturalized Jews—1.6 per cent; and "foreigners," 98.4 per cent. The latter group was in fact sharply differentiated into "foreigners dependent on the state"—i.e., the "native" Jews who had inhabited Rumania for centuries—2.2 per cent; and "foreigners under Rumanian protection," 96.2 per cent. Most of the Jews were scarcely more than "half-Rumanians," as indeed King Carol I himself once said. Under his reign (1881-1916) numerous laws were enacted prohibiting Jews from living in rural districts, barring them from various trades and professions and subjecting them on the pretext of their being foreigners, to all kinds of discriminatory measures.[4] The economic distress these measures caused the Jewish population, and the subsequent peasant revolt which took many Jewish lives in Moldavia, gave a strong impetus to emigration, mostly to America. Between 1899 and 1914, over 60,000 Rumanian Jews immigrated to the United States. Others settled in Western Europe, and a small number went to Palestine.

The situation of the Jews was quite different in the former Hungarian, Austrian, and Russian territories merged with the Old Kingdom in "Greater Rumania." Transylvania (in Hungarian Erdely, in Rumanian Ardeal) was for centuries in the remote past the easternmost province of Hungary. From 1526 to 1691 it was an independent principality. Subsequently it was ruled by Austria, and then in 1868 it was reincorporated into Hungary. The first large group of Jews to settle in Transylvania, at the end of the fifteenth century, were Spanish refugees who came via Turkey; later settlers came from Galicia and Rumania. The complete emancipation of the Jews of Hungary in 1867 enabled them to participate freely in all the economic, cultural, and political activities of the country and led to the rise of strong assimilationist tendencies. By 1910 the 180,000 Jews of Transylvania and the adjacent provinces (Banat and Crishana-Maramuresh) were tightly integrated into the life of the country.[5]

Bucovina was originally part of Moldavia. After having been the theater of numerous invasions, it was finally annexed by Austria in 1774 and thus came under Central European economic and cultural influence. The Jewish population, consisting mainly of settlers from Moldavia and Galicia, were traders in cattle, horses, and agricultural products, as well as artisans and peasants. The decline of the region as a trade center, with its attendant economic distress, led to a Jewish emigration to the United States and Canada. The beginnings of industrialization and an improvement in general economic conditions enabled the Jews to prosper. Jewish capital became active in the important lumber, distilling, brewing, sugar, and oil industries. About 85 per cent of all big landed estates were either owned or managed by Jews. Bucovina's 102,900 Jews constituted more than 12 per cent of the pre-war population of the province. In the early twentieth century they enjoyed full civil rights, both individually and as a community.[6]

Bessarabia was held by Russia until the fifteenth century, when it came under the rule of the Turks. In 1816 it was again taken by Russia, which held it except for a brief interlude of Turkish rule from 1856 to 1878 until 1919. The Jewish population, consisting mainly of settlers from Russia and from Moldavia, was about 20,000 in the middle of the nineteenth century. According to Russian statistics, it had risen to 228,000 at the end of 1897. At this time 43 per cent of Bessarabia's Jews earned their living by commerce and trade, 43.9 per cent as artisans, 7.1 per cent by agriculture, and 6 per cent in the professions. The province was dependent for its existence on the export of its grain and fruit to Russia, and this trade was largely concentrated in Jewish hands. However, there were many small merchants and a large section of the Jewish artisan and agricultural population living in dire poverty; in addition they were harried by recurrent pogroms led by Russian riffraff. But whereas in the Old Kingdom of Rumania the small Rumanian intelligentsia was the instigator of the anti-Semitic-measures, in Bessarabia the Russian intelligentsia viewed the plight of the Jewish population with sympathy and often came to their aid. The Bessarabian Jews came under the influence of Russian literature and Russian political currents. Neither the Jewish intellectuals nor the bulk of the middle class were significantly affected by Rumanian influence even during the period of Rumanian rule after 1919.[7]

The tremendous territorial enlargement of Rumania by the peace treaties of 1919-21 greatly strengthened the economic and political power of the Old Kingdom's ruling classes. The crown, bourgeoisie, and Rumanian administration could now command large industrial resources, mainly in Transylvania, new sources of raw materials, the agricultural products of all the annexed territories, and a much bigger population.

The period between 1920 and 1930 was a prosperous one in the Old Kingdom, with the Liberal Party (representing big business and the bureaucracy of the Old Kingdom) controlling the political life of Greater Rumania. Despite anti-Semitic outbursts, the rigging of elections, and many other evils, this period can be considered the "democratic phase" of the interwar years. In the late twenties a new political force, the National Peasant Party, emerged on the Rumanian political scene. This party was formed by a merger of the National Party of Transylvania and the Peasant Party of the Old Kingdom. The former had a strong following in the Transylvanian towns and countryside because of its opposition to carpet-bag rule and exploitation by the Bucharest ruling circles; the latter party drew its strength from the peasantry of the Old Kingdom and to a lesser extent from the urban middle strata. By 1928 the Peasant Party was so strong that it could successfully challenge Liberal rule, coming to power for a two-year period that ended shortly after the restoration of King Carol II.

The economic crises of the early thirties and the failure of the new leaders to enlarge and strengthen Rumanian democracy led to a rapid displacement of the center of power from the elected parliament to the crown. The palace more and more became a decisive factor in the political life of Rumania, especially after the accession to the throne of King Carol II in 1930. By 1934 the two great parties of Rumania, the Liberals and National Peasants, were seriously undermined by the King, who moved to establish a personal regime. With the assistance of a court camarilla and a wing of the Liberal Party—the so-called "Young Liberals" headed by George Tatarescu—Carol II sought to eliminate the political power of the two great "historic parties." He was helped by the fact that the economic crisis had severely shaken the Liberal bankers in the Old Kingdom and Peasant middle class in Transylvania; the intervention of the state in the economic life of the country secured a strategic economic position to the head of the state, the King.

Out of the crisis of the period arose a new and menacing political force. This was the Nazi-like organization of Corneliu Zelea Codreanu, variously called the Legion, Iron Guard, and later the "All for the Country" movement. A fanatically Orthodox Christian and rabidly anti-Semitic organization openly preaching the massacre of the Jewish population, the Legion of the Archangel Michael was formed by Codreanu and a group of students in 1927 as a wing of A. C. Cuza's anti-Semitic Christian Defense League. In 1929 a group of Legionnaires, impatient at the weakness and inability of the Cuza faction to make any headway, left the League and set up the Iron Guard as an independent political organization. The widespread social distress of the thirties, especially in the countryside, the weakening of the "historic parties," the direct help extended by the state machine to the Legionnaires for many years, and later the repercussions of Hitler's victory in Germany, combined to give the Iron Guard a dominant role in Rumanian political life in the mid-thirties. The elections that took place in 1937 revealed both the new political alignments in the country and the fantastic development of the Codreanu forces. The elections were controlled by the state machine and were supposed to assure the victory of the party already selected by the crown, the Young Liberals. In order to prevent this, Juliu Maniu, leader of the National Peasant Party, made an alliance with Codreanu to "preserve the democratic functioning of the elections against the encroachments of the Tatarescu government." The result was the defeat of the Tatarescu forces and the crown. But Maniu, by dealing with Codreanu's murderous gang, helped it at a critical juncture to become a decisive political factor. At the previous election, in 1931, the Iron Guard had obtained 30,783 votes (or 1.3 per cent of the total vote), while the League of Christian National Defense obtained 113,863 votes (or 4.1 per cent of the votes). This time, the Iron Guard obtained 478,378 votes (or 16.5 per cent of the total vote)—only slightly less than the National Peasant Party itself, which suffered a catastrophic setback—and the League obtained 281,167 votes (or 9.1 per cent of the total).

Carol II, who had helped to undermine the "historic parties" and in the early thirties encouraged the development of the Iron Guard, now saw his own crown menaced by these developments. The Iron Guard also threatened Rumania's system of alliances, based on a defense of the Versailles treaties against the revisionist policies of the Berlin-Rome axis. To check the rise of the Iron Guard the King decided to call to power a government based on the National Christian Party (formerly the League of National Christian Defense), headed by Octavian Goga and A. C. Cuza. This government lasted only six weeks (December 28, 1937-February 10, 1938) and then collapsed. On February 10, 1938, the King decided to set aside the constitution of 1923, dissolve all parties, create a single political organization and concentrate all real power in his own hands.

A new royal government, headed by the chief of the Rumanian Christian Orthodox Church, the Patriarch Miron Christea, was formed in Bucharest, with several "young" political leaders of the old parties (Armand Calinescu, Grigore Gafencu, Alexandru Iamandii, and Mitita Constantinescu) participating in it.

The new government attempted, in foreign affairs, to maintain a balance between the Western Allies and the German-Italian Axis; at home it proposed to check the power of the "uncontrolled forces" of the Iron Guard. But in thirty months' time the royal dictatorship ended in obvious failure.

The new foreign policy—a revived version of the 1914-16 "neutrality" policy of the Old Kingdom—had disastrous results, for it led to the loss, without a military defeat, of a number of Rumanian territories (half of Bucovina and Bessarabia was ceded to Russia, followed by Northern Transylvania and Southern Dobrudja). In 1940 Rumania found itself considerably shrunken in size and totally isolated diplomatically. On the domestic political plane, the royal cabinet was able to strike a heavy blow at the Iron Guard organization. In November 1938 Corneliu Zelea Codreanu and some of his closest associates were murdered in the Zhilava prison by order of the palace. But the physical destruction of the chiefs of the Legionnaires did not mean the steering of a democratic course by the King. The royal dictatorship continued to follow an antidemocratic and harshly anti-Jewish policy. It was one of King Carol's governments which finally enacted the Nazi-like anti-Jewish statutes by which the Jewish population of Rumania was governed during the Second World War. As we shall see later, this policy ultimately paved the way for the return to the fore of the Iron Guard after the collapse of the King's Regime on September 6, 1940.

Status of the Jews in Greater Rumania

At the end of the First World War the Rumanian government had undertaken, in the words of the peace treaties, to "recognize as Rumanian nationals, *ipso facto* and without the requirements of any formality, all Jews inhabiting Rumanian territory who do not possess another nationality." The Rumanian government did not however live up to this obligation. After many delays and subterfuges, the constitution of 1923 was drawn up so as to grant citizenship to the Jews living in the Old Kingdom, but it left the naturalization of the much more numerous Jews of the annexed territories to be accomplished through special legislation. This represented a step backward for the Jews of the annexed territories who had opted for Rumanian citizenship in 1919, and consequently had been naturalized under the law concerning option. In 1924, the Marzescu Law was passed providing for the naturalization, with special limitations, of the inhabitants of the annexed provinces, provided certain conditions were met. Chiefly, it required all applicants to bring proof of their having resided legally in the annexed territories prior to the annexation. The number of naturalizations granted under the Marzescu Law was not published. But as one expert remarks, "there can be no doubt that thousands of Jews who had qualified as citizens under the electoral laws of 1918 were rendered stateless between 1924 and 1927."[8]

The attack on the citizenship of Jews, which was a constant feature of Rumanian political life, reached new heights in the mid-thirties. Old regulations were revised, naturalizations previously granted were cancelled, and innumerable administrative devices were used to deprive individual Jews of their citizenship. Finally, under the short-lived Goga government, a special decree concerning "Revision of Citizenship" (January 21, 1938) was used in conjunction with an anti-Jewish measure to take away the citizenship of a very large part of Rumanian Jewry. According to official figures released in September 1938, of 203,424 heads of family and unmarried adults (totaling, with their dependents, 617,396 persons), 36.7 per cent, or 225,222 persons, were stripped of their citizenship. Moreover, apart from this, 91,570 Jews were classed as "foreigners," which reduced the number of Jewish citizens even further.[9] Rumanian Jewry was thus thrust back, in the twilight days of Greater Rumania, to the inferior civil position it had occupied in the Old Kingdom in 1910.

Antisemitism reached its high point in the thirties; but there had also been numerous anti-Semitic outbursts under the so-called liberal regime, from 1919 to 1929. Anti-Jewish manifestations, the cold-blooded murder of Jewish students (Jassy), and the dissemination of pamphlets advocating the mass murder and wholesale liquidation of Jews were a feature of the mid-twenties, too. A memorandum handed to the Rumanian government in 1925 by the British Jewish Board of Deputies and the Anglo-Jewish Association, stated:

> These anti-Semitic troubles have been going on for years. The propaganda is the work of university professors, teachers in high schools and elementary schools, and priests. After every outbreak the government has issued a communiqué, always to the same effect, that it would sternly repress disorders. It is now something like the fifteenth time. . . .[10]

In spite of these outbursts Jews in both the Old Kingdom and some of the annexed territories, were free to carry on trades and practice the professions; in the Old Kingdom especially the Jewish communities enjoyed relatively prosperous times.

In the thirties, the spectacular growth of the Iron Guard undermined the weak foundations of Rumanian democracy even before Codreanu's success at the polls in 1937. All the Rumanian parties, including the Liberals and the National Peasants, began to ape the anti-Semitic slogans and program of the Iron Guard. One clamorous slogan of the time was the demand for the "Rumanization" of the country. The slogan was meaningless as far as the state administration was concerned: in all the annexed territories Rumanians from the Old Kingdom had long ago taken all posts and positions for themselves. The only thing it could mean was the elimination of Jews from the trades and professions, and even the economy generally. From 1935 on, the Iron Guard seized one Bar Association after another by intimidation, rapidly extended its control over the other professional associations, burned the publications of the pro-Jewish press in the streets until Bucharest's great democratic newspapers were ruined, and increasingly terrorized the Jewish population.

In the late thirties, in the climate created by the Nazi victory in Germany, the "historic parties" were unable to meet the frontal attack of the Iron Guard. Even some National Peasant leaders began to talk about "the Jewish problem," and the need after all to "revise the status of the Israelites," replacing them with "Rumanians trained in corporativist principles." Thus the infamous Goga laws were prepared for by years of anti-Semitic campaigns and by the weak and uncertain opposition of the '"historic parties."

Cultural Patterns in the Various Jewish Communities

Cultural and ideological differences drew visible lines between and within the various Jewish communities of Greater Rumania during the period between 1919 and 1939.

According to the 1939 census, 518,754 persons declared Yiddish to be their mother tongue, out of a total Jewish population of 756,930. The distribution of the Yiddish speaking population is shown in Table II.[11]

TABLE II

JEWS HAVING YIDDISH AS MOTHER TONGUE, 1930 CENSUS

Region		Number	% of total pop. of region
Oltenia	Wallachia	601	0.5
Muntenia		19,842	
Moldavia		109,654	4.5
Dobrudja		1,816	0.2
Bessarabia		201,278	7.0
Bucovina		74,288	8.7
Transylvania		52,008	1.6
Banat		757	......
Crishana-Maramuresh		58,510	4.2
Greater Rumania (total)		518,754	2.9

Table II, taken with Table I, shows that in Wallachia (Oltenia and Muntenia), roughly 20 per cent of the Jewish population had Yiddish for their mother tongue; the rest had Rumanian. In Transylvania and Moldavia, Jews having Yiddish for their mother tongue constituted 60 per cent of the Jewish population, with the rest speaking Hungarian (inTransylvania) and Rumanian (in Moldavia). In Bucovina Yiddish was the mother tongue of 80 per cent of the Jewish population; in Bessarabia, of 97 per cent.

The centuries-old Jewish community of the Old Kingdom, which had fought for and finally achieved emancipation, showed a marked tendency to assimilate with Rumanian society, especially in Wallachia. The prevailing antisemitism arrested but did not halt this development. Jews were members of the traditional parties, played an active part in commerce and industry, and were well-known as writers, journalists, doctors, and lawyers.

The tendency was otherwise in the territories acquired after the First World War, where the Rumanian government's systematically oppressive policy engendered a heightened national consciousness in the Jewish minority, expressed in demands for Jewish cultural autonomy. Zionism, coolly regarded by the Jewish leaders of Old Rumania, gained influence throughout the provinces and won a dominant position in the annexed territories.

The Jews in Northern Transylvania—who had won their emancipation in Hungary—were for the most part highly assimilated to Magyar culture, and spoke Hungarian and German, especially in the cities, as a matter of course. Yiddish was spoken almost exclusively in the part of Transylvania adjacent to Old Rumania.

The Jewish community of Bucovina, though influenced under Austrian rule by German and Ukrainian culture, was nevertheless a center of Yiddishism. The province's chief minorities—Ukrainians, Germans, and Jews—were united against the Rumanizing policy of the Bucharest government and sought to preserve their own languages and ways of life.

Finally, the widespread use of Yiddish in Bessarabia was due in part to a stubborn rejection of the policy of forced Rumanization—ruthlessly pursued by the Bucharest government after 1920—and in part to the impossibility of freely using the Russian language. (A too frequent use of Russian could be looked upon as a "proof" of Communist leanings).

Ruined economically by the loss of their traditional Russian market, plagued by continuous anti-Semitic outbursts that equated Jew with Communist, too poor for the most part to send their sons to universities and into the professions, a minority in a "minority province"—the Bessarabian Jews clung primarily to Yiddish and Yiddish literature, and secondarily to Russian. They used Rumanian, which was considered a "foreign language," only for official business.

Chapter II

War, Pogroms, Deportations

The Second World War shattered the traditional diplomatic position of Rumania. The collapse of Poland and France and the retreat of the British from Europe deprived Rumania of its northern military cover and Western support. At the end of June 1940, the Soviet Union, which now ruled half of pre-war Poland, demanded and obtained from Rumania the immediate cession of northern Bucovina and all of Bessarabia (June 28, 1940). The Russian demand was made in accordance with the Nazi-Soviet pact of August 1939; Germany "advised" Bucharest to submit. The Soviet request touched off a whole series of events which rapidly led Rumania into the camp of the Axis. On July 1, 1940, King Carol, severing Rumania's Anglo-French ties, proclaimed a "reorientation" of her foreign policy.

The months from September 1939 to July 1940 were anything but easy for the royal dictatorship. The crown had killed Codreanu and other Iron Guards in order to keep power in its own hands; at the same time it adopted parts of the Iron Guard program in order to cut the ground from under the Legionnaires; now, after the Nazi victories in Europe, it tried to conciliate both Germany and the Iron Guard. But the King failed in both efforts.

Paying little attention to the Rumanian "reorientation," Berlin and Rome moved to satisfy the revisionist demands of Hungary. On August 30, 1940, Ribbentrop and Ciano for Berlin and Rome and Csaky and Manolescu for Budapest and Bucharest, signed an agreement providing for Rumania's cession to Hungary of the northern part of Transylvania. Less than a week later (September 6, 1940), with the help of the Axis and the Soviet Union, Bulgaria obtained the return of southern Dobrudja, taken by Rumania in 1913 after the Balkan War.

The total collapse of Carol's foreign policy, the shaky position of "rump Rumania" and the virtual isolation of the country, brought about a bloodless palace revolution. On September 4, 1940, Carol II was forced by a military group led by General Ion Antonescu to renounce the prerogatives he had granted himself under the constitution of February 10, 1938. Two days later Antonescu forced his abdication and exile. Carol's son,

Michael I, mounted the throne and Antonescu proclaimed himself the *conducator* (leader) of the country. Basing his power on the army and Iron Guard, with whom he had had secret ties since 1937, Antonescu proclaimed Rumania a "National Legionary State" (*Statul National Legionar*). The Iron Guard was declared the only legal political movement; the government was formed almost exclusively of its members. At the same time the new "ally," Nazi Germany, sent 120,000 of her best troops to Rumania under the guise of a "military advisory mission."

The coalition of Antonescu and the military with the Legionnaire mob (led, after Codreanu's death, by Horia Sima) was an uneasy one. The Guard began to massacre not only Jews but also its political enemies; in the process, it "expropriated" a number of key holdings of influential Rumanians. This provoked strong opposition in the army and the country generally. It apparently also displeased the Germans, who were trying to lay their hands on as much Rumanian property as possible, particularly heavy industries, oil, banks, and the like. From all this resulted the apparent paradox of Nazi Germany's siding with Antonescu and his army against the Iron Guard in the struggle between the two.

The battle between the army and the Guard gave Bucharest the bloodiest period in its history. On January 20,1941, the Iron Guard held a huge demonstration in the streets of the capital against Antonescu's dismissal of two Legionnaires from his cabinet. The next day, the first direct clashes between the Legionnaires and the army took place. The latter evacuated the city and concentrated in its outskirts. On the night of January 21-22, the Iron Guard, now sole master of Bucharest, conducted a terrible massacre of the Jewish population and a number of its other "'enemies." The following noon the army moved in; by January 23 the Iron Guard rebellion was completely quashed, and the organization was declared illegal. All power now passed into the hands of the army, with Antonescu remaining at the head of the government as *conducator*. But the key cabinet posts were in the hands of generals, the supervision of the country's administration was taken over by army officers, and the police, purged of Legionnaires, received an army commandant.[1]

The military dictatorship continued to call for the "Rumanization" of the economy and the seizure of Jewish property, but by the state, not by "adventurers." The military regime sought to make up for the loss of northern Transylvania and southern Dobrudja by recapturing Bucovina and Bessarabia from Russia and taking an additional slice of Russian territory in the southern Ukraine on the western side of the Dniester, inhabited by a population of Moldavian descent. It was this régime, under *conducator* Antonescu, which led Rumania into the war against Russia and down the road to defeat. On August 23, 1944, King Michael I arrested Antonescu and opened Bucharest to the Russian troops.

Massacres and Deportations

From the Goga-Cuza government in 1938 through the royal, Legionnaire, and military dictatorships, the situation of the Jewish population went from bad to worse, at least until 1942. Each political change, each territorial loss, even each taking back of a piece of territory, was a pretext for bloody massacres of the Jewish population.

Table III shows the distribution of the pre-war Jewish population after the cessions of Bessarabia, northern Bucovina, northern Transylvania (North Ardeal) and southern Dobrudja.[2]

TABLE III

THE JEWISH POPULATION IN THE CEDED TERRITORIES AND "RUMP" RUMANIA AFTER THE CESSIONS OF 1940 (BASED ON DATA OF THE 1930 CENSUS)

Region	Number of Jews	% of total pop. of the region
Rumania (after the cessions of 1940)	329,841	2.8
Territories incorporated into the Soviet Union	277,949	8.2
Ceded to Hungary	148,294	6.2
Ceded to Bulgaria	846	0.2
Prewar "Greater Rumania" (total)	756,930	4.2

The cession of northern Bucovina and Bessarabia in June 1940 was accompanied by bloody riots against the Jewish population of these regions.[3] The Guardist rebellion of January 1941 involved the massacre of a significant section of the Jewish population of the capital.[4] The entrance of Rumania into war on the side of Germany was celebrated by one of the bloodiest pogroms in the history of Rumania—the killing of 14,000 Jews in Jassy, the capital of Moldavia, on June 29, 1941.[5]

The conquest of northern Bucovina and Bessarabia by Nazi and Rumanian troops was followed by the destruction of almost three-quarters of the large Jewish population of these provinces. The Jewish population of northern Transylvania, under Hungarian rule from 1940 until the end of 1944, escaped extermination until 1944, when the last-minute victory of the Hungarian Arrow Cross led to its destruction.

The censuses of 1941 and 1942 testify to the extent of these massacres. The first of these war censuses was made in two parts. In April 1941 the Rumanian authorities took a census of the Jewish population of Rumania after the cessions to Russia, Hungary, and Bulgaria. In August and September of the same year, after the reconquest of Bucovina and Bessarabia, a census of the Jewish population was taken in the latter provinces. And in 1942 the newly created Central Office of the Jews of Rumania took a census of the Jewish population of all of Rumania (except northern Transylvania and southern Dobrudja, which were still retained by Hungary and Bulgaria).[6]

TABLE IV

THE JEWISH POPULATION OF RUMANIA (WITHOUT NORTHERN TRANSYLVANIA AND SOUTHERN DOBRUDJA) IN 1941 AND 1942

Region	Census of 1930	Census of 1941	Census of 1942
"Rump" Rumania (after the cessions of 1940)	329,841	314,859	275,068
The "recovered" territories (northern Bucovina and Bessarabia)	277,949	60,692	17,081 (both rows)
Deportation Camps	......	65,742	
Rumania in 1941 (i.e., "Greater Rumania" less northern Transylvania and southern Dobrudja)	607,790	441,293	292,149

Thus the Jewish population of Rumania in 1941 fell to two-thirds of its pre-war number, and in 1942 to *less than one half*.

A breakdown of the above figures, region by region, reveals significant shifts in the location of the Jewish population. Rump Rumania in 1941 shows a sharp fall in the Jewish population of Moldavia and an influx into Bucharest. In northern Bucovina and Bessarabia, as well as in the border region of southern Bucovina, the figures reveal the decimation of the Jewish population through massacres and deportation to the camps of the newly acquired Transnistrian region. As Table IV shows, the Jewish population of northern Bucovina and Bessarabia fell from a pre-war figure of 277,949 to 126,434 at the time of recovery of these territories. In 1942 it was reduced to 17,081 persons—13 per cent of the previous year's figure. In southern Bucovina the Jewish population in 1941 was 29,687; in 1942, 2,495, or a bare 8 per cent of the 1941 figure.

The complete dislocation of the Jewish settlements in the countryside is shown by Table V.[7]

TABLE V

DISTRIBUTION OF THE JEWISH POPULATION BETWEEN TOWN AND COUNTRYSIDE

Region	Loc. of Jewish Pop.	1930	1941	1942
Rump Rumania	Towns	286,747	291,726	272,629
	Countryside	43,094	23,133	2,439
Northern Bucovina and Bessarabia	Towns	163,037	65,463	16,981
	Countryside	114,912	60,971	100
Rumania at the end of 1941	Towns	449,784	357,189	293,610
	Countryside	158,006	84,104	2,539

In 1930 the Jewish population in the countryside amounted to over 25 per cent of the total Jewish population of the area; this percentage fell to 19 per cent in 1941; it went down to less than one per cent in 1942. Massacres, deportations, uprooting—this is the story told by the two war censuses.

Economic Situation

Under the dictatorships of King Carol II, the Iron Guard, and the Rumanian military, the juridical status and economic situation of the Jewish community progressively worsened.

The harsh anti-Semitic legislation enacted in 1940, in the last months in the reign of Carol II, used religion—instead of lack of citizenship, as in 1938—as a basis for discrimination against Jews. This same concept was retained in some of Antonescu's legislation relating to military taxes and compulsory labor in lieu of military service. But in other laws (such as the one transferring Jewish-owned rural real property to the state), race rather than religion was the determining factor.[8] Thus not only the Jewish population proper but baptized Jews of the first and second generation—whose number probably did not exceed some tens of thousands—were systematically driven from their positions in industry and trade, the professions, and handicrafts. In implacable succession these measures often ran the whole gamut from the tragic to the grotesque. Thus the government published special decrees prohibiting the Jews from "breeding carrier pigeons"; Jewish actors from "enacting plays by Rumanian authors"; and Jewish publishers from "editing didactic works."[9] At the end of 1942, virtually all Jews had been driven out of the regular economic life of the country.

This barring of Jews from Rumanian economic life does not mean that all Jews ceased to be gainfully employed. A certain percentage of Jewish doctors, craftsmen, and employees continued to work, but for the most part for the Jewish community itself, which was isolated economically as well as socially from the rest of the country.

In 1940 all Jews were expelled from the army. In lieu of military service, Jewish men and women from the ages of eighteen to fifty were made liable to perform compulsory labor. During the whole war period the Jewish working population was forced to labor without pay both at home and away from home in front zones and bombed areas.

The special census of 1942 listed 108,272 Jews, or 39.4 per cent of the Jewish population of Rumania (excluding northern Transylvania), in the labor force. As a result of the anti-Jewish legislation, only 60,000 or 21.8 per cent of the total Jewish population, were gainfully employed, while 48,271 had lost their normal employment. Economically, 1942 was the worst year in three decades for the Jews of Rumania. In 1912, 37.4 per cent of the Jewish population was gainfully employed; in 1930, 41.3 per cent; in 1942, only one Jew out of five had a source of income. And this source was essentially the impoverished Jewish community itself.

The economic exclusion of Jews was accompanied by an orgy of illegal and "legal" looting of Jewish property. The illegal pillage was carried out during the regime of the Iron Guard, whose members killed and looted at will. Official statistics for the period from September 6, 1940 to January 23, 1941, published after the Iron Guard's fall from power in 1941,[10] record 1,162 acquisitions of property through forced sales; 1,081 cases of illegal confiscations; 260 forcible seizures of real property; 65 large-scale devastations, and others. These are only the *recorded* cases where official complaints were lodged with the courts by the Jewish owners after the fall of the Guard. But thousands of other cases could not even be recorded, the former owners and their families having been killed by the Legionnaires.

According to the records, real property valued at one billion lei was "sold" during the same period at a price of 216 million, of which only 52 million lei were paid. The mass pillage of Jewish property at one time produced a grotesque rivalry between the Iron Guard and local population of German stock in the district of Mediash in Transylvania. The Guardists accused the Germans of having made "a deal with the Jews" by which they acquired Jewish stores at low prices, the basic Jewish aim being "the sabotaging of the Rumanization drive"! Table VI indicates the extent of the Jewish property looted, officially or unofficially, during the war.[11]

The readjusted value of these properties amounted to a total of over 70 billion lei. Of this, 83 per cent was represented by the value of the apartments and buildings taken from the Jewish population. There were also forced contributions. The Jews were obliged during the war to contribute so-called "stocks of clothing for social welfare." The compulsory contribution was fixed according to the estimated gross income of each con-

TABLE VI

JEWISH PROPERTY (EXCEPT FOR THAT IN NORTHERN TRANSYLVANIA) CONFISCATED BY THE RUMANIAN STATE 1940-44

Kind of Property	Hectares[a]	Kind of Property	Number
Arable Land	42,320	Mills	265
Forests	68,644	Sawmills	115
Vineyards	2,062	Other Industries	81
Ponds	78	Boats	152
		Buildings	40,758

[a]A hectare is equal to 2.471 acres.

tributor during 1940-41; the total collected represented at the official prices an additional contribution of two billion lei. Counting other contributions such as the "Reunification Loan" (*Imprumutul Reintregirei*), the total pillage amounted to over one hundred billion lei.[12]

The Rumanian Population and the Jewish Community

For over three years Rumania fought as a partner of the Axis. The alliance with Germany, which led to the loss of Northern Transylvania, the arrival of 120,000 German soldiers in Rumania, the outburst of massacres and pillage during the period of the Iron Guard government, and finally, the entrance of the country into the war, were not very popular with most Rumanians. Still, as long as the German and satellite armies advanced, opposition was not very active. Beginning with 1943, however, Rumanians became more and more concerned over the fate of their country. They could see that the military might of the Allies was growing from month to month, portending the opening up of the second front in Europe. Heavy casualties suffered by the Rumanian Army in the battle of Stalingrad spurred the peasants' resentment. Thus Antonescu faced a difficult domestic as well as military situation.

Even in the darkest days of the persecution of the Jews in Rumania, it was possible to organize aid for those deported to Transnistria or confined in ghettos. A large share of this aid was carried by the Bucharest Jewish community, whose importance grew considerably during the war years. Between the wars this community was only formally the center of the Jewish community in Rumania. The Jewish communities of Bucovina, Bessarabia and Transylvania—with different traditions and cultures—were never too anxious to ally themselves with the community of Old Rumania. The situation changed appreciably during the war, when the Jewish community of Bucharest became the effective center of Jewish life.

On December 17, 1941, the government dissolved the Federation of the Unions of the Jewish Communities (grouping provincial and religious unions), and ordered the creation in Bucharest of the Central Office of the Jews of Rumania as the "sole body authorized to represent the interests of the Jewish community of Rumania." The Central Office, deriving its funds from compulsory contributions from all Jews, became by law the economic center of Rumanian Jewry. Its responsibilities included meeting certain government demands, organizing any paying for the Jewish schools (a task involving in 1942 no less than sixty-eight elementary schools, and twenty-two high schools, professional schools and colleges), and aiding the needy.[13]

Zionist activities were prohibited and the office of the Jewish Agency in Rumania was closed in 1942. Nevertheless, Zionist organizations tried to reorganize on a small scale and were finally able, in co-operation with representatives of the International Red Cross, to help the illegal transport of a limited number of Jews to Palestine.

The first dramatic attempt at illegal flight to Palestine was undertaken in 1942 by 700 Rumanian Jews, on an old boat, the *Struma.* The vessel reached Istanbul, but its passengers were not allowed to disembark. The *Struma* turned back, only to sink in the Black Sea not far off the shores of Turkey, losing all but a few of the passengers aboard. From then on secret preparations for unauthorized emigration by sea were made in close contact with the Jewish Agency's representative in Istanbul. Rumanian Jewish emigrants sailed to Istanbul on all kinds of old boats, a trip of three to four days on a dangerous sea in time of war. In Istanbul at the beginning of 1944 the immigrants received visas and were finally transferred to Palestine by rail via Syria. Nevertheless, this emigration involved only a few Rumanian Jews; most of the Jewish population had to endure their plight down to the last day of the Antonescu regime (August 23, 1944), the long awaited day of liberation.

Chapter III

The Road to a "People's Democracy"

On August 21 and 22, 1944, the Soviet army entered Moldavia and broke through the Jassy defense line. Two Russian armies, one led by Malinovski and the other by Tolbuchin, moved rapidly across Rumanian territory. For Rumania the military situation was now hopeless. On August 23 King Michael and certain of his political advisers, acting on Molotov's declaration of April 2, 1944, that "the Soviet Union has no desire to intervene in the local affairs of Rumania," resorted to a *coup d'etat* in the hope of saving the crown. Antonescu was summoned to the palace, his guards disarmed, and he himself placed under arrest. The king broadcast a proclamation announcing Rumania's withdrawal from the war and asking the mercy of the Allies. Two days later, when Germany retaliated by bombing Bucharest, the palace completed the somersault by declaring war on Germany. The Rumanian army, now under Soviet command, participated in the recapture of northern Transylvania.

After having given northern Transylvania to Hungary, the Germans had "compensated" Rumania by allowing her to recover northern Bucovina and Bessarabia, as well as a slice of the Soviet Union. Now the Russians, after retaking northern Bucovina and Bessarabia, were "compensating" Rumania with northern Transylvania. Almost all the territory involved in these changes had been part of Greater Rumania before 1939.

The *coup d'etat* was followed by the immediate resurgence of all the pre-war parties: the "historic" Liberal and National Peasant parties; some splinter parties; the Social Democratic Party; a Communist front organization, the "Ploughmen's Front"; and the Communist Party itself, illegal in Rumania since the early twenties. All claimed to have waged a strong underground fight against the Nazis during the dark days of the dictatorships. Actually, unlike the Yugoslavs and French, the Rumanians did not take up arms and form a resistance movement. In Rumania the state apparatus was not shattered by a defeat until 1944. No acts of sabotage were known to have been committed by anti-Nazi groups until the last months of the alliance with Germany. Even the effectiveness and the extent of the opposition as a political force prior to 1944 has been disputed. The claim of the left that the underground was well organized and enjoyed popular support was contradicted by the right's assertion that the opposition in Rumania during Antonescu's regime was confined to the political upper crust, i.e., to certain leaders of the disbanded parties and to the king himself.

In fact, however, it was only in 1944, when the end of the Antonescu regime was in plain sight, that the leaders of the traditional parties urged the king to break the alliance with Germany. And only in May 1944 did the few Communist leaders then living in Rumania, some Socialists, and some fellow-travelers from the Ploughmen's Front form a "United Front of Labor"; the latter's best known underground act was the signing, on June 20, 1944, of a declaration asking Antonescu "for the immediate cessation of hostilities against the USSR."

At the moment of the *coup d'état* the palace and army had the situation well in hand. The government appointed by the king was actually a military government under a career officer, General Constantin Sanatescu. The key posts in the government were taken over by eight generals; the leaders of the "opposition" Liberal, National Peasant, Socialist, and Communist parties were apparently happy with four secondary seats as "Ministers of State with no specified departmental duties."

"Conquest" of the State

The re-emergence of the Rumanian Communist Party on the political scene was unspectacular enough; but now that Russian troops were in Rumania, and many Communists had come back from their refuge in the Soviet Union, the reorganized Central Committee of the Communist Party understood quite well that the time had come to aim at higher things than the portfolio of "Minister of State." To the "government of generals" was left the first and the most bitter obligation of defeat: that of signing the armistice clauses returning Bessarabia and northern Bucovina to the Russians, agreeing to the payment of reparations in kind amounting to $300,000,000, promising the "restoration of Russian property moved during the war," and agreeing to pay the costs of Soviet troops stationed in Rumania. Meanwhile, the Communist Party was hastily building a network of party organizations throughout the country, organizing "popular militias" with the help of the Rumanian regiment "Tudor Vladimirescu" (made up of Rumanian war exiles trained in the Soviet army), and building a "National Democratic Front." Under this banner the Communists gathered together, in addition to their own party and the Ploughmen's Front of Petre Groza (a landowner and fellow-traveler, not a farmer), the newly organized trade unions (which reached a membership of 700,000 almost overnight), some very pliable Social Democrats, and various political and professional groups constituted *ad hoc* (e.g., the "Union of Democratic Priests").

The Communist Party quickly extended its influence by recruiting indiscriminately including large numbers of Iron Guardists in search of a political alibi, as well as by employing terror and high-pressure propaganda. Its methodic seizure of the state machine from top to bottom was helped by the Soviet Union and its High Commissioner in Bucharest. The succession of events was rapid. The first Sanatescu cabinet lasted little more than two months: under pressure from the "historic parties," Sanatescu agreed to form a new coalition based not only on the army but on the parties. The second Sanatescu government included Juliu Maniu, leader of the National Peasant Party, Dinu Bratianu, leader of the Liberal Party and Titel Petrescu, leader of the Socialists. The historic parties believed that this government would last until general elections were held. But increasing Communist pressure and Russian "advice" forced it out of office in less than a month.

On December 2, 1944, General Nicolae Radescu, chief of staff of the army, formed a third cabinet. This time it was the Liberal and National Peasant parties, now under heavy attack from the Communist press, which got the insignificant posts. A little over two months after the formation of the Radescu cabinet—in which the Communists were granted the Undersecretariat of the Interior as well as the Ministry of Justice—a huge Communist-led demonstration clashed with Radescu's military force (February 24, 1945). Disturbances occured all over the country following this, and the Communist groups and front organizations demanded Radescu's dismissal.

On February 28, 1945, Andrei Vishinsky, then the Russian Deputy Commissar for Foreign Affairs, flew from Moscow and ordered the king to dismiss Radescu and give the premiership to Petre Groza, nominal leader of the Communist-controlled Ploughmen's Front and the newly organized National Democratic Front. Hoping to save the crown, which had already come under attack during the crisis, the king agreed. General Radescu took refuge in the British embassy and the road was open to the National Democratic Front (March 6, 1945).

The new cabinet was composed of representatives of the Ploughmen's Front, Communist Party, Social Democrats, and Tatarescu faction of the Liberals—the same Tatarescu who led Young Liberals in pre-war days and whom King Carol II used to prepare the way for his dictatorship. The two traditional parties were left out of the government. The Communists took the key post of the Ministry of the Interior, controlling the police and gendarmerie, and left the seemingly important ministeries of defense and foreign affairs to the "bourgeois" members of the coalition.

The nomination of George Tatarescu as Vice Premier and Minister of Foreign Affairs was hailed in some quarters both in Rumania and abroad as a "concession" to the Allies, since Tatarescu was supposed to be, as the

British put it, "a staunch defender of pro-Allied policy." In fact, however, Tatarescu had not even the shadow of real power; his function was to pacify the Allies by his mere presence in the government, and to sign the peace treaty. As in the case of the armistice, Russia wanted Rumanian obligations to the Soviet Union to be endorsed by a Rumanian "bourgeois" leader and not by Rumanian Communists. The Ministry of War was left to General Rascanu—a rival of Radescu—so as not to hamper prosecution of the war. Finally, in order to consolidate the position of Groza's cabinet, Stalin returned the northern part of Transylvania to Rumania (March 10, 1945). Now installed in the key Ministry of the Interior, the Communist Party set about the task of securing complete control of Rumania.

From March 6, 1945, to the end of 1947 the Communist Party and its police arm successively attacked and destroyed all the forces opposing them. On the political plane, it eliminated the "historic parties" as well as other minor groups, and finally did away with the monarchy itself. On the economic plane, it destroyed the foundations of the Rumanian capitalist economy.

The United States and Great Britain accepted the Groza regime only reluctantly. After long discussions at the meeting of the United States, United Kingdom, and Soviet Foreign Ministers held in 1945 in Moscow, the Americans and British agreed to recognize the Groza government provided it was broadened to include genuine representatives of the democratic opposition (Liberal and National Peasant parties), guaranteed civil liberties, and held free elections.

After various postponements the election took place in November 1946. Master of the state machine, the Communist Party conducted an open campaign of intimidation against the Liberals and Peasants, whom it accused of fascist leanings. The Democratic Front included all sorts of camouflaged Communist groups and parties, so that the latter easily carried the 1946 election. But in spite of all manipulations, the National Peasant Party, whose popularity was again increasing because of its opposition to Russia, won twenty-five seats in the new parliament.

The victory of Maniu's Peasant Party did not deter the Communists from attacking it head on. Numerous leaders of the National Peasant Party were arrested on July 15, 1947, the party was dissolved on July 29, and its deputies were expelled from parliament on August 8, 1947. A trial on the charges of "conspiracy, treason and spying" followed; the seventy-year-old Juliu Maniu, Ion Mihalache, and other leaders of the party were sentenced to solitary confinement for life. The Liberal Party of Dinu Bratianu was likewise dissolved, as was the Tatarescu group after it had served its purpose. Tatarescu's signing in Paris of the Rumanian peace treaty, in February 1947, was his last major political act. After that, nothing was heard of him.

Immediately after the destruction of the "bourgeois" parties the Communists turned their police arm against those Socialists who did not accept their leadership: the independent Socialist group of Titel Petrescu was disbanded, and Petrescu was imprisoned.

Thus the field was clear for the Communist Party's absolute control of the political life of the country. On November 7, 1947, the Communists took over all the positions in the government formerly held by the Liberals of the Tatarescu faction. Ana Pauker, secretary of the party, was made Minister of Foreign Affairs; Vasile Luca, assistant secretary of the party, became Minister of Finance. Groza's former under secretary, Emil Bodnarash (a leading Communist from Bucovina, trained in the Soviet Union), was made a general overnight and proclaimed Minister of Defense.

In December 1947 the last official formality consecrating these changes took place at Bucharest without any difficulty: the king was forced to abdicate and Rumania was proclaimed a "people's democracy."

Economic Obligations to the USSR

The postwar Rumanian economy, already burdened with tremendous reparation and restitution obligations, and required to foot the bill for the large Russian military force in Rumania, received its *coup de grâce* when under the peace treaty Russia obtained the ownership of all former German assets in the country. The large German holdings in Rumania, obtained mostly during the war by the robbery and forced sale of Jewish and Rumanian property,[1] were now turned by the Soviet Union to its own benefit. The German assets seized by the Soviets were used as a basis for the formation of so-called Soviet-Rumanian companies. But Russia's contribution to this partnership consisted of shares stolen by Germany from Rumanian and Jewish owners. The joint companies represented a powerful instrument of Soviet pressure on Rumania. They were also a serious factor preventing the restitution of Jewish property looted during the war.

Rumania's economy almost collapsed under her heavy economic obligations to the Soviet Union, the absence of any trade with the West (since her own products had to be sent as reparations to Russia), and two consecutive years of severe drought. The currency plummeted downwards, the standard of living of the population fell lower and lower. Rumania, which formerly exported agricultural surpluses, was now unable to feed its own population and requested relief from the United Nations Relief and Rehabilitation Administration (UNRRA).

Meanwhile, the Groza government launched a series of attacks against private enterprise; it became increasingly hazardous to engage in business of any kind. Finally, on August 15, 1947—at the height of its drive against the "bourgeois" political opponents of the regime—the government struck a decisive blow by sharply devaluing the currency. No individual could obtain more than 150 new lei in exchange for even as much as thirty million old ones. All lei capital was automatically wiped out, and with it all those who relied on liquid assets for carrying on their business. Capital in other forms, such as real estate, still remained unaffected; but the complete uncertainty as to the future paralyzed all private initiative.

The Postwar Jewish Population

According to the figures published in 1947 by the Rumanian section of the World Jewish Congress, the total Jewish population living in Rumania in 1947—i.e., in pre-war Rumania minus Southern Dobrudja, Northern Bucovina, and Bessarabia—was 428,000.[2]

TABLE VII

JEWISH POPUATION IN PRE-WAR AND POSTWAR RUMANIA (1947)
(Not Including Southern Dobrudja, Northern Bucovina and Bessarabia)

Region	1930	1941	1942	1947
Rumania				
Present Boundaries	478,042	466,128	427,296	428,312
Oltenia	3,523	2,841	2,484	3,406
Muntenia	94,216	114,470	108,761	163,144
Moldavia	160,330	135,730	121,131	150,651
Dobrudja				
(without South Dobr.)	3,185	2,885	2,239	3,279
Southern Bucovina	23,844	18,140	179	17,388
Transylvania	18,929	15,720	15,122	15,847
(without North Trans.)				
North Transylvania	148,294	151,125	152,228	44,706
Banat	14,043	14,626	14,009	15,963
Crishana	11,678	10,591	10,497	13,928

A glance at the totals for the entire present territory of Rumania might give the impression that there was only a slight decline and that the Jewish population remained about the same between 1942 and 1947. In reality profound changes occurred both in the composition of the population and in its distribution.

In September 1944, it was estimated that the Jewish population in rump Rumania amounted to around 300,000 persons. In 1947 this population had increased to 428,000. The 128,000 were for the most part Rumanian Jewish survivors from the Transnistrian, Hungarian and German camps, as well as Jewish refugees originally from northern Bucovina and Bessarabia who had managed in the early war period to escape to the Soviet Union. A few might have been new refugees from the adjacent countries, mainly Poland, and a certain number must be imputed to natural increase. Thus around

100,000 *persons* out of this population (if we accept the figure of 28,000 as accounting for the new refugees and natural increase) *represent in fact what remained of the 457,000 Jews of Bessarabia, Bucovina and Transylvania.* In pre-war Rumania there were 757,000 Jews; only 300,000 were to be found in rump Rumania on September 1944; 100,000 more returned to Rumania, not only from northern Transylvania (recovered in 1945), but also, as stated above, from various places including northern Bucovina and Bessarabia.[3]

In 1942, over 152,000 Jews lived in Northern Transylvania under Hungarian occupation. After the massacres of 1944, the recovery of this territory by Rumania and the return of the refugees, the Jewish population in northern Transylvania was only 44,700, or about 30 per cent of the pre-war figure (see Table VII). In southern Bucovina the local settlements were destroyed in 1942 and the Jewish population was deported *en masse*. In 1947, the 1941 level was almost attained, but only by the addition of survivors from northern Bucovina and Bessarabia.

The examination of the 1947 column reveals two further trends. 1. The figures for Crishana, Banat, Southern Transylvania, Moldavia, Dobrudja, and Oltenia suggest a general tendency of the Jewish population to remain in or return to their old settlements. 2. The figures for Muntenia, which includes Bucharest, suggest that there was nevertheless a strong tendency for refugees to concentrate in the capital.

The thousands of returning Jews drawn to Bucharest believed it would be easier to re-establish themselves there; they also hoped that their claims would receive a more favorable hearing if submitted directly in Bucharest. Moreover, it was only natural for the beggared and lonely survivors to seek the shelter of the largest Jewish settlement in the country. For these reasons the Jewish population of Bucharest almost doubled by the summer of 1945; some 150,000 Jews resided there in August 1945, as compared with 85,900 in the pre-war period. With the influx of survivors into the capital, tension developed between the resident Jews and the newcomers which was exacerbated by the acute housing shortage.

Some 29,000 Jews returned to Moldavia, raising its Jewish population to 150,672. The famine-stricken region could offer little to the newcomers; everything was scarce—food, clothing, jobs. Jassy's Jewish population increased by only 4,000 to 38,000 on July 1, 1946. The memories of the massacres of 1941 caused returning Jews to shun that city.

Homecoming was sad and the future unpromising, not only for the repatriates but also for the settled Jews. Government officials were none too friendly, nor were neighbors. As we shall see below, Jews soon began to leave Rumania again. The first wave of mass migration (1947) was the result of hunger; the second wave (1949-50) sprang from a realization that the political and economic situation would not improve and that emigration was the only way out.

Citizenship, Restitution, Economic "Reintegration"

The *coup d'état* of August 23, 1944, coming after years of persecution, aroused hope in the surviving Jewish community for a speedy restoration of their civil rights, restitution of their property and reinstatement in their jobs, businesses and professions. This hope was soon to be frustrated.

An official decree of December 14, 1944, abolished "all the racial laws" previously adopted. But the decree restoring full citizenship to the Rumanian Jews failed to settle the status of the Jewish refugees from the annexed territories. Only after many delays and prolonged negotiation was an agreement reached, at the end of 1946, between the Rumanian Minister of Justice (the then secretary of the Communist Party, Lucretiu Patrascanu) and the leaders of the Jewish community for the granting of citizenship to the refugees who in 1938 had lacked the papers necessary to qualify for it.

Even then, the only positive step taken on behalf of the Jewish refugees returning from deportation or repatriated from the Soviet Union was to exempt them from the registration as *aliens*. Only on May 29, 1947, was a decree issued restoring citizenship to Jews deprived of it by discriminatory legislation during the pro-Nazi regimes, or by territorial changes.

The early expectation that property confiscated by the Antonescu regime would in time be returned to its former owners proved illusory.[4] The decree of December 14, 1944, was ostensibly intended to reinstate the previous Jewish owners in their rights. Paragraph 5 of the decree read:

> All property formerly belonging to Jews, which is now owned by the state or in the possession of any purchaser, is regarded as always having belonged to the dispossessed titular owners and is returned to them without any additional legal procedure. Leases held upon property seized from Jews are automatically canceled on promulgation of this decree.

But the paragraph following it gave a peculiar twist to the question of restitution. It specified that:

> Jews cannot return to buildings owned by them until April 1945, if the buildings are now occupied by factories, schools, or artisan shops, unless the Jewish owners lived there immediately prior to their deportation or forced transfer elsewhere. The following categories of persons are not required to leave property belonging to Jews before April 23, 1945, unless by special agreement: workers and artisans with a monthly income of less than 30,000 lei, and married war widows, invalids, orphans, state employees, and social welfare institutions.

Paragraph 6 left so many loopholes that the practical value of the decree remained questionable. This type of "balanced" law was presented as "justice, not revenge." In fact, actual restitutions were so few that in March 1947 even the Communist Jewish organ *Unirea* was forced to write:

> The wealth, the lost positions, the moral and material rights which have been violated during the regime of racial terror demand rehabilitation and reparation. Thousands of trials, of just claims, lie buried, in doubt of the issue, in the files of the tribunals. Their chances depend on the issue of various "experts' appraisals," the "proof with witnesses," and on "legalistic controversies."[5]

Rapid progress, however, was made in getting back the jobs of survivors. A law of December 19, 1944, revoked the measures taken against the former Jewish employees and reinstated them in both state and private positions. Nevertheless, this solved only part of the problem of the Jewish community, the majority of whom still lived on the margin of the economy. In the period of the comparatively free market (1944-46), the settled Jews worked at their regular trades. But the refugees and former deportees had either to accept low-paying jobs or to depend upon hazardous dealings in the Bucharest black market in the Strada Lipscani.

The economic collapse of 1947 made things extremely difficult, and a decree of April 1947 permitting private entrepreneurs to dismiss their surplus labor led to considerable unemployment. Jews who had found employment in 1945 possessed no seniority rights and were the first to be released. Finally, the decree of August 15, 1947, devaluating the lei ruined the private sector of the country's economy. A large part of the Jewish community found itself again eliminated from virtually all occupation.

At the end of the war, the impoverished Jewish community was faced by a host of problems including the provision of aid to the needy, care of orphan children and establishment of hospitals and dispensaries.

The community lacked the funds to cope with these large tasks and government help was insignificant; officials invariably pointed to the desperate economic plight of the country as a whole as an excuse for their inaction.

There were at the end of 1944 about 150,000 dispossessed Jews in Rumania. They included artisans whose workshops had been confiscated, merchants who had lost their shops, jobless survivors, tenants expelled from their apartments and householders whose homes had been confiscated. The number of the economically dispossessed was reduced when employees were reinstated in their jobs. But the number was swollen again by the waves of refugees returning to Rumania in 1945-46.

The need was great. Thousands of Jewish survivors without any source of income were appealing to the Jewish community for assistance. A great many of the survivors were sick, ill-clad, and suffering from malnutrition. The homes of the repatriates from Transnistria had been stolen and their businesses taken away. Bucharest, Jassy, Dorohoi were crowded with evacuees and refugees.

Because of the difficult financial situation of the Rumanian Jewish community, an appeal was made abroad. The American Jewish Joint Distribution Committee (JDC), which had succeeded in furnishing some measure of relief to Rumanian Jews even during the war, largely financed the postwar activities of the Jewish community. In co-operation with other international Jewish organizations, the JDC allocated funds for a broad network of welfare institutions operating in Rumania.

During the first year following the liberation, the JDC program in Rumania was devoted primarily to emergency relief. In 1946 it shifted "from individual and direct assistance to institutional care and reconstructive aid." In 1946 the JDC and its agencies provided assistance to some 200,000 persons. Some 24,000 refugees, war widows, and foreign Jews (Polish and Hungarian) received cash relief. Because of the drought and inflation, it was found that money relief lagged far behind real needs. The Jewish leaders then decided to enlarge the number of canteens providing meals to persons in distress. The growth in the number of canteens was impressive. During the period January–March 1946, there were 17 Jewish canteens in Rumania feeding some 3,000 persons; one year later, the Jewish community and local organizations operated 105 canteens feeding some 40,000 persons daily.[6]

The problem presented by the orphans and children from destitute families was an appalling one. In 1946 it was estimated that the total of 420,000 Jews included 60,000 children; according to the JDC, two-thirds of the Jewish children in Rumania, i.e., 40,000, were dependent on relief. This problem could not be met by handouts of food and money. The obvious solution was institutional care. The local communities, in co-operation with the World Union for the Protection of the Health of Jews (OSE) and Hechalutz, established a system of homes to provide for all the children's needs, as well as day care centers where the children were fed and supervised, and nurseries for infants. By the end of 1947, some 164 homes and nurseries caring for 21,000 children were functioning in Rumania. Seventeen thousand children living with their families received various kinds of assistance, and 3,200 children suffering from malnutrition were sent to fifteen summer camps.[7]

A survey initiated in the summer of 1947 by the Medical Department of the JDC disclosed that some 340,000 Jews (approximately 79 per cent of the total Jewish population at that time) on relief or with low incomes required medical services. One hundred ninety thousand persons, or 56 per cent of all the Jews for whom medical services were provided, had spent the war years in concentration camps, in special forced labor units, and in the interior of Russia, where they suffered appalling physical hardships. A large number of Rumanian Jews who returned from deportation showed serious pathological symptoms as a result of the lack of shelter, food, and adequate medical care. Tuberculosis and various nervous disorders, particularly among women, were frequent results of the experiences of the war years. The health, mental and physical, of the 150,000 destitute Jews in Rumania proper also suffered during the hostilities from malnutrition and a continuous feeling of insecurity.[8]

The governmental medical institutions could not cope with the needs of either the general or the Jewish population. The droughts of 1945 and 1946 were accompanied by epidemics of spotted typhus and typhoid fever, against which the medical organizations of the state were helpless. The Jewish population was dependent entirely on the importation of medical supplies and equipment from abroad. The JDC's Medical Department shipped quantities of medicine, drugs, and medical instruments to Rumania.

By 1947, the local communities and OSE were operating a network of no less than 158 institutions, consisting of 22 hospitals, 44 dispensaries, 11 dental clinics, and 81 medical centers.

The Jewish community of Rumania was also successful in meeting the problem of economic aid. The *JDC Review* notes:

> Rumania was one of the first countries to start credit co-operative activities after the close of the war. The Jewish community had to its advantage the experience in the field of economic rehabilitation gained in the period between the two World Wars. The loan kassas organized by the JDC in 1922 functioned successfully until 1941, when they were dissolved by the Antonescu regime. Despite the fact that the kassas were inactive for four years, 1942-45 inclusive, the Jewish community was able to rebuild its loan institutions in a short time. Recognizing the importance of the credit co-operatives, the JDC provided the funds needed to grant loans to a constantly increasing membership. On June 30, 1947, the membership totalled 28,020 and the number of loans issued amounted to over 46,000.[9]

Another important aspect of the economic aid program was the development of vocational training. Hechalutz and other Zionist organizations endeavored to provide the prospective emigrants to Palestine with a rudimentary knowledge of agriculture. The ORT rendered great service by helping thousands of Jews to acquire industrial skills needed to get jobs in the nationalized factories. As stated by the *JDC Review:*

> By the end of 1947 some 8,095 had acquired various skills in trades and agriculture. ORT alone established four centers with 55 courses accomodating 1,095 students. In addition, the Hechalutz, other Zionist groups and local Jewish organizations conducted an intensive program of agricultural training in 130 *hachsharoth* with an enrollment of 7,000.[10]

Jewish communal institutions, credit cooperatives, and vocational training centers developed unobstructedly for some three years (1944-47).

When the Communist government turned its attention to the Jewish welfare institutions, restriction after restriction was placed on them. At first these affected only the cooperatives; subsequently the entire Jewish welfare program was taken in hand.

After the problem of feeding the Jewish needy was solved to some extent, it was felt that before expanding welfare activities the local Jewish communities themselves had to be revived and set working. For this purpose, the JDC granted a special allocation. With this grant, the revival of the provincial Jewish communities in Rumania was accelerated, and by April 1, 1947, some 296 communities were functioning. Table VIII shows the distribution, based on incomplete data, of 252 communities in 1947.[11]

TABLE VIII

JEWISH COMMUNITIES IN RUMANIA, 1947

Province	Number
Transylvania	91
Crishana	84
Moldavia	43
Muntenia	11
Southern Bucovina	8
Banat, Oltenia and Dobrudja	15
Total	252

The local communities, with their direct connections with the Jewish population, were best able to minister to immediate Jewish needs. They also participated in planning the establishment of Jewish schools, Talmud Torahs and medical institutions. But when the time came for launching the new program of Jewish welfare activities, the JDC in Bucharest felt that this should be managed by the communities together with the Rumanian branches of the chief Jewish organizations. At the beginning of 1947, Joseph J. Schwartz, then chairman of the European Executive Council of the JDC, visited Rumania and conferred with the representatives of Rumanian Jewry. It was agreed that several organizations would participate directly in the enlarged welfare activities. Hechalutz was to be responsible for the *hachsharah* (agricultural training of Jewish youth in preparation for their settlement in Palestine). The OSE was to provide and maintain homes for Jewish children, and give medical assistance to tubercular persons. ORT was invited to organize and develop a network of vocational training centers. Agudath Israel was to maintain special children's homes and take part in the educational programs of the Talmud Torahs. The Federation of the Union of the Jewish Communities in Rumania was charged with the regulation and co-ordination of all Jewish welfare, cultural, educational, and religious institutions.[12] Within a short period of time the Jewish leaders in Bucharest, working together with representatives of the Jewish population of the provinces, succeeded in reviving communal life and re-establishing Jewish welfare institutions as far as it was possible under the circumstances.

Obviously, care of the needy and the orphans, provision of medical assistance, economic aid and vocational training could solve only the most immediate problems of the community. They could not remedy its "up-rootedness" in an economic situation in which private enterprise was more and more reduced in scope until it approached the vanishing point.

Chapter IV

The Fight for Leadership in the Jewish Community

In order to centralize the administration and control of specifically Jewish affairs, Antonescu had ordered the creation of a "Central Office of the Jews of Rumania." Following the liberation, the pre-war Federation of the Unions of Jewish Communities was restored to its rights (decrees of October 28, 1944 and January 31, 1945). The Unions of Jewish Communities composing the Federation were the following: the Union of Jewish Communists of Old Rumania; the Union of Jewish Communities of the Sephardic Rite; the Orthodox Central Office of Jewish Communities in Transylvania; the Union of Neological Communities of Transylvania and Banat; and, finally, the Union of Jewish Communities of Southern Bucovina. The restored Federation undertook "to represent and defend the interests of the Jewish religion in the country according to its laws, and to help and secure the development of institutions belonging to the communities."

The system of compulsory levies on the Jewish people established by Antonescu to finance the Central Office of the Jews of Rumania was discarded. As before the war, the Federation was supposed to rely for its income on special allocations from community funds, creed and ritual contributions, and remittances from the JDC. But in actuality many Jewish communities were so pauperized and shattered that they had to seek aid from the Federation; without such aid they found it impossible to establish schools, dispensaries, or canteens.

Supplies from abroad came in slowly. In spite of the JDC's efforts to allot Rumania as much foodstuffs, clothing, and medical supplies as possible, there was never enough. The situation of Rumanian Jews in Transylvania, Bucovina, and Moldavia constantly deteriorated and the relief loads grew from year to year; the Rumanian relief program was a race between increased relief supplies and the rising number of the destitute. Innumerable misunderstandings arose between the Jews of the provinces and the Jews of Bucharest, who were better off and more successful in re-establishing themselves. In Bucharest itself a strong hostility grew up between the old community and newly arrived Jewish refugees; the latter lived in overcrowded houses, peddled on the streets, and felt "excluded and unwantd" even in their own community.

The political behavior of the different Jewish groups reflected their social and economic situation. The established inhabitants of the capital were inclined to trust their old Jewish leadership, which had returned to the helm of the Federation. William Filderman, whose name was synonymous with the history of the pre-war Jewish organizations, had their confidence. Moreover, they believed, at least in the early days of the liberation, that some kind of rejuvenated liberalism would prevail; the Allies would surely not abandon Rumania to the Soviet Union. In the provinces and among the masses of refugees, the prevailing sentiment was quite different. The destitute Jews suspected the new government of unwillingness to recognize their rights. Certain ambiguous declarations of the Liberal and National Peasant leaderships seemed to them signs of renascent anti-Semitism. Anti-Semitic incidents, especially in Transylvania in 1946, intensified their fears. The leaders of the Federation advocated "patience and persuasion for the enactment of more effective measures," whereas the destitute Jewish communities felt that the Bucharest leadership was too sanguine about the traditional parties, and hence handicapped in its task of defending the real interests of the community.

The Jewish Democratic Committee

Taking advantage of the opposition of the Jewish communities of northern Transylvania and southern Bucovina to the Bucharest leadership of the Federation, and of the hostility of many Jews, Zionist and non-Zionist, to the past political connections of the leadership of the Federation, the Communists launched a well-calculated attack on the Jewish community.

Before the war the Communists had taken no interest whatsoever in the problems of the community. For them there were no specifically Jewish problems. On the eve of the liberation they had sent one of their representatives—along with representatives of all the other political parties—to a "Jewish General Council" (Consiliul General Evreesc), which was supposed to direct the affairs of the Jewish community upon the collapse of the Antonescu regime. The Council, composed of delegates from the Union of Rumanian Jews, the "historic parties," the Social Democrats, and the Communists, rapidly came to grief after liberation on the rock of political disagreement. The Communists then began to build their own front organization in the Jewish community, appealing to the destitute Jewish strata and the provincial communities, and trying to unite in a political front with the Jewish Social Democrats and the left-wing Zionist organizations. On June 22, 1945, the Communist-dominated Jewish Democratic Committee (Comitetul Democratic Evreesc—CDE) emerged on the political scene. It was based on an alliance between the Jewish Communists and Social Democrats, plus the "bloc of working Palestine" (Mishmar and Ichud), and a very small splinter group from the Union of Rumanian Jews (the traditional party of Old Rumanian Jewry).

The new committee now set about to split the Jewish community. It established a newspaper, *Unirea* ("Union"), for itself; announced its program in the social and economic field (citizenship for the refugees, restitution of Jewish property to its former owners, and economic "productivization" of the Jewish population); and in the political field called for a fight against anti-Semitism and swift justice for pogromists. In the administrative field, the CDE advocated centralization of all revenues in the federation of the Unions of Jewish Communities (i.e., abolition of the autonomy of the synagogues, cemetery funds, etc.) and "democratization" of the Jewish community.

The program seemed to be a compromise among the various groups forming the CDE. But it is interesting to look closer both at the program and the measures taken by the Communists themselves during this period. From August 23, 1944, to March 6, 1945, during the period of the "bourgeois" cabinets, the Ministry of Justice was held by the secretary of the Communist party, Lucretiu Patrascanu. If Patrascanu was unable during the coalition period to enact measures providing for the restitution of Jewish property and the granting of citizenship to all Jews, or to bring to trial at least the known perpetrators of the Jassy pogrom of 1941, certainly the Groza government could have done so in 1945 or at the very latest 1946. But the Groza cabinet did nothing. The reason for this was already clear at the time to many observers. The Communist Party wished to avoid antagonizing those sections of the population which had profited from the anti-Jewish laws and which the party aimed at neutralizing and eventually winning over. While the representatives of the Communist Party in the government were stalling the progress of the citizenship and restitution laws, Jewish Communists were accusing the community leadership of being "complacent" toward the "bourgeois" government and "unfit" to defend Jewish interests.

The same tactic was followed in the so-called "campaign against anti-Semitism." Before the November 1946 elections, the last in which the "bourgeois" parties were permitted to take part, both the "historic parties" and the Communists courted the Iron Guard's old members and sympathizers. The National Peasant leader, Ion Mihalache, bluntly said that Jews were now being "appointed to responsible offices" and decried their "provocative" attitude toward Rumanians. The Communists attacked these anti-Semitic speeches, bidding for the support of the Jews. After the 1946 elections, when the opposition complained of irregularities, the CDE was able to get 80,000 Rumanian Jews to sign a petition addressed to President Truman, Prime Minister Attlee, and Premier Stalin informing them "of the anti-Semitic attitude of the National Peasant and Liberal parties, both of which oppose the democratic bloc that carried the national elections." But at the same time the Communists were admitting former Iron Guardists into their party and delaying the taking of any measures against pogromists. Thus, despite the Communists' control of the Ministry of the Interior from March 1945 on, they commenced no proceedings against those who had murdered 14,000 Jews at Jassy on June 29, 1941.

In June 1947—six years after the pogrom and after no less than two and a half years of Communist control of the Ministries of the Interior and Justice—the organ of the CDE, *Unirea*, came around to declaring:

> The Jewish population is worried about the fact that the trial of the Jassy criminals has not taken place, the assassins stroll about at liberty, the citizenship law has not been voted immediately. . . .[1]

This was published on the eve of the trial of some ninety-four of the Jassy killers, among whom were some generals who were finally arraigned before the tribunal and sentenced to hard labor for life. The Communists, who had waited two and a half years to open the Jassy files, could now pose as the defenders of the Jewish population.

Other points of the "minimum program" of the CDE deserve attention. The demand for restitution, set forth by *Unirea* in 1945, was heard less and less during the Groza regime, until the Communist nationalization of private property rendered it completely pointless. The program of the CDE increasingly centered on the slogan of the "productivization" of the Jewish community. The practical results of this will be discussed in Chapter VI; let us note here only that this program called for the elimination of the Jews from their previous economic positions and activities.

The apparently innocuous proposal in the "administrative field," for the concentration of all the financial resources of the communities and the abolition of the "anomalous autonomous situation of the synagogue and cemetery funds," later justified not only the destruction of the financial independence of these bodies, but the party's totalitarian control of everything from prayers in the synagogue to upkeep of the cemeteries. As *Unirea* put it later, the object of the creation of the Jewish Democratic Committee had been simply to endow the Jewish community "with an organism for the guidance of Jewish political life in the spirit of the National Democratic Front which leads the country."[2]

Two main organized opposition forces faced the CDE in the Jewish community: The Union of Rumanian Jews (Uniunea Evreilor Romani—UER) led by William Filderman (also head of the Federation of the Unions of the Jewish Communities), and the Jewish Party (Partidul Evreesc), led by A. L. Zissu. These forces, traditionally divided over the question of assimilation versus Jewish nationalism, were not able to join hands. An attempt to set up a Jewish National Council failed over a seemingly insignificant issue. Although both parties agreed on its ideological basis, the council never came into being because Filderman wanted the word "national" removed from the title of the new organization, a proposal Zissu would under no circumstances accept.[3] In the end, both Filderman and Zissu were driven from their positions and their organizations dissolved.

The CDE waged its battle for control of the Jewish community by pressure politics, splitting infiltrated organizations, amalgamating with Zionists, near Zionists, or simply fellow-travelers, and finally by getting the government to intervene on its behalf. A violent campaign was waged by *Unirea* against Filderman and Zissu. The Groza government suppressed both the *Curierul Israelit* ("Jewish Courier"), organ of the Union of Rumanian Jews, and *Mantuirea* ("Salvation"), Zissu's organ. Filderman and Zissu soon found themselves isolated in their own parties. Following a pattern used in all the Balkan countries during this period, the Communists forced these parties after a time to discard their own leadership.

In May 1946, both the Union of Rumanian Jews and the Jewish Party agreed to join with the Jewish Democratic Committee in a "Jewish National Bloc" in preparation for the elections to be held in November 1946. Filderman and Zissu voiced public disapproval of this decision. Thereafter Filderman directed all his energies to the work of the Federation, and Zissu resigned from his party (June 6, 1946).

The Jewish National Bloc's co-ordinating committee was composed of Eduard Manulescu, vice president of the Union of Rumanian Jews; Bernard Rohrlich of the Jewish Party; and Angel Dascalu, of the CDE. Undoubtedly at least the two former sincerely believed that the Groza government's promises concerning the Jews would be carried out after the elections. They were encouraged in their hopes by the fact that at this period the government was careful not to interfere in Jewish communal life, and the Jewish press was allowed to advocate the establishment of an independent state in Palestine. Moreover, the National Peasant and Liberal parties were losing ground; a whole epoch seemed to be drawing to a close. What these leaders did not know was that the Communist plan called for getting rid of them as well.

Once the elections were over, the Groza government speedily eliminated the opposition parties, both in the Jewish community and the country at large. In November 1947 a conference of "delegates" of the communities was held in Bucharest by the Jewish Democratic Committee; it vociferously demanded the resignation of Filderman and the whole leadership of the Federation of the Unions of the Jewish Communities, who were accused of having shown themselves to be "opposed to the spirit and the democratic orientation of the Jewish population and in favor of the imperialistic and warmongering cliques."[4]

At the same meeting a delegate explained that

> There are in the world an imperialist bloc and an anti-imperialist bloc . . . by the same token in our 'Jewish street' there are also two blocs. . . . In the same way as the general policy of the country tends towards a complete and real democratization, especially after the reshuffling of the government on November 7, 1947 [i.e., after the imposition of open Communist rule], in the same way it is of immediate urgency to purify the public and political Jewish life.[5]

This "purification" was carried out with the direct aid of the police. Obviously doubting whether the leadership of the Federation of the Unions and the local community leaderships would immediately agree that "in the Jewish street there are two blocs," and that this required the CDE to take everything in its hands, the same meeting asked

> the Minister of Cults to assist the Jewish communities in the normalization of their life by dissolving the present interim commissions and by naming, on our [the CDE's] nomination, new interim commissions corresponding to the democratic orientation of the Jewish population—commissions which would prepare elections and which would give the Jewish communities of Rumania their natural leaders.[6]

The conference touched off a series of events and government actions which in a short time destroyed the basis of Jewish communal life in Rumania.

On November 17, 1947, while the conference was still at work, Filderman announced his resignation from the leadership of the Federation and of the Union of Rumanian Jews (UER); shortly after, he left the country. The UER had to merge with the Sarateanu splinter group which had been allied with the Jewish Democratic Committee since 1945. In November 1948 this reconstituted UER was disbanded.

On December 7, 1947, the Jewish Party "voluntarily" dissolved itself, after sixteen years of activity. It was clear to the executive committee that after the conference the Jewish Party could no longer function as an independent political body.

On December 23, 1947, the Grand Rabbi of Rumania, Rabbi Alexander Safran, fled to Switzerland. On the recommendation of a special committee elected at the November conference, the government installed Sandu Liblich as temporary president of the Federation of the Unions of the Jewish Communities. It soon became apparent that Liblich was a sort of political commissar assigned to enforce the party line. In this he was assisted by Moses Rosen, who subsequently was appointed Grand Rabbi of Rumania.

Mass Emigration

The failure of the Jewish Democratic Committee to gain support of the Jewish Community is seen in the almost universal desire to emigrate.

Immediately after liberation, there were, according to Eliezer Frenkel—a Jewish lawyer who in 1945 interviewed eleven prominent Rumanians as to their views on the Jewish question—two categories of Jews wishing to emigrate at this time. In the first group were about sixty thousand persons who had registered with the Palestine Emigration Office, mainly long-settled Rumanian Jews who had been deprived of all means of livelihood. The second category included refugees and persons liberated from concentration camps; they numbered fifty to sixty thousand and were completely dependent on the JDC relief.[7]

Actual emigration from Rumania to Palestine in 1945 and 1946 was comparatively small. The main barrier was the quota system. Illegal emigration began in the summer of 1946 and rapidly gained momentum. However, emigration priority was given by the Zionist organizations to the large number of Jews living in displaced persons camps in Germany, Austria, and Italy.

When the sixty thousand Rumanian Jews had first registered with the Palestine Emigration Office in 1945, they had looked forward to a "normal" and legal trip to the Holy Land. They were not then prepared for an illegal emigration by the difficult route across the borders of Hungary, Austria, and Italy, and were reluctant to part with their meager belongings.

Although the settled Jews of Rumania were first to register for emigration to Palestine, the first to go were the repatriates and refugees from Bessarabia and northern Bucovina. Their precarious position was recognized by the community and the Jewish leaders were ready to grant them top priority.[8]

As the economic and political plight of the Jewish community worsened, emigration seemed the only escape from Rumanian "popular democracy." In spite of every effort to "persuade" the Jews that their interest lay with the victory of the "Rumanian democratic forces," and in spite of the pressure brought to bear on the prospective emigrants to remain, the desire to emigrate strengthened. Earlier hopes for economic rehabilitation and restitution had not materialized. Gradual nationalization of industry and restriction of the free market had badly affected the Jewish artisans and small traders. The currency reform had deprived them of their small cash holdings. By June 1947, the Jewish Telegraphic Agency reported there were about 150,000 Jews registered for emigration to Palestine, as compared with 70,000 at the end of 1944.[9] More than one-third of the Jewish population made it clear that it did not desire to remain in Rumania.

Impatient to escape, masses of emigrants tried to flee clandestinely from Rumania. It was precisely at this moment that the Communist government of Rumania finally passed the law granting naturalization to the Jewish refugees. But now the refugees had little desire for it. The clandestine emigrants were directed toward Debreczin, at the Hungarian frontier; from Debreczin they sought to reach Czechoslovakia and then Germany, Austria, or Italy.

The Jewish Democratic Committee started a frantic campaign against the "clandestines." It accused "certain individuals" of "exploiting the economic situation of the poor strata of the Jewish population by trying to provoke a panic among them, leading to chaotic emigration";[10] *Unirea* announced in big headlines that a "Zionist organization" (name not given) had aided the clandestine emigration and "swindled billions out of the emigrants."[11] The Zionist organizations, invited "to express their attitude clearly in the face of the chaotic emigration," disclaimed responsibility for the illegal movement. Anxious to keep the road open for regular emigration, the Zionist leaders stated that the Jews wished to leave Rumania because of their determination to build their own national home, and not because of racial persecution. At the European Conference of Zionist Organizations in Prague in October 1947, Mishu Benvenisti, then president of the Rumanian Zionist Council, protested against the cruelties practiced by the British in Palestine and praised the Rumanian government for the "freedom it granted to the Zionist movement."

In the meantime, the Jewish Democratic Committee and the Rumanian press urged those who wished to emigrate to Palestine "to do so in an orderly manner through competent organizations, and in accordance with the law of the land," while Hungarian and Rumanian guards at the border were instructed to stop the "clandestine avalanche." A systematic hunt was started in the fall of 1947 along the Rumanian-Hungarian frontier. Reports multiplied about Jews shot or arrested when trying to cross the border. Hungarian, Czechoslovak, and Rumanian authorities concluded an agreement on the prevention of illegal emigration and transit of refugees. In December 1947, Hungary started to return emigrants to Rumania, where they were arrested and sentenced to prison. In December 1947 Rumanians adopted a law depriving illegal emigrants of citizenship and confiscating their properties.

In 1947, a total of 40,000 Jewish emigrants departed legally or illegally from Rumania, thus signifying their opinion of the "glorious achievements" of the Communist government and its appendage, the Jewish Democratic Committee.

Chapter V

The Jewish Democratic Committee in Power

In order to understand the situation in which the Jewish population of Rumania was placed from 1948 to 1952, we must take into consideration two determining factors: (1) the internal evolution of the Rumanian Communist regime; and (2) Soviet policy toward Israel.

Rumania's evolution followed a pattern common to all the satellite countries. Once the Communists had eliminated all opposing political groups, they started drastic purges of their own party.

In 1944 the Rumanian Communist Party—weakest of all the Communist organizations in the Balkans—numbered between one and two thousand members. By 1947, on its road to complete control of the state apparatus, it had picked up 750,000 people.[1] In this mass former fascists must have represented a substantial section; according to an official statement made during the purge, the party had been "penetrated" by "dishonest, morally corrupt people, careerists, and, lastly, openly hostile elements—fascists, bourgeois nationalists, exploiters, and agents of the bourgeois-landlord repressive apparatus."[2]

In February 1948 the Social Democrats were forced to fuse with the Communists: the new organization took the name of Rumanian Workers Party (Partidul Muncitoresc Roman). This party, the only political organization recognized in Rumania, claimed a membership of 900,000 and more. All other political forces were swallowed up by the new party; there was now nothing to purge except the party itself.

After a few preliminaries—e.g., the purging of Lucretiu Patrascanu, secretary of the party, in June 1948 for having followed "a nationalist policy"[3]—a mass purge, on the pretext of a "verification" of membership cards, started in November 1948 and lasted until May 1949.

> During the verification, nearly 192,000 members were expelled, i.e., more than 20 per cent of the total membership before verification. Of these, more than half were expelled as exploiters, enemies, and elements alien to the working class, as dishonest and morally corrupt people. . . .[4]

This thoroughgoing purge was also part of the campaign against "cosmopolitanism" then going forward in the Soviet world. However, despite its anti-Jewish note, the purge did not at the time imply the elimination of the Jews as such from all public positions. Ana Pauker, who after having been named Minister of Foreign Affairs in November 1947, reached the brief zenith of her career precisely at the climax of the anti-cosmopolitan drive in April 1949.

A second major purge was launched in May 1952. This time, the purge from the outset took on a distinctly anti-Jewish character.

Zionism and Israel

Soviet policy toward Israel explains both the "anti-cosmopolitan" drive, and the positions on Zionism and Israel adopted in the Soviet orbit as a whole. Russia's official attitude toward Zionism changed in the first post-war years (1945-1946) from active hostility to a sort of indifferent neutrality, growing in 1947 into an active interest in the development of Israel—with the aim of eventually securing a foothold on the eastern side of the Mediterranean. During this period Rumanian Communist officials were by and large neutral toward Zionism. Of the six Jewish papers then published in Rumania, three were Zionist. Jewish publishing houses were bringing out books about Palestine and Zionist history. The Jewish Democratic Committee was, as we saw, a coalition of Communists, Social Democrats, and left-wing Zionists. At a Jewish mass meeting in Bucharest in the middle of 1947 the then secretary of the party, Vasile Luca, declared:

> Democratic Zionists, Jewish parties that are not Zionist, Jewish Communists, Jewish Socialists—there is no difference here among us, no difference of interest in regard to the solution of the national problem of the Jewish people. There is no difference because if you go either to Palestine, Brazil, Australia, or any other European country, there is only one way for the Jewish population: the way of democracy and of union with the people among whom you live.[5]

As the "chaotic emigration" of Rumanian Jews attained its climax in July-August 1947, the Jewish Democratic Committee's organ *Unirea* started to stress the theory that "emigration to Palestine can be justified only as a refuge against the anti-Semitic drive in some of the Western European countries."[6]

As far as Israel was concerned, the Jewish press had but one task: to "unmask" the "American and British intrigues" and to present the USSR as the benign "creator" of the Jewish state thanks to her vote at the United Nations session of November 29, 1947. The Communists were fighting in the Jewish community at this time against "bourgeois" organizations, i.e., the Union of Rumanian Jews, and for control of the administration of the communities and their organization, the Federation of the Unions of Jewish Communities.

At the beginning of 1948, *Unirea* and the Jewish Democratic Committee began to stress the "example of the Soviet Jewish population which 'recovered' under socialism from its political and economic diseases." The Jewish Democratic Committee became a more and more uncomfortable place for the left-wing Zionist fellow-travelers.

When in September 1948 the Communist Party of the Soviet Union announced a new anti-Zionist, anti-Israel turn in its policy,[7] the Communist rulers of Rumania quickly jumped on the bandwagon. Furious attacks were launched on Zionism, "Jewish nationalism," and Jewish organizations in general. The fight was carried into the CDE itself. In December 1948 the Politburo of the Rumanian Workers (Communist) Party published a lengthy resolution on minorities containing a special paragraph condemning Zionism and "Jewish nationalism." It declared:

> The attempt of the Jewish bourgeois nationalists to spread the idea of "Jewish unity" and deny the existence of class differentiation among the Jewish population, is the diversion by which they attempt to harness the Jewish working masses to the wagon of reactionary Jewish big business, in the service of the Anglo-American imperialists.

The Jewish working class had participated in the struggle against fascism, the resolution said, but after the war

> . . . the process of re-enrollment of the Jewish working masses for constructive democratic work was hampered by the activities of the Zionists—the Jewish nationalists—who misled parts of the Jewish population with their harmful propaganda. In that action, the Zionists were also aided by other imperialist American agencies in various ways.
>
> Zionism in all its forms is a nationalist, reactionary political movement of the Jewish bourgeoisie, which tries to isolate the Jewish working population from the peoples among whom they live, to hold them back from the ranks of the progressive forces in the fight against capitalism and their own bourgeoisie. As members of the Jewish Democratic Committee, the Zionists have continuously tried to sabotage the strengthening of this committee, have hindered the enrollment of the Jewish working masses in the productive process, have conducted a permanent nationalistic, isolationist propaganda campaign among the Jews, and by all this have put themselves outside the ranks of the Jewish Democratic Committee.

The resolution went on to clear the ground for later purges by accusing "some party members" of having "slid down the road to nationalism";

> Some party members in the Jewish Democratic Committee, although they performed some useful work, were not able to develop a firm struggle against the nationalistic current in the Jewish organizations, thereby helping the nationalistic manifestations of national and cultural isolation in the ranks of the Jewish population; they were themselves sliding down the road to "Bundism."

The resolution concluded that a thorough reorganization of the Jewish Democratic Committee itself was necessary; it should be purged of Zionist elements and reinforced

> with progressive elements able to mobilize Jewish working masses for the fight to consolidate people's democracy against class exploitation and against the agents of Anglo-American imperialism.[8]

The ideas of the resolution were subsequently repeated, elaborated, and applied to all kinds of Zionist organizations and activities. The Zionist movement was accused of having supported the monarchy during "the bloody repression against the peasant uprising" forty-five years before; of having supported the Rumanian National Peasant Party twenty years back; of having made concessions to anti-Semitism; of aiming at cultural "isolationism"; of advocating "double allegiance," subservience to "Jewish capitalism and Western imperialism"; of "disrupting the workers' ranks," "hampering socialist reconstruction," and indulging in "black market activities."

This "ideological campaign" and the repression which accompanied it not only ultimately destroyed all the Zionist organizations, but engulfed even *Unirea* itself and some of the Communists of the Jewish Democratic Committee.

The "Ideological Campaign" and Police Repression

In the general elections of March 25, 1948, five Jewish candidates were nominated by the leadership of the "Democratic Front" to "represent the Jews," and were elected to parliament. Although the Zionists undoubtedly had a majority among the Jewish population, none of the deputies was a Zionist. Bercu Feldman was secretary of the Jewish Committee and very active in the "ideological campaign." Hersh Leibovici-Serban was the Communist-imposed secretary general of the Federation of the Unions of Jewish Communities. They and Marcel Fischer were officially members of the Communist Party; Professor Maximillian Popper, the new chairman of the Federation, was a close fellow-traveler. They were pledged to

> incorporate the Jewish population into productive work, . . . to develop an intense progressive cultural activity, to incorporate the Jewish teaching personnel into the state personnel, to unify the communities administratively, to instill a progressive, truly democratic spirit into the leadership of the community.[9]

The attack on Jewish communal life was now accompanied by police repression against all Zionist organizations and by a violent drive for the eradication of Zionist influence in Jewish life.

The police repression started almost immediately after the publication of Ilya Ehrenburg's September 1948 article in *Pravda.* On November 3, 1948, police raided the offices of the Jewish National Fund and the Palestine Foundation Fund. Four managers, Leon Itscar, Solomon Rosenhaupt, Eugen Cohen, and Michael Leiba, were arrested on charges of "foreign exchange manipulations." The offices were closed and *Unire*a started a violent campaign against Zionists, calling them "black-marketeers," "disrupters of the socialist economy," and "saboteurs of socialist construction."

Early in December, the Communists forcibly occupied the headquarters and offices of Zionist organizations and clubs throughout the country. Some of these offices had been closed by the police, but Communist youngsters broke in, smashed the windows, and tore down the pictures of Israeli leaders. Among the organizations affected were, in addition to the two funds mentioned above, the Poale Zion, Mizrachi, Tarbut, Zionist Women's Organization, B'nai Akiba, and B'nai B'rith. When the Zionist Youth rallied and tried to reoccupy some of the offices, a number of clashes occured in which several persons were injured. The police intervened and a truce was called; the offices remained closed.

On December 23, 1948, the Central Board of the Zionist Organization voted to suspend all activities. It appointed a special committee to notify the affiliated groups throughout the country. Each group was to decide whether it would disband "voluntarily" or try to continue its activities independently. But in reality, there was no choice but to disband. By the beginning of January 1949, the General Zionists, the Mapai, Haoeved Hazioni, Mizrachi, and student group *Hasmonea* had dissolved. The left-wing Mapam reduced its activities to a minimum and disbanded a few weeks later. The Hechalutz movement needed somewhat longer to liquidate its assets. After two or three months, there was not a single Zionist organization in the country. Organizations which had included 110,000 of the 420,000 Rumanian Jews were completely abolished by the Communists.

At the same time the Jewish Democratic Committee organized a series of mass meetings around the country to "educate" the Jewish population against the '"dangers" of Zionism. The tenor of those meetings is evident from reports in *Unirea:*

> Zionism is a dangerous weapon in the hands of the Jewish bourgeoisie, a tool of Anglo-American imperialism—[meeting at Constanza]. A poisoned weapon used by the bourgeoisie to isolate the Jewish masses from the great family of mankind"—[meeting at Galatz]. A hideous instrument . . . of the Jewish bourgeoisie . . . preaching so-called Jewish unity"—[meeting of the CDE in Bucharest].[10]

The "theoretical" aspects of the politburo resolution were further developed with "analyses" such as these:

> Zionism . . . is the political expression of the economic need of the Jewish bourgeoisie to create its own market for exploitation.[11] The tradition of the fight against fascism is carried out in the fight against Zionism.[12]

The Jewish Democratic Committee and its organ *Unirea* now concentrated on proving the "past and present connections" of Zionists with Rumanian reactionaries,[13] Zionist, and fascist collaboration[14] and the Zionists' betrayal of the Jewish population.[15] Any acknowledgement of the existence of Jewish world-wide solidarity and culture was denounced as "nationalist," "reactionary," and "'subservient to the enemies of the working class and the Soviet Union."

In January 1949, a conference of Jewish "activists" from all over the country was called in Bucharest. At this conference, Bercu Feldman declared:

> Among the most important shortcomings in our activities we must count, in the first place, our peaceful, non-militant attitude towards the nationalist-Zionist organizations. We have considered the voluntary dissolution of the Zionist organizations as identical with the political liquidation of their influence. Our belief proved that we were drifting away from the line of the class struggle. . . . This error can be corrected only by vigorous action aimed at the exposure of Zionist nationalism, conducted at meetings as well as in the press, until we achieve the complete liquidation of the Zionist-nationalist influence. . . . This fight must be conducted without compromise, and its result must be the full liquidation of Zionist nationalism in Jewish life.[16]

Jewish communists accused of "lack of vigilance against Zionist influence" began to be expelled from the Jewish Democratic Committee. In February 1949, the regional organizations of the committees of Galatz, Timisoara, and Constanza were completely replaced because of their deficiencies in carrying out anti-Zionist measures.

In July 1949 a new appeal to "continue the fight against Zionist nationalism with increasing vigor" was published in *Unirea*.[17] The purpose of the campaign was "to liberate the Jewish workers from the ideological influence of Zionist nationalism," and special attention was given to the youth who had joined *kibbutzim*. In August *Unirea* complained of a "slackening of vigilance" against Zionism, of Zionist sympathies among school children, and of the fact that some former Zionists still held positions in the nationalized sector of the Rumanian economy.

Theaters, schools, and even synagogues were used to combat "Jewish nationalism." In August 1949 Bernhard Lebli, director of the Jewish State Theater, described the theater's "unmasking of Zionist nationalism." Zionism was also "exposed" in the few remaining Jewish schools. On Rosh Hashanah and Yom Kippur, Jewish Communists forced the recital of special sermons directed against Zionism, the State of Israel, and foreign Jewish organizations. Rabbis who resisted this were threatened with immediate arrest.

In the fall of 1949 the campaign reached a new climax in connection with reports of the trial of former Hungarian Foreign Minister Laszlo

Rajk and his Jewish co-defendants, who were charged with criminal conspiracy and espionage in behalf of "Zionist agents of Western imperialism."

In November the attack was concentrated against religious Jewry, which was described as a "bastion of clerical Zionism." Jewish Communists wearing prayer shawls and skull caps went to synagogues and delivered sharp speeches against Zionism and the State of Israel. A number of Jews who protested against one such speech delivered by Solomon Stern, the chairman of the *kehillah*, in a Bucharest synagogue, were removed from the services and arrested. The first meeting of the Rabbinical Council in November 1949 was forced to adopt a resolution against Zionism and against the former chief rabbi, Alexander Safran.

In March 1950 a new conference of the Jewish Democratic Committee expelled six prominent Jewish leaders for not having conducted the fight against Zionism with sufficient energy; it was the third purge of pro-Communist officials for laxity in this respect. The conference adopted an elaborate plan of propaganda against Israel that included the publication of letters and articles showing the "misery of the masses" in Israel, individual talks against Zionism, street meetings and conferences, and anti-Zionist exhibitions. Special attention was given to authors of Jewish fiction, who were reprimanded for not participating in the "ideological struggle."

In April 1950, Israel was again denounced in the general press and the newspaper *Romania Libera* attacked Israel's Premier Ben Gurion. Chief Rabbi Moses Rosen broadened the denunciation to include other "Jewish warmongers," such as Henry Morgenthau, Jr., Bernard Baruch, and Benjamin Cohen of the United States delegation to the United Nations. The Communist newspaper *Scanteia* castigated Ben Gurion and the "American spy" Morgenthau on May 30, 1950.

In December 1950, Hersh Leibovici-Serban, secretary of the Federation of the Unions of Jewish Communties, wrote in *Unirea* that the influence of Zionism "has been largely removed," but complained of general apathy and the leaders' "remoteness from the masses." In January 1951, special courses in anti-Zionist propaganda were organized for "activists" of the Jewish Democratic Committee.

In July 1950, *Scanteia* wrote that the Americans were building a strategic railroad from Istanbul to Cairo through Israel, which would turn the latter country into a battleground. In September, the Bucharest radio maintained that immigrants in Israel were living "in promiscuity, disease, and starvation," and that the Israel judicial system was comparable to that of "Tito's Yugoslavia, monarcho-fascist Greece, and Franco Spain." In October it announced that the Arab minority in Israel "was receiving worse treatment than the Jews did under Hitler." Special exhibitions, called

"Realities of Israel," were shown about the country. These pictures depicted misery, starvation, and riots.

"New Life" in the Rumanian Republic

A turning point was reached at the beginning of 1951. First, the publication of *Unirea* was discontinued. Its name, adopted in 1945, had underlined the Jewish Democratic Committee's intention to rally around itself all the "progressive" forces in the Jewish community. After the Communists had routed all other forces, the time had come to launch a new organ, called *Viata Noua* ("New Life"), which aimed at the total "integration" of the Jews into the "new life" of the "people's democracy." Second, reference was no longer made to the "Jewish community." The Jewish Democratic Committee and the *Viata Noua* spoke only of "Jewish working people"—no other Jews being supposed to exist in the Rumanian People's Democracy.

Viata Noua stressed the necessity of increasing the productivity of the Jewish working people, of "educating" the Jewish masses to hate Israel, and of developing their "love" for the new regime.

A good notion of the day-to-day activities of the Jewish Democratic Committees throughout the country in 1951 is given us by *Viata Noua's* reports of sessions of the Central Committee of the CDE on February 14 and 15, 1952. The main activity of the various local committees in 1951 had been a campaign to enlighten the Jewish working people about the "poison of Zionism" and the perils of emigration. This campaign was led by young "activists" who visited all the Jewish families in their locality, discussed the questions with them personally, and afterwards reported the concrete results in each case to the local committee of the CDE. The door-to-door campaign ended up with the posting up of permanent placards with anti-Zionist and anti-Israel slogans in the most populous Jewish areas. For the year ahead (1952), the committee defined its program as (1) integration of the Jewish working people, including housewives, into productive work and the encouragement of Jewish youth to attend vocational and technical schools; (2) mobilization of all elements, "including the clergy, the assimilated, and the honest religious elements" in the "fight for peace"; (3) "unmasking" of the Israel leaders as "friends of the Nazis" and tools of "Anglo-American imperialist intrigues in the Near East"; (4) development and strengthening of devotion to the Rumanian People's Democracy, the Rumanian Workers Party, the USSR, and Stalin, "the most beloved friend of the working people of Rumania."[18]

The campaign against Israel became particularly ferocious during the reparation talks between Israel and Western Germany. Zionists were referred to as "fascist spies and Nazi collaborators," Ben Gurion was accused of suppressing the workers of Israel "just as the Nazis had suppressed their workers," and *Viata Noua* regularly published caricatures showing Ben Gurion washing the blood-stained hands of SS men, with a swastika emblazoned on his forehead. There was a systematic denunciation of emigration to Israel. The publication of pledges and letters renouncing emigration, obtained by the "activists" from prospective emigrants, became more and more frequent.

Mass Arrests of Jews

It is difficult to estimate the number of "Zionist agents" now in the jails and camps of the Rumanian People's Democracy. As far back as December 1949, Leo Wolfsohn reported to an annual meeting of the United Rumanian Jews in the United States that 7,500 Zionists were under arrest in Rumania. When the annual meeting asked the Rumanian government to admit a delegation to investigate the situation, Rumanian authorities left the application unanswered.

From 1950 on, reports of the arrest of Zionist and other Jewish leaders became more frequent and more concrete. Several Zionist leaders were detained during the winter and spring, after they had obtained all their emigration papers and were about to board ship for Israel in the port of Constanza. In May about two hundred Zionists, among them forty or fifty prominent leaders, were arrested. A. Dascalu, the secretary of the pro-Communist Hashomer Hatzair, and Zoltan Hirsch, secretary of the left-wing Abdut Haavoda, were released. Among those who were kept in jail were Dr. M. Benvenisti, former president of the Rumanian Zionist organization, Dr. Loewenstein, B. Badi, H. Yakrakner, S. Unger, Dr. Brummer, Dan Iesanu, and Michael Leiba, former manager of the Jewish National Fund. According to some reports, the police officer examining their cases was Eugen Cristescu, a former member of the Rumanian secret police who had worked for the Gestapo under Antonescu and sent eight Zionist youths to jail. Among other things, the Zionist leaders were charged with aiding British agents and parachutists during World War II—which was supposed to prove that they were in the service of British Intelligence.

At the same time Rumanian authorities arrested Marcel Pohne, the Bucharest correspondent of the Jewish Telegraphic Agency, and Leonard Kirscher, the correspondent of the Associated Press.

A new wave of arrests of local Zionist leaders came in September 1951, and continued throughout the winter of 1951-52.

Chapter VI

Decline of Jewish Communal Life

The strongest blow against Rumania's "private sector" was struck in June 1948, when the nationalization of industry was proclaimed. An observer noted:

> Unlike similar measures in Czechoslovakia and elsewhere, the enterprises to be nationalized were not defined by size. Instead, arbitrary lists were published. But in practice almost every enterprise employing more than thirty persons was included. There was not even a pretense of compensation.[1]

The shopkeepers who had survived the "currency stabilization" of August 1947 found themselves caught in a trap:

> Many a merchant would like to close his shop, but cannot. That would require a special authorization from the Minister of Commerce, and up to now very few have been issued. So the merchant must go on paying taxes as best he can. If he falls behind, he is threatened by two to ten years in prison. Some sell furniture and clothes to meet tax deadlines—anything rather than risk a prison sentence in Communist Rumania.[2]

Undoubtedly the measure added to the woes of the Jewish community. In the spring of 1948 the Restratification Department of the Jewish Democratic Committee reported:

> Of the 345,000 Jews in Rumania, about forty per cent were engaged in the commercial field. The new economic and social developments have eliminated elements engaged in speculation from the economic life of the country; a large part of this category has therefore been left without the occupations hitherto practiced by them.[3]

In this context, "elements engaged in speculation" meant people privately engaged in business. Thus 40 per cent of the Jewish population (about 140,000 persons, including dependents)—not taking into account the refugees—had been deprived of any source of regular income. The authors of the statement estimated that one-half of the 345,000 Jewish inhabitants consisted of dependents (children, housewives and elderly people). This left 175,000 people able to work, of whom only 75,000 were said to be gainfully employed at that time. Thus it would appear that there were 100,000 unemployed. But for some reason the Restratification Department estimated the number of persons in need of work at 75,000. This figure was perhaps arrived at by its being estimated that half of the "superfluous" 140,000 were dependents and half employables.

The Restratification Department proposed an ambitious three-year plan of rehabilitation, providing for:

1. Vocational training embracing some 40,000 persons, of whom 32,000 were to be retrained in manual skills, primarily for the steel and electrical industries; the other 8,000 to receive professional training as draftsmen, foremen, and supervisors in industrial plants.
2. Agricultural training and resettlement of 13,500 Jews in 540 farming centers.
3. Establishment of 67 producers' cooperatives, which would absorb 4,875 persons in the first year of the plan [no provision was made for the next two years].[4]

This would have taken care of 58,375 of the estimated 75,000 (or 100,000) unemployed Jews. Nothing was said about the rest.

Still, it was a promising plan. The trouble was that its entire cost (more than 5,000,000,000 lei, equivalent to $25,000,000) was to be paid by the American Joint Distribution Committee. But the JDC could not pay the entire sum, nor was it willing to leave the administration of the plan entirely in the hands of the Communist-dominated Rumanian organizations. The negotiations failed and no comprehensive report was ever made on the result of the plan. Indeed, no detailed statistics on the unemployment or reabsorption of Jews were ever published. Some scattered data of dubious reliability about the number of Jews "provided with jobs" were from time to time released—but there was no possibility of checking them, or of ascertaining how many Jews remained unemployed.

At a national conference of rabbis and community leaders held in July 1949, it was reported that over 13,000 unemployed Jews were placed in jobs in 1948, and that 91 vocational schools had retrained 2,400 adults and 2,700 children. A report of the Jewish Democratic Committee asserted that 18,000 Jews obtained jobs in 1949.[5] Another report from the same source put the number of jobs provided for Jews in 1950 at 13,000. It was, however, impossible to verify the figures, or to find out the nature and duration of this employment, or the number of Jews who remained unemployed at the end of the period. In 1950, unofficial Jewish sources estimated the number of Jewish employables who were either unemployed or had only occasional jobs as unskilled workers at 40,000. With their families, they constituted a large percentage of the Jewish population. In 1952 the secretary of the CDE, Bercu Feldman, reported to its Central Committee that in 1951

> with the help of the state 7,000 Jews have been oriented towards productive work. A turning point has now been reached in this matter,

since the number of those integrated into productive work is larger than the number of those integrated into administrative work.[6]

No figures for the community as a whole were furnished at that time or subsequently.

During this entire period, Jews made up a large percentage of those put in jail for such economic offenses as sabotage of nationalization, tax evasion, black-market dealings, infractions of rationing rules, and illegal trade in foreign exchange.

In 1952 there were repeated reports of large-scale conscription of these economically displaced Jews for forced labor in the construction of roads, railways, and the Danube-Black Sea Canal. All adult citizens of Rumania were now legally subject to conscription for road building and similar heavy labor; in addition, "non-productive" as well as "politically unreliable" elements could be sentenced by administrative order to years at hard labor in concentration camps. These measures of general repression hit the Jews harder than other groups because the percentage of people without "productive jobs" among them was larger.

Dissolution of Jewish Welfare Institutions

The dissolution of Zionist organizations was followed by reprisals against all independent Jewish organizations, including those of a philanthropic character. "Assistance to the needy must cease to be an encouragement to idleness and indolence," the Communist-imposed secretary of the Federation, Leibovici-Serban, proclaimed in 1948.[7] On March 7, 1949, the Bucharest branch of the American Jewish Joint Distribution Committee—which in 1948 was extending aid to 135,000 persons[8]—was closed by the authorities. The closing of ORT and OSE offices followed several days later. The government decided to dissolve all foreign Jewish relief organizations and to transfer their assets to the Communist-dominated Federation of Jewish Religious Communities. Domestic Jewish welfare institutions were simply "nationalized." Nineteen Jewish hospitals were taken over by the state, and in April 1949 the same fate befell 256 Jewish charity institutions—relief kitchens, food distribution centers, orphanages, children's homes, and homes for the aged.

The dissolution of relief organizations left a large part of the community completely destitute. Their despair was expressed in numerous letters which reached the United States. Although it was already dangerous to correspond with the West, a flood of letters from Rumania appealed for help in the face of desperate economic conditions. The writers— mostly former businessmen—were now completely destitute and living on a near starvation diet.

The End of the Jewish Schools

According to the constitution of the Rumanian People's Republic, each national or language minority had the right to educate its children in its mother tongue.

On April 15, 1951, *Romanian News,* the propaganda organ of the Rumanian embassy in Washington, published statistics on "nurseries, kindergartens, and primary schools employing languages other than Rumanian." There were 3,036 such educational institutions conducted in minority languages. Of these 2,163 used Hungarian, 488 German, and 188 Russian or Ukrainian. There were even schools for Tatars (71), for Slovaks (29), Czechs (9), and other small minorities. But the number of institutions with Yiddish as the language of instruction was only 8, including 3 Yiddish primary schools (in Bucharest, Jassy, and Timisoara) and 5 nurseries and kindergartens.[9]

The Jewish Communists, who liked to pose as the "champions of the Yiddish language and literature," and who claimed that they were going to carry Yiddish into the schools,[10] in reality helped to get rid of the Jewish schools.

During the war, when Jewish students were excluded from state schools, the Jewish community developed an important network of Jewish schools. In 1942 there had been 103 Jewish schools in Rumania with six thousand students—three thousand in the elementary schools and three thousand in the high schools and vocational schools.[11] After the war, although Jews could now go to public schools, the Jewish schools continued to enlarge their scope. According to figures published by *Unirea* itself on May 29, 1948, there were then 122 Jewish schools with 12,669 students. These included 30 kindergartens, attended by 1,097 children; 69 Yiddish elementary schools, with 7,504 pupils; and 23 high schools, including 5 vocational schools (one commercial high school and 4 technical schools), with 4,068 students.

Nineteen forty-eight was the last year of independence for the Jewish schools. The constitution adopted on March 28, 1948, charged the state with providing for the teaching of the Jewish population "in their mother tongue." The Jewish schools were simply absorbed into the general school network of the country and reorganized on the Russian pattern.[12] According to the provisional results of the national census of January 25, 1948, 138,795 persons (0.9 per cent of the total population of the country) declared Yiddish to be their mother tongue.[13] This was roughly a third of the total Jewish population of 428,312 (*see* Table VII). Thus for one-third of the Jewish population there were only eight scattered elementary schools.

At the opening of the Bucharest Yiddish school in the spring of 1949, the official speaker declared that the school would teach Rumanian patriotism and wipe out the bourgeois mentality of Zionism, which "is unfortunately widespread among the Jewish youth." He added that the opening of the school "proved" that "for the first time in Rumanian history the Jews were being given equal rights." The main task of the schools, which were now Jewish in name only, was to step up the fight against Zionism, Judaism and Jewish nationalism.

Unofficial reports placed the number of students in Jewish schools at 970 (400 in Bucharest, 320 in Jassy, 250 in Timisoara). In addition, official sources indicated that about 6,000 children were being given some instruction in the Yiddish language in general schools in which there was a large percentage of children whose parents asked for such instruction. According to Polia Barasch, government inspector for Jewish education, there were 90 Jewish teachers on the payroll at the end of the 1948-49 school year. (This compares with 450 Jewish teachers during the war.) Several new Yiddish textbooks were published to ensure the proper "Marxist-Leninist" indoctrination of the children, and a course for the training of Yiddish teachers and kindergarten nurses was opened in Bucharest. (This one course was listed in the previously quoted figures from the *Romanian News* as a "pedagogical institute" and figured among 140 "theoretical, technical, and pedagogical schools" conducted in minority languages.)

Cultural Life

Jewish cultural activity was now limited to two theaters and a number of youth clubs, art groups, and musical societies. These were all associated with the cultural organization IKUF, which was under complete Communist control.

The two Jewish theaters (one in Bucharest and one in Jassy) were "nationalized" in 1948 and 1949. In the summer of 1949, the Bucharest troupe made a countrywide tour and official sources estimated that fifty thousand visitors saw its performances. In 1949-50 it performed three plays by Sholom Aleichem, one by Goldfaden, two plays by Soviet authors, and two by young Rumanian Jewish playwrights. In 1949 the central theme of the play presented in the Jewish theater was the liberation of Rumania by the Red Army. In 1951-52, at the climax of the anti-Israel and anti-Zionist campaign, the theme to be stressed was the unmasking of Zionist propaganda and its agents.[14] One of the plays embodying this new orientation, *Clearing Up* by Paul Isac, centered "on the unmasking of the dealings of various former bourgeois Zionist agents and black-marketeers." It ends with the final repentance of the prospective emigrant, who agrees to hand his uncle over to the police as an "unscrupulous Zionist agent, saboteur and black-market dealer."[15]

A similar spirit prevailed in the thirty-five art groups and orchestras listed by the IKUF in 1950.

Three books in the Yiddish language were published by the state publishing houses in the first half of 1950, according to *Romanian News* of April 15, 1951. Another official report spoke of three "important works in Yiddish on subjects related to party activities" published by the Communist Party. In addition, some of Sholom Aleichem's works appeared in Rumanian translations.

Jewish writers of fiction did not escape ideological *Gleichschaltung*. In April 1949, a conference of Jewish writers was held in Bucharest in order to mobilize them "to combat Zionist, nationalist and reactionary tendencies in Yiddish literature." Soon afterward, in an article in the literary journal *Contemporanul*, T. Faerstein criticised the Jewish writers Jacob Gropper, Simah Snaider, and others for "lack of consistency in the merciless fight against any nationalist tendency and against all mystical and bigoted trends." Gropper, the chairman of the Yiddish Writers Association, was attacked for writing poems that described Jewish sufferings without mentioning "the democratic fighters, the non-Jewish fighters who sympathized with the suffering of the Jews." Even Wolf Tambur, who delivered a "patriotic" speech at the April conference, did not escape censure. He wrote a novel about a Communist heroine, but according to Faerstein he "failed to show the typical qualities of a party member."

At this time the Jewish Democratic Committee also purged the public libraries, banning from them the works of eighteen "nationalist" Jewish writers; among them were Isaac Meier Dick, David Pinsky, H. Leivick, Z. Segalowich, and Jacob Pat. When the purge of Yiddish writers in Soviet Russia became known, the Yiddish theater dropped the plays of Perets Markish and David Bergelson.

There were three periodicals under the control of the Jewish Democratic Committee: *Unirea* in Rumanian, *Ujut* in Hungarian, and *Ikuf Bleter* in Yiddish. In March 1950, the circulation of *Unirea* was officially given as 25,000; *Ujut*, 8,200; and *Ikuf Bleter*, 4,200. As we have noted, *Unirea* was discontinued in January 1951 (after a purge of its staff, some of whose members allegedly intended to emigrate), and *Viata Noua* appeared in its place.

There were also some Yiddish broadcasts on the state radio, mainly devoted to anti-Zionist and anti-Israel propaganda.

Regimentation of the Religious Communities

A law promulgated in 1948 reorganized the Rumanian churches and religious communities. All denominations except the Rumanian Orthodox Church were ordered to apply anew for state recognition. All church officials and clergymen had to be Rumanian citizens and swear allegiance to the People's Republic. They had to be confirmed in their offices by the government. Communications with foreign communities of the same religion had to go through the Ministries of Religion and of Foreign Affairs.

The Jewish religious communities were reorganized under a new statute published in the *Official Gazette* on July 12, 1949. According to this statute, only one Jewish community could exist in each town; it was to include all Jewish religious groups (Orthodox and Reform, Ashkenazic and Sephardic). It was the duty of the unified community "to create, maintain, and supervise the institutions necessary for the fulfilment of the religious needs of its followers." All Jewish communities had to belong to one central body, the Federation of Rumanian Jewish Communities, which was to be their supreme administrative authority. A Supreme Rabbinical Council of twelve members, appointed by the Ministry of Religion on the recommendation of the Federation, was to be the highest spiritual authority. No rabbi or other religious functionary could officiate, and no religious service of any kind could be carried out, without the consent of the reorganized communities, whose leadership was in Communist hands and supervised by the Communist-dominated Jewish Democratic Committee.

Later in July, a national conference of rabbis and representatives of the Orthodox, Sephardic, and Ashkenazic communities was held in Bucharest and effectuated the merger prescribed by the statute. The conference pledged close co-operation with the CDE.

On August 28, the merger was formally proclaimed in Bucharest in a meeting presided over by H. Leibovici-Serban, the Communist secretary general of the Federation. Leon Stern, a Communist, was elected president of the Bucharest community.

In September, the Ministry of Religion appointed the Supreme Rabbinical Council. Chief Rabbi Moses Rosen was appointed its president. At their meeting in November, the Federation leadership and the Rabbinical Council decided to turn over all community buildings in places where communities had ceased to exist to the local Rumanian authorities. There were still 206 local communities in Rumania at that time. Their number diminished subsequently but statistics were never published after that date.

The purpose of the "unification" was to centralize community life and to strengthen the control of all religious institutions by the Communist leaders, who were now strongly entrenched in the central bodies. After the reorganization, the communities were used not only for "peace propaganda," but also in campaigns against Zionism, Israel, and Western Jewry. Rabbis were forced to deliver anti-Zionist sermons and Communists used the synagogues for their political speeches.

Although freedom of religion was guaranteed by the constitution, religious observance became increasingly difficult. Passover food was still provided for religious Jews, but after 1949 it was distributed only to those who could present cards proving that they worked in nationalized enterprises. It was also difficult to observe the Sabbath. Rabbi Jehoshua Aaron Gross, who collected signatures for a petition asking the government to arrange general employment for Sabbath observers, was arrested on the charge of engaging in subversive activities. Special taxes were imposed on religious rituals and ceremonies such as weddings, confirmations, and circumcisions performed in Jewish homes. In many instances the authorities charged religious groups with misusing such ceremonies for political purposes.

Some Orthodox Jewish children's homes were abolished, and attempts were made to force Orthodox children into Communist orphanages, first by cutting off their food supplies and then by direct orders. Many children fled. A number of Orthodox Jews were arrested because of their support of the children's resistance.

Anti-religious propaganda was conducted by the Communist youth. Their organization issued a "catechism" for fighting religious ideologies.

Emigration Meets Increasing Obstacles

It is evident that increasing numbers of Rumanian Jews must have seen emigration as their only salvation in the years 1948-51. Even those who had thought that they might start a new life in Rumania saw themselves dispossessed, unemployed, or underemployed. They were isolated by the destruction of Jewish communal and cultural life, endangered by violent campaigns against "Jewish nationalism," and threatened by mounting anti-Semitism. At the same time, the State of Israel had come into being and its doors were now open to unlimited Jewish immigration.

In 1948, direct emigration to Israel was still permitted, but in many cases tremendous sums were exacted for the issuance of passports and exit visas. At the end of 1948, the Jewish Democratic Committee insisted on its exclusive right to select prospective emigrants and tried to exclude Zionist organizations from any participation in organizing the exodus. When soon afterward the Zionist organizations were dissolved and the offices of foreign Jewish agencies closed, emigration came to an abrupt halt.

In January 1949, the government allowed 1,300 of those registered with the Jewish Democratic Committee to emigrate, but in February only 16 Jews were able to leave the country.[16]

On February 11-17, rumors spread in Bucharest that the Israel legation was registering applicants for emigration. Thousands of Jews jammed the streets and applications were submitted in great numbers. On February 14, ten thousand Jews gathered in front of the legation to celebrate the opening of the Israel Constituent Assembly and to demand free emigration. The Communists attacked the demonstrations in their press as "provocative" and aimed at "hampering the consolidation of people's democracy."

In July and August, the Israel government sent Rumania several diplomatic notes requesting negotiations on the resumption of emigration. In August 1949, the Israel minister to Bucharest, Reuven Rubin, was called to Tel Aviv. Finally in September Shmuel Eliashiv director of the Eastern

European Division of the Israel Foreign Office, arrived in Bucharest. New negotiations, initiated by him, resulted in some relaxation of the ban on emigration.

But when the Israel ship *Eilat* arrived in Constanza in the middle of October, Rumanian authorities refused to permit the embarkation of 246 waiting emigrants. Sixty-three non-Rumanian Jews were eventually allowed to sail but 183 Rumanian Jews were detained. Relatives of the prospective emigrants demonstrated before the Rumanian legation in Tel Aviv, and Israel made new diplomatic representations.

In November, Rubin resigned as Israel minister to Bucharest; the post remained unfilled until March 1951, when the Rumanian government finally accepted a new minister, Ehud Arriel.

In November 1949, the emigration of certain categories, consisting mostly of elderly persons and those with near relatives in Israel, was allowed to resume. The Rumanian government insisted that the Jewish Agency not "interfere" with the organization of emigration and that all emigration be by the Rumanian ship *Transylvania;* exorbitant fares were charged for the passage. In addition, new fees were exacted for exit permits and the emigrants had to leave behind most of their property. Technicians, engineers, skilled workers, and physicians were still barred from leaving, and Zionist leaders were kept in jail. Israel sources complained that the transports were composed mainly of elderly and infirm people.

According to the Research Department of the JDC, 2,574 Jews emigrated legally from Rumania to Israel in 1948; 7,112 in 1949; and 47,213 in 1950. The Statistical Bulletin of Israel reported 24,780 arrivals of Rumanian-born Jews in Israel in 1948; 13,596 in 1949; 46,178 in 1950; and 36,798 from January to September of 1951. In 1948 and 1949 most of the Rumanian Jews who reached Israel came from displaced persons camps in Western Germany, Austria, and Italy. After 1950 the DP camps were empty, so that departures from Rumania and arrivals in Israel were about equal.

In the fall of 1951, pressure against emigration again increased and the *Transylvania* arrived in Israel half empty. Nine to fourteen hundred exit permits had formerly been granted for each voyage; but in October the ship carried 711 emigrants and in November 411. On February 4, 1952, it arrived with only 261 passengers. A second passage in February 1952 had to be cancelled for lack of passengers.

Many Jews who had already obtained exit visas were forced to stay behind. Often they were informed of the ship's departure so late that they could not reach the port in time. In other cases, the Communists obtained the addresses of prospective emigrants and forged their signatures on declarations renouncing emigration. A new devaluation of the lei left others without means to buy a ticket and pay the special exit visa and custom fees. Some emigrants sold the last few belongings they were allowed to take with them and arrived in Haifa not only without baggage but also without overcoats and hats. In numerous cases, exit permits were granted to parents but not to their children, to wives but not to their husbands. Often those who did receive permits did not use them for fear that they would have to part forever from their families. Emigration to Israel was thus reduced to a trickle at the very time the government was preparing for a final "solution" of the question of the Jewish "surplus population" by mass deportations.

Mass Deportations

The first large-scale deportation of Jews in postwar Rumania took place in September 1949. Many Jews from Bessarabia and northern Bucovina had settled inside the boundaries of postwar Rumania, but the Soviet Union claimed them as Soviet subjects. On September 1, 1949, the Rumanian police and militia, co-operating with the Soviet secret police, rounded up Jews born in Bessarabia and northern Bucovina, put them on trucks, and delivered them to railroad stations where they were put in box-cars and shipped to Russia. The operation was meticulously prepared, lists of persons liable to deportation being drawn up from ration-card and police registers. The deportation trains crossed the Russian border or went to the port of Constanza, whence Russian boats transferred the deportees to Odessa. Nothing is known about their further fate.

In the summer of 1951, mass deportations of "bourgeois" and "unreliable" elements, among them many Jews, started in Hungary. Simultaneous purges of Jews in Czechoslovakia and other satellite countries proved that the Hungarian deportations were not an isolated event, but manifestations of a general trend in satellite Europe. Rumania, the satellite country with the largest Jewish population, was the next to introduce the method of mass deportations after the Russian and Hungarian examples.

According to unofficial reports, former middle-class citizens, former officials, and other "alien" and "unproductive" elements were told in February 1952 to be prepared for "compulsory transfer" to remote places and labor camps in the Black Sea region. At the beginning of March reports from Rumania announced that deportations had started. There were estimates that 100,000 people, mostly Jews, were affected. Jews were evacuated from Bucharest, Ploesti, Galatz, Jassy, Timisoara, and other cities and sent to isolated regions. According to one report, former land- and factory-owners were allowed to choose the area to which they were sent and to take their families with them; former political prisoners and persons suspected of opposition to the regime were simply transported to slave labor camps. Many Jewish white-collar workers were dismissed from their jobs; this made them subject to deportation as "unproductive elements."[17]

CHAPTER VII

Postscript

This account of the events that have occurred in Rumania since the liberation belies the alleged free development of the minorities under the regimes of "popular democracy." From the summer of 1944 to the summer of 1952, i.e., in exactly eight years, a whole cycle was completed. The tremendous illusions engendered after the collapse of the Nazi occupation were lost one after the other as the Communist regime solidified. Instead of actually obtaining restitution of looted properties, instead of being able to return to a dignified economic life, instead of recovering the autonomy of its religious, cultural, and welfare institutions, the Jewish minority was trapped in a labyrinth of unsuccessful juridical procedures, rejected from the economic sphere, and barred from any real autonomous development. Finally, the majority of the Jewish community, strongly attracted by the newly created State of Israel, tried desperately to emigrate, but this outlet was rapidly and tightly closed by the watchful Rumanian regime. At the same time a monstrous "anti-cosmopolitan, anti-Zionist and anti-Israel" campaign gained momentum in the whole Soviet orbit.

To this general evolution, which attained its climax in the summer of 1952, history has added a somewhat unexpected epilogue. In the middle of that year, the Political Bureau of the Rumanian (Communist) Workers' Party decided suddenly to discard three of its most unpopular leaders. The purge involved Vasile Luca, Minister of Finance, the person apparently responsible for the monetary reforms that had brought about the systematic ruin of ever-increasing strata of the population; Teohari Georgescu, Minister of Interior and Chief of the dreaded Rumanian Police—the *Siguranza;* and Ana Pauker, well-known Communist leader of Jewish descent.

All the power was henceforth concentrated in the hands of Gheorghe Gheorghiu-Dej. The former Premier Petre Groza, always a figurehead for the Communist machinery, was then reduced to the less important post of President of the Praesidium of the National Assembly. This shake-up (which took place after a somewhat similar purge in the neighboring Czechoslovakia had led first to the exclusion from the Communist Party and later to the execution of the former Secretary General of the Czech Communists, Rudolf Slánský, also of Jewish descent), appeared specially timed to bring to the boiling point the antisemitic sentiments present in the orbit. Ana Pauker had long since severed any ties she may have had with the Jewish community, and had moreover contributed to its destruction. The Communist Party knew quite well that Ana Pauker's downfall at the climax of the "anti-cosmopolitan, anti-Zionist, anti-Israel" campaigns would serve as a catalyst for antisemitic sentiments.

After the death of Stalin in March 1953 and the withdrawal of the charges against the Moscow doctors in April, the prepared trial against Ana Pauker was postponed and it was not clear whether it would ever be held.

Obviously, the fate of Ana Pauker interests us here only in the measure that her trial could heap new fuel on the anti-Jewish campaign. Certainly the regime had shown its true face in its systematic destruction of the economic and spiritual basis of the Jewish community. This regime is clearly, basically, and completely hostile to any group that refuses to fit into the Communist mold. To break down the Jewish resistance, anything is permissible including obviously fabricated campaigns with heavy antisemitic overtones. Thus antisemitism has been turned again into a weapon for terrorizing the remnants of the Jewish communities. Though used overtly only occasionally, the very fact of its presence is a constant threat to the well being of these Jewish communities.

Notes

CHAPTER I

1. Hereinafter the terms "Jews" or "Israelites," if not qualified otherwise, mean persons of the Jewish *faith*.

It has been often contended that the figures of the 1930 Rumanian census concerning the Jews were not "absolutely accurate." The pre-war chief of the anti-Semitic "Iron Guard," Corneliu Zelea Codreanu, wrote in his book *Die Eiserne Garde*, Berlin 1939, that there were between 2 and 2½ million Jews in Rumania. Other odd "estimates" have been made in various quarters, where it was felt that the official figure needed some upward adjustments.

In fact, it does not seem that such adjustments are necessary. The director of the Rumanian Institute of Statistics, as well as the German professor delegated in 1941 for the supervision of the census operation of that year, both indicated clearly that the findings of the 1930 census were completely substantiated by data collected through different means—namely the data of the Ministry of the Interior concerning the demographic movement of the population (birth and death rate of the Jews as compared to the total birth and death rates).

Cf. F. Burgdorfer, *Datele Recensamantului din 1930* (The data of the 1930 census) in *Analele Institutului Statistic al Romaniei*, Vol. I, Bucharest, 1942, p. 340-353.

2. *Recensamantul General al Populatiei Romaniei din 29 Decembrie 1930* (Census of the Population of Rumania, Dec. 29, 1930), Vol. II, Bucharest, 1938.

3. Sabin Manuila & D. C. Georgescu, *Populatia Romaniei* (The Population of Rumania), Bucharest, 1937, Cf. ch. on the ethnic structure of the Rumanian population, p. 49 ff.

4. On the question of civil rights see Joshua Starr, "Jewish Citizenship in Rumania," in *Jewish Social Studies,* Vol. III, No. 1, 1941.

5. For the distribution of the Jewish population (and other "ethnic groups") see, Sabin Manuila, *Aspects Demographiques de la Transylvanie* (Demographic aspects of Transylvania), (Cf. *Annexes Statistics*), Bucharest 1938, p. 70 ff.

6. See the pre-war monograph of Salomon Kassner, *Die Juden in der Bukovina,* (The Jews in Bucovina), Vienna and Berlin, Lowit Verlag, 1917.

7. For the statistical data after the conquest of Bessarabia see *Dictionarul Statistic al Basarabiei* (The Statistical Dictionary of Bessarabia), Directia Generala a Statisticei, Chisinev, 1923.

8. Joshua Starr, *op. cit.,* p. 67.

9. *Monitorul Official* (Official Gazette) No. 283, Dec. 5, 1938. Quoted by Joshua Starr, *ibid.* p. 76.

10. *The Jewish Minority in Rumania*—Correspondence with the Rumanian Government. (*Memorandum on the Anti-Semitic Movement in Rumania,* Joint Foreign Committee of the Board of Deputies of British Jews & Anglo-Jew. Assoc., London, 1928.

11. *Recensamantul General* (Census of 1930) *op. cit.* Vol. II.

CHAPTER II

1. See *Lucretiu Patrascanu: Sous Trois Dictatures* ("Under Three Dictatorships") [tr. from the Rumanian], Ed. Jean Vitiano, Paris, 1946. This analysis was written in 1941 by the secretary of the Rumanian Communists (purged in 1947).

2. *Analele Institutului Statistic al Romaniei* ("The Annals of the Statistical Institute of Rumania") Vol. 1, Bucharest, 1942, p. 340. See also: *Populatia Evraeeasca in Cifre* ("The Jewish Population in Figures") *Memento Statistic*, Ed. World Jewish Congress of Rumania, Vol. I, Bucharest, 1945 (the data of the *Populatia Evreeasca* are the official censuses of 1930, 1941 and 1942.

3. *Marius Mircu: Pogromurile din Bucovina si Dorohoi* ("The Pogroms in Bucovina and Dorohoi"), ed. Glob, Bucharest, 1945.

4. *Cf.* the monumental work of Matatias Carp, *Cartea Neagra, Suferintele Evreilor din Romania 1940-44* (The Black Book: The Sufferings of the Jews of Rumania, 1940-44) 3 vols, Bucharest 1946-48.

5. Carp, *op. cit.*, also *Marius Mircu: Pogromul de la Iasi:* (The Jassy Pogrom), ed. Glob, Bucharest, 1945.

6. Computed from *Populatia Evreeasca,* op. cit.

7. *Ibid.*

8. Joshua Starr, *op. cit.*, p. 69.

9. Data from *Dreptul la Munca, Masurile Impotriva Evreilor 9 August, 1940, 24 August, 1944.* (The Right to Work, the Measures Against the Jews, August 9, 1940-August 24, 1944), a synoptic table published by the *Curierul Israelit,* Organ of the Union of the Jews of Rumania, Series II, No. 2, Sept. 24, 1944.

10. *Pe Marginea Prapastiei* ("On the Edge of the Abyss"); cf. *Cum au fost expropriate Proprietatile evreesti, Curierul Israelit,* as above.

11. Matatias Carp, General Survey of the Period Considered, Vol. I, p. 17-50.

12. Carp values the pillage at a "couple of hundred billion leis" (*ibid*). The lei, at the black market rate was worth 1000 to a dollar; but it was worth many times that in goods and services.

13. *Activitatea Centralei Evreilor din Romania* ("The Activity of the Central Office of the Jews of Rumania"), Bucharest, 1944.

CHAPTER III

1. Lucretiu Patrascanu, in his book written in 1941, notes (p. 281) that the Germans "exercised particular pressure on the Jewish shareholders." Patrascanu mentions particularly the case of the oil distributing company "Sanielevici," taken over under duress by "Mineral Oel A. G." The shares of the latter concern, taken over in 1945 by Russia, now represent part of the Soviet "contribution" to the joint company "Sovrompetrol," which controls the whole Rumanian oil industry.

2. *Asezarile Evreilor din Romania, Memento Statistic* (The Jewish Settlements of Rumania, a Statistical Summary), ed. Rumanian Section of the World Jewish Congress, Vol. II, Bucharest, 1947.

3. Safran (then chief rabbi of Rumania) and William Filderman (then president of the Federation of the Unions of the Jewish Communities) estimated the number of the Jews repatriated up to the summer of 1946 at 97,000 persons. The figures supplied by them are:

Place from which Returned or Repatriated		*Date*	*Number of Jews*
Transnistria	pre-August 23,	1944	18,000
"		1945	21,000
"		1946	23,000
Germany (forced labor)		1945-46	35,000
TOTAL			97,000

The authors added that the figure for 1945 and 1946 also included Jews from northern Bucovina (incorporated into the USSR). Twenty thousand refugees, over and above the figure mentioned, were classified by them as refugees from Poland, Hungary, etc. *Cf.* "Answer to an Inquiry on the Present Number of the Jews in Rumania," Bucharest, 1946.

4. JTA, December 18, 1944.

5. *Unirea,* March 9, 1947.

6. *JDC Review* (JDC Research Department), Vol. III, No. 3, January 17, 1947.

7. *Ibid.*, Vol. III, No. 20, June 20, 1947.

8. *Ibid.*, ("*Medical Aid in Rumania*"), Vol. IV, No. 3, March 1948.

9. *Ibid.*, Vol. IV, No. 3, May 1948.

10. *Ibid.*
11. *Ibid.*, Vol. III, No. 20, June 20, 1947.
12. Report by S. Bertrand Jacobson to J. S. Schwartz, Bucharest, February 17, 1947.

CHAPTER IV

1. *Unirea*, June 2, 1947.
2. *Ibid.*, June 21, 1947 (*cf.* "Celebration of an Anniversary–Two Years Since the Constitution of the CDE").
3. JTA, November 1, 1946.
4. *Viata Evreeasca* (organ of the Jewish Party), November 16, 1947.
5. "Motion Adopted at the Conference of the Delegates of the Unions of Communities and of Jewish Organizations," November 16, 1947.
6. *Ibid.*
7. Eliezer Frenkel, *Le Probleme Juif Vue et Solutionné* par Messrs. Felix Aderca, Tudor Arghezi, N. D. Cocea, I. Flavius, Gala Galaction, Petre Groza, Eugen Horoveanu, Nicolae Lupu, Lucretiu Patrascanu, Mihail Sadoveanu, A. L. Zissu. Jassy, 1945, pp. 95-96.
8. "Rabbi Safran reported that 75,000 returnees from concentration camps and Jewish refugees from other countries among Rumania's 400,000 Jews were anxious to leave immediately for Palestine." JTA, January 19, 1947.
9. JTA, June 5, 1947.
10. *Unirea*, June 2, 1947.
11. *Ibid.*, August 11, 1947.

CHAPTER V

1. Gheorghe Gheorghiu-Dej, "For Purity of the Party." In *For a Lasting Peace, for a People's Democracy*, June 30, 1949.
2. *Ibid.*
3. *Scanteia*, June 20, 1948.
4. Gheorghe Gheorghiu-Dej, *op. cit.*
5. Meeting at the Tomis Theater; cf. *Unirea*, June 2, 1947.
6. *Unirea*, July 2, 1947.
7. *Pravda*, September 21, 1948 (Letter to Alexander R.).
8. *Unirea*, December 15, 1948; *cf.* "The Resolution of the Political Bureau of the Central Committee of the Rumanian Workers Party on the National Question."
9. *Prima Conferinta de Lucru pe Tara a Presedintilor si Secretarilor Comunitatilor Evreesti, Bucuresti* (First Working Conference of the Presidents and Secretaries of the Jewish Communities), Bucharest, February 17-18, 1948). Published by the Federation of the Union of Jewish Communities of Rumania, 1948.
10. *Unirea*, December 18, 1948.
11. *Ibid.*, December 30, 1948 (cf. " '*Socialist-Zionism a Mask of Jewish Bourgeois Nationalism*'').
12. *Ibid.*, January 12, 1949 (*cf.* editorial).
13. *Unirea*, January 15, 1949, reported that a Jew, Aristide Blank, "had been in Goga's Rumanian anti-Semitic movement." The fact that a Zionist leader, Meyer Ebner, was elected in the early twenties on a unity list under the government of General Averescu–of which Goga was a member–was considered sufficient proof that "the Zionists always betrayed the Jewish masses"!
14. *Unirea*, January 22, 1949, (*cf.* "Vaida-Voevod was the supporter of the Iron Guard and of the Zionist movement.")
15. *Ibid.*, January 29, 1949.
16. *Ibid.*, January 12, 1949.
17. Cf. *Unirea* files, 1949-50.
18. "The Meeting of the Central Committee of the Jewish Democratic Committees, February 14-15, 1952," *Viata Noua*, February 26 and Feb. 29, 1952.

CHAPTER VI

1. Camil Ring, "Reds Seen Choking Trade in Rumania," *The New York Times*, March 2, 1949.

2. *Ibid.*

3. The figure used by the Restratification Department of the CDE is at variance with the data of the Rumanian Section of the World Jewish Congress (*cf.* our Table 7; the CDE figure seems to overlook the refugees).

4. *Unirea*, March 1-15, 1948.

5. JTA, March 23, 1950.

6. *Viata Noua*, February 26, 1952.

7. *Prima Conferinta . . . etc., loc. cit.; cf.* speech by H. Leibovici-Serban.

8. *Ibid. cf.* "135,000 persons on relief, of whom 35,000 were receiving partial assistance."

9. *Viata Noua*, April 22, 1951, gives the total of minority schools as 2,439. Of these 2,267 are elementary schools; 79 are intermediate theoretical schools; 92 are intermediate technical schools; and one is a Hungarian university. It is curious that this newspaper, which is the organ of the Jewish Democratic Committee, does not give any figures for Jewish schools.

10. *Unirea*, August 2, 1948.

11. *Activitatea Centralei Evreilor din Romania, loc. cit.*

12. The Russian system comprised elementary schools with a seven-year curriculum and "intermediate" schools with a four-year curriculum. The former high schools were now changed to "intermediate technical and professional schools . . . so as to facilitate immediate entrance into production." Cf. *Unirea*, No. 161, August 1948.

13. A. Golopentia and D. C. Georgescu, *Populatia Republicei Populare Romane la 25 Januarie 1948; Rezultatele provizorii ale Recensamantului* ("The Population of the Rumanian People's Republic on January 25, 1948–Provisional Results of the Census"), Institutul Central de Statistica, Bucharest, 1948, pp. 37-41.

14. *Viata Noua*, June 10, 1952. In his comments on the première of *Cleaning Up*, the reviewer called the play "a piece for the enlightenment of the Jewish working people in the spirit of class vigilance."

15. *Viata Noua*, June 24, 1952, reported that this "admirable finale" was exciting the applause of the Jewish working people, who thus expressed their decision "to fight with greater vigor against the bourgeoisie who use the poisoned weapon of nationalism in order to hamper the construction of socialism in the Rumanian People's Republic."

16. Only 1, 353 Jews were able to leave Rumania during the period from February to October 1949, according to statistics of the Research Department of the American Jewish Joint Distribution Committee. Forty per cent of them were not Rumanian citizens.

17. JTA, February 15, March 4, March 12, 1952.

VI. Bulgaria

BY

PETER MEYER

Chapter I

The Prewar Community

There were about 48,000 Jews in prewar Bulgaria, constituting 0.8 per cent of the entire population. Table I shows the total population of Bulgaria, the number of Jews (adherents of the Jewish faith), and the percentage of Jews in the three censuses taken between the two World Wars:[1]

TABLE I

JEWISH POPULATION OF BULGARIA, 1920, 1926, 1934

Year	Total Population	Jewish Population	Percentage of Jews
1920	4,846,971	43,232	0.90
1926	5,478,741	46,431	0.85
1934	6,077,939	48,398	0.80

As the rate of natural increase of the Jews showed a downward trend, falling behind that of the rest of the population, the ratio of Jews to the total population slowly declined. In 1934, it was only 0.8 per cent for the whole country. At the same time, a process of concentration of Jews in the big cities was going on. In 1920, in towns with more than 10,000 inhabitants, the Jewish ratio was 4.4 per cent of the total population; in cities over 100,000 inhabitants, 6.5 per cent. By 1932, over 45 per cent of all Bulgarian Jews lived in the capital. In 1934, 25,783 Jews (53.3 per cent of all Bulgarian Jews) were counted in Sofia.[2] In 1935, according to another source, the Jewish population of the capital was 26,000 persons, or 55 per cent of all Bulgarian Jews and 9 per cent of Sofia's total population. In addition, there were 7,000 Jews in Plovdiv, 3,100 in Ruse, 1,800 in Varna, and 1,000 in Burgas. Some 90 per cent of the Jews were living in urban communities at that time.[3]

One of the reasons for the growing concentration of Jews in big cities between the wars was their being forced out of the small towns by the multiplying peasant cooperatives. The reduction of the purchasing power of the peasants during the depression was another factor contributing to the movement of Jews to the large cities.[4]

Economic Status

Most Bulgarian Jews were engaged in trade. The census of 1926 recorded 13,444 gainfully employed Jewish persons, forming 29 per cent of the total Jewish population. Their distribution in the economy is shown in Table II:

TABLE II

JEWISH OCCUPATIONAL DISTRIBUTION, 1926[5]

Occupation	Total Number of Jews	Self-employed		Employees	
		Number	Per cent	Number	Per cent
Commerce, credit, insurance	7,373	4,665	63.0	2,708	37.0
Manufacturing, crafts, transportation	4,729	1,736	36.9	2,993	63.1
Professions, civil service	834	204	24.5	630	75.5
Domestic service	213	—	—	213	100.0
Agriculture	63	17		46	
Others	232	10		222	
TOTAL	13,444	6,632	49.3	6,812	50.7

Employees formed more than a half (50.7 per cent) of the gainfully employed Jewish population, but self-employed persons constituted almost two-thirds (63 per cent) of all Jews engaged in commerce.

In 1934, 17,128 Jews were gainfully employed (35.4 per cent of the Jewish population); their distribution is shown in Table III:

TABLE III

JEWISH OCCUPATIONAL DISTRIBUTION, 1934[6]

Occupation	Total No. of Jews	Self-employed		Employees	
		Number	Per cent	Number	Per cent
Commerce, credit, insurance	9,381	5,243	55.9	4,138	44.1
Manufacturing, crafts, etc.	5,165	1,616	31.7	3,549	68.3
Others	2,582	999	38.8	1,583	61.2
TOTAL	17,128	7,858	45.9	9,270	54.1

Of the 9,270 employees, 919 were classified as "laborers" (*pomoshtniki*); 2,367 as officials or white collar workers (*sluzhashti*); and 5,984 as workers. Together, wage and salary earners constituted 54.1 per cent of the gainfully employed Jewish population, as against 50.7 per cent in 1926; and even in commerce the percentage of self-employed dropped to 55.9 (as against 63.1 per cent in 1926). From another source we know that in 1934 there were in Sofia alone 5,421 (57.7 per cent) Jewish employees, and 3,971 (42.3 per cent) self-employed persons.[7]

All these statistics show an increasing percentage of gainfully employed persons; a small trend away from commerce toward manufacturing, crafts, and transportation; and a slight decline in the number of self-employed with a corresponding increase in the number of workers and other employees. But the majority was still engaged in commerce, and the majority of those engaged in commerce was still self-employed.

In commerce, Bulgarian Jews were concentrated in particular branches. The majority worked in the clothing, shoe, and toilet article trades, the second largest group in the food and beverage trade. Many Jews were active as importers and exporters, importing chiefly mass consumption goods and exporting grain, hides, and tobacco. In no branch were the Jews dominant, one of the reasons being that they had to compete not only with the Bulgars but also with Greek and Armenian merchants.[8] In the twenties and thirties the effect of the proliferation of peasant cooperatives and of the depression was to oust many Jews from commerce. Restrictions concerning foreign currency, and state intervention in foreign trade, threatened Jewish importers and exporters. Many became agents of foreign firms or of large domestic enterprises. Private tobacco exporters were eliminated when the state took over this trade. In the state banks and in the major domestic banking corporations using Bulgarian capital, no Jews were employed. Some Jews worked in banks using foreign capital, but rarely in leading positions.[9]

In the crafts, there were, in 1920, 530 self-employed Jewish artisans among the 4,934 artisans of Sofia (11.8 per cent). They were engaged mainly in brushmaking, weaving of tapestries, tinsmithing, and shoemaking.[10]

In the twenties and thirties, a Jewish cooperative movement sprang up with the help of the American Joint Reconstruction Foundation. Cooperative savings banks ("kassas") were founded in most Jewish communities; in 1931 there were 16 such Jewish cooperative banks with about 130,000,000 leva of total assets. Most of the borrowers were tradesmen who used the loans to develop their businesses. A Jewish bank, the Geula, founded in 1920, served as a central organization for all Jewish credit cooperatives.

Communal Life

When Bulgaria was recognized as an independent country by the Congress of Berlin in 1878, it was required to grant equal civil and political rights to all its subjects. The constitution of Trnovo (1879) provided for religious freedom and full equality for all citizens.

The "Provisional Law for the Cultural Administration of Christians, Moslems, and Israelites," promulgated in 1880, recognized the synagogue as a local unit, to be directed by a council of three to five members, "elected with the assistance of the rabbi." The synagogues were to be financed by taxes on meat and wine, by wedding, burial, and circumcision fees, and by donations. Only the Chief Rabbi, the head of Bulgarian Jewry and its representative in relations with the government, was paid by the state. The Central Consistory existed only as an advisory body to the Chief Rabbi.

During the first congress of Jewish communities in 1900, the Zionists proposed the adoption of new, more democratic community statutes. The Chief Rabbi and the so-called notables opposed the reform; the conflict continued for several years, until the Chief Rabbi was forced to resign his office in 1913. The Zionists gradually gained control of all the communities and the second congress in 1920 adopted the new statutes.

Under these statutes, each locality containing thirty or more Jews formed a united community. Thereafter, only united units existed in western Bulgaria; in eastern Bulgaria (Sofia, Varna, Ruse), the Ashkenazim were able to maintain communities separate from those of the Sephardim. Each community had the right to tax its members; in addition to fees for religious ceremonies, an income tax was introduced. The communities were administered by councils elected by all members over twenty-one years of age; the members of the council had to be Bulgarian citizens. The local communities sent delegates to the Sbor, a Jewish central council elected for four years. The Sbor elected a Central Consistory of 21 members, 9 of whom had to be residents of Sofia. The congress of 1920 resolved that the Chief Rabbi was thenceforth to be subordinated to the Central Consistory and was not to negotiate with state authorities unless so authorized.

The new democratic statutes of the communities were never formally recognized by Bulgarian law, although Premier Mushanov promised in 1932 "to study the question." The organs of Jewish self-government, however, were tolerated by the state and continued to administer the religious and cultural life of the Jewish communities.

There were Jewish courts for the settlement of religious controversies, and also of civil (especially family) disagreements brought before them voluntarily by the litigants. Such courts sat in Sofia, Plovdiv, and Ruse, and were composed of three rabbis and two lay consultants, one of whom had to be a member of the bar. Their decisions could be appealed to the Beth-Din-Hagadol in Sofia, consisting of the Chief Rabbi, three other rabbis, and three laymen, one of whom had to be an attorney. The members of the courts were appointed by the Central Consistory. The courts found according to the principles of Jewish law. They had jurisdiction only over matters voluntarily submitted to them by the disputants; but once the latter accepted the courts' jurisdiction, the decision could be enforced with the help of Bulgarian authorities, who recognized them as courts of arbitration.[11]

Jewish Schools

Primary education was compulsory in Bulgaria, and free in the public schools; Jewish children could choose between Bulgarian public and Jewish private schools. In the last decades before the war there was virtually no illiteracy among Jews in Bulgaria, while as late as 1934, 20.4 per cent of the general male population and 42.8 per cent of the general female population were illiterate.[12]

Until the seventies of the last century, there were only traditional Jewish religious schools in Bulgaria; Jewish children rarely attended secular schools. The first modern Jewish elementary schools were founded in the 1870's by the Alliance Israélite Universelle; they taught Bulgarian and French, Hebrew figuring as a religious subject to which only a few hours were allotted. There were 14 such schools. Other schools were founded by the Hilfsverein der deutschen Juden. In 1901, both systems had a total of 3,870 pupils.

At the first Jewish congress in 1900, one of the main points at issue had been the Zionist proposal that the communities renounce the subsidies provided by the Alliance, assume responsibility for their schools, and conduct them in a Jewish national spirit. This was opposed by the group of Jewish notables, supported by the teachers of the Alliance schools.

This controversy, too, was finally resolved at the second Jewish congress in 1920. The schools were reorganized under the supervision of the Central Consistory so as to provide a Jewish education; Hebrew became the language of instruction for all subjects except Bulgarian history, language, and literature, which were taught in Bulgarian.

The Jewish schools received 80 per cent of their financial support from the Jewish communities, and the remainder from local and district authorities. The central government contributed only a nominal sum. All attempts to procure larger public subsidies failed; they were also opposed by a part of the Jewish community which was afraid of increased government intervention in Jewish education. Since 1929-30, the central government discontinued even its nominal subsidies.

There were three grades of Jewish schools: kindergartens, elementary schools, and the so-called "pro-gymnasia." The elementary schools had four grades, the pro-gymnasia three; students graduated from the pro-gymnasia were admitted to public secondary schools.

Except for the inclusion of Jewish subjects, the curriculum conformed to that of the Bulgarian schools. The elementary schools stressed the use of spoken Hebrew; Hebrew grammar began in the second year. In the pro-gymnasium, five hours a week were devoted to modern Hebrew, and six and seven hours to the Bible, Jewish history, and Agadah, also taught in Hebrew. The teachers were at first recruited from abroad, but the Central Consistory organized training courses which turned out an increasing number of Bulgarian Jewish elementary school teachers. In later years some teachers were also invited to Bulgaria from Palestine.

In the twenties, there were twenty-two Jewish elementary schools, two of them in Sofia. Of the seven pro-gymnasia, one was closed in 1929 and a second one later. The number of students is given in Table IV:

TABLE IV

ENROLLMENT IN JEWISH SCHOOLS 1925-31

Year	Total Number of Students	Kindergartens	Elementary Schools	Pro-gymnasia
1925-1926	3,540	734	1,956	850
1927-1928	3,566	651	2,227	688
1930-1931	3,776	673	2,711	392

In 1939, the last prewar year for which data are available, the educational department of the Jewish Consistory supervised fifteen kindergartens, twenty-five primary schools, fifteen sabbath schools, and five pro-gymnasia, with more than 3,000 pupils.[13]

Table V shows the distribution, in 1931, of Jewish children among Jewish schools, Bulgarian public schools, and schools supported by foreign missions. Data are shown in percentages for the three principal cities of Sofia, Plovdiv, and Ruse.

TABLE V

DISTRIBUTION OF JEWISH CHILDREN IN SCHOOLS, 1931

City	Jewish Schools	Bulgarian Public Schools	Foreign-Supported Schools
Sofia	50.0	30.0	20.0
Plovdiv	74.2	4.8	21.0
Ruse	65.8	2.5	31.7

In 1924, the Central Consistory established a program of vocational courses for Jewish artisans. In 1930, a school for apprentices in electrical engineering was founded in Sofia; later on, similar schools were established for tinsmiths, auto mechanics, painters, and decorators. In a *chalutz* farm at Pazardzhik, young men were trained for agriculture, truck-farming, and pomiculture.

In the field of adult education, each Jewish community supported a cultural center, or Beth Ha-am, in which lectures and entertainments were provided. The subjects of the lectures ranged from Zionism and Jewish history and literature to political economy and problems of hygiene. The sports club, Maccabi, which had twenty-four groups and 3,305 members in 1930, organized lectures and entertainments in addition to sports.

Trends in Jewish Life

From the end of the nineteenth century on, a number of Zionist periodicals were published in French, Ladino, and Bulgarian. After the First World War there was a Zionist weekly published in Bulgarian, *Hashofar*, the Revisionist *Razsvet*, and the *Vestnik* of the Central Consistory, the last published in both Bulgarian and Ladino. Attempts to publish a literary and scientific monthly failed. *Hatikvah* (in Ladino) and *Evreiska tribuna* (in Bulgarian), started in 1928, were short-lived. A cooperative publishing firm, *Ivria*, was founded for the publication of Jewish books in Bulgarian and Ladino; but after issuing some pamphlets, it fell victim to the depression.

The contribution of Bulgarian Jewry to Jewish scholarship was minimal, the only important exception being the writings of the historian Solomon A. Rozanes on the history of the Jews in Turkey.

Most Jewish sources categorically assert that Jewish assimilation in Bulgaria was virtually nonexistent. In fact, the number of persons professing Jewish ethnic nationality in 1926 slightly exceeded the number of persons of Jewish religion. There were 46,558 persons of Jewish nationality, compared with 46,431 adherents of the Jewish faith.[14]

But the picture changes when we consider spoken language. Before the First World War, the language spoken by the overwhelming majority of Bulgarian Jews was Ladino, a variant of old Spanish written in the Hebrew alphabet. After 1918, this situation began to change rather quickly. The Bulgarian postwar censuses, in addition to religion and ethnic nationality, registered the spoken language, defined in the census questionnaires as the language in which the person thinks and usually speaks in the family.[15] A comparison of data for 1926 and 1934[16] shows in Table VI.

In 1934, almost two-fifths of the Bulgarian Jews gave Bulgarian as their spoken language, although they considered themselves as belonging to the Jewish nationality. Of the rest, almost all were bilingual, understanding and speaking Bulgarian as well as "Jewish."

TABLE VI

LANGUAGES SPOKEN BY THE JEWISH POPULATION

	1926	1934
"Jewish"[17]	41,523	28,002
Bulgarian	3,535	19,263
German	873	600
Russian	157	151
Hungarian	111	104
Others	232	278
Total persons of Jewish faith	46,431	48,398

Compared with other central or southeastern European countries, the Jews in Bulgaria scarcely played an important role in the political and cultural life of the nation. There were exceptions, of course, the most famous of which was the jurist Dr. Josef Fadenhecht, a baptized Jew of Polish-Austrian origin who was a professor at the University of Sofia. He was the author of important textbooks on Bulgarian law, Dean of the Law School, editor of scholarly and political magazines, and finally, in 1918, Minister of Justice in the cabinet headed by Malinov, which signed Bulgaria's capitulation in the First World War.[18]

There had been several Jewish deputies in the Bulgarian parliament, among them the Russian-born journalist Peter Gabe and the Sofia apothecary Farchi; two Jews were also among the Communist deputies elected in 1920.[19] Among other influential Jews, German sources mention Josef Herbst, son of a Swiss Jew and an outstanding journalist; and the Varna Jew, Menakhem Jakob Fajonov, a lawyer and politician, first a Social Democrat, later connected with the officers' group Zveno, which played an important role in Bulgarian politics.[20]

But these were exceptions; most of the Jews who achieved importance in Bulgarian public life were either foreign-born or descendants of recent immigrants.

Nazi authors of course exaggerated when (probably misled by their Bulgarian colleagues) they asserted that "Jews could never become officers, judges, professors, government officials or journalists";[21] or that "in Bulgaria there are only a few Jewish doctors, only one Jewish lawyer, and Jews have only an indirect influence on newspapers through advertising, as there are no Jewish journalists on the important Bulgarian newspapers."[22] In general, however, the number of Bulgarian intellectuals of Jewish origin was small.

Also, the number of marriages between Jews and Bulgarians was small. A Bulgarian delegate told the Frankfurt meeting of the Nazi Institut zur

Erforschung der Judenfrage in 1941:

> There are no mixed marriages at all. Intercourse between Jews and non-Jews has been considered immoral for centuries. The Bulgarian Jews so far cannot speak correct Bulgarian. They speak Spanish and that has hindered relations with them. . . . In the two last years we have had only seven mixed marriages.[23]

In 1944, another Nazi author, Klaus Schickert, gave the number of existing mixed families as 1,000.[24] Many of these marriages, however, had been concluded during the years 1938-41, when anti-Jewish laws were impending and it was hoped by some to evade them by converting to Christianity or by marrying a non-Jewish partner. In 1938, of every 100 Jewish weddings in Sofia, 5 involved a non-Jewish partner; in 1940, the percentage was 26.[25]

Antisemitism

The beginnings of Bulgarian antisemitism go back to the time of Turkish rule. The Ottoman regime was liberal toward the Jews, and the Jews took no part in the struggle of the Christians for religious and national liberation. During the Russo-Turkish war of 1877-78, Jewish sympathies were rather with the Turkish side, although a number of Jews from Bulgaria fought with the Russians and a Jewish fire brigade saved Sofia from arson and looting by the retreating Turkish troops. The Jews participated in the Bulgarian-Serbian war of 1885, and the Bulgarian regent, Prince Alexander von Battenberg, praised them in an order of the day as "genuine heirs of the Maccabean spirit."[26] Still, the population showed their anti-semitic mood in excesses which took place in Vraca in 1890, in Pazardzhik in 1895, in Lom in 1903, in Kustendil in 1904. In the nineties a project to settle Jews on land in Dobrudzha had to be given up because of resistance from the peasants and local bureaucracy.

The most favorable conditions for the development of the Jewish communities prevailed in the first third of the twentieth century, roughly in the years 1900-1930. In this period there were no anti-Jewish excesses, relatively little open discrimination, and considerable opportunities to develop Jewish cultural life.

After 1933 the atmosphere started to change with the increase of German economic and political influence in the Balkans. An antisemitic movement began among students returning from German universities, and a National Socialist party was founded under the leadership of Khristo Kunchev. It published a newspaper, *Ataka*, and demanded a boycott of Jewish trade, the closing of Jewish banks, and the removal of Jews from "influential positions." The small group of Bulgarian intellectuals that took part in this movement was reinforced by White Russian emigrés and Macedonian nationalist revolutionaries. Other pro-fascist groups with strong antisemitic tendencies were the National Society for Political Renaissance, under Dr. Alexander Stalinski, and the Homeland Defense.

In 1936, a violently antisemitic group, the Ratnitzi, was founded under the leadership of Professor Assen Kantardzhiev. This group spread inflammatory propaganda and later on denounced all governmental anti-Jewish measures as too lenient and inefficient.[27] Another antisemitic organization was the Association of Bulgarian National Legions, led by Ivan Dochev and General Zhekov; Brannik was the organization of antisemitic youth. But according to all Bulgarian and most German sources, the influence of these groups on public opinion was small.

Until 1941 the largest part of the Bulgarian press vigorously protested against antisemitic propaganda. In January 1932, after a mass meeting, most of the political and cultural leaders of the country signed a formal declaration against antisemitism. In December 1932 a number of Bulgarian scholars, writers, politicians, and businessmen formed a pro-Palestine committee.[28] In 1937 the Jewish journalist Buko Piti questioned prominent Bulgarian personalities about their attitudes toward race theories and antisemitism; he obtained statements against antisemitism from 60 persons, among them 16 former premiers and cabinet members. Their contributions were published in a pamphlet.[29] There was even a statement by the Bulgarian pro-fascist politician Alexander Tsankov, who after the Bulgarian armistice in 1944 became "Premier" of the short-lived "Bulgarian Government-in-Exile" in Nazi Germany.[30] Among other contributors of statements against antisemitism were several leaders of the Democratic Party of Malinov; former Premier Nikola Mushanov; Professors G. P. Genov, Dimiter Mihalchev, and Assen Zlatarov; the writers Todor Pavlov and Teodor Traianov; and many others. Most contributors pointed out that the Jews were a national minority and that Bulgarians were tolerant of minorities, that the Jews had made valuable contributions to human culture, and that the authors counted Jews among their best friends.

Under these circumstances, Nazi authors found cause for complaint against the lack of a conscious antisemitic movement in Bulgaria. They were mollified by their Bulgarian colleagues declaring that the Jews had never played any role in Bulgarian life, and that the anti-Jewish steps taken by the Bulgarian government and people had not been publicized. Thus, Peter-Heinz Seraphim, at a time when the extermination of Jews was already going forward in other parts of Europe, wrote:

> In Bulgaria there has been, up to now, no considerable anti-Jewish movement. Jewry is not considered a real danger (to a certain extent, rightly so) because of its small numbers and its weak position in the

> economy. . . . In general, one can say that they do not talk much about antisemitism in Bulgaria but that they act quite efficiently in an antisemitic direction there.[31]

Another Nazi author, Otto Franz Kern, wrote:

> In Bulgaria the Jewish question never played a role comparable to the one it played in other southeastern countries.[32]

These statements were partly based on exaggerated information supplied the German masters by their Bulgarian colleagues.[33] This misinformation was an important factor in helping to save Bulgarian Jews from the extermination that overwhelmed the other Jewries of Eastern Europe. The role of the Jews in the economic and cultural life in the country was not quite so negligible as these sources would have one believe, though it was smaller and less conspicuous than in other southeastern countries. Social distance between Jews and non-Jews was greater in Bulgaria and competition in the same fields was weaker, so that there was less opportunity for direct clashes of interest. Antisemitism did not become a strong indigenous force in Bulgarian life.

Chapter II

Wartime Persecution

The persecution of Jews in Bulgaria began in 1940, one year before Bulgaria's entry into the war. In July, the government announced that it intended to introduce anti-Jewish measures. In August, representatives of Jewish communities and of the B'nai B'rith were officially forewarned. On December 24, 1940, a Bill for the Protection of the Nation was adopted by the Sobranie, and on January 23, 1941, the law was included in the official statutes. On February 17, the first cabinet executive order to implement the law was published. On July 29, another cabinet order set forth detailed regulations governing the enforcement of a *numerous clausus* in the professions; these regulations were revised and supplemented with a list of the remaining Jewish professionals in December 1941.[1]

The Law for the Protection of the Nation[2] was not exclusively devoted to the "solution of the Jewish question." Its first chapter laid a general prohibition on "secret and international organizations." This chapter hit the Jews only obliquely: in the list of prohibited organizations issued by the cabinet on January 15, 1942,[3] are B'nai B'rith, Maccabi, the youth organization B'rith Trumpeldor, the women's association WIZO, the Revisionist Party, the Poale Zion, the ORT, as well as Masonic lodges, Rotarians, the YMCA, the YWCA, and the PEN Club.

Chapter two of the law was especially devoted to "Persons of Jewish Origin." The legal definition of such a person conformed to racist standards: any person with at least one Jewish parent was considered Jewish, and citizenship, religion, and all other "legal and formalistic circumstances" were considered irrelevant. There was one exception. Children of mixed marriages were considered non-Jewish if the following conditions were satisfied: the mixed marriage had been concluded before the promulgation of the law; the non-Jewish partner was a "pure Bulgarian"; the Jewish partner had been converted to Christianity before promulgation of the law; and the child had not had any other religion before baptism.

In addition, some Jews were exempted from the provisions of the law without being declared non-Jews. There were three such categories: (a) Jews born in Bulgaria who had lived there all their lives, were Bulgarian citizens, and had been "converted to Christianity" before September 1, 1940; (b) Jews who had married a "Bulgarian person" before September 1, 1940, and had been "converted to the Christian religion" before promulgation of the law; (c) Jews who had been war volunteers or war invalids and had received a decoration for valor.

The exemptions would seem to have been so restricted that they could have helped only a very small number of persons. But Nazi publications were full of complaints about the enforcement of the law, and even if their exaggerations are set aside, it is apparent that many religious and civilian authorities used the exceptions to sabotage the legislation. As has been mentioned, there was a sharp increase of mixed marriages in 1940, when many persons were able to take advantage of the extended discussion of the anti-Jewish law. Ministers of various Christian denominations engaged in mass "mercy baptisms"; several of them were removed from office because of this. (One of these ministers, with a community of about 200 souls, managed to baptize 200 additional persons between January 1 and September 1, 1940.)[4] High dignitaries of the Bulgarian Orthodox Church declared that "conversion to Christianity" and "formal baptism" were two different acts, the first of which necessarily preceded the second, sometimes by a considerable period; because the law spoke of conversion and not of baptism having to have taken place before September 1, 1940, Jews baptized later could also be saved if the minister declared that they had expressed their will to adopt Christianity before that date. Many courts accepted this reasoning.[5] In this way, a number of baptized Jews and offspring of mixed marriages escaped the provisions of the law.

The rest of Bulgaria's Jews had to submit to the following regulations: They had to register as Jews, use Jewish first names, and were prohibited from having Bulgarian-sounding surnames ending in -ov, -ev, and -ich. If they were aliens, they could not become Bulgarian citizens; if they were citizens, they could neither vote nor be elected to public office or office in non-commercial associations; they could not hold positions in the public service or be supported by public means. They had no right to redeem themselves from military service, but were compelled to serve in labor squads in the army. They were forbidden to marry Bulgarians, to have sexual relations with them, or to employ them in their households. They could move only after having procured special police permission; they could be expelled from certain towns and confined to other places determined by the government. They could not own or rent any real estate or houses in rural communities, and had to sell all such properties in their possession to Bulgarians within a year.[6] All other properties had to be registered with the authorities. The government could exclude Jews from certain types of employment. In July 1941, a new law introduced a special Jewish property tax amounting to 20 per cent of properties between 200,000 and 3,000,000 leva, and to 25 per cent of properties over 3,000,000 leva.[7]

In the summer of 1941 the Ministry of the Interior issued an order making it unlawful for Jews "to spread news" (not just "false rumors" but any news) or to "discuss political questions." At the same time, walking in the streets or frequenting public places, restaurants and places of entertainment between 9 P.M. and 6 A.M. was prohibited. The police were ordered to enforce with great strictness the Law for the Protection of the Nation. On June 24, 1941, another cabinet order decreed the removal of telephones and radios from all Jewish apartments and offices.

On July 9, 1942, a law published in the government's bulletin[8] delegated authority to solve the Jewish question and "all problems connected therewith" to the cabinet. In a memorandum, Alexander Belev, at that time consultant to Minister of the Interior Gabrovski, described the expulsion of all Jews from Bulgaria and the confiscation of their property as the "final solution of the Jewish question."[9] By a cabinet order of August 28, 1942, a Commissariat for Jewish Affairs was established; on September 3, Belev was appointed its head.

This signified the loss by the Jews of all civil rights. They were expelled from all Bulgarian cities, not excepting Sofia. Most of the able-bodied men were sent to labor camps; others were confined to small villages, generally in northeastern Bulgaria.

Expulsion from the cities also meant the expropriation of Jewish homes and businesses; these were taken over by the Commissariat for Jewish Affairs, some of them later being resold to non-Jewish Bulgarians. Movable personal property could be sold by the owners, but the proceeds were placed in blocked accounts from which only limited amounts could be withdrawn monthly.

But—and in this Bulgaria was an exception among the German-occupied and Nazi satellite countries—the Bulgarian Jews escaped deportation to Poland and extermination. Preparations for the "final solution" were made, orders were issued, but the resistance of Bulgarian public opinion delayed their execution, and finally the changed course of the war forced the Bulgarian government to abandon its plan.

In February 1943, a formal contract was concluded between SS-Obergruppenführer Dannecker and the Bulgarian Commissar for Jewish Affairs, Belev, for the deportation to Poland of all Jews from Macedonia and Thrace, "as well as undesirable Jews from the old territory" (Bulgaria proper). The total number of the deportees was not stated; but it was provided that, starting with March 1943, ten to twenty thousand persons would be deported each month.[10] The Cabinet approved the contract.

The Jews were concentrated in camps in provincial towns, from which points they were to be forwarded to deportation centers. However, only Jews from Bulgarian- and German-occupied Yugoslav and Greek Macedonia—some 15,000 persons according to postwar estimates—were in fact deported. In 1943 a German victory seemed very dubious, and the Bulgarians had not forgotten the lessons of 1918. The underground opposition distributed leaflets instructing the partisans "to enter Jewish camps and punish guards who were notorious for maltreating Jews";[11] a storm of protest against the planned deportation arose even in the government camp. Protests were sent to parliament, the cabinet, and the king by the unions of Bulgarian writers, lawyers, physicians, by town meetings, by noted men, and even by some officers of the army. Protesting deputations arrived in Sofia from Plovdiv, Kustendil,Iambol, and other cities. Especially strong protests were made by the Bulgarian Orthodox church and its Exarch, the Metropolitan Stephan of Sofia.[12] Even in the Sobranie, a group of pro-government deputies, headed by the Vice President of the Chamber, Peshev, protested the deportations.

In November 1943, a new cabinet under Dobri Boshilov began to make concessions; it decided on a more liberal interpretation of the term Jew and reaffirmed the exemptions for baptized Jews and children of mixed marriages. On November 5, Jews expelled from Sofia were allowed to return temporarily, in order to settle their affairs. The deadline for their final departure, originally set for November 30, was later prolonged until December 20. In January 1944, mass bombing of Sofia and other Bulgarian cities began, and a capitulatory mood spread quickly. The plan to deport Jews from the country was now quietly dropped; emigration to Palestine was allowed and received support from the government. Criminal proceedings were instituted against the Commissar for Jewish Affairs, Belev, and his aides; they were charged with graft. Belatedly, the authorities discovered that Belev was part Jewish in origin.[13]

In the summer of 1944, the new cabinet under Bagrianov was installed with the avowed purpose of starting peace negotiations; it began a full retreat on the "Jewish front." Throughout July and August secret negotiations were conducted in Istanbul between Ira Hirschmann, representative of the United States War Refugee Board, and the Bulgarian minister Nikola Balabanov. In August, Balabanov addressed to Hirschmann and to John Pehle, Executive Director of the WRB, a letter declaring that the Bulgarian government regretted all anti-Jewish measures and intended to abolish them "at an opportune moment." New instructions mitigating their rigor would be issued immediately, the letter promised.[14]

On July 2, the baptized Jew Dr. Josef Fadenhecht was elected president of the Bulgarian Chamber of Lawyers.[15] On August 17, Bagrianov announced in parliament: "The cabinet declares that, in conformity with the will of the Bulgarian people, it has decided to remove all laws which stand in the way of peace . . . among them those connected with the Jewish question."[16]

Former Premier Mushanov, head of the opposition Democratic Party, declared in a debate that the antisemitic actions of the previous administration would forever shame the Bulgarian nation. Similar declarations were made by Professor Petko Stainov,[17] deputy Peshev, and others. On August 20, Foreign Minister Draganov declared that the attitude of the government changed "not only for reasons of foreign policy, but also in order to remove a situation in which a part of Bulgarian citizenry was treated in violation of the principles of Bulgarian morals and their well-known religious tolerance." On August 24, Minister of the Interior Stanishev received representatives of the Jewish communities and announced the new policy: abolition of the Commissariat for Jewish Affairs, abolition of Jewish stars, freedom for Jews to choose any occupation. Finally, on August 29, the Bagrianov cabinet decided to abolish all anti-Jewish laws.

The decrees of abolition were published in Statute No. 193 on September 5, 1944. This was already under a new cabinet, the premier of which was the agrarian leader and aide of Stamboliski, Konstantin Muraviev, and a member of which was the Democrat Nikola Mushanov. The new cabinet accepted the terms of armistice announced by the British-American delegation to the peace talks in Cairo; one of the conditions was "to restore full rights to Jews and other disfranchised citizens."[18] On September 7, Muraviev signed the armistice terms taking Bulgaria out of war. But at this very moment the Soviet Union, which had been at peace and had maintained diplomatic relations with Bulgaria up to that time, declared war on Bulgaria and the Red Army crossed the Danube. Muraviev declared war on Germany, dissolved parliament, and all pro-German organizations. But this did not stop the Russians. The Red Army arrived in Sofia on September 9, 1944. The same day Muraviev was deposed and a new government of the Fatherland Front installed. This government affirmed the abolition of the anti-Jewish laws previously abolished by the Bagrianov and Muraviev cabinets.[19]

Chapter III

Postwar Economic Conditions, Restitution and Rehabilitation

There had been 48,398 persons of the Jewish faith in Bulgaria in 1934. The average annual rate of increase was 11.1 per 1,000 in the years 1925-1928, but only 5.7 per 1,000 in 1933-1936. So it is unlikely that there was any significant natural increase in the years 1935-1943. This is confirmed by a census of "racial" Jews conducted in 1943 by the Commissariat for Jewish Affairs. There were at that time 47,154 "racial" Jews, including several hundred Jews of Southern Dobrudzha, ceded to Bulgaria by Rumania in 1940.[1]

During the war, according to estimates of the Jewish Central Consistory, 123 Jews were killed while serving with the partisans, 1,100 died in the places of internment, and 3,000 emigrated to Palestine. This would leave a postwar Jewish population of about 44,000, not allowing for natural increase. But after the war the Central Consistory found 49,172 Jews in 34 Bulgarian localities in the fall of 1945.[2] This surprising increase, if the figures of the Consistory are correct, can be explained only by there having been an influx of Jewish refugees from other Balkan countries.

The Jewish population of 1945 is reported to have consisted of 26,921 males and 22,251 females, a ratio of 54.7 to 45.3, whereas in 1934 women had been in the majority (50.9 per cent). Children under 15 years constituted 24.8 per cent of the Jewish population, as against 27.2 per cent in 1934.

Some 56.3 per cent of all Bulgarian Jews lived in Sofia, constituting less than 3 per cent of its total postwar population; 77.1 per cent of all Jews were concentrated in seven large communities. In Sofia there were 27,700;[3] in Plovdiv 5,800; in Ruse, 1,927; in Varna, 1,223; in Kustendil, 1,100; in Iambol, 1,076; and in Dupnitsa, 1,050 Jews. The community was, as always, predominantly Sephardic. The percentage of Ashkenazim, estimated at 10 before the war, seems to have declined; the number of Ashkenazim was reckoned in the postwar census to be 2,200-2,500.

Thus the Bulgarian Jewish community survived the war and Nazi domination with only small numerical losses, which would seem to have been more than compensated for by the natural increase of the Jewish population and by the influx of some refugees from other Balkan countries.

Restitution

As we have seen, the wartime anti-Jewish legislation was already abolished—under pressure from the West—by the Bagrianov and Muraviev administrations. The government of the Fatherland Front, installed on September 9, 1944, issued a decree on October 16, 1944 again abolishing these measures.[4] This was several days before Bulgaria's signing of the armistice treaty, which obliged her to set free immediately all persons imprisoned because of their race or religion, and stated that "discriminatory legislation must be repealed."[5]

In the meantime, on September 13, 1944, a Jew, Isak Frances, was appointed to take charge of and liquidate the Commissariat for Jewish Affairs; liquidation was completed on April 30, 1945, when the remaining archives and assets were transferred to the Central Jewish Consistory. Among these assets was the money that had been extorted from Jews by the "Jewish Community Tax"; 30 million leva of this sum were returned by the Consistory to the Sofia Jewish Community.

Several days after the installation of the Fatherland Front the Minister of Propaganda, Dimo Kazasov, promised in a press conference attended by the correspondents of Jewish newspapers from London, Johannesburg, and Tel Aviv that Bulgarian Jews would get back all their property, concerns, and other assets forcibly sold or confiscated.[6] This promise was repeatedly reaffirmed by spokesmen of the government, but for a long time no action was taken.

The problem of restitution was urgent because the postwar economic situation of the Jews was desperate. In January 1945, Joseph M. Levy, *New York Times* correspondent in Sofia, described it as follows in a dispatch from Istanbul:

> Four months after the liberation, the situation of 45,000 Jews in Bulgaria is deplorable and desperate. They are without clothing, without shoes, and starving. They are existing, not living, under the most unsanitary conditions, 3-4 families sharing a dingy little room, unheated, without windowpanes. Most of them told me that they envy their Macedonian coreligionists who have been exterminated by the Germans. The Bulgarian government has done nothing to help these thousands of destitute Jews.[7]

The dispatch quoted the government's promise to return all confiscated properties to their owners, to release Jewish funds blocked in the banks, to refund extortionate taxes, and to provide tools to impoverished Jewish artisans; and then went on to state that not one of these promises had been fulfilled. It also quoted promises made to the "other side":

> The government announced that no Bulgarian who acquired Jewish property of any description should suffer as a result of the government's decision to restore Jewish belongings.

Mr. Levy summarized his impression in the statement that "the only thing the Jews in Bulgaria are able to do with equal rights and freedom, is to starve and to freeze."

This and similar reports aroused Jewish public opinion abroad. At the end of January the American Jewish Committee appealed to the powers represented on the Armistice Commission for Bulgaria; it charged the Bulgarian government with making promises to the Jews which it does not honor.[8]

Under this prodding the Bulgarian government passed, at the beginning of March, a law providing for the restitution of Jewish properties and rights.[9] It took many months, however, before the Law of Restitution began to be enforced. Not until March 1946 was it announced that confiscated Jewish houses, still in the government's possession, would be returned to their owners without special legal proceedings.[10] Later yet, in August 1946, parliament amended the law to provide for compensation for amounts paid in under the Jewish Property Tax.[11] And finally, in November 1946 the Ministry of Finance issued a regulation providing for the return to Jewish owners of properties confiscated by the state and sold to private persons, the state recompensing the latter for their loans.[12]

There are no statistics—official or otherwise—showing how much Jewish property was really returned. In the other "people's democracies" we know that there was a huge discrepancy between the letter of the restitution laws and enforcement. Since in Bulgaria Jewish organizations were regimented and dominated by the Communists from the very beginning, no public reports, criticisms, or complaints about the enforcement of the laws were carried in the domestic Jewish press. To judge to what extent restitution was really made, we have only the texts of the laws, supplemented and corrected by reports of foreign correspondents and other visitors. Out of these admittedly meager materials we can piece together the following picture.

Real estate and houses under state administration in 1945 were returned. Restitution of houses began in March 1946. It was estimated at that time that 8,288 buildings would be returned, including confiscated properties of non-Jewish Yugoslav and Greek citizens.[13] Many of the houses were in bad condition. If a house had been torn down, six years' rent, without interest, was paid to the owner in compensation.[14]

Properties sold in order to pay the Jewish Property Tax were to be returned; if this was impossible, compensation was to be paid for them. Compensation was to be in cash up to 50,000 leva (*ca.* $100), and the balance in six annual bond installments bearing 3 per cent interest.[15] Stocks, bonds, insurance policies, and bank accounts sequestered by the state were to be released to the owners; these, however, had been greatly reduced in value by the depreciation of the currency which had taken place.[16]

All the foregoing concerns properties still in the possession of the state. The story of Jewish properties and businesses confiscated by the government and resold to private persons was a different one. The government had acquired them for nothing or at a very low price, and had resold them at war-inflated prices. After the war it was decreed that Jews could buy these properties back at the price which the purchaser had paid the state. But these prices were much beyond the reach of the vast majority of Jews, who were impoverished. Later, a new regulation provided that the state would compensate the purchasers; but Jews still found it difficult to recover their property. It was even more difficult to re-establish a business; premises were difficult to rent; rentals were prohibitive.[17] It was repeatedly reported that merchants and artisans were without tools and places of business. The capital available to them sufficed, in the best of cases, only to earn a hand-to-mouth living. Equipment and machinery were almost non-existent.

All individuals in possession of confiscated Jewish property were ordered to report it to the government. But Jewish Telegraphic Agency dispatches and reports of relief agencies agree that this provision was "unenforceable"; very little property was returned in this way.[18] It is true that many of those who had profited from the expropriation of Jewish property were in their turn expropriated. But little of this property found its way back to the original owners. In accordance with a law of April 5, 1946, "Concerning Properties Acquired by Speculation or by Unlawful Means,"[19] all such properties were seized by the state. In the proceedings, the possessors of suspected assets bore the burden of proof; they had to prove that they had acquired them in a lawful way. On the other hand, Jews who had been forced to sell their properties at a ridiculous price figured in these proceedings as creditors. Their claims competed with the claims of the state, and they could get compensation only if they could prove their claims beyond any doubt.[20]

One category of persons was excluded from receiving any compensation: Jewish refugees outside of the country who did not return by March 1946. Such persons lost their citizenship and all their properties. A law, promulgated in March 1945, provided for the expatriation and expropriation of all emigrants who should not have returned to Bulgaria within 12 months; it did not differentiate between fascist and antifascist refugees, between perpetrators and victims of racial persecution. The Jewish Consistory appealed in February 1946 for an extension of the deadline, but without success.[21]

A relief agency report summarizes the effect of the restitution laws in these words: "Notwithstanding the recent favorable laws, only a small part of the Jewish losses will be recovered and the inflation . . . will make that part which is recoverable not much more than a token payment."

Mr. Fishzon, a representative of the JDC who was able to observe the situation in Bulgaria for several months, declared after his return in July 1946 that there was widespread poverty and disease among Bulgarian Jews and that much of their personal property is irretrievably lost.[22] This was the judgment of all independent observers.

Economic Conditions

In the second half of 1946 and at the beginning of 1947—that is, in the period after the adoption of the restitution laws and before the nationalization of commerce and small industry—reports described the economic situation of Bulgarian Jews as most difficult. Almost without exception their current incomes were at best only enough to buy certain foods and to pay rent. Such things as shoes, clothing, sugar, meat, and milk were in the luxury class and could be purchased only by a few.

There was considerable unemployment among the Jews. A tour of the principal Jewish communities, completed by a Jewish Telegraphic Agency correspondent in April-May 1946, "revealed the same picture everywhere; mass unemployment due to the loss of businesses during the fascist regime."[23] It is difficult to estimate the real extent of this unemployment, and of other social transformations in the Jewish population, because the only occupational statistics available, that of the Sofia community, are inaccurate.

According to these figures,[24] there were in Sofia, on May 1, 1947, 26,302 Jews making up 8,551 families. The total number of working members of families, i.e., gainfully employed persons, was given as 9,208, which was a little less than in 1934 (9,392). Their occupational distribution is shown in table VII.

If we add up the number of shop workers, artisan workers, "employees," and unemployed, we obtain 5,497, or 53.8 per cent of all the gainfully employed; this is smaller than the prewar percentage (57.7) of persons working for others. If we leave out the unemployed, wage and salary earners still represent 48.8 per cent of the gainfully employed. Manual workers proper (factory and artisan workers) amount to 2,999, or about 29.4 per cent of the gainfully employed population, as against 35 per cent in 1934. Self-employed persons, including artisans, professionals, merchants, peddlers, commercial agents, etc., amount to 4,234, or more than 41.5 per cent, which approximates the prewar figure of 42.3 per cent. The number of unemployed appears rather small, about 5 per cent of the gainfully employed population. At first glance, it would seem that there had been no major social changes in the community.

But several circumstances call in question the authenticity of this picture. By adding up all categories of the gainfully employed we arrive at a total of 10,213, whereas the statistics of the Sofia Community give a total of

TABLE VII

OCCUPATIONAL DISTRIBUTION, JEWS OF SOFIA, 1947

Occupation		*No.*
Factory workers		548
Workers in small shops		2,451
Employees		
a) in government and public service	643	
b) in private enterprise	1,300	1,943
Independent artisans		1,920
Artisans in cooperatives		81
Liberal professions		391
"Unsettled occupations"		
a) in private enterprise		303
b) in public service		98
Merchants, peddlers, water carriers, commercial agents, etc.		1,923
Unemployed		555
Total		10,213

9,208; even if we understand the expression "working members of families" to mean persons actually working, and exclude the unemployed, we still get a total of 9,658. Thus, the Sofia community's statistics are inconsistent even on paper.

Among the "merchants, peddlers, water carriers, agents, etc.," there are 1,121 "storekeepers"; but a footnote to this says that only an estimated 300 of them are really keeping a store, the rest–about 800–being unemployed. From this we infer that the census-takers were interested not so much in present as in customary occupation and economic status. Many of the merchants were former merchants, many of the artisans former artisans.

In addition to the 555 admittedly unemployed, at least 800 unemployed were concealed in the subdivision of "storekeepers" (under "merchants"); it is probable that other unemployed or irregularly employed persons were counted in other categories, especially in that mysterious division "unsettled occupations." This explains how foreign observers, notwithstanding official statistics, found "mass unemployment" everywhere in the Jewish communities.

In the official Jewish press, the problem of unemployment was rarely discussed. Economic reviews written by the leaders of the communities usually contained specific data only for prewar periods; when they come to the present, they are vague and noncommittal.[25] But occasionally glimpses of the real situation appeared even in the official press. Thus Naim

Shamli, "a former businessman, now a member of a labor union," wrote a letter to the editor of *Evreiski vesti*. It is well known, Shamli declared, that the Bulgarian Jews had the toiling masses to thank for their lives, property, and human dignity.

> But [he continues] one of the greatest wrongs done the Jews by the old regime remains unredressed. A great part of the Jewish population was forced to engage in commerce and speculation because they had no possibility of using their abilities in other fields. Today this category of Jews, *which is by no means small*, remains without work and without means to earn a living, and wanders in the streets and in the cafés of the city full of worries about the next day.

Shamli complained that there were not enough vocational courses. He thought that the Economic Committee of the Jewish Section of the Fatherland Front should solve the problem of these (as he called them) "*luftmenschen*." He ended his letter with this appeal:

> There are people who are inclined to look at former businessmen with a certain contempt; they should understand that they are, with rare exceptions, honorable men who want to be useful to their country, the parents and brothers of our partisans and political prisoners; most of them contribute money to the Fatherland Front, to the party, to the labor unions, to the Antifascist Association "Ilya Ehrenburg," etc.[26]

In the Jewish magazine, *Novi dni*, Eduard Arie wrote:

> The Second World War brought one more difficult problem: the Jewish survivors of the Hitlerite catastrophe were completely ruined economically. In the postwar period . . . the majority of them lack material means and possibilities to continue their usual commercial and middleman activities. In many countries, special economic conditions are developing which limit more and more the opportunities of economic middlemen, and cause many otherwise industrious Jews to be unemployed. This category of Jews, which is, I am sorry to say, rather numerous, staggers helplessly and cannot find its place in the new economy.[27]

Arie as well as Shamli speak of the category of unemployed former businessmen as "by no means small" and "rather numerous."

One indirect proof of the difficult economic situation of the community was the extent of the relief provided by foreign Jewish organizations throughout the postwar period. According to a report in December 1946,[28] 12,000 Jewish families were aided by the JDC during the "last 2-3 years," 8,500 Jewish children being regularly supplied with daily meals. This means that more than three-fourths of all the families and more than two-thirds of the children under 15 years of age received aid from abroad. According to another report, the JDC fed all the children in the Jewish schools.[29] In the winter relief campaign of 1946-1947, the JDC distributed cash, clothing, food, and medical supplies to Jewish families in all the 34 Jewish communities of Bulgaria.[30] The JDC also financed and equipped a Jewish hospital in Sofia of 120 beds caring for Jews and non-Jews,[31] and a clinic serving 3,774 patients. It is fair to say that without this foreign help, many Bulgarian Jews would not have been able to survive their critical economic situation. For the most part, Bulgarian authorities gave only passive assistance to this relief work; they allowed the duty-free import of relief commodities,[32] and supported the relief organizations with their sympathies; but their own positive contributions to relief seem to have been small.

We have been speaking of the time before the final nationalization of commerce and small industry. Former businessmen, even if they were without work and without income, still considered themselves "merchants" and hoped against hope to re-establish their businesses. These hopes were definitely destroyed by the final wave of nationalization at the beginning of 1947.

On January 27, 1947, Premier Dimitrov received the Central Committee of the Association of Bulgarian Merchants and explained the principles of the new commercial policy in the following terms: The government has to coordinate state and national interests with private interests, and private interests must of course yield place when necessary; an example of this is the reconstruction of private commerce, several branches of which will now be transferred to the state or cooperative sector. This transformation will be carried on in successive steps and as painlessly as possible; the government wants to use "honorable and able" businessmen in the nationalized enterprises. But after the reform, government and public enterprises must have priority everywhere. Foreign trade will now become a state monopoly. The government will take over all the larger enterprises. Everybody must acquiesce in this policy.[33]

This declaration caused a panic among the remaining Jewish businessmen, as well as among all who still hoped to rebuild their businesses. The Jewish Communist deputy, Izrael Maier, wrote in *Evreiski vesti*:

> The next day following Dimitrov's interview the newspapers appeared with alarmist headlines which left the impression that the private commercial sector will be closed down almost completely. Confusion reigns everywhere, excitement prevails. . . . Old and honorable merchants come to see me and ask for a frank answer to the following questions: Is this the end of private initiative and does it still make sense to hold on to economic enterprises?[34]

This panic was, according to Maier, injurious to the economic life of the country; he sought to reassure the Jewish merchants. But in a lengthy article he found only two reasons for hope. First, Jewish businesses do not fall into the category of "speculative and parasitic capital": "it is well known that our Jewish merchants have in most cases only poor or middle-sized economic enterprises." And second, the Committee of Economic Ministers, which was directing the reform, was composed of excellent men who would certainly respect all legitimate interests. . . .

Nevertheless, it was clear to all businessmen and former businessmen that their last remaining hopes of continuing in or reviving their businesses were at an end.

The problem before the Jewish community was how to reintegrate the mass of unemployed, underemployed, and impoverished Jews into the economic life of the country. Up to the time of final nationalization, the leaders of the community were inclined to evade this problem; they encouraged hope that there would be a private commercial sector where the former Jewish businessmen could earn their living. Astruk D. Kaleb, a leading member of the Economic Committee of the Jewish Section of the Fatherland's Front, in his report about the merchants' interview with Dimitrov estimated the impact of the new commercial policy on Bulgarian Jews much more realistically:

> A majority of the Jewish businessmen have lost, as a consequence of the anti-Jewish laws, their economic positions, their investments, their warehouses, their inventory, and even the possibility of engaging in enterprise. At the same time unemployment also hit a great number of Jewish wage earners: salesmen, bookkeepers, clerks, etc.[35]

After the war, Kaleb continued, the Bulgarian economy was transformed, and Jews could be reintegrated into economic life only by adapting themselves to the new trends. Therefore, the main tasks of the community were: (1) "productivization of Jewish labor," i.e., retraining of the Jews for industrial work, and especially for skilled jobs; (2) formation of special Jewish producers' cooperatives; (3) employment of Jewish commercial experience and ability in state, public, and cooperative enterprises; (4) employment of "able Jewish cadres" in the state administration.

In a later article,[36] Kaleb stressed that productivization cannot be left to the private initiative of individuals but must be organized by the Jewish communities. In an elaborate "organization plan," he recommended the appointment of special officials in all Jewish communities to see to this, elaboration of "concrete plans" for every community, a broad propaganda campaign for productivization among the Jews, organization of vocational schools and courses and of producers' cooperatives, mobilization of women, youth, etc. The whole campaign would be financed: (a) by appropriations from the budgets of the communities; (b) by "private means," i.e., donations, special taxes, etc.; (c) by contributions from foreign Jewish organizations, "such as the Joint, ORT, etc."; (d) by contributions from the local and central Bulgarian authorities.

This was the plan. What were the results, as far as they can be followed in the Jewish press?

Vocational training courses were organized with the financial help of the ORT. The opening of the first Jewish mechanical-electrotechnical school of the ORT in Sofia, on October 19, 1947, was greeted by the leaders of the community as "a major event on the Jewish front."[37] The school started its first year with 124 pupils, 11 of them non-Jewish Bulgarians. A report at the end of its first year[38] stressed that, in addition to technical abilities, the pupils acquired a "healthy social, political, and anti-fascist education," that they took part in "social actions," organized "socialist competition," and contributed "voluntary labor for social tasks."

As for producers' cooperatives, we saw that according to the Sofia community census of May 1, 1947,[39] there were only 81 "cooperative artisans" in the city at that time. Cooperatives first really got under way when the JDC began to finance them. According to a report by Natan Grinberg,[40] there were, at the end of 1947, 13 cooperatives with 448 members in Sofia, and 13 cooperatives with 209 members in the provinces. This gave a total of 26 cooperatives with 657 members. These cooperatives were financed by the Reconstruction Committee of the JDC. In addition, there were in Sofia 3 additional cooperatives "with a preponderantly [but not exclusively] Jewish membership and leadership" and 130 members. This made a grand total of 29 cooperatives with 787 members. Not all of the members, however, were Jews; there were also in the JDC-financed groups a certain number of Bulgarians, Turks, and gypsies. According to Grinberg, they were "specialists" and their presence helped "to introduce healthy working habits." The exact number of the non-Jewish members was never officially revealed; estimates by relief agencies placed it not far from 50 per cent.

According to a plan cited by Grinberg, the already existing cooperatives were to recruit 695 new members in Sofia and 157 in the provinces; in addition, 5 new cooperatives with 200 members were to be founded in Sofia and 16 new cooperatives with 406 members in the provinces. This would have brought the total number of members to more than 2,000.

But the plan was only partly fulfilled. When a representative of the JDC came to Sofia in September 1948, only 20 cooperatives were able to present reports to a conference called for that purpose. The total number of Jewish cooperatives, as reported at that conference, was 38.[41] The number of their members was not mentioned in this report, but was stated to be about 1,400 by Jewish relief agencies at the end of 1948. The cooperatives were loaned operating capital by the JDC. These "loans," which in reality were subsidies amounting to 80 per cent of total shares, were given mostly in the form of imported equipment, often of the latest design.

Reports of annual meetings and occasional letters of "self-criticism" published in *Evreiski vesti* show the difficulties with which the cooperatives struggled. A typical report concerns the "Ladies' Garment Productive Cooperative Osvobozhdenie" in Sofia.[42] At the time of the report the cooperative had 110 members. After several complaints, a correspondent of the newspaper investigated conditions and found that the managers and supervisors treated the workers rudely; the premises were not properly heated and the cold was often unbearable, thereby undermining labor discipline; a factory kitchen, recently opened, served bad and insufficient food bought on the black market; there were repeated cases of food poisoning; two members had stolen a great deal of material, only being apprehended after several months; a great many of the workers in the cooperative were unemployed for long periods because of lack of raw materials.

There were many such complaints. Under these circumstances it is not surprising that labor discipline was weak,[43] that members of "little faith" sometimes left the cooperatives,[44] and that the cooperative movement, despite all the help from abroad, was not able to embrace a large part of the community.

Producers' cooperatives were a new institution in the life of the Bulgarian Jews. But credit cooperatives and cooperative savings banks had been in existence before the war; there had been 16 of them with total assets of 130 million leva in the thirties. During the war they were forcibly taken over by Bulgarian banks. In July 1946, reports from Bulgarian sources announced that a pending bill to amend the Law of Restitution provided not only for the reconstitution and unification of all Jewish savings banks, but also for a ten-year interest-free government loan of 250 million leva to be granted to the unified Jewish bank.[45] The project, approved by the cabinet, was used to advertise to the world the magnanimity of the Bulgarian government toward the Jews. But then it was quietly abandoned before parliament passed the bill. Instead, attempts were made to get the JDC to finance the bank with 50 million leva.[46]

There remained the possibility of reconstituting the Jewish saving banks if a majority of their former shareholders so resolved. The Economic Committee of the Jewish Fatherland Front conducted a campaign in favor of reconstitution and centralization of the Jewish banks.[47] Finally, six former Jewish institutions in Sofia—Geula, Shalom, Karmel, Toshavim, Naroden Trud, and Tekhia—were revived with "temporary boards of directors" elected not by the members, but appointed by the Economic Committee. These banks were subsequently combined into one Jewish credit institution in Sofia which kept the name of Geula.[48] The Fatherland Front appealed to Jews in the provinces to join the central Jewish bank.[49]

The financing of the producers' cooperatives was stressed as one of the main tasks of the bank. At the end of 1947 the Geula had in fact granted about 60 million leva in loans to the cooperatives.[50] But almost all annual meetings of the cooperatives, as reported in the Jewish press, demanded a large increase in credits from the bank.[51] In general, the support of both institutions, the JDC and Geula, was considered "absolutely indispensable for all the cooperatives."[52]

We lack means to measure the degree of absorption of the Jewish population in the administration of the state and of the nationalized economy, the last two points of Kaleb's program. The Sofia statistics of May 1, 1947, gave the number of Jewish "employees" in government and public institutions as 643, or more than 6 per cent of the total gainfully employed Jewish population. If we add to this 98 persons of "unsettled occupation" listed in the subdivision of "public service," we get 7 per cent. This is a percentage increase as compared with prewar times, when the number of Jews in the public employ was minimal; no doubt many jobs, formerly closed to Jews, were now open to them.[53] But if we take into account the great increase in the "public" as against the private area of the economy, the increase in the number of Jews in public service was relatively small and certainly held forth no hope of helping to solve the economic problem of the Jewish population.

To sum up: although the program of "productivization" and "social transformation" made some progress, it could not solve the problems connected with the expropriation of the Bulgarian Jews. A great many Bulgarian Jews, driven out of the economy by Nazi expropriation, were denied readmittance by the postwar nationalization of private business. They remained in 1948 an impoverished mass, kept alive by foreign philanthropy and seeing no other prospect for themselves save emigration.

Chapter IV

The Jewish Communities

As we have seen, the Bulgarian Jewish communities before the war enjoyed a high degree of religious and cultural autonomy, and possessed a broad network of schools and cultural and social organizations, most of them created and led by a strong Zionist movement. Most of the members and leaders of these organizations survived the war; because persecution and deportation in Bulgaria began later and ended earlier than in most other European countries, conditions for the revival of prewar activities were much more favorable. Soon after the war there were 34 Jewish communities functioning in Bulgaria again, a Central Consistory, a central Jewish weekly, *Evreiski vesti*, Jewish schools and Jewish public libraries. There was also a new organization—the Antifascist Society, "Ilya Ehrenburg," devoted to fighting antisemitism and fascism in general.

The Zionist movement when reorganized was still found to enjoy the support of a majority of Bulgaria's Jews. In 1946 its president, Vitali Haimov, claimed 13,000 active members, or more than 25 per cent of all Bulgarian Jews (if the members' families are counted, 75 per cent).[1]

In Communist Hands

The Jewish communal organizations, however, were from the very beginning in the hands of the Communists and their sympathizers. They were directed by a new institution, the Central Jewish Committee of the Fatherland Front. This committee, subordinated to the Central Committee of the Fatherland Front through the latter's Commission for National Minorities, directed all the activities of the new Central Consistory of Jewish Communities; its official press organ, *Evreiski vesti*, was soon made the official organ of the Consistory. Policy statements were usually signed by the Jewish Fatherland Front Committee together with the Consistory; public meetings and conferences were called by the two institutions acting together; but the Fatherland Front Committee was the policy-making, the Consistory the executive, organ.

At a meeting in Sofia on January 8, 1945, the leaders of the Central Jewish Committee of the Fatherland Front announced Bulgarian Jewry's independence of all international Jewish organizations, Zionist or otherwise. They stated that Bulgarian Jews were simply Bulgarians of Jewish origin having nothing in common with the Jews of the United States or Palestine. The Zionist movement was characterized as bourgeois and chauvinist. The meeting was stormy, with many participants shouting protests from the ranks, but nobody was permitted to take the floor to speak against the proposed resolutions.[2]

Later on, when it became evident that the majority of the Bulgarian Jews still supported the Zionists and the necessity arose to negotiate with international Jewish organizations providing needed relief, it was decided to absorb the Zionists by way of "unification" rather than to exclude them. At the opening of the Second National Conference of the Jewish Section of the Fatherland Front, its president, Zhak Natan, appealed to the Zionists "to join in the common struggle against antisemitism and fascism."[3] In May 1946 the Zionist groups joined the Jewish Section of the Fatherland Front. A formal agreement guaranteed their equal representation in the Central Jewish Committee of the Fatherland Front, in the Central Consistory, and in "all other Jewish communal organizations."[4] In the Central Consistory, the Zionists had, thereafter, the same number of seats as the members of the Communist Party, the balance of power being held by pro-Communist Social Democrats and pro-Communist "non-partisans." In this way the Communist majority in all the institutions was fully assured.[5]

The Communists directed the work of communal organizations through a well-organized faction which conducted its own meetings, often under the direct surveillance of non-Jewish party leaders. Brief announcements about such meetings, with a few general remarks about what was discussed and decided, are found in the Jewish press throughout the postwar years.[6] At these meetings the party line on Jewish questions was handed down to the Communist faction, which then saw to its formal adoption by all Jewish organizations.

Shortly after the Communist faction meeting of April 21, 1948, the Jewish Section of the Fatherland Front was reorganized. The Central Jewish Committee of the Fatherland Front was abolished, the Minority Commission of the Fatherland Front becoming the directing authority for all activities among the national minorities. *Evreiski vesti* ceased to be the organ "of the Jewish Section of the FF and of the Jewish Central Consistory" and became simply the organ of "the Minority Council of the National Council of the FF." A new "Jewish Committee" was appointed by the Minority Council, but only as an advisory body. At the same time the Antifascist Association, "Ilya Ehrenburg," was abolished—because the Fatherland Front was directing the entire antifascist struggle and a special Jewish fight against fascism and antisemitism was no longer considered necessary.

Throughout the postwar period the Communists held all the leading positions in the Jewish Section of the Fatherland Front as well as in the Consistory. The president of the Jewish Committee of the Fatherland Front, Natan, was a Communist; its secretary, Ianko Khershkovich, was a Communist. After the reorganization in 1948, Natan became the chairman of the advisory Jewish Committee of the Minority Council of the FF, and another Communist, Menakhem Koen, became its secretary. The chairman of the powerful Economic Commission of the Jewish Section of the Fatherland Front was the Communist Natan Grinberg; the secretary of this Commission was the Communist Iako Bekhar. The editor of *Evreiski vesti* was the Communist Khaim Benadov, its managing editor the Communist Albert Beni; all the members of the staff and chief contributors were Communists.[7] The President of the Consistory was David Ierokham, a member of the pro-Communist wing of the Social Democrats, who usually took part in the meetings of the Communist Jewish caucuses;[8] but after the reorganization of 1948, Zhak Natan became president of the Consistory in addition to serving as chairman of the Jewish Committee. The secretaries of the Consistory were Communists; Isak Frances, who had been appointed to liquidate the Commissariat for Jewish Affairs after the war, and Isak Moshev, a former officer in the Spanish International Brigade. Two Communist deputies, Izrael Maier and Nastia Naim Isakova, were considered spokesmen of the Jews in the Sobranie. Communists and Communist sympathizers were also at the head of almost all local communities as well as of chapters of the Antifascist Association "Ilya Ehrenburg" and Jewish cultural organizations.

However, the Zionists were allowed to keep their own organizations, and to publish, until 1948, two weeklies, one the organ of the General Zionists, the other of the Poale Zion. These were the only Jewish organs with any degree of independence.

The Jewish organizations were obliged to defend and promote the Communist line on all issues, general as well as Jewish. In general Bulgarian questions they had to give "enthusiastic" support to the administration and violently to denounce any opposition. The official Jewish press never ceased to assert that all pre-Fatherland Front governments in Bulgaria had been fascist and antisemitic; that only the Fatherland Front, under Communist leadership, had saved the Jews from extermination and made them equal citizens; that all opposition served the Western imperialists and was fascist and antisemitic in character.

In its 200th issue, on September 29, 1946, the press organ of the Central Consistory summarized its political achievements in these terms:

Evreiski vesti participated in all important events which took place in our country and abroad; it denounced and unmasked the enemies of Bulgaria abroad and their wicked agents in Bulgaria—the antinational opposition of the followers of Mushanov, Nikola Petkov, Lulchev and others; it took active part in the electoral campaign for the National Fatherland Front Assembly and in the popularization of the candidates of the FF. It contributed to the nationwide enthusiasm for the declaration of the People's Republic and for the unmasking of the monarcho-fascist clique. . . . *Evreiski vesti* leads and will continue to lead a resolute and consistent struggle against the remainders of fascism and antisemitism in our country—the nightmarish heritage of the past. . . . We declare that our newspaper's progressive, democratic line . . . will also continue to be followed in a resolute way, without flinching, in the future.[9]

A good example of the mobilization of Jewish organizations in support of the Fatherland Front is the electoral campaign that took place in October 1946. Thanks to the pressure of the Western powers and in accordance with a three-power agreement, the opposition parties (the Peasant Party led by Nikola Petkov and the Independent Social Democrats under Kostia Lulchev) were allowed to participate in the elections. The Fatherland Front ran a unity list, composed preponderantly of Communist candidates. The electoral campaign "on the Jewish Front" was begun by an article by the Communist deputy Izrael Maier which said:

This is not an ordinary electoral campaign but a decisive political battle. The whole Bulgarian nation is straining all its forces in order to come out with honor from this test. We, the Jews, must . . . throw our forces into the defense of the achievements won by us in the last two years.[10]

In the next issue of *Evreiski vesti* the Jewish candidates of the Fatherland Front were presented to the public. Among these were the Communists Izrael Maier and Nastia Naim Isakova, the pro-Communist Social Democrat David Ierokham, president of the Jewish Consistory, and several other candidates of the minor Fatherland Front parties. (Although the electoral victory of the Fatherland Front was overwhelming, only the two Communists were high enough on the list to be elected.)

A Jewish Youth manifesto for the Fatherland Front was signed by representatives of Hashomer Hatzair, Hechalutz Hatzair, Poale Zion, the Antifascist Association "Ilya Ehrenburg", the Jewish National Reading Room and Library Association, and the Jewish Student Organization, as well as by the Jewish members of the youth organizations of all the FF parties.[11]

A series of public meetings followed. Delegates of the Central Consistory, the Jewish Section of the FF, *Evreiski vesti*, and the Communist Party appeared together and spoke in the same vein.[12] Thus in Khaskovo, on October 23, the Jews, after listening to FF speakers, adopted a resolution holding "persons who rallied to the fascist and antisemitic opposition" responsible for "the degrading state of the country and for the expulsion of Jews." In Kazanlik a resolution was adopted pledging the Jews of this town "unanimously" to vote for the Fatherland Front. Similar pledges were adopted in other towns.[13]

After the election, the Central Committee of the Jewish FF issued a circular thanking all local Jewish units for their contribution to the electoral victory. In this manifesto the Committee expressed solidarity not only with the Fatherland Front in general, but directly with the Communist Party, and criticized the other Fatherland Front parties for their "indecision."

> Many votes were given the FF because the voters saw in the Bulgarian Workers [Communist] Party in particular the most consistent fighter for the realization of the FF program. The loss of seats of the other parties of the FF is due to the fact that in the electoral campaign they did not dissociate themselves sharply enough from the opposition.[14]

The circular stated that the great majority of Jews had voted for the Fatherland Front. "But it is necessary to overcome the doubts of some Jews and to free them from the hostile influence of the opposition because it is known that there are Jewish individuals who voted for the opposition, although everybody could see that the antisemitic elements of the country found refuge in their ranks."

The same problem was dealt with in an article by the secretary of the Central Consistory, Isak Moshev.[15] Earlier, in a plebiscite on the question of Bulgaria's being a monarchy or republic, it had been estimated by *Evreiski vesti* that 97 per cent of the Jews voted for a republic;[16] but now no numerical estimates were made—Moshev reported that the great majority of Jews voted for the Fatherland Front, only a few Jewish votes being given to the opposition. But he felt obliged to consider the reasons for this "influence of the opposition among our conationals." In his opinion, most of the opposition voters were "people with weak nerves" who had "succumbed to foreign pressure." He said that many facts about the antisemitic connections of the oppositionists were not known to all Jewish voters. Moreover, the opposition "demagogically exploited the economic difficulties of the country"; the Jews often suffer the most under these difficulties, being caught in a process of economic transformation. Some of them were "politically backward," some voted for the opposition consciously in order selfishly to protect their narrow class interests. . . .

The first two reasons given by Moshev were patently untrue. A man needed strong rather than weak nerves to vote for the opposition in the circumstances then prevailing. And after the campaign conducted by the official Jewish press and in the communities, no fact—or fiction—about the opposition's association with antisemitism could have escaped the notice of Bulgarian Jews. Undoubtedly the "economic difficulties" mentioned by Moshev were chiefly responsible for whatever Jewish opposition vote there was. Judging by the post-election articles of the Communist Jewish leaders, this vote was by no means negligible.

The fight against the opposition did not end with the election. The Jewish organizations were often used to voice demands for the taking of repressive measures against the opposition parties and leaders. The following resolution was adopted by the local unit of the Antifascist Association in Khaskovo:

> The Jewry of Khaskovo, united in the Antifascist Association "Ilya Ehrenburg" . . . after hearing a report . . . on the behavior of the opposition in the Great National Assembly, declares: that the Jewry of Khaskovo has observed their [the opposition's] provocative and treacherous behavior. Their aims are clear: they want to sabotage the new constitution and all the work of the Assembly. They are trying to compromise our government before the world and to give material to international reaction. They want to bring back the shameful past of fascism and antisemitism. We protest against their gangster-like and treacherous behavior and demand their expulsion from Parliament.[17]

The Jewish Fatherland Front and the Communist-dominated communities regularly celebrated the anniversaries of the Communist uprising of 1923,[18] of the Fatherland Front victory in 1944,[19] of the inauguration of the Bulgarian Republic,[20] of the Russian October Revolution,[21] and of the foundation of the Red Army.[22] Tito, who had been celebrated as the liberator of the Yugoslav nation and of the surviving Yugoslav Jews, was condemned in *Evreiski vesti* immediately following publication of the Cominform resolution against him.[23] Later on Jewish organizations had likewise to condemn the "traitor" Traicho Kostov, who was accused of spying for the Western powers and executed in December 1949. Kostov's successor, Vulko Chervenkov, was praised in every issue of *Evreiski vesti* and celebrated by every orator at every Jewish meeting up to April 1951. Then his name suddenly disappeared from the Jewish press; in a Jewish meeting "for peace" in Sofia on April 12, 1951, not one of the speakers mentioned him; the resolutions expressed thanks and devotion only to Stalin.[24] Three months later, C. L. Sulzberger reported from London that Vulko Chervenkov had fallen into disgrace; though still formally premier of Bulgaria, he was shorn of all real power and authority.[25] When, later on, Chervenkov regained the confidence of Moscow, *Evreiski vesti* celebrated him again as the great leader and hero. Thus in all general political questions the Jewish organizations hewed strictly to the Communist line.

Antisemitism

The policy of the new leadership of the Jewish communities on antisemitism and discrimination can be summarized in the following terms:

Antisemitism is the fruit of capitalism and fascism. In Russia, where socialism has been achieved, no traces of antisemitism remain. In the "people's democracies" only small traces of antisemitism persist as a "heritage from the past"; antisemitism is to be found exclusively in the "fascist" (i.e., opposition) groups and is easily dealt with by law.[26] Special political campaigns against antisemitism are not necessary. Discrimination against Jews by the Fatherland Front authorities is impossible by definition. Hence the dissolution of the Jewish Antifascist Association in 1948: a special fight against antisemitism or fascism from the Jewish point of view was considered superfluous.

No complaints about anti-Jewish discrimination appeared in the official Jewish press. There were no criticisms of the enforcement—or non-enforcement—of the restitution laws, or of the inadequacy of economic assistance given Jews. Except for denunciations of some opposition members for having been connected with antisemitic groups or measures in the past, only one reference to antisemitism in Bulgaria could be found in three (incomplete) volumes of *Evreiski vesti.* It dealt with the expulsion from the Communist Party of a man who "had indulged in antisemitic activities and hostile behavior in the past and abused the confidence of the economic militia."[27]

On the other hand, emigrants from Bulgaria often complained of increasing antisemitism in the country. Their view is summarized in a dispatch of the Istambul correspondent of the London *Jewish Chronicle,* written in September 1950:

> Antisemitism, which has long been absent in Bulgaria, is, according to the refugees, again noticeable among certain sections of the population, and particularly among those dissatisfied with the present regime. The latter tend to blame the Jews in high positions for their plight.[28]

This view was contested in a letter to the editor of the Jewish Chronicle, written by a "British author" who at the end of 1948 had represented "a leading London daily newspaper" in Bulgaria for a month. This correspondent saw Jewish children playing unconstrainedly with other children in the streets, and moreover he was able to quote articles of the constitution proclaiming the equality of religions and nationalities, and prohibiting the preaching of racial hatred.[29] This, of course, did not disprove the contention that antisemitism was growing among certain sections of the population. Whatever the extent of antisemitic tendencies, the Communist-dominated press did not mention their existence and no action was taken against antisemitism. In the official view, such action was unnecessary in Bulgaria.

But the fight against antisemitism continued "on the international front." The main seats of antisemitism were proclaimed to be England, America, and the western parts of Germany. *Evreiski vesti* published many articles about racism in the United States,[30] the plight of the American Jews,[31] and, of course, "imperialist intrigues in Palestine." In September 1946, mass meetings of Bulgarian Jews protested against the verdicts in the war criminals trials at Nuremberg;[32] the Central Consistory proposed to foreign Jewish organizations that an international campaign be conducted to protest the acquittal of some defendants.[33] Not one antisemitic incident in capitalist countries was allowed to pass unnoticed, and a trusting reader of *Evreiski vesti* was supposed to believe that Jews in Western Europe and America trembled for their lives.

A resolution adopted unanimously by the Third Conference of the Jewish Communities of Bulgaria held in Sofia on May 3, 1948, declared:

> 1. The Conference states with joy and satisfaction that the Bulgarian Jews, as well as the whole Bulgarian nation, are living and developing in full freedom and national equality. This was possible thanks only to the victory of the Fatherland Front and people's democracy, thanks to the antifascist popular uprising of September 9, 1944.
>
> 2. The developments after the defeat of Hitler show that only the people's democracies, with the great Soviet Union at their head, guarantee the full political and cultural development of nations and of national minorities.
>
> At the same time, the Conference states with indignation that the so-called "Western Democracies," directed by the imperialist forces in the USA and Great Britain, spread antisemitic and racial ideas in order to promote their warmongering and annexationist plans.
>
> While in the latter countries Jews suffer from persecution and discrimination, and all kinds of obstacles are placed in the way of their developing into a full-fledged nation, in the Soviet Union and in the people's democracies Jews not only are not subject to any limitations, but are rather helped in different ways in their national development.
>
> 3. The Conference acknowledges with infinite gratitude the tremendous contribution of the great Soviet Union to the solution of the Jewish problem and to the realization of the idea of an independent, free and democratic Jewish Republic of Israel. . . .
>
> 4. The Conference states that the Central Consistory of Jews in Bulgaria with all its strength has defended the Bulgarian Jews, who suffered so much under fascism, and that it will lead the Jews to establishing a completely normal life. These results have been achieved with the unlimited fraternal support of the Fatherland Front and its people's government, headed by the Leader and Teacher of the Bulgarian nation, Premier Georgi Dimitrov.[34]

Peace Treaty Guarantees

Since it was absurd to think that Bulgarian Jews might need protection against "their" government, and doubly absurd to look for such protection to the "antisemitic Western imperialists," it is not surprising that the leaders of the Bulgarian Jewish communities violently opposed the idea of an international guarantee of their minority rights in the peace treaties. International guarantees of minority rights have a long tradition in Bulgaria. Such guarantees have been in force ever since the Congress of Berlin in 1878, i.e., since the foundation of the modern Bulgarian state. They were renewed in the peace treaties after the First World War, and the Bulgarian Jews, although they supported the Bulgarian government during the peace negotiations of 1919-20, did not stretch their support to the point of refusing this protection.

The proposal to guarantee the rights of minorities in Bulgaria after the Second World War was made by Great Britain. On September 20, 1946, the Bulgarian Political and Territorial Commission of the Paris Peace Conference adopted it by a vote of 7 to 5. Only the Soviet Union, the Ukraine, White Russia, Yugoslavia, and France voted against the proposal, while Czechoslovakia abstained from voting.[35]

The Bulgarian government considered the minority clause "unnecessary" and "an unjustified affront," and said as much in a memorandum to the Council of Foreign Ministers.[36] It called upon the Bulgarian Jewish organizations, among others, to oppose the proposal.

The Bulgarian Jews had just presented a memorandum at an international conference of the World Jewish Congress in praise of the Bulgarian government's policies. Several delegations objected to this document because of its political and apologetic character. But a special commission composed of American and Italian Jews finally adopted the memorandum with only minor changes.

When David Ierokham, a delegate to this conference, reported on it to a session of the Bulgarian Central Consistory on October 1, 1946, he compared the methods of the Bulgarian and Rumanian Jews:

> While Bulgarian Jews turned with all their material and legal demands to the Bulgarian government, the Rumanian Jews expected improvement of their conditions to come from the peace conference. That course proved to be completely erroneous. There were advocates of such a course among us also. But if we had followed it, the greatest part of our demands would have remained unresolved. . . .[37]

The first result of the Bulgarian memorandum was the formation of a special delegation to the World Jewish Congress; accompanied by Ierokham, this group approached the Bulgarian delegation to the Peace Conference and thanked them for the model treatment given Jews in Bulgaria.

The ground was now prepared for a protest campaign by the Bulgarian Jewish organizations against international protection. At the above-mentioned meeting of the Consistory, Ierokham characterized the British proposal as superfluous and insulting. Bulgarian Jewry, he went on, could not remain silent because it would look as if it were asking for such a protection. It was decided to send to the secretary general of the peace conference a letter in which the Central Consistory, in the name of all Bulgarian Jews, protested against the adoption of any clause for the protection of the Jews or other national minorities.[38] This enabled Novikov, the delegate of the Soviet Union, to declare: "The Jews in Bulgaria showed no signs of worry about their fate. The motive of the British proposal is, perhaps, a desire to divert world opinion from the situation of the Jews in Palestine."[39]

The Bulgarian Jews also opposed British proposals to guarantee the rights of the Jewish minorities in Hungary and Rumania. In a dispatch from Paris, A. Raiski attacked all attempts by international Jewish organizations to influence the results of the peace conference. The Jewish masses, he said, cannot understand the Jewish world organizations, which on one hand struggle against British imperialism, and on the other allow a British delegation to set up as protector of the interests of Jews in Hungary and Rumania.

> Especially adverse is the fact that the World Jewish Congress, which likes to stress its democratic character, identified itself with the policy of well-known elements of the Board of Deputies . . . and of the American Jewish Committee, an organization whose policy is directed by the big capitalist circles. The unity of all Jewish organizations can be achieved only on a democratic platform, and not by capitulation before reactionary elements.[40]

The clause guaranteeing the rights of minorities did not pass. When the peace treaty with Bulgaria was finally signed, *Evreiski vesti* printed a jubilant article by Izrael Maier saying:

> We, the Bulgarian Jews, are proud to recall the heroic struggle which the Bulgarian people conducted for a just and dignified peace. As a matter of fact, we were not alien to this struggle. The memorandum of the Consistory to the peace conference played a great role. Another historical fact was the protest of Bulgarian Jews against the English proposal to include in the peace treaty a protective clause for the Bulgarian Jews.[41]

In 1946 Bulgaria's Jews had already been living for two years under a Communist-dominated regime. They saw many democratic rights abolished and the harsh persecution of all non-conformist elements. Moreover, while the protests against international guarantees were being made, Jewish education was being eliminated from the schools. Even Ierokham admitted that there were among the Jews advocates of international guarantees. But no public discussion of the matter was permitted, and the campaign against such guarantees was conducted in such a way that every voice raised in their favor was made to appear suspect and virtually treasonable.

Even silence on the subject was considered suspect, because, as Ierokham said, it would look as if the Jews were asking for outside protection. The conclusion is inescapable that Bulgaria's Jews were forced by the Communist leadership of their organizations to disavow international guarantees of their rights.

Jewish Communal Life

Meanwhile the Jewish schools were being taken from the communities and placed under government administration. In September 1946 a bill "giving the minority schools the same status as the Bulgarian state schools" was introduced in Parliament.[42] On October 1, 1946, at the same meeting of the Central Consistory at which Jewish protests against the minority clause were adopted, Izrael Maier reported on the school bill.

> Mr. Maier announced that the bill about minority schools passed at the second reading. The bill is favorable to all minorities, which will greet it with joy, the more so as it will come in force during the current school year. The law states that the obligation to pay the expenses will be taken over by administrative authorities.[43]

In other reports it was said that local authorities would pay maintenance expenses, and the central government the salaries of the teachers, who would now have the same pay and pension rights as teachers in the state schools.[44]

But the reform also had another side. In prewar times the language of instruction in Bulgarian Jewish schools was Hebrew; only Bulgarian history, literature and language were taught in Bulgarian. Now the order was reversed: "The Bulgarian language will be used in teaching all subjects except the Hebrew language and Jewish history, which will be taught in Hebrew."[45]

And, even more important,

> the bill provided that the teaching program of the minority schools should be made to conform with that of the Bulgarian national schools. . . . It is really necessary that the program in the minority schools be the same as in Bulgarian national schools. The minorities not only do not object to this, they are proud that their schools will also assume a progressive character and will be freed from all kinds of prejudices which have been common in those schools till now.[46]

This meant the end of Jewish educational autonomy. The Jewish schools became, in administration, curriculum, and ideology, like all other Bulgarian schools, the only difference being that Hebrew was still taught and, for a short time, Jewish history was taught in Hebrew. The educational department of the Jewish Consistory was left with but one task: to recruit and train teachers of Hebrew.

In September 1948, the educational department called a conference of all teachers of Jewish disciplines in Jewish schools. Mati Albukhaire, a teacher in the Sofia Jewish School, spoke on "Methods of Teaching the Hebrew Language."

> In her paper she stressed the Soviet, democratic, and socialist character of the teaching of the Hebrew language in accordance with the educational program of the Fatherland Front. It is necessary that the Hebrew teachers know their specialty, that they be carriers of progressive ideas, that they have a democratic and socialist orientation.[47]

As for the teaching of Jewish history, "the teachers present at the Conference correctly appraised the role of the teaching of Jewish history on the foundations of the materialistic *Weltanschauung*." Since knowledge of Hebrew among the students was weak, the Conference decided that Jewish history would henceforth be taught in Bulgarian. It was also decided that the Hebrew language would be used in kindergartens only to the extent necessary for preparation for elementary school, in accordance with the program of the Ministry of National Education.

In an article written at the beginning of the school year 1948-1949 by Nisim Dzherasi, principal of the Sofia Jewish School, it was emphasized that the task of Jewish schools was the same as that of the Bulgarian schools, namely, to give their students a "socialist education." But the Jewish schools, according to Dzherasi, had an additional problem. In Israel, the Jewish nation conducts a struggle against imperialism which cannot succeed without help from the "democratic forces in the world." The children going to Israel must leave "inspired by the heroic struggle of the Bulgarian people against fascism, by the heroism of its leader, Comrade Dimitrov, and his struggle for a new, democratic world." They must leave "with a clear understanding that the world is divided into two parts, and that one part is trying to subject and annihilate the other.[48]

According to a report written by the Central Consistory in January, 1947, at that time there were Jewish elementary and high schools in four communities (Sofia, Plovdiv, Pazardzhik, Ruse) attended by 1,318 students; there were elementary schools alone in eight communities (Burgas, Vidin, Dupnitsa, Kustendil, Sliven, Khaskovo, Shumen, Iambol) attended by 365 students. Of the total of 1,683, 700 attended the elementary and high school in Sofia. Moreover, the Consistory added that the number of students in Jewish schools was declining.[49]

Compared with prewar days, the number of elementary Jewish schools fell off from 22-25 to 12; the number of high schools (*pro-gymnasia*) from 5-7 to 4; and the number of students from about 3,000 to less than 1,700.[50]

In 1949, all Jewish schools were closed for "lack of pupils."

Information on religious life in the official Jewish press is scant. Synagogues existed in all Jewish communities, and the authorities did not interfere with religious services. The sermons of rabbis were, of course, under the same political surveillance as all other expressions of opinion. In one instance, complaint was voiced in *Evreiski vesti* against a wedding sermon delivered by the Sofia rabbi, Dr. Asher Khanalel; the complaint saw suspicious political implications in a reference to the ruins of the Jerusalem temple.[51] In reply, Rabbi Khanalel admitted that the religious symbols he had used "could have been dialectically connected with present events in Palestine and in our country," and that he was guilty of not seeing all the implications of his word. But he recalled his record as a "faithful servant of the Fatherland Front" and reminded the public of his enthusiastic sermons in favor of the labor brigades.[52]

Replying to an inquiry from abroad about the increase or decrease in religious observance, the Central Consistory characterized the situation as follows:

> Religious traditions have always been [*depuis toujours*] observed by the older groups of our coreligionists. For this reason we cannot speak of an increase or decrease in the observance of Jewish religious traditions. In any case, one can say with certitude that we support an increase of interest in our cultural traditions in all sections of our population.[53]

This statement, with its implication that religious traditions are—and always were—a matter for old people, and with its shift of emphasis from religious to cultural traditions, is of course not an answer one would expect from a Consistory. Nevertheless, it was apparent that religious observance was markedly declining. Foreign correspondents spoke of this repeatedly.[54]

In January 1947, the Office of the Chief Rabbi (*not* the Consistory) called several conferences in order to prepare "a plan for the improvement of religious culture and of the religious education of Bulgarian Jewry."[55] From a report in *Evreiski vesti* we gather that it was stressed in the debate that the Fatherland Front, the Central Consistory, and the Sofia Jewish Community "also supported, along with other cultural expressions, all religious manifestations, the restoration of the Central Synagogue and other *midrashim*." In further discussion at the conferences, it was repeated that the government of the Fatherland Front grants full freedom to religious life; it was demanded that "religious workers" should not limit themselves to the fulfilment of religious functions, but that they should be in contact with the broad popular masses.

The next step was the abolition of the financial maintenance of the synagogues by the Jewish communities. From May 1948 on, religious institutions were to be maintained only by believing Jews. In his report to the Third Conference of Jewish Communities, in May 1948, Professor Zhak Natan declared:

> A certain reorganization of our national communities will be necessary. We have no need for a state within a state. The Bulgarian Jews are equal citizens . . . and have to fulfil all duties, pay all taxes to the National Republic. They also enjoy all rights and privileges. So we cannot burden our co-nationals with special taxes as we have until now. They must be abolished after this conference. . . . From now on, synagogues and religious institutions must be maintained only by believing Jews. Those who believe must pay taxes for the maintenance of the rabbis and synagogues. Of course, we won't cease to aid our religious institutions. But a great part of the burden must be borne by the believers.[56]

Chief Rabbi Daniel Zion and Rabbi Khanalel "expressed fears that the separation of the synagogues from the communities will have bad consequences for religious life and for believers." They appealed to the Conference not to leave religious institutions without support.

The unanimously adopted resolution ordered the transfer of religious activities to a "Rabbinical Institute" and the separation of the synagogue from the community.

In the issue of *Evreiski vesti* commemorating the fourth anniversary of the 1944 victory of the Fatherland Front, its editor, Khaim Benadov, published an article called "The Cultural Achievements of Bulgarian Jews After September 9."[57] Almost two-thirds of the article was devoted to the prewar cultural activities of the Jewish communities in Bulgaria and to their war-time persecution. In the third part, however, the following postwar Jewish cultural achievements were enumerated: the Jewish singing choir, Emil Shekerdzhiiski, which received the title of "choir-brigadeer" for its performances in factories; a Jewish theater collective; a Jewish symphonic orchestra; a literary circle of young Jewish writers; the Jewish weekly *Evreiski vesti;* the newly founded Jewish Scientific Institute; and Jewish libraries (reading rooms) to be found in "all places where compact Jewish masses live." In addition, Benadov mentioned the achievements of the Bulgarian Jewish singer Rafael Arie, and noted generally the fact that writers, artists, composers, and musicians of Jewish origin enjoyed equal opportunities in Bulgarian cultural life. The article, significantly, did not stress Jewish schools or Jewish religious life as components of Bulgarian Jewish culture. It did imply, however, that all cultural expressions and institutions had to conform to the political and cultural line of the Fatherland Front and Community Party.

Compared with the relatively broad cultural autonomy of prewar times, postwar cultural activities were meager in extent and thoroughly conformist.

The word "cultural autonomy" was preserved, however. Its meaning, after regimentation of Jewish schools and separation of the synagogue from the community, was defined by Professor Zhak Natan in his previously quoted report to the Third Conference of Jewish Communities in May 1948:

> I don't think that there are among you persons with conservative views who believe that a national culture could be developed if we shut ourselves up in a kind of a ghetto. Our culture can develop only if we tie the aims of our cultural autonomy with the general progressive cultural tasks of the national culture of the nations among which we live, and if we link the aims of our cultural autonomy to the great successes of the most progressive culture which mankind knows today.[58]

The resolution adopted by the Conference was a trifle more specific. The paragraph concerning the Jewish communities limited their tasks to supervision of Jewish schools and the setting-up of library and reading room associations. As we have seen, the role of the communities in education had been reduced to recruiting and supervising teachers of Hebrew language and Jewish history. The rest of the resolution was vague; it spoke of arousing the national spirit and maintaining healthy national traditions.

As to the welfare work of the communities, the resolution said:

> The social welfare activities of the Jewish communities will be limited to supervision of the proper distribution of the relief which we receive from Jewish relief organizations, the Joint, ORT, OZE, etc.

Very little remained of the broad prewar cultural autonomy enjoyed by Bulgaria's Jews. Except for political indoctrination of the Jewish community in the spirit of the Fatherland Front, distribution of foreign Jewish relief and regulation of emigration were the only *raisons d'être* of the Jewish communities.

The liquidation of autonomous Jewish cultural activities and regimentation of the remaining Jewish organizations was already far advanced at the end of 1948, when the mass departure of Jews from Bulgaria occurred. The decline of the Jewish community cannot therefore be considered a consequence of the decline in the number of Jews in Bulgaria but rather one of the reasons which contributed to the desire to emigrate.

At the close of the exodus of 1948-49, communal life was reorganized on the assumption that those Jews who had not emigrated wished to remain in Bulgaria and to integrate themselves completely with the Bulgarian nation.

The Zionist organizations "voluntarily" liquidated themselves, most of their members leaving for Israel. JDC offices in Sofia were closed in May 1949, when the organization considered its task in Bulgaria fulfilled. The Jewish Section of the Fatherland Front became a mere subcommission of that organization's Council for Nationalities. All remaining Jewish functions were now concentrated in the Jewish communities and their central organization, the Jewish Consistory, completely dominated by the Communists.

On June 6, 1949, a Conference of Jewish Communities, called by the Consistory, completed the reorganization. A resolution by the Conference[59] stated that "the Consistory is the only representative organization of the Bulgarian Jews." Jewish people's communities were to be maintained in the following cities, where there was "a considerable number of Jews": Sofia, Plovdiv, Ruse, Marek, Iambol, Varna, Vidin, Kustendil, Khaskovo, Pazardzhik, Pleven, Sliven, Burgas, Stara Zagora, "and wherever else the Consistory deems it necessary" to have communities. The budgets of all the communities had to be approved by the Consistory. The Consistory was to maintain synagogues "in all places where there is a sufficient number of practising Jews."

The Consistory took over all the assets and liabilities of the JDC; ORT and OZE were to continue their work in Bulgaria "under the direction of the Consistory." The bank Geula, which had been founded with the help of foreign Jewish organizations, was also to continue its work of financing cooperatives. Of all Jewish welfare institutions only two, the Jewish Hospital in Sofia and the Jewish Polyclinic in Plovdiv, remained as institutions of the Jewish communities administered by the Consistory.

All Jewish schools were now closed. The resolution stated:

> In accordance with the laws of the country, which prescribe the [minimum] number of children for each class, the Jewish schools in Sofia and in the provinces shall be closed for lack of a sufficient number of pupils.

The reading rooms and Jewish clubs were permitted to continue. The clubs had to be "centers of cultural activities," the libraries were required to "organize broad Marxist-Leninist enlightenment activities among the Jewish population." In addition, the Jewish Scientific Institute was allowed to continue collecting and publishing "material of historic importance."

Finally, *Evreiski vesti*, now to be published twice a month and not weekly, was ordered "to reflect the spirit of the present conference and the spirit and tasks of socialist reconstruction, as well as to give information about the life of Jews in Israel and other countries."

Little systematic information is available about the communal life of Bulgarian Jews after the exodus. But occasional reports from the communities in *Evreiski vesti*, though written in a tone of official optimism and stressing "achievements," allow some glimpses into what was going on.

Half a year after the exodus *Evreiski vesti* published a report about "The Life of Jews in Plovdiv." Plovdiv is one of the larger Bulgarian cities; it possessed one of the oldest and largest Jewish communities in the country. The report first describes the loneliness and despair felt by the remaining Jews after the departure of the emigrants:

> How shall we live without our milieu, without our relatives, people

> were asking. . . . They seemed to have lost interest in any Jewish work, and the Jewish quarter, the Jewish library, were deserted. Many people thought that only a fragment, a small minority [of the Jewish population], was left in the city, and that it was superfluous and did not make sense to assemble and work together as before for the common cause of peace, socialism, and democracy. . . .
>
> The Jewish Community organized a census of the remaining Jews. The results were surprising. There were still 503 families with 1,364 members, among them about 1,000 people under 50 years. . . .

It is difficult to believe that the Jews in Plovdiv would not have known that a large number of them was still left. It is more likely that they were trying to escape dull endless meetings and "common work" for Communist causes. But they did not succeed. "The activists of the Jewish quarter soon gathered, thought things over, and found new ways for common work. . . ." The first measure taken to revive Jewish life was the transformation of the Jewish library into a general library for that part of the city in which it was located. "Progressive" literature was introduced[60] and "soon the library became a center of Marxist-Leninist enlightenment and of all Fatherland Front campaigns. . . ." Bulgarians as well as Jews now used the library, the reports went on to say, and the Jews "sighed with relief": "The place is not deserted any more; we are not alone. . . ."

Soon the community organized two Jewish meetings: one was an election rally, the other was devoted to the celebration of the seventieth birthday of "beloved Stalin." At the end of the meetings, according to *Evreiski vesti*, the Jews were heard to say:

> It is good to come together again, to feel close to each other in the common fight.
>
> Many of them greeted with special joy the discovery and punishment of the traitorous band of spies of Traicho Kostov[61] and expressed their satisfaction to each other.

Then the article proceeded to enumerate the specific tasks of the Jewish community. The kindergarten, administered by the city, "took over a considerable number of Jewish children." The Community should help to educate them into becoming active participants in "socialist reconstruction." Two vocational courses of the ORT were to be resumed, and a summer camp organized in order to confirm all Jewish children in the spirit of *Septembriichata*, the Bulgarian Communist Pioneer organization.

The Jewish Polyclinic, the best equipped institution of its kind in the city,[62] was to be converted into a "genuine popular medical center" serving patients from the entire city and from neighboring villages. The Jewish community was to give moral and material help to producers' cooperatives.

Finally, Plovdiv Jewry was to fulfil "a great task of international import" in defending peace against capitalist intrigues, under the leadership of the Soviet Union and Stalin. . . .

The report betrayed some important information:

1. Jewish schools had also been liquidated in places where there was a large number of Jewish families and an admittedly "substantial number" of Jewish children.

2. The remaining Jewish institutions (libraries, health centers) had been transformed into institutions serving the whole population, although the Jewish communities still had to support them.

3. Specifically "Jewish" political and cultural work consisted almost exclusively of making Communist propaganda among the Jews.

The cultural activities of the reading rooms and clubs were conducted along the same lines throughout the country. Thus, on December 21, 1949, the Jewish library of the town of Stalin organized a combined celebration of Hanukkah and Stalin's birthday. The chairman said in his address that the Jews of the town of Stalin had several reasons to rejoice in these "Stalin days": first, the death sentence passed against the traitor Traicho Kostov; second, the electoral victory of the Communist Party; third, the renaming of their town in honor of Stalin; fourth, Stalin's seventieth birthday; and fifth, the "militant-national holiday of Hanukkah."[63]

At the annual meeting of the Jewish community in Kustendil, held on February 6, 1950, the chairman of the local library association reported that the activities of the organization had been "comparatively slight" during 1949 because its premises had been used in connection with emigration, then as the Communist Party headquarters. When at last the premises were available, only a small number of members was left to use them.[64]

Sofia was the only scene of any sort of cultural activity. The Library Association of this city, called Emil Shekerdzhiiski after a Jewish partisan, organized a series of concerts and lectures in addition to the usual propaganda activities. The annual meeting of the Association, held on March 26, 1950, listed 15,000 books in the library, and 13,650 books as having been loaned during the year. The number of members was given as 800. The library organized a "Popular University," i.e., a series of lectures on "scientific and political topics," but there were complaints about poor attendance. The library also organized affairs to celebrate the anniversary of the liberation of Bulgaria, Stalin's birthday, and election meetings.[65]

Half a year later the library associations listed 1,200 members (evidently including non-Jews as well), "mostly citizens from the First and from the Dimitrov District of the city." A campaign was organized to win all the Jews in Sofia as members, but it "did not bring the desired result, and a great part of them are still outside the Association." The library acquired the classic works of Marxism-Leninism and many Soviet books. It still had, a report said, "about 15,000 volumes."

In general, the report said, the participation of members and other citizens in the work of the library was not satisfactory. The lectures and meetings did not attract any considerable part of the working population of the quarter.[66] This seemed to be the case with all other library associations. *Evreiski vesti* published repeated appeals to the Jewish public to join the libraries and clubs and to attend their meetings, but the response seems to have been weak.

In the spring of 1950, all books "with a nationalist Jewish tendency" were removed from the libraries:[67] this was probably the reason the number of books in the Sofia library remained stationary although many Communist works had been acquired.

In 1952, it was reported that the Sofia library had 1,395 members, of whom only 387 were Jews. Similar libraries still existed in a few other cities; in most of them, the participation of Jews was minimal.

Of all Jewish institutions, the Jewish Scientific Institute, whose work was devoted mainly to the ancient history of Bulgarian Jews and to the collecting of folklore materials, seems to have been least disturbed in its activities. In 1949, it transferred to the Municipal Archives of Sofia a series of documents on the history of Jews in the capital; but its valuable collection of historical documents seems to have been substantially preserved.

The Istambul correspondent of the London *Jewish Chronicle* interviewed recent Jewish emigrants from Bulgaria and summarized their reports as follows:

> The 7,000 Jews still remaining in that country are gradually losing their connection with Judaism. They are said to be completely absorbed in the life of the country, the vast majority of them being members of the Popular Front, a Communist organization. . . .
>
> Jewish institutions still in existence include the Cultural Society and the Artistic Circle, but these have lost their Jewish character and have become merely centers of Communist propaganda. It is noteworthy that books having a nationalist tendency have been removed from the Jewish community library. The well-known Jewish centre "Beth Ha-am" was recently taken over by the authorities and turned into a Communist office.[68]

In 1951 the government began to limit the activities and budgets of even the regimented Jewish institutions. A plenary meeting of the Consistory, attended by representatives from the provinces, decided on January 21 to reduce the budget for 1951 "in accordance with the general line of our country, as laid down by the party and government." The short communiqué did not say how large the budget was, or give the extent of the reduction. At the same time it was announced that the Consistory had subscribed ten million leva of a Loan for the Development of the People's Economy.[69]

On May 19, 1951, the Directorate for Religious Affairs of the Council of Ministers adopted new bylaws for the Jewish communities. These bylaws made Jewish communities and their Central Consistory lay institutions; to take care of the religious affairs, a Central Israelite Religious Council headed by the Chief Rabbi was established in Sofia, and similar local councils were to be organized in the provinces. Only 5 per cent of the Consistory and Sofia community budget for 1952 was to be spent for subsidies for religious purposes. There were no reports of religious activities at the meetings and conferences of the communities, or in the Consistory's organ, *Evreiski Vesti.* The only activities of the Central Religious Council that were publicized were resolutions for peace, and an address in which the Chief Rabbi greeted the visiting Soviet Russian Orthodox Metropolitan Archbishop Nikolai in June 1952.

After an interval of three years, a conference of Jewish communities was held in Sofia in April 1952. It was announced that as of December 31, 1951, there were 7,676 Jews in Bulgaria; 4,259 of them lived in the capital. There were 19 Jewish communities outside Sofia, 13 being represented at the conference. The conference decided to liquidate communities in all towns with less than 50 Jewish inhabitants. A report presented at the conference made it clear that an important part of the Consistory's income came from the liquidation of funds left by defunct local communities and Jewish institutions.

The activities of the communities were summarized in the resolution of the conference as follows:

> During the period reported [1949-52], the activities of the Consistory and of the Jewish People's Communities were guided by the political line of the government and of the [Communist] Party.

For the future, the resolution promised, the communities would educate Jews

> in love of the Fatherland, and in scorn and hate for its enemies, the American-English imperialists and their Balkan servants, Titoist bandits, Greek monarcho-fascists, and Turkish reactionaries.

The Consistory reported that the Jewish hospital, founded and equipped with American support "had lost its importance as an independent Jewish institute" and had been transferred to the government "for general use." The vocational school, founded by our American ORT and taken over by the Consistory in 1949 to be maintained by remaining ORT funds was taken over by the government and transformed into a model electrotechnical school, named after the Russian Communist leader Sergei M. Kirov. Scholarships and subsidies, given up to 1951 by the Consistory to Jewish students, were abolished in 1951 because they "constituted unearned income" and "gave Jewish students an undue advantage, contrary to the policy of the Party and government." The Jewish Scientific Institute was liquidated because it "had no further value as an independent Jewish institution".[70]

The magazine *Evreiski Vesti*, which had appeared twice a month up to the end of 1951, became a four-page monthly. It was praised at the conference for "expressing the line of the government and of the Party," but criticized for containing too little local news. *Evreiski Vesti* conducted a violent campaign against Israel, making extensive use of the material of the Israel Communist Party, and published many official reports about the "happy life" of Jews in other satellite countries. The Bulgarian material in the magazine consisted mostly of general Communist propaganda and official reports of meetings and demonstrations.

Thus the last Jewish cultural institutions in Bulgaria were eliminated and the "Jewish people's communities" reduced to helpless instruments of Communist propaganda. A small part of the postwar Jewish population was still living in Bulgaria but there was virtually no Jewish communal life.

Chapter V

Israel and Zionism

The attitude of the Bulgarian government, the Communist Party, and the Communist leadership of Jewish communal organizations toward Zionism, Israel, and emigration paralleled the attitude of Soviet foreign policy on these matters.

In the first period after the war, it was openly hostile. At that time Zionism was attacked by the Communist leaders of the Jewish communities as a "bourgeois and chauvinist movement." Bulgarian Jews were defined as Bulgarians of Jewish faith having nothing in common with the Jews of America or Palestine. A demand was made to ban the study of Hebrew in Bulgaria. It was declared that the Jewish communities were opposed to emigration to Palestine; similar declarations were repeatedly made by prominent leaders of the communities.

This line was followed for about two years. In this period the plan for the partition of Palestine was characterized by *Evreiski vesti* as "a new form for the imperialistic enslavement of the country."[1] As late as April 1947 the attitude of the "Bulgarian Jewry" toward Zionism and Palestine was summarized by Izrael Maier, Bulgarian delegate to the WJC Conference in Prague, as follows:

> Care should be taken lest the Congress be transformed into a second edition of the Zionist movement. Here, people speak of Palestine as Eretz Israel. The future of that country lies in the cooperation of Arabs and Jews; it must become a free, democratic state of Jews and Arabs. From this point of view, we must say that the blue-and-white flag which we see here should rather decorate a Zionist manifestation, but not a neutral conference such as this one is. And the Zionist anthem Hatikvah should not be sung here. . . .[2]

The Pro-Israel Period

The first signs of change were seen in the spring of 1946. The beginning of the turn in Russian policies was reinforced in Bulgaria by local considerations of a tactical nature: the Zionist organizations proved to be more influential than expected, and their outright suppression would have jeopardized badly needed foreign relief. So it was decided to absorb the Zionists in the Fatherland Front under the slogan of "Jewish unity." This implied certain concessions which were made easier by the change in Communist policy on emigration. When, in April 1946, at a conference of the Jewish Fatherland Front, its president Zhak Natan appealed to the Zionists to join the Fatherland Front, he declared that the latter had "no objections to emigration to Palestine."[3] At the same time, Premier Kimon Georgiev received JDC representative Arthur Fishzon and promised him "the Government's support for JDC relief," as well as a liberalization of the emigration policy.[4] In the October elections the pro-Communist Social Democratic Party included "sympathy with Zionism, solidarity with Palestinian workers and the Haganah," and "freedom of emigration to Palestine," among the planks of its electoral program.[5] When in December 1946 the new Communist Premier, Georgi Dimitrov, received the Bulgarian delegates to the WJC congress, he promised that, "in principle," emigration to Palestine would be allowed.[6]

In July 1946, Bulgarian Zionists were allowed to hold protest meetings throughout the country against British actions in Palestine; Jewish shops and offices were closed for two hours.[7] Bulgarian delegates were allowed to take part in the Twenty-second Zionist World Congress in Basel. But the Congress was sharply criticized in the Bulgarian Jewish press. Barukh Shamli wrote in *Evreiski vesti*:

> The expectations of world progressive public opinion that Zionism would take a new course in its policy were definitely disappointed. Zionism will continue ... its old game of hide-and-seek with imperialism ... instead of turning its back on imperialism and turning to the enslaved peoples, its faithful allies in the Near East. ...[8]

Throughout this period Zionists, Bulgarian and foreign, were still attacked and denounced in *Evreiski vesti*. The newspaper found an "extraordinary example of Zionist anti-Soviet propaganda" in the Zionist newspaper *Haolam* when it complained of the wartime treatment of Polish Jews in Russia.[9] A Palestinian play performed by a Zionist youth group was the cause of ideological attacks against the Zionist movement.[10]

Zionist speakers at public meetings encountered violent opposition. Thus, on April 18, 1947 a Zionist speaker, Simon Markus, lectured on "The Balfour Declaration and Recent Events in Palestine" in the town of Dupnitsa. This is a description of the meeting in *Evreiski vesti*:

> Great was the disappointment, even among many honest Zionists who listened for almost two hours to so many unfair statements, demagogic tricks, and lies; they heard the speaker contradict his own words from beginning to end. In the whole lecture, there was not one idea about the basic factors upon which the solution of the Jewish problem in Palestine depends, i.e., the Arab factor, the interests of the English imperialists, monopolies, trusts, etc. Not one idea was devoted to the present conditions of the Jewish and Arab masses in Palestine, suffering under the heel of the English administration.

The Communists, according to *Evreiski vesti,* forced a discussion to take place in which their speeches were greeted with "a storm of applause." The report ended with these words: "This ends the story of the unfortunate 'speaker.' Dupnitsa should be proof to him that the people want to hear only those who are sincere, consistent, and honest in their utterances."[11]

This campaign of petty harrassment found its climax in an open warning given by Zhak Natan at a meeting of Jewish Communists on October 12, 1947. Natan

> stressed that our country is taking bold steps toward a serious social transformation, the people's republic is making progress at an unheard-of tempo, the Bulgarian Jews are taking part in it, and the Zionists must, in the fulfilment of these tasks, prove in *deeds* that their Zionism is really of the Fatherland Front variety, that they are resolutely for the country, for the democratic bloc with the Soviet Union at its head, and against the Anglo-American imperialist bloc.[12]

The real turn came with Gromyko's declaration in favor of partition and of the constitution of an independent Jewish state. In a long address before a public meeting of Sofia Jews at the end of May 1947,[13] Natan described the Soviet Union as the only friend of the Jewish nation, which could liberate itself only by fighting "for a free, democratic republic in Palestine against Western imperialism." A telegram to Stalin, sent in the name of this meeting by the Communist deputy Izrael Maier, summarized the new attitude in these words:

> A big public meeting of Sofia Jews expresses its ardent gratitude to you, to the Soviet Government, and to the Soviet representative in the United Nations, Andrei Gromyko, for frank and true support of the oppressed peoples in Palestine, for recognition of the great sacrifices of the Jewish people during the World War, and for recognition of the right of Jews who are persecuted by reactionary regimes or who want to emigrate to their free Fatherland, to go to independent, democratic Palestine.

The new policy matured just before the proclamation of the establishment of the State of Israel. New instructions had to be given to the Jewish Communist faction. On April 21, 1948, the Sofia city committee of the Communist Party called a meeting of Jewish Communist "activists." Some 200 "active participants in Jewish political, economic, and cultural life" were present; the secretary of the city committee, Todor Zhivkov, presided. Natan gave a report on "new factors in our relations to the Palestine problem"; at the same time he spoke about the "new organizational forms" necessary in the "Jewish sector" after the "radical transformation of the organizational structure of the Fatherland Front" and after—to quote literally—"the historical decisions of the historical Congress of the Fatherland Front."[14]

The new line was laid down at the Third Conference of Jewish Communities on May 3, 1948, in the main report by Natan as well as in the unanimous decisions of the Conference. Natan said:

> Today, before the eyes of the whole world, a new nation is being born, a nation constitutes itself which has been dispersed all over the world for thousands of years. Today the Jewish people in Palestine transforms itself into a real nation with all the attributes and qualities proper to the modern nations of the world. And we, the Jews who inhabit other parts of the earth, we cannot but feel spiritually and historically connected with this new nation which is being born in Palestine. . . . Today there cannot be a Jew who would think otherwise about the future of the Jewish people than that the Jewish people has the right to exist in its own independent national state. Today the idea of the erection of a national Jewish refuge in Palestine unites all really patriotic forces in the Jewish people.

For the first time Natan found warm words of praise for Hebrew, that "beautiful, creative language"

> in which one can deliver fighting speeches, in which one can write books which can aid not only the cause of Jewish freedom, but also that of general human emancipation. It is sufficient to say that works of genius, the books of Marx, Engels, Lenin, and Stalin, have been translated into this beautiful language. The Jews are developing today a still richer culture than was developed by our ancestors.

But all the tasks confronting world Jewry could be solved only if the Jews were to achieve "fighting unity" in the camp of the democratic nations under the leadership of the Soviet Union."[15]

The new line was popularized in a series of public meetings and propaganda campaigns. On April 16, 1948, a large public meeting was called at the Sofia synagogue by an improvised "Committee for the Support of the Haganah." The number of participants was too great for the synagogue to accommodate; a large crowd outside the synagogue listened to speeches carried by amplifiers.[16] Similar meetings followed in Pazardzhik, Burgas, Stara Zagora, Razgrad and other communities.[17] Committees for the Haganah were formed and collections of money begun. Jewish communities and groups challenged each other to "socialist contests" in fund raising.

The proclamation of the State of Israel was greeted by a solemn meeting in the Sofia synagogue on May 15, and by another big demonstration on May 16, 1948. Hatikvah was sung, unprotested by Izrael Maier, who was one of the main speakers; blue-and-white flags were shown together with the national colors of Bulgaria; Zionist speakers succeeded Communists and official representatives of the Fatherland Front on the speaker's stand. Such meetings were held in Jewish communities all over the country.[18]

On June 9, a session of the Jewish Committee of the Minority Commission of the FF decided that the Bulgarian public must be "correctly informed" about the events in Palestine. It was planned to create a team of speakers to give reports in FF units, labor unions, cooperatives, etc.; only the Jewish Committee of the Minority Commission would be permitted to send people out to speak on Palestine. The plan for this propaganda campaign called for articles on Palestine to be sent to the Bulgarian press; a special pamphlet on the Haganah to be written by the Communist Isak Moshev; and a special labor brigade to be organized to work in the Haganah's honor.[19]

On June 14-16, a "broader plenum" of the Central Consistory heard a report by Khaim Benadov on "Action for the Support of the New State of Israel and of the Fighters for the Jewish Nation"; the plenum ratified the Jewish Committee's plan.[20] Thereafter all propaganda and collections for Israel were conducted from one center and according to its instructions.

The Campaign Against the Zionists

During this campaign for Israel, attacks against the Zionists in Bulgaria did not cease. Quite the contrary. The same conference of Jewish communities in May 1948 which announced its support of Israel and the Haganah inflicted upon the Bulgarian Zionist movement the most serious blow it had yet suffered in the postwar years; it decided to liquidate its press. A resolution of the conference said:

> In order to further the policy of unifying and consolidating Bulgarian Jewry, be it resolved that in the future only one Jewish newspaper shall appear, namely, the organ of the Minority Commission of the Fatherland Front.

The resolution was adopted unanimously. The Zionist delegates voted for the resolution, with this reservation on the point abolishing their press:

> We think that the resolution on this point is right. We agree that publication of one common Jewish newspaper in Bulgaria can contribute to the unification of Jewish communal forces, which is our wish, too. We think, however, that the publication of the *Tsionisticheska tribuna* and *Poale Tsion* does not contradict the program of the FF, and we are of the opinion that in the interests of common work, they should also continue to publish.[21]

A speech by the Zionist leader Leon Strutti at the meeting in the Sofia synagogue celebrating the foundation of Israel was attacked in *Evreiski vesti* as "untrue" and "factional." Strutti had repeated "rumors which were not confirmed by events," "used news from London broadcasts," and "abused a national holiday for factional purposes."[22] This was followed by a more violent attack against the magazine *Poale Tsion*, now an internal bulletin for members only. Information published by this bulletin, *Evreiski vesti* wrote, "serves only our enemies." Proof? The bulletin published a premature report that 15 states had already recognized Israel, and that Czechoslovakia was giving Israel a train and Chile was giving a boat. ... But most serious was publication of rumors that 20,000 American Jews were ready to go to Israel's aid, and that America had asked Egypt to recall its troops. This was a lie, *Evreiski vesti* said, and everybody including the editors of *Poale Tsion* knew it for a lie. Did the author of the lie mean to say that the Americans are friends of the Jews?[23]

Two months later, in an article entitled "Political Illiteracy or Something Worse?" Barukh Shamli carried the attack further. *Poale Tsion* had reprinted a telegram from Israel's Mapai to a conference of the parties of the Socialist International expressing gratitude "to the great labor movements of the USSR and of the USA and to the two labor organizations in France for their support of Israel." This was enough to arouse Shamli's anger. To thank *both* Russia *and* America? That meant "to burn candles to both God and the Devil." To thank both French labor organizations, the Communist-dominated and the anti-Communist? That was equivalent to solidarity "with such traitors of the French proletariat as Leon Jouhaux and various Trotskyites." And there was still another consideration. The telegram had been published just at the moment of the merger of the Bulgarian Communists with the pro-Communist Socialists. *Poale Tsion*, it is true, had published the report without comment. Nevertheless—

> It is clear that there is something rotten in this whole story. Instead of condemning this document in the name of the Central Committee of the Poale Tsion as hostile to labor unity and to Zionism, the bulletin reprints it *in toto*, which means that it agrees with it. The question is: Is the publication of this document an expression of political illiteracy or something worse? The Jewish community expects a clear answer to this question![24]

The leaders of the Jewish community joined in these attacks, from which the bulletin of the General Zionists was not exempt. The purpose of the campaign was clear: to force the Zionists to stop publication of the remnant of their press. This was accomplished at the end of 1948; soon after the last Zionist organizations in Bulgaria voted to dissolve.

This, and the fact that all active Zionists emigrated to Israel in 1948-1949, did not stop the official campaign against "Zionist influences." A general campaign against Zionism, "Jewish nationalism" and "cosmopolitanism" had just started in Soviet Russia and the other Communist-dominated countries; the Bulgarian Communists had to join in lest they themselves be suspected of nationalist and/or cosmopolitan deviations.

That the campaign against "cosmopolitans" in Russia was aimed at Jews—a fact strenuously denied elsewhere—was openly admitted in Bulgaria. On February 22, 1950, Angel Vagenstein, a Bulgarian Communist just returned from a lengthy visit to the Soviet Union, lectured in the

Jewish Cultural Club in Sofia. Under the headline, "Cosmopolitanism—the International Language of Imperialists," his talk was reported as follows:

Comrade Vagenstein was prepared to explain one aspect of the fight against the cosmopolitans in the Soviet Union. It is characteristic of the Soviet approach to such a fight that it is always concretely pointed out who is the exponent of an enemy ideology. Therefore, if such an exponent has a Russian name and is a Jew, his Jewish name is put in brackets. Is this concrete identification of the exponents of cosmopolitanism to be considered a manifestation of antisemitism? It is clear to any honest man who recognizes the existence and strength of the Soviet Union, which are based on the indestructible foundations of brotherhood among nations and of love for all nations, that there is not even a hint of antisemitic intent in the use of the correct names of the cosmopolitan Jews. One is forced to state frankly that the majority of the small group of cosmopolitans in the Soviet Union are Jews. But millions of Jews in the Soviet Union are proud patriots of their great fatherland. . . .[25]

Bulgaria's attitude toward Israel changed along parallel lines, although more slowly. Bulgaria still maintained "friendly relations" with Israel, concluding trade agreements with it and permitting emigration. At a conference of Bulgarian Jewish communities on June 5, 1949, after the great wave of emigration, it was perhaps felt awkward to describe Israel as a hell when the Bulgarian government had just been praised for its "magnanimous decision" in permitting Bulgarian Jews to go there. So the conference's resolution contained only the following short passage on Israel:

A colossal national liberation movement arose among the nations of Asia, liberating millions of people who had suffered under the imperialist yoke.

The independent Jewish State of Israel was constituted thanks to favorable historical conditions which resulted from the Second World War, thanks to the decisive help given by the Soviet Union, and as a result of the fight of the Jewish people.

This historical development—the foundation of the Jewish State of Israel—will be greeted with joy by Jewish popular masses in all countries as well as in our country, and by all freedom-loving people in the world.

The proclamation of the Jewish State of Israel created a tendency to emigrate in a large section of Bulgarian Jewry, for economic as well as nationalist reasons. The Bulgarian Fatherland Front community did not resist that tendency and gave all those who wished to emigrate the full possibility to do so.

But the same conference reproached the Consistory leadership for laxity in the fight against Zionism, and ended the affiliation of Bulgarian Jews with the World Jewish Congress "in view of the reactionary and pro-Zionist activities of the leadership of this world Jewish organization."[26]

And in March 1950, Isak Moshev wrote:

> All the abominable negative traits characterizing capitalist countries are developed in the State of Israel; racism against the Arabs, artificial fomenting of strife between the Ashkenazim and Sefardim, chauvinism against other nations, religious obscurantism, ideological indoctrination of the masses in order to transform them into cannon fodder for American imperialists, persecution of everything Communist and progressive. . . .[27]

Attacks on Israel and its government, partly drawn from Israeli Communist sources and partly written by Bulgarian Jewish Communists, have abounded in *Evreiski vesti* ever since.

These attacks at the time of the Slánský trial in Czechoslovakia and the frame-up of Jewish "terrorist doctors" in Moscow. Now, "Zionists" and "Jewish nationalists" were treated as traitors and spies, and no Jew was safe from the accusation of "Zionism." In the spring of 1953, it was reported that Jewish officials in the Ministries of Foreign Affairs and of National Defense were dismissed on charges that they had maintained relations with Jews who had emigrated to Israel.[28] As in other satellite countries, the purge was now extended to men who considered themselves completely assimilated.

CHAPTER VI

Emigration

Under the economic, political, and cultural conditions described in previous chapters, emigration must have appeared to the overwhelming majority of Bulgarian Jews as the only solution to their problems. Since the Bulgarian Jewish community had been, from the beginning of the century, overwhelmingly Zionist, with a great part of its younger generation educated in the Hebrew language and culture, the desire to go to Palestine was deeply rooted; this desire was greatly strengthened by wartime and postwar events. All unofficial reports and witnesses agreed that virtually all Bulgarian Jews—including many rank-and-file Jewish "Communists"—were eager to quit Bulgaria for Palestine. Official assertions to the contrary, issued several times during the period when the Communists opposed emigration, were contradicted not only by all independent witnesses, but also by the subsequent exodus of Bulgarian Jews.

The official attitude of the government and of the Communist leaders of the Jewish community toward emigration slowly changed from open hostility to grudging tolerance; tolerance changed to active encouragement under certain conditions. These changes followed the turns in Russian foreign policy.

At the beginning of the regime of the Fatherland Front, Bulgarian Jews had been said to have had nothing in common with the Jews of Palestine; it was declared that the Bulgarian Jewish communities opposed migration to the Holy Land. This stand was affirmed at a meeting of Sofia Jews on January 8, 1945.[1]

The first relaxation of this policy came in April 1946, when at a conference of the Jewish Fatherland Front its president, Zhak Natan, appealing to the Zionists to join, declared that the FF had no objections to emigration to Palestine.[2] At about the same time, Premier Kimon Georgiev promised a JDC representative a more liberal emigration policy.[3]

But the leadership of the Jewish community still officially discouraged emigration. In May 1946, when the Anglo-American Committee on Palestine found that most of the Jews of Eastern Europe wished to go to the Holy Land, the Central Consistory protested that this was not the case in Bulgaria.[4] In August 1946 David Ierokham, chairman of the Central Consistory, declared in a broadcast to England and America that the Bulgarian Jews did not want to go to Palestine.[5] In December 1946, the new Communist Premier, Georgi Dimitrov, promised that in principle emigration to Palestine was permissible. But he warned the Zionists that they would have to purge "reactionary and fascist elements" from their ranks.[6]

The change in Russian policy on Palestine brought about a change in the Bulgarian policy on emigration; active encouragement was now given to the emigration of "fighters against imperialism." After May 1947, the official Jewish press defended the right "of Jews who are persecuted by reactionary regimes" to emigrate "to their free fatherland, the independent democratic Palestine."[7] Later on it maintained, first hesitantly then more resolutely, that "active, fighting elements" ought to go to Palestine to fight against the "feudal Arab rulers and their masters, the Anglo-American imperialists." At all times, however, the Communists sought to control the rate of emigration and the character of the emigrants.

Throughout the postwar period, illegal emigration from Bulgaria to Palestine was considered a crime; if not shot down by frontier guards, those caught attempting to emigrate were given terms at forced labor, with the express consent of the leaders of the Jewish community.

In the spring of 1947, when the policy of tolerating emigration had been in force for some time, a group of Jewish youngsters was overtaken at the border by Bulgarian guards. A special meeting of leading Jewish organizations was called to consider the incident. We quote the official communiqué:

> Some time ago, a group of Jewish youths made an unsuccessful attempt illegally to cross the Bulgarian border on the way to Palestine. This attempt ended in disaster: three youngsters were killed at the frontier; the rest were caught and sent away to forced labor.
>
> This unpardonable breach of the law of the Fatherland Front has profoundly shocked the whole Jewish community, which unanimously condemns the instigators of this action. A joint meeting of the Jewish Committee of the FF and of the Central Consistory of the Jews in Bulgaria was called to consider the question, and the Chairman of the Jewish FF, Professor Zhak Natan, made a detailed report. The spokesman of all groups represented in the Jewish FF and in the Central Consistory participated in the debate. All condemned the illegal crossing of the border; it was unanimously decided to issue a declaration to Bulgarian Jewry.[8]

Although the declaration described the victims as "minors" and "ideologically immature persons," no appeal for clemency was made. The declaration simply said:

> No citizen is allowed to leave the country without the government's permission. The freedom which we enjoy gives us no right to break the laws, the laws of a people's democratic country that shows a deep

> understanding of the Jewish question and belongs to the democratic front headed by the Soviet Union. This democratic front was, in the United Nations, in favor of hearing the Jewish delegation on the Palestine question. . . .
>
> But among our co-nationals there were persons who attempted to cross the border illegally and grossly violated the laws of the country. It is clear that this is not a question of entering Palestine illegally; everybody would condone that in the case of Jews who are persecuted by reactionary regimes or who had lost everything in Europe. But we are dealing here with illegal emigration from Bulgaria which under present international conditions can be used by the enemies of the People's Republic.

The declaration went on to say that the real criminals were the persons who morally, intellectually, and organizationally supported illegal emigration. These people were well known and would not escape the punishment they deserved. The declaration appealed to all Bulgarian Jews to watch their children, to guard them against the influence of irresponsible elements, and to denounce all instigators of illegal emigration.

On May 11, 1947, the Central Committee of the United Zionist Organization, meeting together with representatives of all Zionist organizations and factions in the country, categorically condemned attempts to organize illegal emigration and declared that it would expel from the Zionist organization all persons who organized or in any way supported such attempts.[9]

At the oft quoted Third Conference of the Jewish Communities in May 1948, Zhak Natan defined the new line on emigration in the following terms:

> It is necessary to say that every Jew who had decided to do his duty for the freedom of his nation can and shall go to the Haganah, to Palestine. We demand that only genuine fighting people, who will strengthen the army of resistance against imperialism, be allowed to go to Palestine. There is and can be no place among them for persons who want to flee from the difficulties in Bulgaria, from socialism in Bulgaria, who want to leave in order to secure their personal existence. Fighters, and only fighters are needed there now. . . . The Haganah must be transformed into a genuine fighting national army of the Jewish people for the struggle against American and English imperialism.[10]

A campaign was conducted to popularize this line. Letters, expressing agreements with the decisions of the Conference and of the Consistory, were printed in *Evreiski vesti*. We quote an example, a letter signed by one Aron Nisim Mairov:

> Comrades:
>
> With this letter I want to express my satisfaction with the attitude of the Central Consistory toward emigration to Israel. Its decisions will

cut off the possibility of emigration for persons who are not interested in the fight for freedom of the new State of Israel, for persons who want the return of English capitalism and imperialism to Palestine. The opportunity to emigrate will be given, in the first place, to those who are ready to devote themselves completely to the defense of the Israel state and to the introduction of democracy and socialism in it. . . .[11]

The Great Exodus

Between September 1944 and October 1948, about 7,000 Bulgarian Jews left for Palestine.[12] But in October 1948 the emigration of small groups of selected "fighters" was succeeded by a mass exodus of Jews. The change in policy was probably the result of negotiations with Israel authorities and international Jewish organizations. A similar exodus was allowed, at the same time, from Yugoslavia. Priority was still given to prospective fighters, but the bulk of the communities was allowed to emigrate with them.

In September the Central Consistory appointed a special Emigration Committee responsible for the selection of emigrants, their transportation, and all other arrangements.[13] Among its seven members were Professor Zhak Natan, Deputy Izrael Maier, and the editor of *Evreiski vesti*, Khaim Benadov.

The following information about the organization of the transports is taken from an interview with Izrael Maier and Khaim Benadov published in *Evreiski vesti*:[14]

Final decision on all matters of emigration lay with the above-mentioned Committee, which enjoyed the sympathies of Bulgarian Jewry and the confidence of the government. The Committee was permanent; its task was to introduce justice and order into the emigration, and to avoid the mistakes of the former aliyahs.

According to "an agreement with the Haganah," 10,000 Jews were allowed to emigrate. Nothing had been decided as yet about possible future transports; the leaders of the Committee warned "those of our co-nationals who are leaving their jobs and selling their properties in expectation of being allowed to leave with some future *aliyah*."

The 10,000 Jews allowed to leave were divided into three groups. The first group of 4,000 persons, which was preparing to leave at the time of the interview, was composed of those with the highest priorities, among them parents having children in Israel, victims of the fight against fascism in Bulgaria or Israel, and persons without economic means. A second group, also of 4,000 persons, already selected at the time of the interview, included 2,800 Jews from Sofia and 1,200 from southern Bulgaria. In this group there were families with children under three years of age, families that had suffered casualties in the antifascist fight in Israel or Bulgaria, and young people who were supposed to become soldiers in Palestine. The third group, 2,000 persons, was supposed to be similarly composed of Jews from northern Bulgaria. A general rule excluded all persons over 50 years of age; as an exception, 100 persons between 50 and 60 were to be taken in each of the three groups if they were physically able and had children in Israel. The Committee maintained that persons over 50 were excluded at the wish of the Haganah. The Bulgarian government reserved the right to keep back specialists, such as doctors, nurses, engineers, technicians, and managers of economic enterprises.

The question of whether there would be another *aliyah* after the departure of these 10,000 was answered by Maier and Benadov in the following way:

> After the departure of these 10,000 and considering the fact that 7,000 other persons had already emigrated after September 9 [1944], one must consider the problem of emigration from Bulgaria to Israel as substantially solved. From now on, it will be the task of our institutions and of the Jewish community to work for the security and welfare of all those who have linked their fate to the People's Republic of Bulgaria and to the great work of socialism.

But it would seem that the local Jewish community leaders, who were reluctant to see their "constituency" melt away, were overruled. For new groups of emigrants were allowed to depart for Israel in the winter of 1948 and in spring of 1949. This wave of emigration ended in May 1949. In closing its office in Sofia at that time, the JDC, which had paid the cost of transportation, announced that "less than 4,000 Jews remain in Bulgaria, out of a postwar population of 48,000, while all but 1,000 of those remaining plan to leave."[15] This would make a total of 44,000 postwar Jewish emigrants as of that time; of these 41,000 had departed "since last year," according to the JDC.[16]

But the number of remaining Jews seems to have been underestimated by the JDC. On June 6, 1949, a report to a conference of Jewish communities, called by the Communist-dominated Consistory, estimated the number of Jews in Bulgaria at 10,000. The conference declared emigration over and done with. The activities of the Consistory during the emigration period was generally approved, but the resolution of the conference pointed out the following "weaknesses" in its work:

a. There was insufficient educational work done among the emigrants as to the perspectives of the development of Israel as a capitalist country; this omission makes it possible for a certain number of emigrants to become victims of Zionist demagogy.

b. The policy of keeping back Jewish experts and other skilled workers was not enforced with the necessary strictness.

c. Not enough was done to indoctrinate the Jewish population with proletarian internationalism and with faith in the victory of socialism. This is why some progressive Jews have fallen under the influence of bourgeois Jewish nationalism. The lack of strictness in enforcing exit permission policies, and the long delays, introduced spontaneity into the emigration campaign.[17]

Judging by this resolution, emigration got out of hand the moment the gates were opened. Without strict prohibitions enforced by the government, the Jewish Communists and their organizations were not able to limit the flood of emigrants.

Even among the few thousand Jews remaining, Zionist influences and the desire to emigrate were not extinguished. Attacks against Zionism and "Jewish nationalism" were launched by the Jewish Communists with increasing vigor. Israel was depicted as a country where mass misery existed side by side with violent persecution of workers and "progressive elements." Communist leaders emphatically declared that those Jews remaining in the country were firmly resolved to consider "socialist Bulgaria" their only fatherland. There was no more question of future emigrations.

But the Jewish Communist leaders were again overruled by the government. Bulgaria was anxious to get rid of its national minorities; emigration was one means of making Bulgaria homogeneous. The government not only enforced the emigration of the small Armenian minority to the Armenian Soviet Republic; it also drove out of the country a great part of the Turkish minority. Invoking the Bulgarian-Turkish treaty of 1925, it tried to force Turkey to accept an unlimited number of Bulgarian citizens of Turkish ethnic origin.

This general policy toward minorities explains why Jewish emigration to Israel, "definitely concluded" in 1949, was again permitted to resume in the summer of 1950. The profits derived from the expropriation of the emigrants' properties and from the high prices charged them for transportation in Bulgarian ships were very likely additional reasons for allowing Jews to emigrate.

Several new groups of Jewish immigrants reached Israel in August and September 1950. According to some reports, even doctors and technicians were now allowed to leave the country; the only obstacle to emigration was the destitution of many Jews who were unable to buy steamship tickets. Of the 9,000 remaining Jews, 4,000 applied for emigration permits,[18] but only some of them were able to obtain them. According to Israel immigration statistics, 986 Jews whose principal country of residence had been Bulgaria, immigrated to Israel in 1950.[19] In 1951, the number was 1,148.[20]

Thus, the majority of Bulgarian Jews escaped the Communist totalitarian regime by leaving the country in which their ancestors had been residing for centuries.

Notes

CHAPTER I

1. *Annuaire statistique du Royaume de Bulgarie,* Vol. XXIX (1937), No. 25. See also Leon Shapiro and Joshua Starr, "Recent Population Data Regarding the Jews in Europe," *Jewish Social Studies,* Vol. VIII (October 1946), p. 319.

2. *Tsarstvo Bulgaria. Glavna direktzia na statistikata. Prebroiavane na naselenieto na 31 dekembri 1934. Obshti resultati,* Kniga I, Sofia 1938, p. 45.

3. Peter-Heinz Seraphim, *Die Bedeutung des Judentums in Südosteuropa,* Berlin 1941, p. 36.

4. N. M. Gelber, "Jewish Life in Bulgaria," *Jewish Social Studies,* Vol. VIII (April 1946), pp. 103-126. This excellent study is the main source for the description of the prewar social and cultural life of Bulgarian Jews given in this chapter.

5. *Ibid.,* p. 109. The data are drawn from the records of the Jewish Central Consistory in Sofia.

6. Natan Grinberg, "*Stopanskiat oblik na evreite v Bulgaria,*" *Novi dni,* I, 1 (Sofia 1946), pp. 4-7.

7. *Ibid.,* pp. 4-5.

8. In 1926 there were 27,332 Armenians in Bulgaria according to official statistics. But Armenian leaders maintained that the true number of Armenians in 1926 was 45,000. The Armenians were mostly merchants.

9. Gelber, *op. cit.,* pp. 111-112.

10. *Ibid.,* p. 113.

11. *Ibid.,* p. 123. See also "Jews in Bulgaria," prepared by the Research Institute on Peace and Post-War Problems of the American Jewish Committee, 1943, p. 1.

12. "Jews in Bulgaria," p. 2.

13. *Ibid.*

14. *Tsartvo Bulgaria. Glavna direktzia na statistikata. Prebroiavane na naselenieto na 31 dekembri 1926. Obshti resultati,* Kniga I, Sofia, 1931, p. 16. The German scholar Dr. Richard Busch-Zantner in his book *Bulgarien,* (Berlin 1943, p. 21), erroneously attributes these figures to the census of 1934.

For comparison, we give here the number of persons belonging to the other principal national minorities: Turks, 577,552 (9.5 per cent); Gypsies, 134,488 (2.21 per cent); Pomaks (Bulgarians of the Moslem faith), 102,300 (1.68 per cent); Rumanians, 69,080 (1.13 per cent); Armenians, 27,332 (0.44 per cent); and Greeks, 10,564 (0.17 per cent). Cf. Busch-Zantner, *op. cit.,* p. 30.

15. A facsimile of the questionnaire is attached to the Bulgarian statistical publication mentioned in the preceding footnote.

16. *Tsarstvo Bulgaria, Prebroiavane,* 1926, p. 191; and 1934, pp. 22-23.

17. The census did not distinguish between Ladino, Yiddish, and Hebrew. All three languages were lumped together under the title "Jewish." In most cases, however, Jewish meant Ladino.

18. Klaus Schickert, "Joseph Fadenhecht und der nationale Zusammenbruch Bulgariens," *Weltkampf,* Frankfurt-Munich, No. 3 (September-December 1944), pp. 169ff.

19. Alfred Werner, "Jews in the Land of Attar," *The American Hebrew,* Vol. 154, No. 6 (December 1, 1944), p. 12.

20. Schickert, *op. cit.,* p. 173.

21. Otto Franz Kern, "Das Judentum im Südosten Europas," *Deutsche Arbeit,* Berlin, Vol. 41, No. 11 (November 1941), pp. 379-405.

22. Seraphim, *op. cit.,* p. 71. In reality, there were 123 Jewish physicians and 88 Jewish lawyers in Bulgaria at that time—see Lubomir Vladikin, "Die Judengesetzgebung in Bulgarien," *Weltkampf,* Munich, No. 2 (October-December 1942), p. 288.

23. Address of Peter Schischkoff on Bulgaria in *Weltkampf,* No. 1-2 (April-September 1941), pp. 96-98.

24. Schickert, *op. cit.*, p. 172. Schickert quotes an article by A. Belev, the Bulgarian Commissar for Jewish Affairs, in the *Donauzeitung*, June 18, 1943.

25. Vladikin, *op. cit.*, p. 290.

26. Werner, *op. cit.*, p. 5.

27. Schickert, *op. cit.*, pp. 171-173; see also Liusien Avramov, "Antisemitismut u nas," *Novi dni*, I, 4-5, Sofia (January 1947), pp. 17-20.

28. Gelber *op. cit.*, p. 126.

29. Quoted by Schickert, *op. cit.*, p. 171; see also Vladikin, *op. cit.*, p. 288.

30. Later Tsankov told Schickert that his words had been quoted by Piti "out of context" and "without permission"; however, he made no protest at the time of publication of the pamphlet.

31. Seraphim, *op. cit.*, pp. 86-87.

32. Kern, *op. cit.*, p. 400.

33. For a typical statement of this kind, written by a Bulgarian for German readers, see Christo Ognianoff, "Die Judenfrage in Bulgarien," *Volk im Osten*, May-June 1943, pp. 53-55: "There were no mixed marriages at all. In addition, there never had been any Jewish judges, mayors, ministers, scholars, officers, etc., in Bulgaria." In 1944, after the Bulgarian capitulation, Schickert (*op. cit.*, p. 172) complained bitterly: "One cannot understand what the Bulgarian journalist had in mind when he thought German readers would believe such things. . . ."

CHAPTER II

1. See Vladikin, *op. cit.*, pp. 288-295; Schickert, *op. cit.*, p. 172; and Astruk D. Kaleb, "Pravnoto polozhenie na evreite v Bulgaria," *Novi dni* I, 2 (Sofia 1946), pp. 5-10.

2. For the best summary of its provisions, see Vladikin, *op. cit.*, pp. 288-295, and Kern, *op. cit.*, pp. 379-405.

3. Vladikin, *op. cit.*, p. 289.

4. D. Andreiev in the newspaper *Dnes*, June 24, 1941, as quoted by Vladikin, *op. cit.*, p. 291.

5. *Ibid.*

6. According to a report by the Minister of Finance in July 1941, about 4,000 hectares of land had been "sold" by Jews and distributed among the peasants up to that time. Vladikin, *op. cit.*, p. 293.

7. 25,609 Jews declared properties amounting to less than 200,000 leva; 3,938 Jews declared properties in excess of this limit. Vladikin, *op. cit.*, p. 288.

8. *Derzhaven vestnik*, July 8, 1942.

9. Natan Grinberg, *Dokumenti vuzlaga se na komisarstvoto za evreiskitie vuprosy da izseli za Polsha* 20,000 *Evrei*, Sofia 1945, p. 7.

10. A detailed report by Belev about the contract is published in Grinberg, *op. cit.*, pp. 8-11. The book contains all materials relative to the plan and the initial stages of its enforcement; the documents were found in the Commissariat for Jewish Affairs after the war.

11. N. Petrov, "The Jews Who Survived the Storm," *The Central European Observer*, London, Vol. XXIII, No. 10 (May 10, 1946) p. 156. From this English-language periodical, supported by the Czechoslovak government, the article was translated and published in the Czech language, but without giving the source or even the name of the author, in the *Věstník náboženské obce židovské* (Bulletin of the Jewish Religious Community), Prague, Vol. VIII, No. 7 (July 10, 1946), p. 61.

12. In October 1942, Exarch Stephan published in the official organ of the Bulgarian Orthodox church an order forbidding the wearing of Jewish stars by baptized Jews because "it is incompatible with the wearing of the cross." *Donauzeitung*, November 22, 1942, as quoted by Schickert, *op. cit.*, p. 175.

13. Schickert, *op. cit.*, pp. 173-174.

14 Report by Joseph M. Levy to the *New York Times*, August 23, 1944.

15. Schickert, *op. cit.*, p. 169.

16. *Ibid.*, p. 174.

17. Petko Stainov, a professor of administrative law at the Sofia University, wrote expert articles on Bulgarian anti-Jewish laws in Nazi magazines, for instance, "Die Neue Judengesetzgebung in Bulgarien," published in the *Zeitschrift für osteuropäisches Recht*, Vol. 7, No. 11-12 (May-June 1941), pp. 553-558, and Vol. 9, No. 1-3 (July-September 1942), pp. 51-59. Copies of these are not available in this country, but according to Schickert his treatment of the material indicated that he considered the measures lawful. Later, in September 1944, Stainov spoke of the "unworthy treatment of the Jews" and wrote a jubilant article, "The Stars Are Falling" (meaning the yellow Jewish stars). In October 1944, he flew to Moscow to sign the armistice with Russia. He became Foreign Minister in the first Fatherland Front cabinet of Kimon Georgiev.

18. *New York Post*, August 3, 1944; *New York Times*, September 3, 1944.

19. For the history of the "retreat on the Jewish front," Schickert, *op. cit.*, pp. 174-175. The chronology is rather important because postwar Bulgarian sources usually conceal what happened before the installation of the Kimon Georgiev cabinet, and claim all the credit for the abolition of antisemitic laws for the Fatherland Front. Typical is the assertion of N. Petrov, *op. cit.*, p. 156:

> On the very day on which the Fatherland Front came to power—September 9, 1944—it passed a decree suspending all discriminatory measures against the Jews, and on October 20, 1944, it passed a law abolishing all antisemitic measures taken by the previous governments.

Not a word about the fact that one of the "previous governments," that of Bagrianov, had already abolished the same measures on August 29, and that another previous government, that of Muraviev, had reaffirmed and legally published the decision. Bagrianov, Mushanov, and Muraviev were all sentenced to death or imprisonment for life as war criminals.

CHAPTER III

1. Leon Shapiro and Joshua Starr ("Recent Population Data Regarding the Jews in Europe," *Jewish Social Studies*, Vol. VIII, No. 4 (October 1946), p. 319, give the annual rate of increase as "11.1 per 10,000" for the years "1926-30," and "6.7 per 10,000" for the years "1931-35." They quote as their source L. Hersh in *Algemeyne Entsiklopedye*, Paris 1939, Vol. I, p. 382. An examination of this source revealed that the years were misquoted; Hersh's data refer to the years 1925-28 and 1933-36. Still, the table in the *Algemeyne Entsiklopedye* gives the rates of increase as 11.1 and 6.7 per 10,000, an improbably low ratio. But this turned out to be a mistake which was later corrected in the English translation of Hersh's article ("Jewish Population Trends in Europe," *The Jewish People, Past and Present,* New York 1948, Vol. II, p. 23), where the table is published with the correct heading, "per 1,000 population." The natural increase is still small, but not as insignificant as Shapiro and Starr were led to believe by the error in the *Entsiklopedye.*

2. Another statement by the Consistory, in *Evreiski vesti,* Sofia, May 12, 1946, gave the number as 49, 815.

3. Notwithstanding a steady influx from the provinces, only 26,302 Jews were counted in Sofia in a Jewish community census on May 1, 1947. In seeking to explain the discrepancy, the community asserted that 2,000 Jews, most of them baptized or married to non-Jews, had not registered with the community. But then did such people register in 1945?

4. *Derzhaven vestnik*, October 16, 1944. Petrov (*op. cit.*, p. 156) gives the date of the law abolishing the anti-Jewish measures as October 20, 1944, and mentions another decree as already "suspending" these measures on September 9, 1944. The decree of September 9, however, is not mentioned in other Bulgarian sources and was probably invented only in order to show to the world that the Fatherland Front was solicitous

of the Jews on the first day it came to power. See Astruk D. Kaleb, "Pravnoto polozhenie na Evreite v Bulgaria predi i sled 9 septembri," *Novi dni,* Sofia 1946, Vol. I, No. 2, pp. 5-10. Kaleb gives a list of all laws dealing with the Jewish question and does not mention any decree of September 9, 1944.

5. Article V (*New York Times,* October 30, 1944).

6. United Press dispatch from Sofia; see *New York World-Telegram,* September 23, 1944.

7. *New York Times,* January 20, 1945.

8. *New York World-Telegram,* January 31, 1945.

9. Law concerning the Settlement of Property Claims Arising from the Abolition of the Anti-Jewish Laws (*Derzhaven vestnik,* March 2, 1945). See Kaleb, *op. cit.,* pp. 6-8; see also United Press dispatch in *New York World-Telegram,* March 5, 1945.

10. Jewish Telegraphic Agency (JTA), March 11, 1946.

11. *Ibid.,* August 19, 1946. The text of the amendments is given in *Derzhaven vestnik,* August 13, 1946; cf. *Evreiski vesti,* Sofia, October 6, 1946.

12. JTA, November 22, 1946.

13. *Ibid.,* March 11, 1946.

14. *Ibid.,* June 5, 1946.

15. *Ibid.,* August 19, 1946.

16. *Ibid.,* June 5, 1946.

17. *Ibid.*

18. *Ibid.*

19. *Derzhaven vestnik,* No. 78.

20. Zhak Eshkenazi, "Zakonut za konfiskatsite i ograbenite evreiski imushtestva," *Evreiski vesti,* July 7, 1946.

21. JTA, February 28, 1946.

22. *Ibid.,* July 26, 1946; *New York Times,* July 26, 1946.

23. JTA, May 16, 1946.

24. Census of the Sofia Jewish community (as of May 1, 1947), in the possession of the JDC.

25. A good example of this is Natan Grinberg's "Stopanskiat oblik na Evreite v Bulgaria," *Novi dni,* June 1946.

26. *Evreiski vesti,* February 9, 1947.

27. Eduard Arie, "Profesionalnoto presloiavane i stopanskoto vuzstanoviavane na bulgarskite Evrei," *Novi dni,* Sofia, I, 4-5 (January 1947), pp. 11-13.

28. *New York Times,* December 12, 1946.

29. JTA, January 14, 1947.

30. *New York Times,* December 12, 1946.

31. JTA, January 17, 1947; *New York Herald Tribune,* February 2, 1947. For reports of the opening of the hospital, see *Evreiski vesti,* July 11 and 18, 1948.

32. JTA, April 8, 1946.

33. Astruk D. Kaleb, "Iziavleniata na m.-r. predsedatelia G. Dimitrov pred Ts. K. na bulgarskite turgovtsi," *Evreiski vesti,* February 16, 1947.

34. *Evreiski vesti,* February 16, 1947.

35. Kaleb, *op. cit.*

36. *Evreiski vesti,* February 23, 1947.

37. Zhak Natan, "Edno goliamo subitie na evreiskia front," *Evreiski vesti,* October 19, 1947.

38. *Evreiski vesti,* July 11, 1948.

39. See n. 24 above.

40. *Evreiski vesti,* February 29, 1948.

41. *Ibid.,* September 19, 1948.

42. *Ibid.,* February 22 and March 28, 1948.

43. *Ibid.,* March 7, 1948.

44. *Ibid.,* October 19, 1947.

45. JTA, July 22, 1946.

46. An announcement made in Paris in February 1947 by Manuel Siegel, JDC representative in Bulgaria, promised $250,000 worth of machinery and equipment to the cooperatives, plus a loan of $100,000 to the Jewish Bank (*New York Herald Tribune*, February 7, 1947). These subsidies were subsequently somewhat reduced.

47. See Iako Bekhar, "Evreiskite koop. banki se vuzstanoviavat," *Evreiski vesti*, September 29, 1946; Natan Grinberg, "Vuzstanoviavaneto na banko 'Geula'"; a report on the decisions of the Economic Committee of Jewish Section of the Fatherland Front, *ibid.*, November 17, 1946; and Isak Arueti, "Edina evreiska kooperativna banka," *ibid.*, November 24, 1946.

48. Iako Bekhar, "Na rabota," *ibid.*, February 2, 1947.

49. Iako Bekhar, "Bez uvlechenia," *ibid.*, February 16, 1947.

50. Natan Grinberg, "Podemut na nashite kooperatsii," *ibid.*, February 29, 1948.

51. The cooperative "Dimitri Blagoev" asked for an increase from 20 to 30 million leva (*Evreiski vesti*, March 7, 1948); the cooperative "Svetlina," from 500,000 to 7 million leva, *ibid.*, March 28, 1947.

52. Quoted from a report on the foundation of an opticians' cooperative, *Evreiski vesti*, June 20, 1948.

53. Among Jews in public office, Dr. Nissim Mevorah, the Ambassador to Washington, probably had the highest rank.

CHAPTER IV

1. JTA, March 8, 1946. In 1946, 8,172 members took part in the elections to the Zionist World Congress and gave 5,780 votes to a coalition of General Zionists, Mapai, and Maccabi, and 2,392 votes to *Hashomer Hatzair* (see *Cesta*, Bratislava, November 1946, pp. 2-3).

2. *New Leader*, New York, February 10, 1945.

3. JTA, April 24 and 25, 1946.

4. *Ibid.*, May 17, 1946.

5. Thus the composition of the Central Consistory elected by the Third Conference of Jewish Communities in May 1948 was: 10 Communists, 10 Zionists, 3 pro-Communist Social Democrats, 2 "non-partisans." For names and affiliations, see *Evreiski vesti*, May 9, 1948; see also JTA, September 27, 1948.

6. On October 12, 1947, a meeting of Jewish Communists demanded that the Zionists "prove by deeds" their loyalty to the Fatherland Front (*Evreiski vesti*, October 19, 1947); on April 21, 1948, a caucus of 200 Jewish Communist "activists" received directives about "new elements in our relations to Palestine and new forms of organization in the Jewish sector" (*Evreiski vesti*, April 25, 1948).

7. Among them, Deputy Izrael Maier, who wrote the weekly political review; Eduard Safir, foreign editor of the Communist newspaper *Rabotnichesko delo* and correspondent of the *Daily Worker* in Bulgaria; Khaim Oliver; Isak Moshev; etc. (See *Evreiski vesti*, September 29, 1946).

8. *Evreiski vesti*, October 19, 1947.

9. "Svetul Put," *Evreiski vesti*, September 29, 1946.

10. *Evreiski vesti*, October 6, 1946.

11. *Ibid.*, October 20, 1946.

12. See, for instance, the report on a meeting in Plovdiv in *Evreiski vesti*, October 20, 1946.

13. See a survey of the electoral campaign in *Evreiski vesti*, November 3, 1946.

14. *Evreiski vesti*, November 10, 1946.

15. *Ibid.*

16. *Ibid.*, September 29, 1946.

17. *Ibid.*, February 1, 1947.

18. *Ibid.*, October 6, 1946.

19. *Ibid.*, September 5 and 9, 1948.

20. A solemn service was held in the Sofia synagogue (*Evreiski vesti*, September 29, 1946).

21. The Jewish Fatherland Front collected money for a monument to the Red Army, and signatures for a telegram of thanks to Stalin (*Evreiski vesti*, October 19, 1947).

22. *Evreiski vesti*, February 29, 1948.

23. *Ibid.*, July 4, 1948.

24. *Ibid.*, April 18, 1951.

25. *New York Times*, July 10, 1951.

26. "We shall not allow an increase in antisemitism in Bulgaria," Premier Dimitrov told the delegation of Bulgarian Jews to the WJC Convention in December 1946. "We shall punish severely, even put to death, preachers of racial hatred" (JTA, December 5, 1946). The new Bulgarian Constitution states, in Article 60: "Inciting to racial, national, or religious hatred is punishable by law" (*Evreiski vesti*, October 20, 1946).

27. *Evreiski vesti*, October 13, 1946.

28. *Jewish Chronicle*, September 8, 1950.

29. *Ibid.*, September 29, 1950.

30. *Evreiski vesti*, October 6, 1946.

31. *Ibid.*, July 7, 1946.

32. *Ibid.*, October 13, 1946.

33. *Ibid.*, October 6, 1946.

34. *Ibid.*, May 9, 1948.

35. *New York Times*, September 21, 1946.

36. JTA, November 5, 1946.

37. *Evreiski vesti*, October 6, 1946.

38. Text of letter in *Evreiski vesti*, October 13, 1946.

39. *Ibid.*, October 20, 1946.

40. *Ibid.*, October 13, 1946.

41. "Bulgarskite evrei i mirut," *Evreiski vesti*, February 9, 1947.

42. JTA, September 16, 1946.

43. "Edno interesno zasedanie na konsistoriata," *Evreiski vesti*, October 6, 1946.

44. JTA, October 13, 1946; see also a speech by Izrael Maier in parliament reported in *Evreiski vesti*, October 6, 1946.

45. JTA, October 13, 1946.

46. Speech by Izrael Maier reported in *Evreiski vesti*, October 6, 1946.

47. *Evreiski vesti*, September 19, 1948.

48. "Pred novata uchebna godina," *Evreiski vesti*, September 5, 1948.

49. See letter signed by the secretary of the Central Consistory, Isak Moshev, in the YIVO archives.

50. Cf. chap. I. The comparison is based on the assumption that the number of students given for 1947 did not include kindergarten children. If it did, the decline was still greater.

51. *Evreiski vesti*, March 14, 1948.

52. *Ibid.*, March 28, 1948.

53. See n. 49.

54. See JTA, April 14 and September 29, 1946.

55. *Evreiski vesti*, February 1, 1947.

56. *Ibid.*, May 16, 1948.

57. Khaim Benadov, "Kurturnite pridobivki za bulgarskite evrei ot 9 septembri," *Evreiski vesti*, September 9, 1948.

58. *Evreiski vesti*, May 16, 1948.

59. *Ibid.*, June 11, 1949.

60. The report does not say what happened to the "reactionary" and "nationalist" literature; from other reports it is clear that all such books were eliminated from Jewish libraries.

61. Traicho Kostov, a prominent Bulgarian Communist leader, accused of Titoism, treason, and spying for the Western Powers, was executed in 1949.
62. The report of course did not mention that the Polyclinic had been equipped by American Jewish organizations.
63. *Evreiski vesti*, January 1, 1950.
64. *Ibid.*, March 1, 1950.
65. *Ibid.*, April 1, 1950.
66. *Ibid.*, November 3, 1950.
67. *Jewish Chronicle*, September 8, 1950.
68. *Ibid.*
69. *Evreiski vesti*, February 2, 1951.
70. *Ibid.*, May 1, 1952.

CHAPTER V

1. Samuel Ettinger, "Nova forma na angliiskia imperializum, Planut za razdelaneto na Palestina–nova forma za imperialisticheskoto zarobvane na stranata," *Evreiski vesti*, November 24, 1946.
2. *Evreiski vesti*, May 18, 1947.
3. JTA, April 24, 1946.
4. *Ibid.*, April 14, 1946.
5. *Ibid.*, October 22, 1946.
6. *Ibid.*, December 5, 1946.
7. *New York Times*, July 7, 1946; JTA, July 8, 1946.
8. "Tsionisticheskiat kongres v Basel i negovite reshenia," *Evreiski vesti*, February 9, 1947.
9. "Neobiknoven primer na tsionisticheska antisuvetska propaganda," *Evreiski vesti*, November 24. 1946.
10. *Evreiski vesti*, March 2, 1947.
11. *Ibid.*, April 27, 1947.
12. *Ibid.*, October 19, 1947.
13. "Goreshta priznatelnost na bulg. evreistvo kum velikia Suvetski suiuz za smelata i iskrena zashtita na evreistvo," *Evreiski vesti*, June 1, 1947.
14. *Evreiski vesti*, April 25, 1948.
15. *Ibid.*, May 9, 1948.
16. *Ibid.*, April 25, 1948, and *Tsionisticheska tribuna*, April 30, 1948.
17. *Evreiski vesti*, May 16, 1948.
18. *Ibid.*, May 23, 1948.
19. "Zasedanie na evreiskia komitet na malts. komisia pri NS na OF. Razasnitelna rabota vared bulgarskata obshtestvenost po palestinskite subitia," *Evreiski vesti*, June 20, 1948.
20. "Reshenia na razshirenia plenum na konsistoriata," *Evreiski vesti*, June 20, 1948.
21. *Evreiski vesti*, May 9, 1948.
22. *Ibid.*, May 16, 1948.
23. *Ibid.*, May 23, 1948.
24. *Ibid.*, July 18, 1948.
25. *Ibid.*, March 1, 1950.
26. *Ibid.*, June 11, 1949.
27. *Ibid.*, March 15, 1950.
28. *Israelitsches Wochenblatt*, Zürich, May 15, 1953.

CHAPTER VI

1. *New Leader*, New York, February 10, 1945.
2. JTA, April 24, 1946.

3. *Ibid.*, April 14, 1946.
4. *Ibid.*, May 14, 1946.
5. *Ibid.*, August 3, 1946.
6. *Ibid.*, December 5, 1946.
7. See telegram to Stalin, text of which was published in *Evreiski vesti*, June 1, 1947.
8. *Evreiski vesti*, May 18, 1947.
9. *Ibid.*
10. *Ibid.*, May 9, 1948.
11. *Ibid.*, September 5, 1948.
12. See interview with Izrael Maier and Khaim Benadov, *Evreiski vesti*, October 17, 1948, and an article in the Sofia newspaper *Izgrev*, quoted in a dispatch of the Associated Press from Sofia, October 22, 1948.
13. JTA, September 27, 1948.
14. *Evreiski vesti*, October 17, 1948.
15. Statement by Moses A. Leavitt, JDC Executive Vice-Chairman, see JTA dispatch, May 13, 1949.
16. According to Israeli immigration statistics, 15,676 Jews born in Bulgaria reached Israel in 1948, and 20,008 in 1949. See Dov Tibbon, "Israel: Immigration Statistics," *American Jewish Year Book*, Vol. 52 (1951), p. 399.
17. *Evreiski vesti*, June 11, 1949.
18. *Israelitisches Wochenblatt*, Zürich, August 11, 1950.
19. *Statistical Bulletin of Israel*, Vol. II, No. 2, January-March 1951, p. 115. 1950 is the first full year in which Israeli statistics registered immigrants' "principal country of residence," in addition to their country of birth.
20. *Ibid.*, Vol. III, No. 1-2, January-May 1952, p. 11.

About the Authors

PETER MEYER, Central European economist and editor, arrived in the United States in 1941. He is the author of "The Soviet Union: a New Class Society" in *The Verdict of Three Decades* (Duell, Sloan & Pearce, 1950) and numerous articles on Soviet policy and the Jewish situation behind the Iron Curtain, several of which have been reprinted in the symposium *The New Red Anti-Semitism* (The Beacon Press, 1953).

BERNARD D. WEINRYB was born in Russian Poland and studied at the University of Breslau. He arrived in the United States in 1939. He is the author of more than fifty studies and four volumes dealing with Poland, the most recent being *Texts and Studies in the Communal History of Polish Jewry* (1950). He is on the faculties of the Dropsie College for Hebrew and Cognate Learning, in Philadelphia, Pa., and Yeshiva University, in New York City.

EUGENE DUSCHINSKY was born in Budapest and studied at Budapest, Pressburg and London. He was a member of the Supreme Board of Adult Education in the Hungarian Ministry of Culture and Religion, 1945-48. He left Hungary in 1948 and is at present rabbi of the Cape Town Orthodox Hebrew Congregation in the Union of South Africa.

NICOLAS SYLVAIN is a Rumanian-born economist who came to the United States in 1948 after ten years residence in France. He has studied and written extensively about Soviet Russia and the Iron Curtain countries and is at present engaged in research on this subject at a leading American university.

Index